**books**online

Read this book online today:

With SAP PRESS BooksOnline we offer you online access to knowledge from the leading SAP experts. Whether you use it as a beneficial supplement or as an alternative to the printed book, with SAP PRESS BooksOnline you can:

- Access your book anywhere, at any time. All you need is an Internet connection.
- Perform full text searches on your book and on the entire SAP PRESS library.
- Build your own personalized SAP library.

The SAP PRESS customer advantage:

Register this book today at *www.sap-press.com* and obtain exclusive free trial access to its online version. If you like it (and we think you will), you can choose to purchase permanent, unrestricted access to the online edition at a very special price!

Here's how to get started:

1. Visit *www.sap-press.com*.
2. Click on the link for SAP PRESS BooksOnline and login (or create an account).
3. Enter your free trial license key, shown below in the corner of the page.
4. Try out your online book with full, unrestricted access for a limited time!

Your personal free trial **license key**
for this online book is: hgqk-v6je-bz5w-9ctd

Quick Reference Guide:
Financial Accounting with SAP®

SAP PRESS

SAP PRESS is a joint initiative of SAP and Galileo Press. The know-how offered by SAP specialists combined with the expertise of the Galileo Press publishing house offers the reader expert books in the field. SAP PRESS features first-hand information and expert advice, and provides useful skills for professional decision-making.

SAP PRESS offers a variety of books on technical and business related topics for the SAP user. For further information, please visit our website: *www.sap-press.com*.

Heinz Forsthuber, Jörg Siebert
SAP ERP Financials User's Guide
2009, app. 600 pp.
978-1-59229-190-8

Shivesh Sharma
Optimize Your SAP ERP Financials Implementation
2008, app. 700 pp.
978-1-59229-160-1

Naeem Arif, Sheikh Tauseef
SAP ERP Financials: Configuration and Design
2008, app. 450 pp.
978-1-59229-136-6

Manish Patel
Discover SAP ERP Financials
2008, app. 550 pp.
978-1-59229-184-7

Vincenzo Sopracolle

Quick Reference Guide:
Financial Accounting with SAP®

Galileo Press

Bonn • Boston

Galileo Press is named after the Italian physicist, mathematician and philosopher Galileo Galilei (1564–1642). He is known as one of the founders of modern science and an advocate of our contemporary, heliocentric worldview. His words *Eppur se muove* (And yet it moves) have become legendary. The Galileo Press logo depicts Jupiter orbited by the four Galilean moons, which were discovered by Galileo in 1610.

Editor Stephen Solomon
Developmental Editor Kelly Grace Harris
Copyeditor Julie McNamee
Cover Design Jill Winitzer
Photo Credit Image Copyright dominique landau. Used under license from Shutterstock.com
Layout Design Vera Brauner
Production Editor Kelly O'Callaghan
Assistant Production Editor Graham Geary
Typesetting Publishers' Design and Production Services, Inc.
Printed and bound in Canada

ISBN 978-1-59229-313-1

© 2010 by Galileo Press Inc., Boston (MA)

1st Edition 2010

Library of Congress Cataloging-in-Publication Data
Sopracolle, Vincenzo.
  Quick Reference Guide: Financial Accounting with SAP / Vincenzo Sopracolle. — 1st ed.
      p. cm.
  Includes bibliographical references and index.
  ISBN-13: 978-1-59229-313-1 (alk. paper)
  ISBN-10: 1-59229-313-1 (alk. paper)
  1. SAP ERP. 2. Accounting—Computer programs. 3. Accounting—Data processing. I. Title.
  HF5679.S715 2010
  658.0285'53—dc22

                                                                2010005753

Contents at a Glance

Contents

4   General Ledger Accounts and Postings 155

6   Asset Accounting 359

Appendices 589

Introduction

Purpose of the Book

The aim of this book is to provide practical help to people who work in SAP ERP Financials with Financial Accounting on a daily basis. It puts useful information relevant to any role — end-user, master user, super user, or expert — right at your fingertips, using step-by-step instructions and screenshots that clearly explain how to perform specific activities (creating a master record, posting a document, running a period-end function, performing a customizing task, or simply searching for a table, transaction, or program). Even consultants working on SAP implementation projects will find this to be a helpful resource when designing future systems and testing solutions.

Format of the Book

This book implements a modular format, and, as indicated in the title, is a quick reference book. "Quick reference" does not refer to its size, but rather to its organization; at the beginning of each activity, we provide a Quick Reference box that succinctly lists the relevant information for the activity in question. Although the specific type of information depends on the activity itself, standard details include a menu path, transaction code, table/view, and/or program. (If the section concerns a customizing activity, the menu path always start with IMG.) The text then goes on to describe how to perform the activity using step-by-step instructions and screenshots. At the end of each major section, we provide a collection of frequently asked questions (FAQ) and troubleshooting tips that address the most common concerns and issues incurred when performing the activities discussed in that major section. At the end of the book, we consolidate information about menu paths, transaction codes, tables, views, and programs in four appendices. Finally, the index includes tables, programs, and error numbers to improve the usefulness of the book.

> **Note**
>
> This book is based on SAP ERP 6.0.

SAP General Ledger and Classic General Ledger

SAP General Ledger (more informally known as the New General Ledger) was introduced with SAP ERP 5.0. The previous general ledger SAP solution is called the classic General Ledger. Several functionalities have been introduced with SAP General Ledger (multiple ledgers, document splitting, and segments, among others) to better support companies with complex and multinational requirements.

Companies that start using SAP ERP 5.0 or higher will automatically have SAP General Ledger activated. For all other companies, the upgrade to SAP General Ledger has or will be managed within the framework of a project. At present, there are companies in SAP ERP 6.0 that run SAP General Ledger, and others that still run the classic General Ledger. We have tried, as much as we could, to cover the requirements of both categories of companies. When not explicitly stated, the instructions provided are valid for both SAP General Ledger and the classic General Ledger. If the instructions are valid for just one of the two, we state this clearly.

> **Note on Menu Paths**
>
> If you have activated SAP General Ledger, two similar menus appear under the SAP Customizing Implementation Guide: Financial Accounting and Financial Accounting (New). To a large extent, the two menus contain the same transactions. However, when a transaction is contained in both, we always list the menu path starting with Financial Accounting, as it is available for both users in SAP General Ledger and the classic General Ledger. When an activity is available only under Financial Accounting (New), this is the path we use.

Some configuration needed for the SAP Financials modules is shared with other SAP modules. This chapter is about the customizing that is relevant for Financial Accounting, but is placed under the IMG node titled General Settings.

1   General SAP Configuration for Financial Accounting

The configuration in SAP is organized in a hierarchy that you can access using Transaction SPRO. This hierarchy is called the *implementation guide*, or, more commonly, IMG. Each module has its own configuration node in the IMG; additionally, there are some common nodes that are not tied to specific modules. Countries and currencies are two important configuration objects related to Financial Accounting that are shared among multiple SAP modules. This chapter guides you through the relevant steps necessary to configure both of these objects.

1.1   Countries

You can't work in SAP without configuring countries. They are used in the company code definition, in the plant definition, in customer and vendor master data, and in many other types of master data and customizing objects. Configuring a country means assigning each country a unique key and setting up a number of controls (which are described in detail in this chapter).

Existing countries are already configured in the system at installation. In the standard configuration, each country is identified by its key, which is defined by the International Organization for Standardization (ISO). This should generally not be changed, and, as a result, the customizing of countries isn't a frequent activity. There are, however, some possible cases where you might need to edit country configuration, namely:

- ▸ When new countries are created
- ▸ When you need to make changes to the country-specific controls

> **Note**
>
> Country configuration is a general setting in SAP customizing. Therefore, if you do alter the configuration, it's absolutely necessary that any changes are agreed upon by the parties responsible for the different SAP modules that are implemented in your company.

Country configuration is accessed in customizing via the following menu path: SAP NETWEAVER • GENERAL SETTINGS • SET COUNTRIES. If you are working with older releases, you won't find the upper node called SAP NetWeaver. In this case, the General Settings node will appear immediately under the root node titled SAP Customizing Implementation Guide (Figure 1.1).

New

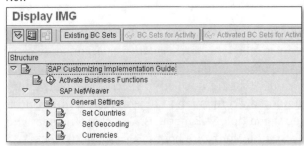

Old

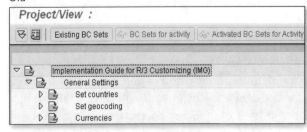

Figure 1.1 General Settings Menu in Newer and Older Releases

The next section discusses the following:

▶ The steps necessary to check the existing configurations for countries and to create a configuration for a new country. The relevant customizing activity for this is Define Country in MySAP Systems.

▶ Country-specific controls for addresses, tax codes, and bank data. The relevant customizing activity for this is Set Country-Specific Checks.

1.1.1 Defining Countries in mySAP Systems

> **Quick Reference**
>
> **Menu path:** IMG • SAP NetWeaver • General Settings • Set Countries • Define Countries in mySAP Systems
>
> **Transaction:** OY01
>
> **Table/view:** T005/V_T005

When configuring countries, you find two customizing activities with similar descriptions (Figure 1.2):

▸ Define Countries in mySAP Systems: view V_T005

▸ Specify Countries in mySAP Systems (CRM, SRM, SCM,...): view V_T005_BAS

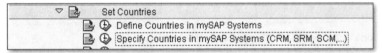

Figure 1.2 Country Definition in IMG

Both these customizing activities are a partial view of the same customizing table, Table T005. Define Countries in mySAP Systems is the customizing activity you need for Financial Accounting. Specify Countries in mySAP Systems (CRM, SRM, SCM,...) is the customizing activity used by your colleagues who work with other SAP systems.

Some fields appear in both views, and others appear just in one view. The important thing to remember is that you are not working with separate objects and separate tables. If you change the name in one view, you see the change in the other view as well (Figure 1.3).

In the example shown in Figure 1.3, we have entered a long description for the country Austria (AT) using the customizing activity Define Countries in mySAP Systems; then we accessed the same country with the customizing activity Specify Countries in mySAP Systems (CRM, SRM, SCM,...). As you can see, the long descriptions appear in both screens. Therefore, any time you need to edit country configuration, you must coordinate the change with your colleagues who work in other areas of SAP.

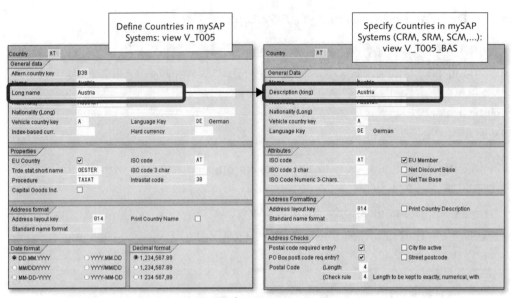

Figure 1.3 V_T005 and V_T005_BAS (Partial Views of Table T005)

Figure 1.4 shows the country settings relevant for Financial Accounting.

Figure 1.4 Country Settings for Financial Accounting

Figure 1.4 contains a number of fields that are very important for the SAP Financials modules, which we explain here:

- **Index-Based Curr.**
  Index-based currency is provided by SAP for group reporting in countries with a high level of inflation; the currency specified here can be used as a parallel currency for the company codes assigned to the country (currency type 50).

- **Hard Currency**
  Hard currency is provided by SAP in addition to index-based currency; it is for group reporting in countries with a high level of inflation, and can be used as a parallel currency for the company codes assigned to the country (currency type 40). (There is no technical difference between the index-based currency and the hard currency; both are available as parallel currencies when configuring a company code that belongs to a specific country. You can choose one or both in the company code configuration; this way, all of the amounts are translated in real-time to the additional parallel local currencies.)

- **EU Country**
  This indicator specifies that the country is part of the European Union.

- **Procedure**
  This is the tax procedure that defines tax rules and tax codes and is used in the system to determine the VAT and the tax on sales and purchases. You can't assign this procedure directly to a company code; rather, you assign it to a country, and then the company code located in that country is automatically assigned to the relevant tax procedure. For example, for the country key DE, Germany, the tax procedure is TAXD. So, if you create a company code and specify that the country is DE, this company code automatically uses the TAXD tax procedure. The configuration of tax procedure and tax codes is accessed via the following menu path: FINANCIAL ACCOUNTING • FINANCIAL ACCOUNTING GLOBAL SETTINGS • TAX ON SALES/PURCHASES • BASIC SETTINGS.

1.1.2 Setting Country-Specific Checks

Quick Reference

Menu path: IMG • SAP NETWEAVER • GENERAL SETTINGS • SET COUNTRIES • SET COUNTRY-SPECIFIC CHECKS

Transaction: OY17

Table/view: T005/V_005_B

In most cases, Set Country-Specific Checks is the customizing activity you must work with if you edit country configurations. We provide a detailed discussion of the fields in this activity here. Before we begin discussing individual fields, though, we must first explain the concept of *field length*.

When setting country-specific checks, many fields in the system require that you specify the *field length* (in digits) and a *checking rule*, which determines how the field length is to be interpreted. The following 10 checking rules are available (Figure 1.5):

1. Maximum Value Length, Without Gaps
2. Maximum Value Length, Numerical, Without Gaps
3. Length to be Kept to Exactly, Without Gaps
4. Length to be Kept to Exactly, Numerical, Without Gaps
5. Maximum Value Length
6. Maximum Value Length, Numerical
7. Length to be Kept to Exactly
8. Length to be Kept to Exactly, Numerical
9. Check Against Country-Specific Edit Format
10. Deactivate Postal Code Check for USA

When specifying the length of the field, keep in mind that the specified length can't exceed the *technical* length of the field. For example, if you specify that the postal code length for a country is 12, the system will ask you to enter a field with a maximum length of 000010 because the technical limit for the postal code field is 10 digits.

Let's now discuss each of the fields in this screen in more detail. To make this explanation as simple as possible, we have grouped the fields into three categories: bank data, address data, and tax data.

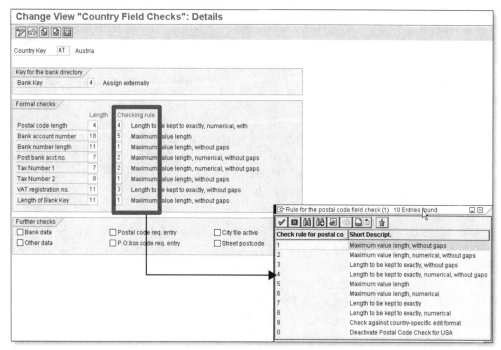

Figure 1.5 Country-Specific Checks: Field Length Controls

Bank Data

The bank data consists of the following fields:

▶ **Bank Key**

This is where you indicate how the banks are identified in the country: with a progressive number, a local bank code, or an external ID (like the SWIFT). This choice has an impact on the manual creation of the banks as well as on the automatic massive creation with programs such as RFBVBIC_0 for the automatic upload of the Bank Identifier Code (BIC) file.

▶ **Bank Account Number**

This refers to the bank account number of the customer, vendor, or house bank. For vendors, the field is LFBK-BANKN; for customers, KNBK-BANKN; for house banks, T012K-BANKN. This field is used if the bank account in question is a regular bank account (as opposed to a post bank account, which we discuss in the next bullet). Note: For this field, you must specify the field length and checking rule.

▶ **Bank Number Length**

This is where you indicate the bank ID with a specific unit key that identifies the physical bank in the country.

▶ **Post Bank Acct. No.**

This also refers to the bank account number but is used if the account in question is a post account (as opposed to a regular account). The system distinguishes between these two accounts by relying on the master data of the bank itself, which has an indicator that defines whether a bank is a post bank or a normal bank. Note: For this field, you must specify the field length and checking rule.

▶ **Bank Key**

This checkbox is relevant only if you choose the option titled 4 Assign Externally in the Bank Key field. In this case, the bank key must respect the format rules defined here. In any other case, it isn't relevant. Note: For this field, you must specify the field length and checking rule.

▶ **Bank Data**

If this checkbox is activated, the system initiates a formal check on the SWIFT code of the bank master data (if entered). For example, if you create a bank (Transaction FI01) for the country AT, then the system checks that the fifth and the sixth characters are "AT." Additionally, the checkbox activates some other country-specific checks for the bank master data. (To see all of the controls available for different countries, check the online help documentation by clicking on the checkbox and pressing F1, as shown in Figure 1.6.)

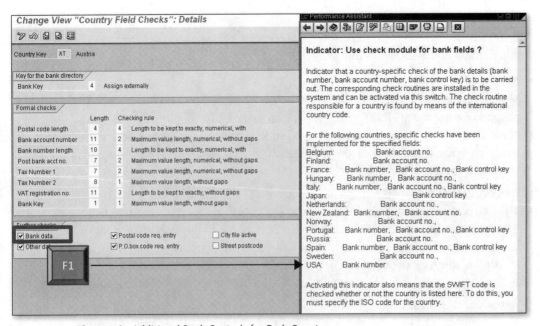

Figure 1.6 Additional Bank Controls for Each Country

Address Data

The address data consists of the following fields:

▸ **Postal Code Length**
This field controls the format of the Postal Code field for any address data in the country (e.g., in the customer master data, the field is KNA1-PSTLZ). Note: For this field, you must specify the field length and checking rule.

▸ **Postal Code Req. Entry**
This checkbox, if selected, means that the field becomes mandatory for any address data that refers to the country.

▸ **P.O. Box Code Req. Entry**
This checkbox, if selected, means that the field becomes mandatory for any address data that refers to the country.

▸ **City File**
This checkbox should be checked if you are using the SAP Regional Structure. This is a feature that allows you to check the accuracy of the address data against an address database stored in the system; the address database can be uploaded into SAP using Report RSADRLSM02. (See SAP Notes 98050 and 132948 for more details.)

▸ **Street Postcode**
This checkbox also refers to the SAP Regional Structure. It should be selected if the postal codes in the country are street specific. If checked, you can enter a postal code and let the system propose a list of permitted addresses.

VAT and Tax Registration Data

The VAT and tax registration data consists of the following fields:

▸ **Tax Number 1**
This control refers to the STCD1 field, which is found in customer vendor master data. Note: For this field, you must specify the field length and checking rule.

▸ **Tax Number 2**
This control refers to the STCD2 field, which is found in customer vendor master data. Note: For this field, you must specify the field length and checking rule.

- ▶ **VAT Registration Number**

  This control refers to the STCEG field, which is found in customer vendor master data. For this field, you must specify the field length and checking rule.

- ▶ **Other Data**

  This checkbox activates some country-specific controls. For example, if you activate the checkbox in the country GB, the system checks that the VAT registration number for vendors and customers located in GB comply with the local coding rule. In some countries, no additional control is available in the system. Check the list of the affected countries on the related online documentation (select the flag and press F1).

1.1.3   FAQ and Troubleshooting Tips

Next we answer some frequently asked questions, and offer helpful troubleshooting tips.

FAQ

1. **Question:** In my SAP implementation, only companies in France are configured. These companies work with customers and vendors in many countries in the world. I have changed the settings for the country FR, putting more strict controls for postcode, VAT code, and so on. Do these settings apply to all of the business partners with whom I work?

   Answer: No. When you create a company code, customer, vendor, plant, or bank, you specify the country in which they are located. Then the system reads the rules to be applied to that country, no matter where your company is located. So, if you are working with a vendor in Germany and you specify its postcode, it must comply with the check control rules specified for the DE country key.

2. **Question:** Is there any way to assign a company code to a tax procedure different from the one assigned to its country?

   Answer: No, the system does not allow this. If two company codes belonging to the same country have different VAT requirements, we recommend that you set up the tax procedure in a way that accommodates both sets of requirements (e.g., by adding all of the necessary tax conditions).

3. **Question:** How can I activate the control of the International Bank Account Number (IBAN) for a specific country?

Answer: You don't activate the formal control of the IBAN code for the country in this customizing activity. To activate the control, use Transaction FIBF and events 3030 and 3040.

4. **Question:** What happens to the existing master data if I introduce or change a control afterwards?

   Answer: The system lets you change the controls, but the new master data (for example, customer, vendors, or banks) must fulfill the control. For existing master data, the control takes effect when you try to change it. You cannot perform any change if the master data does not fulfill the new country-specific settings.

Troubleshooting Tips

1. **Issue:** When I define the length of a field in a specific check for countries, error message BF00407 appears: "Enter field with a maximum length of XXXXX." Why does this happen?

   Solution: You have specified a length that exceeds the technical length of the field. Specify a length shorter than the technical length; for example, for theb bank account number, the technical limit is 18 digits.

2. **Issue:** I have some customers and vendors located in country GB, but their communication address is in country FR. Where should we send dunning letters, interest invoices, and accounts statements? I have created them using the FR address, but now the system won't allow me to put a GB VAT number in the VAT Registration Number field.

   Solution: In the country-specific checks for FR, you can set the controls for the VAT registration (the length and the control rule). In addition, if you select the Other Data flag, the system only allows VAT registration numbers that start with FR, which we strongly recommend. In your case, having activated the Other Data flag, you can't specify a GB VAT number in the VAT Registration Number field; however, you can add the VAT registration number for GB in the general data of the customer or vendor control data by clicking on the Other button next to the VAT Registration Number field. The relevant information is saved in Tables KNAS (for customers) and LFAS (for vendors). However, this information isn't read by the VAT standard report RFUMSV00; for this to happen, you must create an additional customer or vendor with the GB address and the GB VAT registration number, and then connect this customer or vendor to the other one with the Fiscal Address field (under the Control tab) in the customer or vendor master data. After doing this, the VAT registration number of the customer's or vendor's fiscal address will be used in report RFUMSV00.

1.2   Currencies

When your SAP system is created and before any further customizing is done in the implementation project, all of the currencies managed in the commercial world should already be in the system. However, you may need to configure currencies in special situations; for example, as the creation of new countries required new country configuration, it will often also require currency configuration.

The customizing of a currency involves the following:

▸ Rules valid for *exactly one* currency: What is its code? How many decimal places does it have?

▸ Rules valid for *all* currencies: Is it possible to store more than one exchange rate for the same date and pair of currencies?

▸ Rules valid for *pairs* of currency: Which pairs of currencies are allowed? What are the translation ratios?

In this section, we discuss how to introduce a new currency in the system, set decimal places, configure various activities related to exchange rate types, and define translation ratios for currency translation. We also discuss the periodic update of new exchange rates, as well as the difference between manually entering the exchange rate at the time of posting, and letting the system automatically retrieve the suitable exchange rate (for documents posted in foreign currencies).

1.2.1   Creating a New Currency

Quick Reference

Menu path: IMG • SAP NetWeaver • General Settings • Currencies • Check Currency Codes

Transaction: OY03

Table/view: TCURC/V_CURC

The configuration of the currencies in the system isn't in the Financial Accounting menu but rather under SAP NetWeaver • General Settings • Currencies. If you need to create a new currency in the system, we strongly recommend checking in the support portal of SAP for relevant SAP notes. The notes contain a series of recommendations for all of the customizing steps necessary to use the new currency: the definition with the ISO code, the number of decimal places, and the translation ratios with other main currencies. For example, SAP Note 791997 describes how to customize the new Romanian currency (leu): the currency code should be RON; the new currency should have two decimal places; the suggested translation ratios with most of the currencies (e.g., EUR) should be one to one. If a note isn't yet available, we strongly recommend contacting SAP through the support portal.

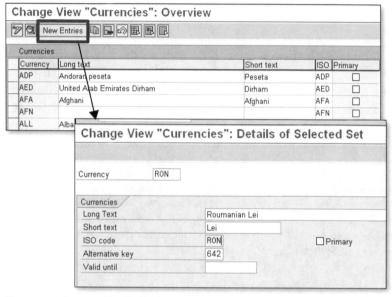

Figure 1.7 Currency Key Definition

Next we explain the first customizing step in creating a currency code (its ISO code) (Figure 1.7).

1. Run Transaction OY04.

2. The system displays a list of the currencies already created in the system. If you double-click on one line, you can check the relevant details.

3. To create a new currency, click on the New Entries button, and specify the currency code (the ISO code), plus a short and long description. The alternative key is useful for companies located in Spain or Belgium.

After you have completed this first step, you can proceed with the configuration settings for the new currency, as described in detail next.

1.2.2 Setting Decimal Places

Quick Reference
Menu path: IMG • SAP NETWEAVER • GENERAL SETTINGS • CURRENCIES • SET DECIMAL PLACES FOR CURRENCIES
Transaction: OY04
Table/view: TCURX/V_CURX

After creating a currency, the next activity is to configure the number of decimal places of the currency (note, though, that this step is needed only if the currency should have other than two decimal places). Check the number of decimal places for currencies via SAP NETWEAVER • GENERAL SETTINGS • CURRENCIES • SET DECIMAL PLACES FOR CURRENCIES. You'll notice that very few currencies are listed here (in Table TCURX); if a currency doesn't appear, it's automatically set to have two decimal places.

Warning!
Changing decimal place configuration for a currency can lead to one of the most catastrophic consequences in a live SAP system. Never make such a change in a live system. The existing values will be incorrect, and you'll most likely need to restore the system to a previous date (with all of the related consequences that this entails). Such a mistake can come at great cost for a company. It bears repeating: Never change decimal place configuration in a live SAP system. Besides, the decimal places customizing is cross-client; so if more than one productive client is present in your SAP installation, they will all be affected by the change of the decimal places for the currency.

If a new currency is created and you need to change its number of decimal places, do the following:

1. Choose the customizing activity SET DECIMAL PLACES FOR CURRENCIES.

2. Confirm the three warning messages that you get from the system (Figure 1.8).

3. Choose New Entries.

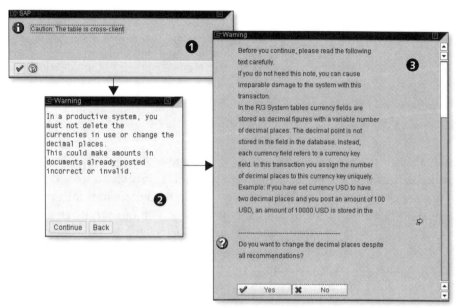

Figure 1.8 System Warnings for Changing Currency Decimal Places

4. Specify the newly created currency and the appropriate number of decimal places (Figure 1.9).

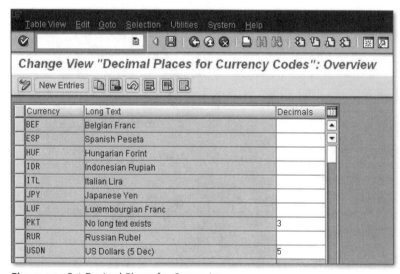

Figure 1.9 Set Decimal Places for Currencies

1.2.3   Checking Exchange Rate Types

> **Quick Reference**
>
> **Menu path:** IMG • SAP NetWeaver • General Settings • Currencies • Check Exchange Rate Type
>
> **Transaction:** OB07
>
> **Table/view:** TCURV/V_TCURV

In SAP, all exchange rates are categorized according to *exchange rate types* that have *validity dates*. Using different exchange rate types, it is possible to store different exchange rates for the same validity date. By default, the system uses the exchange rate type M; however, in the document type settings, you can specify an alternative exchange rate type. If you do this, all postings made with that document type use the alternative exchange rate type, instead of exchange rate type M. You can see the exchange rate types implemented in your system via the menu path provided in the Quick Reference box. This screen is shown in Figure 1.10.

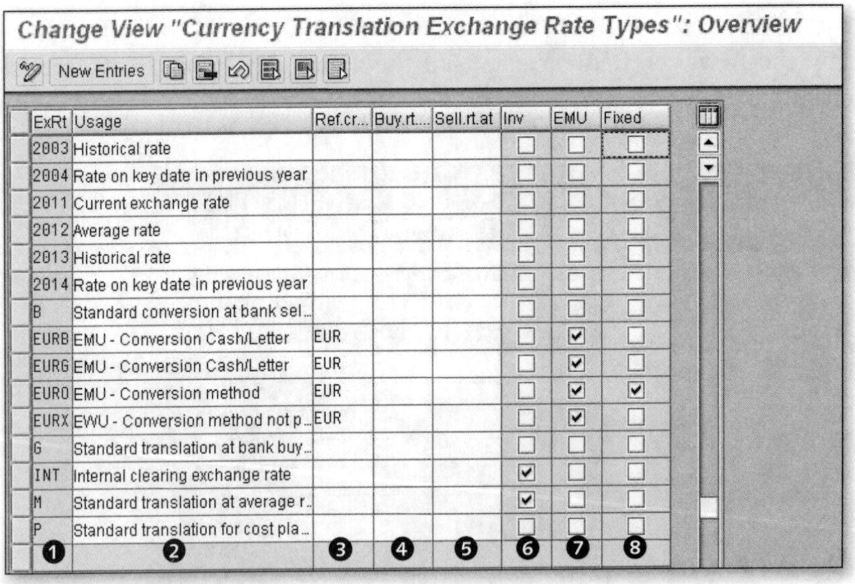

Change View "Currency Translation Exchange Rate Types": Overview

ExRt	Usage	Ref.cr...	Buy.rt...	Sell.rt.at	Inv	EMU	Fixed
2003	Historical rate				☐	☐	☐
2004	Rate on key date in previous year				☐	☐	☐
2011	Current exchange rate				☐	☐	☐
2012	Average rate				☐	☐	☐
2013	Historical rate				☐	☐	☐
2014	Rate on key date in previous year				☐	☐	☐
B	Standard conversion at bank sel...				☐	☐	☐
EURB	EMU - Conversion Cash/Letter	EUR			☐	☑	☐
EURG	EMU - Conversion Cash/Letter	EUR			☐	☑	☐
EURO	EMU - Conversion method	EUR			☐	☑	☑
EURX	EWU - Conversion method not p...	EUR			☐	☑	☐
G	Standard translation at bank buy...				☐	☐	☐
INT	Internal clearing exchange rate				☑	☐	☐
M	Standard translation at average r...				☑	☐	☐
P	Standard translation for cost pla...				☐	☐	☐

① ② ③ ④ ⑤ ⑥ ⑦ ⑧

Figure 1.10   Exchange Rate Types

In a live system, you should never change or delete the existing exchange rate types. Even if you don't use them in Financial Accounting, they are often used in other modules in the system, for example, the CFM module (Corporate Finance Management).

When you access the configuration of the exchange rate types, you see a matrix in which all of the exchange rate types in the system are displayed together with their customizing settings. All of the customizing settings are displayed in the screen; you don't need to double-click and drill down to access further settings.

If you need to create a new exchange rate type, select New Entries (in Figure 1.10), and specify the following:

▶ **ExRt**
This mandatory entry field is for the exchange rate type code.

▶ **Usage**
This mandatory entry field is for the description of the exchange rate type.

▶ **Ref.Crcy**
This optional entry field is for the reference currency. If there is a currency listed in this field, the system uses the *cross-rate exchange rate*. For example, if USD is listed as the reference currency, and you post a transaction that requires a translation from GBP to DKK, the system searches for the following exchange rates: GBP to USD and DKK to USD. It then performs the necessary math to get the correct exchange rate for GPB to DKK. This functionality allows you to maintain a much smaller number of exchange rates in the system; however, you must make sure it's permitted by legislative, accounting, and internal rules.

▶ **Buy.Rt.At**
This optional entry field is for the average exchange rate type for buying rate. You use this field for the exchange rate types whose rates are always derived by another exchange rate type, minus a spread. In this field, you enter the reference exchange rate type from which the rates are derived. You enter the spread under the customizing activity SAP NETWEAVER • GENERAL SETTINGS • CURRENCIES • MAINTAIN EXCHANGE RATE SPREADS. This isn't a very common functionality, so we just mention it for the sake of completeness.

▶ **Sell.Rt.At**
This optional entry field is for the average exchange rate type for selling rate. You use this field for the exchange rate types whose rates are always derived by

another exchange rate type, plus a spread. In this field, you enter the reference exchange rate type from which the rates are derived. You enter the spread under the customizing activity SAP NETWEAVER • GENERAL SETTINGS • CURRENCIES • MAINTAIN EXCHANGE RATE SPREADS. This isn't a very common functionality, so we just mention it for the sake of completeness.

▶ **Inv**
This optional entry field is for the allowed inverted exchange rate. This option allows you to reduce the number of entries for exchange rates. If this checkbox is selected, the system first searches for the specific exchange rate; if the specific exchange rate is missing, the system then uses the inverted exchange rate. As an example to demonstrate the use of inverted exchange rates, say you need to translate USD to EUR, but the specific exchange rate isn't listed in the system. If the Inv checkbox is set, the system searches for the inverted exchange rate, from EUR to USD. If found, it determines the exchange rate based on this inverted exchange rate (1 divided by the inverted exchange rate). If the inverted exchange rate isn't available, the system issues an error message, and you can't go ahead with your financial posting.

▶ **EMU**
The optional EMU (European Monetary Union) setting is typically used for the standard exchange rate types EURX and EURO; the setup of those two exchange rate types was necessary to comply with the introduction of the EURO currency in the years 1999 to 2002. For more information, consult the SAP notes using the two exchange rate types as keywords. You should not change this field after it's set.

▶ **Fixed**
When this optional entry setting is selected, and the correspondent exchange rate type is used, you can't specify in the posting an exchange rate different from the one valid for the date. This setting is typically used for the exchange rate type EURO; from 1999 to 2001, it was used to ensure that the postings between currencies that participated in the monetary union were carried out only at the legal exchange rate. You should not change this field after it's set.

When recording a transaction in Financial Accounting, you can let the system search for the correct exchange rate (based on validity dates) or enter the exchange rate manually (assuming that this option is allowed in your internal accounting policy). We discuss the manual entering of exchange rates later on in this chapter.

In some cases, it's possible to have multiple exchange rate types with the same validity dates. For example, say you have a company code that uses the local currency GBP. You post a transaction in USD with a posting date of 11/12/2009; you don't specify a different translation date, so the system uses the posting date to retrieve the most updated currency exchange rate. In the system, the following three exchange rates are valid for the date 11/12/2009:

▶ Exchange Rate Type M: 1.67

▶ Exchange Rate Type Y1: 1.70

▶ Exchange Rate Type Y2: 1.60

The system is configured so that it always uses exchange rate type M first; so, in this case, the correct exchange rate type is M, 1.67. (There is, however, a way to change this so that an alternative exchange rate type is used first as explained next.)

1.2.4   Defining Translation Ratios for Currency Translations

Quick Reference
Menu path: IMG • SAP NetWeaver • General Settings • Currencies • Define Translation Ratios for Currency Translation
Transaction: OBBS
Table/view: TCURF/V_TCURF

The definition of translation ratios for each pair of currencies (Table TCURF) is a prerequisite to enter the correspondent currency exchange rates for each validity date (Table TCURR). Figure 1.11 shows the connection between the two pieces of information.

In this customizing table (Table TCURF), the following fields appear:

▶ **ExRt**
This is the exchange rate type.

▶ **From**
This is the starting currency, in which the amount is available.

▶ **To**
This is the destination currency, to which the amount has to be converted.

TCURF

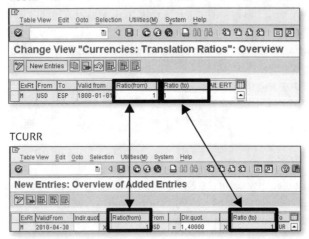

TCURR

Figure 1.11 Translation Ratios and Exchange Rates

▶ **Valid From**
This is the date from which the exchange rate ratios between the two currencies is valid.

▶ **Ratio (from)**
This is the ratio for the starting currency.

▶ **Ratio (to)**
This is the ratio for the destination currency.

▶ **Alt. ERT**
This is the field for the alternative exchange rate type. If another exchange rate type is specified here, the system uses this type. The alternative exchange rate type must have the same translation ratio as the original exchange rate type.

> **Warning!**
>
> You should only edit translation ratios when configuring new currencies: Don't change the translation ratios that are already in the system. The only time you might need to adjust already-existing ratios is if you are working in a currency with extremely high inflation rates. Even in that case, our recommendation is to carefully consider other alternatives. This requirement shouldn't be managed as a simple support request but in the framework of an entire project.

1.2.5 Entering Exchange Rates

Quick Reference

Menu path: ACCOUNTING • FINANCIAL ACCOUNTING • GENERAL LEDGER • ENVIRONMENT • CURRENT SETTINGS • ENTER TRANSLATION RATES – ENTER CURRENCY EXCHANGE RATES USING A WORKLIST

Transaction: OB08/TCURMNT (for the worklist)

Table/view: TCURR/V_TCURR

Transaction OB08 is the standard way of entering exchange rates (Figure 1.12).

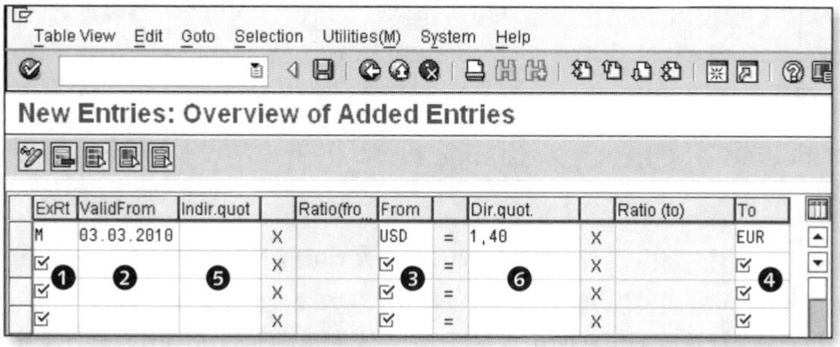

Figure 1.12 Entering Exchange Rates

Select the New Entries button, and enter the exchange rate type (❶), the validity date (❷), and the relevant currencies (❸, ❹). When entering an exchange rate manually, the way you enter it in the system depends on whether the exchange rate is direct (❺) or indirect (❻).

In fact, when making a Financial Accounting posting in foreign currency, you have the option to manually enter the exchange rate between the foreign currency and the local currency; you can use both the direct rate and the indirect rate. If you want to use the direct exchange rate, enter the exchange rate number exactly as it is. If you want to use the indirect exchange rate, put a "/" before the number. The character "/" is the standard protocol; however, the rule can be different if the standard settings have been edited, which may happen due to compatibility issues between SAP and a legacy system. To specify a prefix other than the slash for indirect exchange rates, use the following menu path: SAP NETWEAVER • GENERAL SETTINGS • CURRENCIES • ENTER PREFIXES FOR DIRECT/INDIRECT QUOTATION EXCHANGE RATES. The system will display two columns: "D" for the character to be placed in front of the direct exchange rate, and "I" for the character to be placed in front of the indirect exchange rate. We recommend that you leave the D column blank and to specify, if needed, a character other than "/" in the I column.

This is a general configuration, which isn't valid for a specific currency or currencies.

> **Warning!**
>
> You shouldn't change this setting in a live system. If for some reason it's absolutely necessary that you do, carefully check all of the consequences in the interface and in reporting. Plan a strong test cycle to ensure the consistency of your data.

You can't specify translation ratios here; they are filled automatically by the system based on the configurations found in SAP NETWEAVER • GENERAL SETTINGS • CURRENCIES • DEFINE TRANSLATION RATIOS FOR CURRENCY TRANSLATION, WHICH WE DISCUSSED IN SECTION 1.2.4, Defining Translation Ratios for Currency Translations.

In addition to that method of entering exchange rates, there are also a few other options:

► Using the Worklist functionality, create a worklist for all of the exchange rates that you periodically upload. Then, via SAP NETWEAVER • GENERAL SETTINGS • CURRENCIES • DEFINE WORKLIST FOR EXCHANGE RATE ENTRY, specify the frequency (this information will be used by the system only to help you to carry out the exchange rate update with the correct frequency) and the tolerance (maximum deviation from the last valid exchange rate). Then use Assign Exchange Rate to Worklist to specify all of the exchange rates that belong to the worklist (specify both the exchange rate types and pairs of currencies). Enter the exchange rates with Transaction TCURMNT.

► Create an LSMW and use either the recording function or the business object BUS1093.

► Use the program RFIMPNBS, which uploads EBC exchange rates based on an XML file (see SAP Note 1286897).

► Create a user-defined program.

1.2.6　Manual Entry Versus Automatic Retrieval of the Exchange Rate

When entering a general ledger posting in a currency different from the local currency (i.e., the company code currency) in the system, it's possible to directly specify the exchange rate. The system then compares the manually entered exchange rate with the one that the system would have used automatically. If they are different, the system issues a message about the percentage difference between the two exchange rates (Message F5 212). If the deviation is less than the permitted percentage, no message is issued.

> **Note**
>
> Message F5 212 is a warning only. If you press Enter, you can go ahead. However, you can also configure the message so that it can't be skipped. To do this, use the following menu path: ACCOUNTING • FINANCIAL ACCOUNTING • FINANCIAL ACCOUNTING GLOBAL SETTINGS • DOCUMENT • LINE ITEMS • DEFAULT VALUES FOR DOCUMENT PROCESSING • CHANGE MESSAGE CONTROL FOR DOCUMENT PROCESSING. Choose the area F5, insert a new row for Message 212, and then set the error status for online and batch processing.

You can also configure your system so that this message is issued only if the difference is greater than a certain percentage. This allowed percentage of deviation is specified in the Company Code Global Settings, in the Max. Exchange Rate Deviation field (Table T001, field WAABW). This percentage is unique to the company code. It's also possible to fix a percentage according to the combination of currencies.

The maximum exchange difference is customized via the following menu path: ACCOUNTING • FINANCIAL ACCOUNTING • FINANCIAL ACCOUNTING GLOBAL SETTINGS • DOCUMENT • DOCUMENT HEADER • MAXIMUM EXCHANGE RATE DIFFERENCE • DEFINE MAXIMUM EXCHANGE RATE DIFFERENCE PER COMPANY CODE AND DEFINE MAXIMUM EXCHANGE RATE DIFFERENCE PER FOREIGN CURRENCY (Figure 1.13).

In the customizing activity called Define Maximum Exchange Rate Difference per Company Code, select the company code and specify the percentage; in the customizing activity called Define Maximum Exchange Rate Difference per Foreign Currency, specify the pair of currencies (document currency and local currency) and define the percentage.

The system checks both limits, so the strictest (the lower percentage) will apply.

If you *don't* manually enter an exchange rate, the system automatically retrieves it based on validity dates.

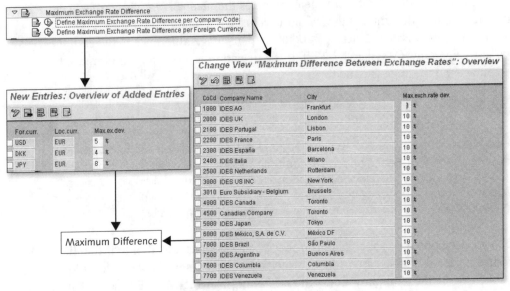

Figure 1.13 Maximum Exchange Rate Difference Configuration

> **Note**
>
> When you carry out a Financial Accounting posting in foreign currency (e.g., with Transaction FB50 or Transaction FB01), the system tries to retrieve the most up-to-date exchange rate between the foreign currency and the company code local currency. In this search, the system uses the translation date. You can manually specify the translation date; if you leave it empty, the system copies the posting date into the translation date.

1.2.7 FAQ and Troubleshooting Tips

Next we answer some frequently asked questions and offer helpful troubleshooting tips.

FAQ

1. **Question:** In a country with high inflation, a new currency has been introduced. Is there an easy way to replace the old currency with the new one?

   Answer: Unfortunately, no. The complexity of necessary changes depends on how you use the currency in your system. Are there company codes that use that currency as local currency? If so, it's necessary to manage the change as a project because it has a very high impact on your system. If, however, the currency is used just as a business partner currency, then the problem is easier to solve. In any case, you can't change the currency and the amount on the posted documents. These are unchangeable data points. Most likely, you'll have to create a new currency, and, at a certain time, require the use of the new one and prohibit the use of the old one. Depending on the amount of open items in the particular currency, a data migration could be necessary to close the open items in the old currency and reopen them in the new currency.

2. **Question:** Why can't I enter exchange rates directly into the production or test systems? It seems that the system recognizes this as a customizing activity. How can I avoid transporting the exchange rates by entering them directly into the test or production systems?

   Answer: This problem is quite common and is described and solved in SAP Note 356483. We suggest that you read this note with your SAP Basis colleagues and implement the proposed solution. Also try using Transaction TCUR-MNT in the production and test systems.

3. **Question:** I have a company outside Europe that uses USD as the local currency. When I post an amount in EUR, the system uses the exchange rate type EURX instead of M. Why?

   Answer: Check the customizing activity called Define Translation Ratios for Currency Translation. Most likely, EURX is listed as an alternative exchange rate type (column Alt. ERT). This is the reason the system searches for the exchange rate under the exchange rate type EURX instead of the exchange rate type M. If the system should not use the EURX exchange rate type, copy the entry and specify a validity date in the future; from the new entry, delete EURX from the field Alt. ERT field.

Troubleshooting Tips

1. **Issue:** When I post in a foreign currency, the system isn't taking the exchange rate from the most recent validity date. Why?

   Solution: When posting to Financial Accounting, the system uses the most recent exchange rate between the foreign currency and local currency stored under the exchange rate type M. However, exchange rates stored under validity dates (Valid From) higher than the translation date are not used because, from the point of view of the system, they refer to future dates.

2. **Issue:** When entering a currency exchange rate, I get the message "Missing translation ratios."

   Solution: In customizing, execute Transaction OBBS, and enter the translation ratios for the exchange rate type and pair of currency used.

1.3 Summary

In this chapter, we discussed some general, cross-application configuration settings that affect the Financial Accounting configuration. We described how countries are set up, and how country-specific controls can be activated for bank, tax, and address data. The second part of the chapter was about customizing currency, where we focused on the setup of a single currency, the exchange rate type functionality that allows you to save parallel exchange rates for the same pair of currencies, and the configuration settings for pairs of currencies. In the next chapter, we discuss the functions related to the global assignment of organizational entities in Financial Accounting.

This chapter covers the functions related to the global assignment of orga-
nizational entities in Financial Accounting, with major emphasis on com-
pany codes and controlling areas.

2   Organizational Structure: Definition and Assignment

In this chapter, we discuss the definition and assignment of the organizational entities relevant to Financial Accounting. The first section focuses on how to define
these entities, and the second section focuses on how to assign them.

2.1   Definition of Organizational Entities Relevant to Financial Accounting

In this section, we explain how to define the following organizational entities relevant for Financial Accounting:

- Company
- Company code
- Credit control area
- Business area
- Consolidation business area
- Functional area
- Controlling area
- Operating concern

> **Note**
>
> For information about segments, please refer to Section 3.6.7; for information about profit centers, refer to Section 3.6.8.

2.1.1   Company

A *company* (also known as an *internal trading partner*) is an organizational unit used for consolidation purposes. In general, you don't post directly to a company; instead, you assign a company code to a company and then post to that company code. By assigning a company to a company code, the company inherits the postings of the other company codes assigned to that company. In addition to being assigned to a company code, a company can also be assigned to customers and vendors, which helps you keep track of the transactions against your business partners. (Company codes will be discussed in more detail in Section 2.1.2, Company Code.)

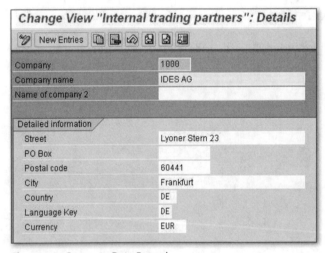

Figure 2.1 Company Data Record

You can create or change companies using Transaction OX15 (Figure 2.1). To create a new company, select the New Entries button, and then specify the name, address, language, and currency. (In general, the naming convention of the companies is defined by the parent company, the holding company of your group; if you don't know it, check with your accounting department.) Then save. No additional activity is required in this step.

Companies in a Global Special Ledger

If you use companies in a global special ledger, you have to assign the company to the ledger. (We discuss this in more detail in Chapter 8, Special Purpose Ledger.)

If the company is used in non-standard tables (i.e., tables that start with a Z or a Y), you may need to update them when you create a new company. You can search for non-standard tables that use the company by following these steps:

1. Run Transaction SE11.

2. Select the Data Type option, and specify the RASSC value. Then select UTILITIES • WHERE-USED LIST.

3. Select the Table Fields option, and click on the Search Area button.

4. In the Object Name field, specify the values Y* and Z*. Confirm the selection, and click the Continue button (✔). The system then displays a list of the non-standard tables that use the company.

Searching the Usage of Company in Tables

In some tables, it's possible to use a data type different from RASSC. To see all similar data types, specify the RASSC data type, and then click on the Display button. In the following screen, the domain to which the data type belongs is displayed; double-click on the domain (for RASSC, it's RCOMP). From UTILITIES • WHERE-USED LIST, select Data Elements. The system displays all of the similar data elements.

The company is also used to keep track of transactions that are performed against a subject that belongs to the same consolidation group. For this purpose, you can manually specify a company in the Financial Accounting document. Alternatively, you can specify the company in the following types of master data (if you do this, the documents that use these master data will automatically contain this information):

▶ Assets (Table ANLA)

▶ General ledger account (Table SKA1)

▶ Customer (Table KNA1)

▶ Vendor (Table LFA1)

2.1.2   Company Code

Quick Reference
Menu path: IMG • Enterprise Structure • Definition • Financial Accounting • Edit, Copy, Delete, Check Company Code
Transactions: OX02 (edit company code), EC01 (copy, delete, check company code)
Table/view: T001/V_T001

You can create a company code in two ways:

▶ Copy an existing company code and then change the necessary settings (e.g., the company code description, the currency, etc.). The system automatically performs most of the necessary customizing settings, copying them from the reference company code.

▶ Create a company code from scratch; in this case, you need to perform all of the company code customizing settings step by step.

When you run Transaction EC01, the system presents two alternatives (Figure 2.2):

▶ **Copy, Delete, Check Company Code**
Due to the large number of customizing steps needed to configure a company code from scratch, we highly recommend using this method. To copy an existing company code to the new one, select the Copy Org. Object button (🗋) and specify the reference company code (From Company Code) and the company code to be created (To Company Code). Confirm. The system asks you two questions:

   ▶ Do you want to copy the general ledger accounts from the reference company code? You should always answer "No" if the new company code must have a different chart of accounts. However, you can always copy the accounts from a reference company using Transaction FS15. In general, we recommend not copying the general ledger accounts.

   ▶ Do you want to create the new company code with a different currency? If yes, specify the new currency.

After the copy is done, review the company code customizing with the transactions listed in Table 2.1. All of the relevant settings are described in detail in subsequent chapters.

> ### Deleting and Renaming Company Codes
>
> In the screen where you copy the company code, you can also perform two additional activities:
>
> - Delete the company code: If you incorrectly created a company code, and you've never used it in a production system, you can use the Delete button (🗑) to erase all of the customizing settings that refer to the specified company code.
> - Rename the company code: If you created a company code with an incorrect ID, and you've never used it in a production system, you can use the Rename button (📇) so that all customizing settings that refer to the specified company code are transferred to a company code with a new ID. (The old company code will no longer exist in the system.)

- **Edit Company Code Data**

  Use this transaction to start the creation of a company code with the step-by-step technique. Specify company code ID, name, and address. Then perform all of the needed customizing settings; you can use Table 2.1 as a checklist. Note that many of the listed transactions may not be needed in your SAP implementation.

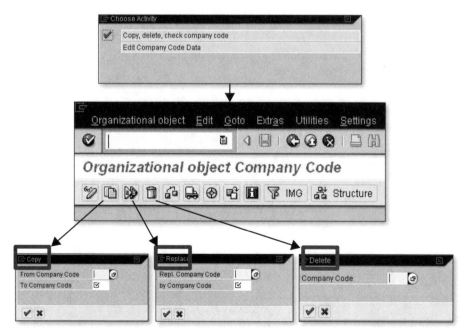

Figure 2.2 Company Code Definition Tools

Non-Standard Tables

If you need to add the company code to non-standard tables and you want to know which tables must be updated, follow the procedure described in Section 2.1.1, Company Code, using the data type BUKRS.

Table 2.1 can be used as a checklist for creating a company code from scratch. Note that only the customizing that involves company-code-specific entries is included. If the new company code belongs to a country for which no specific configuration is already available in the system, you must perform additional steps (e.g., the definition of VAT codes in the new country).

Transaction	Description
OX02	Edit, Copy, Delete, Check Company Code
OX16	Assign Company Code to Company
OB38	Assign Company Code to Credit Control Area
OF18	Assign Company Code to Financial Management Area
OX19	Assign Company Code to Controlling Area
OX18	Assign Plant to Company Code
OVX3	Assign Sales Organization to Company Code
OX01	Assign Purchasing Organization to Company Code
OH05	Assignment of Personnel Area to Company Code
OBB5	Cross-System Company Codes
OBY6	Enter Global Parameters
OB22	Define Additional Local Currencies
OBR3	Set Company Code to Productive
OB37	Assign Company Code to a Fiscal Year Variant
OBB9	Assign Posting Period Variants to Company Code
FBN1	Define Document Number Ranges
OBH1	Copy Number Ranges to Company Code
OBH2	Copy Number Ranges to Fiscal Year
OB28	Validation in Accounting Documents
OBBH	Substitution in Accounting Documents

Table 2.1 Checklist for Creating a New Company Code

Transaction	Description
OB64	Define Maximum Exchange Rate Difference per Company Code
OBC5	Assign Company Code to Field Status Variants
OBA4	Define Tolerance Groups for Employees
OB32	Document Change Rules, Line Item
OB63	Enable Fiscal Year Default
OB68	Default Value Date
OBWJ	Assign Company Code to a Workflow Variant for Parking Documents
SM30/TBUVTX	Transfer Posting of Tax for Cross-Company Code Transactions
SM30/V_T001WT	Assign Withholding Tax Types to Company Codes
SM30/V_T001_EXT	Activate Extended Withholding Tax
OB62	Assign Company Code to Chart of Accounts
OB67	Assign Company Code to Rule Type (Sample Accounts)
OB78	Assign Programs for Correspondence Types
OBYA	Prepare Cross-Company Code Transactions
SM30/V_001_NP	Permit Negative Posting
SM30/V_TACE001_BUKRS	Assign Company Codes to Accrual Engine
sm30/V_TACE_COMBINATN	Accrual Engine: Assign Accounting Principle to Company Code
OB21	Define Screen Layout per Company Code (Customers)
OB24	Define Screen Layout per Company Code (Vendors)
SM30/V_T076B	Assign Company Code for EDI Incoming Invoice
OBBE	Define Reason Codes (Manual Outgoing Payments)
OB60	Prepare Cross-Company Code Manual Payments
FBZP	Automatic Payment Global Setup
OBZO	Define Document Types for Enjoy Transactions
OBA3	Define Tolerances (Customers)
SPRO/V_T076B	Assign Company Code for EDI Payment Advice Notes

Table 2.1 Checklist for Creating a New Company Code (Cont.)

Transaction	Description
OB61	Define Dunning Areas
SM30/T047	Company Code Dunning Control
OBBA	Define Value Date Rules
OBA8	Bill of Exchange Receivables: Define Additional Days for Remaining Risk
OB54	Define Failed Payment Transactions (Bills of Exchange)
OT67	Returned Bills of Exchange Payable: Define Exception Types
OT68	Define Account for Returned Bills of Exchange
OT65	Assign Forms for Returned Bills of Exchange Payable
OT66	Define Sender Details for Form for Returned Bills of Exchange
SM30/V_T018V	Define Clearing Accts. for Receiving Bank for Acct. Transfer
SM30/V_ATPRA_FI	Define Clearing Accounts for Cross-Country Bank Account Transfers
SM30/V_T042Y	Bank Clearing Account Determination
SM30/V_TBKDC	Define Diff. in Days Betw. Value Date of House/Partner Bank
SM30/V_TBKPV	Define Number of Days Between Payment Run Date and Value Date at House Bank
SM30/V_T042EA	Define ALE-Compatible Payment Methods
OBAV	Prepare Payment Authorization/POR Procedure
SM30/V_TCJ_MAX_ AMOUNT	Cash Journal: Amount Limit
FBCJC1	Define Number Range Intervals for Cash Journal Documents
FBCJC0	Set Up Cash Journal
FBCJC2	Create, Change, Delete Business Transactions (Cash Journal)
FBCJC3	Set Up Print Parameters for Cash Journal
OAB1	Assign Chart of Depreciation to Company Code
AO11	Specify Number Assignment Across Company Codes
OBCL	Assign Input Tax Indicator for Non-Taxable Acquisitions
OAYN	Specify Financial Statement Version for Asset Reports
OAB3	Specify Document Type for Posting of Depreciation

Table 2.1 Checklist for Creating a New Company Code (Cont.)

Transaction	Description
OAYR	Assets: Specify Intervals and Posting Rules for Depreciation
ACSET	Specify Account Assignment Types for Account Assignment Objects
OAMK	Assets: Reset Reconciliation Accounts
SM30/V_T093C_APER	Specify Document Type for Periodic Posting of Asset Values
OAYK	Specify Amount for Low Value Assets
OAYO	Specify Rounding of Net Book Value and/or Depreciation
OAYJ	Specify Changeover Amount
OAYI	Specify Memo Value for Depreciation Areas
SM30/V_T093C_06	Specify Other Versions on Company Code Level
OAYP	Define Reduction Rules for Shortened Fiscal Years
SM30/V_T093C_07	Use of Half Months in the Company Code
OAYL	Specify Areas for Individual Period Weighting
OAYH	Define Depreciation Areas for Foreign Currencies
OAYM	Specify Depreciation Areas for Group Assets
AO25	Define Unit-of-Production Depreciation
AFAM_093B	Propose Values for Depreciation Areas and Company Codes
AFAM_093C	Propose Acquisition Only in Capitalization Year for Company Codes
SM30/V_T093C_10	Assign Time-Dependent Period Controls to Dep. Keys
OAW2	Define Maximum Base Value
OAYQ	Reserves for Special Depreciation: Specify Gross or Net Procedure
OAYR	Revaluation of Fixed Assets: Maintain Posting Rules
SM30/J_1AVAA02	Revaluation of Fixed Assets: Revaluation Keys
SM30/J_1AVAA05A	Maintain Additional Settings for Inflation Transaction Types
AO31	Net Worth Tax: Specify Depreciation Area
SM30/V_T093C_16	Assets: Specify Time-Independent Management of Organiz. Units

Table 2.1 Checklist for Creating a New Company Code (Cont.)

Transaction	Description
AOCO	Specify Cost Center Check Across Company Codes
OARC	Assets: Specify Retention Periods for Archiving
OACV	Assets: Define Validation
OACS	Assets: Define Substitution
sm30/V_T093C_NOSKONTO	Prevent Subsequent Capitalization of Discounts
OA01	Determine Asset for Gain/Loss Individually (Substitution)
AO72	Post Net Book Value Instead of Gain/Loss
OAAZ	Asset Under Construction: Assign Settlement Profile to Company Code
OAYU	Specify Capitalization of AUC/Down-Payment
SM30/V_T093C_15	Asset Under Construction: Assign Value Date Variant to Company Code
SM30/V_T093C_09	Assets: Set Company Code Status
OAYE	Asset Data Transfer: Specify Sequence of Depreciation Areas
SM30/V_T093C_08	Asset Data Transfer: Specify Transfer Date/Last Closed Fiscal Year
OAYC	Asset Data Transfer: Specify Last Period Posted in Prv. System (Transf. During FY)
SM30/V_T093C_11	Asset Data Transfer: Specify Entry of Net Book Value (No Accum. Ordinary Depr.)
OAYF	Asset Data Transfer: Recalculate Depreciation for Previous Years
SM30/V_T093C_12	Asset Data Transfer: Recalculate Base Insurable Values
OAYG	Asset Data Transfer: Recalculate Replacement Values
OAYD	Asset Data Transfer: Transfer Foreign Currency Areas
GCL2	Assign Company Code to Ledger
GCVV	Maintain Local Validations (Special Ledger)
GCVX	Maintain Local Substitutions (Special Ledger)
GCP3	Maintain Local Version Parameters (Special Ledger)
GB02	Maintain Local Number Ranges - Plan (Special Ledger)

Table 2.1 Checklist for Creating a New Company Code (Cont.)

Transaction	Description
GB04	Maintain Local Number Ranges - Actuals (Special Ledger)
SM37	Check Variants in Scheduled Programs
SM30	Check Company Code Usage in Non-Standard (Y* or Z*) Tables
SE71	Check Forms (SAPscripts)
SMARTFORMS	Check Smart Forms
SO10	Check Standard Texts

Table 2.1 Checklist for Creating a New Company Code (Cont.)

2.1.3 Credit Control Area

Quick Reference
Menu path: IMG • Enterprise Structure • Definition • Financial Accounting • Define Credit Control Area
Transaction: OB45
Table/view: T014/V_T014

The credit control area is the organizational unit under which the credit management tools of Financial Accounting are managed. It can be company-code-specific, or comprise more than one company code. (See Section 2.2.2, Company Code to Credit Control Area, for more information about the relationship between the credit control area and the company code.)

Use Transaction OB45 to create a new credit control area or to check the settings of existing ones (Figure 2.3). Specify the credit control area code (four digits) and the description.

The following additional customizing settings are available for each credit control area:

► **Currency (❶)**
One credit control area can comprise many company codes. The company codes can have different local currencies, but there is just one credit limit. The currency in which the credit limit is managed is specified here, in the credit control area.

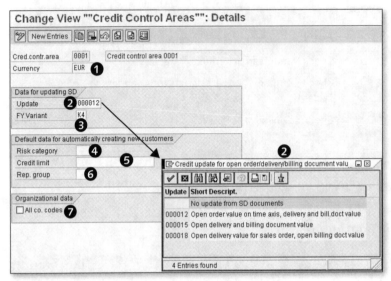

Figure 2.3 Credit Control Area Customizing Settings

- **Data for Updating SD (❷)**

  The settings in this area of Figure 2.3 are extremely important for credit controlling. The Update field specifies which SD (Sales and Distribution) documents update the credit exposure of the customer, which is compared to the credit limit when a new transaction is carried out. The credit exposure is recorded in the customer credit master (Transaction FD32) and is broken down into the following four values:

  - Sales orders

  - Deliveries

  - Billing documents not posted to Financial Accounting

  - Financial Accounting balances

  When a sales order is delivered, the sales order exposure is reduced, and the exposure for the deliveries is increased. The same happens for the other steps in the sales chain. The Update field specifies whether the credit exposure is updated when you receive an order from a customer, or when the goods are delivered. Four options are available:

  - **Blank:** No update from SD. Only the Financial Accounting documents update the credit exposure. SD orders, delivery, and billing documents not yet posted to Financial Accounting don't have any effect on the credit exposure.

- ▶ **000012:** The sales orders, deliveries, billing documents, and Financial Accounting documents update the credit exposure.

- ▶ **000015:** Deliveries and Financial Accounting documents update the credit exposure.

- ▶ **000018:** Sales orders, billing documents, and Financial Accounting documents update the credit exposure.

▶ **FY Variant (❸)**
This is used to update the value for the sales order exposure based on the forecasted delivery date (Table SSSS).

▶ **Risk Category (❹)**
If you specify a value here, all of the newly created customers (in one of the company codes that belong to the credit control area) are automatically assigned to the specified risk category.

▶ **Credit Limit (❺)**
If you specify a value here, all of the newly created customers (in one of the company codes that belong to the credit control area) automatically receive the specified credit limit.

▶ **Rep. Group (❻)**
If you specify a value here, all of the newly created customers (in one of the company codes that belong to the credit control area) are automatically assigned to the specified representative group.

▶ **All Co. Codes (❼)**
If you select this flag, all of the company codes present in the system can post to this credit control area.

2.1.4 Business Area

Quick Reference

Menu path: IMG • ENTERPRISE STRUCTURE • DEFINITION • FINANCIAL ACCOUNTING • DEFINE BUSINESS AREA

Transaction: OX03

Table/view: TGSB/V_TGSB

The business area is an organizational unit that you can use freely for internal or external reporting to depict segmentation of you business within or across company codes. The business area is available in general ledger reporting (in both the classic General Ledger and the new SAP General Ledger), and can be set up in the special ledger tables.

You create a business area using Transaction OX03 (Figure 2.4). Specify the business area code (four digits) and the description, and save your entries.

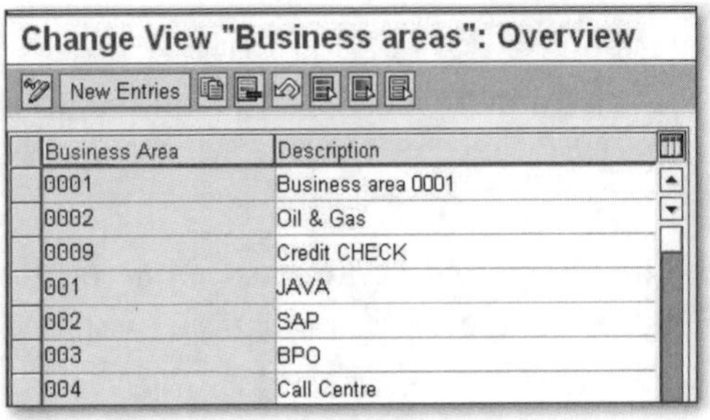

Figure 2.4 Business Areas

If you use the consolidation business areas, you assign the business area to the consolidation business area; see Section 2.2.3, Business Area to Consolidation Business Area, for more details about this.

The business area can be assigned to the following financial and controlling objects:

▶ Asset classes (Table ANKA)

▶ Fixed assets (Table ANLP)

▶ Cost centers (Table CSKS)

▶ Internal orders (Table AUFK)

▶ Investment program positions (Table IMPR)

▶ Project definitions (Table PROJ)

▶ WBS elements (Table PRPS)

If you need to add the business area to non-standard-tables, and you want to know which tables must be updated, follow the procedure described in Section 2.1.1, Company, using the data type GSBER.

2.1.5 Consolidation Business Area

Menu path: IMG • ENTERPRISE STRUCTURE • DEFINITION • FINANCIAL ACCOUNTING • MAINTAIN CONSOLIDATION BUSINESS AREA

Transaction: OCC1

Table/view: TGSBK/V_ TGSBK

You manage company codes and assign them to companies for consolidation purposes. In the same way, you can assign business areas to consolidation business areas for internal consolidation purposes.

Create a consolidation business area using Transaction OCC1 (Figure 2.5). Specify the consolidation business area code (four digits long, according to the naming convention defined in your SAP implementation) and description. Then assign the business areas to the consolidation business areas, as described in Section 2.2.3, Business Area to Consolidation Business Area.

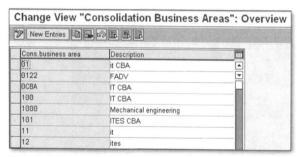

Figure 2.5 Consolidation Business Area

The consolidation business area can be managed in general ledgers, special ledgers, and in the SAP consolidation tools.

2.1.6 Functional Area

Menu path: IMG • ENTERPRISE STRUCTURE • DEFINITION • FINANCIAL ACCOUNTING • DEFINE FUNCTIONAL AREA

Transactions: OKBD (older releases), FM_FUNCTION (new releases)

Table/view: TFKB/V_TFKB

With the functional area, you can keep track of the macro-departments where costs and revenues arise, for example:

▶ Administration

▶ Production

▶ Procurement

▶ Sales

▶ Human Resources

This type of accounting (i.e., accounting by department) is called *cost-of-sales accounting*.

You create functional areas using Transaction FM_FUNCTION (OKBD in older releases). For each of them, specify the functional area ID (16-digit maximum) and the functional area description (Figure 2.6).

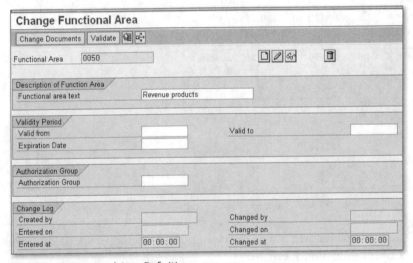

Figure 2.6 Functional Area Definition

Functional area transaction data are updated in real time in the ledger OF (Total Table GLFUNCT, and Line Item Table GLFUNCA). The functional area can also be used in your general ledgers and special ledgers.

You can assign the functional area in the master data of the following objects:

▶ Fixed assets (Table ANLP)

▶ Cost elements (Table CSKA)

- Cost centers (Table CSKS)
- Cost center categories (Table TKA05)
- Internal orders (Table AUFK)
- Investment program positions (Table IMPR)
- Project definitions (Table PROJ)
- WBS elements (Table PRPS)
- General ledger accounts (Table SKA1)

It's also possible to use substitutions for the functional data update:

- Transaction OBZM for functional area substitutions
- Transaction OBBZ for assigning the substitutions to company codes

---

Note on Functional Area Activation

To use the functional data in the master data specified previously and to have the transaction data updated by functional area, you need to activate the cost of sales accounting in customizing. Go to FINANCIAL ACCOUNTING • FINANCIAL ACCOUNTING GLOBAL SETTINGS • COMPANY CODE • COST OF SALES ACCOUNTING • ACTIVATE COST OF SALES ACCOUNTING. You also need to update the settings of the ledger 0F using Transaction GCL2; for example, you need to assign the company code to the ledger. Refer to Chapter 7, Banking, for more details about this.

If you need to add the functional area in non-standard tables and you want to know which tables must be updated, follow the procedure described in Section 2.1.1, Company, using the data type FKBER.

2.1.7 Controlling Area

Quick Reference

Menu path: IMG • ENTERPRISE STRUCTURE • DEFINITION • CONTROLLING • MAINTAIN CONTROLLING AREA

Transaction: OX06

Table/view: TKA01/V_TKA01_GD

The controlling area is the organizational unit under which the Controlling (CO) module works. Cost centers, profit centers, WBS elements, internal orders, and cost elements are all objects whose master data are managed under a controlling area. You assign one or more company codes to a controlling area; see Section 2.2.4, Company Code to Controlling Area, for instructions about how to do this.

> **Note on Controlling Area Creation**
>
> Refer to a SAP Controlling manual for a full description of how to create a controlling area. A brief description is provided in this manual, but a more comprehensive description is beyond the scope of the book.

Create the controlling area using Transaction OX06, and follow these steps:

1. Select New Entries, and specify the controlling area code (four digits, according to the naming convention defined for your SAP installation) and a description. Then select Basic Data.

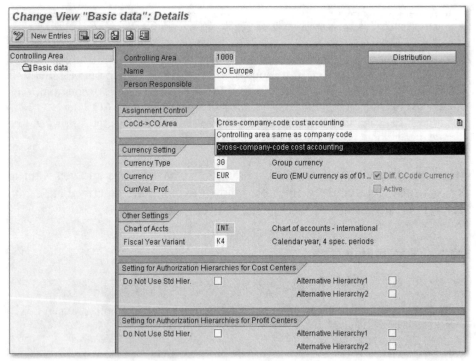

Figure 2.7 Controlling Area Settings

2. In the Basic Data screen (Figure 2.7), specify some of the most important settings of the controlling area; refer to a CO manual for a comprehensive descrip-

tion of the meaning of those settings. For the organizational structure definition, the CoCd → CO Area field is fundamental; here, you specify if the controlling area can be assigned to exactly one company code (Controlling Area Same as Company Code) or to more than one company code (Cross-Company-Code Cost Accounting).

2.1.8 Operating Concern

Quick Reference

Menu path: IMG • Enterprise Structure • Definition • Controlling • Create Operating Concern

Transaction: KEP8

Table: TKEB

The operating concern is the organizational unit that occupies the highest level of the SAP organizational hierarchy. It is used in the Profitability Analysis module, where you can analyze the profit and loss of your company according to multiple dimensions, such as customers, regions, products, and so on. You assign controlling areas to exactly one operating concern; thus, each company code is also assigned to exactly one operating concern. Refer to a CO manual for a comprehensive guide to the creation of the operating concern and the configuration of the COPA SAP module; a more thorough discussion than is provided here is beyond the scope of this book.

Using Transaction KEP8 (Figure 2.8), you can create the operating concern ID and the description. All of the specific customizing settings and the generation of the COPA environment are performed using Transaction KEA0.

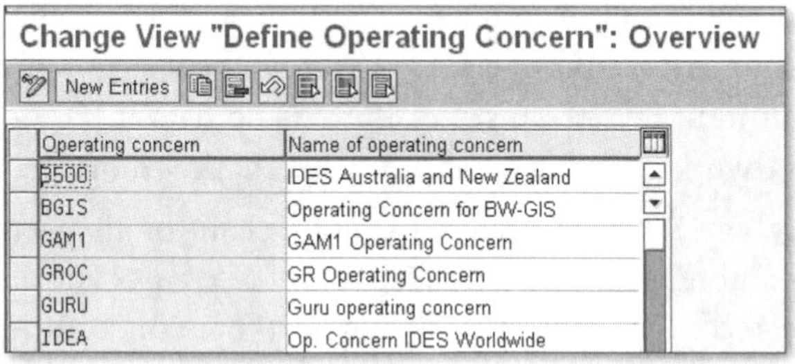

Figure 2.8 Operating Concern

2.1.9 FAQ and Troubleshooting Tips

Next we answer some frequently asked questions and offer helpful troubleshooting tips.

FAQ

1. **Question:** Are the company and the trading partner the same object in SAP?

   Answer: Yes. The terms "company," "trading partner," and "internal trading partner" are synonymous and all refer to the same organizational unit in SAP.

2. **Question:** What is the difference between the company and the global company code?

   Answer: The company is used in your system to keep track of the company code transactions and intercompany transactions from a consolidation point of view; the global company code is needed to exchange information between SAP systems with ALE (Application Linking and Embedding) interfaces.

3. **Question:** When I copy one company code into another, what happens to the number ranges?

   Answer: The number ranges are copied from one company code to the other but not recorded into the transport request. For internal number ranges, the last number used is also copied.

4. **Question:** I've changed the update mode in the credit control area and transported to production. What should I do to have the new settings applied to all of the existing customers?

   Answer: If the update mode is changed, the system has to re-read all of the relevant SD and Financial Accounting documents to get the credit exposure updated. Run Transaction F.28 for the reconstruction of the credit limit.

5. **Question:** I haven't specified any default data for new customers (Risk Category, Credit Limit, and Rep. Group left blank). I expected that the new customers would be set up with a credit limit of zero; instead, there is no data in FD32, and the credit control doesn't work at all for the customer. What's wrong?

   Answer: If you don't specify any default value in the credit control area settings, the new customers are automatically set up as irrelevant to credit controlling (in technical terms, the record in Table KNKK, where the credit control information is stored, isn't created). To make the customer relevant for credit controlling, you must manually process the customer using Transaction FD32. If you want to ensure that new customers are automatically set up for credit controlling, make sure at least one entry in the Default Data for Automatically Creating New Customers area (refer to Figure 2.3) is supplied. This guarantees that the customer is automatically created in Table KNKK.

6. **Question:** If I put a default value for Risk Category and/or Rep. Group, but I don't specify any default credit limit, will the new customers automatically have a credit limit of zero?

   Answer: Yes, exactly.

7. **Question:** What is the relationship between the business area and the company code? Can I specify the possible business areas for each company code?

   Answer: There is no hierarchical relationship between the company code and the business area; as such, there is no standard customizing activity to assign a business area to a company code, or to assign a company code to a business area. If you want to limit the possible business areas in one company code, you can create a validation. If the control requires a complete mapping between several business areas and company codes, it may be worth creating a non-standard table. In this case, you must use a user exit in the validation to use the table for control purposes.

8. **Question:** Can I still use the business area in SAP General Ledger?

   Answer: Yes, the business area can be used as a dimension in SAP General Ledger. If you look at the standard total table for SAP General Ledger, FAGL-FLEXT, the field RBUSA (Business Area) is included, so you don't need to enhance the SAP General Ledger tables using Transaction FAGL_GINS. However, if you are planning to upgrade from the classic General Ledger to SAP General Ledger, you should consider using profit centers and segments instead, as SAP is focusing its development on these two dimensions for segment reporting.

9. **Question:** Is table group GLFUNC* still available if I use SAP General Ledger?

   Answer: Yes, it can be used as a dimension in SAP General Ledger. If you look at the standard total table for SAP General Ledger, FAGLFLEXT, the field RFAREA (Functional Area) is included, so you don't need to enhance the SAP General Ledger tables using Transaction FAGL_GINS.

10. **Question:** If I change the assignment of an object to a functional area, does it affect the old postings or only the newly created postings?

    Answer: In general ledger accounting tables and in the GLFUNC* tables, the system updates the records with the functional area available at the time of the postings. The reporting that reads these tables reads the historical assignment to the functional area, not the assignment at the time the report is run.

11. **Question:** In my SAP implementation, SAP General Ledger isn't active. I'm trying to run Program RFBILA00, but I can't get the functional area in the output.

    Answer: The functional area isn't updated in Table GLT0, where the transaction data is read from Program RFBILA00. The function isn't supported.

12. **Question:** What does the generation of the COPA environment mean?

    Answer: The COPA tables are specific to each operating concern; in other words, the COPA table names include the name of each operating concern. Therefore, the COPA tables are created by you, online, after you have completed the COPA customizing. The COPA environment generation is the creation of the COPA operating-concern-specific tables.

13. **Question:** Why is it possible to create the operating concern with Transaction KEP8 with minimal settings (operating concern code and ID)? Wouldn't it be better to create an operating concern using Transaction KEA0, where a complete COPA setup is possible?

    Answer: The system allows the creation of an operating concern with minimal settings so that the user can build up the enterprise structure, including the assignment of controlling areas to operating concerns, in an early stage of the SAP implementation project. At this point, it's likely that high-level decisions on the structure of the controlling have been made, but all of the details about the building of the COPA module (characteristics, key figures, etc.) aren't yet defined.

Troubleshooting Tips

1. **Issue:** The extended withholding tax customizing isn't copied.

    Solution: Create the customizing manually. Maintain views (Transaction SM30) V_T001WT and V_T001_EXT with the company-code-relevant data.

2. **Issue:** I receive error message TK455, "Enter numeric values only," when copying the company code.

    Solution: The error and the relevant solution is described in SAP Note 494490.

3. **Issue:** I receive message FC125, "Certain data was not copied," when copying the company code.

   Solution: This is just an information message. The following assignments aren't copied from the source to the destination company code:

   ▶ Assignment of company code to company. Perform this assignment using Transaction OX16

   ▶ Assignment of company code to FM area. Perform this assignment using Transaction OF18.

   ▶ Assignment of company code to cross-system company code (or global company code). Perform this assignment using Transaction OBY6.

   ▶ Assignment of company code to controlling area. Perform this assignment using Transaction OX19.

4. **Issue:** I receive error message FC158 when copying the company code.

   Solution: If the source company code is assigned to profit center ledger 8A, the destination company code inherits the same assignment — even though the assignment to the controlling area isn't copied. You can't use profit center accounting in a company code without assigning the company code to a controlling area; to avoid this error message, make sure this is done.

2.2 Assignment of Organizational Entities Relevant to Financial Accounting

Now that you understand how to define the organizational entities relevant for Financial Accounting, we explain how to assign them. In this section, we discuss the following assignments:

▶ Company code to company

▶ Company code to credit control area

▶ Business area to consolidation business area

▶ Company code to controlling area

▶ Controlling area to operating concern

▶ Plant to company code

▶ Sales organization to company code

▶ Personnel area to company code

(Refer to the appropriate manuals for information about the creation of plants, sales organizations, and personnel areas; because they aren't Financial Accounting or Controlling organizational entities, we don't discuss them here.)

2.2.1 Company Code to Company

> **Quick Reference**
>
> **Menu path:** IMG • ENTERPRISE STRUCTURE • ASSIGNMENT • FINANCIAL ACCOUNTING • ASSIGN COMPANY CODE TO COMPANY
>
> **Transaction:** OX16
>
> **Table/view:** T001/V_001_Y

For consolidation purposes, each company code can be assigned to a company. Use Transaction OX16 (Figure 2.9) for this purpose. The system automatically presents all of the company codes available, and you specify the company to which they belong in the Company column. Save your settings. Note that this step can also be performed in Transaction OBY6, together with all of the most relevant settings of the company code.

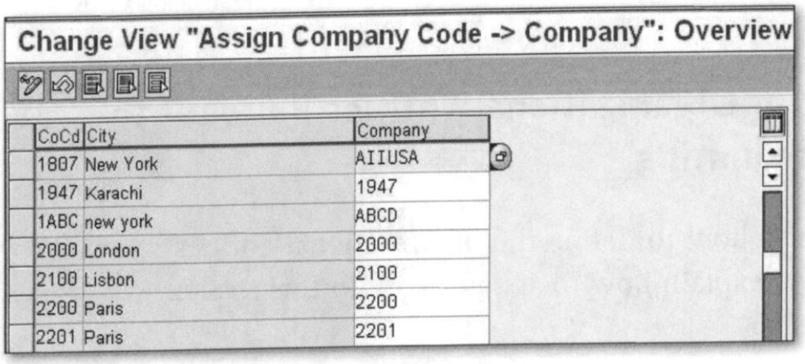

Change View "Assign Company Code -> Company": Overview

CoCd	City	Company
1807	New York	AIIUSA
1947	Karachi	1947
1ABC	new york	ABCD
2000	London	2000
2100	Lisbon	2100
2200	Paris	2200
2201	Paris	2201

Figure 2.9 Assign Company Code to Company

2.2.2 Company Code to Credit Control Area

> **Quick Reference**
>
> **Menu path:** IMG • ENTERPRISE STRUCTURE • ASSIGNMENT • FINANCIAL ACCOUNTING • ASSIGN COMPANY CODE TO CREDIT CONTROL AREA
>
> **Transaction:** OB38
>
> **Table/view:** T001/V_001_X

The SAP Credit Management module allows you to keep track of the credit exposure of customers and also to set credit limits. You can also issue warnings or error messages if the credit exposures overrun a certain percentage of the credit limit. The credit management isn't performed at the company code level but at the credit control area level, and you must assign each company code to a credit control area. The same credit control area can have one or many company codes assigned to it. Each time a transaction relevant for the credit control is performed in the company code, the credit exposure in the connected credit control area is updated, and the credit limit set in the connected credit control area is checked.

You assign the company code to the credit control area in customizing using Transaction OB38. The system presents all of the company codes, and you specify the connected credit control area in the relevant column (Figure 2.10). In addition, you can specify whether it's possible to use a different credit control area in the document itself by selecting the Overwrite CC Area flag in the last column of the screen.

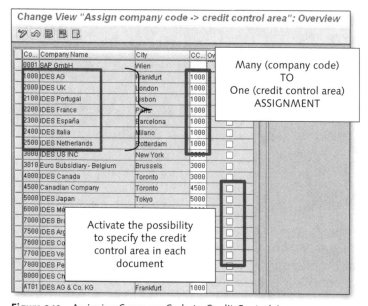

Figure 2.10 Assigning Company Code to Credit Control Area

2.2.3 Business Area to Consolidation Business Area

> **Quick Reference**
>
> **Menu path:** IMG • ENTERPRISE STRUCTURE • ASSIGNMENT • FINANCIAL ACCOUNTING • AS-SIGN BUSINESS AREA TO CONSOLIDATION BUSINESS AREA
>
> **Transaction:** OBB6
>
> **Table/view:** TGSB/V_GSB_A

You assign each business area to a consolidation business area using Transaction OBB6. The system presents all of the business areas available in the system and allows you to assign them to a consolidation business area in the Cons.Bus.Area column. This is all you need to do under the Enterprise Structure definition.

Note that the consolidation business area has a very limited use in the SAP environment; as such, you should make an in-depth investigation before deciding to use this organizational unit in your SAP implementation. For example, unlike the business area, the consolidation business area isn't updated in the general ledger total tables GLT0 and FLAGFLEXT, so it's not available in most of the standard Financial Accounting reports.

2.2.4 Company Code to Controlling Area

> **Quick Reference**
>
> **Menu path:** IMG • ENTERPRISE STRUCTURE • ASSIGNMENT • CONTROLLING • ASSIGN COMPANY CODE TO CONTROLLING AREA
>
> **Transaction:** OX19
>
> **Table/view:** TKA02/V_TKA02

You assign each company code to a controlling area to manage your internal controlling in an integrated way. Note that activities such as internal allocations of costs can be performed between objects (such as cost centers) that belong to different company codes only if the two company codes belong to the same controlling area.

To assign a company code to a controlling area, use the path specified in the preceding box and follow these steps (Figure 2.11):

1. Select a Controlling area, and double-click the Assignment of Company Code(s) folder (❶).

2. In the right side of the resulting screen, you can see the company codes assigned to the controlling area you have selected (❷). To assign a new controlling area, select New Entries.

3. If you click on the matchcode for the company codes, the system displays all of the company codes not yet assigned to a controlling area. Select the company code you want to assign, and save your entries.

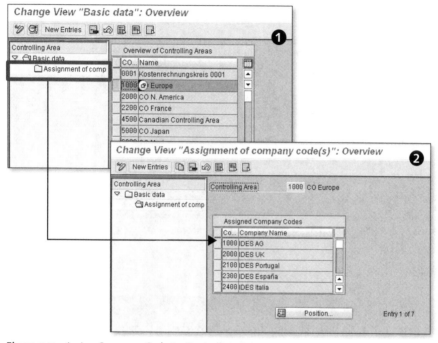

Figure 2.11 Assign Company Code to Controlling Area

2.2.5 Controlling Area to Operating Concern

Quick Reference

Menu path: IMG • ENTERPRISE STRUCTURE • ASSIGNMENT • CONTROLLING • ASSIGN CONTROLLING AREA TO OPERATING CONCERN

Transaction: KEKK

Table/view: TKA01_ER/TKA01_ER

You can assign several controlling areas to one operating concern using Transaction KEKK (Figure 2.12). The system displays all of the controlling areas available in the system and allows you to assign them to the operating concern in the OpCo column. That's all you need to do under the Enterprise Structure definition.

In assigning a controlling area to an operating concern, you also indirectly assign the company code to the operating concern. Refer to a Controlling manual to fully understand the consequence of this assignment; a more thorough discussion is beyond the scope of this book.

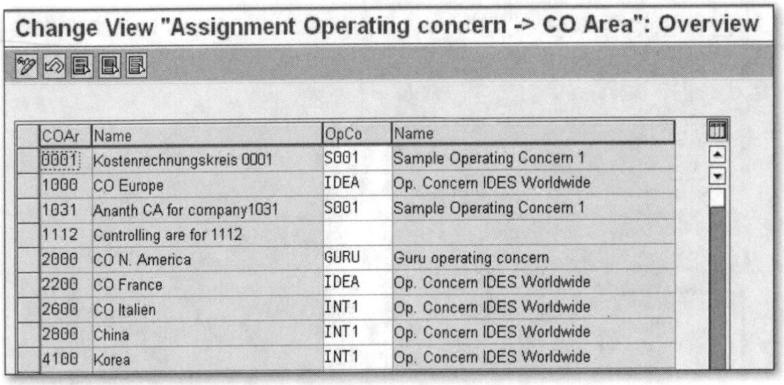
Change View "Assignment Operating concern -> CO Area": Overview

COAr	Name	OpCo	Name
0001	Kostenrechnungskreis 0001	S001	Sample Operating Concern 1
1000	CO Europe	IDEA	Op. Concern IDES Worldwide
1031	Ananth CA for company1031	S001	Sample Operating Concern 1
1112	Controlling are for 1112		
2000	CO N. America	GURU	Guru operating concern
2200	CO France	IDEA	Op. Concern IDES Worldwide
2600	CO Italien	INT1	Op. Concern IDES Worldwide
2800	China	INT1	Op. Concern IDES Worldwide
4100	Korea	INT1	Op. Concern IDES Worldwide

Figure 2.12 Assigning Controlling Area to Operating Concern

2.2.6 Plant to Company Code

Quick Reference

Menu path: IMG • Enterprise Structure • Assignment • Logistics General • Assign Plant to Company Code

Transaction: OX18

Table/view: T001K_ASSIGN/V_T001K_ASSIGN

The plant is the basic organizational unit in the Logistics modules and can represent a factory, branch, or any physical segmentation of a legal entity. Each plant is assigned to exactly one company code. The assignment of the plant to a company code can be performed by a Materials Management (MM) expert or by a Financial Accounting expert, depending on the organizational rules defined in your company. To perform the assignment, follow this procedure:

1. Select Transaction OX18 (Figure 2.13). The system displays a list of all of the company codes present in the system and all of the plants assigned to each of them.

2. If you need to assign a new plant to an existing company code, position the cursor on the company code, and click the Assign button.

3. The system displays a list of the plants not yet assigned to any company code. Select your plant, and click the Continue button (✔). Save your entries.

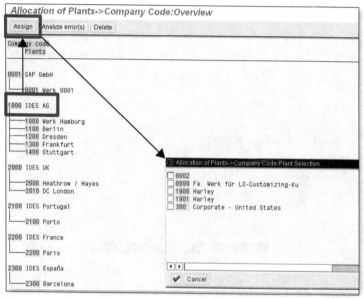

Figure 2.13 Assign Plant to Company Code

If you make a mistake in the assignment and the plant has never been used, you can correct the mistake by positioning the cursor over the plant and pressing the Delete button. Then follow the procedure just described to perform the correct assignment.

2.2.7   Sales Organization to Company Code

Quick Reference

Menu path: IMG • ENTERPRISE STRUCTURE • ASSIGNMENT • SALES AND DISTRIBUTIONS • AS-SIGN SALES ORGANIZATION TO COMPANY CODE

Transaction: OVX3

Table/view: TVKO/V_TVKO_ASSIGN

Each sales organization is assigned to exactly one company code. The assignment of the sales organization to a company code can be performed by an SD expert or by a Financial Accounting expert, depending on the organizational rules defined in your company. To perform the assignment, follow these steps:

1. Select Transaction OVX3 (Figure 2.14). The system displays a list of all of the company codes present in the system and of the sales organization assigned to each of them.

2. If you need to assign a new sales organization to an existing company code, position the cursor over the company code, and click Assign.

3. The system displays a list of all of the sales organizations not yet assigned to any company codes. Select your sales organization, and confirm the selection. Save your entries.

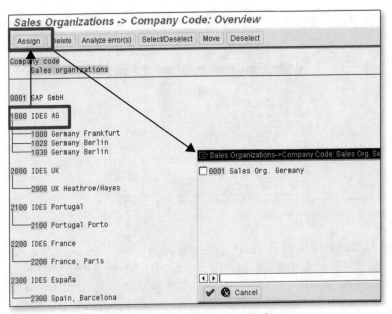

Figure 2.14 Assign Sales Organization to Company Code

If you make a mistake in the assignment and the sales organization has never been used, you can correct the mistake by positioning the cursor over the sales organization and pressing the Delete button. Then follow the procedure just described to perform the correct assignment.

2.2.8 Personnel Area to Company Code

The personnel area is an organizational unit used in SAP Human Resources Management (SAP HRM). Each personnel area must be assigned to exactly one company code. Because the assignment requires an in-depth knowledge of SAP HRM, we strongly recommend that this customizing activity is performed by, or in coordination with, an SAP HRM consultant. A more thorough description of this process is beyond the scope of this book.

2.2.9 FAQ and Troubleshooting Tips

Next we answer some frequently asked questions and offer helpful troubleshooting tips.

FAQ

1. **Question:** What happens if I change the assignment of a company code to a company when the company code is already productive?

   Answer: You shouldn't change assignments when a company code is already in use in a production system. If you do, all of the tables (e.g., global special ledgers) that derive the company from the company code master data (field T001-RCOMP) will adopt the new assignment from a certain point in time, which will result in data inconsistencies. Reports that read the assignment from Table T001 will present one result (all of the data will be presented with the new assignment), while reports that read the line items or the total record will present the historical assignment (some data on the old company, and other data on the new company). The investigation and correction of such inconsistencies can be very time consuming, and you can never be certain that they have all been reconciled. Therefore, we strongly recommend not making this type of change in a production system.

2. **Question:** Can I change the assignment of a company code to a controlling area?

Answer: You can't change the assignment of a company code to a controlling area after the company code is productive and has postings. If you need to reassign a company code to a different controlling area, you have two viable options. The first is to create a new company code and perform a traditional data migration; the second is to use the services from the dedicated SAP team (contact the SLO [System Landscape Optimization] service reference from SAP). In any case, the reassignment of a company code to a different controlling area is a complex activity that should be managed as a dedicated project.

3. **Question:** Can I change the assignment of a plant to a company code?

   Answer: You can't reassign the plant to another company code if the plant is productive. If you need to reassign a plant to a different company code, you have two viable options. The first is to create a new plant and perform a traditional data migration; the second is to use the services from the dedicated SAP team (contact the SLO service reference from SAP). In any case, the reassignment of a plant to a different company code is a complex activity that should be managed as a dedicated project.

4. **Question:** Can I assign a controlling area to an operating concern for which the environment generation hasn't taken place?

   Answer: Yes, this is possible. Transaction KEP8 allows you to create an operating concern with just the ID (four digits) and the description, without any generation of the relevant environment. This allows the assignment of the operating concern to controlling areas.

Troubleshooting Tip

1. **Issue:** I can't assign a company code to a controlling area.

   Solution: This means that the Controlling area has the Controlling Area Same as Company Code option selected; see Section 2.1.7, Controlling Area, for more details. If you want to assign more than one company code to the Controlling area, change the setting in the Controlling area using Transaction OX06.

2. **Issue:** Can I change the assignment of a sales organization to a company code?

   Solution: You can't reassign the sales organization to another company code if the sales organization is productive. If you need to reassign a sales organization to a different company code, you have two viable options. The first is to create a new sales organization and perform a traditional data migration; the second is to use the services from the dedicated SAP team (contact the SLO service reference from SAP). In any case, the reassignment of a sales organization to a different company code is a complex activity that should be managed as a dedicated project.

2.3 Summary

In this chapter, we covered the definition and assignment of those entities relevant to Financial Accounting. In the first section, we explained the definition of the following entities:

- Company
- Company code
- Credit control area
- Business area
- Consolidation business area
- Functional area
- Controlling area
- Operating concern

In the second section, we explained how to make the following assignments:

- Company code to company
- Company code to credit control area
- Business area to consolidation business area
- Company code to controlling area
- Controlling area to operating concern
- Plant to company code
- Sales organization to company code
- Personnel area to company code

In the next chapter, we discuss the configuration of SAP General Ledger.

SAP General Ledger is the core module of SAP; most of the transactions created in other SAP components, such as Sales and Distribution and Materials Management, end in a general ledger document. In this chapter, you will learn how to configure SAP General Ledger.

3   General Ledger Configuration

SAP General Ledger was introduced with the release of SAP ERP 5.0 and allowed companies that already run SAP to migrate from their previous solution (which we refer to as "the classic General Ledger") within the framework of a project. Because certain companies run SAP General Ledger while others continue to run the classic General Ledger, we discuss both components in this chapter and state explicitly when a certain functionality applies only to SAP General Ledger or to the classic General Ledger. If we don't specify one or the other, you can assume that the functionality applies to both.

In this chapter, we discuss the main activities in configuring a ready-to-run general ledger. The following main areas of configuration are covered:

- Company code settings
- Fiscal year variants
- Chart of accounts and general ledger accounts configuration
- Configuration of general ledger postings
- Specific configurations steps valid only for SAP General Ledger
- Validation and substitutions
- Automatic account determination

3.1   Company Code Settings

Quick Reference

Menu path: IMG • FINANCIAL ACCOUNTING • FINANCIAL ACCOUNTING GLOBAL SETTINGS • COMPANY CODE • ENTER GLOBAL PARAMETERS

> **Transaction:** OBY6
>
> **Table/view:** T001/V_001_B

In Chapter 2, Organizational Structure: Definition and Assignment, we described how to define a new company code with minimal information (company name, currency, address, and language) when customizing the enterprise structure. In this section, we describe the more detailed configuration of a company code, which is performed using Transaction OBY6.

To begin, you must perform some customizing to create objects that are successively assigned to the company code. These objects are mapped in Figure 3.1, together with their customizing transactions.

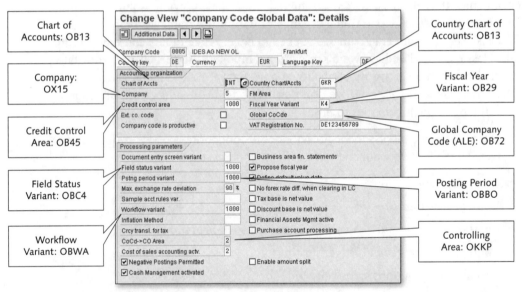

Figure 3.1 Company Code Settings: Main Assignments

The following list explains a bit more about each of these objects:

▶ **Chart of Accts**
This is the *operational chart of accounts*; when you post, you can choose among the accounts that belong to this chart of accounts and those that are created in this company code.

- **Company**

  Here you assign your company code to the company, which is the entity that is used for consolidation purposes. In general, the assignment is one to one.

- **Credit Control Area**

  Multiple company codes can be assigned to one credit control area. In Transaction FD32 (where you specify the credit management information for each customer), you specify the credit limit for customers at the credit control area level, not at the company code level.

- **Field Status Variant**

  In each general ledger account, you specify a field status group that, together with the posting key, determines which fields are suppressed, optional, or mandatory during postings. You can choose among the field status groups created within the field status variant assigned to the company code.

- **Workflow Variant**

  This setting is relevant if you use workflow for some of your postings. It's usually used together with the parking functionality, especially for incoming invoices.

- **Country Chart/Accts**

  You have the option to assign the company code to a country chart of accounts, which then allows you to assign each operational general ledger account to an alternative account (chosen from the accounts created in the country chart of accounts and in the company code). The relevant field for this is SKB1-ALTKT. When you post, you can choose general ledger accounts from the operational chart of accounts. You post country charts of accounts indirectly, as you assign accounts from the country chart of account in the master data of accounts of operational chart of accounts. Country chart of accounts can be used (optionally) to produce local reporting with accounts that follow a country-specific naming convention.

- **Fiscal Year Variant**

  This is used to map the posting dates to posting periods and fiscal years; you can use a calendar fiscal year, where the posting periods match the months (apart from the special posting periods) or a non-calendar fiscal year (year-dependent or year-independent fiscal year variant). See Section 3.3, Fiscal Year Variant, for more details.

- **Global CoCde (global company code)**

  This entry is necessary to allow the exchange of data via ALE (IDocs) between two SAP installations. The global company code must be the same in the sending and receiving systems. In general, the global company code and the company code are the same, but you must create the global company code entity and assign it to the company code to use the ALE connection.

▶ **Posting Period Variant**
This assignment is necessary to open and close posting periods in Transaction OB52; you don't open and close posting periods directly for each company code but indirectly through the posting period variant.

▶ **CoCd → CO Area**
Many company codes can share the same controlling area for an integrated, cross-company code controlling area. However, you can also decide that your controlling area should contain just one company code (a one-to-one assignment); if this is the case, specify the value 1 in this field. If, as is more common, you want to allow many company codes to be assigned to the controlling area (a many-to-one assignment), specify the value 2.

Figure 3.2 highlights further detailed settings of the company code that, unlike the ones just listed, don't require a preceding customizing step.

Figure 3.2 Company Code Settings: Other Relevant Configuration

The following list describes the settings in Figure 3.2 in more detail.

▶ **Company Code is Productive (❶)**

After you've started using the company code in the productive system (after successful go-live), we highly recommend that you set this indicator. When set, the system prevents the use of certain programs to delete test data:

- ▶ Program SAPF020 to delete document data
- ▶ Program SAPF019 to delete master data (general ledger accounts, customers, and vendors)

▶ **VAT Registration No. (❷)**

If the company code is part of the European Union, here is where you specify the VAT registration number that the company has obtained from the VAT authority of the country in which it's legally located.

▶ **Max. Exchange Rate Deviation (❸)**

When you post an accounting document, you can leave the system to automatically calculate the applicable exchange rate; alternatively, you can also manually specify an exchange rate. If you manually specify the exchange rate, the system checks that the rate doesn't deviate more than the percentage specified here (in percentage terms). If the deviation is bigger, then you see the following message: "F5212 Exchange rate NNN deviates from table rate MMM by XX%," (where NNN, MMM, and XX are replaced with the appropriate data). When customizing, you can specify if the message is a warning or an error by using Transaction OBA5 (application area F5 and message 212).

▶ **Negative Postings Permitted (❹)**

With negative postings, you can specify a negative sign in the lines, allowing you to reduce the debit or credit transaction figures (i.e., the total data per period). For example, if you have an account with a balance of 1.100 Euros, and you want take the balance to zero, you can post – 1.100 on the debit side or 1.100 on the credit side. In both cases, the balance is zero, but in the first case, you see 0 on both the debit and credit sides, while in the second case, you see 1.100 on the debit side and 1.100 on the credit side. You need to carefully consider the need for this setting and discuss the topic with your accounting department before making a decision. You should also consider your audit requirements.

▶ **Cash Management Activated (❺)**

If activated, you can use the cash management functionality for the management of the cash position and the liquidity forecast. Refer to a SAP treasury manual to get more details on this functionality.

▶ **Business Area Fin. Statements (❻)**
If you activate this indicator, the business area is always available, no matter what the field status.

▶ **Propose Fiscal Year (❼)**
This indicator is relevant only for the transactions that display and change Financial Accounting documents (FB02 or FB03).

▶ **Define Default Value Date**
If selected, the default value date is the same as the system date. (*Value dates* are typically used in bank accounts for the calculation of interest on balances.)

▶ **No Forex. Rate Differences when Clearing in LC (local currency) (❽)**
This indicator is relevant when clearing items with different document currencies, and the clearing document is posted in the local currency. If the indicator is set, the system uses the historical local currency value for clearing (i.e., the local currency value recorded in the items to be cleared); if it isn't set, the system recalculates the local currency value according to the exchange rate valid for the date of the clearing document.

▶ **Tax Base is Net Value (❾)**
By default, the tax base doesn't include cash discounts. Setting this indicator means that the base amount on which the sales tax is calculated is reduced by the possible cash discounts agreed upon in the invoice.

▶ **Purchase Account Processing (❿)**
This indicator is relevant for companies located in countries in which, when you post an incoming invoice, you're required to post to an appropriate expense account. By default, SAP posts to the stock account. If this indicator is set, the system creates two postings for invoices with goods receipts; one to the purchase account (which shouldn't be set as a cost element, so as not to duplicate the values in Controlling) and offsetting purchase account, and one to the stock account. Discuss this setting with your Materials Management expert.

3.2 Parallel Currencies

In this section, explain how to define a maximum of two additional local currencies for each company code and then move on to describe how to create more than two additional local currencies (a functionality allowed only in the classic General Ledger).

3.2.1 Defining Additional Local Currencies (Maximum of Two)

In addition to company code currency 10 (which is mandatory, as the first local currency for the company code), you can set up to two additional local currencies for each company code. To do this, execute Transaction OB22. The system presents a screen listing only the company codes for which an additional currency has been set up (Figure 3.3).

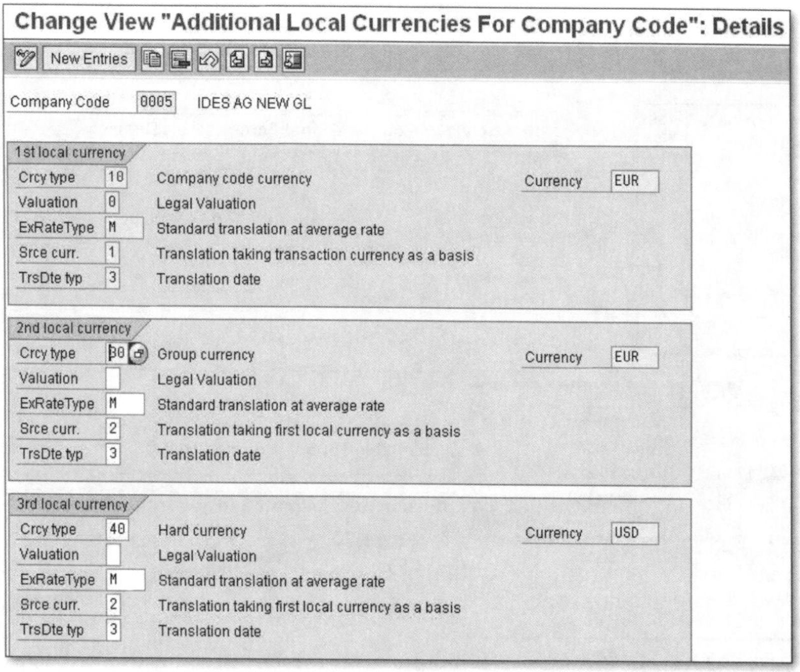

Figure 3.3 Parallel Currencies for Company Code

If you want to set up additional local currencies for another company code, select the New Entries button. The first currency type is always 10 and can't be changed; for the second local currency, select the currency type from the matchcode. When you add the local currencies, specify the currency type, and the currency code is automatically set by the system. See Table 3.1 and Figure 3.4 to understand the source of the currency code.

Currency Type	Defined In...
10 Company code currency	Company code global settings, Table T001, field WAERS
30 Group currency	Client: Table T000, field MWAER
40 Hard currency	Country the company code belongs to: Table T005, field CURHA
50 Index currency	Country the company code belongs to: Table T005, field CURIN
60 Global Company Currency	Company to which the company code is assigned: Table T880, field CURR

Table 3.1 Currency Type Definitions

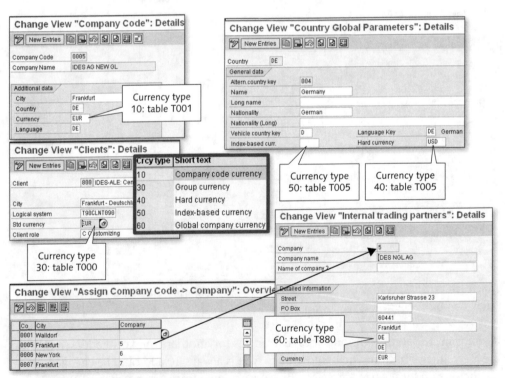

Figure 3.4 Origin of Currency Types

After choosing the currency type, the right side of the screen displays the currency code associated with that type. At this point, you must specify the following additional mandatory settings:

▶ **ExRate Type (exchange rate type)**
Choose M. You can also specify that the system uses another exchange rate type to take the most recent exchange rate from Table TCURR. See Chapter 1, General SAP Configuration for Financial Accounting, for more details.

▶ **Srce Curr. (source currency)**
Specify the currency from which the translation takes place:

▶ **1: Translation Taking Transaction Currency as a Basis:** In this case, the system searches for the exchange rate between the document currency and the additional local currency.

▶ **2: Translation Taking First Local Currency as a Basis:** In this case, the system searches for the exchange rate between the first local currency (currency type 10) and the additional local currency.

▶ **TrsDte Typ (translation date type)**
Here you define the date in the header of the Financial Accounting document that is used in the search for the most recent exchange rate. The following options are available:

▶ 1: Document Date

▶ 2: Posting Date

▶ 3: Translation Date

Additional Local Currencies: SAP General Ledger

The currencies defined in Transaction OB22 automatically become the parallel currencies of the leading ledger. You also have the option of assigning the currencies assigned to the leading ledger to the non-leading ledgers. However, it isn't possible to assign local currencies not already present in the leading ledger.

3.2.2 Defining Additional Local Currencies with Additional Ledgers (Classic General Ledger)

Quick Reference

Menu path: IMG • FINANCIAL ACCOUNTING • FINANCIAL ACCOUNTING GLOBAL SETTINGS • COMPANY CODE • MULTIPLE CURRENCIES • DEFINE ADDITIONAL LOCAL CURRENCIES FOR LEDGERS

Transaction: OBS2

Table: T881

If you want to manage more than two local currencies for your company code in the classic General Ledger, you must create a new ledger for Table GLT0. By default, there is just one ledger in GLT0: ledger 0. However, with Transaction OBS2, you can create an additional ledger with the same settings as ledger 0 and assign different currencies.

Follow these steps:

1. Execute Transaction OBS2.

2. Select LEDGER • CREATE (Figure 3.5).

3. Specify an ID for the ledger (two digits long, alphanumeric, can't begin with numbers from 1 to 9), and press Enter.

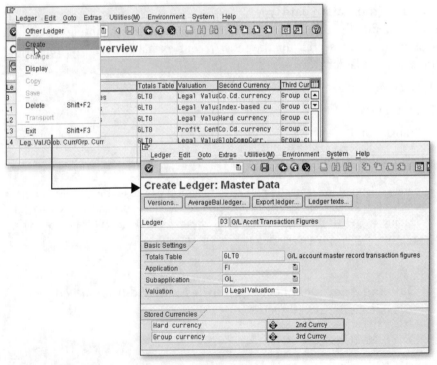

Figure 3.5 Parallel Currencies in a New GLT0 Ledger

4. In the resulting screen (Figure 3.5), select the additional local currencies you want to update in this ledger. (You can't directly specify the currency code, only the currency type.)

5. Save the new ledger.

3.3   Fiscal Year Variants

> **Quick Reference**
>
> **Menu path:** IMG • FINANCIAL ACCOUNTING • FINANCIAL ACCOUNTING GLOBAL SETTINGS • FISCAL YEAR • MAINTAIN FISCAL YEAR VARIANT (MAINTAIN SHORTENED FISC. YEAR)
>
> **Transaction:** OB29
>
> **Tables:** T009 (fiscal year), T009B (posting period of the fiscal year), T009Y (shortened fiscal year)

The fiscal year variant settings answer the following question: When I post to a specific posting date, which posting period and fiscal year are updated? The answer can be different for each company code; in fact, you assign company codes to the fiscal year variant.

Execute Transaction OB29 to access the fiscal year variant definition. The configuration is performed in one or two steps (one step if you select the Calendar Year indicator, discussed next; two steps in all other cases).

In the first step, you create the fiscal year variant and specify a two-digit ID (Figure 3.6). You must specify the following pieces of information:

▶ **Description**
Provide a brief description of the fiscal year variant. For example, "Calendar Year 4 special periods."

▶ **Year-Dependent**
Set this flag if the start date and finish date of each posting period varies for each calendar year.

▶ **Calendar Year**
Set this flag if the posting periods are months (with the exception of the special periods). If you flag this, you can't also flag the Year-Dependent option.

▶ **No. Posting Periods**
If you have chosen the Calendar Year option, you're forced to specify 12 here; otherwise, specify the number of normal posting periods.

▶ **No. Special Periods**
If you post with a posting date that falls in the last normal posting period, you can specify an alternative special period. Here you specify the number of allowed special periods. The maximum number of periods (i.e., normal plus special) is 16.

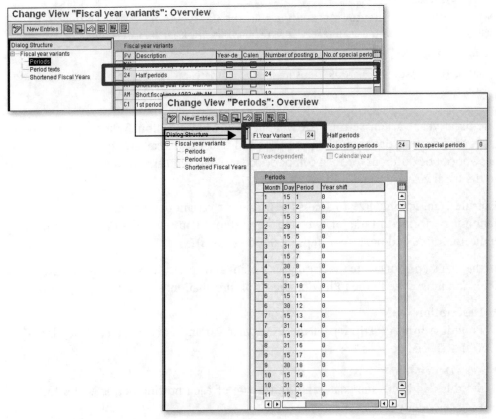

Figure 3.6 Fiscal Year Variant Definition

In the second step (which is necessary *only* if you haven't selected the Calendar Year indicator), do the following to map calendar dates to posting periods:

1. Select your fiscal year variant, and double-click on the Periods folder on the left side of the screen (Figure 3.6).

If the fiscal year variant is year dependent, the system asks you for the fiscal year for which you want to maintain the periods. If the fiscal year variant isn't year dependent, you're taken to the screen where you define the start and final date of all of the periods with validity for all of the fiscal years.

2. Define the final date of each posting period (Figure 3.6).

For example, specify the following combination for the year 2010: month 1, day 15, period 12, year shift – 1. You read this combination in this way: January 15, 2010 is the last day of the twelfth period of fiscal year 2009. With the year shift you can assign a portion of a calendar year (in the example above, January 1 until January 15, 2010) to a different fiscal year (in the example above, 2009).

3.3.1 FAQ and Troubleshooting Tips

Next we answer some frequently asked questions and offer helpful troubleshooting tips.

FAQ

1. **Question:** Can I assign special periods to fiscal year variants with the Calendar Year indicator?

   Answer: Yes. If the posting date is in December, you're allowed to specify a special posting period (the system will propose 12 as a default value).

2. **Question:** How can I ensure that the posting to special periods takes place only in the last day of the fiscal year?

   Answer: A standard control ensures that you can only post to special periods if the posting date falls in the last normal period of the fiscal year variant. If, for example, the last normal period of the fiscal year variant corresponds to December, you can specify a special posting period for any posting with a posting date in December. If you want to make it possible only to specify a special posting period on the last day of the fiscal year, you can create a validation. (Prerequisite: The posting period must be a special period. Control: The posting date should start with 31.12, for example, if the last date of the fiscal year is December 31).

3. **Question:** When I post to Financial Accounting, the posting period can be entered manually. What happens if I specify a posting period that doesn't match the rules of the fiscal year variant assigned to the company code?

Answer: The system automatically changes the posting period according to the posting date and the rules of the fiscal year variant.

Troubleshooting Tip

1. **Issue:** Message appears: "Periods can't be maintained for calendar-dependent financial year variants."

   Solution: You're trying to define the posting periods of a calendar fiscal year. This doesn't make sense because the posting periods are the same as the months.

3.4 Configuring Charts of Accounts and General Ledger Accounts

Accounts are created within a container that is called the *chart of accounts*. For each company code, one chart of accounts must be assigned. Therefore, each account has two sets of information:

▶ Data on the chart of accounts level (Table SKA1): Applies to all company codes assigned to the chart of account.

▶ Data on the company code (Table SKB1): Applies only to the particular company code.

Next we describe the steps necessary to create the needed general ledger accounts.

> **Note**
> If the standard functionalities and controls to create and manage general ledger accounts aren't sufficient, you can develop improvements using enhancement SAPMF02H.

3.4.1 Defining Charts of Accounts

> **Quick Reference**
> **Menu path:** IMG • FINANCIAL ACCOUNTING • GENERAL LEDGER ACCOUNTING • G/L ACCOUNT • MASTER RECORDS • PREPARATION • EDIT CHART OF ACCOUNTS LIST
> **Transaction:** OB13
> **Table/view:** T004/V_T004

Three types of charts of accounts can be assigned to a company code:

▸ Operational chart of accounts

▸ Country chart of accounts

▸ Group chart of accounts

Each company code is assigned to exactly one operational chart of accounts. The operational chart of accounts is the collection of the accounts that are used when posting to the company code; for example, if you're posting with Transaction FB50 and select the matchcode to look after a specific account, the matchcode searches through the accounts of the operational chart of accounts. You assign the operational chart of accounts to the company code using Transaction OBY6.

The alternative chart of accounts can be used to create a financial statement version with local, country-specific accounts. Assign the company code to the alternative chart of accounts in customizing, Transaction OBY6. Then, in each operational account created in the company code, specify the corresponding alternative local accounts, selected from the alternative chart of accounts assigned to the company code. When posting, you post only to the operational chart of accounts; however, it can be reported by alternative accounts or group accounts. In reporting (specifically in the financial statement version, report RFBILA00), you can use the alternative accounts.

The group chart of accounts is assigned directly to the operational chart of accounts and can be used for consolidation purposes.

This section is about the creation of a chart of accounts; the process is the same regardless of the type of chart of accounts.

Use Transaction OB13, and specify a chart of accounts (four digits long, alphanumerical) and a description. Then specify the following additional customizing settings (Figure 3.7):

▸ **Maint. Language (maintenance language) (❶)**
When you maintain the description of an account in Transaction FS00, the description isn't saved in the logon language but in the language specified here. If you want to translate the description to other languages, indicate this in the Key Word/Translation tab of Transaction FS00. Now, when you use the account, the description is the one in the logon language.

- **Length of G/L Account Number (❷)**

  Here you specify the maximum length of the account number belonging to the chart of accounts.

- **Controlling Integration (❸)**

  Here you decide how primary cost elements are defined. (A *primary cost element* is a Controlling object with a one-to-one relationship with a general ledger account that must first be created in the Financial Accounting chart of accounts; it is used to transfer cost and revenues from Financial Accounting to Controlling.) There are two possible options:

  - **Manual Creation of Cost Elements:** When you save a P&L account, no associated primary cost element is created. You must create the cost element manually (individually or collectively).

  - **Automatic Creation of Cost Elements:** In this case, when you save a P&L account automatically, a primary cost element is created based on the customizing of Table TKSKA.

- **Group Chart of Accts (❹)**

  Here you associate the operational chart of accounts with the group chart of accounts.

- **Blocked (❺)**

  This setting prevents the creation of accounts at the company code level, but not the chart of accounts level.

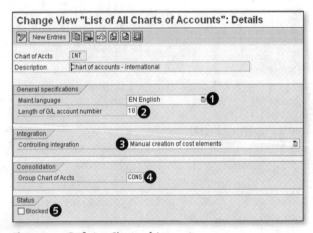

Figure 3.7 Defining Charts of Accounts

3.4.2 Defining Account Groups

Quick Reference

Menu path: IMG • FINANCIAL ACCOUNTING • GENERAL LEDGER ACCOUNTING • G/L ACCOUNT • MASTER RECORDS • PREPARATION • DEFINE ACCOUNT GROUP

Transaction: OBD4

Table/view: T077S/V_T077S

When you create an account, first specify the account number and the account group. The account groups are created depending on the chart of accounts and represent a segmentation of the chart of accounts with the following two functions:

▶ **Number range**

You must specify the range within which the accounts created in the specific account group of the specific chart of accounts should fall. Number ranges can be external (user-assigned: numeric or alphanumeric) or internal (system-assigned: numeric).

▶ **Field status group**

This setting determines the rules for creating the company code data of the accounts belonging to the account group. We'll focus on this topic here because it involves a complex configuration activity, while the range of allowed accounts is simply specified in the first screen of the account group configuration (as described next).

To create an account group, run Transaction OBD4, select the New Entries button, and specify the following:

▶ The chart of accounts

▶ The account group ID

▶ A meaningful description of the account group (e.g., "IFRS gross profit accounts")

▶ The range in which the accounts belonging to the group can be created

Then select the account group, and click on the Field Status button (Figure 3.8); the system brings you to another screen where you can define the field status for each possible field available at the company code level. To get a report of the statuses for each field, click on the Print Field Status (Figure 3.8).

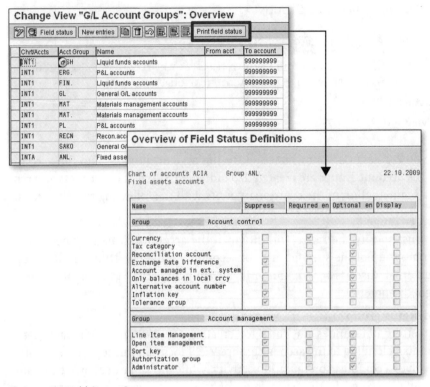

Figure 3.8 Field Status Groups

Your field status options are as follows (Figure 3.9):

▸ **Suppress (❶)**
The field isn't shown in the screen, and no value can be entered.

▸ **Req. Entry (required entry) (❷)**
The field is displayed, and you're required to enter a valid value.

▸ **Opt. Entry (optional entry) (❸)**
The field is displayed, and you're allowed but not required to enter a valid value. You can't enter an invalid value; for example, in the Currency field, you can't enter a currency code that hasn't been defined in Table TCURC.

▸ **Display (❹)**
The field is displayed with its content, but it can't be changed.

When processing the company code data of a general ledger account, the status for each available field doesn't depend only on the account group to which the account is assigned but also on the activity you're performing: creating, changing, or displaying an account. We describe how to customize field statuses for each of these activities in the next section: Configuring Screen Layout for Creating, Displaying, and Changing General Ledger Accounts.

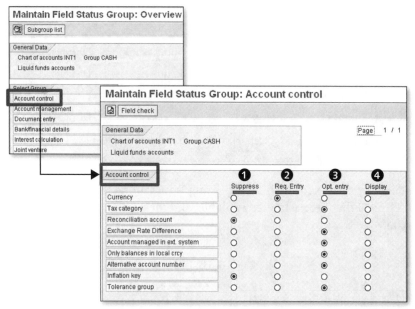

Figure 3.9 Field Status Group Customizing

3.4.3   Configuring Screen Layout for Creating, Displaying, and Changing General Ledger Accounts

Quick Reference

Menu path: IMG • FINANCIAL ACCOUNTING • GENERAL LEDGER ACCOUNTING • G/L ACCOUNT • MASTER RECORDS • PREPARATION • ADDITIONAL ACTIVITIES • DEFINE SCREEN LAYOUT FOR EACH TRANSACTION

Transaction: OB26

Field status rules can be defined for the activities of creating, displaying, and changing general ledger accounts. The combination between the rules defined in the account group and the rules defined for each activity determine the final status of each field, that is, determines the screen layout that appears to the user each time he tries to create, display, or change a general ledger account. The rules from the two sources are combined according to the matrix displayed in Table 3.2.

> **Note**
>
> The combination of Required and Suppressed leads to an error issued when you run the transaction to maintain the general ledger accounts.

	Suppressed	Required	Optional	Display
Suppressed	Suppressed	Error	Suppressed	Suppressed
Required	Error	Required	Required	Display
Optional	Suppressed	Required	Optional	Display
Display	Suppressed	Display	Display	Display

Table 3.2 Field Status Combinations for Creating, Displaying, and Changing General Ledger Accounts

Define the field status rules for each activity using Transaction OB26 (Figure 3.10). Double-click one of the three activities available, and then assign the field statuses as appropriate.

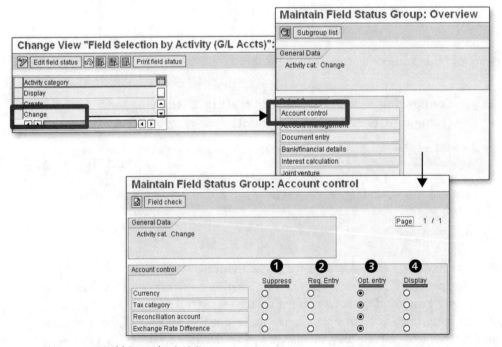

Figure 3.10 Field Status by Activity

We recommend not changing the predefined standard settings delivered by SAP (in which all of the fields have the Opt. Entry status). Refine the rules by means of the account groups only.

3.4.4 Defining Retained Earnings Accounts

> **Quick Reference**
>
> **Menu path:** IMG • FINANCIAL ACCOUNTING • GENERAL LEDGER ACCOUNTING • G/L ACCOUNT • MASTER RECORDS • PREPARATION • DEFINE RETAINED EARNINGS ACCOUNT
>
> **Transaction:** OB53
>
> **Table:** T030 (transaction key BIL)

At the end of the fiscal year, you perform the carryforward of the balance for each account:

▶ The balance of the balance sheet accounts is carried forward to period 0 (the carryforward period) against the same account in the new fiscal year.

▶ The balance of the P&L accounts is carried forward to one or more cumulated retained earnings accounts.

In customizing Transaction OB53, you define the possible retained earning accounts for each chart of accounts. Then in the master data of each P&L account (in the chart of accounts segment), you must specify the retained earnings account the account belongs to. To create or change a retained earnings account, follow these (Figure 3.11):

1. Run Transaction OB53.

2. Specify the chart of accounts, and click on the Continue button.

3. In the P&L Statmt Acct Type column, specify a two-digit indicator that identifies a retained earnings account; this indicator has to be specified in all of the P&L accounts at the chart of accounts level.

4. In the Account column, specify a balance sheet general ledger account; the balances of all of the P&L accounts assigned to the P&L statement account type are summarized in the carryforward under the account specified here.

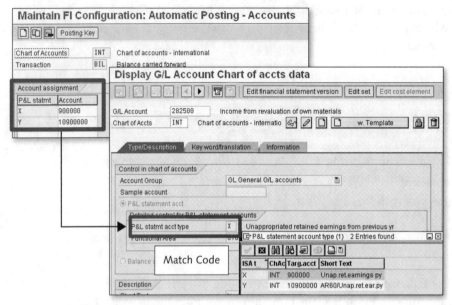

Figure 3.11 Defining Retained Earnings Accounts

3.4.5 FAQ and Troubleshooting Tips

Next we answer some frequently asked questions and offer helpful troubleshooting tips.

FAQ

1. **Question:** Is it possible that in one company code, one chart of accounts is used as an operational chart of accounts, and in another company code, the same chart of accounts is used as an alternative chart of accounts?

   Answer: Yes, this is possible.

2. **Question:** For the display activity, what happens if I define one field as ready for input?

   Answer: In the display activity, optional and required fields automatically take the status displayed.

3. **Question:** Can I change the retained earnings account in the master data of a P&L account that already has postings (and worse, in different fiscal years)?

   Answer: Yes, this is possible. However, it's then necessary to re-run the balance carryforward for all of the affected company codes and fiscal years. Start with the oldest fiscal year and perform all of the carryforwards in sequence. Always carefully consider the consequences for closed fiscal years, for which a financial statement version has already been produced and issued, either internally or externally. Remember, you're changing the distribution of the retained earnings between different accounts.

Troubleshooting Tip

1. **Issue:** The field status of an account group has been changed, and some fields are hidden. How can I see the content of those fields? Is changing the field status the only way?

   Solution: To see the content of hidden fields, use Transaction SE16 for the table that contains the field (SKA1 for data at the chart of accounts level, and SKB1 for data at the company code level).

3.5 Configuring General Ledger Settings for Postings

In this section, we describe the main configuration objects that directly affect general ledger postings; in particular:

- Document type
- Posting key
- Field status groups
- Number ranges

3.5.1 Defining Document Types

Quick Reference

Menu path: IMG • FINANCIAL ACCOUNTING • GENERAL LEDGER ACCOUNTING • G/L POSTING • CARRY OUT AND CHECK DOCUMENT SETTINGS • DEFINE DOCUMENT TYPES

Transaction: OBA7

Table/view: T003/V_T003

The document type is the most important control information specified when posting a Financial Accounting document. It can be typed manually, as in the case of direct postings, or it can come from customizing settings, as in the case of postings coming from Materials Management or Sales and Distribution transactions.

Document types are defined using Transaction OBA7. Begin by specifying the ID (two digits, alphanumeric) and document type description.

Document Type Naming Conventions

Because the document type is the main information used to classify financial documents, we strongly recommend defining a consistent and logical naming convention that allows you to easily recognize the type of posting simply by reading the document type for each transaction.

Note that the description you enter should be in the logon language. If more than one language is used in the system, it's necessary to translate the description. Follow these steps (Figure 3.12):

1. In the list of the document types, select one or more document types and then GOTO • TRANSLATION.

2. Click the box next to each of the languages into which you want the description translated.

3. For each document type and language, specify a suitable description.

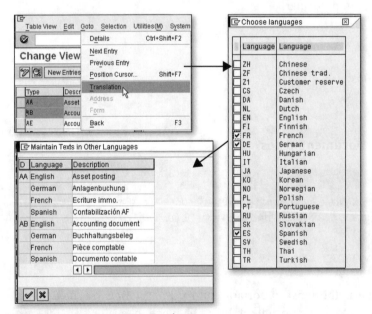

Figure 3.12 Document Type Translation

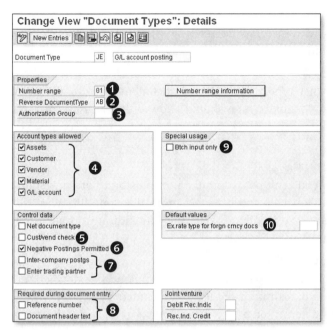

Figure 3.13 Defining Document Types

In addition to the ID and description, the following main settings are available in the document type configuration (Figure 3.13):

▶ **Number Range (❶)**
Here you specify one of the number ranges you defined in Transaction FBN1 (see Section 3.5.4 Defining Number Ranges, later in this chapter, for more details). Many document types can be assigned to the same number range. Consider the local legal requirements in the assignment; for example, if you define three different document types with the same number range, and only two of them are printed in the purchase VAT report, you're mining the progressive numbering of the VAT report.

▶ **Reverse Document Type (❷)**
This is the document type that the system automatically uses when reversing a document with Transaction FB08 or FBRA. You can leave this field blank; in this case, the system uses the same document type for the reversal.

▶ **Authorization Group (❸)**
This field allows you to assign all of the document types for manual purchasing invoices to the same authorization group, and then assign the authorization

group to the users that work with incoming invoices. In this way, you can prevent them from posting with incorrect document types or posting transactions outside their responsibilities.

▶ **Account Types Allowed (❹)**
Here you specify with which type of accounts the document type can work. For example, a depreciation document type should allow only the usage of asset and general ledger accounts. This allows you to prevent the incorrect usage of the document type.

▶ **Cust/Vend Check (❺)**
If you set this indicator, you can't post more than one customer or one vendor in the same document. However you can post more than one line with the same customer or vendor. We recommend setting this indicator in all of the document types to be used in VAT reporting.

▶ **Negative Postings Permitted (❻)**
You can prevent the use of negative postings in the company code detailed settings (Table T001). Here you can limit the use by document type. To be used, negative postings must be permitted both at the company code and at the document type level.

▶ **Inter-company Postgs (❼)**
Select this indicator to allow more than one trading partner (field BSEG-VBUND) in the same document.

▶ **Enter Trading Partner (❼)**
If selected, you can manually enter a trading partner (for the whole document if the Intercompany Postings indicator is set; for each row if it isn't). If deselected, the trading partner can only come from the general ledger, vendor, or customer master data.

▶ **Required During Document Entry (❽)**
Here you specify if the header text or the Reference field are mandatory when posting with this document type. For example, it's typical to make the Reference field mandatory for all incoming invoices. In this type of transaction, the reference field carries the number of the vendor invoice.

▶ **Btch Input Only (❾)**
If selected, the document type can't be used in any online transactions but only in interfaces that post to Financial Accounting through the batch-input technique (not with IDocs).

▶ **Ex. Rate Type for Forgn Crncy Docs (⑩)**
By default, the system translates amounts in the document currency to the first local currency by means of the M exchange rate type. If you leave this field empty, the document type automatically uses M. If you indicate a different exchange rate type, the system uses the exchange rate type specified.

3.5.2 Defining Posting Keys

Quick Reference
Menu path: IMG • FINANCIAL ACCOUNTING • GENERAL LEDGER ACCOUNTING • G/L POSTING • CARRY OUT AND CHECK DOCUMENT SETTINGS • DEFINE POSTING KEYS
Transaction: OB41
Table: TBSL

Posting keys are necessary in any row of the Financial Accounting document and have the following three main functions:

▶ Specify whether the posting is debit or credit.

▶ Specify which account type (asset, customer, vendor, material, or general ledger) can be used (must be one and only one).

▶ Specify, in combination with the field status group coming from the general ledger account of the row, which fields are available for posting and, among them, which are optional and which are mandatory.

Use Transaction OB41 to customize the posting keys. In general, you don't need to create new posting keys because almost all SAP installations use only the SAP standard-delivered posting keys; instead, customize their field status to adapt the screens of the postings to the requirement of your installation.

When you run Transaction OB41, you see a list of the available posting keys in the system. The customizing of the posting key affects the definition of some basic settings and the definition of the field status. Next we discuss the basic settings and the field status management for posting keys.

Basic Settings for Posting Keys

When you run Transaction OB41 and double-click on a row, you see a screen where the following settings must be configured for each posting key (Figure 3.14):

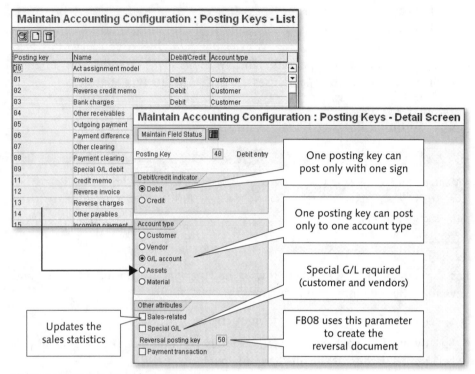

Figure 3.14 Basic Settings for Posting Keys

▶ **Debit/Credit Indicator area**

You don't decide the sign of the posting by putting plus or minus signs in front of the amount; instead, you enter the amount without the sign (the absolute value), and the posting key determines whether you have posted a debit or credit to the account specified in the row. As an exception, you can specify a negative amount if the negative postings are allowed in the company code and in the document type. In this case, the posting key decides if you're updating the debit or credit total figures for the account; if you specify a negative amount, these figures are reduced instead of increased.

▶ **Account Type area**

Each posting key can be assigned to exactly one account type. If, when posting a document with Transaction FB01, you specify a posting key (e.g., 15, the customer posting key) and type the account number, the system searches to see whether the account exists in Tables KNA1 and KNB1.

▸ **Sales-Related**

If you mark this indicator, the system updates the total sales in Table KNC1 (customers; field UMXXU, where XX is the period) and Table LFC1 (vendors; field UMXXU, where XX is the period). The standard reports RFDUML00 (customers) and RFKUML00 (vendors) are used to present the sales data based on these settings.

▸ **Special G/L**

This indicator can be set only for posting keys for customers and vendors. In this case, you must specify a special general ledger indicator in the posting (the allowed indicators are listed in Table T074U). As a result, the posting doesn't update the reconciliation account of the customer or the vendor but the alternative reconciliation account specified in Table T074.

▸ **Reversal Posting Key**

Here you enter the posting key that the system should use to generate the automatic reversal document with Transaction FB08 or Transaction FBRA.

▸ **Payment Transaction**

For some SAP business transactions, the system needs to know if the posting is or isn't a payment. For example, you can clear an invoice not for a payment but because you issued a credit note. Here you specify if the posting key is used with payment-related transactions.

Posting Key Field Status Management

When you post to a general ledger account, there are many fields with different field statuses. The field status is different for each row in the document, and depends on the following two factors:

▸ The posting key of the row

▸ The field status group

Both the factors contain rules for each field, specifying whether the field is suppressed (i.e., hidden), mandatory, or optional.

However, the final result depends on the combination of the two rules, according to the matrix shown in Table 3.3.

	Suppressed	Required	Optional
Suppressed	Suppressed	Error	Suppressed
Required	Error	Required	Required
Optional	Suppressed	Required	Optional

Table 3.3 Field Status Combinations for Posting Keys

Here we describe how to make the field status settings for posting keys. From Figure 3.14, select the Maintain Field Status button, and the system presents a list of the fields for which you're allowed to control the status. For technical reasons, some fields aren't subject to the field status customizing, for example, the posting key itself, the account number, and the amount. All other fields are displayed.

The fields are further grouped into groups and subgroups (Figure 3.15). One subgroup can sometimes contain just one field; in this case, the subgroup generally has the same description as the contained field. If you customize field statuses at the subgroup level, that status is valid for all of the fields contained in the subgroup.

Double-click on a group and specify, for each of the subgroups, whether all of the fields belonging to the subgroups should be suppressed, mandatory, or optional (Figure 3.16).

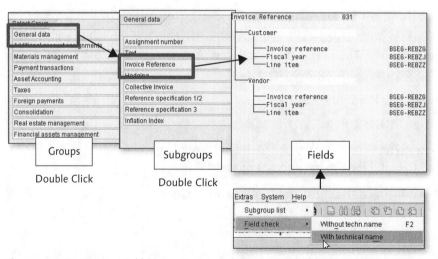

Figure 3.15 Posting Key Field Status: Groups, Subgroups, and Fields

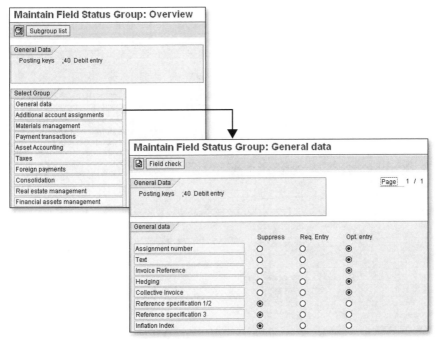

Figure 3.16 Posting Key Field Status: Groups, Subgroups, and Fields (Continued)

3.5.3 Maintaining Field Statuses from the General Ledger Account

Quick Reference
Menu path: IMG • FINANCIAL ACCOUNTING • GENERAL LEDGER ACCOUNTING • G/L POSTING • CARRY OUT AND CHECK DOCUMENT SETTINGS • MAINTAIN FIELD STATUS VARIANTS
Transaction: OBC4
Tables: T004V (field status variants) and T004F (field status groups of each variant)

As previously explained, the combination of the field status rules contained in the posting key and the field status group specified in the general ledger account master data determines which fields are mandatory, optional, and suppressed in each row of a Financial Accounting posting. This section describes how to customize the field status groups.

The field status group is assigned to each general ledger account at the company code level. In each account, you can choose among the field status groups contained in the field status variant assigned to the company code.

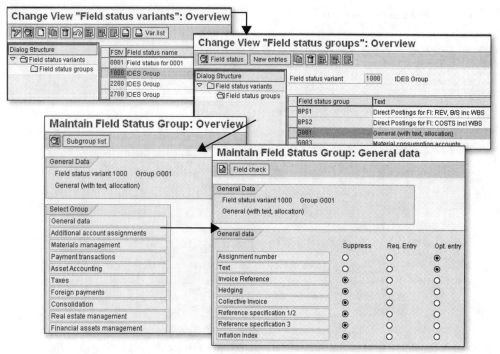

Figure 3.17 Field Status Variants (Field Status from the General Ledger Account Master Data)

Follow these steps:

1. Define the field status variant with Transaction OBC4.

   It's possible to assign all company codes to the same field status variant; in this case, you still must create one field status variant.

2. Within the field status variant, create the field status group (Figure 3.17).

   The groups should be created based on your Financial Accounting and Controlling model, so we can't make any general recommendations.

3. Double-click on one group to branch to the field status definition.

   Proceed exactly as described in the previous Posting Key Field Status Management section.

4. General rules (i.e., mostly fields that are optional) are generally set at the posting key level.

5. Detailed rules (i.e., specific definitions, field by field, of those fields that are hidden and mandatory) are generally set at the field status group level.

6. Refine the rules in the field status group so that the posting screen is adjusted to the requirements of your Financial Accounting and Controlling model.

For example, if you aren't using the WBS elements, you should hide this field in the postings to help users work more efficiently.

7. Assign the field status group in the general ledger account maintenance.

Use Transactions FS00 or FS01/FS02, or take advantage of the mass maintenance tool available in Transaction MASS.

3.5.4 Defining Number Ranges

Quick Reference

Menu path: IMG • Financial Accounting • Financial Accounting Global Settings • Document • Document Number Ranges • Define Document Number Ranges

Transactions: FBN1 (Financial Accounting number ranges for each company code), OBH1 (copy number ranges from company code to company code), OBH2 (copy company number range from fiscal year to fiscal year)

Programs: RFNRIV10 (copy number ranges from company code to company code), RFNRIV20 (copy company number range from fiscal year to fiscal year)

Table: NRIV (OBJECT: RF_BELEG)

Each Financial Accounting document can be uniquely identified in the system by the following three fields:

▶ The company code (field BKPF-BUKRS)

▶ The document number (field BKPF-BELNR)

▶ The fiscal year (field BKPF-GJAHR)

You specify the company code when you post directly in Financial Accounting. The fiscal year is derived by the posting date through the fiscal year variant assigned to the company code. Either you specify the document number (external numbering), or it's assigned automatically by the system; in any case, the document number must be within the number range assigned to the document type.

To define a number range, follow these steps (Figure 3.18):

1. Run Transaction FBN1.

2. Specify the company code.

Remember that the number range (a two-digit code) is assigned to the document type; this assignment doesn't depend on the company code, but the specification of the number range does.

3. Click on the Intervals button (Figure 3.18).

The system presents a list of all of the number ranges created for the different fiscal years.

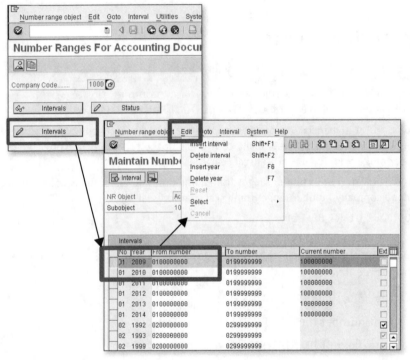

Figure 3.18 Defining Number Ranges for Company Codes

4. If you want to create a record for a new fiscal year for a number range that already has at least one record, first select one number range/fiscal year, and then select EDIT • INSERT YEAR.

Specify the fiscal year and the same initial and final number (usually you specify the same numbers as the previous fiscal year). Note that the internal/external status isn't ready for input; the system automatically takes the status from the former fiscal year range.

5. If you want to create a brand new number range, click on the Interval button.

   Specify the number range (two digit, alphanumeric), the year (9999 if year independent), initial and final number, and current number (by rule, leave the field blank). If the number range is external and therefore must be explicitly specified in each posting, click the Ext. indicator.

6. If you want to change the last number, click on the Status button, and change the number in the Current Number column. This is possible only for external number ranges and should be done only in exceptional cases.

Next we discuss the processing of copying number ranges from company code to company code, followed by copying number ranges from fiscal year to fiscal year.

Copying Number Ranges from Company Code to Company Code

When a new company code is created, number ranges can be copied from a similar company code with the help of Transaction OBH1 (Figure 3.19). Note that you can copy number ranges from exactly one reference company code to one or more destination company codes and one or more fiscal years. Any already-existing number range (in a specific year) in the destination company code isn't overwritten.

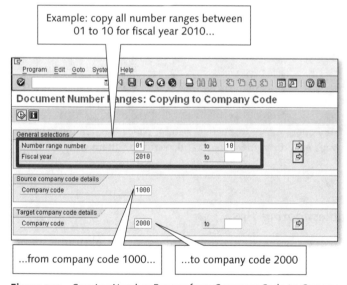

Figure 3.19 Copying Number Ranges from Company Code to Company Code

Copying Number Ranges from Fiscal Year to Fiscal Year

When a new fiscal year is approaching, you must define all number ranges for the new fiscal year for the year-dependent number ranges. You don't need to do this manually; instead, use Transaction OBH2. You can specify more than one company code (Figure 3.20).

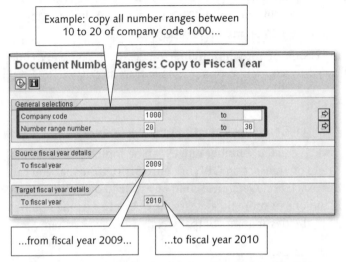

Figure 3.20 Copying Number Ranges from Fiscal Year to Fiscal Year

> **Number Range Transport**
>
> We strongly recommend never transporting number ranges. However, when you create a new company code by copy, the number ranges of the reference company code are automatically copied and transported together with all of the other settings. Before starting to use the company code in the productive system, check the number ranges. We advise deleting the transported number ranges and recreating them with the help of Transaction OBH1.

3.5.5 FAQ and Troubleshooting Tips

Next we answer some frequently asked questions and offer helpful troubleshooting tips.

FAQ

1. **Question:** What happens if I log on in a language to which a document type has not been translated? How is it displayed?

   Answer: The document type appears in the matchcode with an empty description. This could be used to avoid using document types in specific countries. However, we recommend putting a specific description such as "DO NOT USE" to prevent unwanted usage of document types and to set up specific validations for this purpose.

2. **Question:** One document type is used in different company codes. Can the number range be set up differently?

   Answer: You should assign the document type to exactly one number range; however, you can define each number range (initial number, final number, external or internal setting) at the company code level. In this case, the answer is yes.

3. **Question:** Is it possible to manage the field status of some of the fields not contained in any of the groups?

   Answer: No. The fields that aren't ready for field status customizing aren't displayed for technical reasons, either because it's always necessary to input some data (e.g., the amount or the account number) or because they are updated automatically by the system (e.g., the clearing document and the clearing date). In both cases, they aren't part of the field status customizing because of their role in assuring the consistency of data in the system.

4. **Question:** Is it possible to manage the field status group at the subledger level? In other words, is it possible to assign different field status groups to customers, vendors, or assets?

   Answer: No. The assignment of the field status group is limited to the general ledger accounts. Customers, vendors, and assets inherit different field status groups if they are assigned to different reconciliation accounts with different field status groups. Of course, alternative reconciliation accounts for special general ledger postings (defined in Table T074) can have field status groups different from the normal reconciliation account specified in the customer or vendor master record.

5. **Question:** When should a number range be set as external?

   Answer: Typically, number ranges are set as external when the posting comes from an interface, and it's important to keep the same document number as in the external system (e.g., in the case of outgoing invoices). It's also possible, but not mandatory, to set up external number ranges for Sales and Distribution invoices.

6. **Question:** If a number range is external, does the system check if the number you input is in sequence (no skipped numbers)?

   Answer: No. If the number range is external, the system only checks if the number falls within the range and if the number is already assigned.

7. **Question:** What happens when all of the numbers in the internal number range are used?

   Answer: The system starts from the beginning of the number range. If the number has already been assigned in the same fiscal year, you see an error message.

8. **Question:** Consider a situation where there are two entries for the same number range, one for fiscal year 2010 and one for fiscal year 9999. If I post with a posting date that falls in fiscal year 2010, which number range is used?

   Answer: The system selects the range for fiscal year 9999 only if there is no number range for the fiscal year in which you're posting. In the example specified in the question, the system would use the range for fiscal year 2010. However, you should always be consistent in clearly defining the number ranges as either year dependent (no number ranges in year 9999) or year independent (only one number range in year 9999).

9. **Question:** Is it possible that the same number range is external for one year and internal for another year?

   Answer: Yes, this is possible. However, the change from external to internal affects all fiscal years.

10. **Question:** How do I change a number range from year independent to year dependent?

    Answer: Simply create a new record for the number range for the fiscal year from which it will start to be year dependent. The system selects the specific fiscal year range, if it does exist, and not the record with year 9999. Remember to set up the last assigned number correctly, taking into consideration eventual numbers already assigned in the year. Use Transaction SE16, and specify Table BKPF to find the last assigned number.

Troubleshooting Tips

1. **Issue:** When I am updating a posting key, error message F4858 appears: "No special G/L transactions are to be updated for G/L accounts."

Solution: Special general ledger transactions are possible only for account types K and D, not for account type S (general ledger accounts).

2. **Issue:** When I'm posting a reversal, error message F5522 appears: "Reverse posting key specification is missing for posting key."

Solution: In the posting key configuration, the Reversal Posting Key field is empty. Specify a reversal posting key with the same characteristics, apart from the sign (debit or credit). In this way, you ensure that the reversal offsets all of the effects of the original posting.

3. **Issue:** When I try to make a normal Financial Accounting posting, error message F5272 appears: "Rules for posting key XX and acct AAAAAAAAAA set incorrectly for 'FFFFF' field."

Solution: There is a conflict between the field status rules of the posting key and the ones from the field status group assigned to the general ledger account. One rule says that the field is suppressed, and the other rule says that the status is mandatory; the two rules are in conflict, and the system can't post. If you need to post with the specific posting key and the specific account, you must solve the problem in customizing. Either the rule must be changed from suppressed to optional or mandatory, or the other rule must be changed from mandatory to optional or suppressed. The change has to be done either in Transaction OB41 for the posting key, or in Transaction OBC4 for the field status group. To understand which field status group you need to change, you need two pieces of information: the field status variant (find the field status variant assigned to the company code in Table T001, field FSTVA) and the field status group assigned to the account (Table SKB1, field FSTAG). Then change the field status with Transaction OBC4; first select the field status variant, and then the field status group.

4. **Issue:** When creating a new number range, the system stops me, saying that it overlaps with an existing number range without specifying which number range. How can I find this information?

Solution: Use Transaction SE16 in Table NRIV, and fill in the fields as follows:

- **Object Name:** "RF_BELEG"
- **Subobject Value:** Your company code
- **Number Range:** Leave blank
- **To Year:** Specify the year in which you're making the update

This results in a list of all of the existing number ranges for the company code and the year, allowing you to easily identify the overlap.

3.6   SAP General Ledger Settings Only

In this section, we analyze the configuration setting available only for SAP General Ledger, such as parallel ledgers, ledger groups, document splitting, and segments. If you're working with the classic General Ledger, you can skip this section.

3.6.1   Defining General Ledgers

Quick Reference
Menu path: IMG • Financial Accounting (New) • Ledgers • Ledger • Define Ledgers for General Ledger Accounting
Table/view: T881/V_FAGL_T881

In the SAP General Ledger environment, unlike in the classic General Ledger environment, you can manage one or more ledgers. The total table for reporting is no longer GLT0, but FAGLFLEXT, where more dimensions can be managed (ledgers, segments, profit centers, cost centers, etc.). One of the main functionalities of SAP General Ledger is the possibility to manage parallel accounting with multiple ledgers. In the classic General Ledger, the possible solutions were the following:

▸ Parallel accounts

▸ Special ledgers

▸ Parallel company codes

The definition of a new ledger isn't a routine activity but should be managed within the framework of a project because it's a considerable change in your Financial Accounting and Controlling model. Define ledgers with the path specified in the Quick Reference box. In this step, you only define the following settings (Figure 3.21):

▸ **Ld (ledger code)**
This field should be two-digits and alphanumeric.

▸ **Ledger Name**
For example, "Leading Ledger."

▸ **Total Table**
Use the total table predefined by SAP for the SAP General Ledger total data: FAGLFLEXT.

▶ **Leading**

This indicator is set once at the beginning of your SAP installation, and can't be changed after you've made postings to the system. The leading ledger has certain characteristics that distinguish it from all other ledgers:

- ▶ All of the postings of the leading ledger are contained in Table BSEG. If a document doesn't post to the leading ledger, it updates Table BSEG_ADD instead.

- ▶ The leading ledger is integrated with Controlling. No integration with Controlling is possible for the other ledgers.

- ▶ The leading ledger is integrated with depreciation area 01.

- ▶ The leading ledger automatically inherits some of the settings defined at the chart of accounts level (e.g., the fiscal year).

- ▶ The leading ledger defines the set of local currencies that can be used in a company code; in other words, the non-leading ledgers can use some or all of the parallel currencies defined for the leading ledger.

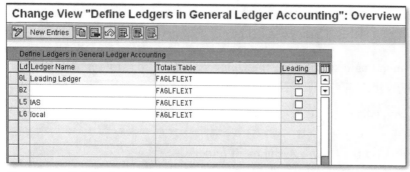

Figure 3.21 Defining Ledgers

3.6.2 Defining Ledger Groups

Quick Reference

Menu path: IMG • FINANCIAL ACCOUNTING (NEW) • FINANCIAL ACCOUNTING GLOBAL SETTINGS (NEW) • LEDGERS • LEDGER • DEFINE LEDGER GROUP

Tables: FAGL_TLDGRP (ledger groups), FAGL_TLDGRP_MAP (ledgers assigned to the ledger group)

When you post directly in Financial Accounting, you can't directly specify the ledger to post to; instead, you specify the ledger group, which is simply a collection of ledgers. The same ledger can be contained in more than one ledger group.

For example, say you have the following three ledgers:

- A0 (group ledger)
- A1 (local ledger)
- A2 (tax ledger)

And you've defined the following four ledger groups with the assigned ledgers:

- 0001: Group and local (ledgers A0 and A1)
- 0002: Group and tax (ledgers A0 and A2)
- 0003: Local and tax (ledgers A1 and A2)
- 0004: Tax (ledger A2)

Note

If you want to post to all of the ledgers, leave the ledger group blank; the system automatically updates all ledgers.

Follow the menu path specified in the Quick Reference box. To define the ledger groups, follow these steps (Figure 3.22):

1. Define the ledger group ID (four-digit max long, alphanumeric) and the description.
2. Double-click on the Ledger Assignment folder.
3. Click on New Entries, and assign all of the necessary ledgers.

   The system displays all ledgers, whether or not they are contained in other ledger groups. One ledger can be assigned to many ledger groups.

4. Specify which is the representative ledger within the group (if the leading ledger is contained in the ledger group, then it must be the representative ledger).

   The representative ledger has the following roles within the ledger group:

   - When you post a Financial Accounting document, the system checks whether the posting date falls in an open posting period. To make this check, the system accesses Table T001B and uses the posting period variant assigned to the representative ledger. If the period is open in the representative ledger, you can go ahead and post.

▶ The number range used to post to the ledger group is the one assigned to the representative ledger.

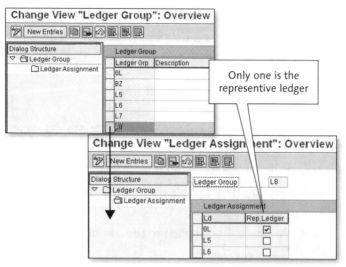

Figure 3.22 Defining Ledger Groups

3.6.3 Leading and Non-Leading Ledger Settings

The main characteristics of the leading ledger are the same that you define at the company code level (and then in Table T001, in most cases):

▶ The fiscal year variant is the one assigned to the company code in Transaction OBY6, field T001-PERIV.

▶ The posting period variant is the one assigned to the company code in Transaction OBY6, field T001-OPVAR.

▶ The parallel currencies (if defined) are the ones specified at the company code level in Transaction OB22.

The non-leading ledger settings, however, are different and are discussed in more detail next.

Quick Reference
Menu path: IMG • FINANCIAL ACCOUNTING (NEW) • FINANCIAL ACCOUNTING GLOBAL SETTINGS (NEW) • LEDGERS • LEDGER • DEFINE AND ACTIVATE NON-LEADING LEDGERS **Table/view:** T882G/V_FAGL_T882G

The non-leading ledger can differ from the leading ledger for the dimensions that are updated in the ledger. For example, in the total data table FAGLFLEXT for ledger Z1, the profit center is present and therefore can be used in the reporting, while for ledger Z2 it isn't updated.

In addition to this, the following characteristics can differ in the leading ledger and the non-leading ledger (Figure 3.23). You can maintain the different characteristics in Table T882G.

To perform this task, follow these steps:

1. Follow the menu path specified in the Quick Reference box; the system issues a pop-up where you can specify the ledger.

2. Enter the ledger, and click on the Continue button.

3. In the following screen, click on the New Entries button, and, in the first column, specify the company code.

4. Enter the following settings that should be applied to the combination ledger/company code (Figure 3.23):

▶ **Additional local currencies**
Assign the local currency of the company code in Table T001; this is assigned to all ledgers and can't be changed in any ledger. In Transaction OB22, define up to two additional local currencies in the company code; these automatically become the additional local currencies of the leading ledger. In the non-leading ledger, you can decide whether to manage only the local currency assigned to the company code (in Table T001), or to add one or two additional local currencies. In the latter case, you can't freely choose additional local currencies but rather pick up only the ones assigned to the company code/leading ledger.

▶ **Fiscal year variant**
Here you can assign a fiscal year variant different from the one in the leading ledger. If you leave the field blank, the fiscal year variant of the non-leading ledger is automatically the same as the leading ledger.

▶ **Posting period variant**
Here you can assign a posting period variant different from the one in the leading ledger. If you leave the field blank, the posting period variant of the non-leading ledger is automatically the same as the leading ledger.

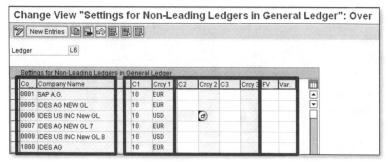

Figure 3.23 Non-Leading Ledger Settings

3.6.4 Assigning Scenarios

> **Quick Reference**
>
> **Menu path:** IMG • FINANCIAL ACCOUNTING (NEW) • FINANCIAL ACCOUNTING GLOBAL SETTINGS (NEW) • LEDGERS • LEDGER • ASSIGN SCENARIOS AND CUSTOMER FIELDS TO LEDGERS
>
> **Tables/views:** FAGL_SCENARIO/V_FAGL_SCENARIO (scenarios), FAGL_SCEN_FIELDS/V_FAGL_SCE_FIELD (fields assigned to the scenario), FAGL_LEDGER_SCEN (assignment of scenarios to ledgers)

In the SAP General Ledger environment, you can manage parallel accounting with parallel ledgers. The total data of the ledgers is updated in Table FAGLFLEXT, but, like in the special ledger, only some dimensions are available for each ledger in FAGFLEXT (e.g., ledger S1 has a profit center and business area that aren't available in ledger S2).

Instead of directly specifying the fields in the ledger definition, you assign scenarios to the ledgers and then assign fields to these scenarios. This ensures that the ledger is updated in FAGLFLEXT with all of the fields assigned to the scenarios that are in turn assigned to the ledger.

Figure 3.24 illustrates the linkage between the scenarios (the six scenarios displayed in the figure are pre-delivered by SAP; you cannot define your own scenarios) and the assigned fields; Figure 3.25 illustrates the assignment of scenarios to ledgers. As you can see, many scenarios can be assigned to one ledger. The same scenario can be assigned to many ledgers.

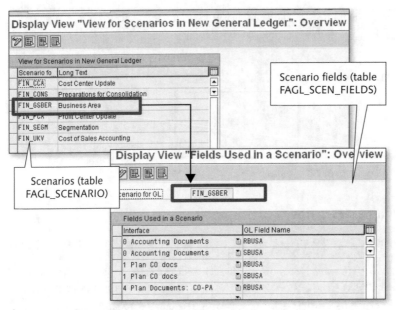

Figure 3.24 Scenarios and Assigned Fields

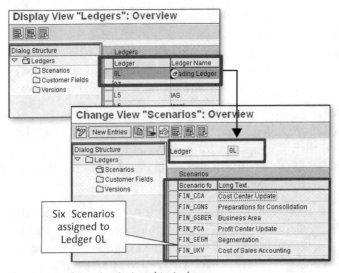

Figure 3.25 Scenarios Assigned to Ledger

3.6.5 Configuring Document Splitting

To explain document splitting, we begin with an example. When you post an incoming invoice for services, there is only one vendor open item but potentially many cost items with different cost centers and profit centers. If you want to have your debts split according to the correct profit center, the split functionality "explodes" the vendor line item in many items in proportion to the amount of the costs for each profit center. The same happens when the item is cleared.

The system performs the split in the background. For users that post invoices and payments, nothing changes because they continue to work with a single line item. In fact, the vendor invoice continues to generate one line item in Tables BSEG and BSIK, but in the background, the system generates linked multiple items in Table FAGLFLEXA. When you look at a posted document, you can see the unique vendor line item in the entry view, and the split items in the general ledger view.

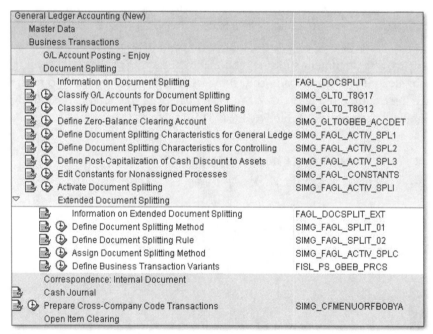

General Ledger Accounting (New)	
Master Data	
Business Transactions	
G/L Account Posting - Enjoy	
Document Splitting	
Information on Document Splitting	FAGL_DOCSPLIT
Classify G/L Accounts for Document Splitting	SIMG_GLT0_T8G17
Classify Document Types for Document Splitting	SIMG_GLT0_T8G12
Define Zero-Balance Clearing Account	SIMG_GLT0GBEB_ACCDET
Define Document Splitting Characteristics for General Ledge	SIMG_FAGL_ACTIV_SPL1
Define Document Splitting Characteristics for Controlling	SIMG_FAGL_ACTIV_SPL2
Define Post-Capitalization of Cash Discount to Assets	SIMG_FAGL_ACTIV_SPL3
Edit Constants for Nonassigned Processes	SIMG_FAGL_CONSTANTS
Activate Document Splitting	SIMG_FAGL_ACTIV_SPLI
Extended Document Splitting	
Information on Extended Document Splitting	FAGL_DOCSPLIT_EXT
Define Document Splitting Method	SIMG_FAGL_SPLIT_01
Define Document Splitting Rule	SIMG_FAGL_SPLIT_02
Assign Document Splitting Method	SIMG_FAGL_ACTIV_SPLC
Define Business Transaction Variants	FISL_PS_GBEB_PRCS
Correspondence: Internal Document	
Cash Journal	
Prepare Cross-Company Code Transactions	SIMG_CFMENUORFBOBYA
Open Item Clearing	

Figure 3.26 Document Splitting Customizing

The customizing and activation of the splitting functionality has a high level of complexity (Figure 3.26) and can be managed only within the framework of a project where the business requirements for the splitting are clearly identified, and a coherent design of the splitting functionality is established. Any change to the splitting configuration requires an intensive check of the consequences on the internal Financial Accounting business transactions and on the interfaces; as such, it requires a strong test effort.

This section aims to provide some tips for understanding the customizing steps required for document splitting but can't be exhaustive given the dimension of the topic. For the sake of clarity, we describe the customizing steps in the form of questions and answers.

Where Can I See if Splitting is Activated?

Quick Reference
Menu path: IMG • Financial Accounting (New) • General Ledger Accounting (New) • Business Transactions • Document Splitting • Activate Document Splitting
Table/view: FAGL_ACTIVEC/V_FAGL_ACTIVEC_2

When you activate document splitting, you make the setting at the client level (it is active by default for all company codes) by assigning a splitting method to the client (see the example in Figure 3.27). You can deactivate the document splitting at the company code level in Table FAGL_SPLIT_ACTC.

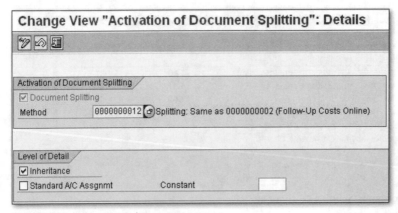

Figure 3.27 Document Splitting Activation

Which Fields Are Used for Splitting?

Quick Reference

Table/view: FAGL_SPLIT_FIELD/V_FAGL_SPLIT_FLD

In Table FAGL_SPLIT_FIELD, the fields you're using in the splitting functionality are defined at the client level.

Figure 3.28 displays an example of the configuration; *zero balance* means that the documents in which the split has to take place must balance to zero according to this dimension; with the Mandatory flag, you specify whether the field must always be present.

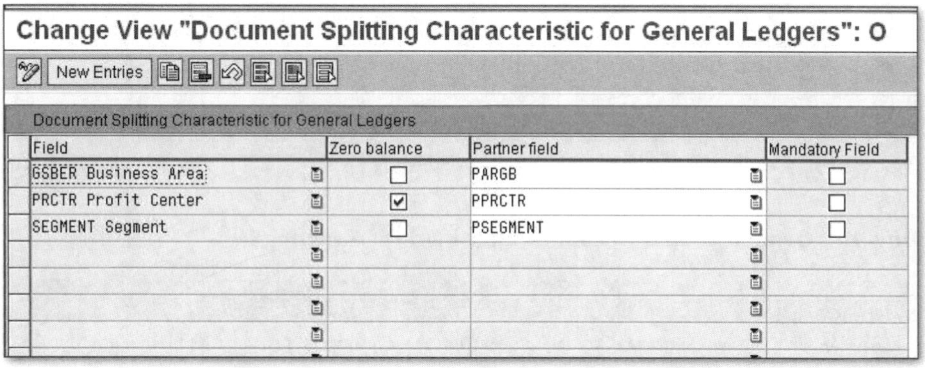

Field		Zero balance	Partner field		Mandatory Field
GSBER Business Area	🖹	☐	PARGB	🖹	☐
PRCTR Profit Center	🖹	☑	PPRCTR	🖹	☐
SEGMENT Segment	🖹	☐	PSEGMENT	🖹	☐
	🖹			🖹	
	🖹			🖹	
	🖹			🖹	
	🖹			🖹	

Figure 3.28 Fields Relevant for Splitting

How Are Document Types Classified for Splitting?

Quick Reference

Menu path: IMG • FINANCIAL ACCOUNTING (NEW) • GENERAL LEDGER ACCOUNTING (NEW) • BUSINESS TRANSACTIONS • DOCUMENT SPLITTING • CLASSIFY DOCUMENT TYPES FOR DOCUMENT SPLITTING

Table/view: T8G12/V_ T8G12

In Table T8G12, document types are assigned to business transactions and business transaction variants (Figure 3.29). This classification, with the item categories assigned to the accounts, is used in the actual splitting functionality.

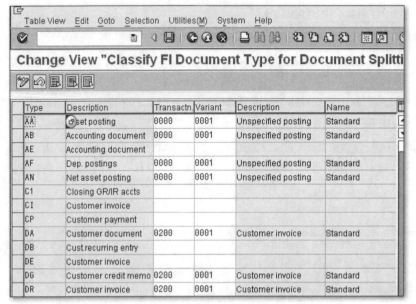

Figure 3.29 Classification of Document Types for Splitting

How Are General Ledger Accounts Classified for Splitting?

Quick Reference
Menu path: IMG • FINANCIAL ACCOUNTING (NEW) • GENERAL LEDGER ACCOUNTING (NEW) • BUSINESS TRANSACTIONS • DOCUMENT SPLITTING • CLASSIFY G/L ACCOUNTS FOR DOCUMENT SPLITTING
Table/view: T8G17/V_ T8G17

If a document is subject to splitting, all of the accounts in the document must be classified for splitting and assigned to an item category, which is defined in Table TG802. The classification of the accounts in item categories is necessary to let the system know which accounts must be split and which accounts are the basis for splitting (e.g., customer accounts are split according to the amounts in the revenue and cost accounts, so the system must know which accounts belong to the customer, cost, and revenue categories). See Figure 3.30 for an example of the customizing for document splitting.

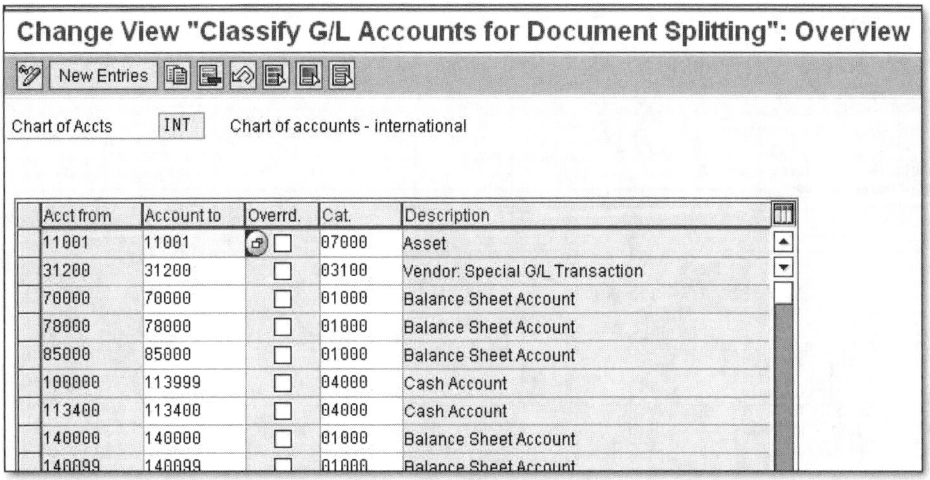

Acct from	Account to	Overrd.	Cat.	Description
11001	11001	☐	07000	Asset
31200	31200	☐	03100	Vendor: Special G/L Transaction
70000	70000	☐	01000	Balance Sheet Account
78000	78000	☐	01000	Balance Sheet Account
85000	85000	☐	01000	Balance Sheet Account
100000	113999	☐	04000	Cash Account
113400	113400	☐	04000	Cash Account
140000	140000	☐	01000	Balance Sheet Account
140099	140099	☐	01000	Balance Sheet Account

Figure 3.30 Classification of General Ledger Accounts for Document Splitting

How Do Item Categories and Business Transactions/ Variants Generate the Split?

Quick Reference

Menu path: IMG • Financial Accounting (New) • General Ledger Accounting (New) • Business Transactions • Document Splitting • Extended Document Splitting

For each splitting method (❶ of Figure 3.31), you must assign business transactions and business transaction variants. For each combination of splitting method/ business transaction/business transaction variant (❷ of Figure 3.31), you must specify the item categories to be split (❸ of Figure 3.31) and, for each category to be split, the item categories that form the basis of the splitting (❹ of Figure 3.31). The system gets the needed information from the financial document, and the following actions occur:

- The document type is assigned to a combination of business transaction and business transaction variant.
- The accounts are assigned to an item category.

Only one splitting method is activated at the client level.

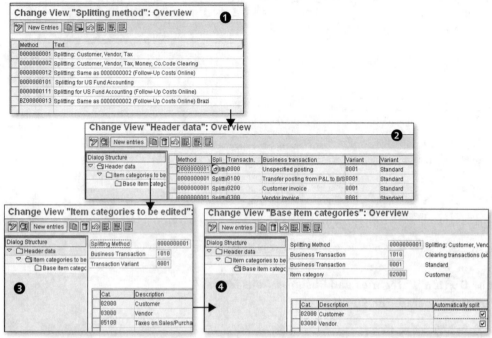

Figure 3.31 Logic of the Splitting Functionality

3.6.6 Configuring Document Types and Number Ranges for Non-Leading Ledger Postings

Quick Reference

Menu path: IMG • FINANCIAL ACCOUNTING (NEW) • DOCUMENT • DEFINE DOCUMENT TYPES FOR ENTRY VIEW IN A LEDGER/DEFINE DOCUMENT TYPES FOR GENERAL LEDGER VIEW

Tables/views: FAGL_BELNR_LD/V_FAGL_BELNR_LD and FAGL_DOCNR_LD/V_FAGL_DOCNR_LD

If you want to post to a ledger group that doesn't include the leading ledger, you must perform this customizing activity. When you post to a ledger group, the representative ledger determines the number range according to the following rules:

▶ If you post to a ledger that includes the leading ledger, the number range comes from the leading ledger and depends on the document type (field T003-NUMKR).

▶ If you post to a ledger group that doesn't include the leading ledger, the number range depends on a combination of the representative ledger and document type.

To use a document type without the leading ledger, there must be an entry in Table FAGL_BELNR_LD that includes the representative ledger and the document type (see Figure 3.32 for the customizing details).

The same activity must be performed in Table FAGL_DOCNR_LD, but only if the fiscal year variant of the non-leading ledger differs from the fiscal year variant of the leading ledger.

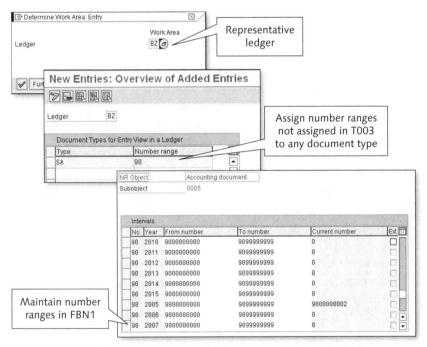

Figure 3.32 Number Range Assignments for Posting to a Non-Leading Ledger

3.6.7 Defining Segments

Quick Reference

Menu path: IMG • ENTERPRISE STRUCTURE • DEFINITION • FINANCIAL ACCOUNTING • DEFINE SEGMENT

Table/view: FAGL_SEGM/V_FAGL_SEGM

SAP General Ledger offers a segments functionality, which helps to fulfill IFRS reporting requirements. You define segments in customizing using view V_FAGL_ SEGM; click on the New Entries button, and define the segment ID and description (Figure 3.33). That's all that is needed in this step.

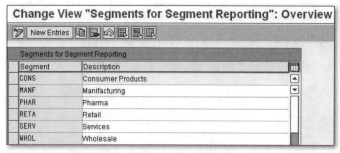

Figure 3.33 Defining Segments

3.6.8 Defining Profit Centers

Quick Reference
Menu path: IMG • ENTERPRISE STRUCTURE • DEFINITION • FINANCIAL ACCOUNTING • DEFINE PROFIT CENTER
Transaction: KE51
Table: CEPC

Profit centers are integrated in the SAP General Ledger environment; therefore, Table GLPCT (profit center ledger) should no longer be updated. The profit center dimension can be integrated within the new SAP General Ledger total table, FAGL-FLEXT. Profit centers are directly assigned to a controlling area and can be allowed in one or more company code, just as in the classic General Ledger environment.

You can also define profit centers in customizing, within the enterprise definition, or directly with Transaction KE51. To create a profit center, follow these steps (Figure 3.34):

1. Run Transaction KE51.

2. If you're working with a controlling object (such as a cost center or profit center) for the first time since you logged on to SAP, the system asks you for the Controlling area. Specify the Controlling area, and click on the Continue button. For the rest of your logon session, you can change the Controlling area you're working with using Transaction OKKS.

3. In the next screen, specify the profit center number and, optionally, a reference profit center to use to copy the relevant data. Press Enter.

4. In the resulting screen, specify the following information:

   ▶ **Analysis Period:** This is the period in which the profit center is valid.

   ▶ **Name (short text) and Long Text:** Provide a meaningful description of the profit center.

   ▶ **Profit Center Group:** Each profit center has to be assigned to a special hierarchy (or *profit center group*) called a *standard hierarchy*. The standard hierarchy can be multilevel and contain several nodes; in this field, you must specify one of the nodes contained in the standard hierarchy.

   ▶ **Segment:** Specify a segment. This information is used by the system to automatically derive the segment from the profit center at the time of posting.

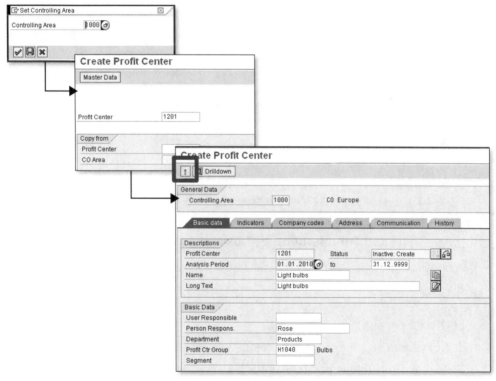

Figure 3.34 Profit Center Creation

After you've completed these steps, click on the Company Codes folder, and assign the profit center to one or more company codes (you can use Transaction KE56 to collectively change the assignment of profit centers to company codes, as illustrated in Figure 3.35).

When all of the needed information is updated in the profit center master data, click on the Activate button to immediately use the profit center.

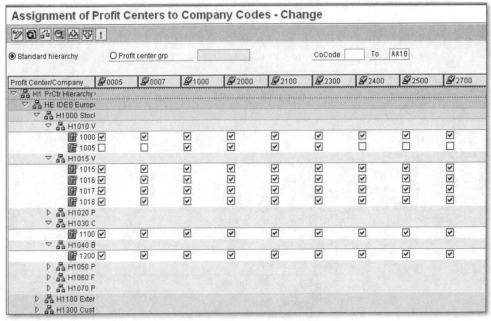

Figure 3.35 Mass Assignment of Profit Centers to Company Codes

3.6.9 FAQ and Troubleshooting Tips

Next we answer some frequently asked questions and offer helpful troubleshooting tips.

FAQ

1. **Question:** Can a ledger group contain only one ledger?

   Answer: Yes, this is possible and is actually necessary if you need to post to exactly one specific ledger because only the ledger group is available in the posting header.

2. **Question:** Is it possible to not assign a company code to the leading ledger?

   Answer: No. All company codes are automatically assigned to the leading ledger, and the assignment can't be broken.

3. **Question:** Are the company codes automatically assigned to all ledgers? In this case, how can I deactivate the assignment?

   Answer: Each company code is assigned to the leading ledger, and this can't be changed. The assignment to a non-leading ledger isn't mandatory. A company code is assigned to a ledger in view V_FAGL_T882, as described in this section. If a specific ledger in a company code isn't present in this view, it means that the company code isn't assigned to the ledger.

4. **Question:** Can I create my own scenario?

   Answer: No. You cannot create your own scenario.

5. **Question:** How can I find the number ranges assigned to the leading ledger?

   Answer: The number ranges assigned to a document type in its configuration data (Table T003, field NUMKR) are the number ranges used by the leading ledger.

6. **Question:** Should the segment be posted directly in the Financial Accounting documents, or can it be derived?

   Answer: The segment is generally derived by Profit Center Accounting. In Transaction KE51 (profit center creation) or KE52 (profit center change), you can assign the profit center directly to a segment. You can also use substitutions to automatically fill in the segment based on your user-defined prerequisites.

   Another option is BAdI FAGL_DERIVE_SEGMENT, which is available for the segment derivation: Financial Accounting (New) • Financial Accounting Global Settings (New) • Ledgers • Tools • Customer Enhancements • Segment Derivation. In the same area, BAdI FAGL_DERIVE_PSEGMENT is also available for the derivation of the partner segment.

7. **Question:** What does "Analysis Period" mean in the profit center master data?

   Answer: When you change the data in a profit center you can specify that the new data will be valid from a certain date onward. In this way, you're creating multiple records in Table CEPC for the same profit center under the same controlling area. When you post to a profit center the validity period will be chosen on the basis of the posting date.

8. **Question:** Can the same profit center exist under two different company codes? And under different controlling areas?

Answer: Each profit center is defined at the controlling area level. Therefore, in one controlling area, one profit center can be used in some or all of the company codes assigned to that controlling area. The assignment is made using Transaction KE51 or KE52 or, collectively, using Transaction KE56 (refer to Figure 3.35). The same profit center code can exist in two different controlling areas.

Troubleshooting Tips

1. **Issue:** Error message FAGL_LEDGER_CUST013 appears: "Changes cannot be made to leading ledger."

   Solution: This means that you tried to change the leading ledger after it has already been posted to, which isn't possible. If you're in a test or development system and still in the implementation phase of your SAP project, reset the data for the company code using report SAPF020. If you're in a productive system (i.e., if there are already company codes with data in the system), you can't perform this activity.

2. **Issue:** Error message FAGL_LEDGER_CUST012 appears: "Define exactly one leading ledger."

   Solution: This means that you tried to set the Leading indicator for more than one ledger in the list. This isn't possible. Only one leading ledger is possible in the system.

3. **Issue:** An error message appears: "The leading ledger must be the representative ledger in a ledger group."

   Solution: This means that you're updating a ledger group that contains the leading ledger and have assigned the role of representative ledger to another ledger. This isn't possible; if a ledger group contains the leading ledger, the representative ledger must be the leading ledger.

4. **Issue:** Message FAGL_LEDGER_CUST093 appears: "Doc. type XX: Number range NN is used for ledger LL with doc. type XX."

   Solution: This means that you're trying to assign a document type in a non-leading ledger to the same number range as in the leading ledger, which isn't possible. If you want to use a document type to post to a non-leading ledger, you must assign a separate number range to the representative ledger of the ledger group you're using.

5. **Issue:** I've created a profit center without activating it. Can I activate it afterwards?

Solution: Yes, you can run Transaction KE52 and activate the profit center with the Activate button (🔲). You can also use Transaction KCH5N to change the standard hierarchy, and then perform mass activation of all of the profit centers with an inactive status.

3.7 Validations and Substitutions

In this section, we discuss *validations* (user-defined controls that are triggered when a specific prerequisite is met) and *substitutions* (which allow you to replace the value that was specified in a field on the basis of rules you define in the system). Validations and substitutions are treated together because the ways you build them are very similar.

3.7.1 Validations

Quick Reference

Menu path: IMG • Financial Accounting • General Ledger Accounting • Business Transactions • G/L Posting • Carry Out and Check Document Settings • Validation in Accounting Documents

Transaction: OB28

SAP has some basic controls necessary to ensure the consistency of data in the system. Examples of standard controls are listed here:

- To save an accounting document, it must balance to zero; the system doesn't allow you to post unbalanced documents.
- You can't specify a document number already assigned in the company code and fiscal year.
- If the account is created as a cost element, the system requires an additional account assignment (such as cost center, profitability analysis segment, or WBS element).
- You can't specify a document number if the number range is internal.

In addition to the standard controls in Financial Accounting documents, you can add specific controls using the *validation* technique. Here we discuss the setup of validations in Financial Accounting, although it's also possible to set up validation in Controlling as well.

> **Validations in Controlling**
>
> Validations in Controlling affect Financial Accounting in the following way: if the Controlling document that should be generated together with the Financial Accounting document can't be posted because of a validation in Controlling, you can't post the Financial Accounting document. Of course, if you're posting a document within Controlling with no effect on Financial Accounting, the Controlling validation is relevant only within the Controlling module.

Validations are set up in two main phases. We give a brief summary of each phase in the following list, and then go into more detail about the steps involved in each phase.

1. Create the validation.
   Specify the point in the document in which the control should take place (after entering the header data, after entering each line item data, or before saving the entire document), and perform all of the necessary steps. Each step is a control, and all of the steps are carried out in the specified order.

2. Assign the validation to each company code.
   You can assign the same validation to all company codes, or you can create different validations for different groups of company codes (e.g., one validation for each of the company codes that belong to the same country).

In the first phase, creating the validation, follow these steps. (See Figure 3.36 for an example of a validation, and Figure 3.37 for an example of how to use the validation working area.):

1. Run Transaction OB28, and follow this menu path: ENVIRONMENT • VALIDATION.

2. Position the cursor on one of the three possible levels to which validations are designed to work (refer to Figure 3.36):

   ▶ **Document Header:** The validation is triggered after you correctly enter all of the document header data and press Enter.

   ▶ **Line Item:** The validation is triggered for each line item after you correctly enter all of the line item data and press Enter.

   ▶ **Complete Document:** The validation is triggered after you enter all line items and the document balances to zero; to trigger the validation, you must save or simulate the document.

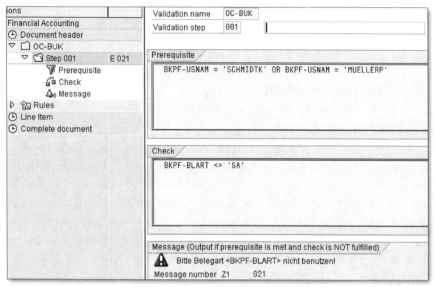

Figure 3.36 Example of a Validation

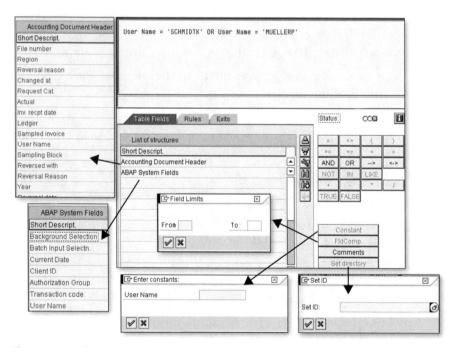

Figure 3.37 Validation Working Area

3. Enter the validation code (maximum of seven digits, alphanumeric) and a brief meaningful description.

4. Create the first step (i.e., the first control) contained in the validation.
   Click on the Step button, and specify a brief but meaningful description for the step. The description is very important, especially if the Boolean rules are long and complex; it helps the people that rework the validation in the future to understand the purpose of the step.

5. Double-click on the Prerequisite button, which you can find under the step. Here you define the rule that has to be satisfied to have the control performed. If the prerequisite isn't met, no control is performed in this step. In general, you start with the field. For example, if you want to specify that the cost center must start with 100, double-click on the Structure BSEG row, and find the Cost Center field. Double-click on the field, and it appears in the prerequisite. Now click on the LIKE button on the right side of the screen.

6. Specify the value that should be compared with the content of the field.

7. When the prerequisite is created, save it and click on the control.
   Create the control with the same logic as the prerequisite. Just keep in mind the following differences:

   ▶ The prerequisite must be met for the system to perform the control.

   ▶ The control must be passed in order not to get the message (which can be an error, warning, or information message).

8. Click on the Message button (see Figure 3.38).
   This allows you to specify which message the user receives when the control isn't passed.

9. Specify the message type.
   You have several options for the message type:

   ▶ **Type E (error):** The user sees an error message, meaning that he can't go ahead until he has addressed the error.

   ▶ **Type W (warning):** The user sees a warning message and must decide whether to change some data to comply with the control or to simply skip the control by pressing Enter.

   ▶ **Type I (information):** The user sees an information message and can still complete or post the document.

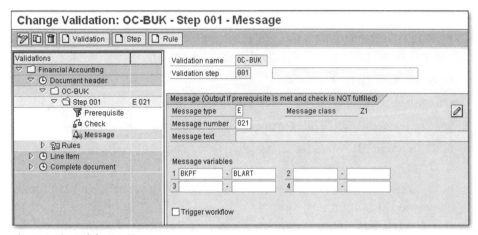

Figure 3.38 Validation Message

10. Specify the message number (Figure 3.38).

    Note that you can't simply type the message; instead, you must choose a message that you've already defined in customizing using Transaction SE91. The messages are created within a message class; the link between the validation and the message class is defined in Table GB02C.

11. For each message, you can specify up to four message variables.

    For this to work, the message must allow the variables. For example, the message "Combination cost center &1 and account &2 incorrect" will have the &1 and &2 replaced by real values when you post. To do this, enter variable 1 as "BSEG – KOSTL" and variable 2 as "BSEG – HKONT". Remember to think about the callup point of the validation; the combination described in the example won't work for header level validations, as both the account and the cost center aren't available at the header level. It also won't work at the document complete level because more than one line item exists, and the system won't know which line item to choose.

    After the validation is created, you can perform the second step and assign it to the company code. You do this in Transaction OB28 (Figure 3.39):

1. Select the New Entries button.

2. Specify the company code that should use the validation.

3. Define a callup point (this is the moment in the document when the validation is triggered, as already described in the first step):

- ▸ **0001** – Document Header
- ▸ **0002** – Line Item (validation triggered for each line item after you correctly enter all of the line item data and press Enter)
- ▸ **0003** – Complete Document

4. Using the matchcode, select the validation just created.

5. Specify the activation level. Three choices are available:

- ▸ **0 – Inactive:** The validation is assigned to the company code, but the controls aren't activated.
- ▸ **1 – Active:** All of the controls in the validations area are active for both manual and batch input postings.
- ▸ **2 – Active, No Batch Input:** All of the controls in the validations area are active for just manual postings.

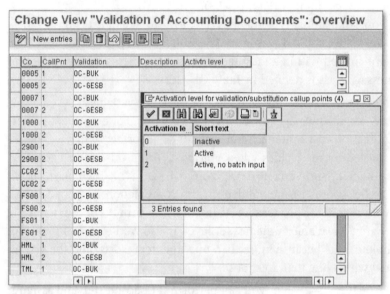

Figure 3.39 Assigning Validations to Company Code

Next we explain some of the functionalities available for building complex validation rules. We begin by explaining the meaning of the many different buttons available in the validation working area; then we clarify the usage of sets in validations; and, finally, for the most complex validations, we briefly describe the usage of user exits.

Buttons for Building Validations

In the validation working area, you can directly enter the formula of the prerequisite or of the control, or you can choose the fields from the lists available and complete the Boolean statement with the help of the interactive buttons (Figure 3.40).

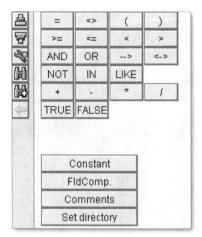

Figure 3.40 Buttons for Building Validations

The following buttons are used to build the formula (Boolean statement) in the prerequisite or in the control:

▶ =, <>, >=, <=, <, >
  Used for comparison between two values.

▶ (,)
  The parentheses are used to create nested complex controls.

▶ AND
  Indicates that two conditions must be met at the same time.

▶ OR
  Indicates that at least one of the two conditions must be met.

▶ ->
  See Table 3.4. If the result is TRUE in the prerequisite, the control is made; if the result is TRUE in the control, the control is passed.

Statement A	Statement B	A – -> B
TRUE	TRUE	TRUE
TRUE	FALSE	FALSE
FALSE	TRUE	TRUE
FALSE	FALSE	TRUE

Table 3.4 Truth Table I

▶ <->: – >

See Table 3.5. If the result is TRUE in the prerequisite, the control is made; if the result is TRUE in the control, the control is passed.

Statement A	Statement B	A <-> B
TRUE	TRUE	TRUE
TRUE	FALSE	FALSE
FALSE	TRUE	FALSE
FALSE	FALSE	TRUE

Table 3.5 Truth Table II

▶ **NOT**

At the beginning of a statement, specifies that a condition must not be met.

▶ **IN**

Use this button before specifying a set. For example, if, in the prerequisite, you want to specify that the cost center must be contained in set Y_CC_ALLOWED, type: "BSEG – KOSTL IN Y_CC_ALLOWED".

▶ **TRUE**

If defined in the prerequisite, the control is always done; if defined in the control, it's always passed.

▶ **FALSE**

The condition is never met. If defined in the prerequisite, the control is never done (as such, it doesn't make any sense to put FALSE in a prerequisite); if defined in the control, it's never passed.

▶ **Constant**

Use this button to specify a single value for one field.

► **Comments**

Use this button to enter some descriptive comments that don't affect the logic of the validation but might be useful to understand the background of the control.

► **Set Directory**

Use this button to search the appropriate set to specify after the operator IN.

The following buttons are used to search fields from the list:

► 🖨 sorts the listed fields in ascendant order.

► 🖨 sorts the listed fields in descendant order.

► 🔍 shows or hides the technical names of the fields.

► 🔍 searches fields by the technical name or field description.

► 🔍 continues a search (started with the previous button).

► ⬅ allows you to branch from the field list to the list of available tables.

Sets

With the Boolean rule IN, you can work with sets or groups (which technically are a specific form of sets and are contained in the same tables as the sets; SETHEADER for the header data and SETLEAF for the line item data). Use the following transactions to create sets and groups:

► GS01 to create sets. In the creation of sets, we recommend that you use Tables BKPF and BSEG and the fields available there.

► KDH1 to create account groups.

► KCH1 to create profit center groups.

► KSH1 to create cost center groups.

► KAH1 to create cost element groups.

► KOH1 to create order groups.

User Exits

Sometimes the normal interactive functions and rules that you can use to create a validation aren't sufficient to completely build your specific rules. In this case, you may need the help of ABAP code and user exits. You don't have to create one program for each user exit; there is one unique ABAP program that functions as a user exit "container," where you create all of the user exits to be used in all of the validations. This ABAP program is accessed via the following customizing path: FINANCIAL ACCOUNTING • SPECIAL PURPOSE LEDGER • BASIC SETTINGS • USER EXITS • MAINTAIN CLIENT-SPECIFIC USER EXITS. Work with your ABAP expert to build the necessary user exits.

Validation Transport

There are two steps in transporting validations and the assignment of validations to company codes.

▶ First, transport the validation. From the validation working area (not from the screen where you assign each company code and callup point for a validation), double-click on a validation, and select VALIDATION • TRANSPORT. In the following screen, don't select the indicator sets and run the program; instead, select or create a new transport request.

▶ Second, transport the assignment of the validation to the company code and the callup point; do this in the first screen of Transaction OB28. Proceed as you would with any other customizing table.

If the validation uses sets or user exits, be sure that both are in the destination system before the transport takes place. For sets, we strongly recommend not transporting them, and instead recreating them in the destination system. It's good practice to define the production system as the master for all of the sets created in the system. From the production system, you can export the sets to the test system and to the development system via the export/import function (no transport and then no STMS involved).

For user exit transport, you must transport the entire user exit pool. Work with the ABAP programmer who created the user exit to ensure that the relevant transport takes place before the transport of the validation.

Generation of Validations

When a validation is changed and saved, the system generates it. If the validation is transported into the destination system, the validation is generated when the first document is posted. It's possible to force the generation of validations after the transport by running program RGUGBR00; select the Financial Accounting application area and the Validations flag (you can also select all of the flags, as it's just a generation program).

Warning on Validation Generation

If there is any problem in the validation generation (e.g., sets missing or missing user exits), generation will fail. In this case, no accounting document is posted in the company codes assigned to that validation until the error is corrected. For this reason, you should be very careful to ensure that all of the set's groups and user exits recalled by the validation are available in the destination system before the transport takes place.

If the validation is transported and a generation message occurs, you will get the information of the missing object. Create the object and re-run the validation generation with program RGUGBR00.

3.7.2 Substitutions

Substitutions allow you to automatically replace the value of one or more fields; the replacement takes place if the conditions you specify are satisfied (see Figure 3.41 for an example of a substitution). Each substitution is made of one or many steps; each step allows you to replace the content of one or more fields and is made of the following two components:

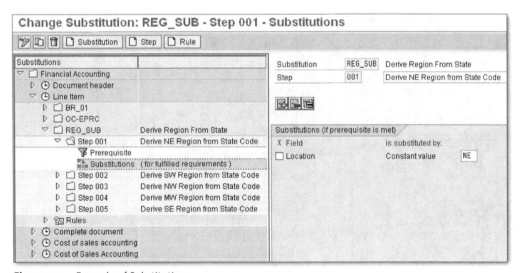

Figure 3.41 Example of Substitutions

► **Prerequisite**
The condition that must be met so that the replacement takes place.

▶ **Substitutions (For Fulfilled Requirements)**
Here the fields to be replaced are specified, and the target value or the rule to determine the target value is established.

Manage substitutions using Transaction OBBH (Figure 3.42). As with validations, substitutions are customized in two phases. These are briefly explained here, and then described in more detail.

1. Define the substitutions.

   Each substitution is created for exactly one level in the document posting logic (header, line item, or document complete). Each substitution can be made of one or more steps.

2. Assign exactly one validation to each combination of company code/callup point. The callup points are the following:

   ▶ **0001: Document Header.** This is triggered by pressing Enter after you correctly enter all of the header details.

   ▶ **0002: Line Item.** This is triggered for each line item by pressing Enter after you correctly enter all of the necessary information.

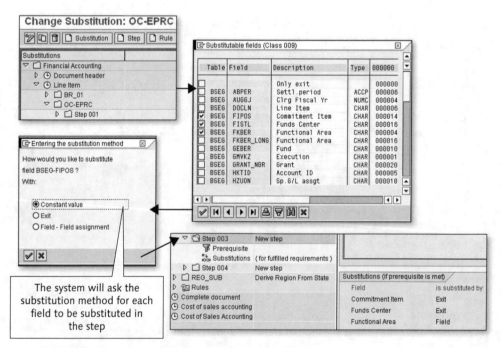

Figure 3.42 New Step in Substitution

▶ **0003: Document Complete.** This is triggered by posting or simulating the posting of the document, after you correctly enter all line items and the document balances to zero.

In the first phase, each substitution is made of one or more steps, and each step is made of two components: the prerequisite and the replacement. When you create a new step in the substitution, the system asks you which field you want to replace. Specify exactly one prerequisite in each step; if the prerequisite is satisfied, one or more replacements occur.

You create the prerequisite with the same logic as in the validation; refer to Section 3.7.2, Substitutions, for instructions on how to do this.

To create the substitution (i.e., to determine which field is replaced and how), double-click on the Substitutions (For Fulfilled Requirements) button. The system asks you which fields you want to replace; select one or more fields. When you confirm your choice, the system asks you, for each field, which substitution method you want to use. You have the following three alternatives:

▶ **Constant Value**
Specify a fixed value (for example, cost center = 12000).

▶ **Exit**
In this case, you must specify a user exit selected from the ones available in the program (the "exit pool"), declared in transaction under the following menu path: FINANCIAL ACCOUNTING • SPECIAL PURPOSE LEDGER • BASIC SETTINGS • USER EXITS • MAINTAIN CLIENT-SPECIFIC USER EXITS.

▶ **Field-Field Assignment**
With this method, you specify that the content of the field to be substituted should be replaced by the content of a second reference field.

If the step is already created, and you want to change the field to be replaced, change the substitution method, or add a new field, by following these steps:

1. Double-click on the Substitutions (For Fulfilled Requirements) button.

2. If you want to add a new field to be replaced, select the Insert Substitution Entry button (🔲), and proceed as described previously to define the field to be replaced, the method and the constant value, the reference field, or the user exit.

3. If you want to add or delete the replacement for a field, select the field and then the Substitution Entry button (🔲).

4. If you want to change the validation method for a field (e.g., from Constant Value to Exit), select the field, click the Move Substitution Entry button (🔢), and specify the new method and the constant value, the reference field, or the user exit.

Substitution: Only Exit

When you define a new step, the system proposes the fields to be replaced. The first choice is Only Exit, which means that the fields to be replaced and the rules for the replacement are all contained in the user exit. We recommend not using this method because it makes it difficult to understand the background of the substitution in the future; to understand which field has to be replaced and the way the replacement takes place, you would always need to look at the ABAP program that contains the user exit.

3.7.3 FAQ and Troubleshooting Tips

Next we answer some frequently asked questions and offer helpful troubleshooting tips.

FAQ

1. **Question:** Can I transport one step of the validation?

   Answer: No. When you transport the validations, you're always transporting the whole validation, including all of the steps contained within it.

2. **Question:** How can I enter the formulas without using the buttons?

   Answer: You can manually write the prerequisite and controls by following SETTINGS • EXPERT MODE.

3. **Question:** I want to see the technical names (table and field) instead of the field description. How can I get it?

   Answer: Choose from the menu SETTINGS • TECHNICAL NAMES.

4. **Question:** I want to replace one field with the first four digits of the content of a second field. Can I use the field-field assignment?

   Answer: No. With the field-field assignment, the whole content of the second field is used to replace the content of the first field. If you want to make a replacement with only a part of the content of the second field, you're forced to create a user exit.

5. **Question:** Can I replace the value of a header field with the content of a line item field?

Answer: Yes, this is possible. However, you should consider the following:

▸ You can't use a header substitution because the line item fields aren't available when this type of substitution is triggered.

▸ You can use a line item substitution; however, keep in mind that this substitution is repeated for each line item. As such, it could be useful to limit the substitution with the prerequisite; for example, if you want to replace the header text with the due date only for the vendor items, you should specify in the prerequisite that the account type of the line item (BSEG-KOART) is K.

▸ You can use a substitution for the callup point 0003 (document complete), but in this case you must create a user exit.

Troubleshooting Tips

1. **Issue:** In validations and substitutions I've created steps in the incorrect order. How can I change the order? Should I recreate the steps?

   Solution: When you click on one validation or substitution in the working area and select the Step button, the system adds the new step after all of the existing steps. If, instead, you click on one existing step and then click on the Step button, the system adds the new step before the selected step. If you created the steps in the incorrect order, simply use the mouse to drag and drop the steps until they are in the correct order.

2. **Issue:** The field that I want to replace isn't available in the list that the system provides. Why? How can I add the field that I need to the list?

   Solution: Some fields aren't displayed because the substitution of those fields could be dangerous for the consistency of data. For example, if you want to substitute the posting period, the system always ensures that the posting period is consistent with the posting date, based on the rules of the fiscal year variant assigned to the company code (or to the ledger/company code combination in SAP General Ledger). Substitution, however, can break this rule and lead to inconsistent postings.

   The fields that are allowed for substitutions are contained in Table GB01. Be very careful when changing Table GB01; you should do this only in exceptional cases when it's absolutely necessary. Be aware of the risk of data inconsistencies. Read SAP Note 42615 and other related notes before making any change in Table GB01.

3.8 Automatic Account Determination

When an accounting document is created, the accounts to be posted are selected manually by the user. However, under certain circumstances, the accounts can be selected automatically by the system. This is typical when a document is generated in Financial Accounting from other component (e.g., invoices generated through Sales and Distribution, or Materials Management documents); in this case, the rules to determine the accounts to post to are generally defined in the customizing of that component.

However, in certain cases, automatic account determination also takes place for postings generated automatically in Financial Accounting. Next we discuss the main steps in customizing account determination for Financial Accounting direct postings.

3.8.1 Differences in General Ledger Account Clearing

Quick Reference
Menu path: IMG • FINANCIAL ACCOUNTING • GENERAL LEDGER ACCOUNTING • BUSINESS TRANSACTIONS • OPEN ITEM CLEARING • CLEARING DIFFERENCES
Transactions: OBXZ (accounts for clearing differences), OBA0 (tolerances groups for accounts), OBA4 (assign users to tolerance groups)
Tables: T030 (accounts for automatic differences, Transaction DSA), T043S (tolerance groups for general ledger accounts), T043T (tolerance groups for employees), T043 (assignment of tolerance groups to users)

If you try to clear a general ledger open item with an offsetting account that has a lower amount than that of the open item, the system doesn't allow the posting of the clearing document. However, there is a way to clear the open items and to automatically post the difference to a difference account. There are two prerequisites for this process, though:

▶ The difference between the payment and the open item must be below the tolerances limits defined in customizing.

You can define tolerances rules to be assigned to users, and separate tolerances rules to be assigned to accounts. Both the rules must be respected during posting, so the more restrictive rule is applied (Figure 3.43). You assign the tolerance rules to the users in Customizing, with Transaction OBA4; you assign the tolerance rules to the general ledger accounts in the general ledger account master data, under the Control Data tab (Figure 3.44).

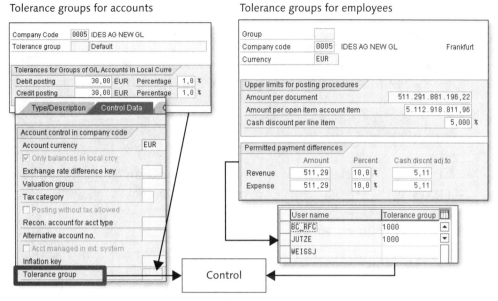

Tolerance groups for accounts

Tolerance groups for employees

Figure 3.43 Tolerance Groups for Clearing Differences

▸ You must have defined the accounts for the difference using Transaction OBXZ.

The assignment must be done for each chart of accounts (Figure 3.44).

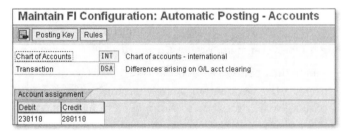

Figure 3.44 Accounts for General Ledger Clearing Differences

Recommendation for Tolerance Rules

If you customize accounts for clearing differences, we strongly recommend that you define tolerance rules. You can also define a "blank" tolerance rule for users and accounts that will apply to all of the accounts and users.

3.8.2 Exchange Rate Differences

Exchange rate differences arise in two cases: open item clearing, and the valuation of open items in a foreign currency. We discuss both of these cases next.

General Ledger Open Item Clearing

When you post to an account managed on an open item basis in a currency different from the local currency, the system translates the amount in the local currency based on the exchange rate difference you enter in the posting; or, if you don't specify an exchange rate difference, it's automatically retrieved by the system. When you clear the open item posting with a different exchange rate, you usually offset the open item by posting the same amount in the foreign currency, and a different amount in the local currency. As a result, the document balances to zero in the foreign currency but doesn't balance to zero in the local currency; therefore, an additional item with an amount of zero in the document currency and the difference amount in the local currency is automatically created by the system.

Valuation of General Ledger Open Items in Foreign Currency

At period-end, you can evaluate the open items in foreign currencies by using program SAPF100; the system posts the devaluation or revaluation to P&L accounts and to a balance sheet account (which can be the same general ledger account valuated, or an adjustment account).

The accounts to be posted for both cases are defined in customizing using Transaction OB09. Follow these steps (Figure 3.45):

1. When you run Transaction OB09, specify the chart of accounts, and select New Entries.

2. In the resulting screen, specify the general ledger accounts with open items you want to clear and then make these settings:

   ▸ **Currency:** Specify an entry here only if you need separate exchange rate accounts depending on the currency of the open items.

   ▸ **Currency Type:** This is relevant only if you're working with additional local currencies. In this case, you can post the revaluation to the same accounts, regardless of whether the exchange rate arises in the first local currency (currency type 10) or in any of the other local currencies; as such, leave the field blank. Alternatively, you can decide to post the revaluation to different accounts depending on the currency type that is evaluated; in this case, create one entry for each currency type with separate accounts.

   If you leave these fields blank, the entry is valid for all currencies and currency types.

3. Specify the following accounts (in the order in which they appear in Figure 3.45):

   ▸ **Loss for realized exchange rate differences (P&L account):** The account that should be used for exchange rate differences that arise during clearing.

   ▸ **Gain for realized exchange rate differences (P&L account):** The account that should be used for exchange rate differences that arise during clearing.

   ▸ **Loss for valuated exchange rate differences (P&L account):** The account that should be used for exchange rate differences that arise when running the evaluation program SAPF100.

   ▸ **Gain for valuated exchange rate differences (P&L account):** The account that should be used for exchange rate differences that arise when running the evaluation program SAPF100.

   ▸ **Balance sheet account for the exchange rate differences:** The balance sheet account that will be used for exchange rate differences that arise when running the evaluation program SAPF100. When you valuate general ledger accounts open items, it's the same general ledger account that is valuated; however, you can also specify a different general ledger account (known as an *adjustment account*).

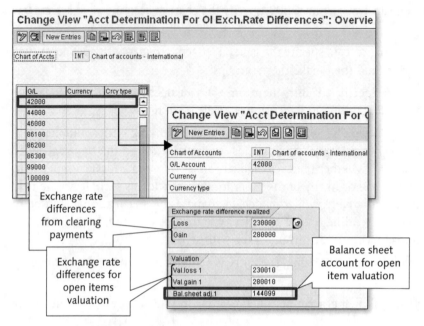

Figure 3.45 Exchange Rate Differences Accounts (Open Items)

3.9 Summary

In this chapter, we went through the main customizing settings needed to get General Ledger up and running. Most of the configuration is the same regardless of whether you're running SAP General Ledger or the classic General Ledger; however, when a configuration activity was relevant for just one of the components, we clearly stated it in the section. In the next chapter, we continue our discussion of General Ledger, with a focus on master data and postings.

In the previous chapter, we described how to configure the general ledger. In this chapter, we discuss the creation of master data and documents within the general ledger.

4   General Ledger Accounts and Postings

In this chapter, two main topics are discussed in detail:

- **General ledger accounts**
  This is the central type of master data in general ledger accounting. A correct setup of general ledger accounts is of primary importance for the correct functioning of general ledger postings and of the integration between general ledger accounting and other modules such as Sales and Distribution (SD) and Material Management (MM). When discussing this topic, we also discuss the creation of primary cost elements; this is Controlling master data, but given the strict relationship between general ledger accounts and primary cost elements, we thought it useful to provide some details on the topic.

- **General ledger postings**
  Also in this chapter, we introduce the functionality for directly posting within General Ledger; changes between posting in the classic General Ledger and SAP General Ledger are discussed in detail. The chapter discusses both the technique of posting with the traditional transaction, FB01 (FB01L if you want to specify the ledger group), as well as the technique of posting with Enjoy transactions (FB50 and FB50L). The chapter also provides some insights on posting via batch-input session and IDocs, two techniques used by interfaces between external systems and SAP.

In the last part of the chapter, we discuss Value Added Tax (VAT) in general ledger accounting.

4.1   General Ledger Accounting Master Data

This section is made up of three subsections. In the first, we discuss how to create and change general ledger accounts, individually and collectively; some details are provided on the alternative technique of creating accounts through the sample accounts. In the second, we explain how to create primary cost elements. We conclude this section by discussing general ledger account master data reports and offering some tips on the creation of queries for accounts.

4.1.1 General Ledger Account Management

Next we discuss the functionalities used to create and change general ledger accounts. We discuss both individual and mass maintenance.

General Ledger Accounts: Individual Maintenance

Quick Reference
Menu path: ACCOUNTING • FINANCIAL ACCOUNTING • GENERAL LEDGER • MASTER RECORD • INDIVIDUAL PROCESSING
Transactions: FS00 (chart of accounts and company code data), FSP0 (only chart of accounts data), and FSS0 (only company code data)
Tables: SKA1 (chart of accounts data), SKB1 (company code data), and SKAT (account descriptions)

The instructions discussed here are based on Transaction FS00 but also apply to Transactions FSP0 and FSS0. Select G/L ACCOUNT • CREATE, and specify the chart of account and company code. The fields of the general ledger account master data are grouped in four tabs; next we discuss the main fields in each.

Chart of Accounts Data: Type/Description Tab

When you create a new general ledger account, you must first define the information at the chart of accounts level in the Type/Description tab. The information contained here is valid for all company codes that use the chart of accounts to which the company code belongs. This tab is always the same; in other words, the information you see when you manage the chart of accounts information of a general ledger account doesn't depend on field status.

The following is a brief description of the main fields available at the chart of accounts level (Figure 4.1):

▶ **Account Group (❶)**
   The account group defines the allow range for the account number and the field status for the company code level information. See Section 3.4.2, Defining

Account Groups, in Chapter 3, Error! Reference source not found.for more details on account groups.

▶ **P&L Statmt Acct Type (❷)**
If the account is a P&L account, you specify the retained earnings account to which it belongs here; see Section 3.4.4, Defining Retained Earnings Accounts, in Chapter 3, Error! Reference source not found.for details on the retained earning account.

▶ **Balance Sheet Account (❸)**
Mark this indicator (and leave the P&L Statement Account Type field blank) if the account is a balance sheet account.

▶ **Short Text, G/L Account Long Text (❹)**
Specify the texts of the general ledger account. Keep in mind that the text you type here is updated in the language specified in the chart of accounts configuration (not the logon language). If the system uses other languages, perform the translation in the Key Word/Translation tab.

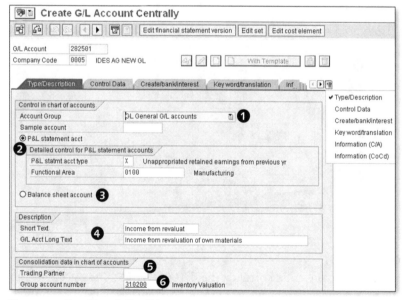

Figure 4.1 Type/Description Tab

▶ **Trading Partner (❺)**
Specify a trading partner only if the account will be used with a specific company of your group. For example, if the account has the description "Stock of

company AAAA," specify the trading partner corresponding to company AAAA. As a result, the trading partner is automatically copied from the general ledger account to the posting. (However, you should read the document type configuration fields to find out how the trading partner in the account is copied into the document.)

▶ **Group Account Number (❻)**
If the chart of accounts is assigned to a group account, you can specify that here.

Company Code Level Data: Control Data Tab
Figure 4.2 shows an example of the content of the fields in the Control Data tab of the general ledger account master record. The following list provides a brief description of the most important fields:

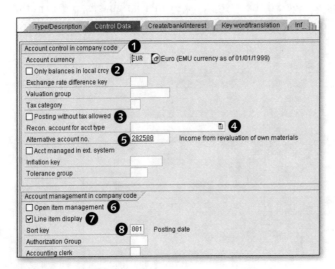

Figure 4.2 Control Data Tab

▶ **Account Currency (❶)**
If you enter the company code currency (field T001-WAERS), the account can be posted in any currency. If you specify another currency, you can post only in the specified currency (e.g., this can be the case of a bank account in a foreign currency or a loan in a foreign currency).

▶ **Only Balances in Local Crcy (❷)**
If you choose this indicator, the system doesn't update the total data (transac-

tion figures) of the account in the foreign currency. We recommend the following:

▶ Don't set the indicator if you need to revaluate the account on a balance basis.

▶ Always set the indicator for the GR/IR account, and, in general, for accounts that are posted in different currencies and cleared in local currencies.

▶ **Tax data (❸)**
The tax code (field BSEG-MWSKZ) isn't included in the field status customizing; instead, you decide in the general ledger account master data if the field should appear in the posting and whether it's optional or mandatory. For the Tax Category field, you have the following choices:

▶ **Leave the field blank:** The tax code is hidden in the line item.

▶ ***:** The tax code appears in the screen, and any value is allowed.

▶ **+:** Only output tax is allowed. With this tax category, you can only post to accounts with tax codes classified as output tax codes (field MWART in Table T007A).

▶ **-:** Only input tax is allowed: With this tax category, you can only post to accounts with tax codes classified as input tax codes (field MWART in Table T007A).

▶ **>:** This is a VAT output account (the debit against local authorities is posted in this general ledger account).

▶ **<:** This is a VAT input account (the credit against local authorities is posted in this general ledger account).

▶ **Any specific tax code:** The account can be posted only with the specific tax code.

▶ **Posting Without Tax Allowed (❸)**
If you have not left the Tax Category field blank, the tax code is displayed in the document. If you flag this indicator, it's optional; otherwise, it's mandatory.

▶ **Recon. Account for Acct Type (❹)**
In this field, you specify the reconciliation account. In this case, the account can't be posted directly but only through the subledger accounts. The following options are available:

▶ **Asset:** The linkage between the asset and the account is through the account determination (field ANLA-KTOGR).

▶ **Vendor:** Each vendor is assigned to one reconciliation account in its master data (field LFB1-AKONT).

▶ **Customer:** Each customer is assigned to one reconciliation account in its master data (field KNB1-AKONT).

▶ **Alternative Account No. (❺)**
Here you can assign the general ledger account to an alternative account selected from the alternative chart of accounts assigned to the company code (see field T001-KTOP2).

▶ **Open Item Management (❻)**
If this indicator is selected, you can manage the account on an open item basis; each item has two possible statuses: open (stored in Table BSIS) or cleared (stored in Table BSAS).

▶ **Line Items Display (❼)**
If you select this indicator, the line items are stored in Table BSIS (and BSAS if managed on an open item basis). If the account is managed on a line item basis, you can run report FBL3N. This report reads just from Tables BSIS/BSAS, not from Table BSEG (where all of the line items are stored, regardless of the settings of the general ledger accounts; selecting line items from Table BSEG leads to poor performance).

▶ **Sort Key (❽)**
Here you define how the field assignment is automatically filled when you save the document. The rules are contained in the sort key indicator that is maintained in customizing (Transaction OB16).

Note

When an account is created at the charts of account level and you want to use it in a company code, use the Create activity, and not the Change activity, because you are creating the company code segment.

Company Code Level Data: Create/Bank/Interest Tab
Next we describe the main fields you can find in this section of the general ledger account master data (Figure 4.3):

▶ **Field Status Group (❶)**
This field, together with the posting key, determines which fields in the document line items are hidden, optional, or mandatory.

▶ **Post Automatically Only (❷)**
If selected, you can post to this account only through automatic account determination (e.g., based on customizing Tables T030 or T030H). Note that in this
context, postings coming from batch-input or from IDocs aren't considered
automatic postings.

▶ **Supplement Auto. Postings (❸)**
Select this indicator if you want to allow manual changes to automatic postings
to this account (e.g., VAT, bank charges, or exchange rate differences). You can
use this indicator, for example, if you want to add the cost center manually.

▶ **House Bank and Account ID (❹)**
If the general ledger account is a bank account, here is where you specify the
correspondent house bank and house bank account ID.

▶ **Interest Indicator (❺)**
If the account is subject to interest calculations with Transaction FINT, this field
is where you specify the interest indicator you defined in customizing. Note
that this is valid only for the balance sheet accounts that aren't reconciliation
accounts; for customers, you specify the interest indicator directly in the customer master data, not in the master data of the connected reconciliation
account.

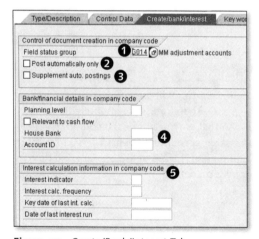

Figure 4.3 Create/Bank/Interest Tab

Company Code Level Data: Key Word/Translation Tab
The description that you specify in the Chart of Accounts section of the general
ledger account master data is automatically assigned to the language that you

have assigned to the chart of accounts in Transaction OB13 (field T004-DSPRA). If a user logs on to the system in a different language, the account has an empty description. To translate the account into another language, go into the general ledger account master data and perform the needed translations in the Key Word/ Translation tab (Figure 4.4).

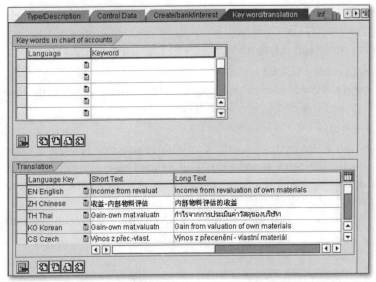

Figure 4.4 Key Word/Translation Tab

> **Warning for General Ledger Account Translation**
>
> If the system is used in many languages, then each user will use the account based on the description translated in the logon language. Therefore, it's extremely important that the translations are carried out carefully so that each user in each country will use the account in the same context and for the same accounting event. Transactions not carried out carefully can lead to a misunderstanding of the use of the account and therefore can mine the homogeneity of the consolidation data.

Blocking Indicators

If you want to prevent an account from being posted to, you can set a block in the master data. To block an account, run Transaction FS00, and select G/L ACCOUNT • BLOCK; the following blocks are available (Figure 4.5):

▶ Chart of accounts level blocks (valid for all company codes that use the chart of accounts):

▸ **Blocked for Creation:** The account can't be created in any company code.

▸ **Blocked for Posting:** The account can't be posted (actual data) in any company code.

▸ **Blocked for Planning:** No planning posting can be made against the account in any company code.

▸ Company code level block:

▸ **Blocked for Posting :** You can't make any actual postings against the account in the specified company code.

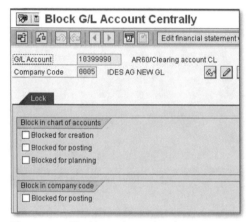

Figure 4.5 Blocking a General Ledger Account

Flagging Master Data for Deletion

After an account is created, you can't delete it. Instead, you mark it for deletion; the accounts marked for deletion can be deleted with the archiving functionality. Discuss the details of the archiving activity with your SAP Basis colleagues.

To flag one account for deletion, run Transaction FS00, and select G/L ACCOUNT • SET DELETE FLAG. Two flags are available (Figure 4.6):

▸ **Mark for Deletion (at chart of accounts level)**

If this indicator is selected, the chart of accounts data of the general ledger account master record is deleted with the next archive run, assuming the prerequisites for the archiving are met. One prerequisite is that the archiving of the company code level data has already been performed; of course, the company code segment can't exist for one account (record in SKB1) without the chart of accounts segment (record SKA1).

▶ **Mark for Deletion (at company code level)**
If this indicator is selected, the chart of accounts data of the general ledger account master record is deleted with the next archive run, assuming the prerequisites for the archiving are met.

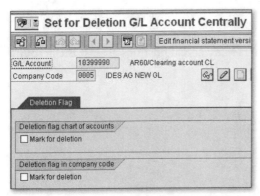

Figure 4.6 Flags for Deletion

General Ledger Accounts Deletion

Quick Reference

Program: SAPF019

As already discussed, you can't delete a general ledger account after it's created. Instead, you mark the account for deletion, and it's removed in the next archiving run. Note that the first archiving run is managed within a project framework, and, in general, the archiving process is managed in collaboration with SAP experts.

However, you might need to perform the cancellation of one or more general ledger accounts within the initial SAP implementation or within a SAP rollout for a new company code; for example, if you incorrectly created general ledger accounts and want to delete them before the go-live. In this case, provided that the company code doesn't have the Productive flag selected (field T001-XPROD), you can use program SAPF019 to cancel the accounts. Run program SAPF019 with Transactions SA38 or SE38 (Figure 4.7).

The following are the most important fields on the screen in Figure 4.7:

▶ **Delete G/L Accounts/Process Sample Accounts Also**
In these fields, specify whether you want to delete the general ledger accounts and the sample accounts.

▸ **Only General Master Data**

If this indicator is selected, only accounts that don't exist in any company code can be deleted.

▸ **With General Master Data**

If this indicator is selected, you can delete company code master data at the chart of accounts level, provided the account doesn't exist in other company codes.

▸ **G/L Account Detail Log**

In this indicator is selected, only accounts that have the Deletion flag selected can be deleted.

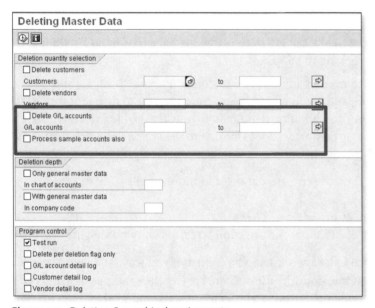

Figure 4.7 Deleting General Ledger Accounts

Copying General Ledger Accounts from Company Codes

Quick Reference

Menu path: ACCOUNTING • FINANCIAL ACCOUNTING • GENERAL LEDGER • MASTER RECORD • COMPARE COMPANY CODE

Transactions: FS15 (sending data) and FS16 (receiving data; necessary if the receiving company code is in another client or SAP system)

Programs: RFBISA10 (sending data) and RFBISA20 (receiving data; necessary if the receiving company code is in another client or SAP system)

With this tool, you can copy some or all accounts from one sending company code to one or more receiving company codes. In particular, you can do the following:

- Copy accounts from company code A to company code B, C, and so on, where all of the company codes are located in the same SAP client.

- Copy accounts from company code A to company code A (the sending and receiving company code can be the same; for example, you may want to copy the general ledger accounts of company code A from the production client to a test client), B, C, and so on, where the sending and receiving company codes belong to different clients but are in the same instance (see Table T000 for a list of all clients that belong to an instance).

- Copy accounts from company code A to company code A, B, C, and so on, where the sending and receiving company codes belong to different instances. In this case, you need an additional program to transfer the file from the instance in which the sending company code is located to the system in which the receiving company code is located.

Now let's examine these three different cases in more detail.

Case 1: Company Codes in the Same Client

Run Transaction FS15 and fill in the selection screen as shown in Figure 4.8.

1. Specify the general ledger accounts to be copied; if you leave the field blank, all accounts are taken into consideration. Then, specify the sending company code in the Company Code field. Note that if you specify accounts that don't exist in the sending company code, they are simply ignored by the program (❶).

2. Specify whether you want to copy the general ledger account company code normal data (Transfer Master Data), the company code level blocking indicator (Transfer Blocking Indicator), or the company code level deletion indicator (Transfer Deletion Flags) (❷).

3. Specify the target company code or codes that should receive the selected general ledger master data (❸).

4. Define the way the master data should be created in the target company codes (**❹**):

- ▶ **Update File Immediately:** If you select this indicator, the system immediately creates accounts in the target company codes. A batch input session isn't created, unless for some reason some accounts can't be created directly. Thus, the batch input session contains only the accounts that could not be created automatically. You can see errors and correct them when processing the session online.

- ▶ **Batch Input Session Name:** Here you specify the batch input session that the system creates. Go to Transaction SM35 to process the session.

- ▶ **Check File Only:** If you select this indicator, no update is performed. The system only checks the formal correctness of the input file.

5. Leave the File Name field blank (**❺**).

The next step is to run Transaction SM35 and process the batch-input session created. You don't need to perform this step if, in Transaction FS15, you selected the Update File Immediately option (unless, for some reason, some accounts could not be created; the relevant transactions are put in a batch-input session for postprocessing).

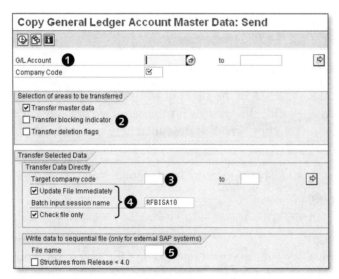

Figure 4.8 Copying General Ledger Accounts from Company Code: Send Data

Case 2: Company Codes in Different Clients of the Same Instance

In this case, you need to perform the activity with Transaction FS15 in the sending client, Transaction FS16 in the receiving client; use Transaction SM35 for processing the batch-input session. First run Transaction FS15 in the client in which the sending company code is located (e.g., instance KRP, client 500), filling in the selection screen according to the following instructions (Figure 4.8):

1. Specify the general ledger accounts to be copied (the G/L Account field in Figure 4.8); if you leave the field blank, all accounts are taken into consideration. Specify the sending company codes in the Company Code field; if you specify accounts that don't exist in the sending company code, they are simply ignored by the program.

2. Specify whether you want to copy the general ledger account company code normal data (Transfer Master Data), the company code level blocking indicator (Transfer Blocking Indicator), or the company code level deletion indicator (Transfer Deletion Flags).

3. Leave the Target Company Code field blank. You specify the receiving company codes in Transaction FS16.

4. Leave the following fields empty:
   - Update File Immediately
   - Batch Input Session Name
   - Check File Only

5. Specify a four-digit file name in the File Name field.

In a second step, run Transaction FS16 in the client in which the target company codes are located (e.g., instance KRP, the same as for the sending company code and client 501), and fill in the selection screen as described here (see Figure 4.9):

- **File Name (❶)**
  Specify the same file name you have entered in Transaction FS15.

- **Target Company Code (❷)**
  Specify the receiving company code or company codes.

- **Program Control area (❸)**
  See the Case 1: Company Codes in the Same Client section for how to set these fields.

Now the system, in the destination client, creates a batch input session that you process with Transaction SM35. If you've chosen the Update File Immediately option, the accounts are created immediately; a batch-input session is created only if some accounts can't be created automatically.

Figure 4.9 Copying General Ledger Accounts from Company Code: Receiving Data (Company Codes in Different SAP Clients or Systems)

Case 3: Company Codes Located in Clients of the Different Instances

If you want to copy accounts from company codes located in one SAP instance (e.g., instance KRP and client 500) to another instance (e.g., instance KRQ and client 500 or 501), you can follow the same procedure as Case 2, but you need an additional step between FS15 and FS16.

The steps are as follows:

1. Run Transaction FS15 as described in the Case 2: Company Codes in Different Clients of the Same Instance section (fill in the File Name field, and leave the Target Company Code field blank).

2. Use a program to download the data from the sending instance to the destination instance (we assume that they are located in different servers). Identify a suitable program that allows the transferring of the data from the server to the PC and vice versa; usually, this process is done by temporarily placing the file in your local disk.

3. Run Transaction FS16, following the instructions in Case 2: Company Codes in Different Clients of the Same Instance.

To perform step 2, you need to know the following:

▸ The exact name of the file that is created in the server by Transaction FS15. This name is FBIS plus the content of the File Name field.

▶ The location of the file to be downloaded in the sending server. This location can be retrieved in the sending client using Transaction FILE:

   ▶ Double-click on Logical File Name Definition, Cross Client.

   ▶ Double-click on the logical file FI_COPY_COMPANY_CODE_DATA_FOR_GENERAL_LEDGER, and find the logical path.

   ▶ Select Logical File Path Definition, select the logical path retrieved in the former step, and then double-click on Assignment of Physical Paths to Logical Paths.

   ▶ Double-click on the syntax group of your server (UNIX or Windows), and you've found the location of the file.

▶ The location in the receiving server where the file should be uploaded. To locate this directory, repeat the steps outlined in the previous bullet point in the destination server.

General Ledger Accounts: Mass Changes

Quick Reference

Menu path: ACCOUNTING • FINANCIAL ACCOUNTING • GENERAL LEDGER • MASTER RECORD • COLLECTIVE PROCESSING

Transaction: MASS (object BUS3006)

Using Transaction MASS, you can update many general ledger accounts at the same time (e.g., you can change the sort code for a large number of accounts). The transaction is very powerful, so ordinary users should not be authorized to use it.

To perform a mass change on general ledger accounts, proceed as follows:

1. Run Transaction MASS, and enter the value "BUS3006" in the Object Type field; you can use the matchcode to see what other objects can be modified in the mass change. Leave the Variant field blank, and click the Execute button (❶) (❶ of Figure 4.10).

2. Read the informative message delivered by the system, and click Continue.

3. Select the table where the field or fields to be changed are stored (SKA1 for chart of accounts level data; SKB1 for company code level data; and SKAT for description in multiple languages), and continue by clicking the Execute button (❷ of Figure 4.10). Confirm the following message, which informs you that the changes will take place immediately and can't be reversed.

4. Fill in the selection criteria to select the record to be modified, and go ahead with the Execute button (❸ of Figure 4.10). You can also save the selection screen as a variant with the Save button (🖫). Reuse the variant with the Get Variant button.

5. In the next screen, the system displays the selected record; add the fields that have to be modified to the list by using the Select Fields button (🎛).

6. Specify the new value for the records to be modified (if the new value is different for different records), or use the procedure illustrated in ❹ and ❺ of Figure 4.11 to assign the same value to all of the records. Click the Carry Out a Mass Change button (🎛) after you select the relevant columns and specify the new value in the first row.

7. Click the Save button to perform the change (❻ of Figure 4.11); the system displays a list with all records modified (green light) and those that could not be modified (red light) (❼ of Figure 4.11).

8. If you don't leave the transaction, you can reset the changes with the Undo Changes button (🖉), and then save the new changes with the Save button.

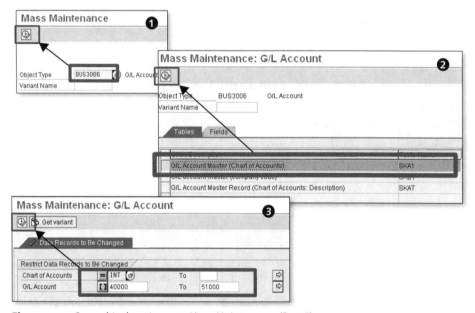

Figure 4.10 General Ledger Account Mass Maintenance (Part 1)

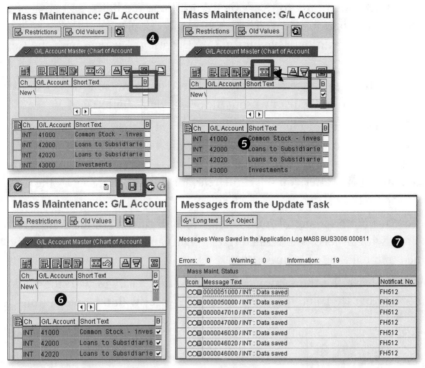

Figure 4.11 General Ledger Account Mass Maintenance (Part 2)

General Ledger Accounts Maintenance with the Sample Account

Using the sample account functionality, you create template accounts with Transaction FSM1. These accounts are stored in Table SKM1. Each sample account contains template data for the company code segment of the general ledger account. Next we discuss how to define the rules for sample accounts and how to create sample accounts.

Defining Rules for Sample Accounts

> **Quick Reference**
>
> **Menu path**: IMG • FINANCIAL ACCOUNTING • GENERAL LEDGER ACCOUNTING • GENERAL LEDGER ACCOUNTS • MASTER DATA • ADDITIONAL ACTIVITIES • SAMPLE ACCOUNTS
>
> **Transactions**: OB15 (maintain list of rule types), FSK2 (define data transfer rules), and OB67 (assign company code to rule type)
>
> **Tables**: T004R (list of sample account rules), T004M (details, field by field, of sample account rules), and T001 (assignment of sample account rules to company code)

Customize the sample account functionality by following these steps (Figure 4.12):

1. Run Transaction OB15 to create the variant (specify a four-digit ID and a brief description).

2. Run Transaction FSK2, specify the variant just created, and define whether and how the fields flow from the sample account to the real accounts.

3. Run Transaction OB67, and assign the variant (Rules Var. column) to company codes.

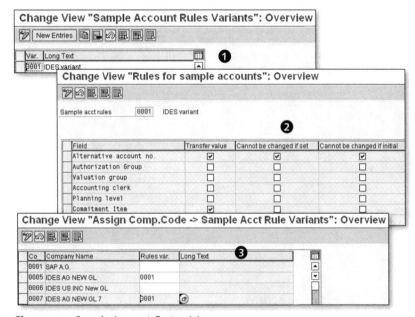

Figure 4.12 Sample Account Customizing

Creating Sample Accounts and Related Real Accounts

Quick Reference

Menu path: ACCOUNTING • FINANCIAL ACCOUNTING • GENERAL LEDGER • MASTER RECORDS • G/L ACCOUNT • SAMPLE ACCOUNT • CREATE

Transaction: FSM1

Table: SKM1 (sample accounts)

Create the sample account with Transaction SKM1, and create the general ledger account at the chart of accounts level, assigning it a sample account (Figure 4.13). Then, when you create the account at the company code level, the system copies the information from the sample account to the real account, based on the configuration that is valid for the specific company code.

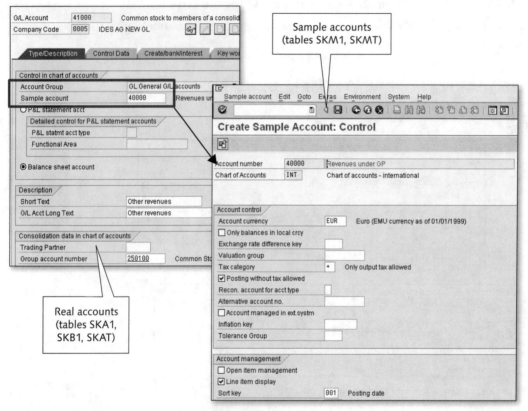

Figure 4.13 Sample Accounts and Real Accounts

4.1.2 Primary Cost Elements

For each P&L general ledger account, it's possible to create a primary cost element, which allows the transfer of costs or revenues from Financial Accounting to Controlling. A primary cost element can be created only if the corresponding general ledger account has already been created. There are three ways of creating primary cost elements:

► Automatically, when the corresponding general ledger account is created

► Manually, from the general ledger account master data (Transaction FS00) or with Transaction KA01

► Collectively, with Transaction OKB3

Next we describe all three options in more detail.

Configuring Automatic Creation of Primary Cost Elements

Quick Reference

Menu paths: IMG • FINANCIAL ACCOUNTING • GENERAL LEDGER ACCOUNTING • G/L AC-COUNTS • MASTER DATA • PREPARATIONS • EDIT CHART OF ACCOUNTS LIST (FOR CHART OF ACCOUNTS SETTING)

OR

CONTROLLING • COST ELEMENT ACCOUNTING • MASTER DATA • AUTOMATIC CREATION OF PRIMARY AND SECONDARY COST ELEMENTS (FOR COST ELEMENT CREATION CONFIGURATION)

Transactions: OB13 (chart of accounts setting) and OKB2 (cost element creation configuration)

Table/view: T004/V_T004 (chart of accounts setting) and TKSKA/V_TKSKA CSKB (cost element creation configuration, controlling area data)

With this option, the primary cost element is created when the corresponding general ledger account is created. Activate this option with the following two customizing steps:

1. When customizing the chart of accounts, run Transaction OB13. In the Controlling Integration field, select Automatic Creation of Cost Elements (Figure 4.14).

2. In Transaction OKB2, define the cost element type to which each range of account is assigned (Figure 4.15).

As a result of these steps, every time a P&L account is created, a cost element account is automatically created with the same description as the general ledger account and the same cost element category as defined in Transaction OKB2.

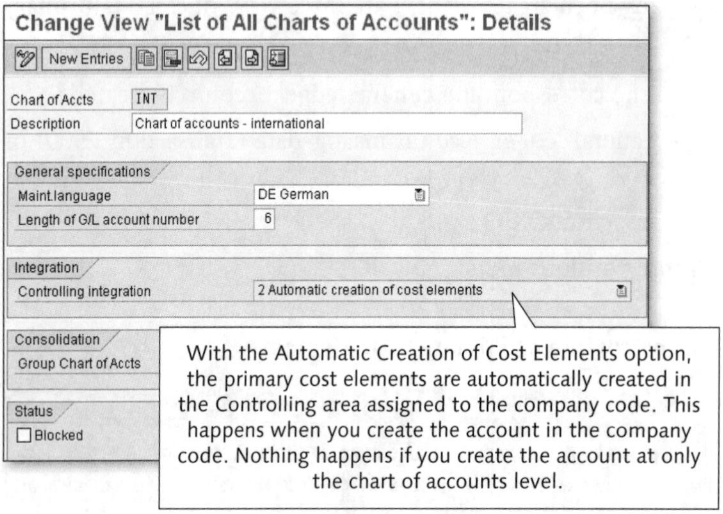

Change View "List of All Charts of Accounts": Details

Chart of Accts	INT
Description	Chart of accounts - international

General specifications

Maint.language	DE German
Length of G/L account number	6

Integration

Controlling integration	2 Automatic creation of cost elements

With the Automatic Creation of Cost Elements option, the primary cost elements are automatically created in the Controlling area assigned to the company code. This happens when you create the account in the company code. Nothing happens if you create the account at only the chart of accounts level.

Consolidation

Group Chart of Accts	

Status

☐ Blocked

Figure 4.14 Automatic Creation of Primary Cost Elements

Creating Primary Cost Elements Manually

> **Quick Reference**
>
> **Menu path**: ACCOUNTING • FINANCIAL ACCOUNTING • GENERAL LEDGER • MASTER RECORD INDIVIDUAL PROCESSING • IN COMPANY CODE
>
> **Transaction**: FSS0
>
> **Tables**: CSKA (chart of accounts data), CSKB (controlling area data), CSKT (description)

From the account master data, select the Edit Cost Element button. The system proposes a cost element with the same description as the general ledger account, and a cost element category depending on the setting made in the transaction. You don't need to create cost elements using this method if they are created automatically by the method discussed immediately before this.

Creating Primary Cost Elements Automatically

> **Quick Reference**
>
> **Menu path**: IMG • CONTROLLING • COST ELEMENT ACCOUNTING • MASTER DATA • AUTOMATIC CREATION OF PRIMARY AND SECONDARY COST ELEMENTS
>
> **Transactions**: OKB2 (customizing settings), OKB3 (cost elements mass creation)
>
> **Table/views**: TKSKA/V_TKSKA (customizing settings), CSKA (chart of accounts data), CSKB (controlling area data), CSKT (description)

In Transaction OKB2, specify the customizing that determines which cost element category belongs to each P&L general ledger account (see a Controlling manual to fully understand the meaning of the cost element category). Then run Transaction OKB3 to collectively create the corresponding primary cost elements (Figure 4.15).

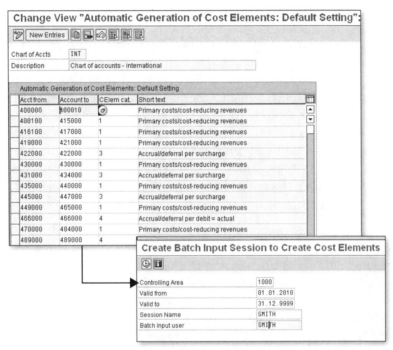

Figure 4.15 Automatic Creation of Cost Element

4.1.3 Master Data Reporting and Utilities

SAP doesn't provide many standard reports for general ledger master data, and the ones available provide very basic information. If you don't have special reporting requirements, these reports may be sufficient for you. Next we discuss the two standard reports, one that is used only for the chart of account segment (RFSKPL00), and one that can be used for both the chart of accounts segment and the company code segment. If you have more complex reporting requirements, we suggest creating an SAP query. We provide some tips that may be useful for queries on general ledger accounts, but a comprehensive discussion is beyond the scope of the book.

General Ledger Account Standard Reports

The availability of master data reports for general ledger account master data is quite limited. To get a list of the general ledger accounts belonging to a specific chart of accounts, you can use report RFSKPL00; the report lists all accounts with a code and description, and you can double-click on a line to drill down to the general ledger account master data. No company code level data can be displayed with this report. Note that the list is fixed (no ALV); you can't add columns, sort, or easily download to Excel (but you can still use the menu function SYSTEM • LIST • SAVE • LOCAL FILE). If you need a more flexible report in ALV format and easily downloadable to Excel, we recommend creating a SAP query (use Table SKA1 for this purpose).

To get a list of the general ledger accounts with company code level data, use report RFSKVZ00; the report lists all of the accounts with codes, descriptions, and the data you choose to display in the selection screen. You can't drill down to the general ledger account master data. Note that the list is fixed (no ALV); you can't add columns, sort, or easily download to Excel. To create a more flexible report on company code data for general ledger accounts, we recommend again creating a SAP query (use Tables SKA1 and SKB1 for this purpose).

Queries on General Ledger Accounts

To get a flexible report on the general ledger account master data with all ALV functionalities included, we suggest creating SAP queries. A comprehensive discussion of this process is beyond the scope of this book, but here are some quick tips:

- Before creating a query on general ledger master data, create an infoset with Transaction SQ02. The infoset defines the logic used to retrieve the data and the fields that can be used in the queries assigned to the infoset.

- There is no logical database that includes only the general ledger master data. Logical databases SDF and BRF include the general ledger tables but also the document tables.

- We suggest creating the infoset with the option Table Join Using Basis Table, and specifying Table SKA1.

- The tables you are most likely to use are the following:

  - **SKA1:** General ledger accounts data, chart of accounts level.

  - **SKB1:** General ledger accounts data, company code level.

  - **SKAT:** Description of the accounts in different languages.

4.1.4 FAQ and Troubleshooting Tips

Here we answer some frequently asked questions and offer helpful troubleshooting tips.

FAQ

1. **Question**: Is there any program to delete an incorrectly created general ledger account?

   Answer: Program SAPF019 can be used to delete Financial Accounting master data (general ledger accounts, customers, and vendors), if the company code doesn't have a productive status (i.e., if indicator T001-XPROD isn't flagged). After the company code has a successful go-live, we strongly recommend that the flag be set, and not be reset for any reason. If accounts have been created incorrectly, they should be flagged for deletion and deleted with the first archive run.

2. **Question**: Are the changes to general ledger accounts performed with Transaction MASS recorded in the same way as manual changes?

   Answer: Yes, all changes are recorded in Tables CDHDR and CDPOS. You can retrieve the changes to general ledger accounts with report RFSABL00.

3. **Question**: What is the advantage of using the sample account functionality?

   Answer: The main advantage is to ensure the homogeneity of the company code level data. The tool is flexible because it allows specifying mandatory fields that are copied from the sample account and transferred to the real account, as well as "free fields" for which you can specify a default changeable value or no value at all.

4. **Question**: When running Transaction OKB3 for automatic creation of cost elements, what happens if a cost element already exists?

   Answer: All of the cost elements that already exist remain unchanged. The transaction creates only the primary cost elements for which a P&L general ledger account listed in Transaction OKB2 has already been created.

5. **Question**: Can I limit the creation to specific cost elements?

   Answer: No. The transaction works only at the controlling area level. Note that all company codes belonging to a controlling area must share the same operational chart of accounts.

6. **Question**: What is the difference between SAP queries and quick views?

   Answer: Creating quick views doesn't require the creation of infosets and user groups; you must also keep in mind that quick views can be run and modified only by the user that created them. Quick views can be converted into queries, but only by the user that created them.

7. **Question**: How can I find the logical databases that use a specific table?

   Answer: Run Transaction SE11, specify the table, and click on the Where-Used List button (🔁). In the resulting screen, select Logical Databases, and confirm your choice with the Continue button (✅). You get a list of all of the logical databases that include the specific table.

Troubleshooting Tips

1. **Issue**: When I use Transaction FS00, the system automatically takes me to the change activity. How can I get to the create activity by default?

   Solution: From the menu, choose SETTINGS • START ACTIVITY. Choose the activity titled "Create G/L Account," or "Create G/L Account with Reference."

2. **Issue**: I have incorrectly created an account without the Line Item indicator. I have now activated the indicator, but it only affects subsequent postings. All of the postings made before the activation of the indicator aren't displayed in Transaction FBL3N.

   Solution: You can recreate the line items using report RFSEPA01. Read the note about the report (in the selection screen, click the Program Documentation button).

3. **Issue**: I have incorrectly created an account without the Open Item indicator. I have activated the indicator, but it only affects subsequent postings; only these postings are displayed when I try to clear the open items. The postings made before the activation of the indicator are displayed in Transaction FBL3N as "open" but aren't displayed in clearing transactions.

   Solution: In former releases, report RFSEPA02 was designed to perform this transaction. However, in the current release, due to inconsistency issues, the report can't be run. When you run the report, you get the following message, which explains how to perform the activity correctly: "Do not use the report program to set up open item management for the account. Create a new account with the correct account assignment. Post your items to the new account. If you want to use the original account number, you must bring the account balance to zero, change the account assignment, and repost the items. You can remove the old items by archiving the documents." Some companies have made a copy of report RFSEPA02 and continue to use it; however, we strongly recommend using the procedure described by SAP instead of creating your own copy of RFSEPA02 to bypass the message.

4. **Issue**: I need to change a large number of accounts. The list is in Excel, and I uploaded the list in the selection screen of Transaction MASS using the Multiple Selection button (⇨), and then copied the list from Excel and pasted it into SAP using the Upload From Clipboard button (📋). The result was error message M&169: "Too many individual values in where condition, selection not possible."

   Solution: There is a limit to the number of records that SAP can manage with the copy and paste functionality; the limit is about 8000 records in SAP ERP 6.0 and is generally lower for older releases. If needed, split the list into smaller lists and perform multiple mass changes.

5. **Issue**: I have changed the description in the general ledger account. However, the description in the connected primary cost element isn't automatically changed.

   Solution: The text in the primary cost element is automatically changed and synchronized with the text in the corresponding general ledger account only if Transaction OB13, the Automatic Creation of Cost Elements option, is set to Controlling Integration in the chart of accounts. However, if you can still change the text in the cost element master data maintenance, the text is synchronized again the next time you change the linked general ledger account.

6. **Issue**: I run Transaction KA01 and get a message saying that the corresponding general ledger account isn't created. What does this mean?

Solution: Each primary cost element must be created only after the corresponding general ledger account has been created. The general ledger account must be a P&L account, and the general ledger account and cost element must have the same code.

4.2   General Ledger Accounting Postings

In this section, we describe the different ways to post general ledger accounting documents; note that posting to subledger accounts (customers, vendors, and assets) isn't included in this chapter but is discussed in detail in Chapter 5, Accounts Receivable and Accounts Payable (for customer and vendors), and in Chapters 6, Asset Accounting (for assets).

In particular, the following topics are included in this section:

- ▶ Postings in the classic General Ledger, with traditional Transaction FB01 and the more recent and user-friendly Transaction FB50. Note that Transaction FB01 is commonly used by interfaces when posting to General Ledger via the batch-input technique.

- ▶ Postings in SAP General Ledger, with traditional Transactions FB01 and FB01L (FB01L, unlike FB01, allows you to specify the ledger group if you want to post to some ledgers only), Enjoy Transactions FB50 and FB50L (FB50L, unlike FB50, allows you to specify the ledger group if you want to post to some ledgers only).

- ▶ Some information on batch input sessions and IDocs, as the daily control of interfaces is often part of the job of master users and SAP Financials experts.

- ▶ How to change general ledger documents.

- ▶ How to automatically clear general ledger account open items.

- ▶ The individual and mass reversal of general ledger documents.

4.2.1   Posting with the Classic General Ledger

Quick Reference

Tables: BKPF (header data), BSEG (line item data), BSIS (secondary index for line items; only if account is managed on line item basis), GLT0 (total data by company code, business area, year, period, and account)

If you haven't activated SAP General Ledger, use Transactions FB01 or FB50 to create ordinary Financial Accounting documents with general ledger accounts. You can also use other transactions to post to Financial Accounting; these transactions are discussed in other parts of this book. Here we focus on manual postings within Financial Accounting using account type S; in other words, we don't address postings to subledger accounts (customers, vendors, assets, and materials) or postings that come from other components (such as Materials Management or Sales and Distribution).

Transactions FB01 and FB50 are only different in the user interface; the way the documents look after you create them is exactly the same, as is the way the two transactions update the database tables (BKPF, BSEG, GLT0, etc.). We discuss each transaction in more detail next.

Basic Transaction (FB01)

> **Quick Reference**
>
> **Menu path**: ACCOUNTING • FINANCIAL ACCOUNTING • GENERAL LEDGER • DOCUMENT ENTRY • GENERAL POSTING
>
> **Transactions**: F-02 or FB01

Transaction FB01 is used for manual posting within Financial Accounting and for batch-input postings. It can be used to enter most type of Financial Accounting documents for all account types. However, given the more user-friendly interface, we recommend using Enjoy transactions (see the "Enjoy Transaction (FB50)" section later in this chapter for more on enjoy transactions).

When you run Transaction FB01, you must first correctly supply the necessary fields of the header (Figure 4.16). Note that the Reference and Header Text fields can be mandatory if the corresponding settings are set in the Document Type customizing.

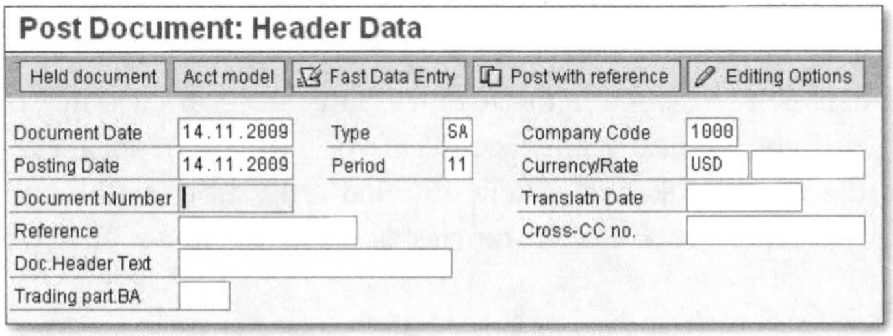

Figure 4.16 Transaction FB01: Header Data

Fill in the following fields to complete the header data and continue with the line items data:

▶ **Document Date**
In general, this represents the date of the original document (the date printed on the invoice, the date of the bank statement, etc.). No particular control is made for the document date; however, the system issues a warning message if the document date and posting date are in different fiscal years.

▶ **Type**
This information is needed to classify the Financial Accounting transaction; it determines the number range. The importance of the document type has been emphasized in the SAP General Ledger environment, due to the role that it plays in document splitting (see Section 3.6.5 for more details). For the details of document type customizing, refer to Section 3.5.1.

▶ **Company Code**
Here you specify the company code in which the document is updated.

▶ **Posting Date**
This is the most important date in any Financial Accounting document. Based on the fiscal year variant, the system automatically derives the posting period and the fiscal year associated with the specified posting date and updates the transaction figures. (The document date has no role in this context.) The system also checks that the posting period is opened based on the posting period variant. You open and close posting periods in Transaction OB52.

▶ **Period**
In general, you leave this field blank, as the posting period is automatically derived from the posting date. The only case in which it makes sense to specify a posting period is when the posting date falls in the last posting period of the fiscal year; then you are allowed to specify one of the special posting periods.

▶ **Currency**
This is the document currency. A currency for the document must always be specified, even if the document is posted in a local currency.

▶ **Rate**
The exchange rate between the document currency and the local currency is stored here. The field is automatically filled with 1 if you post in the local currency. If you leave the field blank, the system automatically supplies the rate based on the translation date, the pair of currencies, and the exchange rate type

(usually M, but this can be different based on the customizing of the exchange rates and on the customizing of the document type).

▶ **Document Number**
Leave this field blank if the number range is internal. Otherwise, specify a document from the external number range associated with the document type.

▶ **Translation Date**
This date is used by the system to retrieve the exchange rate to apply to the document (or to compare with the manually entered exchange rate). If you leave this field blank, the system automatically uses the posting date.

When you press Enter, the system checks the correctness of the entered values. There are three types of accuracy checks:

▶ **Formal correctness**
For example, the document type exists, the date is entered in the correct format, and so on.

▶ **Correctness according to standard rules**
For example, the document number must be empty if the number range is external.

▶ **Correctness according to user-defined rules**
For example, the validations must be passed successfully.

If all data is correct, you are prompted to enter the first line item. In the same screen in which you specify the header data, specify the following (see ❶ of Figure 4.17).

▶ **Pstky (posting key)**
Enter "40" for debit and "50" for credit. The other available posting keys are used for other account types and are described in other sections of this book.

▶ **Account**
Enter an account, selected from the accounts that belong to the chart of accounts assigned to the company and created in the company code.

Now press Enter. The system takes you to the detailed screen for the first line item (❷ of Figure 4.17). The minimum mandatory information is the amount in the document currency; the amount in local currency is then automatically calculated based on the exchange rate. Technically, you can also enter the amount in the local currency, so the line item exchange rate can be different from the exchange rate specified in the header of the document; however, this should happen only in exceptional cases and only for legally mandatory reasons. In general, we highly recommend that you let the system calculate the amount in the local currency.

Figure 4.17 Line Item Details

All other fields can be mandatory, depending on the field status resulting from the configuration of the line item and of the field status group assigned to the general ledger account.

You can search for additional account assignment objects by clicking the More button. Other fields and information are available by clicking the More Data button (Figure 4.18).

When you press Enter, the system checks the correctness of the entered values. When the controls are passed, you can enter the next line item, starting from the posting key and account number on the bottom of the screen (refer to ❸ of Figure 4.17).

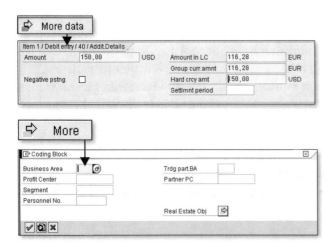

Figure 4.18 Additional Screen Fields for Line Items

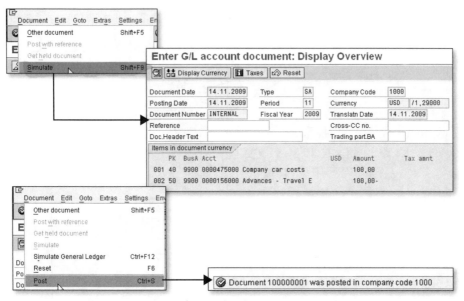

Figure 4.19 Simulation and Posting of General Ledger Documents with Transaction FB01

After you've completed all line items, you can have the system simulate the posting of the document (Figure 4.19). At this point, some additional checks are performed. For example, the system checks that the document balances to zero in the document currency and in all of the local currencies; it also performs the substitutions and validation of callup point 3 (document complete). Note that no tables are updated with the simulation functionality. If the simulation is successful, you can save your document. (The simulation is an optional step in posting a general ledger accounting document; in other words, you can save without simulating.) The system displays the document number assigned; without leaving the transaction, if you select DOCUMENT • DISPLAY, the system immediately displays the document just created.

Figure 4.20 shows some useful tools available in Transaction FB01:

▸ **Account Assignment Model (❶)**
This uses the same functionality as fast data entry, but some data in the screen are precompiled.

▸ **Post with Reference (❷)**
With this function, you can copy data from an existing document, and then edit data as necessary, or simply save the document without any changes.

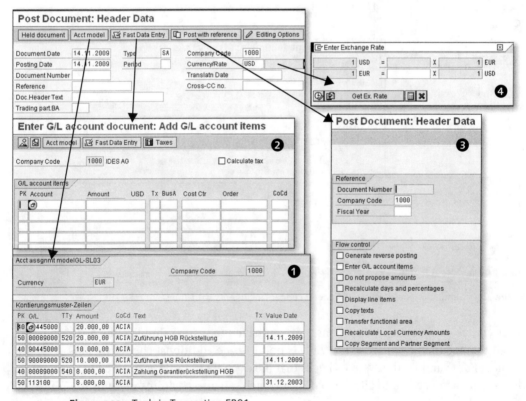

Figure 4.20 Tools in Transaction FB01

▶ **Fast Data Entry (❸)**

With this function, you can post several line items in one screen.

▶ **Get Ex. Rate (❹)**

Use this function to provide the correct exchange rate, entering the amount in local currency for one unit of document currency.

Enjoy Transaction (FB50)

Quick Reference

Menu path: ACCOUNTING • FINANCIAL ACCOUNTING • GENERAL LEDGER • DOCUMENT ENTRY • ENTER G/L ACCOUNT DOCUMENT

Transaction: FB50

With Enjoy transactions, you can post documents with the same information as those you can enter with Transaction FB01 but with a more user-friendly interface. The following Enjoy transactions are available in Financial Accounting:

▶ **FB50:** GL Acct Pstg: Single Screen Trans.

▶ **FB60:** Enter Incoming Invoices

▶ **FB65:** Enter Incoming Credit Memos

▶ **FB70:** Enter Outgoing Invoices

▶ **FB75:** Enter Outgoing Credit Memos

Here we illustrate only Transaction FB50, which allows you to post only to general ledger accounts with posting keys 40 (debit) and 50 (credit). The main difference in Transaction FB01 is that you create all postings in one screen. However, you must always specify the header and line item information, following the same rules as with Transaction FB01.

The following information is useful to understand the main differences between FB50 and FB01 (Figure 4.21).

▶ **Company Code button (❶)**

When you run the transaction, the system asks you for the company code. This information is retained in your session for the next postings with FB50. If you want to change company codes, simply click the Company Code button.

▶ **Hold button (❷)**

You can use the hold function to save the document as it is, completed or uncompleted, under an identification key. No update is made in the transaction figures or in BKPF, BSEG, or BSIS. You can subsequently post the held document using Transaction FB11.

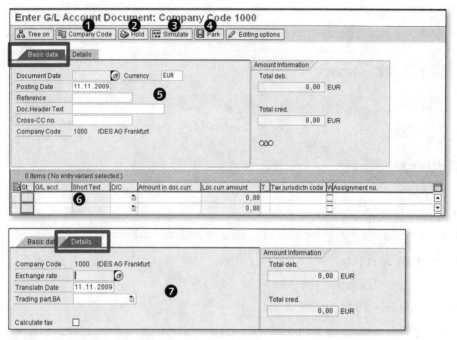

Figure 4.21 Transaction FB50 Working Area

- ► **Simulate button (❸)**
  The Simulate button triggers the document simulation. It works in the same way as described in FB01.

- ► **Park button (❹)**
  This button allows you to park the document. In this case, the system assigns a real document number within the number range associated with the document number. You can then post the document with Transaction FBV0 or FV50.

- ► **Basic Data tab (❺)**
  Enter the document and posting date, reference, and header text. Specify the currency of the document. For the exchange rate, see the next point.

- ► **Line item details (❻)**
  In the center of the screen, you enter the information for each line item. Here all of the considerations that are true for Transaction FB01 are still valid. Note that you can't directly specify the posting key but only whether the posting is a

debit or a credit. However, in the background posting key, 40 (debit) and 50 (credit) will work with the consequent field status rules.

► **Details tab (❼)**

In the Details tab, you don't need to specify anything if you want the system to automatically calculate the exchange rate. Use this section if you want to enter a specific translation date (different from the posting date) or a specific exchange rate.

For each line item, all possible fields are displayed. It's likely that in your Financial Accounting model, few fields are allowed because working in the standard screen with dozens and dozens of fields isn't efficient for your accountants. We recommend setting up screen variants for the most frequent type of postings, as illustrated in Figure 4.22. After the screen variants are set up with only the necessary fields, each accountant can select the suitable one from this menu: EDIT • SCREEN VARIANT • SELECT SCREEN VARIANT.

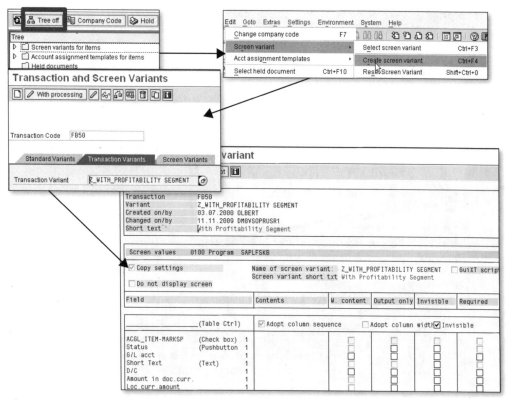

Figure 4.22 Screen Variant for Items

If you need to make frequent postings with repetitive data, you can use the account assignment template. Create a template in this way by following these steps (Figure 4.23):

1. Select an appropriate screen variant with only the necessary fields.

2. Compile all line items with the necessary information and, if needed, the amounts.

3. Select EDIT • ACCT ASSIGNMENT TEMPLATES • SAVE ACCOUNT ASSIGNMENT TEMPLATE.

4. When you need to use the template, select EDIT • ACCT ASSIGNMENT TEMPLATES • SELECT ACCOUNT ASSIGNMENT TEMPLATE, and complete or change the proposed values.

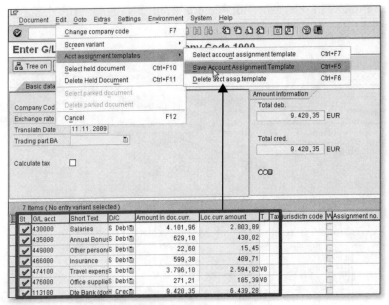

Figure 4.23 Account Assignment Template

4.2.2 Posting with SAP General Ledger

Quick Reference

Menu paths: ACCOUNTING • FINANCIAL ACCOUNTING • GENERAL LEDGER • DOCUMENT ENTRY • ENTER G/L ACCOUNT DOCUMENT FOR LEDGER GROUP

AND

ACCOUNTING • FINANCIAL ACCOUNTING • GENERAL LEDGER • DOCUMENT ENTRY • ENTER GENERAL POSTING FOR LEDGER GROUP

Transactions: FB50L and FB01L

Posting within SAP General Ledger offers the following two additional functionalities:

▶ The possibility to specify a ledger group

▶ The possibility to simulate the document in the entry view and in the general ledger view

You can post in SAP General Ledger with Transactions FB01 and FB50, the same transactions that are used in the classic General Ledger; however, when you use these old transactions in SAP General Ledger, you can't specify a ledger group, so the posting updates all ledgers. You can also use two new transactions in the SAP General Ledger, FB01L and FB50L, which differ from FB01 and FB50 in that you can specify a ledger group (see Figure 4.24); in this case, the system updates only the ledgers that belong to the ledger group.

Apart from the specification of the ledger group, you post with Transactions FB01L and FB50L in the same way as you post with Transactions FB01 and FB50.

When you specify the ledger group, the following things happen:

▶ The system checks whether the posting period is open or not; the posting period variant associated to the representative ledger is used.

▶ If the leading ledger isn't included in the ledger group, the number range is taken by a combination of the representative ledger and the document from Table FAGL_BELNR_LD. If the leading ledger is included, the number range associated with the document type in Table T003 is used.

▶ Table BKPF is always updated with the additional information from the ledger group. BSEG is updated only if the leading ledger is included; if the leading ledger isn't included, Table BSEG_ADD is updated instead.

▶ Totals data is updated in Table FAGLFLEXT only for the ledgers included in the ledger group. If the ledger group has been left blank, all ledger groups are updated in FAGLFLEXT.

▶ A Controlling document is created only if the leading ledger is included in the document and if a cost element is included in at least one line item.

Table 4.1 shows which tables are updated when you post within SAP General Ledger.

Table	No Ledger Group (All Ledgers)	Ledger Groups That Include the Leading Ledger	Ledger Groups That Don't Include the Leading Ledger
BKPF	X	X	X
BSEG	X	X	
BSEG_ADD			X
FGALFLEXT	X	X	X
FGALFLEXA	X	X	X

Table 4.1 Tables Updated When Posting in SAP General Ledger

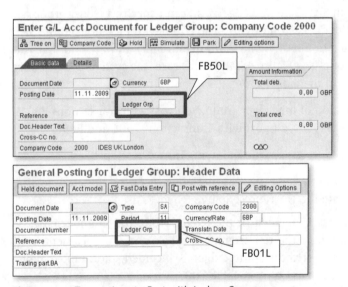

Figure 4.24 Transactions to Post with Ledger Group

4.2.3 Financial Accounting Documents Generated from IDocs

When postings are made to general ledger accounts through IDocs, they usually come from an interface between an external system (either a SAP system or a non-SAP system) and your SAP system where the financial transactions are recorded. The design and implementation of interfaces and ALE connections is a discussion that is beyond the scope of this book. However, as the daily monitoring and troubleshooting of IDoc postings are often part of the tasks of super users or SAP ERP Financials experts, we think it would be useful to provide some quick and practical information about IDoc functionality.

> **ALE Connections**
>
> ALE connections refer to the exchange of data between SAP systems. For example, you could have Sales and Distributions running in instance KSP, and Financial Accounting and Controlling running in instance KFP; in this case, it's common for invoices generated in KSP to be sent to KFP through IDocs to generate the related Financial Accounting and Controlling documents.

The following list provides some useful transactions for working with IDocs:

- ▶ **BALA:** ALE application distribution.
- ▶ **BALM:** ALE master data distribution.
- ▶ **BD87:** Reprocess IDocs in error or waiting for action.
- ▶ **WE05:** View IDocs.
- ▶ **WE09:** IDoc lists according to content. Search for IDocs based on field content.
- ▶ **WE19:** EDI test tool. Use to test inbound function module changes.
- ▶ **WE20:** Partner profile configuration. Add partner detail together with inbound and outbound relationships.
- ▶ **WE30:** Create IDoc extension types.
- ▶ **WE31:** Create segments.
- ▶ **WE57:** Assign function modules to logical messages and IDoc types.
- ▶ **WE60:** IDoc type documentation tool.
- ▶ **WE82:** Link release detail to the extension IDoc type.

Financial Accounting Documents Generated from Batch Input Sessions

> **Quick Reference**
>
> **Transaction**: SM35
> **Table**: APQI

When postings are made to general ledger accounts through batch input sessions, they often come from an interface between a non-SAP external system (e.g., an invoicing system or a payroll system) and SAP; however, batch input sessions are also generated from SAP transactions such as foreign currencies, open items, and balances valuations. Each interface is designed individually, and a discussion of the design and implementation of interfaces is beyond the scope of this book. However, as the daily monitoring and troubleshooting of batch input postings is often part of the tasks of super users and SAP ERP Financials experts, we've provided some quick and practical information about the batch input functionality.

▶ To process or review the batch input sessions created, use Transaction SM35.

▶ You can process a batch input session in three ways:

  ▶ **In the background:** The system creates a background job and tries to post all transactions. If one transaction can't be processed, then it's placed in an error list ready to be reprocessed (online or in the background).

  ▶ **Online (process/foreground):** In this case, you process the session screen by screen. The system simulates a manual processing. You can skip one transaction with the command /n; you can end the session with command /bend. Transactions not processed or in error are kept in the batch input session for later processing.

  ▶ **With the Display Error Only option:** In this case, the system doesn't display a screen until it encounters an error; then it stops on the screen that has an error and shows the error message. You can correct the error or skip the transaction with the command /n, or end the session with command /bend.

▶ You can continue to process one session until all of the transactions contained are processed, and no transaction is in error.

▶ To block one session not fully processed, follow these steps:

  ▶ Mark the session.

  ▶ Select SESSION • LOCK.

  ▶ Specify the date until which the session is locked.

  To unlock a session, follow these steps:

  ▶ Mark the session

  ▶ Select SESSON • UNLOCK.

▶ Each time a batch input session is processed, a log is generated. To print a log of each processing, select the session, and click on the Log button; double-click on the line to get the complete log. When you try to print the log, a preview in

ALV is created and can be easily downloaded into Excel. To see only the error messages for each transaction, filter or sort the log in SAP or Excel according to the Log Message column or T column (message type, where E means "error").

▶ You can see the content of each transaction (which fields are contained; e.g., the document type, the posting date, etc.) if you mark one session and select the Analysis button. Double-click on one transaction to see the screens included; double-click on one screen to see a preview of the online process of the screen. Alternatively, you can get a list of all of the fields included in the transaction if you select the Field List button from the list of screens.

4.2.4 Editing General Ledger Documents

When a Financial Accounting document is created, some fields can't be changed due to rules designed to guarantee the consistency of data. For example, the posting date, the account number, and the amount in both the document and local currency can't be changed after a document is posted (different rules apply for parked documents). This is the list of the main fields that can't be changed:

▶ Header fields:
  ▶ Document Type
  ▶ Document Number
  ▶ Currency
  ▶ Posting Date
  ▶ Document Date
  ▶ Translation Date
  ▶ Exchange Rate
  ▶ Company Code
  ▶ All of the fields updated internally by the system (the user that created the document, the reference key, and the transaction code)
▶ Line item fields:
  ▶ Posting Key
  ▶ Account
  ▶ Amount in Local Currency
  ▶ Amount in Document Currency

▶ Business Area

▶ All account assignment objects (cost center, profit center, internal order, COPA segment, WBS element, etc.)

▶ Functional Area

▶ Consolidation Transaction Type

▶ Asset Number

▶ Asset Transaction Type

▶ Clearing Data

Next we discuss two important topics in editing general ledger documents: the fields that you can change, and how to execute a mass change for general ledger account line items.

Changeable Fields

Quick Reference
Menu paths: IMG • FINANCIAL ACCOUNTING • FINANCIAL ACCOUNTING GLOBAL SETTINGS • DOCUMENT • DOCUMENT HEADER • DOCUMENT CHANGE RULES, DOCUMENT HEADER (FOR HEADER DATA); FINANCIAL ACCOUNTING • FINANCIAL ACCOUNTING GLOBAL SETTINGS • DOCU- MENT • LINE ITEM • DOCUMENT CHANGE RULES, LINE ITEM (FOR LINE ITEM DATA)
Transactions: OB32 (header data), OB32A (line item data)
Table/view: TBAER/V_TBAER

When you define the fields of the financial documents that can be changed and the prerequisites to change them, you do it in two separate transactions, one for the header fields (fields in BKPF) and one for the line item fields (fields in BSEG BSEG_ADD). We discuss both of these processes next.

Header Fields

Run Transaction OB32 to get a list of fields belonging to Table BKPF. If a field isn't in this list, this means that the field can't be changed after the document has been created. For such fields, it's possible to define different rules depending on the following factors (see ❶ of Figure 4.25):

▶ **Account Type**
For header data, this field isn't relevant, so it's always blank.

▶ **Transaction Type**
Leave this field blank.

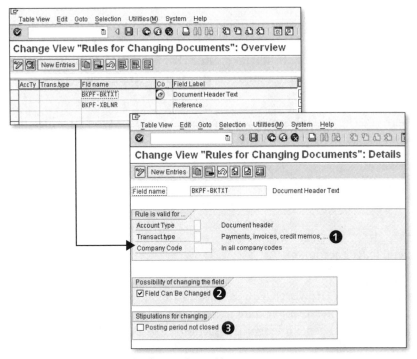

Figure 4.25 Changing Rules for Header Fields

▶ **Company Code**
Leave this field blank if you want to specify rules that are valid for all of the company codes in the client.

To define the rules for a field, follow this procedure:

1. Double-click on one line if the combination field/account type/transaction type/company code is already in the list, or select the New Entries button and specify the field (for header data the fields are contained in Table BKPF) and the combination of the account type, transaction type, and company code, as specified earlier.

2. Specify the following:

   ▶ If the field can be changed, select the Field Can Be Changed flag (❷ of Figure 4.25).

   ▶ If it can be changed, a prerequisite is that the posting period is open (❸ of Figure 4.25). For the header data, what matters is the entry in OB52 with the account type "+".

Line Item Fields

Run Transaction OB32A to get a list of fields belonging to line item tables (you can't select BKPF fields). If a field isn't in the list, this means that the field can't be changed after the document has been created. For such fields, it's possible to define different rules depending on the following factors (❶ of Figure 4.26):

- **Account Type**
  You can leave this field blank; otherwise, specify the account type for which the rule is valid:
    - **A:** Assets
    - **D:** Customers
    - **K:** Vendors
    - **M:** Material
    - **S:** General ledger accounts

- **Transaction Type**
  Leave this field blank. However, you can use this field to define specific rules for defined special general ledger transactions. The value that you specify here is the group of special general ledger transactions (e.g., A for down payments, W for bill of exchange).

- **Company Code**
  Leave this field blank if you want to specify rules that are valid for all company codes in the client.

To define the rules for a field, follow this procedure:

1. Double-click on one line if the combination field/account type/transaction type/ company code is already in the list, or select the New Entries button.

2. Specify the following:
    - If the field can be changed (❷ of Figure 4.26), select the Field Can Be Changed flag.
    - If it can be changed, specify whether there is a prerequisite requiring that the posting period is open for the account type specified (❸ of Figure 4.26).
    - If it can be changed, specify whether there is a prerequisite requiring that the line item isn't cleared (❹ of Figure 4.26). This is relevant only for customer and vendor line items, and for general ledger accounts managed on an open item level.

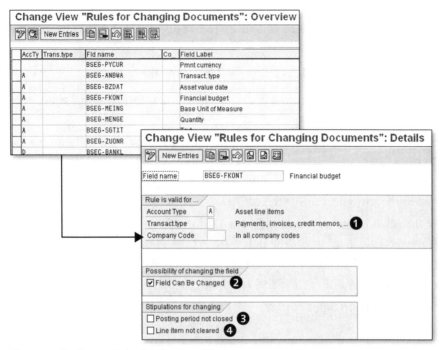

Figure 4.26 Change Rules for Line Item Fields

Mass Change of General Ledger Account Line Items

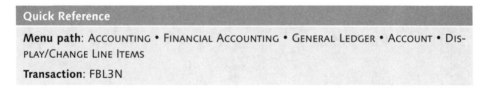

Quick Reference

Menu path: ACCOUNTING • FINANCIAL ACCOUNTING • GENERAL LEDGER • ACCOUNT • DIS-PLAY/CHANGE LINE ITEMS

Transaction: FBL3N

If you need to perform a mass change for many line items in one or more general ledger accounts (e.g., to change the Sort Key field), you can choose one of two options:

▸ **Use the Legacy System Migration Workbench (LSMW) for the scope**
This is particularly useful if you need to specify a different value for each line item (e.g., if you need to replace the assignment field BSEG-ZUONR with the document number). Refer to a specific manual to become familiar with the LSMW tool; it doesn't require any ABAP knowledge and doesn't require a development key.

▶ **Use Transaction FBL3N**

This tool is useful if you need to specify the same value for all items or for a large amount of items; the procedure is described in this section.

To change line items with FBL3N (Figure 4.27), follow these steps:

1. Run Transaction FBL3N with the necessary selection information to select only the line items to be changed.

2. If necessary, use the filter criteria to further restrict the line items to be changed.

3. Mark the line items to be changed. If you need to mark all of the line items displayed in the list, select EDIT • SELECT ALL.

4. Click the Mass Change button (🔣), and, in the following screen, specify the new value for the field or for the fields subject to the mass change. If you need to erase the content of a field, fill in the field with spaces.

5. Don't specify any value (or a space) for the fields that must be left unchanged.

6. Click the Execute Changes button.

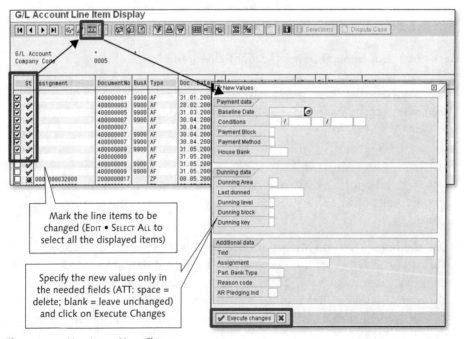

Figure 4.27 Line Items Mass Change

After the mass change has taken place, the system highlights the lines that couldn't be changed in red. Follow the procedure shown in Figure 4.28 to see the error log (which lists the reasons why the mass change couldn't be performed). Correct the errors, and perform the mass change again.

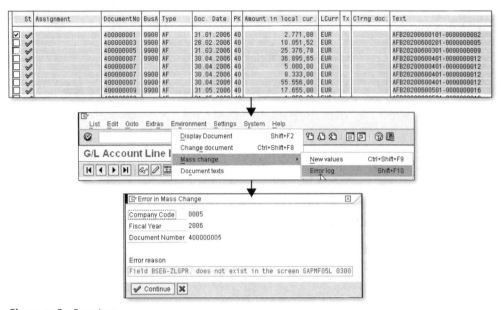

Figure 4.28 Error Log

4.2.5 Clearing General Ledger Open Items

All customer and vendor accounts are managed on an open item level. SAP General Ledger accounts are managed on the open items level if the account is a balance sheet account (SKA1-XBILK = "X") *and* if the Open Item Management indicator is selected (SKB1-XOPVW).

There are three ways to clear open items:

- Match open items with Transaction F-03. Specify the account, select the open items, and save the document.

- Clear an open item posting at the same time as an offsetting posting using Transaction F-04 or FB05.

- Run program SAPF100, and automatically clear based on the matching conditions specified in customizing.

With the automatic clearing function (program SAPF124), you can run or periodically schedule a program that clears all open items grouped together on the basis of customizing grouping criteria and whose total amount is zero in the document currency.

Next we describe the customizing behind automatic clearing and the use of program SAPF124 to collectively clear open items for several general ledger accounts.

Customizing Automatic Clearing Rules

Quick Reference

Menu path: IMG • Financial Accounting • General Ledger Accounting • Business Transactions • Open Item Clearing • Prepare Automatic Clearing

Transaction: OB74

Table/view: TF123/V_TF123

In this transaction, you specify the fields that can be used to group the open items to be cleared according to the following keys:

- **Chart of Accounts**
  If you leave this field blank, the rule is valid for all listed accounts, no matter to which chart of accounts they belong.
- **Account Type**
  For general ledger accounts, choose S. The entry is mandatory.
- **From Account/To Account**
  In these two fields, specify the range of accounts that share the same rule.

For each record (Figure 4.29), you can specify up to five clearing criteria. The more criteria you specify, the smaller the number of open items grouped together becomes; they must have the same value in all of the specified fields to be cleared together.

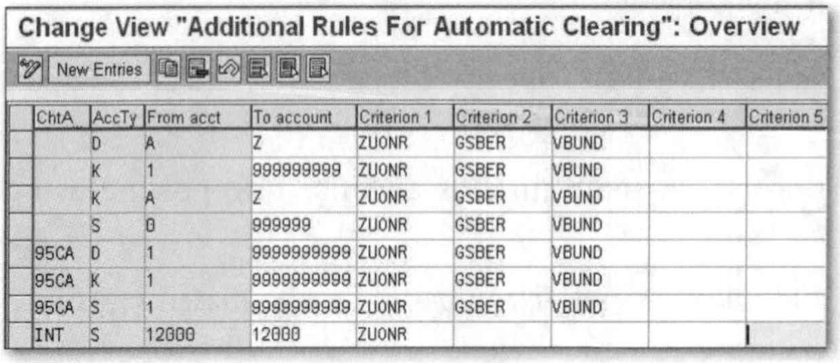
Change View "Additional Rules For Automatic Clearing": Overview

New Entries

ChtA	AccTy	From acct	To account	Criterion 1	Criterion 2	Criterion 3	Criterion 4	Criterion 5
	D	A	Z	ZUONR	GSBER	VBUND		
	K	1	999999999	ZUONR	GSBER	VBUND		
	K	A	Z	ZUONR	GSBER	VBUND		
	S	0	999999	ZUONR	GSBER	VBUND		
95CA	D	1	9999999999	ZUONR	GSBER	VBUND		
95CA	K	1	9999999999	ZUONR	GSBER	VBUND		
95CA	S	1	9999999999	ZUONR	GSBER	VBUND		
INT	S	12000	12000	ZUONR				

Figure 4.29 Rules for Automatic Clearing

For example, if for general ledger account 12000 in chart of accounts INT, the grouping criterion is ZUONR, program SAPF124 groups together the items with the same value in field ZUONR. If the total value of the items in a group is zero in the document currency, the items are cleared together and receive the same clearing number and clearing date.

Running Automatic Clearing

Quick Reference
Menu path: ACCOUNTING • FINANCIAL ACCOUNTING • GENERAL LEDGER • PERIODIC PROCESSING • AUTOMATIC CLEARING
Transaction: F.13
Program: SAPF124

Program SAPF124 is used for automatic clearing, provided that the account with open items has the clearing rules defined in Table TF123. Figure 4.30 shows the selection screen of program SAPF124.

Note the following about the selection screen:

▶ **General Selections**
Here you identify the documents for which open items should be selected; in general, you should specify the company code and leave the following fields blank: Fiscal Year, Assignment, Document Number, and Posting Date (unless for specific reasons you want to identify precisely some open items to be cleared).

▶ **Select G/L Accounts**
Click this indicator to clear open items in general ledger accounts. If you leave the range of accounts blank, the system selects all of the accounts with open item management; however, it clears the relevant open items only if the account is customized in Table TF123.

▶ **Posting Parameters**
Here you specify the posting date of the clearing document (clearing date); alternatively, you can select the Date from Most Recent Document indicator; in this case, the clearing document has the posting date equal to the latest posting date of the documents cleared together. Select the Include Tolerances flag if you want the clearing to take place even if the total amount of the items grouped together isn't zero but is below the tolerance specified in Transactions OBA0 (define tolerance groups for general ledger accounts), OBA4 (define tolerance

groups for employees), OB57 (assign users to tolerance groups), and OBXZ (create accounts for clearing differences).

▶ **Test Run**
With the Test Run indicator, you can preview the results of the run.

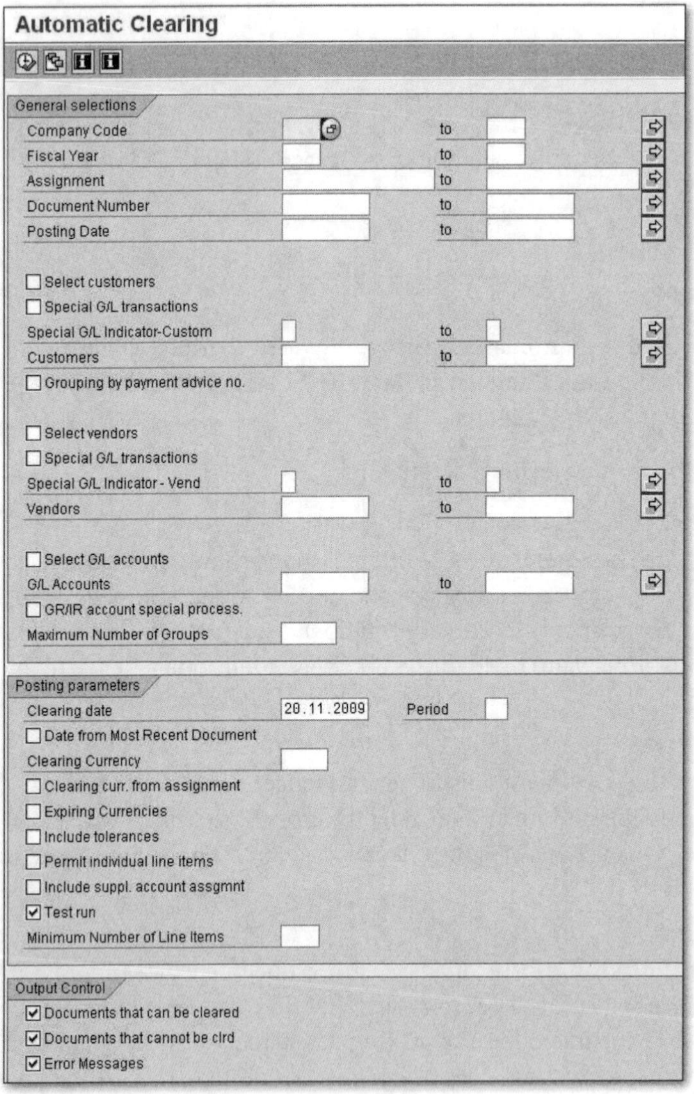

Automatic Clearing

General selections

Company Code		to	
Fiscal Year		to	
Assignment		to	
Document Number		to	
Posting Date		to	

☐ Select customers
☐ Special G/L transactions
Special G/L Indicator-Custom | | to |
Customers | | to |
☐ Grouping by payment advice no.

☐ Select vendors
☐ Special G/L transactions
Special G/L Indicator - Vend | | to |
Vendors | | to |

☐ Select G/L accounts
G/L Accounts | | to |
☐ GR/IR account special process.
Maximum Number of Groups

Posting parameters

Clearing date | 20.11.2009 | Period |
☐ Date from Most Recent Document
Clearing Currency
☐ Clearing curr. from assignment
☐ Expiring Currencies
☐ Include tolerances
☐ Permit individual line items
☐ Include suppl. account assgmnt
☑ Test run
Minimum Number of Line Items

Output Control

☑ Documents that can be cleared
☑ Documents that cannot be clrd
☑ Error Messages

Figure 4.30 Automatic Clearing Program

▸ **Output Control**
With Output Control, you can choose whether you want to have a complete list of the items to be cleared or just those that can't be cleared and the relevant errors that prevent the clearing.

4.2.6 Reversal of Financial Accounting Documents

You can only reverse a financial document in Financial Accounting if the document has been created in Financial Accounting. If, for example, the document has been generated from a cash journal posting, it has to be reversed from the cash journal component; the same principle is valid for documents created in Sales and Distribution, Materials Management, and any component external to Financial Accounting.

However, no matter whether the document has been created within Financial Accounting or within an external SAP module, it isn't possible to delete a document; you can only reverse the document and create an identical document with opposite amounts.

Next we explain how to perform reversals in several different cases.

Reversing Documents with Cleared Items

Quick Reference
Menu path: ACCOUNTING • FINANCIAL ACCOUNTING • GENERAL LEDGER • DOCUMENT • RESET CLEARED ITEMS
Transaction: FBRA

A clearing document can't be reversed with Transaction FB08; instead, you must use Transaction FBRA to first reset the clearing and then reverse the document. If document A contains an item whose clearing document is document B, you must first reset document B (with FBRA), and then reverse document A.

Proceed as follows (Figure 4.31):

1. Run Transaction FBRA.

2. Specify the document number of the document to be reversed, the company code, and the fiscal year

3. If you want to see the accounts included in the document, click on the Accounts button. If you want to see all of the items cleared with the document that you want to reverse, click on the Items button.

4. Select CLEARING • RESET CLEARED ITEMS, or click on the Reset Cleared Items button (🖫).

5. The system asks you the reason for reversal (which will be recorded in the reversing document) and the posting date that the reversal document should take. If you leave the posting date blank, the reversal document is created with the same posting date of the document to be reversed.

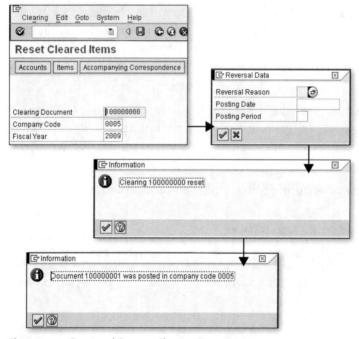

Figure 4.31 Reset and Reverse Clearing Documents

After these steps are completed, the system issues a message of confirmation that the reset of the open items has been carried out and provides the document number of the reversal document.

Reversing Documents Without Cleared Items

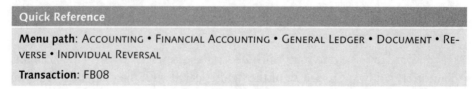

Quick Reference

Menu path: ACCOUNTING • FINANCIAL ACCOUNTING • GENERAL LEDGER • DOCUMENT • REVERSE • INDIVIDUAL REVERSAL

Transaction: FB08

If a document has been created in Financial Accounting and doesn't contain any open items, you can use Transaction FB08 for the reversal. Simply specify the document number, company code, and fiscal year of the document to be reversed, and click the Post button (🖫). The system asks you the reason for the reversal (which is recorded in the reversing document; reasons for reversal are maintained in Table T041C) and the posting date of the reversal document. If you leave the posting date blank, the reversal document is created with the same posting date of the document to be reversed. The system automatically displays the document number of the reversal document.

If, before the reversal, you want to see the document being reversed, click on the Display Before Reversal button. If you want to search the document to be reversed, click on the Document List button.

Mass Reversal of Financial Accounting Documents

Quick Reference

Menu path: ACCOUNTING • FINANCIAL ACCOUNTING • GENERAL LEDGER • DOCUMENT • RE-
VERSE • MASS REVERSAL

Transaction: F.80

Program: SAPF080

You can use Transaction F.80 to reverse more than one accounting document at a time. Note the followings restrictions on the use of the program:

▸ You can't use this transaction to reverse documents created outside Financial Accounting.

▸ You can only reverse documents that can be reversed individually with Transaction FB08.

▸ You can't reverse documents that contain open items.

When using the mass reversal program:

1. Use the selection parameters (Figure 4.32) to identify the documents to be reversed. If the parameters displayed aren't sufficient, click on the Dynamic Selections button (⌶) to access all of the document header fields (from Table BKPF).

2. Specify a reason for the reversal (this is mandatory).

3. Run the program in test mode, which results in a list of the documents that can't be reversed, followed by a list of the documents that can be reversed. If you don't use the test mode, the system reverses all documents that can be reversed and displays the corresponding reversal document for each of them.

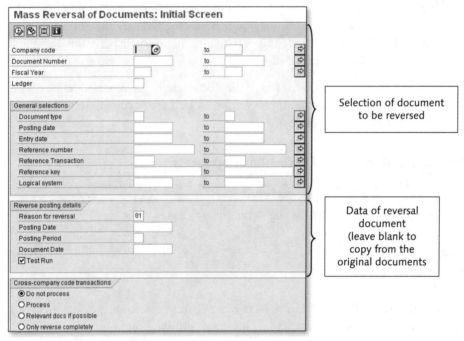

Figure 4.32 Mass Reversal of Financial Accounting Documents

4.2.7 FAQ and Troubleshooting Tips

Next we answer some frequently asked questions and offer helpful troubleshooting tips.

FAQ

1. **Question**: I have to post a document with several line items, and the last item has the amount needed to balance the document to zero. How can I have the system automatically calculate this amount?

   Answer: First specify the correct posting key, and then enter an asterisk for the amount. The system automatically calculates the necessary amount to balance the document to zero.

2. **Question**: Is it mandatory to execute a simulation before saving the document?

   Answer: Not at all. But it's useful to have a preview of the final document without any update to the database table. The simulation has no effect on the document numbering (in other words, no document number is taken).

3. **Question**: In Transactions FB50 and FB50L, all fields are displayed in the line items. Does this mean that the field status rules are ignored in Transactions FB50 and FB50L?

   Answer: No. If you specify a value in a field that should be hidden according to the field status rule coming from the posting key and the field status group, the system issues an error message, and you're forced to delete the value. To avoid this inconvenience, we recommend working with a suitable screen variant.

4. **Question**: How can I find an IDoc with a specific transaction?

   Answer: Use Transaction WE10. In the bottom of the screen, use the parameters contained in the Criteria for Search I Data Records option to select IDocs with specific values in selected fields. You can use up to two fields in one selection run.

5. **Question**: What IDoc type should I use to post to Financial Accounting?

   Answer: Refer to SAP Note 114814 for a comprehensive illustration of the different IDocs available to transfer Financial Accounting document data.

6. **Question**: Is there a standard SAP program that creates batch input sessions for Financial Accounting documents based on a text input file?

   Answer: Yes, the standard program is RFBIBL00.

7. **Question**: Is there a program to automatically submit (process) the batch input session created?

   Answer: Yes, it's program RSBDCSUB.

8. **Question**: Is it possible to limit the user access only to certain batch input sessions?

   Answer: Yes, it's possible based on the name of the batch input session. Work with your authorization expert to build proper profiles.

9. **Question**: Are postings using batch input techniques subject to the same controls as manual postings?

   Answer: Yes, with one exception: A message might be an error message if you process a transaction online, and a warning when you process the transaction via batch input (and vice versa). This is established in customizing via the message control.

10. **Question**: How can I distinguish the fields that are transferred from the batch input session from the ones that are provided by the system (e.g., the value date)?

    Answer: You can only see this difference when processing online; the value passed from the batch input session is displayed in red, and all others are displayed in black.

11. **Question**: When I have to define the rule for changing header or line items of a Financial Accounting document, how can I know to what category the line item belongs? Is this a setting that is defined in the configuration of the document type or in the posting key?

    Answer: Not at all. This indicator refers to special general ledger transactions that take place only when you post to customers with the special posting keys 09 and 19, or to vendors with the special posting keys 29 and 39. In such cases, you must specify a special general ledger indicator, and, depending on the customizing settings, the reconciliation account can be different.

12. **Question**: Is it possible to reverse the mass change made to general ledger account line items?

    Answer: Not directly; in other words, there is no button to automatically restore the values of the fields. The quickest way to do this is to perform another mass change that neutralizes the effects of the incorrect one. You can get a report of all of the changes made to the document by field, date, and user. You can also download the report to Excel to use the information as an input for the mass change, either via FBL3N or with a specifically created LSMW.

13. **Question**: Can I clear items from different accounts with SAPF124?

    Answer: No. You can use this function only with manual clearing.

14. **Question**: Are there fixed criteria that the system uses besides those specified in Table TF123?

    Answer: Yes. For clearing general ledger open items, the system always uses the company code, the account number, and the currency key, together with the additional criteria specified for the general ledger account in Table TF123.

15. **Question**: What is the difference between Transactions F.13 (program SAPF124) and F.13E (program SAPF124E)?

Answer: The only difference is that with SAPF124E, you can specify a clearing currency.

16. **Question**: Which document type takes the reversal document?

    Answer: The document type assigned to the reversal document depends on the configuration of the document type of the document to be reversed (field T003-STBLA). If the field is blank, the reversal document type is the document type itself.

17. **Question**: What is the linkage between the reversed and reversing document?

    Answer: In the reversed document, field BKPF-STBLG (document number) and field BKPF-STJAH (fiscal year) store the reference to the reversing document, and vice versa. You can branch to the reversal document with the Reversal Document button.

18. **Question**: What happens if I incorrectly run the program for mass reversal (program SAPF080, Transaction F.80) twice?

    Answer: Nothing. The same document can't be reversed twice. If you run the program with the same selection options, the system tells you that the documents are already reversed and can't be reversed again.

Troubleshooting Tips

1. **Issue**: Error FX213: "Acct assignment model can't be selected; different currencies."

    Solution: When an account assignment model is created, it's assigned to a specific currency. This message means that you've entered a document currency in Transaction FB01 and then selected an account assignment model assigned to a different currency. This isn't possible.

2. **Issue**: Error Message KI235: "Account AAAAAAAAAA requires an assignment to a CO object."

    Solution: When an account is created as a primary cost element (this is possible only for P&L accounts, not for balance sheet accounts), you must enter a real account assignment object (e.g., a statistical internal order isn't sufficient) to pass the amount to Controlling. Refer to a Controlling manual to understand which are the real account assignment objects and which become the real object if more than one is specified (e.g., a cost center and a WBS element).

3. **Issue**: Error Message FS219: "G/L account AAAAAAAAAA is relevant to tax; check code."

Solution: This means that you've specified a tax code (or *, +, –) in the account master record, but you haven't flagged the Posting Without Tax Allowed indicator. If the account can be posted with or without a tax code, flag the indicator. Alternatively, you can use a tax code designed as "not relevant" for sales taxes. Check this point with your tax and accounting department.

4. **Issue**: What happens if the posting period specified manually doesn't match the posting period derived from the posting date?

   Solution: The system automatically changes the posting period based on the posting date and on the fiscal year variant.

5. **Issue**: After the document has been posted, I selected DOCUMENT • DISPLAY, but the system says that the document doesn't exist in the database and asks me to search in the archive.

   Solution: The system immediately issues the document number, and this number is definitive. However, depending on the speed of your system, it could take some seconds for the system to update the tables in the physical database. Just wait for a minute and then try again.

6. **Issue**: I can't delete an old IDoc within BD87. Is there a standard transaction to delete the IDocs?

   Solution: Use Transaction WE11 for this purpose.

7. **Issue**: In one batch input session, there are around 100 transactions in error. I want to directly process transaction number 55. Must I go through all of the previous transaction to get to number 55?

   Solution: Yes. When you process a batch input session online, the process is sequential; you can't branch directly to a specific transaction. Skip one transaction with the command /n.

8. **Issue**: One batch input session is displayed as in process, but no one is actually processing it.

   Solution: This happens when someone is processing a transaction and leaves SAP without first exiting the batch input session (e.g., due to a computer crash). To solve the issue, mark the batch input session, and select SESSION • RELEASE from the menu. The session appears then with the status "New."

9. **Issue**: Error message SV033 appears: "Specify the key within the work area."

   Solution: This means that you are working with Transaction OB32 (header data) but have specified a field from line items. You must specify a field from Table BKPF. The same message can appear in Transaction OB32A if you specify a field from the header data.

10. **Issue**: Error message FC447 appears: "You do not need to enter account type for the document header field."

    Solution: When you run Transaction OB32 (header data), you must leave the Account Type field blank. The account type can only refer to a line item, not to header information.

11. **Issue**: I often get error messages such as "Field BSEG-ZLSPR does not exist in the screen SAPMF05L." What do they mean?

    Solution: In general, they mean that you are trying to change the content of a field that isn't ready for input; either the posting key or the field status of the general ledger account specifies that the field is suppressed.

12. **Issue**: I want to include the field item text (BSEG-SGTXT), but I can't find it in the matchcode. If I specify the field manually, I get error message FC221: "Field SGTXT is too long."

    Solution: There is a limitation in the fields that you can use for automatic clearing: Only fields with a length up to 20 characters are allowed. The field BSEG-SGTXT has a length of 50 and therefore can't be used. Read SAP Note 117393 about this issue and potential workaround.

13. **Issue**: When running the program for the automatic clearing of general ledger open items, the system isn't considering documents with posting dates in former fiscal years.

    Solution: This means that you've specified a fiscal year in the General Selections area of the selection screen. This criterion is often misunderstood; it's used to select open items, not to determine the date of the posting of the clearing document. Therefore, unless there are specific reasons to limit the selection of the open items to a specific year, leave this field blank.

14. **Issue**: The following error message appears when running automatic clearing: "Account was selected, but is not entered in Table TF123."

    Solution: The account is in the range specified in the selection screen but isn't contained in any record in Table TF123. Therefore, the system is missing the rules to clear the account open items. This may not be a problem if you want to manage an account on an open item basis but you want to perform the clearing manually in a more controlled way. If you do want to use automatic clearing for the account, customize Table TF123 accordingly, using Transaction OB74.

4.3 Tax on Sales/Purchases for Financial Accounting Documents

In this last section of Chapter 4, we discuss the configuration necessary to post documents with tax on sales/purchases, as well as program RFUMSV00, which covers most of the requirements for carrying out tax on sales/purchases reporting for local tax authorities.

4.3.1 Tax on Sales/Purchases Configuration

When you store sales and purchase data information in one document, you have to work with tax codes. Each tax code provides three basic pieces of information:

- Whether it's an input or output tax
- The percentage of the tax
- The account to which the tax should be posted

Each tax code is created within one country, and each country is assigned to a tax procedure that contains the possible rules for the tax code. Each company code is also assigned to a country and therefore inherits the tax rules assigned to the country; the company code can use the tax codes assigned to the country in which it's located. These concepts are shown in Figure 4.33. Tax procedures are very rarely changed, and it's likely that you'll never have reason to change them.

> **Warning!**
>
> If a tax procedure *does* need to be changed, we strongly recommend that you don't handle it as part of daily maintenance but as extraordinary maintenance or within the framework of a small project with an extensive test cycle that also includes the interfaces that create tax-relevant documents in SAP ERP Financials.

Next we explain two of the most important elements of VAT configuration: creating tax codes, and defining accounts for tax codes.

Creating Tax Codes

> **Quick Reference**
>
> **Menu path**: IMG • FINANCIAL ACCOUNTING • FINANCIAL ACCOUNTING GLOBAL SETTINGS • TAX ON SALES/PURCHASES • CALCULATION • DEFINE TAX CODES FOR SALES AND PURCHASES

Transaction: FTXP

Table: T007A

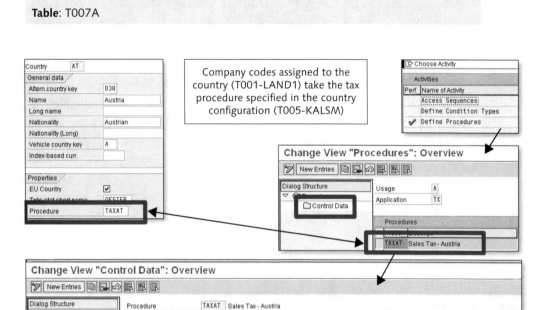

Figure 4.33 Procedure Configuration

To create a tax code, run Transaction FTXP, and follow these steps:

1. Specify the country and the tax code according to your naming convention (❶ and ❷ of Figure 4.34).

2. Specify the description and the characteristics; in particular, you must specify if the code is for output tax (Tax Type A) or input tax (Tax Type V) (❸ of Figure 4.34).

3. Specify the percentage in the correct line (❹ of Figure 4.34). Note that for tax-exempt codes, you must specify a zero rate. Any tax code without a percentage (including a percentage of zero) in at least one item is considered deactivated and can't be used in any transaction.

4. When specifying the percentage, keep in mind that the base to which the percentage applies depends on what you specify in the From Level field.

5. Click on the Accounts button (❺ of Figure 4.34). If the field is editable (i.e., white and not gray), specify an account. More details on this step are offered next.

The tax code is now ready to use.

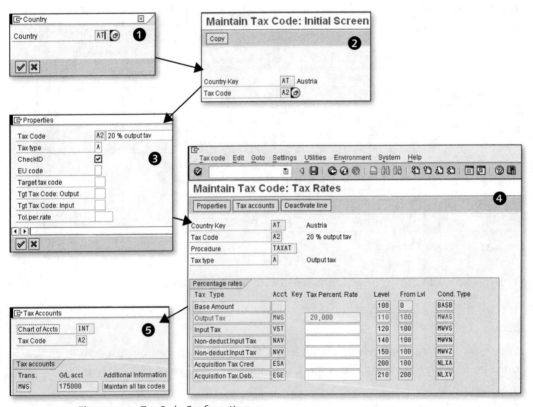

Figure 4.34 Tax Code Configuration

Defining Accounts for Tax Codes

Quick Reference

Menu path: IMG • FINANCIAL ACCOUNTING • FINANCIAL ACCOUNTING GLOBAL SETTINGS • TAX ON SALES/PURCHASES • POSTING • DEFINE TAX ACCOUNTS

Transaction: OB40

Table: T030

In some cases, it's possible to specify accounts in the tax code; in other cases, it isn't possible because the account is already specified and can't be changed (the field appears in gray). Why is this the case?

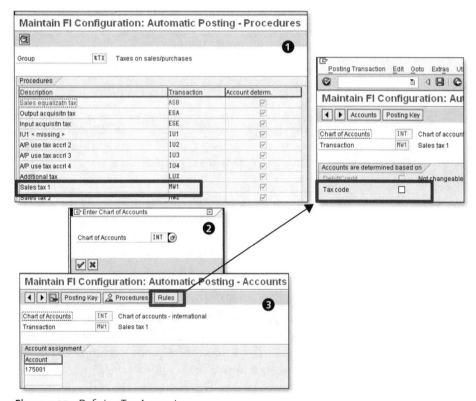

Figure 4.35 Defining Tax Accounts

The answer to this question depends on the settings specified in Transaction OB40. See the example in Figure 4.35; the accounting transaction in this case is MW1 (this information is in the tax code in each line, under the Account Key column; see ❶). The customizing for MW1 specifies that the account determination doesn't depend on the tax code (upper right of Figure 4.35). In this case, you can't specify the account in Transaction FTXP but only in Transaction OB40 (❷ and ❸ of Figure 4.35). This is valid only for the tax lines that have the account key MW1. If the Tax Code indicator is selected instead, the account determination for MW1 depends on the tax code. The accounts can be specified in two ways:

▶ Directly in the tax code for lines that have the account key MW1

▶ In Transaction OB40

The settings configured for account key MW1 (as an example) are applied to all other account keys. The decision depends on your accounting model; discuss the relevant requirement with your accounting department.

4.3.2 Tax Reporting

Quick Reference

Menu path: Accounting • Financial Accounting • General Ledger • Reporting • Tax Reports • General • Advance Return for Tax on Sales/Purchases

Program: RFUMSV00

Tax data is stored in Table BSET on the document level. A special program has been designed to report the tax data; it first reads the documents in BSET and then assigns each document to a business partner (vendor or customer): report RFUMSV00.

In our experience, this report is generally sufficient to cover local tax requirements. However, if it isn't, you can create your own Y or Z report; in this case, we strongly recommend that you make a copy of report RFUMSV00 and add the necessary adjustments. Figures 4.36 and 4.37 show you the selection screen available for the report (we had to split the screen into two figures due to the large number of fields available). Use the fields shown in ❶ of Figure 4.36 to select the documents to be included in the report. If you want to generate a posting to summarize all the credit and debit versus the tax authorities in one tax payable account, use the fields shown in the Tax Payable Postings section (❷ of Figure 4.36, upper right). You can customize your own output lists, as displayed in Figure 4.37 (❸). In the Output Lists section, specify a layout, and click on the Configure button. In the resulting screen, build the list with the ALV technique. You can also generate a Data Medium Exchange (DME) file to be sent to the local authorities (❹ of Figure 4.37).

RFUMSV00: Selection Screen

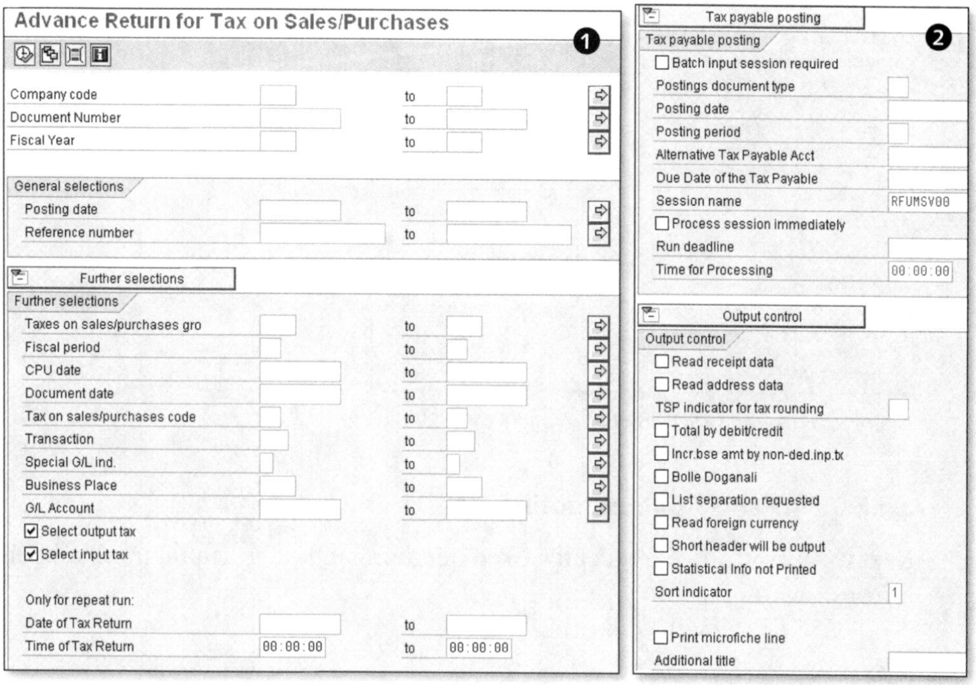

Figure 4.36 Selection Screen of Program RFUMSV00 (Part 1)

Given the large number of fields available in the selection screen of the report, we recommend reading the report documentation for a full description of the characteristics of the report. (Some of the fields are applicable only in specific countries, such as the Bolle Doganali flag that you can see in the Output Control section in Figure 4.36; this flag is only relevant for Italy.)

RFUMSV00: Selection Screen

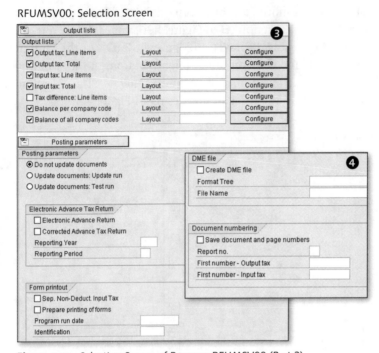

Figure 4.37 Selection Screen of Program RFUMSV00 (Part 2)

4.3.3 FAQ and Troubleshooting Tips

Next we answer some frequently asked questions and offer helpful troubleshooting tips.

FAQ

1. **Question**: The government has changed the percentage on a tax code. Should I change the tax percentage in FTXP?

   Answer: We strongly recommend that you don't change the percentage in tax codes if they've already been used in at least one document. Instead, create brand new tax codes, and adapt the Sales and Distribution condition records and any interface tables that use the tax codes.

2. **Question**: I want to prevent the incorrect use of a now-invalid tax code without deleting it (for audit reasons, and to ensure the correct printout of the tax code description in report RFUMSV00, in case a printout of old data is necessary). How can I do this?

Answer: You can deactivate the tax code. Note that it isn't sufficient to delete the percentage because this makes the tax code a zero percent code. Instead, for each line that appears in red, click on it, and then click the Deactivate Line button.

3. **Question**: Is it possible to have the same tax code in many countries? If so, must it have the same percentage?

   Answer: Yes, it's possible, unless you use the plant abroad procedure. The tax codes in different countries are completely independent of each other and can have completely different meanings.

4. **Question**: How can I get program RFUMSV00 to automatically number the documents and pages? In particular, the next time I run the report, I need the program to remember both pieces of information without starting from the beginning. For example, if the last page of the report from March 2010 was 1456, the report in April must start with page 1457.

   Answer: In the Document Numbering area of the selection screen, select the Save Document and Page Numbers indicator. If you need to print more than one report with separate paging, use the Report No. field, for example, output tax is report 01, input tax is report 02, and so on. The system saves separates numbers for each report and remembers the last page and document number for the next run.

Troubleshooting Tips

1. **Issue**: When I run Transaction FTXP, I get a message with warning instructions on the transport of tax codes.

   Solution: When you save and transport a tax code, all of the characteristics of the tax code are transported in the destination system but not the percentage. In other words, the tax code appears as deactivated with no percentage in any line. We recommend re-updating the percentage in the destination system after the transport has been performed.

2. **Issue**: I can't see the VAT number of the business partner in the lists of program RFUMSV00.

   Solution: In the Output Control area of the selection screen, select the Read Address Data indicator.

4.4 Summary

In this chapter, we focused on how to create and change general ledger accounts and documents. The last section of the chapter was dedicated to VAT configuration and reporting. In the next chapter, we discuss the configuration and usage of the subcomponents Accounts Receivables (customers) and Accounts Payables (vendors).

Customer receivables and vendor liabilities usually originate in Sales and Distribution and Materials Management. In Financial Accounting, you must ensure the correct settlement and management of the connected financial transactions.

5   Accounts Receivable and Accounts Payable

The focus of this chapter is the Financial Accounting processes that involve interaction with partners *to which* your company sells goods and services (customers), and partners *from which* your company purchases goods and services (vendors). The following areas of Accounts Receivable and Accounts Payables are discussed in detail:

- **Configuration and management of customer master data**
  In addition to being relevant to Financial Accounting, this topic is also important for sales and distribution; as such, it's good practice to collaborate with your Sales and Distribution colleagues.

- **Configuration and management of vendor master data**
  In addition to being relevant to Financial Accounting, this topic is also important for purchasing; as such, it's good practice to collaborate with your Materials Management colleagues.

- **Business transactions, postings, and period-end processes in Accounts Receivable and Accounts Payable**

We discuss the configuration and execution of all of these topics.

5.1   Customer Master Data

In this section, we discuss customer master data as it relates to Accounts Receivable and Accounts Payable. Specifically, we cover its configuration, management, and reporting.

5.1.1 Configuring Customer Master Data

Here you will learn about the following topics that affect the configuration of customer master data:

▶ Account groups, which affect the screen layout and number ranges

▶ Screen layout rules at the company code level, which affect the status of the available fields when you try to create, change, or display customer master data

▶ Screen layout rules at the activity level, which affect the status of the available fields for the customer master records

▶ The creation of number ranges for customer master data and the link between the account group and the number range

▶ The accounting clerk, an object used in customer master data to manage communication with the customer

Defining Customer Account Groups

Quick Reference
Menu path: IMG • FINANCIAL ACCOUNTING • ACCOUNTS RECEIVABLE AND ACCOUNTS PAYABLE • CUSTOMER ACCOUNTS • MASTER DATA • PREPARATION FOR CREATING CUSTOMER MASTER DATA • DEFINE ACCOUNT GROUPS WITH SCREEN LAYOUT (CUSTOMERS) **Transaction:** OBD2 **Table/view:** T077D/V_T077D

When you create a customer account, you must assign it to an account group. The account groups are created in customizing and control the following:

▶ The number range within which the customer is created

▶ The field status of the customer master data, in combination with the rules defined at the company code and activity levels (discussed later in this chapter)

To define the customer account groups in customizing, use Transaction OBD2, and then use Transaction OBAR to assign the account group to a number range. After these steps are completed, follow these steps (Figure 5.1):

1. Specify the new account group with the New Entries button, and define the new account group according to your naming convention. Specify a short

description. If you want to change an existing account group, double-click an existing one.

2. In the next screen, flag the One Time Account field if the customer account will be used for several real customers. In this case, specify the address at the document level; this means that you can specify a different address for each posting to the one-time account. The relevant address will be picked up and displayed in the VAT report, RFUMSV00.

3. To define the value for the Output Determination Procedure field, ask your Sales and Distribution colleagues.

4. To define the field status, double-click on one of the following three rows:

   ▶ General Data (stored in Table KNA1 and unique for each customer)

   ▶ Company Code Data (stored in Tables KNB1 and KNB5 and dependent on the company code)

   ▶ Sales Area Data (data relevant for Sales and Distribution; in general, this section of the customer master data is the responsibility of Sales and Distribution experts)

5. The system shows all groups divided into the fields for each level. Double-click on a single group to jump to the field status definition.

6. Each row represents a field or a subgroup of fields. If it represents a subgroup of fields, you can only define the field status rule for the subgroup, not for the single fields contained in the subgroup. The field statuses you can define are Suppressed (❶ of Figure 5.1), Required (❷ of Figure 5.1), Optional (❸ of Figure 5.1), and Displayed (❹ of Figure 5.1).

When you process the customer, however, the final result depends not only on the account group but also on the combination of rules specified for the activity in Transaction OB20 (whether it's created centrally, created at the company code level, changed centrally, etc.) and at the company code level with Transaction OB21; the following sections describe this type of customizing.

Table 5.1 shows how the system combines the rules from the three different types of customizing (account group Transaction OBD2, company code screen layout Transaction OB21, and activity screen layout Transaction OB20), to define the final field status for each field in the customer master data.

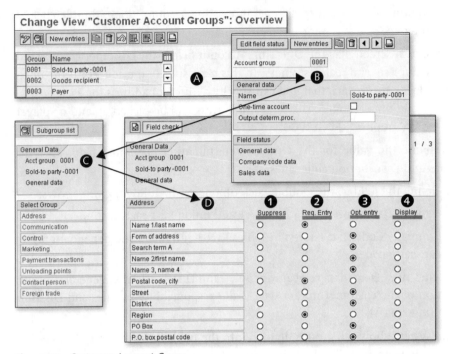

Figure 5.1 Customer Account Group

	Suppressed	Required	Optional	Display
Suppressed	Suppressed	Error	Suppressed	Suppressed
Required	Error	Required	Required	Display
Optional	Suppressed	Required	Optional	Display
Display	Suppressed	Display	Display	Display

Table 5.1 Field Status Combinations for Customer Master Data

Account Groups Between Financial Accounting and Sales and Distribution

Financial Accounting and Sales and Distribution share customer master data; specifically, both components use the general data. As such, it's important that any change to the account group configuration is made in collaboration with experts in both components.

Defining Screen Layout per Company Code

> **Quick Reference**
>
> **Menu path**: IMG • FINANCIAL ACCOUNTING • ACCOUNTS RECEIVABLE AND ACCOUNTS PAYABLE • CUSTOMER ACCOUNT • MASTER DATA • PREPARATION FOR CREATING CUSTOMER MASTER DATA • DEFINE SCREEN LAYOUT PER COMPANY CODE (CUSTOMERS)
>
> **Transaction**: OB21

As stated in the former section, the field status for the fields of the customer master record depends on the combination of the rules defined for the account group, the company code, and the activity. However, the rules at the company code level don't affect the field status of the fields at the general data level or the sales area level; they affect only the status of the field at the company code level (e.g., the accounting clerk and the reconciliation account). The field status rules at the company code level are maintained in customizing using Transaction OB21 (Figure 5.2).

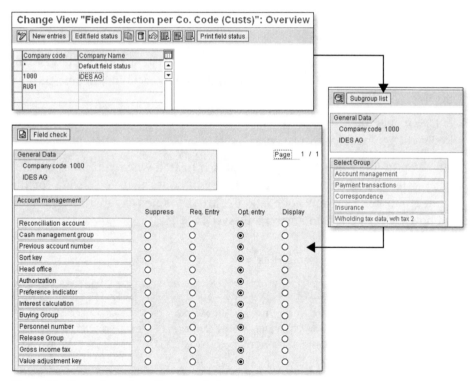

Figure 5.2 Screen Layout per Company Code

It isn't mandatory to define different rules for different company codes. If you don't want to make any differentiation, simply define just one rule, and, in the first screen of Transaction OB21, specify the company code as "*" (see Figure 5.2, on the top left). This special character indicates to the system that the set of rules applies to all of the company codes; however, if you create a later entry with a specific company code, this company code will take its specific rules, not the ones defined under the generic rule. In the example illustrated in Figure 5.2, the company codes 1000 and RU01 have their specific set of rules; all other company codes take the rules specified under the entry with company code "*".

To define the field status rules in this transaction, follow these steps:

1. If you create rules for a specific company code, start with the copy of the generic entry "*"; if you want to change the settings for an existing record, double-click it. In the example illustrated in Figure 5.2, we change the settings for the record that refers to company code 1000.

2. The system presents the group of fields that belong to the company code segment of the customer (Tables KNB1 and KNB5). Note that in this customizing step, you can't make any field status setting related to the general data segment and the sales area segment.

3. Double-click on one of the groups to define the field status for the fields or subgroup of the fields. To see the field contained in each line, double-click on the line.

4. For each subgroup, you can have one of the following statuses: Suppressed, Required, Optional, or Displayed.

Again, keep in mind that the way the status is treated when you process a customer master record depends on the field status rules that you define for the account group, the company code, and the activity. Refer to Table 5.1 to understand how the rules are combined by the system.

Defining Screen Layout for Activities

Quick Reference

Menu path: IMG • FINANCIAL ACCOUNTING • ACCOUNTS RECEIVABLE AND ACCOUNTS PAYABLE • CUSTOMER ACCOUNT • MASTER DATA • PREPARATION FOR CREATING CUSTOMER MASTER DATA • DEFINE SCREEN LAYOUT PER ACTIVITY (CUSTOMERS)

Transaction: OB20

As stated in the former sections, when processing the customer master data, the field status depends on the combination of the customizing made in the following three activities:

▸ **OBD2:** Customer account group

▸ **OB21:** Screen layout per company code

▸ **OB20:** Screen layout for activities

We discussed Transactions OBD2 and OB21 in the previous two sections; in this section, we describe how to perform the configuration for Transaction OB20 (Figure 5.3).

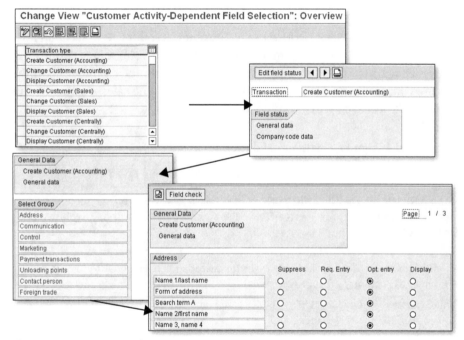

Figure 5.3 Screen Layout for Activities

In the first screens of this customizing step, SAP presents a list of the possible transaction that manage customer master data. There is a basic distinction between the following two groups of transactions:

▸ **XD01, XD02, XD03**

These transactions are used to create, change, and display customers centrally. With these transactions, you can process the screens for all three segments of the customer master record (general data, such as the address; company code data, such as the reconciliation account; and sales data, such as the invoicing currency).

- ▶ **FD01, FD02, FD03**
  These transactions are used to create, change, and display the customer up to the company code level. With these transactions, you can process the screens for only two segments of the customer master record (general data and company code data).

For all six transactions, you can specify different field status rules, which the system combines with the field status rules defined when creating customer account groups and defining the screen layout for company codes.

When you select one of the six transactions, the way you carry out the configuration is exactly the same as described in the Customer Account Group section under Section 5.1.1, Configuring Customer Master Data, so refer to that section to get step-by-step instructions. Just remember that to maintain the customer up to the company code level, no field status can be defined for the sales area fields; this segment isn't displayed when running those transactions.

Creating and Assigning Customer Number Ranges

Quick Reference
Menu path: IMG • Financial Accounting • Accounts Receivable and Accounts Payable • Customer Account • Master Data • Preparation for Creating Customer Master Data • Create Number Ranges for Customer Accounts/Assign Number Ranges to Customer Account Groups
Transactions: XDN1 (create number ranges for customer accounts), OBAR (assign number ranges to customer account groups)
Table/view: NRIV (Object DEBITOR), XDN1 (create number ranges for customer accounts), T077D/V_077D_B (assign number ranges to customer account groups)

Each time you create a customer, you must first specify the account group. The account group will then define the following:

- ▶ Whether you are allowed to specify a customer number, or the system will automatically assign it
- ▶ The number range within which you can specify the customer, or within which the customer number will be automatically assigned

To create customers within one account group, you must assign a customer number range to the account group. This customizing transaction is performed in two steps:

1. Run Transaction XDN1 in the production system, and define the new number range (Figure 5.4). Click on the Intervals button, and specify a new number range ID, as well as the first and final number. Then specify whether the number range is external; in this case, every time you enter a new customer, you are requested to specify a customer number. If you leave the Ext field blank, the number range is internal; every time you create a customer in the account group, the system assigns the first number available in the range. In exceptional cases when you need to redefine the last number for the internal number range, you can click on the Status button.

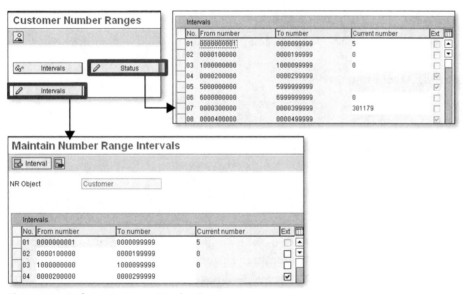

Figure 5.4 Defining Customer Number Ranges

2. Assign a number range to each account group using Transaction OBAR (Figure 5.5). Account groups without an assigned number range can't be used in the customer creation. A subsequent deletion of an assigned number range doesn't affect the customers already created but prevents the creation of new customers in the affected account group.

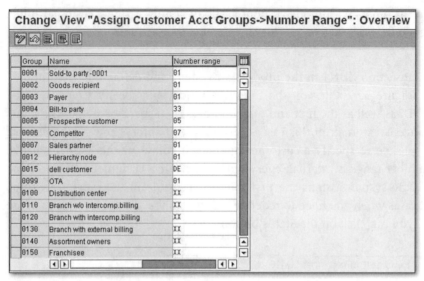

Figure 5.5 Assigning Number Ranges to Customer Account Groups

Entering Accounting Clerks

The accounting clerk is typically used in conjunction with the customer and can be further used as a selection criterion in customer and vendor reports. In general, an accounting clerk corresponds to a specific user in the system. The connection between the accounting clerk and the SAP user allows the use of some fields that are stored at the user level (e.g., telephone number and email).

Note also that when you send correspondence by email, the sender is the one specified in the user ID connected to the accounting clerk. If you don't enter an accounting clerk identification code for customers, the email won't be issued and won't appear in Transaction SOST.

To create an accounting clerk, run Transaction OB05 (Figure 5.6), and select the New Entries button. Then specify the following:

- The company code to which the accounting clerk belongs.
- The accounting clerk ID (two digits, alphanumeric).
- The name of the accounting clerk.
- The SAP user of the accounting clerk. You can see the user created in the system using Transaction SU01.

Enter the accounting clerk in the customer and vendor master data, at the company code level, in the Correspondence tab.

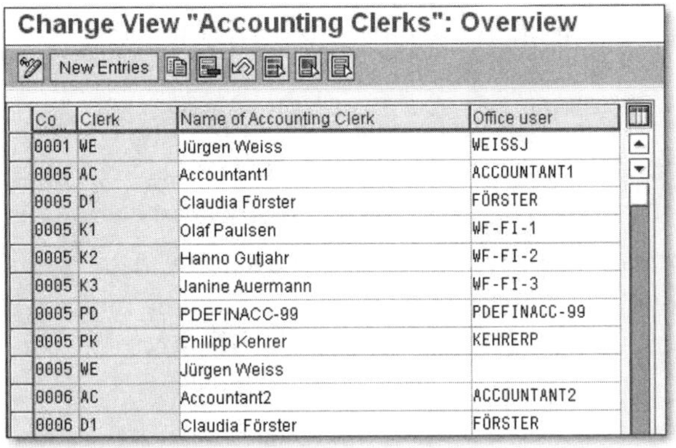

Change View "Accounting Clerks": Overview

Co	Clerk	Name of Accounting Clerk	Office user
0001	WE	Jürgen Weiss	WEISSJ
0005	AC	Accountant1	ACCOUNTANT1
0005	D1	Claudia Förster	FÖRSTER
0005	K1	Olaf Paulsen	WF-FI-1
0005	K2	Hanno Gutjahr	WF-FI-2
0005	K3	Janine Auermann	WF-FI-3
0005	PD	PDEFINACC-99	PDEFINACC-99
0005	PK	Philipp Kehrer	KEHRERP
0005	WE	Jürgen Weiss	
0006	AC	Accountant2	ACCOUNTANT2
0006	D1	Claudia Förster	FÖRSTER

Figure 5.6 Accounting Clerks

5.1.2 Managing Customer Master Data

Quick Reference

Menu path: ACCOUNTING • FINANCIAL ACCOUNTING • ACCOUNTS RECEIVABLE • MASTER RECORDS • CREATE

Transactions: FD01 (general and company code data), XD01 (general, company code, and sales data)

Tables: KNA1 (general data), KNB1 (company code data), KNBK (bank data), KNB5 (dunning data), KNKK (credit management data), KNAS (VAT registration number in different countries), KNVV (sales area data)

To create a customer, you can use the following two transaction codes:

- Transaction FD01 (Figure 5.7), in which you can create the following:

▸ A customer with general data only. In the initial screen, specify the account group and the customer number (only if it belongs to an external number range). Leave the company code blank.

▸ A customer with both general and company code data. In the initial screen, specify the account group, the customer number (only if it belongs to an external number range), and the company code.

▸ The company code segment of an already existing customer. In the initial screen, specify the customer number and the company code.

▸ Transaction XD01, in which you have all of the options as in Transaction FD01. Leave the Sales Organization, Distribution Channel, and Division fields blank. In addition, you can also create the following:

▸ A customer with general data and sales area data only. In the initial screen, specify the account group, the customer number (only if it belongs to an external number range), and sales area. Leave the company code blank.

▸ A customer with general data, company code data, and sales area data. In the initial screen, specify the account group, the customer number (only if it belongs to an external number range), the company code, and the sales area.

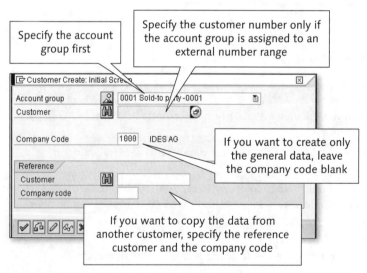

Figure 5.7 Creation of a Customer: Initial Screen

The sales area is a combination of the following Sales and Distribution organizational units: sales organization, distribution channel, and division. The configuration necessary to update the customer data at the sales area level is the responsibility of Sales and Distribution experts.

> **Customer Creation: The Matchcode of the Account Group**
>
> When creating a new customer, you must first select an account group. You can do this from the matchcode, though you may only be able to see the description of the account groups and not the four-digit code. This isn't an error; it can be changed from any screen or transaction by following Option • Expert and selecting the Customize Local Layout button (🖳). In the Control section, select the Show Keys in All Dropdown Lists flag. The next time you create a customer, the system always displays the four-digit keys together with the account group description. If you want the records to be sorted according to the key instead of the description, select the Sort Items by Key flag. Note that both settings affect the same types of matchcodes, and not only on the account group selection when you create a customer master record (Figure 5.8).

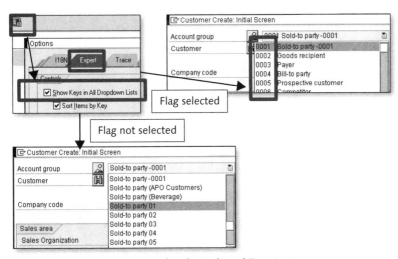

Figure 5.8 Account Group Matchcode: Code and Description

Next we describe the maintenance of the customer master record at the general data and company code levels, including some special functions. (If you're looking for information about maintenance at the sales area level, consult an appropriate SAP Sales and Distribution manual.) We also discuss three additional activities that are relevant for managing customer master data in Accounts Receivable and

Accounts Payable: blocking customer accounts, deleting customer accounts, and changing account groups.

Maintaining General Level Data

General data stores customer information that is valid for all company codes, such as addresses, bank accounts, and trading partners (if the customer is intercompany). The main groups of information are: address, control data, and payment transaction. We describe each of these groups next.

Address Tab

Figure 5.9 show an example of the address data of a German customer.

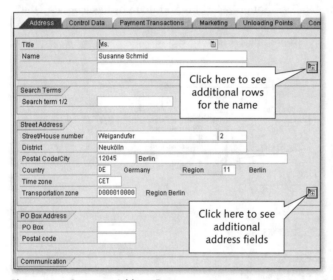

Figure 5.9 Customer Address Data

Note the following when updating the address data of a customer:

- The name can be stored in up to four lines; all of these lines correspond to different fields in Table KNA1.

- The postal code can be controlled by country-specific rules that you define when customizing the country.

- The region is available only for countries in which it has been defined; in other words, its presence depends on the country's local administrative organization.

▶ In the Communications section (Figure 5.10), pay attention to the Language field; there could be communication programs that read this field to select a form in specific languages. Forms are maintained with Transaction SE71; SAP Smart Forms are maintained with Transaction SMARTFORMS.

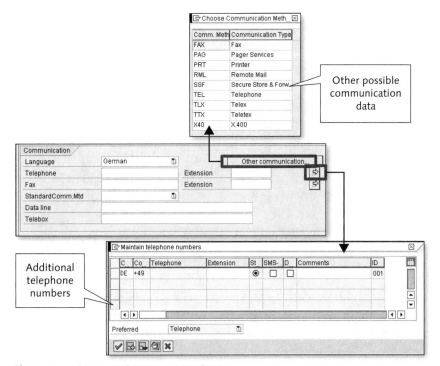

Figure 5.10 Customer Communication Data

▶ You can enter many communication methods (e.g., telephone, fax, and email). Some programs can send the data using different methods; this choice is usually made on the basis of the specification of the main method in the Standard-Comm.Mtd field.

Control Data Tab

Figure 5.11 shows an example of fields available on the Control Data tab.

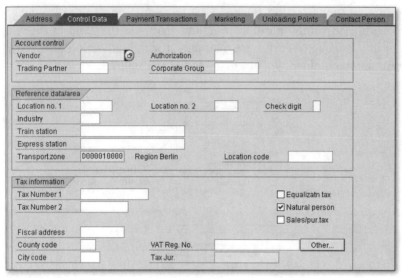

Figure 5.11 Control Data (Cross-Company Code)

Next we explain the most important fields available here:

▶ **Vendor**

If the customer also has a vendor master record, you can specify the vendor number here. The effects of specifying the vendor account are as follows:

▶ When you run the open item report for customers (Transaction FBL5N), you have the option to also see the line items of the connected vendor; on the bottom of the selection screen, select the Vendor Items flag.

▶ The reference to the customer is placed in the corresponding vendor master data.

▶ In the customer master data, the Clearing with Vendor field can be activated (if the vendor isn't specified, SAP hides this field). If you do this, the vendor line items are used in the automatic payment program (Transaction F110) and in manual clearing.

▶ **Trading Partner**

If the customer is intercompany, specify the company/trading partner here (configure the companies/trading partners with Transaction OX15). When you post to the customer, the trading partner is automatically added into the document. The way the trading partner updates the document depends on the settings at the document type level.

▶ **Tax Number 1 and Tax Number 2**
These two fields have different meanings in different countries; click on the field, and then press F1 to get more information. Note that the length of the two fields can be controlled for each country (Transaction OY17).

▶ **Fiscal Address**
In this field, you can specify another customer whose address and VAT number is printed in the VAT reporting. Note that this customer must already exist in the system.

▶ **VAT Reg. No.**
The VAT registration number is the identification number recognized throughout the European Union. In general, it's determined by the country ISO code (e.g., FR) and the local VAT identification number.

Payment Transactions Tab
The main information that you enter in the customer master data is the bank information for the customers. This kind of information can be necessary in the following two cases:

▶ When you send a bill of exchange to the customer, or carry out a direct debit

▶ When you want to pay the customer using automatic payment program credit notes (instead of clearing with issued invoices)

You can update more than one bank account for the customer. Note that this is the account of the customer's own bank; don't confuse it with the house bank account, which is the bank account of the company code. For each bank account, specify the following information (Figure 5.12):

▶ **Bank Country and Bank Key**
These two pieces of information identify the branch where the customer has opened the current account. Table BNKA must have an entry for each of these fields; they are the only key fields in the table. If these entries don't exist, the system opens a window to create the bank in Table BNKA. We recommend checking your internal procedure about bank creation; in general, banks are created by a specific department that ensures the correct naming convention and that periodically carries out a mass update of the master records in each country.

▶ **Bank Account**
This is the bank number of the account the customer keeps. Make sure to update this field carefully and precisely. Speak with your treasury department about the rules for each country.

- **Acct Holder**

  Leave this field blank if the owner of the account is the customer itself. If not, you can specify the name here. In the case of the latter, the name you specify is used when creating the payment file.

- **Control Key**

  This field is used to control the coherence between the bank key and the bank account. It isn't relevant for all countries; click on the field, and then press F1 to see a list of the different meanings of the field for different countries (the relevant country here is the country of the bank, not the country of the customer).

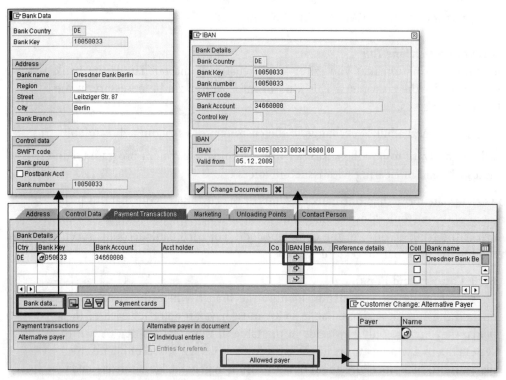

Figure 5.12 Payment Transactions

- **Bank Type**

  If you create multiple bank accounts here, you can assign a freely defined four-digit code to each of them (the system doesn't check what you enter here). Then, in the customer line items, you can assign one of the bank accounts by selecting one of these codes; the result is that the line items are assigned to the specified bank in the automatic payment process. If you don't specify any bank time in the line item, the automatic payment assigns the line item to the first bank account listed in the customer master data.

▶ **IBAN**
If you click on the IBAN button, the system opens a new window where you can specify the IBAN information. The system proposes an IBAN code based on the country of the bank, the bank number, and the control key (if specified). You should check the proposed IBAN and change it if necessary.

▶ **Coll. (Collection Authorization)**
If you want to perform a direct debit, click this field. Otherwise, the payment method for the automatic collection skips the customer invoices.

It's also possible to specify an alternative payer (Figure 5.12), which is another customer account whose bank information will be used. You can also differentiate the alternative payer in the line item, but you must first specify a list of the possible alternative payers and then select the payer from the list when updating the single customer line item. You can also specify a payer at the company code level, which then has precedence over the payer specified at the general data level.

To specify the company code level data, click on the Company Code Data button.

Maintaining Company Code Level Data

The information you store at this level can be different for each company code. Remember that if you need to open an existing customer in a company code where you haven't created the master data before, you shouldn't use the transaction for changing the customer master record (FD02 or XD02) but rather the transactions for creating the customer master record (FD01 and XD01).

The most important fields available in the company code segment of the customer master record are grouped in the following tabs: Account Management, Payment Transactions, and Correspondence. We discuss each of these tabs in more detail next.

Account Management Tab

The main information you store in the Account Management tab is about the reconciliation account. This is the general ledger account where all postings to a customer are replicated at the general ledger level. The only exception to this rule is when you post to a customer with a special general ledger indicator; in this case, it's possible to specify another general ledger account (which must be marked as a reconciliation account). When you specify the reconciliation account in the customer master record, you can use the matchcode. In this particular context, SAP doesn't display all general ledger accounts — only those marked as reconciliation accounts for customers in their general ledger account master record (Figure 5.13).

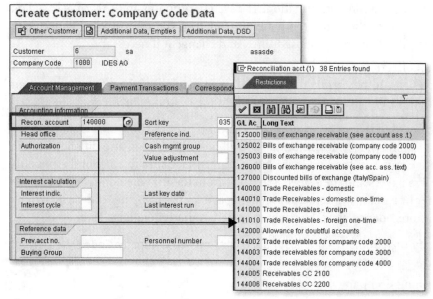

Figure 5.13 Account Management Tab

Other important fields available in this tab are the following:

▶ **Sort Key**
This field determines the way the field assignment (BSEG-ZUONR) is filled when you post to the customer; you can maintain the sort keys through Transaction OB16. The field assignment is a key in the table of customer open items (BSID) and closed items (BSAD), so it can be used for a quick selection and sort of the line items.

▶ **Head Office**
This is another customer account where the line items are automatically posted. If the field is left empty, the line items are created on the customer account. If a head office is specified, the line items are created on the customer account specified in the Head Office field. The branch account is noted in the line items in field BSEG-FILKD.

▶ **Interest Indic.**
Specify an interest indicator if you want to calculate interests on a customer account for invoices paid or unpaid after the due date. The interest indicator controls the rules for calculating interest.

▶ **Interest Cycle, Last Key Date, and Last Interest Run**
See Section 5.6.3 for information about using these fields.

Payment Transactions Tab

In this tab, you can set how payments are to be collected from the customer. In particular, you can specify the following (Figure 5.14):

▶ **Terms of Payment**
This important information provides a default term of payment when creating an invoice against the customer. Invoices created in Sales and Distribution give priority to payment terms defined in the customer master record at the sales area level. If the payment term isn't available at the sales area level, the one specified at the company code level is used. See Section 5.3.1, Maintaining Payment Terms, later in this chapter, to learn about the payment terms configuration.

▶ **Payment Methods**
Here you can define, at the customer master level, allowed payment methods for the customer. When you run the automatic payment program to create bills of exchange or direct debits, one prerequisite is that the relevant payment method is specified in the invoice or in the customer master record.

▶ **Payment Block**
If this indicator is set, the open items of the customer aren't used in the automatic payment run.

▶ **Alternat. Payer**
If you specify an alternative payer, the system uses the bank information of the alternative payer (i.e., another customer) when you carry out the automatic payment program with Transaction F110. The alternative payer specified here has priority over the alternative payer specified at the general data level.

▶ **House Bank**
In the automatic payment configuration (Transaction FBZP), you define the rules for the selection of a house bank. However, you can force the open items of a specific customer to be collected through a specific house bank through the specification that you make here.

▶ **Single Payment**
This indicator, if selected, means that the customer open items aren't grouped together in automatic payments; each invoice produces one bill of exchange.

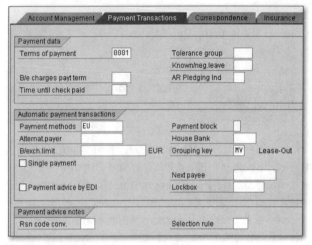

Figure 5.14 Payment Transactions Tab

Correspondence Tab

In the Correspondence tab (Figure 5.15), you can specify information necessary to automatically carry out correspondence with the customer.

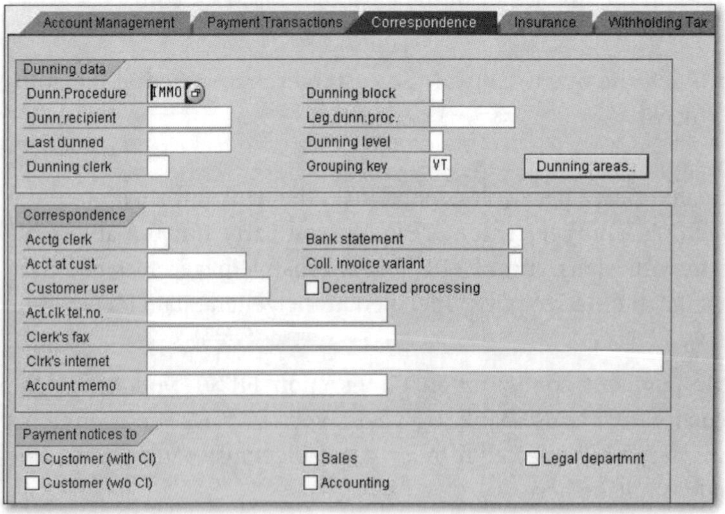

Figure 5.15 Correspondence Tab

Specifically, you can determine the dunning process (in the Dunning Data area) and the correspondence procedure (in the Correspondence area). The use of dunning areas allows you to carry out separate dunning letters for the same customer and dunning level. As a result, you can have different dunning data for the same customer in the same company code but in different dunning areas.

In the Dunning Data area, specify the following:

- **Dunn. Procedure**
  The dunning procedure defines the rules of the dunning (dunning level, dunning charges, tolerance days, etc.). If a customer isn't assigned to a dunning procedure, that customer isn't taken into consideration by the dunning run carried out with Transaction F150.

- **Dunning Block**
  You can temporarily block a customer from being dunned by setting a dunning block here. Note that the dunning block can also be set at the single open item level.

- **Dunn. Recipient**
  Here you can specify a customer whose address data should be used for the dunning instead of the main customer.

- **Last Dunned**
  In general, this field is set automatically by the dunning program and shouldn't be changed manually.

- **Dunning Clerk**
  If often happens that different groups of customers are, for collection purposes, under the responsibility of different clerks. Here you can link the customer to one accounting clerk. This way, the dunning run can select just the customers belonging to one or more specific accounting clerks, and the accounting clerk information can be used in the sending data (if the accounting clerk is linked to a SAP user).

In the Correspondence area, you can specify details about correspondence other than dunning letters. This information is generally used to fill in the various types of correspondence you send to customers and is recalled in the SAPscripts that you create using Transaction SE71, or the SAP Smart Forms that you create using Transaction SMARTFORMS.

Blocking Customer Accounts

Menu path: ACCOUNTING • FINANCIAL ACCOUNTING • ACCOUNTS RECEIVABLE • MASTER RE-CORDS • BLOCK/UNBLOCK

Transaction: FD05

Tables: KNA1 (all company codes), KNB1 (selected company code)

The blocking function ensures that no posting can be made to a customer. You can block the customer for all company codes present in the system or for specific company codes. After the customer is blocked, neither invoices nor incoming payments can be posted against the customer.

To block a customer, use Transaction FD05, and specify the customer number and (optionally) the company code; then select the block for all of the company codes or just for the company code you've selected.

Marking Customer Accounts for Deletion

Menu path: ACCOUNTING • FINANCIAL ACCOUNTING • ACCOUNTS RECEIVABLE • MASTER RE-CORDS • SET DELETION INDICATOR

Transaction: FD06

Table: KNA1 (all company codes), KNB1 (selected company code)

You can't delete customers in the system if they are already used in productive company codes. Instead, mark the customers that you want to delete, and, in a second step, archive them. Archiving in SAP means to save the selected data to a sequential file and subsequently delete it from the system. You should discuss the archiving process with your Basis colleagues. Implementation of the archiving functionality isn't part of ordinary maintenance; it can be managed only within the framework of a project.

Using the blocking function means that no posting can be made to the customer; instead, the system issues a warning message. If you have to post to the customer, you should investigate whether maintaining the deletion flag still makes sense for this customer. You can mark a customer for deletion for all company codes present in the system or for specific company codes.

To mark a customer for deletion, use Transaction FD06, and specify the customer number and (optionally) the company code. Then select the deletion indicator for all of the company codes or just for the company code you've selected.

Changing Account Group

You can change account groups using Transaction XD07 (Figure 5.16).

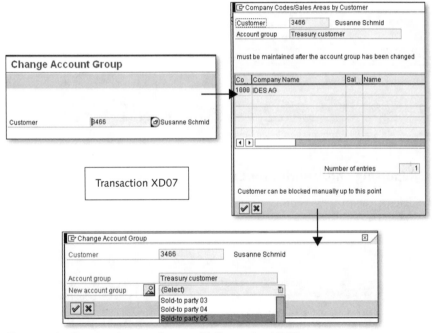

Figure 5.16 Changing Account Groups with Transaction XD07

Changing an account group for a customer is subjected to the following restrictions:

▶ The old and new account group must have the same number range.

▶ The new account group must have a field status "wider" than the old account group. In other words, the new account group must not suppress any field that is mandatory or displayed in the old account group; otherwise, you'll get the error message shown in Figure 5.17.

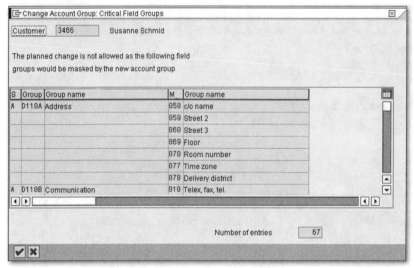

Figure 5.17 Field Status Configuration Error Message

5.1.3 Reporting and Utilities for Customer Master Data

Next we discuss the processes of reporting, deleting, and performing mass changes on customer data.

Reporting

Quick Reference

Menu path: ACCOUNTING • FINANCIAL ACCOUNTING • ACCOUNTS RECEIVABLE • INFORMATION SYSTEM • MASTER DATA

Reporting on customer master data is quite weak in the standard SAP system. Figure 5.18 shows an example of report RFDKVZ00,, which provides a list of the customer master records, with the option to choose different groups of information in the selection screen, both at the general data level and at the company code level. The resulting list isn't in ALV format, however, so it can't be easily downloaded into Excel for further analysis.

We strongly recommend creating queries to analyze customer master data. These queries are naturally built to produce ALV lists where flexible sorting, filtering, and the defining of specific layouts can be performed.

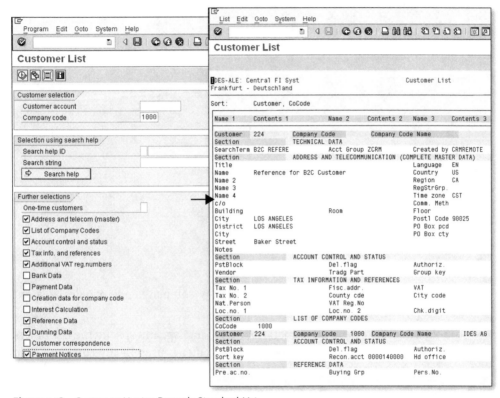

Figure 5.18 Customer Master Records Standard List

Deleting Customer Master Data

Quick Reference
Menu path: IMG • FINANCIAL ACCOUNTING • ACCOUNTS RECEIVABLE AND ACCOUNTS PAYABLE • CUSTOMER ACCOUNTS • MASTER DATA • DELETE CUSTOMER MASTER DATA
Transaction: OBR2
Program: SAPF019

You can use program SAPF019 to delete customer master data (Figure 5.19).

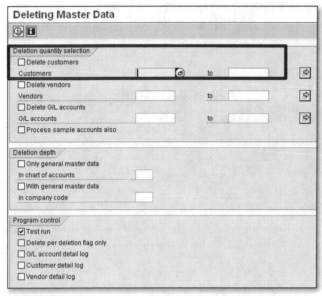

Figure 5.19 Customer Master Data Deletion

Specifically, you can do the following:

▶ Delete customers that don't have data in any company code or sales area but only in general data.

To do this, select the Only General Master Data flag, and specify the customers to be deleted. If the system finds that a customer is used in any company code or sales area, it won't proceed to the deletion of that customer.

▶ Delete the customer at the company code level only.

To do this, specify the company code in the selection screen. If the company code is productive, no deletion takes place. If it isn't productive, the customers' information for the specific company code is deleted. You can also delete general data using the With General Master Data flag, but the deletion is performed only if the customer isn't used in any other company code or sales area.

You can limit deletion to the customers that have the deletion flag by selecting this option in the selection screen (Figure 5.19).

Remember, the general data of a customer can never be deleted if the customer is used in any sales area.

Mass Changes

Quick Reference

Transaction: MASS (OBJECT KNA1)

To perform a mass change to customer master data, we suggest using one of the following two tools:

▶ Create a LSMW (Legacy System Migration Workbench) recording using Transaction FD02 or XD02.

▶ Use Transaction MASS.

This section describes the use of Transaction MASS. Refer to a specific manual to understand the LSMW tool.

Run Transaction MASS and follow the steps described next (Figure 5.20 and Figure 5.21).

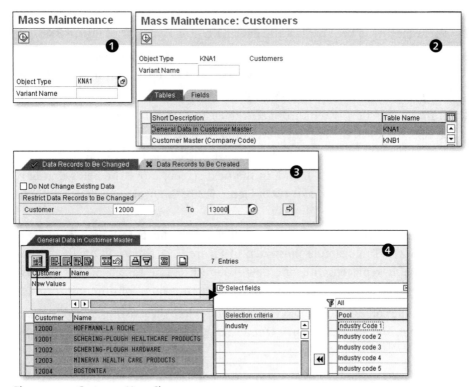

Figure 5.20   Customer Mass Change

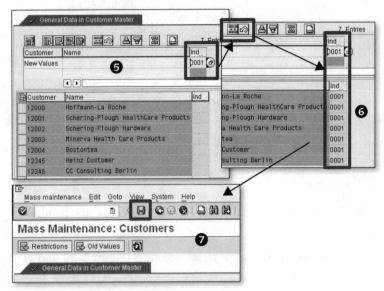

Figure 5.21 Customer Mass Change (Cont.)

1. Select object type KNA1. Click the Execute button (❖) (❶ of Figure 5.20).

2. Select the table that contains the fields to be modified (❷ of Figure 5.20). For example, specify Table KNB5 if you want to modify the accounting clerk for the dunning procedure. Click the Execute button.

3. Fill in the selection criteria to select the customers you want to modify (❸ of Figure 5.20). Click the Execute button to go ahead.

4. In the next screen, specify which field or fields you want to modify. Click the Select Fields button (🔳), and, in the next screen, move the fields that have to be modified to the left side (❹ of Figure 5.20). Confirm your choice with the Continue button.

5. In the next screen, specify the new values for the fields to be modified (❺ of Figure 5.21). The example illustrated in Figure 5.21 shows all of the existing values being replaced with one new value (the same for all of the records). However, you can also manually specify different values for different records.

6. Click on the columns for which you want to replace the existing record with the new value, and select the Carry Out a Mass Change button (🔳) (❻ of Figure 5.21).

7. Select the Save button to carry out the change (❼ of Figure 5.21). Just after the change, without leaving the screen, you can change back to the old values with the Undo button (🗁). This function isn't available if you exit the transaction.

5.1.4 FAQ and Troubleshooting Tips

Next we answer some frequently asked questions and offer helpful troubleshooting tips.

FAQ

1. **Question**: I want to suppress a field for an already existing account group. What will happen to the existing customers created in that account group?

   Answer: First you must check that the field isn't mandatory according to the field status defined in Transactions OB21 (company code level field status) and O20B (activity level field status). When you change the configuration and make the field Suppressed, it won't appear any longer in the selection screen, regardless of whether you create, change, or display the customer. But if some values have been specified for the already-created customers, these values remain in the database, and you can see them with Transaction SE16 (specifying the table in which the field is contained).

2. **Question**: I want the field status to be determined only by the combination of the rules defined for the account group and the activity. How should I make the setting in Transaction OB21?

   Answer: You should create only one entry with company code "*". Then, for all of the possible fields, set the field status as Optional Entry.

3. **Question**: Can I assign multiple account groups to the same number range?

   Answer: Yes.

4. **Question**: Can I assign multiple number ranges to the same account group?

   Answer: No. Only one number range can be assigned to each account group.

5. **Question**: How does the system control customers that use an external number range?

Answer: The system checks that the customer number you enter is within the number range and that no other customer already exists with the same number specified.

6. **Question**: Why should I use an external number range?

Answer: The use of external number ranges is typical when the master system for customer master data is an external system because the master data is transferred through an interface from the external system to SAP. It's important that the customer keeps the same number in the external system and in SAP, especially when changes are transferred through the interface (so the external system knows the SAP number has been changed).

7. **Question**: How can I store different addresses for the same customer? I need to send the goods to one address, the invoices to another address, and the communication to a third address.

Answer: If you generate the invoices in Sales and Distribution, you have partner functions in the customer master data; create different customer's accounts with different addresses for different purposes (sending the goods, sending the invoices, and posting to accounting; the address for posting to accounting is used for communication sent from Financial Accounting). All three accounts should be linked together; discuss this point with your Sales and Distribution expert. In Financial Accounting, you can have a different account for tax reporting by using the Fiscal Address field in the customer master data (KNA1-FISKN); the Dunning Recipient field (KNB5-KNRMA) can be used as an alternative account to send the dunning letters.

8. **Question**: How can I ensure that the reconciliation account is always filled when a customer is created but isn't changed after the creation?

Answer: You do this through the configuration of the screen layout for the activity. For the creation activities (company code and central), specify that the field is mandatory; for the change activities, specify that the field is displayed (and therefore not changeable).

9. **Question**: What happens if I change the reconciliation account of a customer that still has open items?

Answer: The new items are posted against the new reconciliation account. However, when you clear the open items, the clearing posting is generated under the same reconciliation account of the item that is cleared.

If at period end, you have open items under the old and new reconciliation account, you can use report SAPF101 (or Transaction F101) to make the necessary adjustment postings (to an adjustment account of the reconciliation account defined in Transaction OBBW).

10. **Question**: Is it possible to see who removed a posting block and when it was done?

    Answer: Yes. As with all changes to a customer account, this information is recorded in Tables CDHDR and CDPOS and retrieved through report RFD-ABL00 or Transaction FD04.

11. **Question**: Using program SAPF019, is it possible to find out who deleted customer master records and when it was done ?

    Answer: Unfortunately, no. The master records are completely deleted from the database, together with the change logs. The deleted numbers can be reused to create new accounts.

12. **Question**: Are the changes recorded with Transaction MASS logged in the system in the same way as the changes performed with Transactions FD02 and XD02?

    Answer: Yes. They are written in Tables CDHDR and CDPOS, and retrieved via report RFDABL00 or Transaction FD04.

Troubleshooting Tips

1. **Issue**: In Transaction OB21, I have deleted the entry for a specific company code. What happens with the customers already created for this company code?

   Solution: If you delete the company code-specific rules, the rules defined for the generic entry "*" automatically apply for all future transactions.

2. **Issue**: I'm trying to enter an alphanumeric range for customer master records, and I get a message that reads: "Please enter numeric number."

   Solution: If the number range is internal, then you must specify a numeric value for the From Number and To Number fields.

3. **Issue**: I get the following error message when I update the number range: "Enter intervals without overlap." How can I easily retrieve the existing number ranges to see which slots are available?

   Solution: Download data from Table NRIV for the DEBITOR object. This provides all existing number ranges, which you can sort by the initial number.

4. **Issue**: In field STCEG, when I try to store a VAT number starting with a country different from the country specified in the address of the customer, I get error message AR 191: "ISO code XX is not correct in the VAT registration number."

Solution: You'll get this error message in most cases. However, in recent releases, the function is allowed. For more information, read SAP Note 889691.

5. **Issue**: When I try to change the account group of a customer, I get an error message stating that some fields will be suppressed, but my customer has no values in those fields.

Solution: The control made by the system doesn't consider whether or not the fields are used in the involved customer; it simply makes a comparison between the field status of the old account group and the new account group. Unfortunately, at this point, there is no SAP note that can be applied to this case.

5.2   Vendor Master Data

As in the previous section, we divide this section into three parts that discuss the configuration, management, and reporting and utilities available in vendor master data.

5.2.1   Configuring Vendor Master Data

Next we discuss the following topics that affect the configuration of vendor master data:

▶ Account groups, which affect the screen layout and number ranges

▶ Screen layout rules at the company code level, which affect the status of the available fields when you try to create, change, or display vendor master data

▶ Screen layout rules at the activity level, which affect the status of the available fields for the vendor master records

▶ The creation of number ranges for vendor master data and the link between the account group and the number range

▶ The accounting clerk, an object used in vendor master data to manage communication with the vendor

> **Note**
>
> The configuration for vendor master data is very similar to that of customer master data; therefore, unless specific consideration is needed for vendors, you can refer to the corresponding topic in Section 5.1, Customer Master Data.

Defining Vendor Account Groups

Menu path: IMG • Financial Accounting • Accounts Receivable and Accounts Payable • Vendor Accounts • Master Data • Preparation for Creating Vendor Master Data • Define Account Groups with Screen Layout (Vendors)

Transaction: OBD3

Table/view: T077K/V_T077K

When you create a vendor account, you must assign it to an account group. The account groups are created in customizing and control the following:

▶ The number range within which the vendor is created

▶ The field status of the vendor master data, in combination with the rules defined at the company code and activity levels

To define the vendor account groups, execute Transaction OBD3, and use Transaction OBAS to assign the account group to a number range. The subsequent procedures are the same as those for defining customer account groups. See Figure 5.22, and consult the Defining Customer Account Groups section under Section 5.1.1, Configuring Customer Master Data, for more details.

Defining Screen Layout per Company Code

Menu path: IMG • Financial Accounting • Accounts Receivable and Accounts Payable • Vendor Account • Master Data • Preparation for Creating Vendor Master Data • Define Screen Layout per Company Code (Vendors)

Transaction: OB24

Defining the screen layout per company code for vendors is done using Transaction OB24 (Figure 5.23). The instructions for this process are the same as for customers. For detailed instructions, see the Defining Screen Layout per Company Code section under Section 5.1.1, Configuring Customer Master Data.

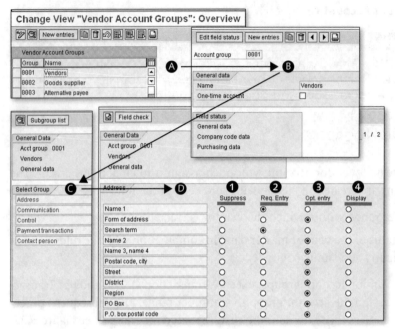

Figure 5.22 Defining Vendor Account Groups

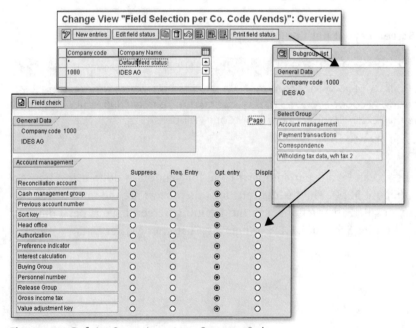

Figure 5.23 Defining Screen Layout per Company Code

Defining Screen Layout for Activities

Quick Reference

Menu path: IMG • FINANCIAL ACCOUNTING • ACCOUNTS RECEIVABLE AND ACCOUNTS PAY-ABLE • VENDOR ACCOUNT • MASTER DATA • PREPARATION FOR CREATING VENDOR MASTER DATA • DEFINE SCREEN LAYOUT PER ACTIVITY (VENDORS)

Transaction: OB23

When processing vendor master data, the field status depends on the customizing in the following three activities:

▶ **OBD3:** Vendor account group

▶ **OB24:** Screen layout per company code

▶ **OB23:** Screen layout for activities

Here we describe how to perform the configuration for Transaction OB23 (Figure 5.24).

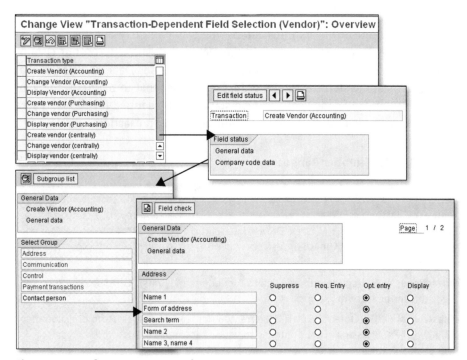

Figure 5.24 Defining Screen Layout for Activities

In the first screen, SAP presents a list of the possible transactions that allow you to manage vendor master data. There is a basic distinction between the following two groups of transactions:

▸ **XK01, XK02, XK03**
These are transactions used to create, change, and display the vendor centrally. With these transactions, you can process the screens for all three segments of the vendor master record (general data, such as the address; company code data, such as the reconciliation account; and purchasing organization data, such as the incoterms).

▸ **FK01, FK02, FK03**
These are transactions used to create, change, and display the vendor up to the company code level. With these transactions, you can process the screens for only two segments of the vendor master record (general data and company code data).

For all six transactions, you can specify different field status rules that the system will combine with the field status rules defined when creating a vendor account group and defining the screen layout for company codes.

When you select one of the six transactions, the way you carry out the configuration is exactly the same as described in the Defining Customer Account Groups section under Section 5.1.1, Configuring Customer Master Data, so refer to that section to get step-by-step instructions. Just remember that to maintain the vendor up to the company code level, no field status can be defined for the sales area fields; this segment isn't displayed when running those transactions.

Assigning Vendor Number Ranges

> **Quick Reference**
>
> **Menu path**: IMG • FINANCIAL ACCOUNTING • ACCOUNTS RECEIVABLE AND ACCOUNTS PAYABLE • VENDOR ACCOUNT • MASTER DATA • PREPARATION FOR CREATING VENDOR MASTER DATA • CREATE NUMBER RANGES FOR VENDOR ACCOUNTS/ASSIGN NUMBER RANGES TO VENDOR ACCOUNT GROUPS
>
> **Transactions**: XKN1 (create number ranges for vendor accounts), OBAS (assign number ranges to vendor account groups)
>
> **Tables/views**: NRIV (Object KREDITOR) (create number ranges for customer accounts), T077K/V_077K_B (assign number ranges to vendor account groups)

The instructions for defining number ranges for vendors are the same as those for customers. For step-by-step instructions, see the Defining Customer Number Ranges section under Section 5.1.1, Configuring Customer Master Data. The only differences are the menu path, transaction, and table/view, as shown in the Quick Reference box. See Figures 5.25 and 5.26 for more details.

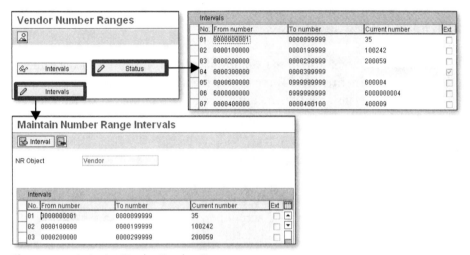

Figure 5.25 Assigning Vendor Number Ranges

Group	Name	Number range
0001	Vendors	01
0002	Goods supplier	XX
0003	Alternative payee	XX
0004	Invoice presented by	XX
0005	Forwarding agent	XX
0006	Ordering address	XX
0007	Plants	XX
0010	Special vendor	02
0012	Hierarchy nodes	01
0020	Vendor-BP-Commission Recipient	04
0099	One-time vendors	01
0100	Vendor distribution center	XX
1111	Insurance Vendor Group	
BR01	Nacional Brazilian Vendors	XX
CPD	One-time vend.(int.no.assgnmt)	02

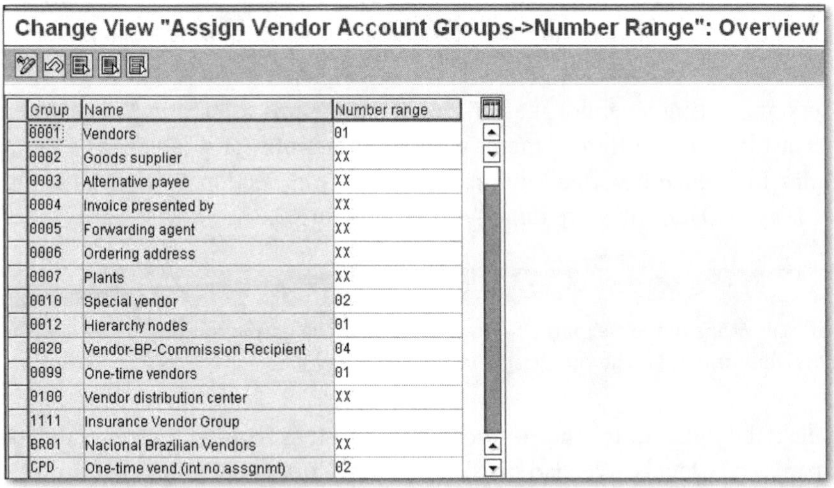

Figure 5.26 Assigning Number Ranges to Vendor Account Groups

Defining Accounting Clerks

Quick Reference

Menu path: IMG • FINANCIAL ACCOUNTING • ACCOUNTS RECEIVABLE AND ACCOUNTS PAYABLE • VENDOR ACCOUNT • MASTER DATA • PREPARATION FOR CREATING VENDOR MASTER DATA • DEFINE ACCOUNTING CLERKS

Transaction: OB05K

Table/view: T001S/V_T001S

The accounting clerk you use in the vendor master record is exactly the same as in the customer master records. There is only one table for the accounting clerks: T001S. For more details about the maintenance of accounting clerks, refer to Section 5.1.1, Configuring Customer Master Data.

5.2.2 Managing Vendor Master Data

Quick Reference

Menu path: ACCOUNTING • FINANCIAL ACCOUNTING • ACCOUNTS PAYABLE • MASTER RECORDS • CREATE

Transactions: FK01 (general and company code data), XK01 (general, company code, and sales data)

Tables: LFA1 (general data), LFB1 (company code data), LFBK (bank data), LFAS (VAT registration number in different countries), LFM1 (purchasing organization data)

The process of creating a vendor master record is the same as creating a customer master record but with different menu paths, transactions, and tables (as shown in the Quick Reference box). Follow the instructions in Section 5.1.2, Managing Customer Master Data, for more details, and see Figure 5.27.

Note

Your Materials Management experts are responsible for the configurations necessary to update the vendor data at the purchasing organization level.

Next we describe the maintenance of the vendor master record at the general data and company code levels. We also discuss three additional activities that are relevant for managing vendor master data in Accounts Receivable and Accounts Payable: blocking vendor accounts, deleting vendor accounts, and changing account groups.

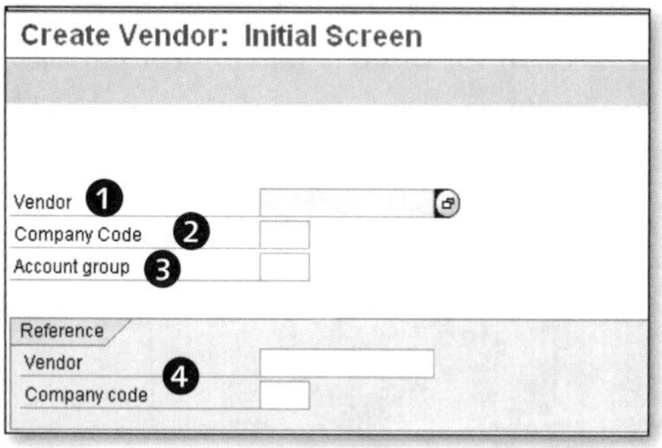

Create Vendor: Initial Screen

Vendor **(1)**

Company Code **(2)**

Account group **(3)**

Reference

Vendor

Company code **(4)**

Figure 5.27   Creation of a Vendor: Initial Screen

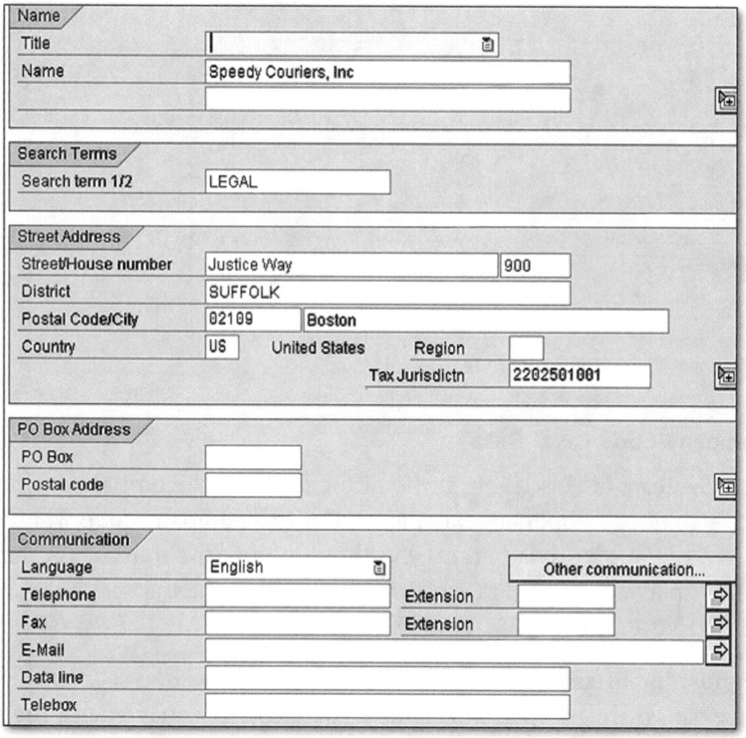

Name

Title	
Name	Speedy Couriers, Inc

Search Terms

Search term 1/2	LEGAL

Street Address

Street/House number	Justice Way	900
District	SUFFOLK	
Postal Code/City	02109	Boston
Country	US	United States	Region
	Tax Jurisdictn	2202501001

PO Box Address

PO Box	
Postal code	

Communication

Language	English		Other communication...
Telephone		Extension	
Fax		Extension	
E-Mail			
Data line			
Telebox			

Figure 5.28   Vendor Address Data

Maintaining General Level Data

Similar to the general data for customers, the system stores vendor information that is valid for all company codes and separates this information into three tabs: Address (Figure 5.28), Control Data (Figure 5.29), and Payment Transactions (Fig-

265

ure 5.30). They are very similar to the tabs discussed in Section 5.1.2, Managing Customer Master Data, so please see that section for more detailed information.

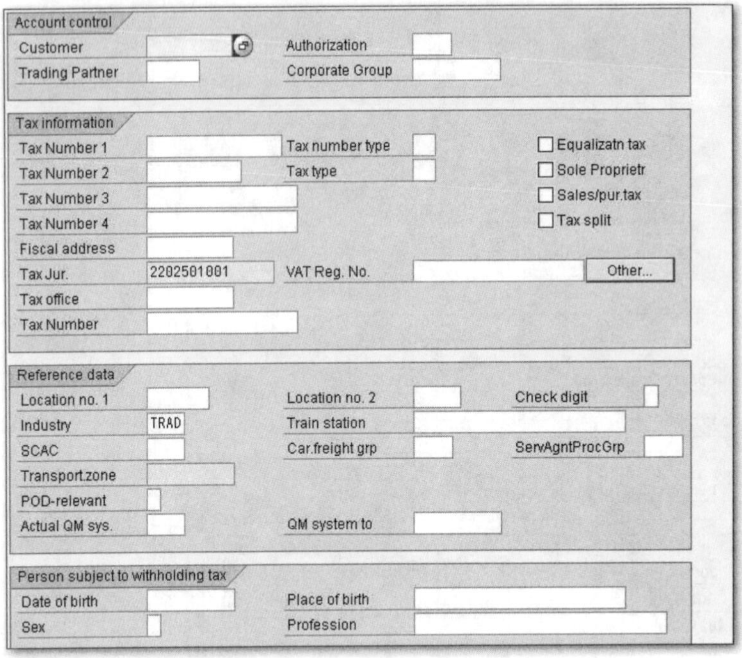

Figure 5.29 Control Data (Cross-Company Code)

Maintaining Company Code Level Data

The information you store at this level can be different for each company code. Remember that if you need to open an existing vendor in a company code where you haven't created the master data before, you shouldn't use the transaction for changing the vendor master record (FK02 or XK02) but rather the transactions for creating the vendor master record (FK01 and XK01).

Once again, the most important fields available in the company code segment of the vendor master record are grouped into three tabs: Account Management, Payment Transactions, and Correspondence. We discuss each of these next.

Account Management Tab

The instructions here are the same as those discussed in the Account Management Tab section under Section 5.1.2, Managing Customer Master Data. See that section, and Figure 5.31, for more details.

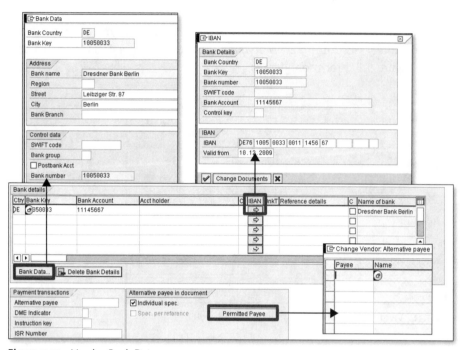

Figure 5.30 Vendor Bank Data

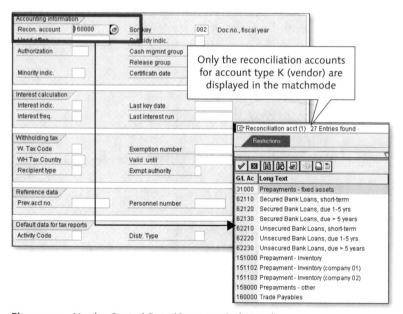

Figure 5.31 Vendor Control Data (Company Code Level)

Payment Transactions Tab

The instructions here are the same as those discussed in the Payment Transactions Tab section under Section 5.1.2, Managing Customer Master Data. See that section, and Figure 5.32, for more details.

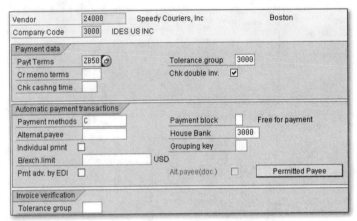

Figure 5.32 Vendor Payment Data (Company Code Level)

Correspondence Tab

The Correspondence tab (Figure 5.33) contains information necessary to automatically perform correspondence with the vendor. Dunning information can be entered also at the vendor level; however, as it makes little sense to carry out dunning letters against vendors, we suggest suppressing these fields in the vendor master data.

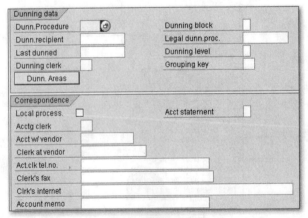

Figure 5.33 Vendor Correspondence Data

In the Correspondence area in the Correspondence tab, you can specify details for all correspondence other than the dunning letters. This information is generally used to fill in the various type of correspondence you send to the vendor and is therefore used in the SAPscripts you create with Transaction SE71, or the SAP Smart Forms you create with Transaction SMARTFORMS.

Blocking Vendor Accounts

> **Quick Reference**
>
> **Menu path**: ACCOUNTING • FINANCIAL ACCOUNTING • ACCOUNTS PAYABLE • MASTER RECORDS • BLOCK/UNBLOCK
>
> **Transaction**: FK05
>
> **Tables**: LFA1 (all company codes), LFB1 (selected company code)

The blocking function for vendor accounts is similar to the blocking function for customer accounts. See the Blocking Customer Accounts section under Section 5.1.2, Managing Customer Master Data, for more information.

Deleting Vendor Accounts

> **Quick Reference**
>
> **Menu path**: ACCOUNTING • FINANCIAL ACCOUNTING • ACCOUNTS PAYABLE • MASTER RECORDS • SET DELETION INDICATOR
>
> **Transaction**: FK06
>
> **Tables**: LFA1 (all company codes), LFB1 (selected company code)

Deleting vendor accounts is similar to deleting customer accounts. See the Deleting Customer Accounts section under Section 5.1.2, Managing Customer Master Data, for more information.

Changing Vendor Account Group

> **Quick Reference**
>
> **Transaction**: XK07
>
> **Table**: LFA1

The process for changing vendor account groups is the same as the process for changing customer account groups. See the Changing Customer Account Groups under Section 5.1.2, Managing Customer Master Data, for more details, as well as Figures 5.34 and 5.35.

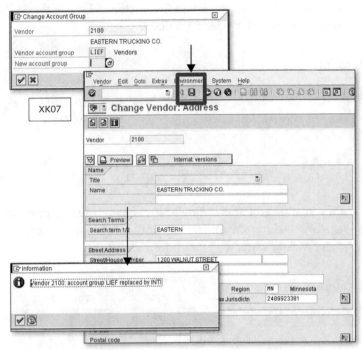

Figure 5.34 Changing Vendor Account Groups

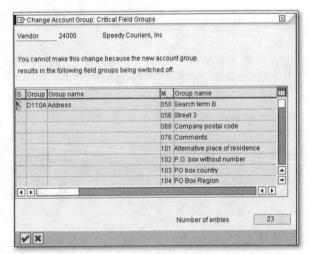

Figure 5.35 Error Message When Changing Vendor Account Group

5.2.3 Reporting and Utilities for Vendor Master Data

Next we provide some information about reporting, deleting, and performing mass changes on vendor master data.

Reporting

Reporting on vendor master data is similar to reporting on customer master data. See that discussion in Section 5.1.3, Reporting and Utilities for Customer Master Data, for more details, as well as Figure 5.36.

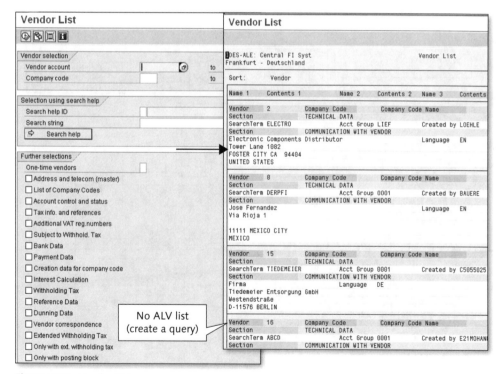

Figure 5.36 Vendor List

271

Deleting Vendor Master Data

Quick Reference

Menu path: IMG • FINANCIAL ACCOUNTING • ACCOUNTS RECEIVABLE AND ACCOUNTS PAYABLE • VENDOR ACCOUNTS • MASTER DATA • DELETE VENDOR MASTER DATA

Transaction: OBR2

Program: SAPF019

The process for deleting vendor master data is similar to the process for deleting customer master data. See that discussion in Section 5.1.3, Reporting and Utilities for Customer Master Data, for more details.

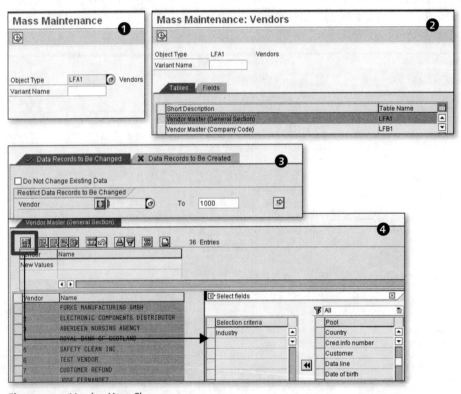

Figure 5.37 Vendor Mass Change

Mass Changes

Quick Reference

Transaction: MASS (Object LFA1)

Performing a mass change to vendor master data is similar to performing a mass change to customer master data. See this discussion in Section 5.1.3, Reporting and Utilities for Customer Master Data, for more details, as well as Figures 5.37 and 5.38; just remember to use object LFA1 instead of KNA1.

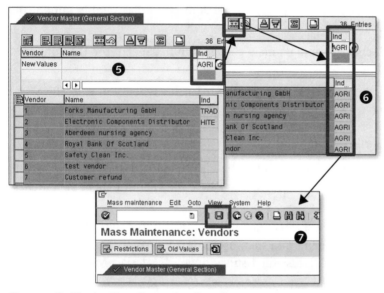

Figure 5.38 Vendor Mass Change (continued)

5.2.4 FAQ and Troubleshooting Tips

Next we answer some frequently asked questions and offer helpful troubleshooting tips.

FAQ

1. **Question**: Is it possible to block an account for certain transactions only?

   Answer: The posting block prevents any posting to the vendor account. If you want to prevent certain types of postings to some vendors, you should create a validation. (The document type can be used to select the transactions you want to allow or prevent, and the vendors to be blocked should be placed in a set.)

2. **Question**: Is the deletion indicator a prerequisite to deleting the vendors with program SAPF019?

    Answer: No. However, you can use Delete per Deletion Flag Only in program SAPF019; this means that only vendors with the deletion flag are deleted.

3. **Question**: Which type of selections should I use when I create an infoset for a query on vendor master data? Should I use a logical database?

    Answer: There is no logical database just for vendor master data. We recommend creating the infoset with the Table Join Using Basis Table option; the Basis table should be LFA1.

4. **Question**: When performing a mass change, can I change more than one field at the same time?

    Answer: Yes, simply select all of the needed fields when you click the Select Fields button (📇).

Troubleshooting Tips

1. **Issue**: I can't delete vendor accounts because there is data at the purchasing organization level. Is there a program to delete the vendor data at the purchasing organization level?

    Solution: No. Instead, use the archive functionality to delete the purchasing organization level segment, and then use program SAPF019 for the company code and general data. Discuss the issue with your Materials Management and Basis experts.

2. **Issue**: I get an error message stating that the VAT code is incorrect; however, I'm modifying a different field. How can I override this issue?

    Solution: When you run the MASS transaction, the system ensures that all of the controls you encounter online are checked in the mass change. For example, if you're trying to modify a field (such as a name), SAP checks all of the fields of the master record, not just the modified ones. The error due to the VAT code could be the result of a change in the country-specific controls; perhaps existing data in the system isn't compatible with the new changes.

5.3 Configuring Business Transactions in Accounts Receivable and Accounts Payable

When posting to customer and vendor accounts, all of the rules that apply to general Financial Accounting documents are still applicable. The created documents are updated in the same tables as the documents posted just to general ledger accounts. Tables BSID (open items) and BSAD (cleared items) are updated for the customer line items, and Tables BSIK (open items) and BSAK (cleared items) are updated for the vendor line items.

This section describes the additional customizing settings needed to post to customer or vendor accounts.

5.3.1 Maintaining Payment Terms

> **Quick Reference**
>
> **Menu paths**: IMG • FINANCIAL ACCOUNTING • ACCOUNTS RECEIVABLE AND ACCOUNTS PAYABLE • BUSINESS TRANSACTIONS • INCOMING INVOICES/CREDIT MEMOS • MAINTAIN TERMS OF PAYMENT
>
> **AND**
>
> IMG • FINANCIAL ACCOUNTING • ACCOUNTS RECEIVABLE AND ACCOUNTS PAYABLE • BUSINESS TRANSACTIONS • INCOMING INVOICES/CREDIT MEMOS • DEFINE TERMS OF PAYMENTS FOR INSTALLMENT PAYMENTS
>
> **Transactions**: OBB8 (maintain terms of payment), OBB9 (define terms of payment for installment payments)
>
> **Table/views**: T052/V_T052 (single term of payment), T052S/V_T052S (terms of payment for installment payments)

Payment terms are used in customer master data (at the company code and sales area levels), in Sales and Distribution invoices (the specification at the sales area level takes precedence), and vendor master data (at the company code and purchasing organization levels; in Material Management invoice verification, the specification at the purchasing organization level takes precedence). Then the payment terms are copied from the master data to the customer and vendor line items, where the default value can be changed.

Payment terms are used to determine the due date and discounts that a customer can obtain or that a company can obtain payment from a vendor in a specific framework of time.

When creating a vendor or customer line item, the baseline date indicates the point from which to calculate the due date. You can specify up to three numbers and attach them to two discount percentages. The last number has no discount and indicates the net due date. The net due date is the sum of the baseline date and the day number without a discount.

For example, you may specify the following:

▶ Document date: 5/31/2010

▶ Baseline date: 5/31/2010

▶ Days 1: 30, discount 5% (this applies if the payment is completed by 6/30/2010)

▶ Days 2: 45, discount 2% (this applies if the payment is completed by 7/15/2010)

▶ Days 3: 60; no discount.

In this example, the net due date is 5/31/2010 + 60 = 7/30/2010. If you don't supply any numbers of days, the baseline date is the net due date.

An example of payment terms is shown in Figure 5.39.

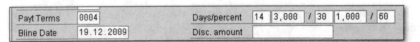

Figure 5.39 Fields in the Customer and Vendor Line Items Affected by Payment Terms

Figure 5.40 shows an example of a payment term. Each payment term is a four-digit alphanumeric code for which you can specify the following settings with Transaction OBB8:

▶ **Day Limit**
Use this indicator if you want to specify different settings for the same payment term, depending on the baseline date. For example, if you create two records for the payment term 0015, one with a day limit of 16, and another with a day limit of 31, the items that have a baseline date up to the 16th of any month take the configuration from the first record (0015/16), while all of the others take the configuration of the second record (0015/31). If you don't want to use this functionality, simply leave the Day Limit field blank.

- **Account Type area**
  You must decide if the payment term is to be used for both customers and vendors, or only for one of the two account types. Note that if you specify a payment method in the payment term, you should usually allow just one account type (e.g., if the payment method is a bill of exchange, the payment term should be used only by customers).

- **Default for Baseline Date area**
  First, specify the source of the baseline date; you can choose among the posting date, the entry date, the document date (the most common choice), or no default, which means that it must be specified manually.

- **Baseline Date Calculation area**
  In this area, you can define whether the default value provided for the baseline date (see the previous bullet point) should be automatically modified by adding a specific number of months (the Additional Months field), or by shifting to a specific date in the month (the Fixed Day field). For example, if the baseline date is automatically provided as the document date, the Fixed Day field is 31, the Additional Months field is 2, and you specify the document date as 6/15/2010, the baseline date automatically becomes 8/31/2010.

- **Block Key and Payment Method**
  These two fields are particularly important for automatic payments because they can be automatically supplied from the payment terms. If they should be provided not just when creating the invoice but also when changing the payment terms, click on the checkbox to the right of both fields.

- **Payment Terms area**
  The last date an invoice must be paid is called the *net due date*. If, for a specific term of payment, the net due date is equal to the baseline date, you leave all of the fields in this area empty.

  If you want to use the baseline date as a starting date instead (usually the date of the invoice) and specify a number of days that represent the delay in payment granted to the customer or by the vendor, use the fields here. You can also use these fields if you want to specify a discount percentage when the invoice is paid before the net due date. In this area, there are three rows (Figure 5.40); you can use one, two, or all three.

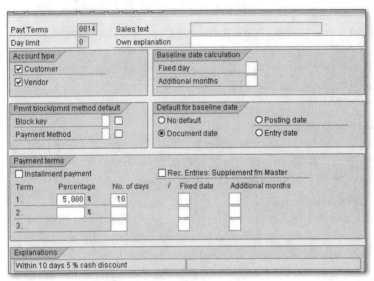

Figure 5.40 Terms of Payment Configuration

If you use one row, you can't specify any discount percentage; you just define the number of days of delay in payment granted to the customer. The sum of the number of granted delay days and the baseline date is the net due date.

If you use two rows, specify in the first one a discount percentage and a number of days; if the payment is made within the specified number of days, the discount is applied. In the second row, specify a number of days that is higher than the first row, and no discount percentage; the sum of the number of days specified here and the baseline date is the net due date.

If you want to use all three rows, specify two discount percentages (the discount percentage in the first row must be higher than the discount percentage in the second row) and two associated number of days (the number of days in the first row must be lower than the number of days in the third row). In the third row, specify a number of days higher than the first and second row, and no discount percentage; the sum of the number of days specified here and the baseline date is the net due date; next we provide a description of each field available in this area:

▶ **Percentage:** Specify the discount rate that the customer can get or you can get from your vendor when the payment is completed before a specified number of days. You can do this specification in two rows, which correspond to a different number of days for the payment delay.

▸ **No. of Days:** Define the maximum number of days of delay to obtain the discount specified in the previous bullet point. If you specify this in the last used row, no percentage of discount can be specified, and the number of days here is the maximum delay granted without a cash discount associated.

▸ **Fixed Date/Additional Months:** Use these parameters instead of the Number of Days to get the delay (in days) granted. The starting point is the baseline date; the final date is the baseline date modified by the fixed date (e.g., 31, which means the last day of the month) and the additional months specified. The difference between the calculated final date and the baseline date is the number of days of delay granted for each row.

If the payment term is an installment payment, select the Installment Payment indicator, and leave all of the other fields in this area blank; you can further customize the installment payment terms in Transaction OBB9.

In certain cases, you may create a single invoice where the total amount is to be paid/received in installments that have different payment terms. For example, say you have to post an outgoing invoice of $1000, where $300 must be paid within 60 days, $350 within 70 days, and the remaining $350 within 80 days. The normal term of payment can't satisfy this requirement, so SAP offers the following solution: Create one line item for the total amount, and specify one single term of payment in the invoice. This term of payment should have a specific configuration and be linked in percentage to two or more terms of payments. When you save the invoice, the system expands the single line item you've entered into two or more line items, depending on the configuration of the installment term of payment.

Figure 5.41 shows an example of an installment term of payment. In Transaction OBB8, you create the MF01 term of payment and specify that it's an installment term of payment. Then, in Transaction OBB9, you assign the MF01 payment term to three different terms of payment for three portions of the invoice (they must total 100%, of course).

When you create the invoice, enter the MF01 term of payment. When the document is created, you'll see three line items for the vendor or customer: one with term of payment 0002 (50% of the total), one with term of payment 0004 (30% of the total), and one with term of payment 0005 (20% of the total).

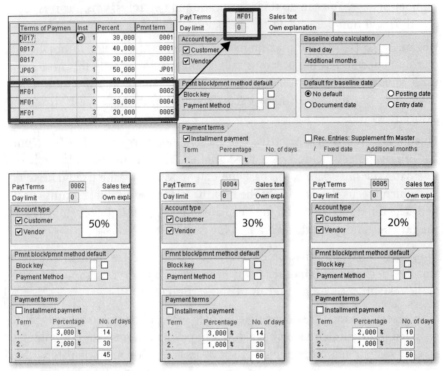

Figure 5.41 Installment Terms of Payment

5.3.2 Defining Default Document Types for Enjoy Transactions

> **Quick Reference**
>
> **Menu path**: IMG • FINANCIAL ACCOUNTING • ACCOUNTS RECEIVABLE AND ACCOUNTS PAYABLE • BUSINESS TRANSACTIONS • INCOMING INVOICES/CREDIT MEMOS • INCOMING INVOICES/ CREDIT MEMOS – ENJOY • DEFINE DOCUMENT TYPES FOR ENJOY TRANSACTION
>
> **Transaction**: OBZO
>
> **Table**: T003D

When you post incoming invoices or outgoing invoices directly into Financial Accounting, you'll usually use Enjoy transactions, which are the most user friendly and, unlike classic transactions, allow you to post documents all in one screen. Each time you run an Enjoy transaction, a document type is automatically provided. The specification of this document type is made using Transaction OBZO for all possible Enjoy transactions, as listed here (Figure 5.42):

- Customers credit memo: Transaction FB75
- Customers invoice: Transaction FB70
- Vendors credit memo: Transaction FB65
- Vendor invoice: Transaction FB60

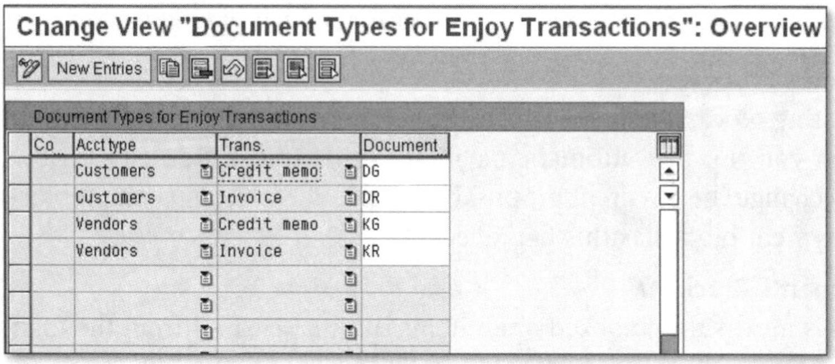

Co.	Acct type	Trans.	Document
	Customers	Credit memo	DG
	Customers	Invoice	DR
	Vendors	Credit memo	KG
	Vendors	Invoice	KR

Figure 5.42 Default Document Types for Enjoy Transactions

As specified previously, in all Enjoy transactions, the document type is automatically provided based on the customizing in Transaction OBZO; however, you can also change the document type. To perform this change, check the editing options: Select SETTINGS • EDITING OPTIONS, and then check that Doc. Type Option isn't set to Document Type Hidden or Document Type Will Be Displayed.

5.3.3 Defining Payment Block Reasons

Quick Reference

Menu path: IMG • FINANCIAL ACCOUNTING • ACCOUNTS RECEIVABLE AND ACCOUNTS PAYABLE • BUSINESS TRANSACTIONS • OUTGOING PAYMENTS • OUTGOING PAYMENTS GLOBAL SETTINGS • PAYMENT BLOCK REASONS • DEFINE PAYMENT BLOCK REASONS

Transaction: OB27

Table/view: T008/V_T008

To prevent posting payments to a customer or a vendor, you can use the payment block functionality. The payment block can be put in the following:

- The customer and vendor master data, and affect only automatic payments (Transaction F110)

▶ The customer and vendor line items, and affect both automatic and manual payments

The payment block is a one-digit alphanumeric code that can be customized with Transaction OB27. The payment blocks aren't technically differentiated between customers and vendors.

Figure 5.43 shows the customizing settings available for each payment block:

▶ **Change in Pmnt Prop. (❶)**
All of the posting blocks cause the blocked open items to be put in the exception list when you run the automatic payments with Transaction F110. However, you can change the payment proposal and select/deselect a payment block only if the payment block has this flag selected.

▶ **Manual Payments Block (❷)**
If selected, this means that blocked open items can't be cleared from the manual payment postings (e.g., with Transaction FBZ1). The item is displayed but can't be selected.

▶ **Not Changeable (❸)**
If selected, this means that after the payment block is set in an open item, it can't be deleted outside the workflow.

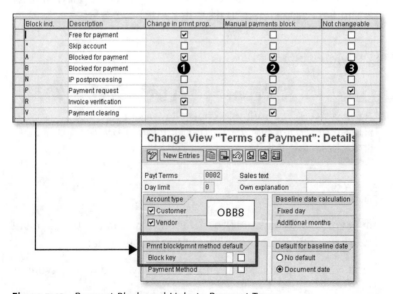

Figure 5.43 Payment Blocks and Links to Payment Terms

5.3.4 Configuring Automatic Payments

With automatic payment programs, you can do the following:

► Automatically post payments that clear open items.

► Create output to be sent to the bank, such as letters or DME.

► Create bills of exchanges.

To use the automatic payment function (Transaction F110), you have to carry out the relevant configuration. We suggest using Transaction FBZP, which allows you to branch to all of the different steps and screens necessary to customize the function. Next we describe the six main steps to customize the automatic payment program (see Figure 5.44 for the initial screen of Transaction FBZP and for the six buttons used to perform the six steps).

Step 1: All Company Codes

This section of the configuration of automatic payments refers to the company code where the open items are posted; this company code can be different from the paying company code (the company code that executes the payment from its own bank account and can pay its own open items or open items of other company codes) (❶ of Figure 5.44):

In particular, define the following:

► **Paying Company Codes (under the Control Data area)**
Usually, this field should be filled with the company code itself. However, if the payments are to be made from the bank account of another company code in your group, this is where you would specify the different company code. When you perform the payment postings, the open items are cleared in the company code in which they are posted. Note, though, that the offsetting account isn't a house bank account but rather the intercompany account defined in Table T001U (Transaction OBYA) for the pair of companies involved. In the payment

283

company code, the house bank account defined in Transaction FBZP is debited; the offsetting account is the intercompany account, which is always defined in OBYA.

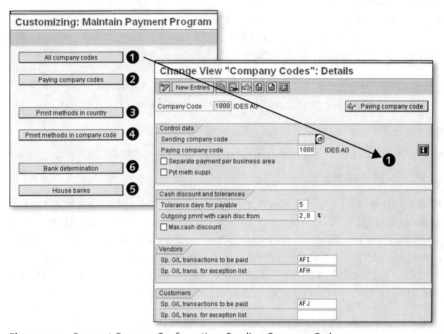

Figure 5.44 Payment Program Configuration: Sending Company Codes

▶ **Sending Company Code**
If this field is left empty, the sending company code is the same as the paying company code; otherwise, you can specify a different company code. The sending company code is noted in the payment advice and in the DME files. Note that if the sending company code is different from the paying company code, this affects the payment grouping: The sending company code items aren't grouped together with other items of the same vendor belonging to different sending company codes (of course, this is relevant only if another company code pays your company code items).

▶ **Separate Payment per Business Area**
With this indicator, open items posted in the same company code but in different business areas, aren't grouped and paid together.

▶ **Tolerance Days for Payables**
The days specified here are added to the dates for payment (dates for discounts

and net due date) to vendors. In other words, you're forcing the system to always pay later.

▶ **Outgoing Pmnt with Cash Disc. From**
This indicator is needed for the system to understand when to pay if there are cash discounts (i.e., whether to pay in advance to get a better cash discount, or to pay at the net due date). The system pays earlier to get a cash discount *only* if you can get a cash discount that is equal to or greater than the percentage fixed here. Otherwise, the system pays at the net due date.

▶ **Sp. G/L Transactions to be Paid**
Usually, the open items with special general ledger indicators (see Section 5.3.8 for more details on special general ledger indicators) aren't taken into consideration by the payment run. Here you can specify the indicators that are an exception to this rule.

Step 2: Paying Company Code

The settings specified here are valid only for paying company codes (company codes that pay for their own open items or for open items of another company code). The main settings available are shown in Figure 5.45.

▶ **Minimum Amounts for Incoming/Outgoing Payments**
The payments (not the open items that can be grouped into a unique payment) that don't reach the amounts specified here aren't carried out, and the relevant open items aren't cleared.

▶ **No Exchange Rate Differences**
If you want to post an amount in local currency that is equal to the total historical amount in local currency of the cleared open items, select this indicator; no exchange rate is generated. Be careful in setting this indicator because it may not be in line with the accounting rules followed by your company. Check the consequences of this configuration with your accounting department.

▶ **Bill of Exchange area**
When grouping invoices for the same customer in a bill of exchange, three choices are possible:

  ▶ One bill of exchange per invoice

  ▶ One bill of exchange per due date

  ▶ One bill of exchange per payment run

Discuss this setting with your Accounts Receivable and Treasury departments because it impacts the costs of issuing bills of exchanges.

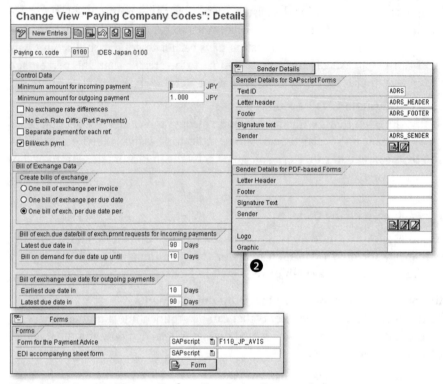

Figure 5.45 Payment Program Configuration: Paying Company Code

Step 3: Payment Method in Country

The settings you make here are valid for all company codes assigned to a specific country. These are the only payment methods you can use in the company codes assigned to that country. (However, to use the payment method in one company code, you also have to perform step 4, described next.)

At the country level, make the following settings for the payment method (Figure 5.46):

▶ **Payment Method For area and Payment Method Classification area**
Specify whether the method is for an outgoing or incoming payment. Depending which you select, you have different options for the payment method classification. The most common classifications are listed here:

- ▶ Bank transf. (bank transfer of checks for outgoing payments)
- ▶ Bill/ex (bill of exchange for incoming payments)

▶ **Required Master Record Specifications area**
Enter the necessary information in the customer or vendor master record to perform the payment. For example, for a payment to foreign customers, you usually specify that the SWIFT and IBAN are required in the master record (note that the IBAN is specific to the business partner, while the SWIFT is assigned to the bank where the business partner has opened an account). Collection authorization is generally required for direct debit to customers.

▶ **Posting Details area**
You can make the following specifications about the document type:

- ▶ **Document Type for Payment:** This is the document type where the bank posting is made. If the sending and paying company codes are the same, this is the only document type used.

- ▶ **Clearing Document Type:** Specify here whether the paying and sender document type are different. This is the document type used in the sender company code to clear the customer and vendor open items against the intercompany clearing account.

▶ **Payment Medium area**
This is one of the most important settings for the payment program. The settings here determine the output file that is generated by the payment program; speak with your treasury department to understand your specific requirements. Check SAP Notes for suggested settings for each country, or compare the standard data provided by SAP. Work with your developer to find the correct program (RFFO*) or to copy an existing program to adapt to your specific local requirements. You can also use the payment medium workbench and the functionalities of the DME engine to build the DME file in an alternative way.

▶ **Currency Allowed**
If you don't specify any currency here, the payment method is valid for all currencies. Otherwise, it's valid only for the currencies specified. To reach the screen where you specify the currencies, double-click on the Currencies Allowed folder on the left side of the screen (Dialog Structure, see Figure 5.46 on the top right).

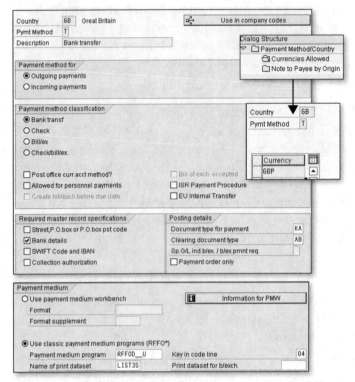

Figure 5.46 Payment Program Configuration: Payment Method (Country-Dependent Configuration)

Step 4: Payment Method in Company Code

After you've defined the payment method at the country level, you must make some additional specifications at the company code level to use the payment method in customer and vendor master data, as well as for line items in a specific company code.

The main settings are as follows (Figure 5.47).

▶ **Amount Limits area**

Here you can specify the minimum and maximum amounts for each payment to be issued. These parameters apply to the payment, not to the single open items included in the payment. The Distribution Amnt. field is where you enter a maximum amount for the payment; however, in this case, the system acts actively, trying to split the payment into smaller groups according to the open items. The target is to pay all of the selected items in several payments (the minimum necessary) with an amount less than the maximum.

▶ **Grouping of Items area**
If selected, the Single Payment for Marked Items checkbox ensures that items with the payment method specified are paid individually. If the Payment per Due Day checkbox is selected, items are grouped according to their due date. If you want to group as many open items as possible in the same payment, don't select either of these checkboxes.

▶ **Foreign Payments/Foreign Currency Payments area**
In this area, specify whether foreign business partners, foreign currencies, and/ or foreign bank accounts are allowed.

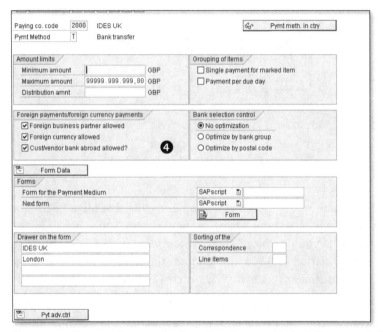

Figure 5.47 Payment Program Configuration: Payment Method (Company-Code Dependent Configuration)

Step 5: House Banks and House Bank Accounts

To make any payment or issue any bill of exchange, you must create house banks and house bank accounts (Figure 5.48).

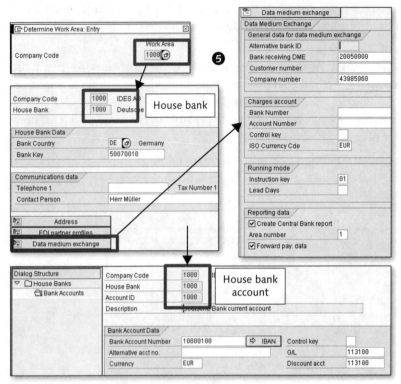

Figure 5.48 House Bank and House Bank Account

The house bank is defined by a five-digit alphanumeric code that must be unique within each company code. The house bank is then assigned to a bank already created in Table BNKA. If you download the payment data with a DME file, you can find additional information to be compiled under the Data Medium Exchange section; the required information can vary for each DME file, which is usually country-specific.

For each combination of company code and house bank, you can assign multiple house bank accounts, each identified by a five-digit alphanumeric code. For each bank account, the following main fields must be filled:

- **Bank Account Number**
  This is the account number assigned to your company by the bank.

- **IBAN**
  If the bank is located within one of the countries that use the IBAN code to uniquely identify each bank account, you can specify the relevant code by click-

ing on the IBAN button. The system proposes an IBAN based on the local code of the bank and on the account number. Check the IBAN proposed with the one provided by the bank.

The IBAN can't be generated if the local code isn't present in the Bank Number field (BNKA-BNKLZ) of the bank master data, regardless of how the bank is identified with the bank key.

▶ **Control Key**
This is a field used in some countries (such as Italy) to make sure the local bank number and the bank account match.

▶ **Currency**
This is the currency of the bank account.

▶ **G/L**
This is the general ledger account where all of the bank transactions on the account are recorded. We strongly recommend that each house bank account has its own general ledger account (of course, there can be clearing accounts for each house bank account). The balance of the house bank account and of the corresponding general ledger account should correspond.

If, for example, you keep five accounts in five different currencies by Bank AAA on Chiswick High Street in London, you should create one house bank for the branch in Chiswick (Bank AAA). Then create five house bank accounts under this house bank.

Step 6: Bank Determination

When making a payment, the transaction is carried out by a bank (the house bank) from your company code's account to the bank account of the vendor. The bank account of the vendor is specified in the vendor master data. However, if your company has many bank accounts, which will be chosen by the automatic payment program to carry out the payment? The answer is in the configuration of the payment program in the Bank Determination section (Figure 5.49).

First, specify a ranking order of the house banks for each combination of payment method and currency (you can also leave the Currency field blank, which means that the record will be valid for all currencies).

Then, for each house bank, specify which house bank account should be used for each combination of currency and payment method. Also specify the general ledger account to be posted to. This account can be different from the general ledger account specified in the house bank account configuration; this is because the house bank account is usually posted by the electronic bank statement only, to ensure perfect reconciliation with the information coming from the bank. The payment to vendors is posted in SAP *before* the actual payment is carried out, and the information is also contained in the bank statement. Thus, if you post the payment to the same general ledger account, the amount is duplicated because the same information comes from the bank statement. You should customize the bank statement postings so that the vendor payments are posted to the same bank clearing account that is posted by the automatic payment program.

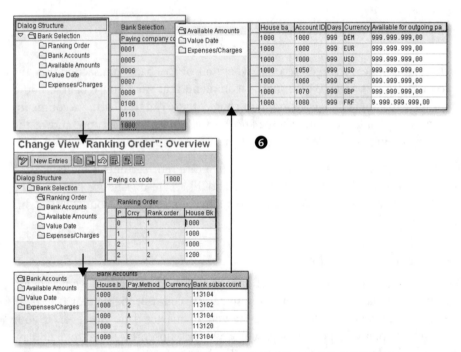

Figure 5.49 Payment Program Configuration: House Bank Account Determination

For each house bank account, also specify the available amount for outgoing payments. If the amount won't be sufficient, the system selects the following house bank in the ranking order. You can update the available amounts from the application menu: ACCOUNTING • FINANCIAL ACCOUNTING • ACCOUNTS PAYABLE • ENVIRONMENT • CURRENT SETTINGS • ENTER AVAILABLE AMOUNTS FOR THE PAYMENT PROGRAM. Note that you can update the table only if the client (Table T000) has the Production role; discuss this with your Basis colleagues.

5.3.5 Configuring Dunning Procedures

Quick Reference

Menu path: IMG • FINANCIAL ACCOUNTING • ACCOUNTS RECEIVABLE AND ACCOUNTS PAYABLE • BUSINESS TRANSACTIONS • DUNNING

Transactions: OB61 (define dunning areas), OB18 (define dunning blocks), FBMP (define dunning procedures)

Tables/views: T047M/V_T047M (dunning areas), T040S/V_T040S (dunning blocks), T047A (dunning procedures), T047B (dunning levels), T047C (dunning charges), T047H (dunning minimum amounts)

To create dunning letters for a customer, you must assign a dunning procedure to that customer that establishes the rules for carrying out the dunning. Dunning procedures are defined with Transaction FBMP and are independent of company codes.

For each dunning procedure, define the following main settings (Figure 5.50):

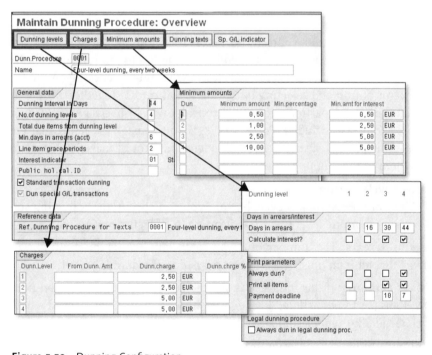

Figure 5.50 Dunning Configuration

- ▶ **Dunning Interval in Days**

  This is the minimum number of days between each dunning run (the system compares the dunning date of each run).

- ▶ **No. of Dunning Levels**

  Each time an invoice is dunned again, the system increases the dunning level; for different dunning levels, there are different forms for the letters. Here you specify the maximum number of levels. Generally, when an item reaches the maximum dunning level, the legal process to recover the credit begins.

- ▶ **Min. Days in Arrears (Acct)**

  This is the minimum number of days in arrears that at least one item must have to have the whole customer dunned.

- ▶ **Line Item Grace Periods**

  Here you can specify a minimum number of days that an item must be overdue to be included in the dunning.

- ▶ **Standard Transaction Dunning**

  You should always set this indicator, unless you want to dun only the customer open items posted with a special general ledger indicator.

- ▶ **Dun Special G/L Transactions**

  You can't set this indicator yourself; it's automatically set by the system if you decide to include any special general ledger transaction in the run. Specify the special general ledger indicators relevant for the dunning by clicking on the Sp. G/L Indicator button and selecting one or more indicators. Together with your credit management department, carefully consider which special general ledger indicators should be included. For example, if you manage the items that are under legal action with a special general ledger indicator, it makes no sense to include them in the dunning run.

- ▶ **Dunning Levels button**

  By clicking on the Dunning Levels button, you can specify the following settings for each dunning level (see the bottom right of Figure 5.50):

  - ▶ **Days in Arrears:** The number of days you specify here is the minimum in arrears that an item must reach to be assigned to the dunning level.

  - ▶ **Always Dunning:** If this indicator is set, the customer is dunned, even if no new items are to be included in the letter, and no items have reached a new level. Generally, a letter similar to the former letter is generated.

  - ▶ **Minimum Amount:** The amount you specify here refers to the total for the dunning level; if, for a customer, the total of items assigned to this dunning level doesn't reach the minimum amount, they are assigned to a lower level.

You can make further settings for each company code by selecting ENVIRONMENT • COMPANY CODE DATA in the window of the dunning procedure configuration.

Create the dunning form as an SAPscript (Transaction SE71) or SAP Smart Form (Transaction SMARTFORMS). Then assign the form to each combination of dunning procedure/company code/dunning level under FINANCIAL ACCOUNTING • ACCOUNTS RECEIVABLE AND ACCOUNTS PAYABLE • BUSINESS TRANSACTIONS • DUNNING • PRINTOUT • ASSIGN DUNNING FORMS.

You can create a dunning block to exclude customers or open items from the dunning run under FINANCIAL ACCOUNTING • ACCOUNTS RECEIVABLE AND ACCOUNTS PAYABLE • BUSINESS TRANSACTIONS • DUNNING • BASIC SETTINGS FOR DUNNING • DEFINE DUNNING BLOCK REASONS.

5.3.6 Configuring Interest Calculations

Quick Reference

Menu path: IMG • FINANCIAL ACCOUNTING • ACCOUNTS RECEIVABLE AND ACCOUNTS PAYABLE • BUSINESS TRANSACTIONS • INTEREST CALCULATION

Transactions: OB46 (define interest calculation types) OB82 (prepare interest on arrears calculation), OBV1 (A/R: calculation of interest on arrears (postings)), OBAC (define reference interest rates), OB81 (define time-based terms), OB83 (define time-based terms (reference rate))

Tables: T056/V_T056 (calculation types), T056U (interest terms), T056X (additional interest data), T033F (posting configuration), T056R (reference interest rates), T056A (interest rates), T056P (interest rates for reference rate)

To use the interest program and calculate interest on unpaid invoices at their due dates, three major steps are required:

1. Define interest indicators where the rules to calculate the interest are defined. Use Transaction OB46 and OB82.

2. Specify an interest indicator in the master data of the customer, at the company code level in the Account Management section.

3. Define the interest rates valid for specific periods, and, if necessary, create reference interest rates if your interest percentage is linked to the percentage of a

reference rate (like the discount rate of the local central bank). Use Transaction OBAC to create reference interest rates, Transaction OB81 to specify the interest rate for each interest rate indicator, and Transaction OB83 to specify the rate for the reference rate.

In Transaction OB46, define the interest indicator, specify an ID (alphanumeric, two digits long), a short description, and the interest calculation type, which is P for customer items (the other possible value is B, which is on the balance, and not applicable for customers) (see Figure 5.51).

Change View "Interest Settlement (Calculation Type)": Overview

Int ID	Name	Acct no.as IntClcInd	Int calc. type	Name
01	Standard itm int.cal	☐	P	Item Interest Calculatic
02	Standard bal.int.cal	☐	S	Balance Interest Calcula
03	Bal.int.calc.term 2	☐	S	Balance Interest Calcula
04	Item int.calc.term 2	☐	P	Item Interest Calculatic
05	Bal.int.calc.term 3	☑	S	Balance Interest Calcula
10	Pjct interest calc.	☐	S	Balance Interest Calcula
IM	Inv. proj. interest	☐	S	Balance Interest Calcula

Figure 5.51 Transaction OB46 to Define Interest Rate Indicator

In Transaction OB82 (IMG • FINANCIAL ACCOUNTING • ACCOUNTS RECEIVABLE AND ACCOUNTS PAYABLE • BUSINESS TRANSACTIONS • INTEREST CALCULATION • INTEREST CALCULATION GLOBAL SETTINGS • PREPARE INTEREST ON APPEARS CALCULATION), specify the detailed configuration of each interest indicator. These are the main settings (see Figure 5.52, left side of the figure):

- **Selection of Items area**
  You can calculate the interest for the following:
  - Open and all cleared items (regardless of whether the clearing happened because of a payment or because of a different transaction, such as a credit note)
  - All open items and items cleared by a payment transaction.
  - All cleared items, excluding the calculation on open items
  - Items cleared by a payment, excluding open items and items cleared by a transaction different than a payment

- **Calendar Type**
  You can choose among the commercial calendar (all months are considered as 30 days), the exact number of calendar days, or the options 30/365 (all months are considered as 30 days but to calculate the interest, the days in arrears are

divided by 365) or real calendar days/360. Discuss this point with your Accounts Receivable department because this will affect interest amounts and could have legal implications.

▶ **Transfer Days**
The number of days specified here is relevant for paid items, not for open items. This is the amount of days that a payment takes to go from the payer to the payee, and it's usually different in different countries. In practice, the interest on cleared items is calculated on a specific number of days, minus the transfer days.

▶ **Tolerance Days**
This is the minimum number of days an item is overdue and charged interest. The tolerance days determine whether or not to calculate interest on an item; if an item is overdue for more than the tolerance days set, the interest is calculated on the total period overdue, without subtracting the tolerance days.

▶ **Calculate Interest on Items Paid Before Due Date**
If a customer pays before the due date, you may decide to pay the customer the interest. If so, select this indicator. If no interest has to be paid or deducted for invoices paid in advance, don't select the indicator.

▶ **Only Calculate Interest on Debit Items**
Select this indicator if you want to calculate interest on credit notes and, in general, on items posted to the credit side of a customer.

▶ **Amount Limit**
You can specify the minimum amount of the interest on an invoice to be issued (not for single items). Sometimes, if the invoice amount is very small, the cost of issuing an invoice can be bigger than the invoice amount.

▶ **No Interest Payment**
Select this indicator if you don't want to generate interest credit notes. This only happens if you choose to calculate the interest on credit amounts (i.e., if the Only Calculate Interest on Debit Items indicator isn't selected).

▶ **Output Control**
Each interest invoice has an internal number range that is put on the reference field of the connected Financial Accounting document. The number range you specify here must be defined in Transaction FBN1 and not used by any other document type.

▶ **Terms of Payment**
The interest invoice has its due date and terms of payment specified here.

▶ **Tax Code**

If the revenue account is subjected to tax, you specify the tax code here.

In a subsequent step (IMG • FINANCIAL ACCOUNTING • ACCOUNTS RECEIVABLE AND ACCOUNTS PAYABLE • BUSINESS TRANSACTIONS • INTEREST CALCULATION • INTEREST CALCULATION GLOBAL SETTINGS • PREPARE ITEM INTEREST ON APPEARS CALCULATION), you can make some further specifications necessary to make Transaction FINT (program RFINTITAR) work correctly (Figure 5.52):

▶ The option to have interest calculated only on open items, not on cleared items

▶ The option to specify the reference date for the start of interest calculation (this should be the net due date)

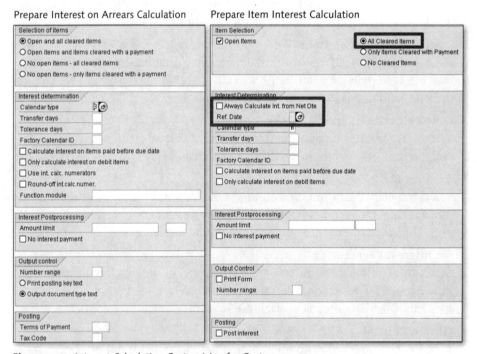

Figure 5.52 Interest Calculation Customizing for Customers

The last step is to define the posting scheme that determines the general ledger accounts used by Transaction FINT to post the interest invoices to Financial Accounting. Execute Transaction OBV1, and follow these steps (see Figure 5.53):

1. Define the account symbols (the posting scheme contains only the account symbols, not the real general ledger accounts). When you run Transaction FINT, the posting scheme is read, and the account symbols are replaced by the real general ledger accounts, based on the chart of accounts and the currency (see the next step). Click on the Symbols button to create the account symbols.

2. Specify which general ledger accounts replace the account symbols, based on a combination of the chart of accounts and currency. Click on the Accounts button to perform this step. Keep in mind that if you want to define a replacement valid for all of the currencies you specify, use the value "+" instead of the country code. If the account symbol refers to the customer account, don't specify any general ledger account; use "+".

3. Build the posting specification (or posting scheme). Each scheme is valid for a combination of business transactions (1000 for interest received, and 2000 for interest granted), interest indicators, company codes, and business areas. If you don't want to differentiate the postings by interest indicator, company code, or business area, use "+" instead of a real value. In each posting specification, define the credit and debit posting key (for interest received, the credit posting key is 50, and the debit 01), and the credit and debit account symbols.

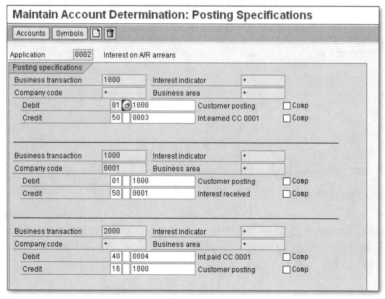

Figure 5.53 Posting Configuration for Interest

To specify interest rates, follow these steps (Figure 5.54):

1. If the interest rate in linked to a reference rate (plus or minus spread), define the percentage of the reference rate with Transaction OB83. Then specify the interest term in Transaction OB81, where you define the reference interest rate and the spread to add or deduct to the reference rate.

2. If the interest isn't linked to a reference rate, specify the amount of interest in Transaction OB82. In this case, leave the Ref. Interest Rate field blank.

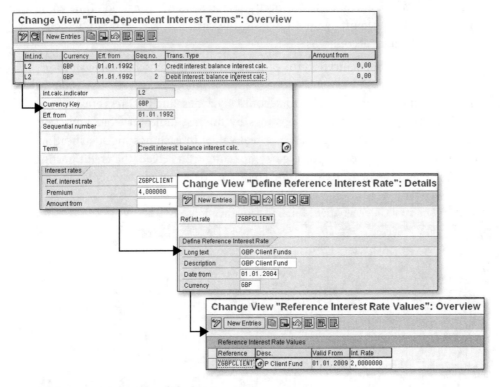

Figure 5.54 Interest Rates Calculation

In any case, all percentages are time dependent. If the days in arrears fall into two or more periods in which different interest percentages apply, the system correctly calculates the interest for each portion.

5.3.7 Customizing Exchange Rate Calculations

Menu paths: IMG • FINANCIAL ACCOUNTING • FINANCIAL ACCOUNTING GLOBAL SETTINGS • GENERAL LEDGER ACCOUNTING • BUSINESS TRANSACTIONS • CLOSING • VALUATE • FOREIGN CURRENCY VALUATION

OR

IMG • FINANCIAL ACCOUNTING (NEW) • FINANCIAL ACCOUNTING GLOBAL SETTINGS (NEW) • GENERAL LEDGER ACCOUNTING (NEW) • PERIODIC PROCESSING • VALUATE

Transactions: OB59 (define valuation methods), OBA1 (prepare automatic postings for foreign currency valuation), SM30 (view V_T033) (define valuation areas), SM30 (view V_TACC_BWBER_PR) (assign valuation areas and accounting principles), SM30 (view V_FAGL_TRGT_LDGR) (check assignment of accounting principle to ledger group)

Tables/views: T044A/V_T044A (valuation method), T030H (accounts for exchange rate valuation), T030HB (accounts for exchange rate valuation with valuation area (new G/L)), T033/V_T033 (valuation areas), TACC_BWBER_PR/V_TACC_BWBER_PR (assign valuation areas and accounting principles), V_FAGL_TRGT_LDGR (assignment of accounting principle to ledger group)

You can revaluate customer and vendor open items posted in foreign currencies using program SAPF100 (Transaction F.05), or with Transaction FAGL_FC_VAL if you're using SAP General Ledger (the new General Ledger). You must perform two main steps to carry out this function:

1. Set up a valuation method using Transaction OB59.

2. The account determination must be specified for all general ledger accounts to be revaluated (for customer and vendors, this is the reconciliation account). This is done via Transaction OBA1; some additional steps are required within the new SAP General Ledger environment.

The first step just mentioned involves defining the valuation method that is specified in the selection screen of Transaction F.05 (if you're using the classic general ledger; the valuation method is linked to the valuation area in the new SAP General Ledger); follow these steps (Figure 5.55):

1. Run Transaction OB59. If you create a new method, click on the New Entries button, and specify a four-digit alphanumeric code and a meaningful description. If you want to check or modify an existing method, simply double-click on the corresponding line.

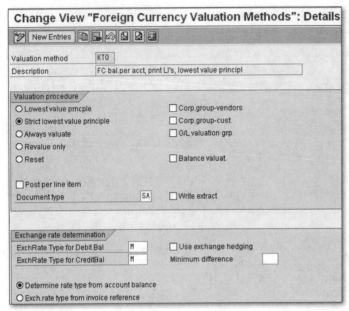

Figure 5.55 Foreign Currency Valuation Method

2. Specify the valuation principle. The most common is Always Valuate; in this case, the valuation is always carried out, no matter whether it's a revaluation or devaluation.

3. Don't select the Post Per Line Item option unless you want to generate one posting for each open item valuated; this could lead to a large number of postings, depending on the size of your portfolio of open items in foreign currencies.

4. Specify the document type for the posting. Be aware that the posting never takes place directly on customers or vendors but on an adjustment account (which isn't a reconciliation account) of the reconciliation account. The document type must, in its configuration settings, be allowed to post to general ledger accounts (account type S).

5. Specify the exchange rate type that should be used to retrieve the exchange rate valid at the time of valuation. If you don't specify an exchange rate type, the standard exchange rate type, M, is used.

6. If you've specified a different exchange rate type for debit and credit, specify whether the balance to be used is the total by customer and currency, or the total by invoice reference (in this case, the system totals all open items with the same invoices referenced in field REBZG; you use this field to link credit notes or partial payment to an existing invoice).

The second step is to specify the general ledger accounts to which to post the following:

▶ The revenue arising from the valuation

▶ The cost arising from the valuation

▶ The balance sheet account to be posted (this account can't be the same as the one valuated in the case of reconciliation accounts for customers and vendors)

If you have the classic general ledger, perform this step by following these instructions (Figure 5.56):

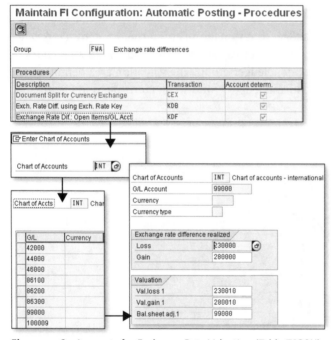

Figure 5.56 Accounts for Exchange Rate Valuation (Table T030H)

1. Run Transaction OBA1, and double-click on the line of Transaction KDF.

2. Specify the chart of accounts.

3. In the resulting screen, make individual specifications for each account. Keep in mind that if an account to be revaluated isn't in the list, you must carry out the specification for the account to be able to carry out a successful foreign currency valuation.

4. In the detailed screen of each account, there are five places to specify the accounts to be posted. The first two refer to the realized exchange rate differences, and arise when you clear the open items (they aren't relevant for program SAPF100). The last three contain the following:

▶ **Val. Loss 1:** This is the cost account where the valuation is posted if it leads to a loss.

▶ **Val. Gain 1:** This is the revenue account where the valuation is posted if it leads to a gain.

▶ **Bal. Sheet Adj. 1:** This is the balance sheet account where the valuation is posted; it can be the same account valuated only if the account valuated isn't a reconciliation account.

If you're using SAP General Ledger, the valuation is performed according to valuation areas; each valuation area is linked to a valuation method and to an accounting principle that, in turn, is linked to a ledger group. The valuation area definition and the link to the valuation method and ledger group are demonstrated in Figure 5.57.

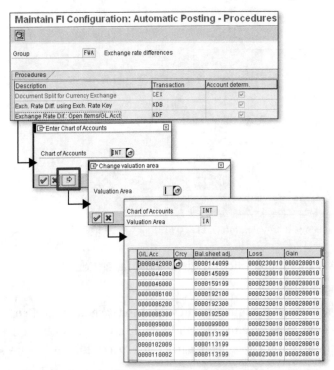

Figure 5.57 Accounts for Exchange Rate Valuation by Valuation Area (Table T030HB)

The Quick Reference box at the beginning of this section lists the corresponding customizing tables.

If you're using SAP General Ledger, assign the general ledger accounts using Transaction OBA1. The difference between SAP General Ledger and the classic general ledger is that you do this by valuation area (Figure 5.58). However, it's optional, not mandatory, to specify different accounts per valuation area.

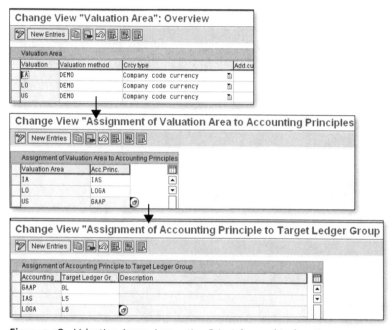

Figure 5.58 Valuation Areas, Accounting Principles, and Ledger Groups

5.3.8 Configuring Special General Ledger Indicators for Accounts Receivable Posting

Quick Reference

Menu paths: IMG • FINANCIAL ACCOUNTING • ACCOUNTS RECEIVABLE AND ACCOUNTS PAYABLE • BUSINESS TRANSACTIONS • POSTINGS WITH ALTERNATIVE RECONCILIATION ACCOUNT • DEFINE ALTERNATIVE RECONCILIATION ACCOUNT FOR CUSTOMERS

OR

IMG • FINANCIAL ACCOUNTING • ACCOUNTS RECEIVABLE AND ACCOUNTS PAYABLE • BUSINESS TRANSACTIONS • POSTINGS WITH ALTERNATIVE RECONCILIATION ACCOUNT • DEFINE ALTERNATIVE RECONCILIATION ACCOUNTS FOR VENDORS

Transactions: OBXR (define reconciliation accounts for customer down payments) OBYR (define alternative reconciliation account for down payments [vendor]), OBXY (define alternative reconciliation account for customers [other]), OBXT (define alternative reconciliation account for vendors [other]), OBYN (define alternative reconciliation account for bills/exchange receivable), OBYM (define alternative reconciliation account for bills of exchange payable)

When you post to a customer or a vendor account, the posting is automatically made to the reconciliation account specified in the customer or vendor master data at the company code level. However, it's possible to post to a different account if you specify a special general ledger indicator in the posting. In this case, the posting key must be marked as relevant for special general ledger transactions (the posting keys are 09 and 19 for customers, and 19 and 29 for vendors).

The following categories of special general ledger transactions are possible in the system:

► **Customers**

  ► Down payment received

  ► Bill of exchange receivable

  ► Other (vendor)

► **Vendors**

  ► Down payment made

  ► Bill of exchange payable

  ► Other (customer)

Figure 5.59 shows the steps necessary to set up a special general ledger indicator for customers belonging to the Other category.

For each special general ledger indicator, the following specifications are needed:

► **Special G/L Ind.**
This should be a unique one-digit, alphanumeric ID. The same indicator can be created with different meanings for customers and vendors.

► **Posting Key**
The posting keys to be used to post debit and credit are 09 and 19 for customers, and 29 and 39 for vendors.

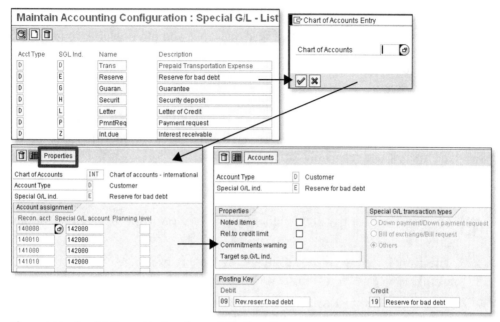

Figure 5.59 Special General Ledger Account Configuration

- ▶ **Noted Items**

  This indicates whether the posting belongs to a noted item; noted items don't in any way update transaction figures and can't be considered postings from an accounting point of view. They are created with Transaction F-57 for vendors, and F-49 for customers, and they can be used, for example, to pay a vendor before the invoice receipt with the automatic payment program.

- ▶ **Rel. to Credit Limit**

  Discuss this field with your Accounts Receivable department; should the posting with the specific general ledger indicator update the credit limit that can be displayed with Transactions FD32 and FD33?

- ▶ **Target Sp. G/L Ind.**

  The target special general ledger indicator makes sense only with noted items, when the noted item should be picked up by the automatic payment program to generate a posting to another item marked with a special general ledger indicator (e.g., a completed down payment).

- ▶ **Special G/L Account**

  The account to be posted to should be specified for each reconciliation account. The new reconciliation account can be the same or different.

5.3.9 FAQ and Troubleshooting Tips

Next we answer some frequently asked questions and offer helpful troubleshooting tips.

FAQ

1. **Question**: How can I specify interest rates valid for all invoice currencies?

   Answer: You can't specify an interest rate valid for multiple currencies. Specify the interest rate separately for each currency.

2. **Question:** Is it possible to create a payment method to be used for both incoming and outgoing payments?

   Answer: No. Each payment method can be used *either* for incoming *or* for outgoing payments.

3. **Question:** I need to create a complex DME file to exchange payment data with a bank. How can I access the DME engine?

   Answer: Access the DME engine with Transaction DMEE. Work together with an ABAP developer and in collaboration with the bank to build the specific DME structure.

4. **Question**: An invoice has been partially paid, and we've posted the payment as a partial payment (with an invoice reference on the BSEG-REBZG field). Is the interest calculated on the net amount?

   Answer: Yes, but only if the Only Calculate Interest on Debit Items indicator isn't set.

Troubleshooting Tip

1. **Issue**: I have put the payment block on customer and vendor line items, and the payment block is set to have an effect on both automatic and manual payments. However, I can clear the open items with Transaction FB05 (by selecting the Transfer Posting with Clearing option), and with Transactions F-44 or F-32 to clear the vendor and customer open items, respectively. Is this as it should be?

   Solution: Yes. The payment block only affects the transactions marked as payments. Transaction FBZ1 posts incoming payments, Transaction F-53 posts outgoing payments, and Transaction FB05 posts either.

2. **Issue:** In the dunning configuration, I don't see the option to define the posting of the dunning charges.

   Solution: This functionality isn't designed in the standard dunning procedure; the system can calculate the dunning charges and print them in the dunning letters but can't post them. If you want to post the dunning charges, you must build an ABAP program or work with a business transaction event. Identify the proper solution together with an ABAP expert.

3. **Issue:** I'm testing the automatic payments, and I want to change the available amounts for each bank account. When I try to update view V_T042D to change the amounts, I get the message "Client XXX has status 'not modifiable.'"

   Solution: Discuss this issue with your Basis colleagues. If you change the Client Role of client XXX to "Production" in Table T000, you'll be able to carry out this activity, even though the customizing isn't allowed in the client XXX.

5.4 Accounts Receivable Postings

In this section, we offer detailed instructions for the most common types of posting to customers. In particular, you'll learn how to the following:

▶ Post incoming invoices and credit notes within Financial Accounting, both with classic and Enjoy transactions.

▶ Post incoming payments and down payments.

▶ Post with special general ledger indicator.

We conclude the section by describing the standard reporting transaction on customer line items (FBL5N).

5.4.1 Financial Accounting Outgoing Invoices

Quick Reference

Menu paths: ACCOUNTING • FINANCIAL ACCOUNTING • ACCOUNTS RECEIVABLE • DOCUMENT ENTRY • INVOICE – GENERAL

OR

ACCOUNTING • FINANCIAL ACCOUNTING • ACCOUNTS RECEIVABLE • DOCUMENT ENTRY • INVOICE

Transactions: F-22 (invoice – general), FB70 (invoice)

Next we discuss how to post incoming invoices directly within Financial Accounting, using both the classic transaction, Transaction F-22, and the more user-friendly Enjoy transaction, Transaction FB70.

Classic General Ledger Transaction (F-22)

The instructions for using Transaction F-22 are the same as those for Transaction FB01, so consult Section 4.2.1, Posting with the Classic General Ledger, in Chapter 4, for more details. This section only discusses specific instructions about using Transaction F-22 to post a customer invoice directly into Financial Accounting.

In the header data of the invoice, the document type is particularly important. In general, outgoing invoices are posted with specific document types dedicated only to these types of transactions. When specifying the posting date and document date for outgoing invoices, note that they are usually, but not always, the same. If you want to ensure that all of the manual Financial Accounting invoices are always created with a document date equal to the posting date, create a validation step in Transaction OB28 (callup point 1, header data).

After the header information is entered, you can specify the line items, which include the customer, revenue, and tax lines. In general, the first line is the customer line. Follow these steps (Figure 5.60):

1. In the first screen, after you enter the header data, specify the posting key (01 for customer invoices) and the customer account number, and press Enter to move to the next screen.

2. In the following screen, specify the amount in the document currency (the system automatically calculations the local currency). If you post in the local currency, the system displays only this field.

3. Specify the tax data. If the invoice contains an amount subjected to different tax codes, then enter "**" in the tax code field; otherwise, specify the unique tax code of the invoice, and then specify the tax amount of the invoice, or select the Calculate Tax indicator. The tax is calculated on the general ledger account items where a tax code has been specified.

4. The other mandatory information in this screen relates to the payment:
   - **Pmt Method:** This is automatically provided from the customer master record but can be changed in the document.
   - **Bline Date:** The baseline date is calculated from the system based on the payment method and can be changed.

▶ **Days/Percent:** This data is also provided from the payment method and can be overwritten. The net due date is determined by adding the highest number of days to the baseline date. The net due date isn't a date written in the database but is automatically calculated by the system in transactions or in reporting.

5. Complete the customer item with any further information required by your accounting model, and then specify the posting key of the revenue item (50) and the revenue account. Press Enter to go to the next screen, which is where you can specify information about the revenue item.

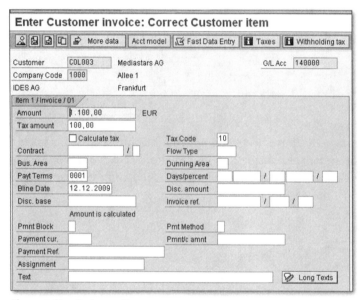

Figure 5.60 Customer Item

In the revenue item, specify the following:

▶ The amount in the document currency.

▶ The tax code. Note that if you have to use the same account with two different tax codes, you must create two line items.

▶ A real Controlling account assignment. The Controlling object to be used depends on your specific Controlling model. In the example specified in Figure 5.61, the revenue account has been created as a primary cost element of category 1 and has been posted to a cost center. (Please note that revenues above gross profit are more often created with cost element category 11, and, in that case, cannot be posted with the cost center as real account assignment objects, but should be posted to profitability segments or other real account assignment objects allowed for category 11.)

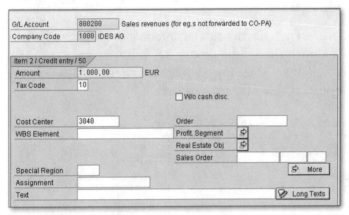

Figure 5.61 Revenue Item

After all of the revenue items have been entered, you can simulate the document. In the simulation, the system also displays the automatically created tax items (Figure 5.62). If no error occurs and the document in the simulation view appears as expected, you can post the document.

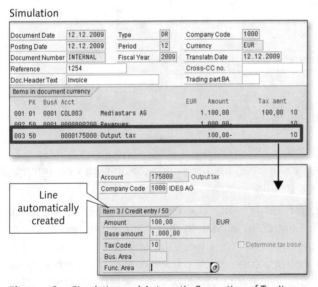

Figure 5.62 Simulation and Automatic Generation of Tax Item

Enjoy Transaction (FB70)

Using Transaction FB70, you can post outgoing invoices within Financial Accounting with the same information as those that you can enter in Transaction F-22 but with a more user-friendly interface. Documents created with FB70 and F-22 look the same after they are posted.

The main difference with Transaction F-22 is that you create everything in one screen. With FB70, you must always specify the header and line item information following the same rules for Transaction F-22.

The following information will help explain the main differences between FB70 and F-22 (see Figures 5.63, 5.64, and 5.65 to locate the corresponding sections in the FB70 working area):

▸ When you run Transaction FB70, the system asks you for the company code. This information is retained in your session for the next postings with FB70. If you want to change company codes, click the Company Code button (❶ of Figure 5.63).

▸ With the Hold button (❷ of Figure 5.63), you can use the hold function, which allows you to save the document as it is, completed or incomplete, under a user-created identification key. No update is made in the transaction figures or in BKPF, BSEG, and BSID.

▸ The Simulate button (❸ of Figure 5.63) triggers the document simulation. It works in the same way as described in Transaction F-22.

▸ The Park button (❹ of Figure 5.63) allows you to park the document. In this case, the system assigns a real document number within the number range associated with the document type. You can then post the document with Transactions FBV0 or FV70.

▸ In the Basic Data header (❺ of Figure 5.63), you enter the customer, document and posting date, and reference and header text. Also specify the currency of the invoice, the total amount of the invoice, and the tax amount and related tax code. However, if the invoice contains more than one tax code, leave the tax fields empty. For the exchange rate, see the next point.

▸ In the Payment section of the header (❻ of Figure 5.64), you can specify payment details for the customer line item. In general, you have to specify at least the information required to calculate the due date.

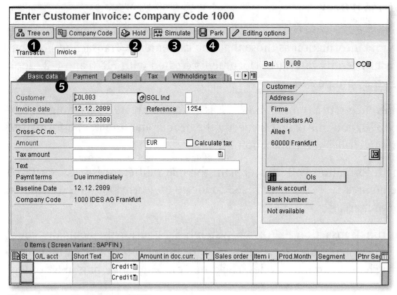

Figure 5.63 Transaction FB70

▸ In the Details section of the header (❼ of Figure 5.64), you can specify additional information that applies only to the customer line item, such as the dunning block or the assignment. The same information for other line items must be entered on the lines below the header information.

▸ In the Tax section of the header (❽ of Figure 5.64), you can enter the tax amounts for different tax codes.

▸ In the Local Currency section of the header (❾ of Figure 5.64), you don't need to specify anything if you want the system to automatically calculate the exchange rate. Use this section if you want to enter a specific translation date (different than the posting date) or a specific exchange rate.

▸ Below the header and customer data, you enter the information for each line item that is different from the customer item (❿ of Figure 5.65). All of these items can only refer to general ledger accounts, and post with a posting key of 40 for debit and 50 for credit. All of the considerations valid for Transaction F-22 are also valid here, but you enter all needed values in one line and not in fields positioned around the screen. Note that you can't directly specify the posting key, only whether the posting is debit or credit. However, in the background, posting keys 40 (debit) and 50 (credit) work with the consequent field status rules.

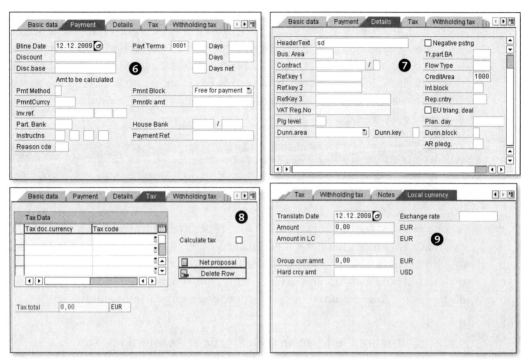

Figure 5.64 Transaction FB70 (Cont.)

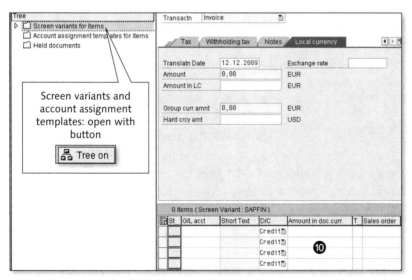

Figure 5.65 Transaction FB70 (Cont.)

For each line item, all possible fields are displayed. It's likely that in your accounting model, few fields will be allowed because to work with the standard screen with dozens and dozens of fields would be not efficient for your accountants. We recommend setting up screen variants for the most frequent types of postings, as illustrated in Figure 5.65. After the screen variants are set up with only the necessary fields, each accountant can select a suitable one from the menu: EDIT • SCREEN VARIANT • SELECT SCREEN VARIANT.

Screen Variants for Transaction FB70

The screen variants that you define for Transactions FB50 and FB60 are also valid for Transaction FB70, and vice versa.

If you need to make frequent postings with repetitive information, you can use the Account Assignment Template functionality. Refer to the instructions for Transaction FB50 (Section 4.2.1, Posting with the Classic General Ledger, in Chapter 4) to understand how to maintain screen variants and account assignment templates. All of the instructions provided in that section also apply to Transaction FB70.

5.4.2 Outgoing Credit Memos in Financial Accounting

Quick Reference

Menu paths: ACCOUNTING • FINANCIAL ACCOUNTING • ACCOUNTS RECEIVABLE • DOCUMENT ENTRY • CREDIT MEMO

OR

ACCOUNTING • FINANCIAL ACCOUNTING • ACCOUNTS RECEIVABLE • DOCUMENT ENTRY • CREDIT MEMO – GENERAL

Transactions: FB75 (credit memo), F-27 (credit memo – general)

When you create a credit memo within Financial Accounting, you can run either Transaction FB75 or Transaction F-27. Transaction FB75 works in the same way as Transaction FB70, and Transaction F-27 works in the same way as Transaction F-22. The only differences are the following (Figure 5.66):

▶ When you use Transaction FB75, the amount specified in the header is automatically interpreted as negative and posted with posting key 11. In other words, you should specify the amount in absolute value, without any sign, and the system interprets it as a credit posting to the customer. Remember to post debit to the revenue or cost account.

▶ When you use Transaction F-27, the system automatically provides posting key 11 in the first row.

▶ To create a physical link between the credit note and the invoice (if the credit note refers to exactly one invoice item), you can use the Invoice Reference fields (Figure 5.66) that identify uniquely one customer line item in the system (the company code is the same). The three boxes should be filled with the following information, in this order:

  ▶ Invoice reference document number

  ▶ Invoice reference year

  ▶ Invoice reference line item

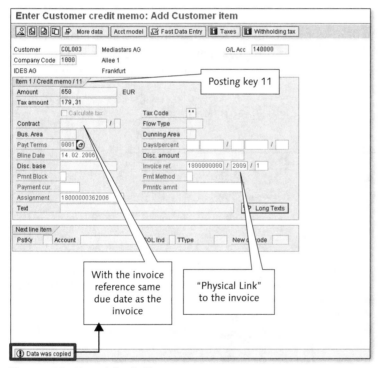

Figure 5.66 Manual Credit Notes

The result is that the net due date is copied from the reference invoice to the baseline date of the referred credit memo. In this way, when you run the automatic payment transaction, the amount of the credit note is automatically deducted from the amount of the reference invoice.

5.4.3 Manual Incoming Payments and Clearings

When posting incoming payments from a bank account statement, the information contained in the note to the payee could be enough to automatically clear related invoices, but this changes from country to country. In some contexts, the quality of information isn't as good, so you may prefer to post incoming payments to a bank clearing account, and then manually clear customer open items. To manually register an incoming payment, you usually run Transaction F-28 or Transaction FBZ1.

The initial screen is made of four sections (Figure 5.67).

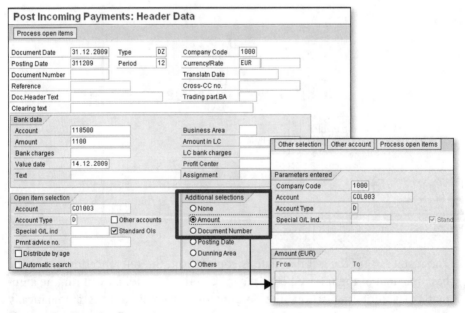

Figure 5.67 Incoming Payment

▶ **Header data**

Shown at the top of Figure 5.67, here is where you specify the usual header information, such as the posting date and document date, currency of the payment, and document type, among others. Be sure to use a document type dedicated to customer incoming payments.

▶ **Bank Data area**

Here you specify the general ledger bank clearing account (not the bank account, as this is posted by the bank statement), the amount of the payment, and the value date, plus any additional information required by your accounting model.

▶ **Open Item Selection area**

In this area, specify the customer number in the Account field (the account type is already set to D and shouldn't be changed). Click on the Standard OIs flag to select the open items not posted with a special general ledger indicator and, if needed, any special general ledger indicator. You can also select items of more than one customer account by clicking on the Other Account button; in the resulting screen, specify the account whose open items should be selected.

▶ **Additional Selections area**

In this section, you have the option of using additional selection criteria to restrict the search of the open items (e.g., the amount, as displayed in Figure 5.67). The possible criteria and the order in which they are displayed are defined in Transaction O7F1.

After you've completed the information in the initial screen and specified additional selections (if needed), you can select open items with the Process Open Items button. The system displays the selected open items in the resulting screen (Figure 5.68).

In this screen, you can mark the items you want to clear by simply double-clicking on the amount of each item. The items with the amount in blue are selected for clearing (or marked as "active"), while the items with the amount in black color aren't selected (or marked as "inactive"). You can mark or activate items with the Activate Items button (![Items]) and deactivate them with the Deactivate Items button (![Items]). You can also mark all items with the Select All button (![icon]) and unmark all items with the Deselect All button (![icon]). If you haven't chosen Selected Items Initially Inactive in the Editing Options (see the Editing Options button), the items are initially displayed as all activated.

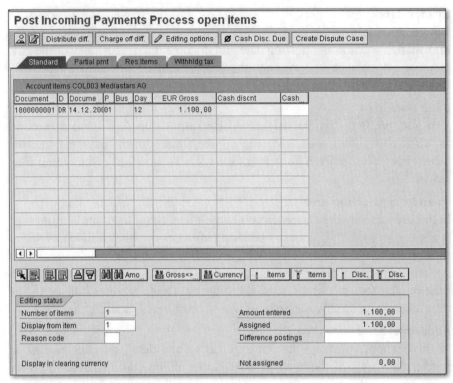

Figure 5.68 Incoming Payment (Cont.)

The system automatically recognizes the cash discount (if the items are posted with the possibility of a cash discount in the payment terms) based on the payment terms of the item and on the date of payment; you can, however, change or deactivate the proposed cash discount.

From the screen shown in Figure 5.68, you can immediately save the document if the balance in the document currency is zero. The amount in the document currency of the selected items is translated into the currency specified in the header of the document at the current rate (even though the currency specified in the header is the local currency). However, if the No Forex Rate Diff. When Clearing in LC flag is set in the company code global settings, the historical value in local currency is used instead. If the total amount isn't zero, you can charge the difference against a cost or revenue account.

You can also post a partial amount to open items that don't clear the total amount of the invoices; to do this, click on the Partial Pmt button, and specify the payment amount for each item. The system then posts a partial payment item for each item, physically linked to the original invoice through the RBZEG field. Alternatively, you can clear the open item even though the amount of the payment is less than the amount of the invoice, and post the residual to a new open item as a clearing difference (a cost). To do this, click on the Res. Items button and double-click on the Residual Items field. The system automatically assigns the remaining amount necessary to post the document to a newly created open item (you can also specify the residual amount manually). The newly created items (residual items) aren't physically linked to the assigned items but inherit the terms of payment.

When the document is posted, immediately select Document Display from the menu to see an overview of the document just created (Figure 5.69). To see which open items have been cleared by the displayed document, select Environment Payment Usage.

Entry view

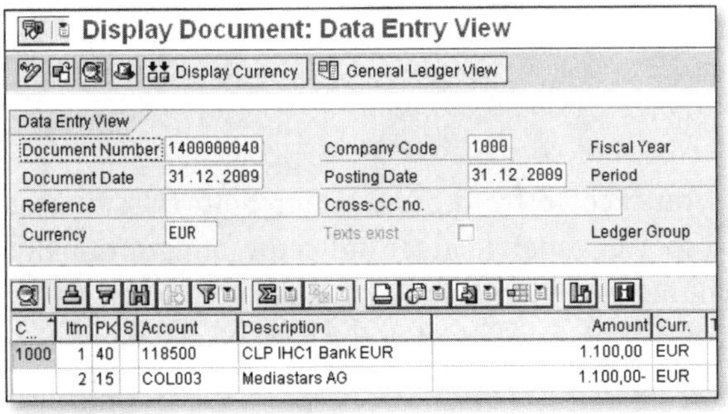

G/L view

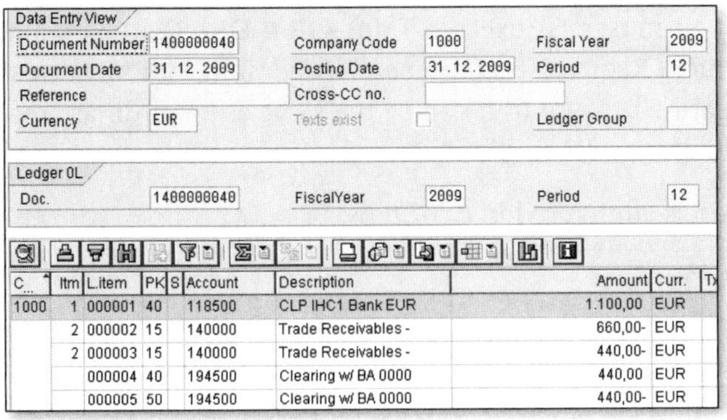

Figure 5.69 Incoming Payment (Cont.)

If you're using SAP General Ledger, you can see the document in the entry view (without document splitting). In the general ledger view, you can see where the customer item is split according to the split criteria (provided that splitting is active in your client).

When posting a payment to a customer open item, you can only process the document in the entry view. In other words, you can't select the split items but only the open items integer. When saving the document, the passive split is automatically triggered, and the customer items are split according to the splitting customizing settings.

5.4.4 Posting and Clearing Down Payments

> **Quick Reference**
>
> **Menu paths**: Accounting • Financial Accounting • Accounts Receivable • Document Entry • Down Payment • Down Payment
>
> **OR**
>
> Accounting • Financial Accounting • Accounts Receivable • Document Entry • Down Payment • Clearing
>
> **Transactions**: F-29 (down payment), F-39 (clearing)

Down payments are payments you receive from a customer before issuing an invoice. They are recorded with a special general ledger indicator (and, optionally, with a special reconciliation account) and then charged against the invoice after the invoice is issued. Having down payments marked with the special general ledger indicator allows you to control them more effectively and to easily distribute payments among one or more invoices at a later stage.

To use this functionality, you must first execute Transaction OBXR; at least one Down Payment/Down Payment Request special general ledger indicator must exist and be linked to a reconciliation account (this can be the same as the ordinary reconciliation account, or a different one).

The down payment function is configured in two steps:

1. Post the down payment.
2. Assign the down payment to one or more issued invoices (i.e., clear the down payment).

Both of these steps are discussed in more detail next.

Posting Down Payments

You can post down payments using Transaction F-29 (Figure 5.70), which offsets the amount you received from the customer on the bank account or bank clearing account. Specify an appropriate document type according to your naming convention and accounting manual. Then specify the customer account and the special Down Payment/Down Payment Request general ledger indicator. Complete the information with the bank or bank clearing account and related details, and the amount of the payment received. Then post the document.

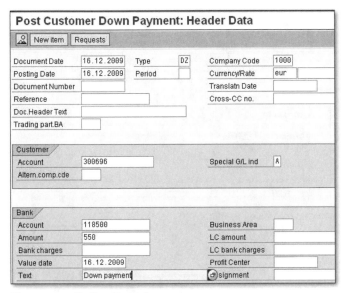

Figure 5.70 Posting Down Payments

When you run Transaction FBL5N, you can see the down payment received but not yet distributed to invoices by selecting the Special G/L Transaction flag on the bottom of the selections screen. To exclude other Special G/L Transactions (such as the bill of exchange), you can select the specific special general ledger indicator by using dynamic selection (⯐).

Clearing Down Payments

Perform this second step after you've sent the invoice or invoices related to the down payment. To do so, run Transaction F-39 (one time for each invoice you want to assign to a down payment), and then follow these steps (Figure 5.71):

1. Specify the dates of the transaction and other header details.

2. Specify the customer number.

3. Specify the invoice details (document number, year, and item number). The payment is displayed as a partial payment linked to the invoice specified in the Ref. field, so if you perform an automatic payment run, the down payment is automatically deducted from the invoice.

4. Select the Process Down Pmnts button, and specify the amount that you want to deduct from the down payment and assign to the invoice.

5. Save the document.

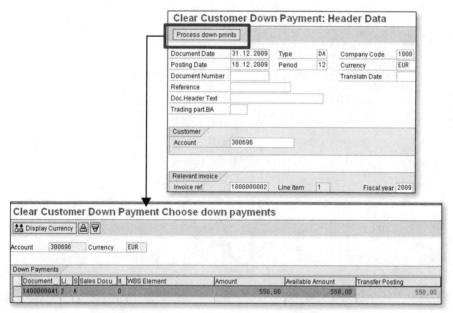

Figure 5.71 Clearing Down Payments

5.4.5 Posting with Special General Ledger Indicator

You can make postings to customer accounts with a special general ledger indicator other than the down payment or bill of exchange, which means that the posting is made in the customer account but marked specifically with the special general ledger indicator in the BSEG-UMSKZ field. You can also define a different reconciliation account when posting with special general ledger indicators, but this is optional.

In any case, related postings can be retrieved and listed separately in the customer line items report (FBL5N). Simply select the Special G/L Indicator flag in the selection screen; if you want to see just the items posted with the specific indicator, you can use dynamic selections (⌗). Then, in the Documents group, click the Sp. G/L Trans. Type button, double-click on the field, and specify the value.

5.4.6 Reporting Customer and Vendor Line Items

> **Quick Reference**
>
> **Menu paths**: Accounting • Financial Accounting • Accounts Receivable • Account • Display/Change Line Items (customer line items)
>
> **AND**
>
> Accounting • Financial Accounting • Accounts Payable • Account • Display/Change Line Items
>
> **Transactions**: FBL5N (customer line item), FBL1N (vendor line item)
>
> **Programs**: RFITEMAR (customer line item), RFITEMAP (vendor line item)

The most-used transactions for customer line item and vendor line item reporting are FBL5N and FBL1N, respectively. With these transactions, you get a list in the flexible and user-definable ALV format, and you can make mass changes to selected items.

The two transactions work exactly the same. Here we explain the functionality of Transaction FBL5N, but all of the instructions we provide can be easily applied to Transaction FBL1N.

The selection screen has four sections (Figure 5.72):

▸ **Customer Selection area**
In this section, you specify the customers and the company code (one or more).

▸ **Selection Using Search Help area**
In this section, you can use dynamic selections to use fields from the customer master data and from the document header and line item data; these fields aren't immediately displayed in the selection screen but can be used as further selection criteria.

▸ **Line Item Selection area**
Here you specify whether you want to select open items or cleared items. You have three options:

▶ **Open Items:** The system selects the open items (items in Table BSID) with posting dates before or equal to the key date specified in the Open at Key Date field, or cleared items (items from Table BSAD) with clearing dates after the key date specified.

▶ **Cleared Items:** The system selects only items from Table BSAD, cleared in the interval specified or opened at the specified date.

▶ **Open and Cleared Items:** The system selects items from Tables BSID and BSAD according to the range of posting dates specified in the Posting Date fields.

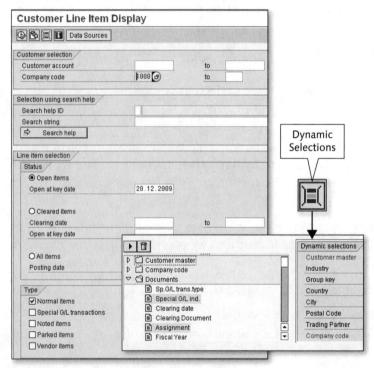

Figure 5.72 Customer Line Items Selection Screen

▶ **Type area**

In this section, you specify which category of items should be selected. You can choose one or more of the following categories:

   ▶ **Normal Items:** Items posted on the customer without any special general ledger indicator. This is the default choice proposed by the system.

▸ **Special G/L Transactions:** Includes the items posted with a special general ledger indicator.

▸ **Noted Items:** Items posted with a special general ledger indicator marked as relevant for noted items. The noted items aren't real accounting postings; in general, they don't affect the balance sheet or transaction figures. You should never mark this indicator when you're running the report for reconciliation purposes.

▸ **Parked Items:** Like the noted items, parked documents don't affect transaction figures or balance sheets. However, parked documents can be transformed into real documents.

▸ **Vendor Items:** If the customer is also a vendor and this information has been specified in the customer master data, the system also reads the vendor items.

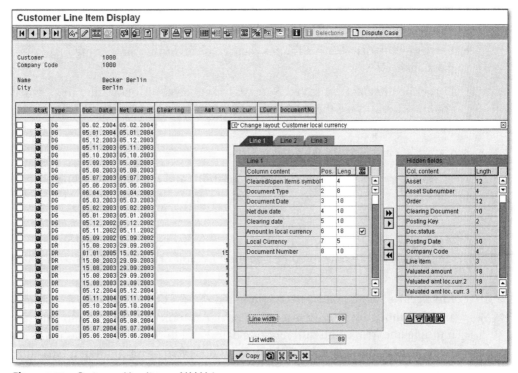

Figure 5.73 Customer Line Items: ALV List

When you run the program online, with the Execute button (⊕), the system displays the data in ALV format (Figure 5.73). For performance reasons, we recommend using the ALV layout (indicate this at the bottom of the selection screen in the Layout field). You can create the ALV layout in advance by selecting a small number of line items using the Maximum Number of Items selection field.

In the ALV list display you can use, among others, the following interactive buttons and functions:

▶ 🔢: Collectively modify the selected items.

▶ 🔲: Jump to the customer master data of the selected item.

▶ 🔽: Filter the selected items according to chosen fields.

▶ 🔲🔲🔲: Buttons to change, select, or save a layout.

▶ Σ: Use a field for totaling (only for currency and quantity fields).

▶ 🔳: Use the selected columns to calculate subtotals. The subtotals are in the order in which you selected the columns.

▶ EDIT • SELECT ALL: Mark all items displayed for further processing (e.g., for a mass change).

▶ EDIT • SUMMARIZATION LEVEL: Suppress some level of totalization (e.g., when you only need to see the total lines).

5.4.7 FAQ and Troubleshooting Tips

Next we answer some frequently asked questions and offer helpful troubleshooting tips.

FAQ

1. **Question**: Is it possible to enter a vendor account or an asset account in Transaction FB70?

   Answer: No. Transaction FB70 is designed to post one line item to a customer account (though if you use particular payment terms, the system can generate multiple line items with different due dates) and to general ledger accounts for all remaining lines. If you need to post a document with a different structure (e.g., if you want to include a vendor account in the subsequent lines), we suggest using Transaction F-22 where such limitations aren't present.

2. **Question**: Is there a different Enjoy transaction for posting customer invoices to specific ledgers?

   Answer: No. Outgoing invoices should be posted to all ledgers.

3. **Question**: Is there a transaction for clearing open items with the new SAP General Ledger?

   Answer: No. Use the same transactions as in the classic general ledger.

4. **Question**: When paying invoices automatically, some customers deduct the invoices they sent, posted in the vendor subledger. How can I clear the customer open items and the open items of the corresponding vendor together, if the business partner is both a customer and a vendor?

   Answer: When selecting open items, the system automatically proposes the vendor open items if, in the customer master data, the vendor is specified in the KNA1-LIFNR field, and if the Clearing with Vendor option is selected in the company code section of the customer master record (KNB1-XVERR).

5. **Question**: When will the down payment be cleared and appear in the cleared items instead of the open items?

   Answer: This will happen when the remaining amount in the down payment is assigned to an invoice.

6. **Question**: What is the meaning of the Amount and Available Amount columns in Transaction F-39?

   Answer: The Amount column displays the total amount of down payment posted with Transaction F-29. The Available Amount column displays the amount that hasn't yet been distributed to invoices in former postings.

7. **Question**: Not all of the document fields are available for selection in FBL1N or FBL5N. Can I add more fields?

   Answer: The fields available for selection come from Tables BSID/BSAD. However, you can add additional fields from Table BSEG via Transaction OBVU. Note that the selection will become slower, though.

Troubleshooting Tips

1. **Issue**: Error message F5555 appears: "Delete tax amount or don't let the system calculate the tax."

   Solution: This means that, in the customer line item, you've specified the tax amount and selected the Calculate Tax flag. This doesn't make sense. If you select the Calculate Tax flag, the system calculates the tax amount based on the tax code and amount of line items that don't refer to account types D (customer) or K (vendor) — you don't need to enter it manually.

2. **Issue**: Error message FF707 appears: "Tax entered incorrect...".

   Solution: This means that you've specified different tax amounts in the customer and revenue line items. Check the information you've entered. Was the total tax amount in the customer line item correct? Or was there a mistake in the line item information?

3. **Issue**: Error message F5118 appears: "Transaction key MWS XX chart of account CCCC not defined in table T030K."

   Solution: This means that tax code XX isn't linked to any general ledger account of chart of accounts CCCC. Select Transaction FTXP, enter the country to which the company code belongs, and enter the tax code XX. In the next screen, click on the Tax Accounts button, and enter the chart of accounts as CCCC and the tax general ledger account.

4. **Issue**: When I try to post a document to clear customer or vendor open items, some of my open items aren't selected and available for clearing.

   Solution: This is usually because the affected open items are contained in a payment run that still has a "proposal created" status. Use Transaction SE16, Table REGUS, to see the customer accounts blocked by one proposal. Then, from Table REGUP, you can use the payment run date and ID to see which invoices are blocked by the proposal.

   Then, either complete the proposal making the payment run in Transaction F110, or delete the proposal.

5. **Issue**: Some of my open items are displayed, but can't be activated or cleared.

   Solution: This usually happens when the open items have a payment block that is set to also work with the manual payment. If it's okay from a business point of view, you can sometimes remove the block and carry out the activity outside the workflow (it depends on the payment block configurations; see Section 5.3.3, Defining Payment Block Reasons, for more details).

6. **Issue**: When I post a payment, the system selects items in different currencies. How can I clear only items with the same currency?

Solution: First, specify the currency in the header data (e.g., USD). Then use the Additional Selections tool to use the document currency as a further selection criterion; specify only the currency. The correct foreign rate differences are posted in the local currency.

5.5   Accounts Payable Postings

In this section, we provide detailed instructions for the most common types of posting to vendors. In particular, you'll learn how to do the following:

- Post outgoing invoices and credit notes within Financial Accounting, both with classic and Enjoy transactions.
- Post outgoing automatic payments.

5.5.1   Financial Accounting Incoming Invoices

Quick Reference

Menu paths: ACCOUNTING • FINANCIAL ACCOUNTING • ACCOUNTS PAYABLE • DOCUMENT ENTRY • INVOICE

OR

ACCOUNTING • FINANCIAL ACCOUNTING • ACCOUNTS RECEIVABLE • DOCUMENT ENTRY • INVOICE – GENERAL

Transactions: FB60 (invoice), F-43 (invoice – general)

In general, posting incoming invoices is a step in invoice verification; use the logistic invoice verification transaction that allows you to recognize and manage any deviation between the invoice and the goods receipt, or between the invoice and the order. However, for some types of purchases, it's common to post incoming invoices directly into Financial Accounting. You may also do this if you don't have an integrated Materials Management/Financial Accounting solution.

The following two sections describe how to post an incoming invoice directly into Financial Accounting, through the classic transactions (F-43 or FB01), or through the more user-friendly Enjoy transaction (FB60).

Classic General Ledger Transaction (F-43)

The instructions for using Transaction F-43 are the same as those for Transaction FB01. First read Section 4.2.1, Posting with the Classic General Ledger, in Chapter 4, which contains only the specific instructions for using the classic transaction to post a vendor invoice directly into Financial Accounting.

In the header data, the document type is of particular importance; incoming invoices are generally posted with specific document types dedicated only to these types of transactions. The posting and document dates are usually not the same, unlike outgoing invoices; the document date corresponds to the date printed on the paper invoice, while the posting date corresponds to the date when the invoice was received. To ensure that an incoming invoice isn't posted twice, select the Check Double Invoice indicator (LFB1-REPRF) in the vendor master data, at the company code level. The system then issues a message if it finds that the following information matches:

► If the Reference Number field (which stores the number of the invoice as printed by the vendor) is filled in:
  ► Company code
  ► Vendor
  ► Currency
  ► Document date
  ► Reference number
► If the Reference Number field isn't filled in:
  ► Company code
  ► Vendor
  ► Currency
  ► Document date
  ► Amount in document currency

After the header information is entered, you can specify the line items, which include the vendor, cost, and tax lines line. In general, the first line is the vendor line. Then follow the same instructions we gave for using Transaction F-22, as discussed in the Classic General Ledger Transaction (F-22) section of Section 5.4.1, Financial Accounting Outgoing Invoices, and see Figures 5.74 and 5.75.

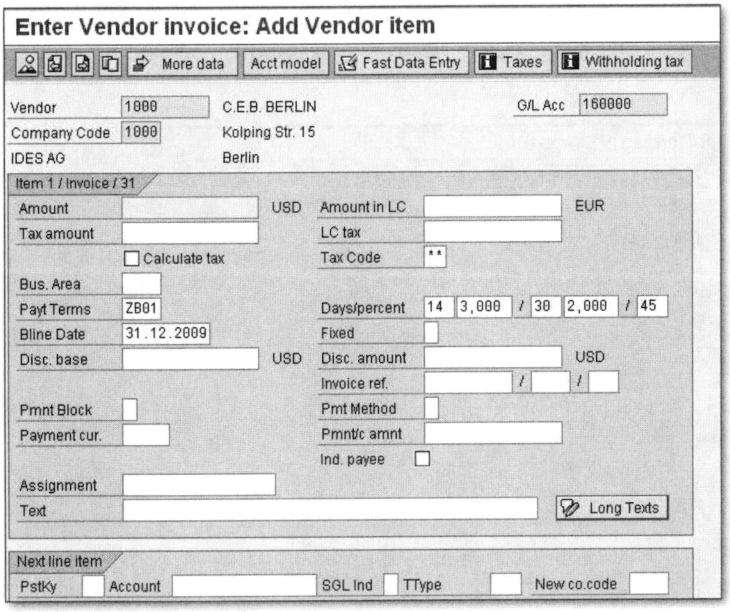

Figure 5.74   Vendor Item

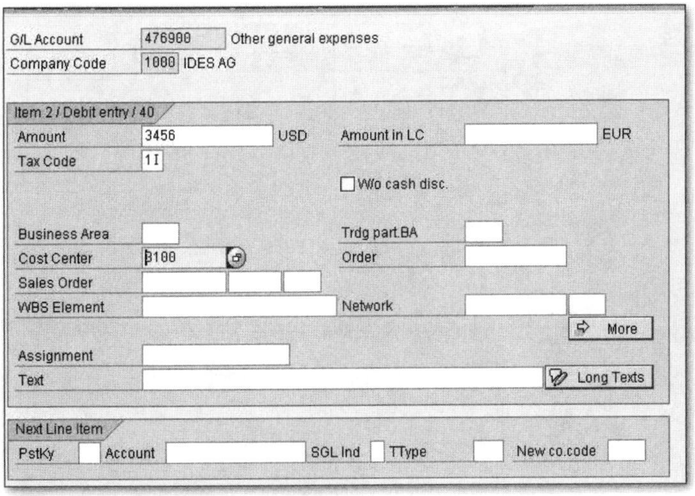

Figure 5.75   Cost Item

Enjoy Transaction (FB60)

The instructions for using Transaction FB60 are the same as the instructions for using Transaction FB70, which we discussed in the Enjoy Transaction (FB70) section of Section 5.4.1, Financial Accounting Outgoing Invoices. Refer to that section, as well as Figures 5.76, 5.77, and 5.78, for more details.

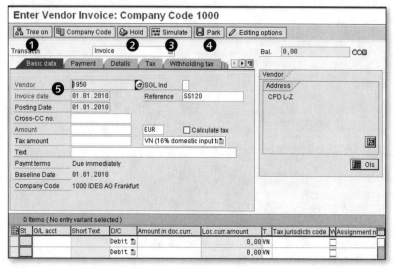

Figure 5.76 Vendor Invoice Header Data

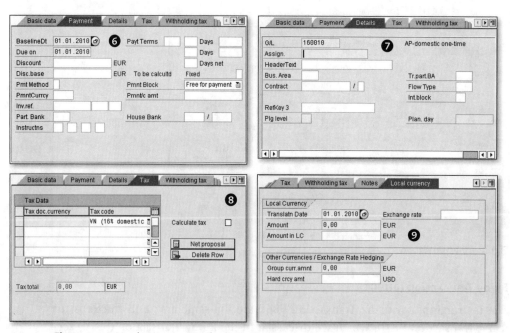

Figure 5.77 Vendor Invoice Header Data (Cont.)

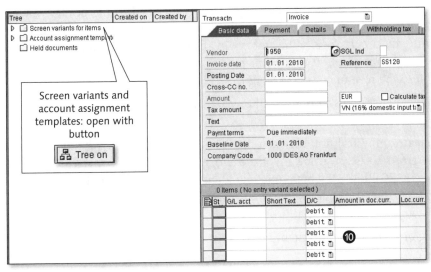

Figure 5.78 Screen Variants for FB60

Screen Variants for Transaction FB60

The screen variants that you define for Transactions FB50 and FB70 are also valid for Transaction FB60, and vice versa.

5.5.2 Financial Accounting Incoming Credit Memos

Quick Reference

Menu path: ACCOUNTING • FINANCIAL ACCOUNTING • ACCOUNTS PAYABLE • DOCUMENT ENTRY • CREDIT MEMO

OR

ACCOUNTING • FINANCIAL ACCOUNTING • ACCOUNTS PAYABLE • DOCUMENT ENTRY • CREDIT MEMO – GENERAL

Transactions: FB65 (credit memo), F-41 (credit memo – general)

When you create a credit memo within Financial Accounting, you can run Transaction FB65 (Enjoy) or Transaction F-41 (classic). Transaction FB65 works in the same way as Transaction FB60, and Transaction F-41 works in the same way as Transaction F-43. The only differences are as follows:

▶ When you use Transaction FB65, the amount specified in the header is automatically interpreted as negative and posted with posting key 21. In other words, you should specify the amount in absolute value, without any sign, and the system interprets it as a debit posting to the vendor. Remember to post credit to the revenue or cost account.

▶ When you use Transaction F-41, the system automatically proposes the posting key 31 in the first row.

▶ To create a physical link between the credit note and the invoice (if the credit note refers to exactly one invoice item), you can use the Invoice Reference fields (BSEG-REBZG), which uniquely identify one vendor line item in the system (the company code is the same). The three boxes should be filled with the following information, in this order:

  ▶ Invoice reference document number

  ▶ Invoice reference year

  ▶ Invoice reference line item

As a result, the net due date is copied from the reference invoice to the baseline date of the referred credit memo; when you run the automatic payment transaction, the amount of the credit note is automatically deducted from the amount of the reference invoice.

5.5.3 Automatic Outgoing Payments

> **Quick Reference**
>
> **Menu path**: ACCOUNTING • FINANCIAL ACCOUNTING • ACCOUNTS PAYABLE • PERIODIC PROCESSING • PAYMENTS
>
> **Transaction**: F110
>
> **Program**: SAPF110V
>
> **Tables**: REGUH (header of payments), REGUP (line items (paid) or each payment), REGUS (accounts blocked by payment proposal)

To use program F110, you need to perform the step-by-step configuration of this functionally, as described in Section 5.3.4, Configuring Automatic Payments.

The automatic payment run involves the following major steps:

1. Filling in the selection screen and the parameters

2. Running, reviewing, and, if necessary, modifying, deleting, or rerunning the payment proposal

3. Running the payment and the printout

Filling Selection Screen and Parameters

To begin, create a unique ID for your new payment run (Figure 5.79), which is identified by the following:

▶ Run Date

▶ Identification (alphanumeric, five digits)

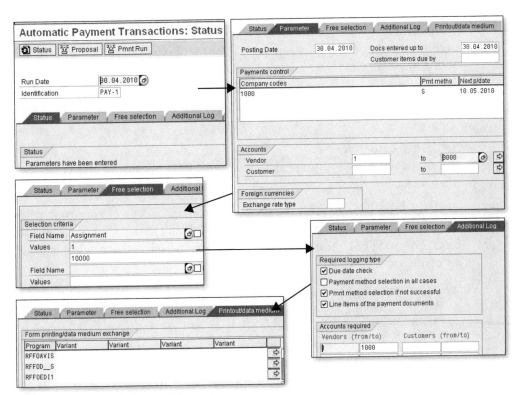

Figure 5.79 Automatic Payment Parameters

In the Parameter tab, specify the following:

▶ **Posting Date**
This is the posting date of the payment document and the clearing date of the items that are paid in the run.

- ▶ **Documents Entered Up To**
  This is the latest entry date (BKPF-CPUDT) a document can have for it to be included in the run.

- ▶ **Company Codes**
  Specify one or more sending company codes (separated by commas).

- ▶ **Pmt Meths**
  Select one or more from the matchcode. All of the invoices that can't be paid through the method but that are selected with other criteria, finish in the exception list (they aren't excluded by the run).

- ▶ **Next P/Date**
  Specify the next payment date. All invoices with due dates after this date (plus the tolerance days defined at the company code level in FBZP), or that lose cash discounts (according to the rules defined in FBZP for the company code), are included in the run. Other items are excluded and not displayed in the exception list.

- ▶ **Vendor**
  In this field, enter vendors to be included in the run. You can't leave the field empty.

- ▶ **Exchange Rate Type**
  Specify whether the posting has to be done with an exchange rate type other than M (or EURX).

In the Free Selection tab, you can restrict the selection of open items using fields belonging to the document tables (BKPF and BSEG) and to the vendor master data tables (LFA1 and LFB1). You can use up to three fields. Select the matchcode to see a list of all available fields.

In the Additional Log tab, you can choose to see an extended log on the payment run. Without selecting one or more of the additional logs available, the log provided by the run is quite poor, and it can become very difficult to correct errors. You can freely select the four logs; however, the system doesn't allow you to select the Payment Method Selection In All Cases flag at the same time as the Payment Method Selection If Not Successful flag. Remember to specify the vendors for which the log is valid.

In the Printout/Data Medium tab, specify the variant for the programs that create a DME file (a file that you can send to the bank and that has a specific format in different countries and bank systems), print the payment advices, and print checks. You can't freely enter the name of the program here because it comes from the payment configuration performed in FBZP.

On the bottom of the screen, you can add additional programs and variants for the payment proposal list.

Running the Payment Proposal

When all of the parameters are ready, save them and click the Proposal button (Proposal). The program only runs in background, and you can decide to schedule the run at a specific time or to make it run immediately by selecting the Start Immediately flag in the pop-up shown in Figure 5.80.

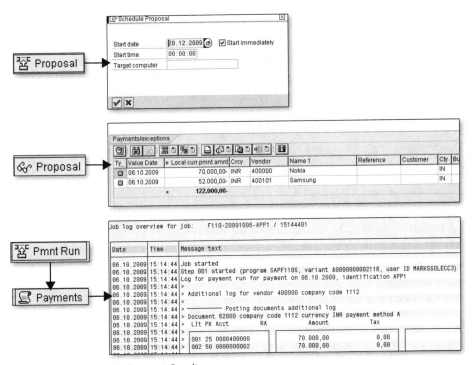

Figure 5.80 Automatic Payment Result

After the job starts, you can update the status simply by pressing Enter or by clicking on the Status button. When the job finishes, the system has created a payment proposal only; no document has been posted, and no items have been cleared. However, the vendor open items contained in the payment proposal can no longer be included in another payment proposal, nor can they be cleared manually; they are locked by the payment proposal. This lock disappears if you delete the payment proposal or if the payment is finally executed.

To see the proposal, click on the Proposal button (🔍 Proposal); the system lists the proposed payments with a green icon. As more than one vendor open item can be grouped into a payment, you must double-click a single payment to have a list of the open item contained in the payment. The payments displayed in red are in the exception list (again, double-click to see the open items contained); they can't be paid. To understand why, click on the Proposal button (💲 Proposal), and search for the specific vendor or document number with the Search button (🔍).

You can also change the proposal with the Proposal button (✏️ Proposal). If you want to include an open item that is in the exception list into a payment, double-click the item. The system displays all of the vendor open items; mark one item, and click on the Change button. Remove the payment block, if allowed (this is a customizing setting of the block); then, in the following pop-up, click on the Real-locate button, and assign the open item to an existing payment for the same vendor (this is possible only if some invoices in the proposal have been successfully selected in the same proposal), or assign it to a combination of payment methods, house banks, and house bank accounts by selecting the New Payment button. The combination you enter here must be defined and assigned to a general ledger account in FBZP (the customizing of the automatic payments).

If you want to remove some invoices, double-click the item, and then double-click one of the open items contained. You can set the payment block, which reduces the payment amount by the amount of the newly excluded invoice. If you want to reassign the entire payment to a different combination of payment methods, house banks, and house bank accounts, select the payment item (not one of the open items included), and click on the Change button; then specify a new combination that must be valid according to the customizing in FBZP (bank determination).

If you want to delete the proposal and recreate it again (e.g., because you've changed something in customizing or in the vendor master data), select EDIT • PROPOSAL • DELETE, and reprocess the proposal from the beginning, changing the selection parameters, if necessary.

After the proposal contains all of the items you want to pay, you can perform the payment run (Figure 5.80). Click the Status tab, and then click on the Pmnt Run button (🏃 Pmnt Run). The system opens a pop-up similar to the one of the payment proposal, where you can trigger the job that performs the payment run. You can choose between scheduling the job for later or running the job immediately. After the job starts, you can update the status simply by pressing Enter or by clicking on the Status button.

As a result of the payment run, all payments listed in the proposal are carried out, the posting documents are created, and the open items are cleared. However, at this stage, only the SAP booking is updated; the information about the payment to be performed is still within SAP and hasn't yet been communicated to the bank. Click on the Payments button (⬛ Payments) to see a log of the payment run; the log is similar to the one for the payment proposal, but it also displays the document numbers created (as shown in the bottom of Figure 5.80).

To communicate payment information to a bank and give the instructions necessary to actually carry out a payment to the vendor, it's generally necessary to extract a payment file (also known as a DME file) created according to a specific record description provided by your bank. SAP provides standard programs (starting with "RFFO...") specific for each country and bank system. Check to see if there is a standard program, and, if necessary, make a copy to adapt it to your specific requirements. Assign the program to the payment method using Transaction FBZP, in the Payment Method in the Country section. Alternatively, you can use the DME engine tool.

To create the DME file (if the payment method is set up to generate a DME file), click on the Printout button, and schedule the related job. To see the DME file, select ENVIRONMENT • PAYMENT MEDIUM • DME ADMINISTRATION. This result in a list of the files created with the payment run. Select one file, and click the Download button (🖹) to export the file to your local PC. If you need to automatically transfer the file to your banking system, speak with your Basis colleagues.

SAP also provides standard program RFFOUS_C for printing checks in the US.

5.5.4 FAQ and Troubleshooting Tips

Next we answer some frequently asked questions and offer a helpful troubleshooting tip.

FAQ

1. **Question**: When items are included in a payment proposal, they can't be cleared or included in another proposal. Is this true for both the items in the proposal and those in the exception list?

   Answer: No; this isn't true for the items in the exception list.

2. **Question**: Is there a standard workflow to transfer the DME file from the SAP server to the banking system?

Answer: No. Check with your workflow expert to see if it's possible to build a user-defined workflow.

3. **Question**: Is it possible to pay down payments with the automatic payment program? I need to pay a specific amount but haven't yet received an invoice.

   Answer: Yes. You can create noted items with an appropriate special general ledger indicator. The special general ledger indicator must be able to be paid in the company code configuration.

Troubleshooting Tip

1. **Issue**: The payment proposal could not be carried out.

   Solution: Check the log. For example, you may see the following message: "For company code XXXX posting period PP/YYYY has not been opened." In this case, simply use Transaction OB52 to open the posting period (if correct). Then delete the payment proposal and run it again.

5.6 Accounts Receivable and Accounts Payable Period-End Functions

In this section, we explain how to carry out the most common period-end functionalities within Accounts Payable and Accounts Receivable accounting:

▶ Automatic clearing of customer and vendor open items

▶ Dunning the customers that are late with payments

▶ Calculating and invoicing interest for invoices not paid at the due date

▶ Revaluating customer and vendor open items in foreign currencies

5.6.1 Automatically Clearing Open Items

Quick Reference

Menu path: ACCOUNTING • FINANCIAL ACCOUNTING • GENERAL LEDGER • PERIODIC PROCESSING • AUTOMATIC CLEARING

Transactions: F.13 (without specification of clearing currency), F13E (with specification of clearing currency)

Program: SAPF124 (in Transaction F.13, the clearing currency isn't displayed and therefore can't be selected)

To automatically clear open items, use program SAPF124. It's common practice to schedule the program as a daily night job. In the selection screen (Figure 5.81), specify the following main parameters:

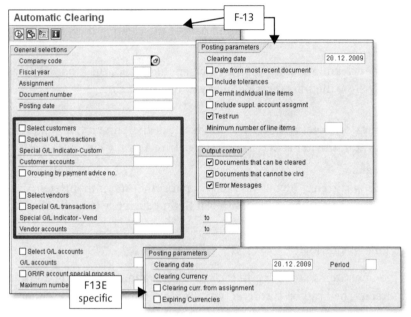

Figure 5.81 Open Item Clearing Selection Screen

▶ **Company Code, Fiscal Year, Assignment, Document Number, and Posting Date**
If you're performing a mass clearing in a scheduled run, just the company code and posting date are sufficient. Use the other parameters for targeted runs.

▶ **Select Customers, Select Vendors, Select G/L Accounts**
Select the Select Customers indicator to run the clearing on customer open items; if you want to restrict the selection only to specific customer accounts, specify the accounts using the Customer Accounts field.

Select the Select Vendors indicator to run the clearing on vendor open items; if you want to restrict the selection only to specific vendor accounts, specify the accounts using the Vendor Accounts field.

You can include customer, vendor, and general ledger account open items in the same run; to also include general ledger accounts open items, select the Select G/L Accounts indicator.

When selecting vendor and customer open items, explicitly specify whether you want to clear special general ledger transactions.

▶ **Clearing Date/Date From Most Recent Document**
Specify the clearing date or, alternatively, select the Date From Most Recent Document flag. If you do the latter, the latest posting date of the cleared items becomes the clearing date and the posting date of the clearing document.

▶ **Include Tolerances**
Specify whether clearing can be performed when the total of the grouped items isn't zero but below the tolerances defined when customizing.

▶ **Test Run**
Select this indicator to get a preview of the result of the program; if you don't select the indicator, the items that can be cleared are actually cleared.

▶ **Clearing Currency**
Specify a clearing currency if you want to group together items in different currencies, and then convert the amount into a different currency (i.e., the clearing currency).

The program follows this logic:

1. It selects the open items according to the selection parameters specified in the selection screen. They can be customer, vendor, or general ledger open items.

2. The open items are grouped according to the following criteria:
   ▶ Company code
   ▶ Currency (only if the clearing currency isn't selected)
   ▶ Customer, vendor, or general ledger account
   ▶ Reconciliation account
   ▶ Special general ledger indicator

   All further grouping criteria are specified in Table TF123 (the more criteria specified in Table TF123, the smaller the number of items grouped together will be).

3. The items grouped together are summarized in the document currency or in the clearing currency (if specified). If the amount is zero, they are cleared. If it isn't zero, they aren't cleared, unless you've selected the Include Tolerances flag; in this case, the clearing can be done if the difference is below the tolerances defined. The difference is posted against the clearing difference account.

If the clearing currency is also the local currency, the amount in the local currency is recalculated. However, if the No Forex Rate Diff. When Clearing in LC indicator is set in the company code global settings (field T001-XSLTA), the original value is used instead. (By "original value," we mean the amount in the local currency specified at the time of the posting and recorded in the database in field BSEG-DMBTR.)

In the output list, the system displays a summarized statistic of the selected and cleared items. In addition, it's possible to see the following:

▶ A detailed list of the cleared items, if you select the Documents That Can Be Cleared indicator (at the bottom of the selection screen).

▶ A detailed list of the items that can't be cleared, if you select the Documents That Cannot Be Clrd indicator (at the bottom of the selection screen).

▶ A list of the error messages related to the items that can't be cleared, if you select the Error Messages indicator.

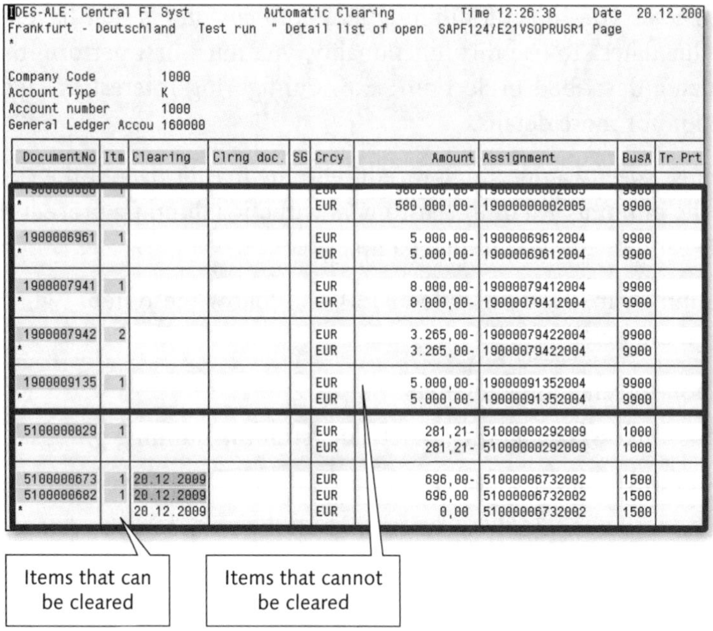

Figure 5.82 Automatic Clearing Result

Figure 5.82 shows a detailed list issued by the program; the items grouped together are summarized, and, if they can be cleared, the clearing date and clearing document (not displayed if in test mode) are displayed in green. At the end of the list, some error messages can be displayed; for example, an error message saying that items in a foreign currency aren't cleared because the exchange difference accounts aren't specified in Table T030H or Table T030HB (relevant only for SAP General Ledger if you use a valuation area).

5.6.2 Dunning

Quick Reference

Menu path: ACCOUNTING • FINANCIAL ACCOUNTING • ACCOUNTS RECEIVABLE • PERIODIC PROCESSING • DUNNING

Transaction: F150

Program: SAPF150V

Tables: MHND (dunning data at customer level), MHNK (dunning data at document level), MAHNS (accounts blocked by the dunning selection)

Transaction F150 allows you to send dunning letters to customers that haven't paid within their due dates. To use this functionality, you must first perform the necessary customizing described in Section 5.3.6, Configuring Interest Calculations; see that section for more details.

In addition, you must specify a dunning procedure in the master data of the customers subject to the dunning. All of the customers without a dunning procedure in a company code can't be dunned in that company code.

To perform the dunning run, use Transaction F150, and follow these steps (which we then discuss in more detail):

1. Fill in the selection screen and parameters.
2. Run, review, and, if necessary, modify, delete, or rerun the dunning proposal.
3. Make a test print of the dunning letters.
4. Make a productive test of the dunning letters, and, at the same time, update the customer master records and the dunned open items.

Filling the Selection Screen and Parameters

Begin by creating a unique identification for your new dunning run (Figure 5.83). This is identified by the following fields:

▶ Run Date

▶ Identification (alphanumeric, six digits)

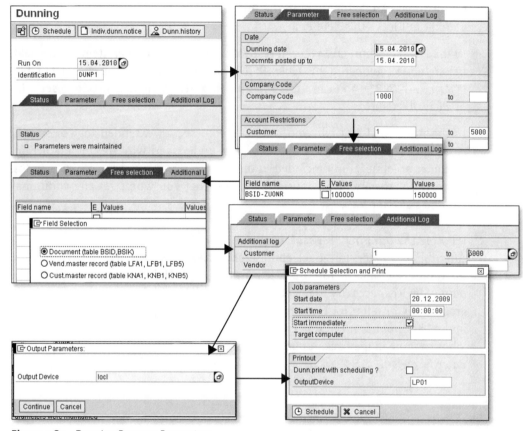

Figure 5.83 Dunning Program Parameters

In the Parameter tab, specify the following:

▶ **Dunning Date**
This is the date of the dunning letters and the date up to which the days in arrears are calculated (in other words, the date on which the number of days that the payment is late is calculated).

▶ **Documents Posted Up To**
This is the latest posting date (BKPF-BUDAT) that a document can have to be included in the run. Unlike the automatic payment run, this date doesn't refer to the entry date but to the posting date.

▶ **Company Code**
Specify one or more company codes; of course, the dunning letters are created separately for each company code.

▶ **Customers To Be Included in the Run**
You can't leave this field empty.

In the Free Selection tab, you can restrict the selection of open items using fields belonging to the open items table (BSID) and to the customer master data tables (KNA1 and KNB1). You can use up to 20 fields. Select the matchcode to see a list of all available fields.

In the Additional Log tab, you can choose to see an extended log for specific customers. The extended log allows you to understand why specific invoices or customer accounts aren't included in the dunning, as expected. Note that, in this context, not specifying any customer means that you won't get any additional, customer-specific logs.

Running the Dunning Proposal

After the parameters in the selection screens have been completed, you can create the dunning proposal. To do this, click on the Schedule button, and specify the output device (necessary to format the dunning list) and the start date of the background job (or tell it to run immediately). The dunning program can only be run in the background; it can't be run online. When you've run the proposal and the job is running in the background, you can refresh the status of the job by pressing Enter (see Figure 5.84).

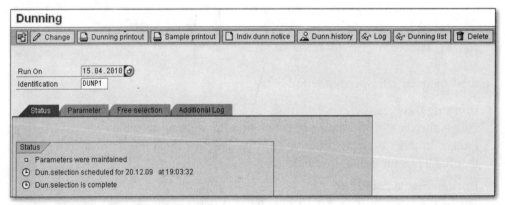

Figure 5.84 Dunning Program Status

You can also choose to immediately perform the dunning printout and therefore the generation of the dunning letters. To do this, select the Dunning Print with Scheduling flag. (The dunning print is the productive one, not the test one.) If you select this flag, the proposal is no longer modifiable, and the customer accounts and documents are updated with the dunning information. For our example, we assume that you haven't selected the productive dunning print flag and that you can still modify or delete the dunning run.

To see the content of the dunning run click on the Dunning List button (Dunning list). The system automatically proposes the program RFMAHN21. You can specify the output variant (if you leave it empty, a default ALV list is used).

The dunning list displays all of the documents selected in the run. Some of them will be dunned, and others won't be (e.g., perhaps because some of them have a dunning block). We recommend that you customize a list in which the following fields are shown both if a customer account is dunned and if a specific document is dunned:

- **Ind: Account Is Dunned**
  In this field, you'll see an "X" if the customer account is to be dunned; if the field is empty, it means that the customer has been selected in the dunning run, but for some reason, no dunning letter will be produced (e.g., you might have set a dunning block at customer level).

- **Document To Be Dunned**
  In this field, you'll see an "X" if a specific customer open item is to be dunned; if the field is empty, it means that for some reason, the document won't be included in the dunning letter (e.g., you might have set a dunning block at the document level).

The list is made of a header section, which contains the information about the customer and the dunning level of the letter (if dunned), and a line item section, which contains a list of all of the documents that will be dunned for the combination of customer and dunning level.

To understand why some documents aren't being dunned, click on the Log button. Following are the main reasons why a customer is excluded from a dunning run:

- The customer is blocked for dunning in the master data (company code level, Communications section).

- The customer has no dunning procedure specified in the master record.

▶ The last dunning for the account was not older than the minimum number of days between the dunning runs (specified in the customizing of the dunning procedure).

Following are the main reasons why some documents (or, to be more precise, some open items) aren't included in the dunning:

▶ The line item has been cleared.

▶ The line item has a dunning block.

▶ The number of overdue days (taking into consideration the tolerances defined in the customizing of the dunning procedure) is less than the minimum defined in customizing.

If you want to modify the parameters and regenerate the proposal, you must first delete it using the Delete button. You can't perform this step if you've already run the dunning printout (not the sample printout).

If you want to change the proposal dunning, click on the Change button and then specify, if needed, some criteria in the selection screen. Click the Execute button (⊕). In the next screen, the system shows a list with all of the items included in each dunning notice (or excluded items). Select a dunning notice (or documents excluded from the dunning), marking the field and clicking on the Change Dunning Notice button. In the following screen, you can block or unblock a customer and include or exclude single documents. Note that everything you do in this specific function won't change the customer master data or the single items but will remain "internal" in the dunning run. To change a customer master record, use the Change Master Data button; in this case, you're directly changing the customer master data.

Test Printing Dunning Letters

To perform a test print of the dunning, select the Sample Printout button. You can perform this function many times. The dunning run remains modifiable, and the dunning information (last dunning run and dunning level) aren't updated in the customer master data or in the documents.

Productive Printing of Dunning Letters

If you don't want to make any further modification of the dunning run, and you're ready to generate the dunning letters, click on the Dunning Printout button. The system asks for the printer, date, and time to run the job, or allows you to run the job immediately. The job generates the dunning letters and updates the customer master data in the Last Dunned fields (with the date of the dunning run) and the Dunning Level (the latest in the dunning run). It also updates the dunned items with the date of the dunning run and the dunning level reached.

5.6.3 Calculating Interest and Invoicing

Quick Reference
Menu path: ACCOUNTING • FINANCIAL ACCOUNTING • ACCOUNTS RECEIVABLE • PERIODIC PROCESSING • INTEREST CALCULATION • ITEM INTEREST CALCULATION
Transactions: FINT (item interest calculation), FINTSHOW (interest run display)
Program: RFINTITAR
Tables: INTITHE and INTITIT

When an invoice isn't paid by a customer at the due date, you can charge the invoice with interest costs, provided it's allowed by local law and by a specific agreement between your company and the customer. Use Transaction FINT to calculate the interest and generate and post the interest invoice.

Interest can be calculated on the following:

- Overdue open items
- Cleared items with a payment transaction that occurred after the due date
- Overdue cleared items

The way the system chooses these categories depends on the interest indicator. Set the interest indicator in each customer master record; if no indicator is specified in the master record, no interest is calculated for the items.

In the selection screen of Transaction FINT, you must specify the following main parameters (Figure 5.85).

- **Customer Account and Company Code**
  If you leave these fields blank, the program calculates the interest for all customers in all company codes.
- **Interest Indicator**
  Specify something here if you want to restrict the run to customers that have specific interest indicators in the master data (e.g., you may have different indicators, and thus different calculation rules, for national and foreign customers).

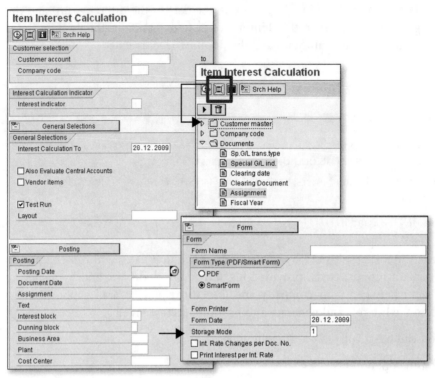

Figure 5.85 Interest Calculation Selection Screen

▶ **Interest Calculation To**
This is the date used as a reference for calculating days in arrears. Only items with posting dates prior to this date are selected. If they are open items, they must be overdue before this date; otherwise, they are excluded.

▶ **Test Run**
Select this flag if you don't want to generate or post interest invoices.

▶ **Posting Date and Document Date**
These are the dates written in the corresponding fields in the Financial Accounting document. There is no control in the system to ensure that these dates are the same as those in the Interest Calculation To and From Date fields; as such, we recommend creating a suitable variant where the dates are unchangeable and automatically set as the entry date, using the variable function.

▶ **Cost Center**
If you post the interest revenue to a P&L account, here is where you specify a cost center.

▶ **Form Type**

Here you can select a PDF or SAP Smart Form. Specify the name and the form date. Usually the form date is the date of the invoice; however, this depends on how the form has been created.

You can use dynamic selections to further restrict the selection of the customers or of the items (the right side of Figure 5.85).

When you run the program, the items of customers with interest indicators are selected according to the customizing specification of each interest indicator. The interest is calculated, and the items are grouped together to generate the relevant interest invoices. In the resulting screen, the system displays any errors encountered. In the following screen, the complete list of the selected items is displayed. Those marked in red could not generate an interest calculation for a specific error; those marked in yellow appear just in the test run and are okay for the interest invoice; those marked in green will appear just in the productive run and are cleared for the interest and included in one invoice.

Document Generation

Posting takes place online without generating any batch-input invoices. The system immediately displays the document number, which means that the document number can also be picked up in the SAP Smart Form or PDF.

You can see an example of a generated list in Figure 5.86.

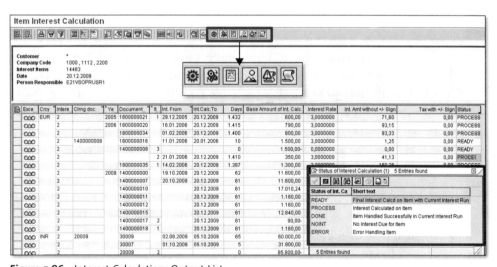

Figure 5.86 Interest Calculation: Output List

The list shown in Figure 5.86, is interactive, and the following buttons have specific functions within the list:

▶ ⚙: Generates and prints an invoice for items that you've specifically marked in the list. This also generates the Financial Accounting document for the specific items.

▶ 🐾: Generates all forms for all items in the list. This also generates the Financial Accounting document for the specific items.

▶ 📄: Creates a print preview of an invoice for selected items.

▶ ⚖: Generates a print preview for all invoices in the list.

▶ 📠: Creates an error log.

▶ 🖥: Creates an extended log for all items in the list; this log shows you the complete logic, followed by the calculation of the interest.

5.6.4 Foreign Currency Valuation

Quick Reference

Menu path: Accounting • Financial Accounting • General Ledger • Periodic Processing • Closing • Valuate • Foreign Currency Valuation

Transactions: F.05 (if the new SAP General ledger isn't activated), FAGL_FC_VAL (if the new SAP General Ledger is activated)

Programs: SAPF100 (if the new SAP General Ledger isn't activated), FAGL_FC_VALUATION (if the new SAP General Ledger is activated)

When you run the program to revaluate open items in a foreign currency, you must use one of the two different transactions listed in the Quick Reference box, depending on whether you've activated the new SAP General Ledger. The selection screen of the two programs is exactly the same; however, Transaction FAGL_FC_VAL can post different values to different ledgers. This is accomplished via the connection of the valuation area to the ledger group.

Here we describe the functionality based on Transaction FAGL_FC_VAL; we'll specifically explain when the use of Transaction F.05 differs.

▶ **General Data Selection area** (❶ of Figure 5.87)
When running the exchange rate revaluation, you must first specify the company code (one or more) and the valuation key date. The valuation key date is necessary to identify the items that should be processed:

- ▸ The open items with a posting date up to the valuation key date
- ▸ The cleared items with a clearing date later than the valuation key date (i.e., items that were open at the date of the valuation)

In addition, specify the valuation area that should determine the valuation method and the ledgers to be posted (if you use Transaction F.05, you must directly specify the valuation method). The valuation method controls the document type, the exchange rate type, and other important parameters of the function.

- ▸ **Postings tab (❷ of Figure 5.87)**
  In the Postings tab of the selection screen, select the Create Posting flag, which specifies that you're running the program to create a posting, and not in the test mode. Specify the parameter for the posting and the reversal. Note that in the new SAP General Ledger environment, you can no longer run the program without reversal. In other words, there is *no delta mode*, which is when the system remembers the valuations already made in the past, and posts only the delta necessary to adapt the values of the already revaluated items to the new revaluated value. This option is possible only within the classic general ledger by selecting the Balance Sheet Preparation Valuation flag.

- ▸ **Open Items tab (❸ of Figure 5.87)**
  This can be used to revaluate customers, vendors, and general ledger open items (if managed on an open items basis) posted in foreign currencies. You can make an overall run or split the run into separate sessions to separately process, for example, customers, vendors, and general ledger items. You can also select or exclude specific business partners, reconciliation accounts, documents, and currencies.

- ▸ **Miscellaneous tab (❹ of Figure 5.87)**
  In this tab, you can specify and configure the list variants for open items. The system first issues a list with all open items selected, and their relevant valuation; this is the list that you can configure here. A second list is displayed with the postings. This list can be configured but not in the selection screen.

When running in test mode, the system displays a list of all items to be valuated, and compares the historic value with the revaluated value. When running the system in productive mode, we strongly recommend that you save the list in an Excel file as an audit trail for the postings made.

Clicking on the Postings button (Figure 5.88) gives you a preview of the postings to be made. If you run the program in productive mode, the system also shows the document number and whether the postings were successful; if any errors occurred, the postings are placed in a batch input session.

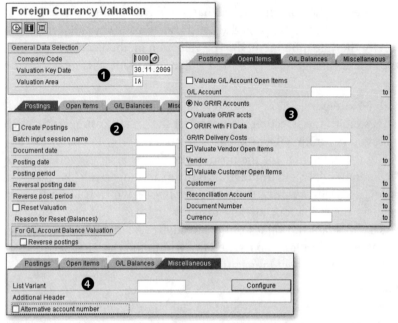

Figure 5.87 Foreign Currency Valuation Selection Screen

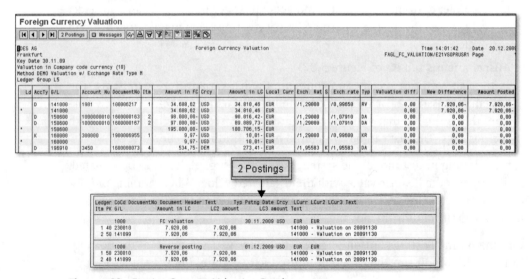

Figure 5.88 Foreign Currency Valuation Result

Clicking the Messages button shows you the error (red), warning (yellow), and information (green) messages issued by the run. We recommend first running the program in test mode and carefully reading all error message issued. Then make the necessary corrections (a typical example is accounts missing in Table T030H or T030HB) and rerun the program in test mode until all of the errors have disappeared. Then run the program in productive mode.

5.6.5 FAQ and Troubleshooting Tips

Next we answer a frequently asked question and offer helpful troubleshooting tips.

FAQ

1. **Question**: How can I create a SAP Smart Form? A PDF?

   Answer: To create a SAP Smart Form, use Transaction SMARTFORMS (you can use the standard form F_INTITAR_SF as a template to copy and adapt). To create a PDF, use Transaction SPF. Work with an ABAP developer to build a form that meets your requirements.

Troubleshooting Tips

1. **Issue**: The following error message appears: "Account was selected, but is not entered in Table TF123."

   Solution: This means that there are no clearing rules defined in Table TF123 for the specific account. Carry out the relevant customizing using Transaction OB74.

2. **Issue**: Error message MSINT177 appears: "Maintain the Customizing for the new interest program."

   Solution: This means that entries in Table T056UX are missing. Run SM30 and view V_ T056UX.

3. **Issue**: Error message MSINT361 appears: "No time-dependent conditions for II/EUR/Cred. Int. Rate/from DD.MM.YYYY."

   Solution: Specify the interest rate for the interest indicator, the currency, and the specific validity date in Transaction OB81.

4. **Issue**: Error message FR606 appears: "Company code XXXX is in new general ledger; use transaction FAGL_FC_VAL."

Solution: You're using Transaction F.05 on company codes that use the new SAP General Ledger. In this environment, Transaction FAGL_FC_VAL is designed to carry out the valuation according to the valuation areas configuration. Use the new transaction instead.

5. **Issue**: I need to rerun the valuation program because the exchange rates were incorrectly defined.

   Solution: First run the program with the Reset Valuation flag. Then rerun the valuation.

6. **Issue**: The program has created a batch input session, but the account is listed as "missing."

   Solution: This means that the account determination for the account to be valuated is missing. Check and customize Table T030H or, in the new SAP General Ledger, Table T030HB. Associate the valuation accounts to the account to be valuated.

5.7 Summary

The chapter focused on configuring and using the Accounts Payable and Accounts Receivable submodules of Financial Accounting. We discussed customer and vendor master data configuration and management, customer and vendor posting configuration and execution, plus the most common period-end functionalities. In the next chapter, we discuss another submodule of Financial Accounting, Asset Accounting.

Every company owns fixed assets, which are assets that will be used in the production process for many years. The Asset Accounting component is designed to support the automated handling of assets throughout their lifetime in a company.

6   Asset Accounting

This chapter is divided into five main sections that go through the steps in configuring the Asset Accounting submodule and main functions provided by SAP to manage the fixed assets of your company. In Section 6.1, Configuring Asset Accounting, you learn the main objects that need to be configured to run Asset Accounting. Section 6.2, Asset Master Data Management, is about the functionalities used to manage asset master data, including advanced tools such as validations and mass changes. In Section 6.3, Posting Transactions to Assets, we describe the principal transactions that can affect the life of an asset. In Section 6.4, Depreciation and Other Periodic Postings, the focus is on the periodic activities in Asset Accounting, with special attention dedicated to depreciation. Finally, in Section 6.5, Year-End Activities, we discuss the year-end activities for the Asset Accounting submodule.

6.1   Configuring Asset Accounting

The main steps necessary to have an Asset Accounting submodule ready to run are discussed in detail in this section. You'll find instructions to customize the following objects:

- ▶ Chart of depreciation
- ▶ Asset classes
- ▶ Number ranges for asset master data
- ▶ Account determination
- ▶ Screen layout rules
- ▶ Evaluation groups

- ▸ Validation, substitutions, and enhancements

- ▸ Depreciation areas

- ▸ Posting key and document types for asset postings

- ▸ Depreciation keys

- ▸ Activation of Controlling objects for Asset Accounting postings

- ▸ Posting rules for depreciation

- ▸ Transaction types

- ▸ Asset history sheet

6.1.1 Copying Charts of Depreciation

Quick Reference

Menu path: IMG • Financial Accounting • Asset Accounting • Organizational Structure • Copy Reference Chart of Depreciation/Depreciation Areas

Transaction: EC08

Table/view: T096/V_T096_00

The chart of depreciation is the main organizational structure in Asset Accounting; it stores most of the Asset Accounting configuration. You assign each company code to exactly one chart of depreciation, and there are two types of charts of depreciation:

- ▸ **Standard**
  Standard charts of depreciation are provided by SAP, and their names always start with 0. For example, chart of depreciation 0AT is the chart that SAP has created for companies located in Austria. Standard charts of depreciation cannot be assigned to company codes, but only used as a template to create user-defined chart of depreciations.

- ▸ **User-defined charts of depreciation**
  User-defined charts of depreciation are created by copying a standard chart and making edits; you can't create a chart of depreciation from scratch.

You can create, change, and assign user-defined charts of depreciation (not standard charts of depreciation) to company codes. To do this, run Transaction EC08, and follow these steps (see Figure 6.1):

1. Click on the Copy Org. Object button (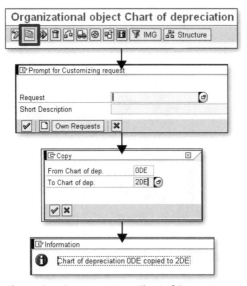).

2. Specify both the chart of depreciation to be copied and the new chart of depreciation, following your naming convention.

3. Confirm your choice.

4. Specify a transport request, and click the Continue button (✔). The system copies all customizing entries that depend on the chart of depreciation.

Figure 6.1 Creating a New Chart of Depreciation

If you want to delete an incorrectly created chart of depreciation, execute Transaction EC08, and click the Delete button (🗑). Never perform this step for a chart of depreciation already assigned to a company code or for which data has already been created. The reassignment of company codes to a different chart of depreciation can be managed only within the framework of a project, not as a maintenance activity.

Table 6.1 shows which main customizing objects in Asset Accounting depend on the chart of depreciation.

Customizing Object	Dependent on Chart of Depreciation	Independent of Chart of Depreciation
Asset classes		X
Account determination keys		X
Depreciation areas	X	
Depreciation keys	X	
Insurance types		X
Integration with SAP General Ledger (rules and accounts)	X	
Investment measures	X	
Leasing keys		X
Posting keys used for depreciation or transaction postings		X
Revaluation measures	X	
Screen layout rules		X
Transaction types		X

Table 6.1 Asset Accounting Customizing Objects and Dependency on the Chart of Depreciation

6.1.2 Setting the Chart of Depreciation for Customizing

Quick Reference

Menu path: IMG • Financial Accounting • Asset Accounting • Valuation • Set Chart of Depreciation

Transaction: OAPL

When you work with Asset Accounting customizing, the system asks you to specify a chart of depreciation and remembers this specification for all your working sessions. This means that every time the customizing is dependent on the chart of depreciation, you continue to work within the specified chart of depreciation. If, at any time, you want to work with another chart of depreciation, use Transaction OAPL to specify the new one (Figure 6.2).

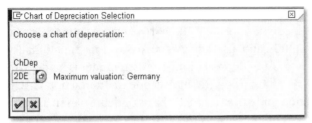

Figure 6.2 Setting the Chart of Depreciation for Customizing Activities

6.1.3 Assigning Charts of Depreciation

Change View "Maintain company code in Asset Accounting": Overview

CoCd	Company Name	Chrt dep	Description
1100	AS INC LTD	1US	Sample chart of depreciation: USA
1111	Renz Masterbind Pty Ltd		
1112	BIRLA SUGAR LTD	COD2	Chart of depreciation for 1112
1113	PATEL MACHINERY LTD		
1500	AAIDES US INC		
1807	Anusree Industries Inc.		
1ABC	1abc pvt ltd	COD1	chart of depreciation for india
2000	IDES UK	1GB	Sample chart of depreciation: Great Britain
2100	IDES Portugal	1DE	Sample chart of depreciation: Germany
2200	IDES France	1FR	Sample chart of depreciation: France
2201	IDES France affiliate	1FR	Sample chart of depreciation: France
2300	IDES España		
2400	IDES Filiale 1 IT Ko.1000		
2500	IDES Netherlands		
2600	IDES IDES Italia		
2700	IDES Schweiz	1DE	Sample chart of depreciation: Germany
2800	China		
2900	Schweden	1DE	Sample chart of depreciation: Germany
2ABC	2abc pvt ltd		
3000	IDES US INC	1US	Sample chart of depreciation: USA
3010	Euro Subsidiary - Belgium	1DE	Sample chart of depreciation: Germany
3050	IDES Subsidiary UK	1GB	Sample chart of depreciation: Great Britain
3399	ARTS Company		

Chart of depreciaton for asset valuation (1) 46 Entr

ChD	Name
1AR	Sample chart of depreciation: Argentina
1AT	Sample chart of depreciation: Austria
1AU	Sample chart of depreciation: Australia
1BE	Sample chart of depreciation: Belgium
1BR	Sample chart of depreciation: Brazil
1CA	Sample chart of depreciation: Canada
1CH	Sample chart of depreciation: Switzerland
1CL	Sample chart of depreciation: Chile
1CN	Sample chart of depreciation: China
1CO	Sample chart of depreciation: Colombia
1CZ	Sample chart of depreciation: Czech Republic
1DE	Sample chart of depreciation: Germany
1DK	Sample chart of depreciation: Denmark
1ES	Sample chart of depreciation: Spain
1FI	Maximum valuation: Finnland
1FR	Sample chart of depreciation: France

Figure 6.3 Assignment of Chart of Depreciation to Company Code

Every company code has to be assigned to exactly one chart of depreciation; company codes not assigned to a chart of depreciation can't use the Asset Accounting component. For example, looking at Figure 6.3, company code 2201 is active in Asset Accounting because it's assigned to the 1FR chart of depreciation. On the other hand, company code 2300 can't use any Asset Accounting functionality because it isn't assigned to any chart of depreciation. The assignment is made with Transaction OAOB (Figure 6.3). When using the matchcode in Transaction OAOB to select the chart of depreciation, only user-defined charts of depreciation appear; you can't assign a standard chart of depreciation to a company code.

Multiple company codes can be assigned to one chart of depreciation. Typically, all of the company codes of the same country are assigned to one chart of depreciation, but this isn't mandatory.

6.1.4 Defining Asset Classes

> **Quick Reference**
>
> **Menu path:** IMG • FINANCIAL ACCOUNTING • ORGANIZATION STRUCTURES • ASSET CLASSES • DEFINE ASSET CLASSES
>
> **Transaction:** OAOA
>
> **Table/view:** ABKA/V_ANKA_00

Assets classes are used to group together assets with similar characteristics (like depreciation terms and account determination), and are necessary to create any new assets in the system; it isn't possible to create an asset without specifying to which asset class it belongs. Create the asset class with Transaction OAOA, but first make sure the following customizing objects are present because they are mandatory in each asset class (Figure 6.4):

▶ **Number Range (❶)**
The number range of the asset master data.

▶ **Scr. Layout Rule (❷)**
Defines the rules for creating and changing asset master data, such as which fields are mandatory, hidden, or optional. The values of the fields are provided by default from the asset classes.

▶ **Account Determ. (❸)**
This field is used in a different customizing step to define the SAP General Ledger accounts to which depreciation and transactions post.

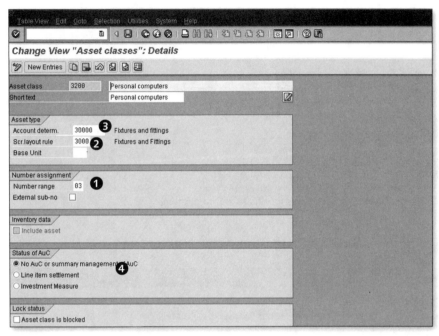

Figure 6.4 Asset Class Customizing

Another important setting in the asset class is highlighted by ❹ of Figure 6.4, where you specify whether the asset class contains assets under construction, or normal assets.

6.1.5 Deactivating Asset Classes in Charts of Depreciation

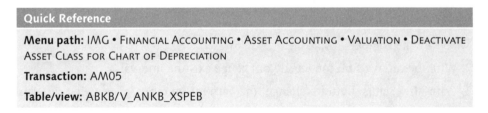

Quick Reference

Menu path: IMG • FINANCIAL ACCOUNTING • ASSET ACCOUNTING • VALUATION • DEACTIVATE ASSET CLASS FOR CHART OF DEPRECIATION

Transaction: AM05

Table/view: ABKB/V_ANKB_XSPEB

Asset classes are independent of charts of depreciation; however, it's possible to prevent an assets class from being used in a chart of depreciation. Use Transaction AM05 (Figure 6.5) to lock an asset class in all depreciation areas.

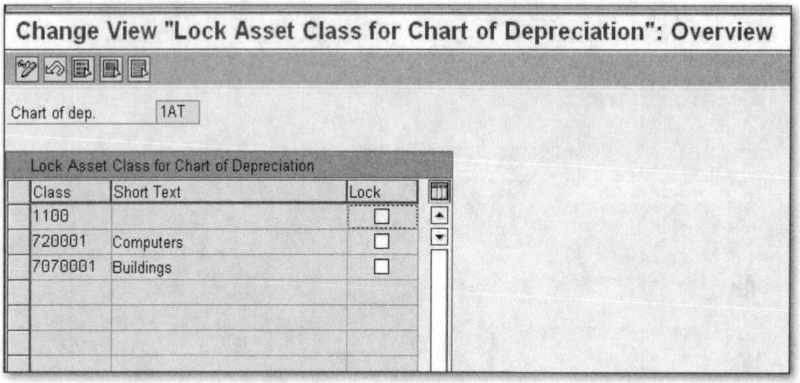

Figure 6.5 Deactivating Asset Classes for Charts of Depreciation

6.1.6 Defining Number Ranges for Asset Master Data

Quick Reference

Menu path: IMG • FINANCIAL ACCOUNTING • ASSET ACCOUNTING • ORGANIZATIONAL STRUCTURES • ASSET CLASSES • DEFINE NUMBER RANGES INTERVAL

Transaction: AS08

Table/view: NRIV (OBJECT ANLAGENNR)

Assets are assigned to asset classes, and asset classes are assigned to number ranges; thus, every time you create an asset, the system either assigns the number range (for internal number ranges) or checks the number range you specified (for external number ranges) based on the number range assigned to the asset class.

Create asset master data number ranges for each company code using Transaction AS08 (6.6). Follow these steps:

1. Specify the company code.

2. With the Intervals button, create or change existing intervals.

3. With the Status button, change the current number of existing internal intervals.

4. With the Overview button (![icon]), open a list of all number ranges created in all company codes.

5. With the Copy button (![icon]), copy all of the asset number ranges of one company code to the target company code.

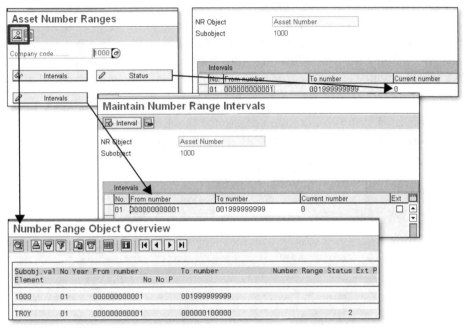

Figure 6.6 Asset Master Number Ranges

If you want multiple company codes to share the same number range, create a number range in a reference company code, and then assign the other company codes to the reference company code using Transaction AO11. Note that, in this case, there is no progressive numbering of the assets within a company code; for example, the first asset you create in class 0001 in company code 1000 may be 1051, and the second one in the same class may be 1074 because the numbers between 1052 and 1073 have already been taken by assets created in other company codes.

6.1.7 Specifying Account Determination

Quick Reference

Menu path: IMG • Financial Accounting • Asset Accounting • Organizational Structures • Asset Classes • Specify Account Determination

Table/view: T095A/V_T095A_01

Before creating an asset class, you must create account determination keys. In this customizing step, you only define the key and the description; in a later customizing step, you will use the account determination keys to assign general ledger accounts to different type of postings (this is discussed in more detail in Section 6.1.17, Specifying General Ledger Accounts for APC Posting and Depreciation).

When you create the account determination, keep in mind that many asset classes can be assigned to the same account determination. However, you can also have a one-to-one relationship between asset class and account determination.

6.1.8   Creating Screen Layout Rules

Quick Reference

Menu paths: IMG • FINANCIAL ACCOUNTING • ASSET ACCOUNTING • ORGANIZATIONAL STRUCTURES • ASSET CLASSES • CREATE SCREEN LAYOUT RULES

AND

IMG • FINANCIAL ACCOUNTING • ASSET ACCOUNTING • MASTER DATA • SCREEN LAYOUT • DEFINE SCREEN LAYOUT FOR ASSET MASTER DATA

Tables/views: T082A/V_T082A_01 and V_T082A_10

When creating an asset, there are fields that are mandatory, optional, and hidden. For example, leasing information is relevant only for cars, so specific customizing rule should be created for assets that belong to the asset class for cars. These rules should make mandatory all leasing-related fields for the car asset class but hide the leasing-related fields for all other asset classes.

These screen layout rules are maintained using the Screen Layout function in the system. In the first customizing step, which you access via IMG • FINANCIAL ACCOUNTING • ASSET ACCOUNTING • ORGANIZATIONAL STRUCTURES • ASSET CLASSES • CREATE SCREEN LAYOUT RULES, only the key is created, nothing more; the screen layout rule is assigned to the asset class when creating or changing the asset class (Transaction AM01). In the second customizing step (Figure 6.7), specific rules are defined.

All of the fields available in the asset master record are grouped into 14 groups, called *logical field groups*:

▸ General data
▸ Posting information

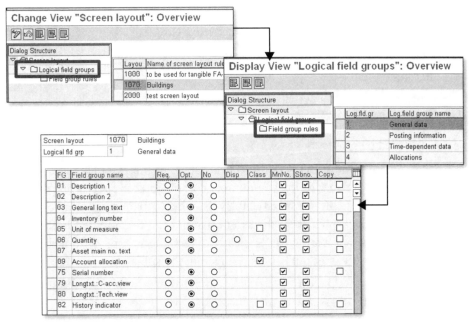

Figure 6.7 Screen Layout Rules for Master Data

- ▶ Time-dependent data
- ▶ Allocations
- ▶ Leasing
- ▶ Net worth valuation
- ▶ Real estate and similar rights
- ▶ Insurance
- ▶ Origin
- ▶ Inventory account assignment
- ▶ Inventory
- ▶ Investment support measures
- ▶ Equipment
- ▶ Depreciation

The fields belonging to one group are displayed together in the asset master record. To define the screen layout rules, use Transactions OA77 (groups 1 to 13) and OA78 (group 14). Then follow these steps:

1. Select one screen layout rule.

2. Select a logical field group (only in Transaction OA77).

3. For each field, specify whether the field is

   ▶ Required (Req.)

   ▶ Optional (Opt.)

   ▶ Hidden (No)

   ▶ Displayed (Disp)

4. Specify whether the value is defined at the level of the asset class (Class), the main number (MnNo.), or the sub-number (Sbno). You can specify one or more levels. For example, if you specify all levels, when a main asset number is created, the value is copied from the asset class and can be modified in the main number; also, when a sub-asset is created, the value is copied from the main number to the sub-asset but can be changed in the sub-asset.

5. Click the Copy checkbox if the field should be copied from the reference asset when you create an asset with reference.

6.1.9 Defining Evaluation Groups

Quick Reference

Menu path: IMG • FINANCIAL ACCOUNTING • ASSET ACCOUNTING • MASTER DATA • USER FIELDS • DEFINE 4-CHARACTER EVALUATION GROUPS AND DEFINE 8-CHARACTER EVALUATION GROUPS

Transactions: OAVA (define four-character evaluation groups), OAV8 (define eight-character evaluation groups)

Tables/views: T087/V_T087 (four-character evaluation groups), T087G/V_T087G (eight-character evaluation groups)

The evaluation groups are a series of fields that can be used in the asset master data for reporting, validations, and substitutions. No other functionality is linked to user fields.

The four evaluation groups are four digits long, and you can customize them with Transaction OAVA. Run the transaction, click on the New Entries button, and specify the following (Figure 6.8, left side):

▶ **No.**
Specify a number between 1 and 4 that corresponds to one of the four-digit-long evaluation groups.

▶ **Evalat. Grps 1-4**
Specify a freely defined four-digit-long value for the field. Only the values specified here can be used in the account master data.

▶ **Description**
Provide a meaningful description (see the examples in Figure 6.8).

There is just one eight-digit-long evaluation group, which you can customize with Transaction OAV8. Run the transaction, click on the New Entries button, and specify the following (Figure 6.8, right side):

▶ **Evaluation Group 5**
Specify a freely definable value that is, at maximum, eight digits long (it can be shorter); only the values specified in this customizing step can be assigned in asset master data.

▶ **Name**
Specify a meaningful description (see Figure 6.8 for some examples).

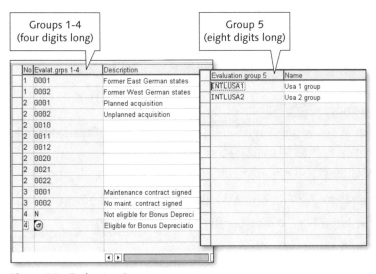

Figure 6.8 Evaluation Groups

6.1.10 Defining Validations for Asset Master Data

In Asset Accounting, just as in SAP General Ledger, it's possible to create validation and substitutions; however, the settings are slightly more complex. Validations and substitutions in Asset Accounting cover both documents and master data.

We recommend creating and changing validations and substitutions using Transactions GBB0 and GBB1, respectively. To begin, execute Transaction GBB0, and identify the area for Asset Accounting. You can create two types of validations: one for master data, and one for postings. In the master data validations, you can use fields from the following tables:

▶ ANLA: Asset Master Record Segment (e.g., description, asset class)

▶ ANLB: Depreciation Terms (e.g., depreciation key, useful life)

▶ ANLV: Insurance Data

▶ ANLZ: Time-Dependent Asset Allocations (e.g., cost center)

▶ SYST: ABAP System Fields (this isn't a physical table, and all of the fields refer to dynamic values, e.g., transaction code, current date)

In the posting validations, you can use fields from the following tables:

▶ ANEA: Asset Line Items for Proportional Values (in case of retirement)

▶ ANEP: Asset Line Items (e.g., transaction type, asset value date)

▶ ANLB: Depreciation Terms

▶ ANLC: Asset Value Fields (e.g., cumulative acquisition value up to the current fiscal year)

- ANLZ: Time-Dependent Asset Allocations

- ANTS: Sub of Asset Master Record (ANLA) (this is technically a structure, not a table, but it contains the fields from Table ANLA that can be used in validations)

- SYST: ABAP System Fields

As for the general ledger validations, it's possible to use user exits.

After the validations are created, they can be assigned to company codes in Transaction OACS. The same transaction allows you to activate or deactivate them at the company code level. Assigning a validation begins with specifying for which company code it's valid. Then it's necessary to specify whether it applies to normal data (independent of depreciation areas) or depreciation data (specific to depreciation areas), as well as its logical field group (Figure 6.9).

In Figure 6.9 and Figure 6.10 you can see an example of a validation step for asset master data, complete with prerequisite, check, and message.

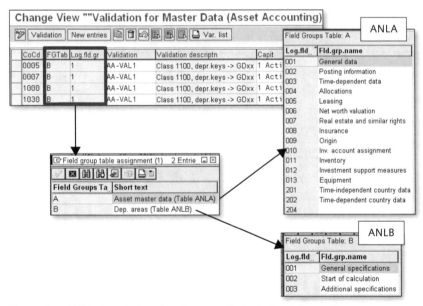

Figure 6.9 Validations Assigned to Company Codes in Asset Accounting

You can create one unique validation with many steps and assign the same to all different logical field groups. Alternatively, it's possible to create separate validations for one or more logical field groups.

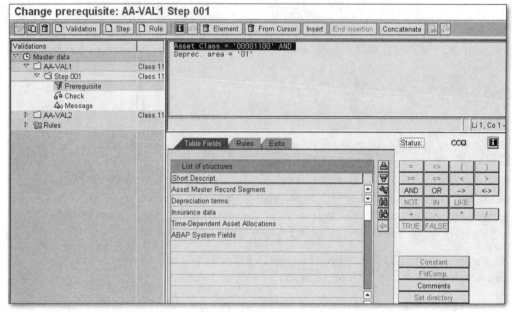

Figure 6.10 Asset Master Data Validation: Prerequisite

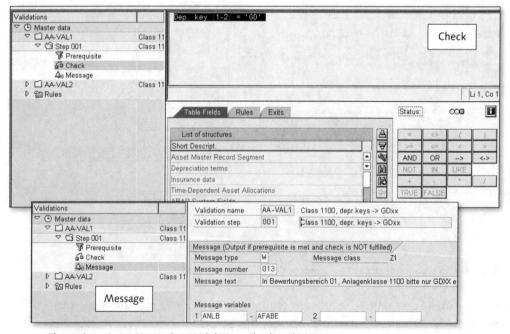

Figure 6.11 Asset Master Data Validation: Check and Message

6.1.11 Substitutions for Asset Master Data

> **Quick Reference**
>
> **Menu path:** IMG • FINANCIAL ACCOUNTING • ASSET ACCOUNTING • MASTER DATA • DEFINE SUBSTITUTIONS
>
> **Transactions:** OACS (asset master data substitutions), GBB1 (all substitutions)
>
> **Table/view:** T093SB/V_T093SB

You can create two types of substitutions for master data:

▶ Substitutions that work only with transactions that create assets (such as Transaction AS01)

▶ Substitutions that work with a mass change of assets

There is no substitution that works with the individual change of one asset (Transaction AS02). The substitution for mass changes of assets works just with the specific transaction for the mass change of asset master data, which is Transaction AR31. The general transaction for the mass change, Transaction MASS, doesn't work with asset master data.

The process to create a substitution is as follows (Figure 6.12):

1. Run Transaction OACS, and select GOTO • SUBSTITUTION.

2. In the resulting screen, create a new substitution with the Substitution button.

3. Put your cursor on the substitution just created, and select the Step button.

4. For the new step, define one or more fields that will be substituted in the step (selecting them from the proposed list).

5. For each field, specify the substitution technique:

   ▶ **Constant Value:** If selected, this means that you replace the field with a fixed valid value (e.g., if you substitute the cost center, you can specify a fixed value such as 10100).

   ▶ **Exit:** If selected, you can specify one of the user exits created for the asset master data substitutions.

   ▶ **Field – Field Assignment:** If selected, you can substitute the field with the whole value coming from another field.

6. After you confirm the substitution technique, define the prerequisite that must be met to trigger the substitution. For a full description of the way you can

build your rules in the prerequisite, refer to the instructions for creating validations in SAP General Ledger (Section 3.7.1, Validations, in Chapter 3).

7. Specify the way the substitution should take place. Depending on the choice you made in step 5, you may specify

- ▶ A constant value
- ▶ A user exit
- ▶ A reference field

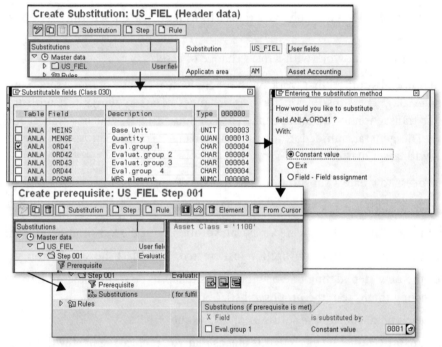

Figure 6.12 Asset Master Data Substitution (Creation)

6.1.12 Defining Depreciation Areas

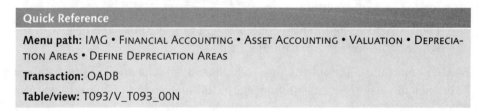

Quick Reference

Menu path: IMG • FINANCIAL ACCOUNTING • ASSET ACCOUNTING • VALUATION • DEPRECIATION AREAS • DEFINE DEPRECIATION AREAS

Transaction: OADB

Table/view: T093/V_T093_00N

To manage the value and history of each asset according to all possible accounting principles, the solution provided by SAP is the management of several depreciation areas. In each depreciation area, the asset can have different acquisition, depreciation, and net book values.

The configuration of the depreciation areas depends on the chart of depreciation. To create new depreciation areas, use Transaction OADB, and specify the chart of depreciations. In the following screen, select one existing depreciation area and the Copy As button. In the resulting screen, specify the new depreciation area, and, if necessary, change the following settings (which are copied from the depreciation area used as a reference) (Figure 6.13 and Figure 6.14):

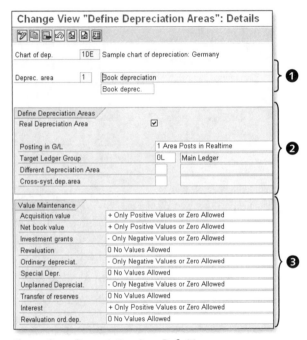

Figure 6.13 Depreciation Area Definition

- ▶ **Deprec. Area (❶ of Figure 6.13)**
  In this field, specify the number and description of the depreciation area.

- ▶ **Real Depreciation Area (❷ of Figure 6.13)**
  This checkbox indicates whether the depreciation area is real or derived. A real depreciation area has its own values for each transaction or depreciation; a derived depreciation area has values that come from values of other deprecia-

tion areas (Figure 6.14). For example, you can define depreciation area 03 as equal to two times depreciation area 01, minus depreciation area 02. All of the values of the derived depreciation areas are calculated according to the formula defined in customizing.

▶ **Posting in G/L (❷ of Figure 6.13)**
In this field, specify whether the area posts to the SAP General Ledger. Table 6.2 outlines your options. Options 4 to 6 were introduced with the latest versions of SAP ERP and the new SAP General Ledger.

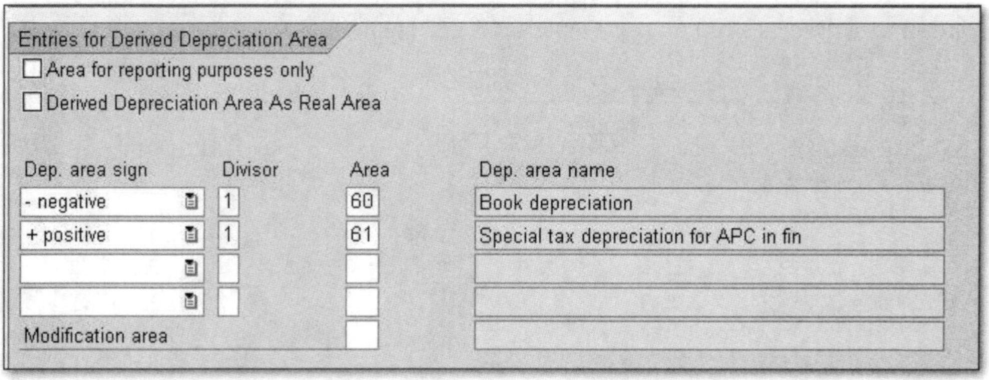

Entries for Derived Depreciation Area				
☐ Area for reporting purposes only				
☐ Derived Depreciation Area As Real Area				
Dep. area sign	**Divisor**		**Area**	**Dep. area name**
- negative 📋	1		60	Book depreciation
+ positive 📋	1		61	Special tax depreciation for APC in fin
📋				
📋				
Modification area				

Figure 6.14 Additional Customizing for Derived Depreciation Areas

Posting Rules in SAP General Ledger	Acquisition and Production Costs (APC) Transactions	Depreciation
0: Area does not post	No posting	No posting
1: Area posts in real time	Online	With AFAB/AFABN
2: Area posts APC and depreciation on periodic basis	With ASKB/ASKBN	With AFAB/AFABN
3: Area posts depreciation only	No posting	With AFAB/AFABN
4: Area posts APC directly and depreciation	With AFABN	With AFABN
5: Area posts APC only	With ASKB/ASKBN	No Posting
6: Area posts only APC directly	With AFABN	No Posting

Table 6.2 Posting Rules for General Ledger

As described in the table, if depreciation has to be posted, it's always posted periodically, with the normal depreciation run. There is a technical restriction when creating derived depreciation areas: In their formulas, you can only use depreciation areas with a number ID less than the derived one. For example:

- Allowed: Area 22 = Area 21 – Area 01
- Not allowed: Area 22 = Area 21 – Area 23

▶ **Value Maintenance area (❸ of Figure 6.13)**
Specify which values are possible (positive, zero, and negative) for Acquisition Value, Net Book Value, and the rest of the fields in this area. If a transaction violates any of the rules specified here, the system issues an error message and doesn't allow you to continue.

6.1.13 Specifying Transfer of APC Values to Another Depreciation Area

Quick Reference
Menu path: IMG • Financial Accounting • Asset Accounting • Valuation • Depreciation Areas • Specify Transfer of APC Values
Transaction: OABC
Table/view: T093A/V_T093A_03

When you post an acquisition to an asset, you're required to specify the acquisition value for all of the depreciation areas involved. However, you can specify that certain depreciation areas automatically take values from another depreciation area. To do this, execute Transaction OABC (Figure 6.15), and specify the following:

▶ **ValAd (❶)**
This is the area from which the values are automatically adopted.

▶ **Ident. (❷)**
If you mark this indicator, you can't change the adopted values; if you don't mark the indicator, the values are proposed and can be changed.

Note that depreciation area 01 can't adopt APC (acquisition and production cost) values from another depreciation area.

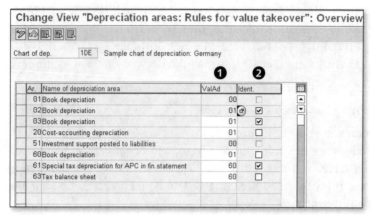

Figure 6.15 Adoption of APC Values from Another Depreciation Area

6.1.14 Specifying the Transfer of Depreciation Terms from Another Depreciation Area

Quick Reference

Menu path: IMG • FINANCIAL ACCOUNTING • ASSET ACCOUNTING • VALUATION • DEPRECIATION AREAS • SPECIFY TRANSFER OF DEPRECIATION TERMS

Transaction: OABD

Table/view: T093A/V_T093A_04

In the definition of an asset, you're required to specify the depreciation terms for all of the depreciation areas used by the asset. However, you can specify that certain depreciation areas should automatically take the depreciation terms from another depreciation area. To do this, execute Transaction OABD (Figure 6.16), and specify the following:

▶ **TTr (❶)**
This is the area from which the depreciation terms are automatically adopted.

▶ **Identical (❷)**
If you mark this indicator, you can't change the adopted depreciation terms; if you don't mark this indicator, the terms are proposed and can be changed.

Note that depreciation area 01 can't adopt depreciation terms from another depreciation area.

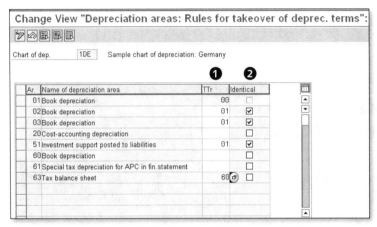

Figure 6.16 Adoption of Depreciation Terms from Another Depreciation Area

6.1.15 Integrating Depreciation Areas and the SAP General Ledger

In the SAP General Ledger environment, depreciation areas 01 posts to the leading ledger and to Controlling. Other depreciation areas can post to different ledgers but not to the depreciation ledger or Controlling.

To set up integration between depreciation areas and ledgers other than the leading ledger, use the menu path that appears in the Quick Reference box (Figure 6.17). All of the settings you make are valid for the chart of depreciation that you have set with Transaction OAPL. Follow the six steps presented in Figures 6.17 and 6.18.

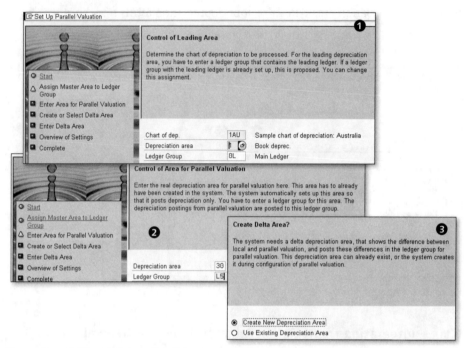

Figure 6.17 Setting Up Integration Between Depreciation Areas and Ledger Groups

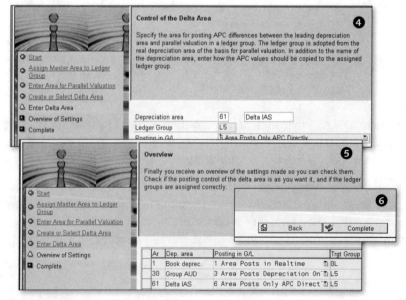

Figure 6.18 Setting Up Integration Between Depreciation Areas and Ledger Groups (Cont.)

6.1.16   Deactivating Depreciation Areas in Asset Classes

Quick Reference

Menu path: IMG • FINANCIAL ACCOUNTING • ASSET ACCOUNTING • VALUATION • DETERMINE DEPRECIATION AREA IN ASSET CLASSES

Transaction: OAYZ

Table/view: ANKB/V_ANKB_00

It's possible to specify that assets belonging to specific asset classes can't manage certain depreciation areas in a chart of depreciation. For example, you can limit a depreciation area for the calculation of insurance only for the asset class for buildings. To do this, execute Transaction OAYZ and follow these steps:

1. Select an asset class (❶ **of** Figure 6.19).

2. On the left side of the screen, double-click the Depreciation Areas folder (❷ of Figure 6.19).The system displays all depreciation areas defined in the chart of depreciation with which you're working (you set the chart of depreciation with Transaction OAPL).

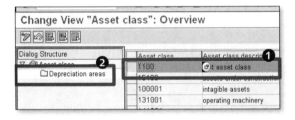

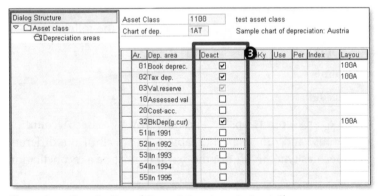

Figure 6.19   Deactivation of Depreciation Areas in Asset Classes

3. Click on the Deact flag to specify that the relevant depreciation area isn't relevant for the assets belonging to the specified asset class (❸ of Figure 6.19).

6.1.17 Specifying General Ledger Accounts for APC Posting and Depreciation

Quick Reference

Menu path: IMG • FINANCIAL ACCOUNTING • ASSET ACCOUNTING • INTEGRATION WITH THE GENERAL LEDGER • ASSIGN G/L ACCOUNTS

Transaction: AO90

Tables/views: T095, T095B, T095P/V_T095_MASTER (balance sheet), V_T095B_MASTER (depreciation), V_T095P_MASTER (special reserves)

The general ledger account determination depends on the following:

▸ **Chart of depreciation**
This information comes from the company code; remember, each asset is assigned to one company code.

▸ **Chart of accounts**
This information also comes from the company code.

▸ **Depreciation area**
One transaction can generate different postings depending on the depreciation area; the same principle is valid for the depreciation.

▸ **Account determination key**
This information comes from the asset class to which the asset belongs.

▸ **Type of transaction or depreciation**
These types are predefined in the system and grouped into the following:

  ▸ Balance sheet accounts

  ▸ Depreciation accounts

  ▸ Special reserves accounts

Some of the general ledger accounts posted automatically by Asset Accounting are reconciliation accounts, and others aren't. Table 6.3 lists all of the different accounts posted and specifies whether or not the account must be a reconciliation account.

Account For....	Non-Reconciliation Account	Reconciliation Account
Acquisition: Acquis. and production costs		X
Acquisition: Down payments		X
Contra account: Acquisition value	X	
Down-payments clearing account	X	
Acquisition from affiliated company	X	
Revenue frm post-capitaliz:	X	
Loss made on asset retirement w/o reven.	X	
Clearing acct. revenue from asset sale	X	
Gain from asset sale	X	
Loss from asset sale	X	
Clear.revenue sale to affil.company	X	
Revaluation acquis. and production costs		X
Offsetting account: Revaluation APC	X	
Cost elem. for settlmt AuC to CO objects	X	
Capital. difference/non-operatng expense	X	
Clearing of investment support	X	
Acc.dep. accnt.for ordinary depreciation		X
Expense account for ordinary depreciat.	X	
Expense account for ord. dep. below zero	X	
Revenue from write-up on ord.deprec.	X	
Accumulated dep. account special dep.		X
Expense account for special depreciation	X	
Expense account for spec.dep.below zero	X	
Revenue from write-up on special deprec.	X	
Accumulated dep. account unpl. deprec.		X
Expense account for unplanned deprec.	X	
P&Lact.unpl.dep.below 0		

Table 6.3 General Ledger Accounts Automatically Posted in Asset Accounting

Account For....	Non-Reconciliation Account	Reconciliation Account
Revenue from write-up on unplnd. deprec.		
Val. adj. acct. for transfer of reserves		X
Contra account for transferring reserves	X	
Revenue from w-up transfer of reserves	X	
Reval. accumulated ord. depreciation		X
Offsetting accnt: Reval. ordinary deprc.	X	
Expense account for interest	X	
Clearing interest posting	X	
Intrst expense when book val.below zero	X	
Special reserves balance		X
Expense: Allocation to spec.reserves	X	
Write-off special reserves (gross)		X
Revenue: Amortiz. special reserves	X	
Write-off spec.reserves after retiremn		X
Write-up on special reserves		X
Gain from asset sale	X	
Loss from asset sale	X	
Clear.revenue sale to affil.company	X	

Table 6.3 General Ledger Accounts Automatically Posted in Asset Accounting (Cont.)

You should customize account determination only for processes that you will actually use; for example, you definitely need to specify the account determination for the acquisition of assets, but you may not need the account determination for special reserves. To customize the account determination, run Transaction AO90, and then do the following (Figure 6.20):

1. Select a chart of accounts, and double-click on the Account Determination folder (Figure 6.20, ❶). Remember that you assign assets to asset classes and asset classes to account determination.

2. On the right side of the screen (Figure 6.20, ❷), select one account determination and, on the left side, one of the three folders (Balance Sheet Accounts, Depreciation, Special Reserves).

3. The system displays the depreciation areas that post to the general ledger; double click one of them (Figure 6.20, ❸). The system displays all of the possible types of accounts that can be posted to; specify a general ledger account. In ❹ of Figure 6.20, you can see, for example, that account 11000 will be posted to when you use a transaction for the acquisition of an asset that has account determination 13000 in a company code assigned to chart of depreciation 1DE and chart of accounts INT.

4. Repeat the process for all needed accounts.

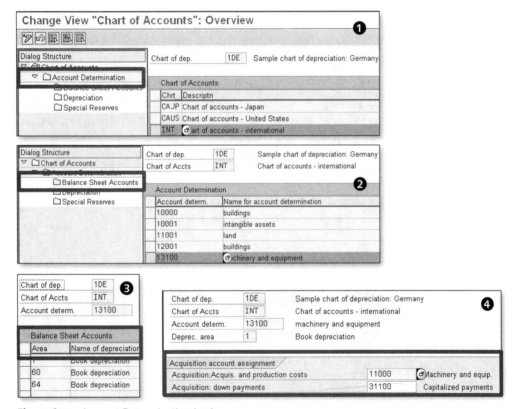

Figure 6.20 Account Determination Logic

6.1.18 Specifying Posting Keys for Asset Posting

> **Quick Reference**
>
> **Menu path:** IMG • FINANCIAL ACCOUNTING • ASSET ACCOUNTING • INTEGRATION WITH THE GENERAL LEDGER • SPECIFY POSTING KEY FOR ASSET POSTING
>
> **Transaction:** OBYD
>
> **Table:** T030B

There are two types of postings that come from Asset Accounting:

- **Posting to asset reconciliation accounts**
  Transaction ANL (asset posting). Default: debit 70, credit 75. Note that, in this case, you will post indirectly to those accounts through a fixed asset.

- **Posting to normal general ledger accounts (non-reconciliation)**
  Transaction ANS (GL account posting from asset posting). Default: debit 40, credit 50.

In general, there is no reason to change the default posting key. Acquisition and retirements use the postings keys of the first type of postings (70/75). Depreciation uses the posting keys of the second type of postings (40/50) for P&L accounts, and the first rule for the accumulated depreciation account.

You can check the default posting keys by running Transaction OBYD (Figure 6.21). Double-click on Transaction ANL to see the posting keys to post to asset reconciliation general ledger accounts, or double-click on Transaction ANS to see the posting keys to post to non-reconciliation general ledger accounts.

6.1.19 Specifying Document Type for Depreciation

> **Quick Reference**
>
> **Menu path:** IMG • FINANCIAL ACCOUNTING • ASSET ACCOUNTING • INTEGRATION WITH THE GENERAL LEDGER • POST DEPRECIATION TO GENERAL LEDGER • SPECIFY DOCUMENT TYPE FOR POSTING OR DEPRECIATION
>
> **Transaction:** OAB3
>
> **Table/view:** T093C/V_T093C_01

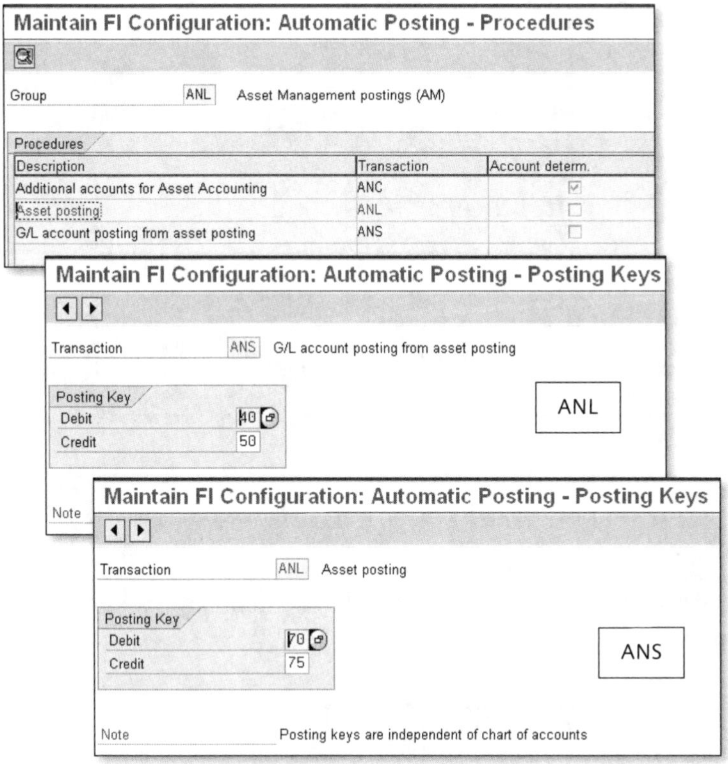

Figure 6.21 Posting Keys for Asset Accounting Postings

Using Transaction OAB3, specify the document type that should be used by the depreciation to post to the general ledger. Make the specification at the company code level (Figure 6.22). Note that the document type specified here must allow posting to account types S and A.

6.1.20 Defining Depreciation Area Currency

Quick Reference

Menu path: IMG • FINANCIAL ACCOUNTING • ASSET ACCOUNTING • VALUATION • CURRENCIES • DEFINE DEPRECIATION AREAS FOR FOREIGN CURRENCIES

Transaction: OAYH

Table: T093B/V_T093B_05

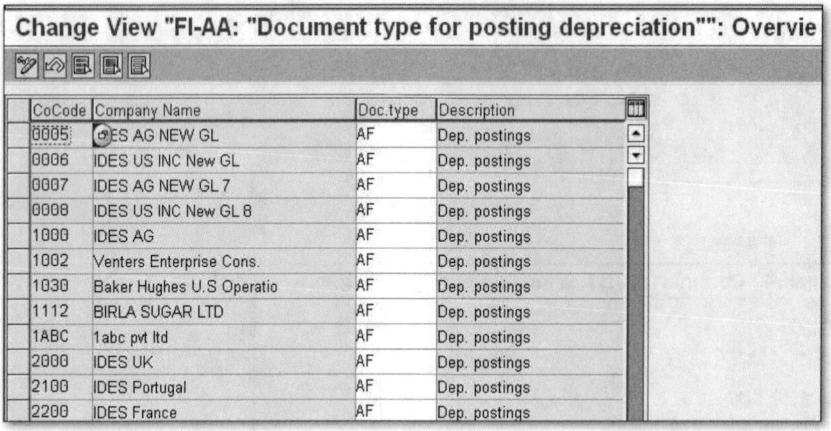

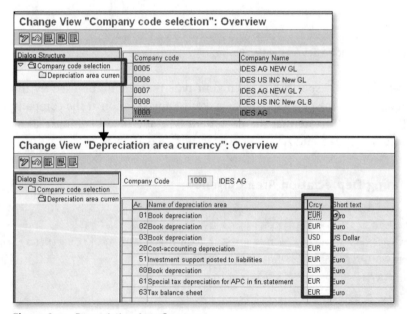

Figure 6.22 Document Type for Depreciation

Specify the currency of each depreciation area using Transaction OAYH. Follow these steps (Figure 6.23).

1. Select a company code (depreciation areas in different company codes can have different currencies).

Figure 6.23 Depreciation Area Currency

2. Click on the Depreciation Area Currency folder.

3. Specify the currency for each depreciation area.

6.1.21 Maintaining Depreciation Keys

> **Quick Reference**
>
> **Menu path:** IMG • Financial Accounting • Asset Accounting • Depreciation • Valuation Methods • Depreciation Keys • Maintain Depreciation Key
>
> **Transaction:** AFAMA
>
> **Tables:** T090NA (depreciation keys), T090NAZ (assignment of calculation methods to depreciation keys)

All of the rules for controlling depreciation (calculation technique, period control, etc.) are contained in the depreciation key, which is why you must assign a depreciation key to each asset (usually this information is automatically supplied based on the asset class to which the asset belongs). The depreciation key assigned to an asset can be different in each depreciation area; alternatively, in the configuration of the depreciation area, you can specify that the key is the same as that of another depreciation area. The only information not defined in the depreciation key is the useful life, which is specific to each asset. In general, the useful life is provided by default from the asset class and doesn't need to be changed.

Configuring depreciation keys is a highly technical step in Asset Accounting customizing. A large number of depreciation keys are already available in your chart of depreciation; we recommend that you first check these available depreciation keys before creating a new one. If you do need to create a new one, we strongly recommend creating the new depreciation key as a copy of an existing one, changing only the needed settings.

Let's now explore how to create a depreciation key as a copy of depreciation key LINR, which is used for ordinary depreciations posted with the same percentage in all of the posting periods contained in the useful life of an asset. Follow these steps:

1. Run Transaction AFAMA, and specify, upon request, the chart of depreciation.

2. In the resulting screen, you see a list of the depreciation keys that already exist in the chart of depreciation. Select depreciation key LINR, and click on the Copy Entries button (🖺) (❶ of Figure 6.24).

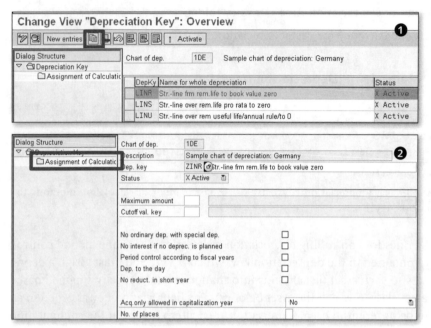

Figure 6.24 Depreciation Key Definition

3. In the following screen (❷ of Figure 6.24), specify a destination depreciation key — for example, ZINR — and change the description copied from the reference depreciation key. Specify the status (active or inactive), and then check the other settings copied from the reference depreciation key. Pay particular attention to the following two settings (❷ of Figure 6.24):

   ▶ **Dep. To the Day (depreciation to the day):** If you select this indicator, the depreciation is calculated exactly in proportion to the calendar dates.

   ▶ **Acq. Only Allowed in Capitalization Year (acquisition only allowed in capitalization year):** If you select this setting, you can't post subsequent acquisitions in fiscal years different from the year of the capitalization date.

4. Press Enter, and double-click the Assignment of Calculation Methods folder on the left side of the screen; the system displays the calculation methods assigned to the depreciation key (❸ of Figure 6.25). The calculation methods are the most important setting of the depreciation key and controls, among the following:

   ▶ Whether the depreciation is calculated according to the straight-line method (the same amount for all of the periods included in the useful life) or the declining balance method (the depreciation amount per period declines period by period).

▶ How the asset value date of each transaction affects the starting and ending point of the depreciation.

The following is a brief explanation of the fields contained in this screen (Figure 6.25):

▶ **Dep./Int**
In this column, specify whether the depreciation key affects the ordinary depreciation, the special depreciation, or the fictions interest.

▶ **Phase**
Specify a progressive number for each type of depreciation. For example, in Figure 6.25, you can see two lines for the ordinary depreciation. The system starts with the depreciation rules contained in the first line, and then, when the conditions specified in the Chnge. Method and Changeover%Rate columns are fulfilled, switches to the rules contained in the second line (see the corresponding bullet points in this list).

▶ **Base Method**
From the proposed list, select a method by which to carry out the depreciation with the straight-line technique.

▶ **Decl.-Bal. Method (declining-balance method)**
From the proposed list, select a method by which to carry out the depreciation with the declining balance technique. In depreciation key LINR, this method is 001—which means, in practice, that no declining balance technique is applied.

▶ **Prd Control (period control)**
From the proposed list, select the period control — that is, the way different types of transactions affect the starting and ending points of the depreciation. You can see the detailed customizing of period control using Transaction AFAMP.

▶ **Multilev. Meth. (multilevel method)**
This setting can be used for complex depreciation rules that imply different percentages of depreciation in different phases of the useful life of an asset. It's very unlikely that you will use this functionality. In the example shown in Figure 6.25, you can see that method 001 has been assigned to phase one, and method 013 to phase two. Both methods 001 and 013 mean that no multilevel method will be used.

▶ **Chnge. Method (changeover method)**

Specify the rule according to which system switches to the next phase. In the example shown in Figure 6.25, the first phase has changeover method 5, which means that the switch happens at the end of the useful life. You can open the matchcode and select one of the methods available in the proposed list.

▶ **Changeover%Rate**

This is an alternative to the changeover method and allows you to specify a percentage of the acquisition value. For example, if you specify 60%, when the accumulated depreciation has reached the 60% of the acquisition value, the system switches to the depreciation rules specified in the next phase.

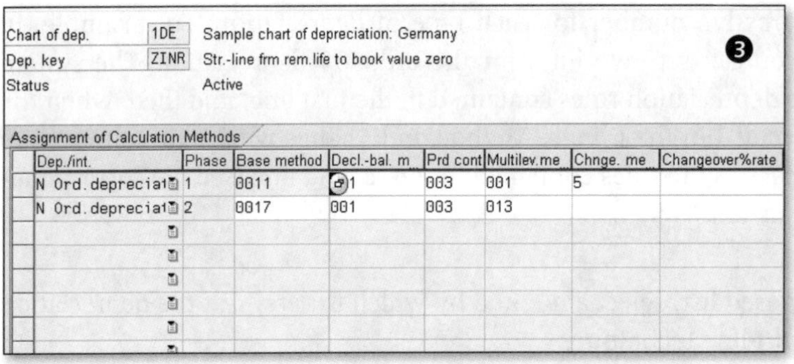

Figure 6.25 Depreciation Key: Assignment of Calculation Methods

6.1.22 Activating Controlling Objects for Posting in Asset Accounting

Quick Reference

Menu path: IMG • FINANCIAL ACCOUNTING • ASSET ACCOUNTING • INTEGRATION WITH THE GENERAL LEDGER • ADDITIONAL ACCOUNT ASSIGNMENT • VALUATION METHODS • ACTIVATE ACCOUNT ASSIGNMENT OBJECT

Table/view: T093_ACCOBJ/V_T093_ACCOBJ

The possible Controlling objects that can be posted to from Asset Accounting are defined in the customizing activity we discuss here. This activity is valid for the whole client.

Figure 6.26 shows the screen in which this customizing step is carried out, which displays all of the possible Controlling objects that can be posted from Asset Accounting. Following is a brief explanation of the columns on that screen:

▶ **Active (❶)**

Select this flag to indicate that the object should be posted in the asset transactions. If the object isn't active, you still can use it in the asset master record, but the information isn't transferred to accounting in the depreciation or transactions.

▶ **Bal. Sheet column (❷)**

If you select this flag, you can no longer change the assignment in the asset master record after the asset is capitalized.

▶ **Agreement (❸)**

If you select this flag, the objects in the asset and in the posting are always the same.

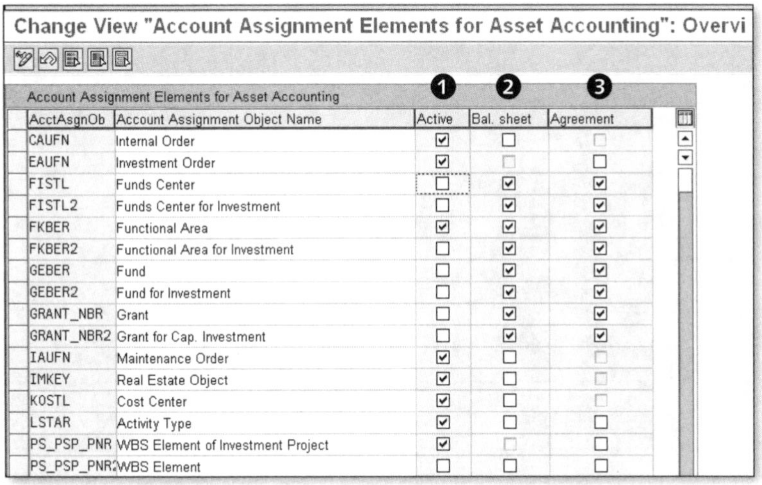

AcctAsgnOb	Account Assignment Object Name	Active	Bal. sheet	Agreement	
CAUFN	Internal Order	☑	☐	☐	
EAUFN	Investment Order	☑	☐	☐	
FISTL	Funds Center	☐	☑	☑	
FISTL2	Funds Center for Investment	☐	☑	☑	
FKBER	Functional Area	☑	☑	☑	
FKBER2	Functional Area for Investment	☐	☑	☑	
GEBER	Fund	☐	☑	☑	
GEBER2	Fund for Investment	☐	☑	☑	
GRANT_NBR	Grant	☐	☑	☑	
GRANT_NBR2	Grant for Cap. Investment	☐	☑	☑	
IAUFN	Maintenance Order	☑	☐	☐	
IMKEY	Real Estate Object	☑	☐	☐	
KOSTL	Cost Center	☑	☐	☐	
LSTAR	Activity Type	☑	☐	☐	
PS_PSP_PNR	WBS Element of Investment Project	☑	☐	☐	
PS_PSP_PNR2	WBS Element	☐	☐	☐	

Figure 6.26 Activation of Controlling Objects in Asset Accounting

To actually post to a Controlling object in a specific company code, you must also activate the assignment at the company code level. This is described next.

6.1.23 Activating Controlling Objects for Posting in Asset Accounting per Company Codes

Quick Reference

Menu path: IMG • FINANCIAL ACCOUNTING • ASSET ACCOUNTING • INTEGRATION WITH THE GENERAL LEDGER • ADDITIONAL ACCOUNT ASSIGNMENT • VALUATION METHODS • SPECIFY ACCOUNT ASSIGNMENT TYPE FOR ACCOUNT ASSIGNMENT OBJECT

Table/view: AAACC_OBJ/V_AAACC_OBJ_01

Transaction: ACSET

If you want to post to a Controlling object (e.g., the cost center) through Asset Accounting, you must first carry out the activity described in the previous section and then perform activation at the company code level. To do this, run Transaction ACSET, and then follow these steps (Figure 6.27):

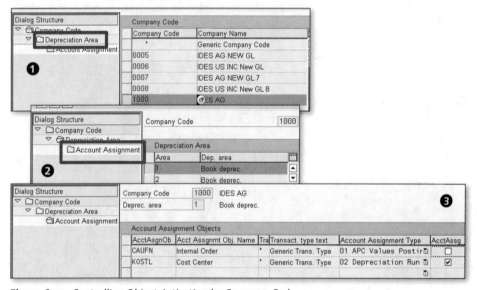

Figure 6.27 Controlling Object Activation by Company Code

1. Select a company code, and click on the Depreciation Area folder (❶).

2. Select one of the depreciation areas that posts to the general ledger, and double-click on the Account Assignment folder (❷).

3. In the resulting screen (❸), specify the Controlling object that is posted in the company code through Asset Accounting, and click on the AcctAssg flag.

4. To activate the Controlling object for all transactions, enter "*" in the column related to the transaction types.

Warning!

The settings here have to be consistent with the characteristics of the related accounts. For example, in depreciation area 01, the ordinary depreciation posts to account 601000, which is also a primary cost element; however, depreciation area 01 doesn't post to any account assignment objects. This means that when running ordinary depreciation, the system will issue an error message saying that account 601000 requires a Controlling object. However, depreciation area 01 doesn't post to any Controlling object, meaning that it isn't possible to post to Financial Accounting.

6.1.24 Specifying Posting Rules for Depreciation

Quick Reference

Menu path: IMG • Financial Accounting • Asset Accounting • Integration with the General Ledger • Post Depreciation to the General Ledger • Specify Intervals and Posting Rules

Transaction: OAYR

Table/view: T093D/V_T093D_00

Typically, depreciation is posted at the end of each posting period. However, this isn't fixed in the system; you can define it via Transaction OAYR. The specification is valid at the company code and depreciation area levels (Figure 6.28):

1. Run Transaction OAYR, and select one of the company codes displayed on the right side of the screen. Double-click the Posting Rules folder on the left side of the screen.

2. A list of the available depreciation areas for the company code appears on the right side of the screen. Skip the depreciation areas with the description ">>> No entries for acct. assgnmt. possible <<<" because they don't post to the general ledger. Double-click one of the other depreciation areas.

3. If the fiscal year variant assigned to the company code contains 12 normal posting periods (they can be the same as or different from calendar months), you have one of the following choices:

   ▸ **Monthly Posting:** Depreciation is posted every posting period.

   ▸ **Bi-monthly Posting:** Depreciation is posted every two periods.

▶ **Quarterly Posting:** Depreciation is posted every three periods.

▶ **Semi-Annual Posting:** Depreciation is posted every six periods.

▶ **Annual Posting:** Depreciation is posted every year, on period 12.

Alternatively, you can select the Enter in Expert Mode button, and specify the period interval. This is allowed for both fiscal year variants with 12 periods or with a different number of posting periods. For example, if your company code is assigned to a fiscal year variant with 24 posting periods, and you want to post 4 depreciations a year, select 6 in the Period Interval field.

In the same customizing step, there is an important option called *Smoothing*; this option determines how the system behaves if settings like the depreciation key or useful life have changed in the asset, resulting in a too-high or too-low calculated depreciation. If the Smoothing option is selected, the difference is distributed equally among the remaining posting periods of the year; if the Smoothing option isn't selected, the entire difference is posted to the current period (this is known as *catch-up*).

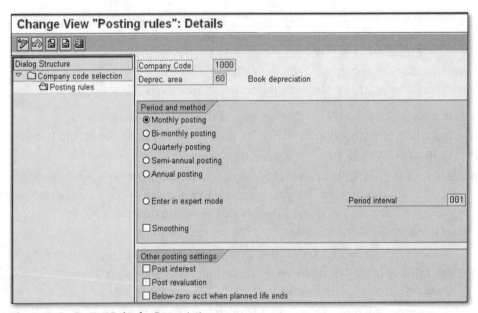

Figure 6.28 Posting Rules for Depreciation

6.1.25 Transaction Types

Transaction types are managed in the customizing transactions specified in the Quick Reference box. We have provided the transaction codes for the most common transaction type groups:

- Acquisitions
- Retirements
- Transfers
- Unplanned depreciation

Next we describe the creation of an acquisition transaction type and then the additional settings specific to each category (retirements, transfers, and unplanned depreciation). We recommend creating transaction types only when needed; first check the existing transaction types to see if they already fulfill your needs.

Creating a Transaction Type for Acquisitions

To create an acquisition transaction type, follow these steps (Figure 6.29):

1. Run Transaction AO73. The system doesn't ask you to specify a chart of depreciation because the transaction types are chart-of-depreciation independent.

2. In the following screen, select the New Entries button.

3. In the next screen, fill in the settings for the new transaction type for acquisitions. These are the most important fields:

   - **Transaction Type:** This is the three-digit, alphanumeric ID of the new transaction type. Follow the naming convention for your company.

   - **Description:** Provide a meaningful description; keep in mind that the end users will choose the transaction type based mainly on its description.

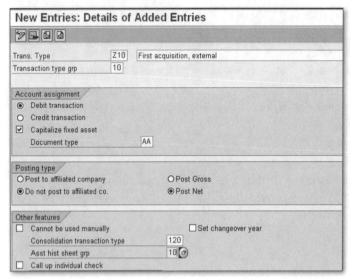

Figure 6.29 Transaction Type for Acquisition

▶ **Debit Transaction/Credit Transaction:** Choose one of the two fields to specify whether the transaction type should increase or reduce the value of the asset.

▶ **Capitalize Fixed Asset:** If you select this indicator, one of the effects of the transaction is that the asset value date is copied into the capitalization date in the asset master data.

▶ **Document Type:** When you post with a transaction type in Asset Accounting, a Financial Accounting document is generated. In this field, specify the document type used for that Financial Accounting document.

▶ **Post to Affiliated Company/Do Not Post to Affiliated Co.:** Choose exactly one of the two indicators to specify whether or not a trading partner is required when using the transaction.

▶ **Post Gross/Post Net buttons:** If you choose Post Gross, you can post both acquisition values and accumulated depreciations; if you choose Post Net, you can post only acquisition values. In general, you post gross when you acquire an asset from an intercompany partner; however, consult your accounting department to decide which of the two buttons to choose.

▶ **Consolidation Transaction Type:** Assign the asset transaction type to one of the consolidation transaction types that you have maintained with Transaction OC08.

▶ **Asst Hist Sheet Grp (asset history sheet group):** Assign the transaction type to an asset history sheet group; consult Section 6.1.26, Configuring the Asset History Sheet, for more details.

Creating a Transaction Type for Retirements

You create a transaction type for retirements in the same way you create a transaction type for acquisitions; just use Transaction AO74 instead of Transaction AO73. However, some fields are specific to retirement (Figure 6.30):

▶ **Deactivate Fixed Asset**
If you select this indicator, when you post the retirement, the system automatically updates the deactivation date in the affected asset master data using the asset value date of the transaction.

▶ **Debit Transaction/Credit Transaction**
These buttons don't appear in the screen because the transactions for retirement are always credit transactions.

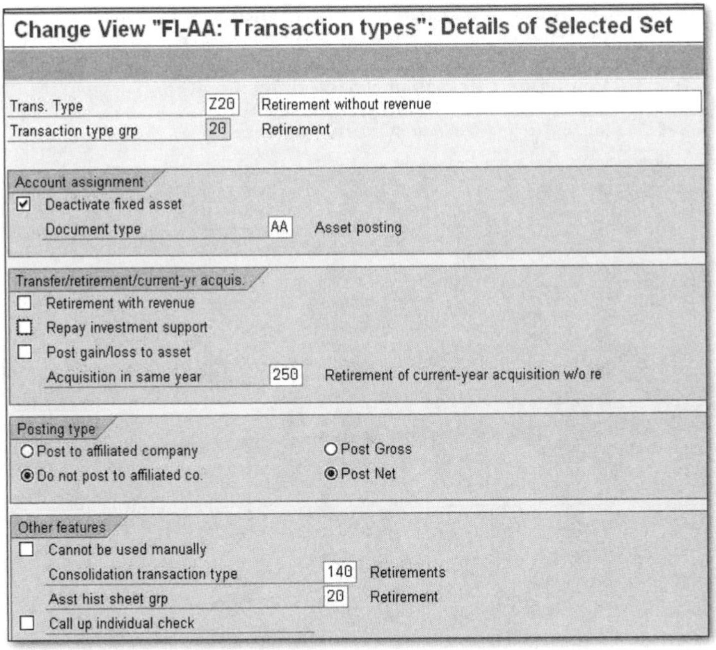

Change View "FI-AA: Transaction types": Details of Selected Set

Trans. Type	Z20	Retirement without revenue
Transaction type grp	20	Retirement

Account assignment
☑ Deactivate fixed asset
Document type   AA   Asset posting

Transfer/retirement/current-yr acquis.
☐ Retirement with revenue
☐ Repay investment support
☐ Post gain/loss to asset
Acquisition in same year   250   Retirement of current-year acquisition w/o re

Posting type
○ Post to affiliated company   ○ Post Gross
◉ Do not post to affiliated co.   ◉ Post Net

Other features
☐ Cannot be used manually
Consolidation transaction type   140   Retirements
Asst hist sheet grp   20   Retirement
☐ Call up individual check

Figure 6.30 Transaction Type for Retirement

▶ **Retirement with Revenue**
If you select this indicator, you can specify a revenue when posting the retirement. If the indicator isn't set, the remaining net book value is posted as a loss.

▶ **Acquisition in the Same Year**
Use this indicator when your asset has had different acquisition transactions in the current year and in previous years; the system uses the alternative transaction type specified here to post the retirement of the acquisition value posted in the current fiscal year.

Creating a Transaction Type for Transfers

You create a transaction type for transfers in the same way you create a transaction type for acquisitions; just use Transaction AO76 instead of Transaction AO73. However, some fields are specific to transfers (Figure 6.31):

▶ **Transfer Adopting Dep. Start Date**
If you select this indicator, the depreciation start date and the capitalization date are copied from the retired asset to the new-receiving asset.

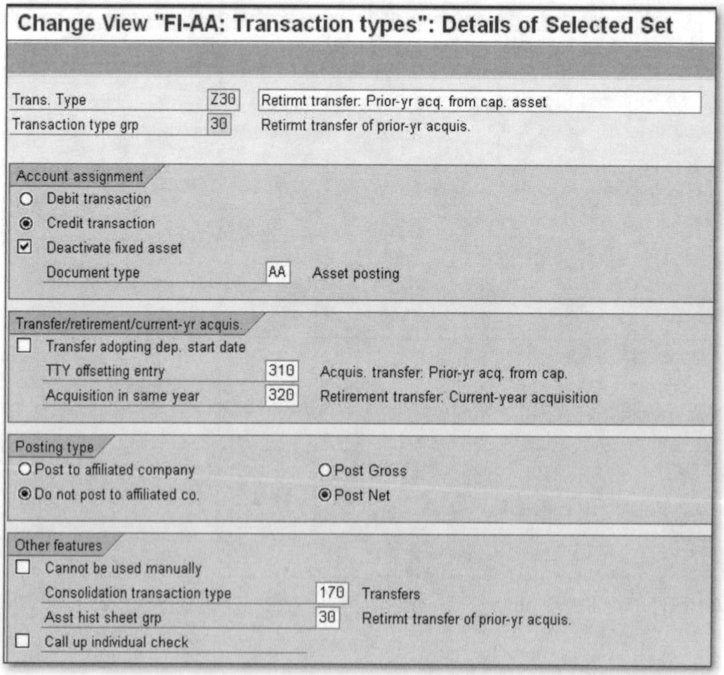

Figure 6.31 Transaction Type for Transfer

► **TTY Offsetting Entry/Acquisition in Same Year**

When you post a transfer, you post a retirement to the old asset and an acquisition to the new-receiving asset. The transaction type used for the old asset is the one that you specify when posting the transaction; the transaction type used in the new-receiving asset comes from the customizing specified here:

► The transaction type specified in the TTY Offsetting Entry field is used for prior-year acquisition postings.

► The transaction type specified in the Acquisition in Same Year field is used for current-year acquisition postings.

Creating a Transaction Type for Unplanned Depreciation

You create a transaction type for unplanned depreciation in the same way you create a transaction type for acquisitions; just use Transaction AO78 instead of Transaction AO73. In unplanned depreciation, a limited number of fields (compared to acquisitions) is required (Figure 6.32). The important fields have already been explained in the sections about the creation of transaction types for acquisitions.

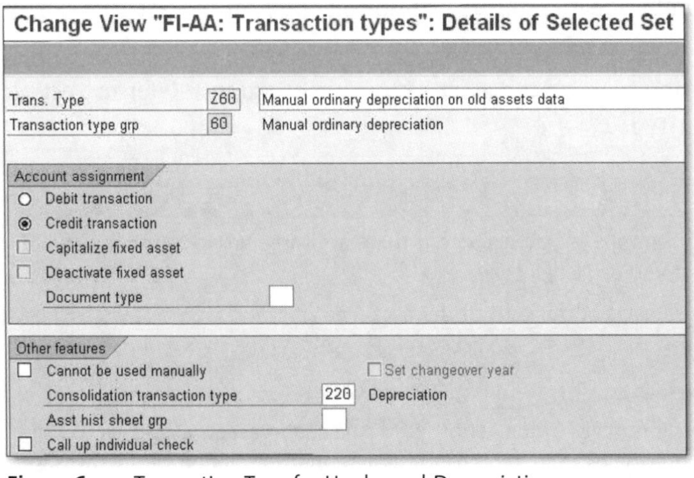

Change View "FI-AA: Transaction types": Details of Selected Set

Trans. Type	Z60	Manual ordinary depreciation on old assets data
Transaction type grp	60	Manual ordinary depreciation

Account assignment
- ○ Debit transaction
- ◉ Credit transaction
- ☐ Capitalize fixed asset
- ☐ Deactivate fixed asset
- Document type

Other features
- ☐ Cannot be used manually   ☐ Set changeover year
- Consolidation transaction type   220 Depreciation
- Asst hist sheet grp
- ☐ Call up individual check

Figure 6.32 Transaction Type for Unplanned Depreciation

Technical Insight

Every time you use a transaction type in Asset Accounting, a document is recorded in Tables ANEK (header) and ANEP (line items). Depreciation postings aren't recorded in these tables.

6.1.26 Configuring the Asset History Sheet

The asset history sheet is a specific report that allows you to represent the values of one or more assets in a matrix, and it is, to some extent, configurable. To configure the asset history sheet, you need to perform two steps.

In the first step, use Transaction OAV9 to create the asset history sheet groups. Many groups are already created, so create a new one only if necessary (Figure 6.33). To do this, follow these steps.

1. Select the New Entries button.

2. Specify the group ID in the Grp field (two-digit, alphanumeric; we recommend starting with Z), and a meaningful description in the Name Asset Hist. Sheet Group column.

3. Assign the transaction types to the asset history sheet groups. Refer to Section 6.1.25, Transaction Types.

Special Asset History Sheet Groups

You can create as many groups as you want, but there are three groups already defined in the system (and that you can't delete):

▶ **YA:** Accumulative values as of the start of the fiscal year

▶ **YY:** Annual values

▶ **YZ:** Accumulative values as of the end of the fiscal year

These groups are used internally in the report to display total accumulated values independent of transaction types. You should not assign any transaction types to these predefined asset history sheet groups.

Note that the report can display detailed information on the basis of the transaction type only for the chosen fiscal year. For the previous fiscal year, you can display the accumulated values (carryforward values to the chosen fiscal year) only in cumulated form.

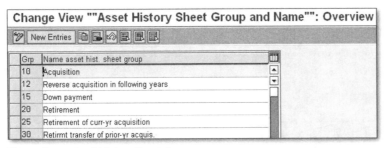

Figure 6.33 Asset History Sheet Groups

In the second step (Figure 6.34), you create the asset history sheet version, which is the matrix in which the values in the asset history sheet report are displayed. (You can create more than one asset history sheet version.) Follow these steps:

1. Run Transaction OA79; the system displays all of the existing versions. Never create a version from scratch; instead, identify the one that is closest to your requirements, copy it, and adapt it as needed.

2. Select the version you want to copy, and click on the Copy History Sheet Version button ( ). In the pop-up, specify the new asset history sheet ID (four digits, starting with Z), and confirm by clicking the Copy History Sheet Version button again.

3. The system displays a matrix where you can specify which value should be contained in each cell (History Sheet Position). To do this, double-click the position you want to modify.

4. In the next screen, on the left side, you can see a list of all of the history sheet groups (remember, you assign transaction types to asset history sheet groups). On the right side, you can define which values of the asset history sheet group are included in the selected position. Descriptions of the possible values are as follows:

   ▶ **Trn:** The transaction value.

   ▶ **Acc Dep – Ord:** Proportional ordinary depreciation associated with the transaction (if it exists).

   ▶ **Acc Dep – Spc:** Proportional special depreciation associated with the transaction (if it exists).

   ▶ **Acc Dep – Upl:** Proportional unplanned depreciation associated with the transaction (if it exists).

405

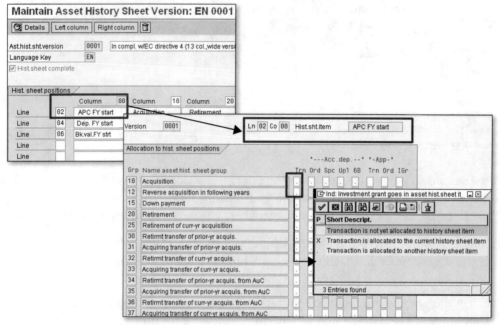

Figure 6.34 Asset History Sheet Variant

- ▶ **Acc Dep – 6B:** Proportional transferred reserves associated with the transaction (if it exists).

- ▶ **App – Trn:** Proportional revaluation of APC associated with the transaction (if it exists).

- ▶ **App – Ord:** Proportional revaluation of accumulated depreciation associated with the transaction (if it exists).

- ▶ **IGr:** Investment grant associated with the transaction (if it exists).

For each value, three indicators are available:

- ▶ **Space:** This means that the value isn't assigned to any position in the asset history sheet.

- ▶ **Period (.):** This means that the value is assigned to another position.

- ▶ **X:** This means that the value is assigned to this position.

5. If necessary, change the settings of all of the positions included in the asset history sheet version that you created by copying. Specifically, ensure that all of the asset history sheet groups that you use are correctly mapped in the version.

> **Note**
>
> Don't confuse the asset history sheet with the asset history (FINANCIAL ACCOUNTING • FIXED ASSETS • INFORMATION SYSTEM • REPORTS ON ASSET ACCOUNTING • HISTORY • ASSET HISTORY, report RAHIST01). The asset history report generates a printout of all information about an asset, including master data fields and changes, transactions posted, and depreciations carried out.

6.1.27 Using Asset Accounting Enhancements (User Exits)

If you need a specific function that can't be achieved via the customizing tools, a user exit may be available. In this case, you aren't changing the standard system (the standard ABAP programs); instead, you're putting your own ABAP code in a placeholder made available by SAP; that is, a *user exit*.

Below is a list of the user exits available for the asset master data in the Asset Accounting module:

- Automatic assignment of inventory number: AISA0001
- Determination of base value for depreciation calculation: AFAR0001
- Calculation method for depreciation calculation: AFAR0002
- Changeover method for depreciation calculation: AFAR0003
- Calculation of proportional values during asset retirement: AFAR0004
- Definition of revaluation: ARVL0001
- Output of descriptions in reporting: ANLR0001
- Currency translation in asset reporting: AMGS_001
- Output of asset number in reporting: BADA0002
- Changing posted line items: AINT0004
- Checks during posting: AINT0001
- Company code relationship for intercompany transfers: AMSP0002
- Distribution of revenue for mass retirement: WFOB0001
- Account determination during posting: AINT0002
- Checks during legacy data transfer: ALTD0001
- Repayment percentage or amount: AINT0003
- Number range for master data maintenance: AIST0001

▸ Determination of asset value date while posting: AMAV0001

▸ Defining your own fields for asset master record: AIST0002

▸ Integration of Asset Accounting with Plant Maintenance (PM): AAPM0001

Work together with your ABAP colleagues to check the possibilities and implement the needed enhancements. Don't confuse the user exits available for substitutions and validations with the user exits for enhancements.

6.1.28 FAQ and Troubleshooting Tips

Next we answer some frequently asked questions and offer helpful troubleshooting tips.

FAQ

1. **Question:** How can I translate the chart of depreciation into different languages?

   Answer: Use Transaction EC08 to copy a reference chart of depreciation. In the resulting box, select Specify Description of Chart of Depreciation. Select one chart of depreciation, and then choose GOTO • TRANSLATION.

2. **Question:** Can I create a chart of depreciation from scratch, instead of copying an existing one?

   Answer: No, this isn't possible.

3. **Question:** Can I copy a non-standard chart of depreciation (i.e., one that I created before)?

   Answer: Yes.

4. **Question:** What should the naming convention be for the chart of depreciation?

   Answer: We suggest keeping a naming convention that includes the country ID. Remember, all of the standard charts of depreciation have the following naming convention: 0 + Country ID (e.g., 0DE for Germany).

5. **Question:** In practice, what is a chart of depreciation?

   Answer: In very simple words, it's a container of customizing within the Asset Accounting component. After a new chart of depreciation is copied from another one, you proceed with customizing all of the other Asset Accounting objects.

6. **Question:** Can I have different number ranges for the same asset class in different company codes?

   Answer: Yes. For example, asset class 1000 points to the number range 01. You can create the number range 01:

   ▸ In company code 1000: from 0100000000 to 0199999999.

   ▸ In company code 2000: from 0200000000 to 0299999999.

7. **Question:** I have a large number of company codes in the system, and I want to have one unique number range for all of them. Is this possible?

   Answer: Yes. Open FINANCIAL ACCOUNTING • ASSET ACCOUNTING • ORGANIZATIONAL STRUCTURES • SPECIFY NUMBER ASSIGNMENT ACROSS COMPANY CODES, and assign all of the company codes to one reference company code. Then maintain the number range only under the reference company code. In such a situation, there will be no sequence to the assets numbers in each company code; for example, asset 1 may be in company code 1000, while asset 2 may be in company code 3000.

8. **Question:** Does the validation for asset master data work both when I create the asset *and* when I change it?

   Answer: Yes.

9. **Question:** In which program are the user exits for Asset accounting validations stored?

   Answer: In the same program where general ledger validations are stored: FINANCIAL ACCOUNTING • SPECIAL PURPOSE LEDGER • BASIC SETTINGS • USER EXITS • MAINTAIN CLIENT-SPECIFIC USER EXITS (or Transaction GCX2). The application area is GBLR (Val/Sub: Exit for Rules).

10. **Question:** In my situation, depreciation area 11 must always have the same acquisition value as area 01 but can have its own depreciation terms. How should I perform this configuration?

    Answer: First, depreciation area 11 must be a real depreciation area. If this is the case, go to: FINANCIAL ACCOUNTING • ASSET ACCOUNTING • VALUATION • DEPRECIATION AREAS • SPECIFY TRANSFER OF APC VALUES. For depreciation area 11, specify 01 under the ValAd column, and select the Ident. Flag. In this way, you ensure that the APC values in area 11 are exactly the same as in area 01. Now go to FINANCIAL ACCOUNTING • ASSET ACCOUNTING • VALUATION • DEPRECIATION AREAS • SPECIFY TRANSFER OF DEPRECIATION TERMS. Leave the TTr and Identical columns blank for Area 11.

11. **Question:** Can I create or modify a transaction type group?

    Answer: The transaction type group is predefined in the system and can't be changed.

12. **Question:** Does the system use only the value date to determine the connected posting period?

    Answer: No. The asset value date is the starting point for determining how and when the transaction affects the depreciation, but the system also uses another important configuration object: the period control specified in the depreciation key.

13. **Question:** When should a number range be external?

    Answer: Either during migration or when the asset master record numbering is externally determined (very rare).

14. **Question:** In which table are the asset master data number ranges stored?

    Answer: All number ranges are maintained in Table NRIV. For asset master data, the object name is ANLAGENNR.

Troubleshooting

1. **Issue:** When running the depreciation, an error message states that the company code has a parallel currency, but no depreciation area manages that parallel currency.

   Solution: If a company code uses one or more parallel currencies, at least one depreciation area must be set up with the parallel currencies. You specify the currency of the depreciation area in Transaction OAYH.

2. **Issue:** Error F5557 appears when running Transaction OAYZ to maintain asset classes in depreciation areas: "Local currencies for company code 2900 cannot be completely determined."

   Solution: One of the company codes assigned to the chart of accounts in which you're working has a problem with the local currency or parallel currencies. First check the parallel currencies. This error can happen if, for example, the company code has been assigned a hard currency in Transaction OB22, but the hard currency isn't defined in the country to which the company code is assigned.

3. **Issue:** Error ACC_AA029 appears: "Leading ledger depreciation area 01 post to ledger group YY without leading ledger."

Solution: Depreciation area 01 is the leading depreciation area and must be assigned to a ledger group that contains the leading ledger. You're trying to assign that area to a ledger group that doesn't contain the leading ledger.

4. **Issue:** When assigning validations to company codes, error message SV074 appears: "Enter a floating point number."

   Solution: Use just letters and numbers in the validation name, avoiding special characters. If necessary, copy the validation to a new one and assign the new one to the company codes.

6.2   Asset Master Data Management

In this section, the creation and change of asset master data is described in detail. We focus on seven functions related to the management of fixed assets master data:

- Creating a main asset
- Creating a sub-asset
- Blocking an asset for further acquisition
- Deleting an asset
- Creating asset master data directly inside the transaction to post the asset acquisition
- Carrying out mass changes to asset master data
- Using standard reporting for asset master data

6.2.1   Creating a Main Asset

Quick Reference

Menu path: Accounting • Financial Accounting • Fixed Assets • Asset • Create • Asset

Transaction: AS01

Tables: ANLA (asset data depending only on the company code), ANLB (depreciation terms), ANLZ (time-dependent data)

When creating and changing an asset, running a report, or posting is necessary, specify the asset ID in the following form:

ASSET NUMBER (max 10 digits) + SUB-ASSET NUMBER (max 3 digits).

Creating a main asset means to create an asset with sub-number "0". The main asset can be used to create subsequent sub-assets to which data are copied and can be changed or not depending on the customizing specified for the screen layout rules in view V_T082A_10. This section is about creating a main asset; we will focus on creating sub-assets in Section 6.2.2, Creating Sub-Assets.

To create a main asset, use Transaction AS01, and follow these steps:

1. In the initial screen (Figure 6.35), specify the asset class and the company code. Also specify the number of similar assets you want to create; the system provides 1 by default, but you can change this. Press Enter.

2. If the number range assigned to the asset class is external, the system asks you the asset number. Supply this information.

3. In the General tab, fill in the following information:
   - **Description:** Enter a description for the asset.
   - **Acct. Determination:** This information comes from the asset class and can't be changed.
   - **Inventory Number:** Enter the internal identification number, which is usually physically marked on the asset.
   - **Capitalized On:** For consistency reasons, we recommend letting the system automatically fill this field with the first acquisition, unless there are legal or company reasons to set the date differently.
   - **Deactivation On:** This field is automatically updated with the posting of an asset retirement but can also be filled manually.
   - **First Acquisition On:** This is the date of the first acquisition posted to the asset (more than acquisition posting is possible for the same asset).

4. When you first create an asset, the system automatically creates a time interval from 01.01.1900 to 31.12.9999 in which the information is valid (Figure 6.36). When you change the asset and add or change any information in the time-dependent data, the system asks if you want to overwrite the existing information for the validity period (if so, click Yes), or create a new validity period when the new data is valid (if so, click New Time Interval, and specify the from date). The time-dependent information is managed in Table ANLZ.

5. In the Allocations tab (Figure 6.36), assign the asset to one or more of the allocation groups that you've defined in Transactions OAVA or OAV8. You use the evaluation groups for classification and reporting purposes.

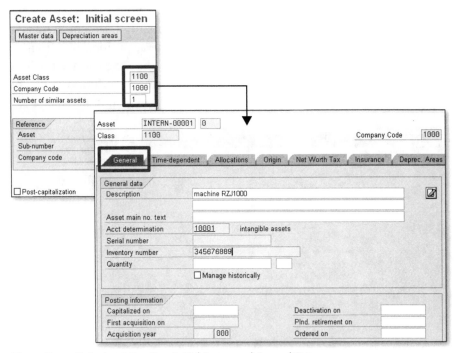

Figure 6.35 Main Asset Creation: Initial Screen and General Data

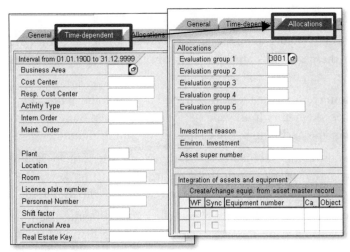

Figure 6.36 Main Asset Creation: Time-Dependent Data and Allocation (User Fields and Equipment)

6. In the Origin tab (Figure 6.37), the Vendor field is automatically filled if the asset was posted via Transaction F-90. Otherwise, specify the value manually. The same is true for the Trading Partner field, if the acquisition was from an affiliated company (Transactions ABZP or ABT1N). The Original Asset field is filled automatically if the asset was created through a transfer (intracompany or intercompany); this field is also typically used for the migration of old assets.

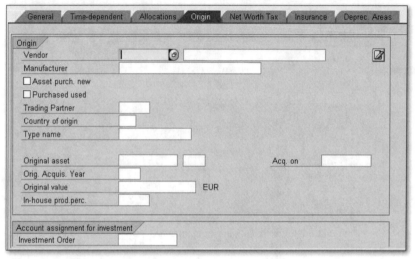

Figure 6.37 Main Asset Creation: Origin Data

7. In the Deprec. Areas tab (Figure 6.38), enter the depreciation terms, which are usually defined in the asset class and automatically transferred to the assets belonging to it. They include the following fields:

  ▶ **DKey:** This column controls the technical method by which the depreciation is carried out; that is, whether it uses the straight-line method (same amount in each period), or the declining balance method (declining amount).

  ▶ **UseLife:** This stands for "useful life in years and periods" and is the period in which the depreciation occurs. With the standard depreciation key, LINR, the acquisition cost is spread equally in all of the periods of the useful life.

  ▶ **ODep Start:** You usually leave this field blank when you create the asset; the field is automatically filled by the asset value date of the first acquisition posting.

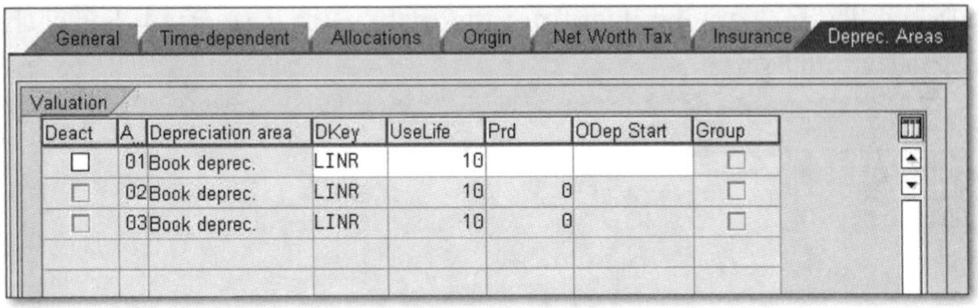

Figure 6.38   Main Asset Creation: Depreciation Terms

You can also copy the asset from another one. In this case, don't choose the asset class; it's automatically provided based on the asset class of the reference asset. Technically, it's possible to specify an asset class and copy from an asset that belongs to another asset class, but we strongly advise against this because it can lead to unwanted and inconsistent data in the new asset master record. The fields that are copied from the reference asset are defined for the screen layout rules in view V_T082A_10 (the field is copied if the Copy flag is activated).

6.2.2   Creating Sub-Assets

Quick Reference

Menu path: ACCOUNTING • FINANCIAL ACCOUNTING • FIXED ASSETS • ASSET • CREATE • SUB-NUMBER • ASSET

Transaction: AS11

Tables: ANLA (asset data depending only on the company code), ANLB (depreciation terms), ANLZ (time-dependent data)

To create a sub-asset, run Transaction AS11 (Figure 6.39), and specify the following:

► The asset number of an existing main asset.

► A sub-number different from zero (zero is reserved for the main asset number). Keep in mind that you should do this only if the asset class specifies that the sub-number assignment is external; otherwise, leave the sub-number blank, and the system automatically uses the first sub-number available for the main asset.

In all of the screen's tabs (General, Time-Dependent, etc.), the system proposes information based on the main asset number for fields for which, in view

V_T082A_10, the flag for copying data from the main asset is selected. For each field, the Copy flag is activated.

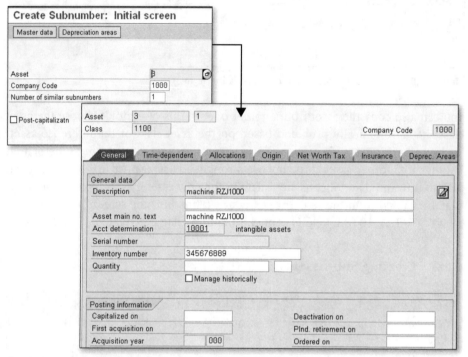

Figure 6.39 Asset Sub-Number Creation

6.2.3 Blocking Assets

Block an asset by running Transaction AS05 and selecting the Locked to Acquis. flag (Figure 6.40). The result of the asset block is that no further acquisition is possible on the asset; depreciation and retirement, however, can still be performed.

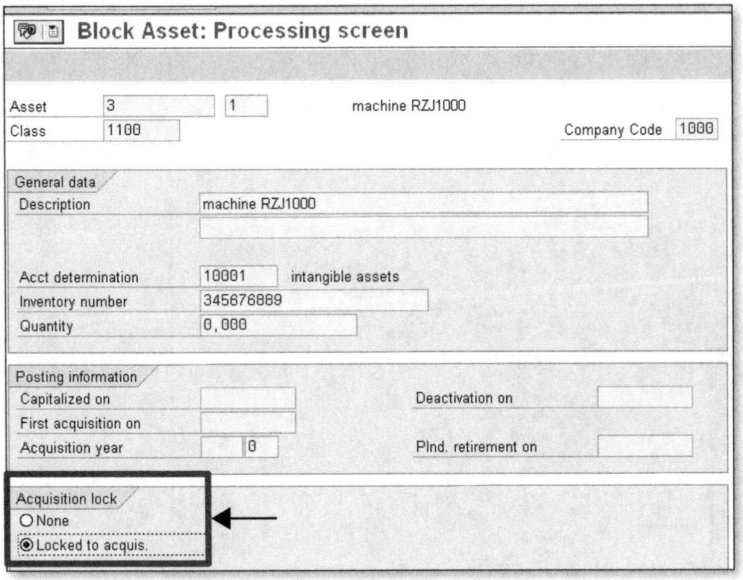

Figure 6.40 Blocking an Asset for Further Acquisitions

6.2.4 Deleting Assets

Quick Reference

Menu path: ACCOUNTING • FINANCIAL ACCOUNTING • FIXED ASSETS • ASSET • DELETE • ASSET

Transaction: AS06

Unlike with general ledger accounts, customers, and vendors, there is a menu transaction available to physically delete assets from the database. The prerequisite for this action is that no transaction, and therefore no depreciation, has been posted against the asset.

To delete a single asset, use Transaction AS06 (Figure 6.41), select the Physically Delete Asset flag, and click the Save button (💾). The system asks for a final confirmation for the deletion; if you click the Yes button, the asset is physically deleted. The number won't be reused automatically.

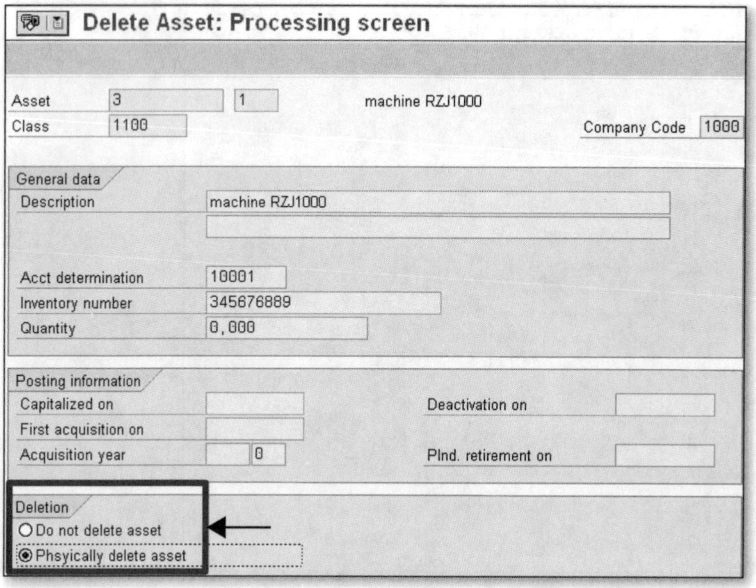

Figure 6.41 Physical Deletion of an Asset

6.2.5 Creating Assets with Acquisition or Transfer Transactions

Quick Reference

Transactions: ABZON (acquisition with automatic offsetting entry), ABUMN (transfer within company code), ABT1N (intercompany asset transfer)

Tables: ANLA (asset data depending only on the company code), ANLB (depreciation terms), ANLZ (time-dependent data)

There may be a situation where you need to create an asset for technical reasons but don't want new master data that refers to a new physical asset. In this case, you can create the new asset using a posting transaction. This function is available in the following posting transactions:

▶ **ABZON:** Acquis. w/Autom. Offsetting Entry

▶ **ABUMN:** Transfer within Company Code

▶ **ABT1N:** Intercompany Asset Transfer

Figure 6.42 shows how the functionality can be used within Transaction ABZON. Click on the New Asset option instead of the Existing Asset option, and then specify a description, asset class, and cost center. If additional information is required, click on the Master Data button; a new screen opens where you can add values for other fields. If there are still other fields that must be filled in, click on the Additional Data button, and the system displays the same screens available for creating an asset with Transaction AS01.

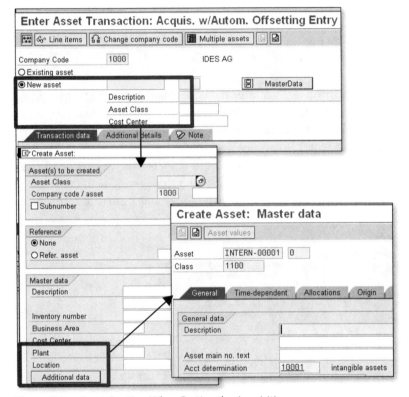

Figure 6.42 Asset Creation When Posting the Acquisition

6.2.6 Reporting on Asset Master Data

Next we discuss two standard master data reports and also offer some brief instructions on how to create queries.

Standard Reports

Quick Reference

Menu paths: ACCOUNTING • FINANCIAL ACCOUNTING • FIXED ASSETS • INFORMATION SYSTEM • REPORTS ON ASSET ACCOUNTING • ASSET BALANCES • BALANCE LISTS • SAMPLE FOR ADDRESS DATA FOR ASSETS

AND

ACCOUNTING • FINANCIAL ACCOUNTING • FIXED ASSETS • INFORMATION SYSTEM • REPORTS ON ASSET ACCOUNTING • PREPARATION FOR CLOSING • INTERNATIONAL • CHANGES TO ASSET MASTER RECORDS

Transactions: S_ALR_87010125 (sample for address data for an asset), S_ALR_87012037 (changes to asset master records)

If you need a good report on asset master data, we suggest creating a query and using the ADA logical database. Most of the standard reports in Asset Accounting are about values, not master data; however, there are two master data reports available, as listed in the Quick Reference box. With the first transaction, you can see a list of assets with address data (see Figure 6.43 for the selection screen). With the second transaction, you can see a list of the changes made to the selected assets (see Figure 6.44 for an example of the list). The changes are read from Tables CDHDR and CDPOS.

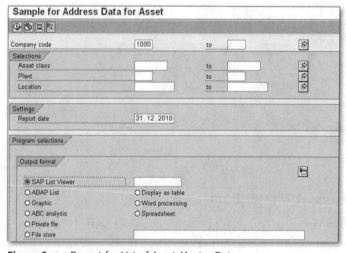

Figure 6.43   Report for List of Asset Master Data

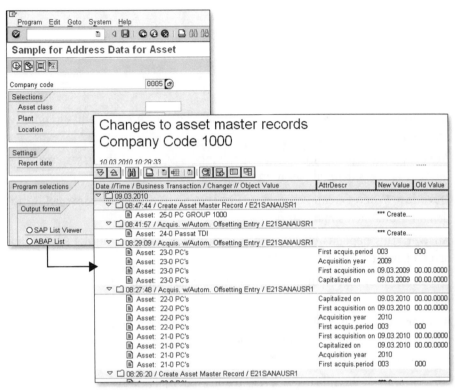

Figure 6.44 Report for Master Data Changes

Queries

Menu path: ACCOUNTING • FINANCIAL ACCOUNTING • FIXED ASSETS • INFORMATION SYSTEM • TOOLS • AD HOC REPORTS

Transaction: ARQ0

Create queries using Transaction SQ01. Before creating a query, you must define the infoset with Transaction SQ02, where you specify the tables involved in the query and the logic of extraction of data. For queries on asset master data, we suggest creating an infoset that starts reading the data from Table ANLA. Remember to maintain the infoset assignment to a user group using Transaction SQ03.

6.2.7 FAQ and Troubleshooting Tips

Next we answer some frequently asked questions and offer helpful troubleshooting tips.

FAQ

1. **Question:** When I create a new asset using Transaction AS01, what number is assigned to it?

   Answer: This depends on the number range assigned to the asset class. The number range is defined based on company code.

2. **Question:** When I create, change, or display an asset, why are some fields hidden and some fields mandatory?

   Answer: This depends on the screen layout rules; see Section 6.1.8, Creating Screen Layout Rules, for more information.

3. **Question:** The Depreciation Terms field is already filled. Where do they come from?

   Answer: They are default values that come from the combination of asset class and depreciation area. Technically they can be changed, but this may not be allowed in your company's accounting policy.

4. **Question:** Does the substitution for creating assets also work when I change an existing asset using Transaction AS02?

   Answer: No; such substitution works only with Transaction AS01.

5. **Question:** In two different periods of fiscal years, I purchased two machines that are logically or technically linked. Should I create one asset with two acquisition postings, two sub-assets with the same asset number, or two completely separate assets?

   Answer: Table 6.5 provides an overview of the most important practical consequences of the three different choices.

6. **Question:** Can an asset be deleted even though the company code is productive?

   Answer: Yes.

7. **Question:** In an asset class, is it possible to specify that one or more depreciation areas can't be used?

Answer: Yes. Use the customizing activity FINANCIAL ACCOUNTING • ASSET ACCOUNTING • VALUATION • DETERMINE DEPRECIATION AREA IN THE ASSET CLASS.

Consequence of Activity...	One Asset, Two Acquisitions	Two Sub-Assets with Same Asset Number	Two Separate Assets
Depreciation	The duration of depreciation doesn't change, even if the new acquisition is posted in a new fiscal year.	The second sub-asset will have a separate planned depreciation. No connection between the depreciation of the two sub-assets.	The second asset will have a separate planned depreciation. No connection between the depreciation of the two assets.
Reporting	There is only one asset.	The two sub-assets can be displayed together in reporting.	The two assets are displayed separately. However, if they have the same asset class, they can be displayed together at the asset class display level.
Master data creation	There is no new sub-asset.	The second sub-asset can take some values from the main asset (first asset with sub-number = 0). This depends on the customizing of the asset class.	The new asset can be copied from the other. The new asset will have restrictions based on the customizing of the asset class.

Table 6.4 Acquisition of Assets and Sub-Assets

Troubleshooting Tips

1. **Issue:** Error message AA130 appears: "Asset class XXXX cannot be used in company code YYYY" when creating a new asset.

   Solution: This means that the asset class is deactivated in the chart of depreciation to which the company code belongs. You can unlock the asset class in the chart of depreciation using Transaction AM05.

2. **Issue:** Error message AA203 appears: "Number range XX not in the number allocation range."

Solution: This means that you haven't created the number range assigned to the asset class in the company code. Create the number range.

3. **Issue:** Error message AB059 appears: "Fiscal year change not yet made for company code XXXX."

   Solution: This means that the system (server) date is a new fiscal year, but you haven't yet done the fiscal year change. Run Transaction AJRW to carry out the fiscal year change.

4. **Issue:** When trying to display the master data of an asset with Transaction AS03, error message AY237 appears: "Invalid screen layout rule in asset class 1100, ch. of deprec. 1DE."

   Solution: Run Transaction OAYZ, and check that the layout is specified in all of the depreciation areas.

6.3   Posting Transactions to Assets

In this section, we explain the most common transactions used to post to assets. All transactions automatically create a Financial Accounting document for the depreciation area, which posts in real time to the general ledger (usually general ledger 01). For other areas that post to the general ledger, the posting takes place periodically using Transaction ASKB.

6.3.1   Posting Acquisitions with Automatic Offsetting Entries

Quick Reference
Menu path: ACCOUNTING • FINANCIAL ACCOUNTING • FIXED ASSETS • POSTING • ACQUISITION • EXTERNAL ACQUISITION • ACQUISITIONS W/AUTOM. OFFSETTING ENTRY
Transaction: ABZON
Tables: ANEK (asset document header), ANEP (asset document line items)

Use Transaction ABZON to post the acquisition of an asset against an offsetting account; the offsetting account is automatically determined based on your customization of Transaction AO90 (balance sheet accounts, contra account: acquisition value); however, you can also manually specify the offsetting account in the Additional Details tab, using the Offsetting Acct No field (Figure 6.45). You can use Transaction F-91 to clear the offsetting account.

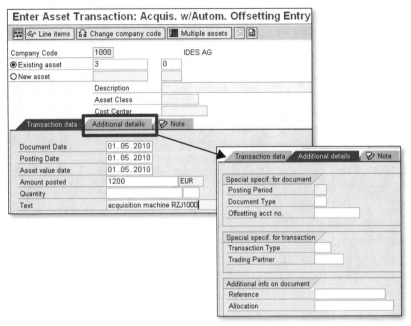

Figure 6.45 Transaction ABZON

Follow these steps to post the acquisition with Transaction ABZON (Figure 6.45):

1. In the initial screen, decide whether you want to post to an existing asset (select Existing Asset) or create an asset from within the transaction (select New Asset) (see Section 6.2.5, Creating Assets with Acquisition or Transfer Transactions, for more details).

2. Specify the document and posting date that will be transferred to the Financial Accounting document. Also specify the asset value date, which is modified by the period control in the depreciation key and determines the date on which the depreciation starts. This can be different in different depreciation areas because you can specify different posting keys in different depreciation areas.

3. Specify the acquisition value in the Amount Posted field. If you click on the Line Items button (🔗 **Line items**), you can see the asset value in the different depreciation areas managed in the asset.

4. Click on the Additional Details button, and specify the following:
   ▸ Trading partner, if the asset was acquired by an affiliated company, and if needed and allowed by the transaction type.

▶ Document type, if you want to post with a document type different from the one specified in the transaction type configuration. We don't recommend using this option.

▶ Clearing account, if you want to post to a different offsetting account than the one that is automatically determined. We don't recommend using this option.

▶ Transaction type, if you don't want to post with the default transaction type specified for this transaction.

After saving, the system posts an Asset Accounting document and a general ledger Financial Accounting document (this is for the depreciation area that posts in real time to the general ledger; for the other depreciation area, the general ledger document is generated by Transaction ASKB) (Figure 6.46). On the debit side of the general ledger document, the system posts to the asset; on the credit side the system posts to a general ledger offsetting account. The offsetting account is specified in the customizing related to the account determination under the Contra Account: Acquisition Value Denomination field, unless you have specified a different account.

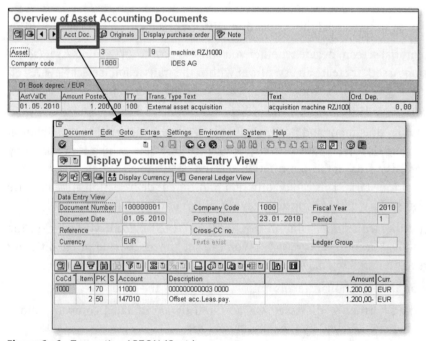

Figure 6.46 Transaction ABZON (Cont.)

You can use Transaction F-91 to clear the offsetting account. If the acquisition comes through a Financial Accounting invoice, you post the invoice against the same offsetting account and then clear the account via Transaction F-91.

6.3.2 Posting Acquisitions with Financial Accounting Vendor Invoices

Quick Reference
Menu path: ACCOUNTING • FINANCIAL ACCOUNTING • FIXED ASSETS • POSTING • ACQUISITION • EXTERNAL ACQUISITION • WITH VENDOR
Transaction: F-90
Tables: ANEK, ANEP

For acquisitions with a Financial Accounting vendor invoice, use a Financial Accounting transaction to post directly to the asset. The screen is similar to the ones displayed in the standard transaction, FB01, which can also be used to post to assets.

Post the invoice as you usually would. The only difference compared to a normal, vendor invoice is in recording the cost on the account; here you don't specify a P&L general ledger account, but an asset.

When posting to an asset within a Financial Accounting transaction, you must use specific posting keys dedicated to that purpose. In a standard SAP system, posting keys 70 (debit) and 75 (credit) are used for posting to assets. Figure 6.47 shows the configuration for posting key 70; the Account Type radio button indicates that it can be used only with asset accounts.

Together with the asset-specific posting key, specify the asset number (main number plus sub-number; e.g., 1122-0) and the transaction type. When the asset posting keys are used, a specific screen is available in the Financial Accounting transaction, allowing you to record the different transaction values for the different depreciation areas.

From an Asset Accounting point of view, the only difference between acquisition within Asset Accounting and acquisition through a Financial Accounting invoice is that, in acquisition through Financial Accounting, the number of the vendor is automatically recorded in the asset master record.

427

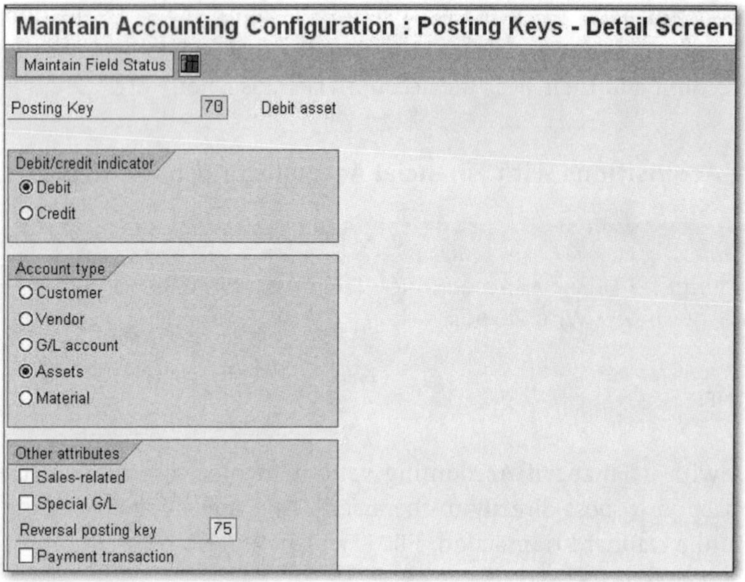

Figure 6.47 Posting Key 70 for Assets

6.3.3 Posting Acquisitions from Logistics (Settlement from WBS or Internal Order)

If you're using Materials Management for the company's purchasing, you probably manage the acquisition of assets in an integrated process that starts with the creation of a purchase order. Keep in mind that no asset is included directly in the purchase order; instead, you enter either the WBS or the internal order. In this way, it's possible to carry out the budget availability control during purchase order creation; in a separate step within Controlling, the costs posted to the WBS or internal order with the invoice verification will be settled to the asset under construction and then to the final asset.

If the acquisition of capital assets must be subjected to a budgeting control, SAP provides an integrated solution that involves the following modules:

▶ Investment Management, to carry out planning and budgeting at a high level

▶ Controlling-Project System or Controlling-Internal Orders, to manage a detailed budgeting availability control for each specific investment measure

▶ Asset Accounting, through the creation of assets under construction that are *physically linked* to WBS or internal orders

A comprehensive discussion of the management of the integrated chain is beyond the scope of this book. However, we've provided a quick list of the main customizing activities and the transactions necessary to carry out the process.

- **Inventory Management configuration**
    - **Investment program types:** INVESTMENT MANAGEMENT • MASTER DATA • DEFINE PROGRAM TYPES
    - **Budgeting profile:** INVESTMENT MANAGEMENT • BUDGETING IN PROGRAM • DEFINE BUDGET PROFILES FOR INVESTMENT PROGRAMS AND ASSIGN BUDGET PROFILE TO PROGRAM TYPE

- **Controlling-Project System configuration**
    - **Budget profile for projects:** PROJECT SYSTEM • COSTS • BUDGET • MAINTAIN BUDGET PROFILE AND STIPULATE DEFAULT BUDGET PROFILE FOR PROJECT DEFINITION
    - **Tolerance limit:** PROJECT SYSTEM • COSTS • BUDGET • DEFINE TOLERANCE LIMITS

- **Controlling-Internal Orders configuration**
    - **Budget profile:** CONTROLLING • INTERNAL ORDERS • BUDGETING AND AVAILABILITY CONTROL • MAINTAIN BUDGETING PROFILE
    - **Tolerance limit:** CONTROLLING • INTERNAL ORDERS • BUDGETING AND AVAILABILITY CONTROL • DEFINE TOLERANCE LIMITS FOR AVAILABILITY CONTROL

- **Asset under construction configuration (Asset Accounting)**
    - **Set the asset class as relevant for assets under construction:** FINANCIAL ACCOUNTING • ASSET ACCOUNTING • ORGANIZATIONAL STRUCTURE • ASSET CLASSES • DEFINE ASSET CLASSES
    - **The other steps are contained in the following customizing menu:** FINANCIAL ACCOUNTING • ASSET ACCOUNTING • TRANSACTIONS • CAPITALIZATION OF ASSETS UNDER CONSTRUCTION

- **Process transactions**
    - Inventory Management program definition: IM01
    - Inventory Management creation of top position: IM11
    - Inventory Management program structure: IM22
    - Inventory Management program budgeting: IM32
    - Project definition: CJ06

- WBS creation: CJ01
- Internal order creation: KO01/KO04
- WBS direct budgeting: CJ30
- Internal order budgeting: KO22
- Settlement of costs from WBS to AuC/final asset: CJ88/CJ8G/CJIC
- Settlement of costs from internal order to AuC/final asset: KO88/KOB5

When the final asset is created and the acquisition costs settled to it, the process continues entirely within the Asset Accounting module, just as for all of the other assets.

> **Note**
>
> It's possible to settle acquisitions from WBS or internal orders without using the Logistics invoice verification. In this case, the posting takes place directly in Financial Accounting. Apart from the initial step of acquisition, the process is exactly the same.

6.3.4 Posting Acquisitions from Affiliated Companies

> **Quick Reference**
>
> **Menu path:** ACCOUNTING • FINANCIAL ACCOUNTING • FIXED ASSETS • POSTING • ACQUISITION • EXTERNAL ACQUISITION • FROM AFFILIATED COMPANY
>
> **Transaction:** ABZP
>
> **Tables:** ANEK, ANEP

Transaction ABZP is used to post to an asset with the trading partner information as mandatory; unlike Transaction ABZON, in Transaction ABZP, you can't create the master data inside the posting screen.

When you run Transaction ABZP, follow these steps (Figure 6.48):

1. In the first screen, specify the asset identification data (number, sub-number, and company code) and the document and posting date that will be transferred to the subsequent Financial Accounting document.

2. Use the transaction type automatically proposed by the system, or change it to another suitable one. Press Enter.

3. In the following screen (shown in the bottom of Figure 6.48), specify a trading partner, which is recorded in the Financial Accounting document and in the asset master data (in the Origin field).

4. Specify the amount and the asset value date. The asset value date determines, in combination with the depreciation key, the depreciation start date.

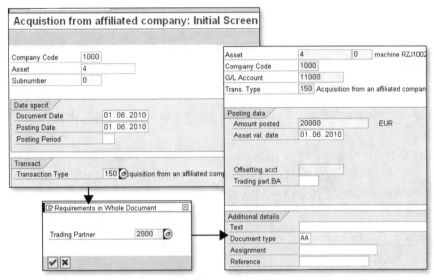

Figure 6.48 Acquisition from Affiliated Company (Posting with Trading Partner)

The system generates an asset accounting document (recorded in Tables ANEK and ANEP) and a related Financial Accounting document for the area that posts in real time to the general ledger. For the other depreciation areas that post to the general ledger, the posting takes place with Transaction ASKB.

6.3.5 Transferring Assets from Company to Company (in the Same Client)

Quick Reference

Menu path: ACCOUNTING • FINANCIAL ACCOUNTING • FIXED ASSETS • POSTING • TRANSFER • INTERCOMPANY ASSET TRANSFER

Transaction: ABT1N

Tables: ANEK, ANEP

Use Transaction ABT1N to transfer an asset between two different company codes available in your client. Don't use this transaction if one of the company codes is managed in another SAP system or in an external system.

Run Transaction ABT1N, and, if needed, change the sending company code with the Company Code Change button. Then follow these steps (Figure 6.49):

1. Specify the asset that is transferred (❶).

2. Define the document date, posting date, and asset value date (2).

3. Specify (❸) whether the transfer is carried out

   ▸ Without revenue in depreciation area 01

   ▸ With a specified manual revenue

   ▸ With revenue equal to the net book value from a specified depreciation area

4. Specify the receiving company code and whether the posting is made against an asset that you already created previously, or to a new asset that will be created together with the posting transaction (❹).

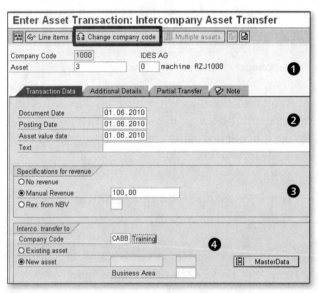

Figure 6.49 Intercompany Asset Transfer (Between Company Codes of the Same Client)

When you save the transaction, two posting are created in Asset Accounting, which you can retrieve with Transaction AB03 (Figure 6.50):

▸ A retirement in the sending company code; the asset that is transferred is deactivated in this company code.

▸ An acquisition in the receiving company code.

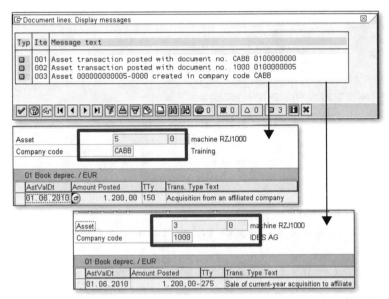

Figure 6.50 Intercompany Asset Transfer (Between Company Codes of the Same Client) — Asset Documents Created

In both the classic general ledger and the new SAP General Ledger, two documents are created, one in the sending and one in the receiving company code. The documents are physically linked through the Cross-CC No. field, which has the same value in both documents (Figure 6.51).

Note

The use of this transaction must comply with the group policy and local fiscal rules. No invoice is created; if tax-related invoices must be created (which is usually the case), you need to create them separately.

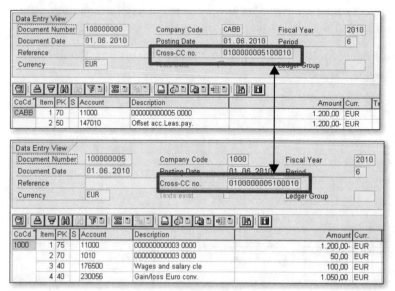

Figure 6.51 Intercompany Asset Transfer (Between Company Codes of the Same Client) — Financial Accounting Documents Created

6.3.6 Transferring from Asset to Asset Within Company Codes

Quick Reference

Menu path: ACCOUNTING • FINANCIAL ACCOUNTING • FIXED ASSETS • POSTING • TRANSFER • TRANSFER WITHIN COMPANY CODE

Transaction: ABUMN

Use Transaction ABUMN to post the transfer of APC values and accumulated depreciation from one asset to another within the same company code. You can do the following:

▸ Transfer the values from an old asset to an existing asset. The existing asset can be brand new or be an old asset itself, with existing values.

▸ Transfer the values to a brand new asset. If the new asset should be exactly the same as the old one, don't make any further specifications; the system automatically creates a new asset with the same master data. The new asset references the sending asset in the Original Asset field.

The system posts the following:

▶ Two transactions in Asset Accounting for the two assets involved. Two different transaction types are used.

▶ One common accounting document.

To post a transfer within one company code, follow these steps:

1. Run Transaction ABUMN, and specify a company code (see Figure 6.52, on the top left).

2. In the next screen (Figure 6.52, bottom right), specify the asset to be transferred, the document date, posting date, asset value date, and a meaningful text description.

3. Choose between transferring the values to an existing asset that you have already created (the Existing Asset button) or to a brand new asset that is automatically created by the system as a copy of the existing one (the New Asset button).

4. To post the transaction, click the Save button.

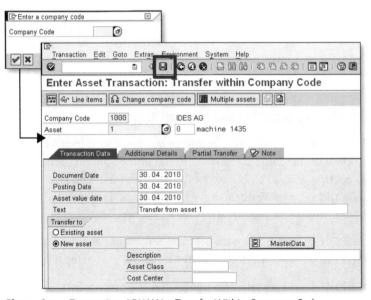

Figure 6.52 Transaction ABUMN – Transfer Within Company Code

6.3.7 Posting a Retirement

When an asset is fully depreciated, its net book value is zero, but it doesn't disappear from reports. The accumulated depreciation is equal to the acquisition value, and both appear separately in the Asset Explorer, balance sheet, and any Asset Accounting or SAP General Ledger reports.

If an asset is sold or scrapped (i.e., if it's retired), you must post this event with one of the following transactions:

▶ **F-92**
For an asset sale with a customer, post the retirement within a Financial Accounting transaction.

▶ **ABAON**
For an asset sale without a customer, the retirement takes place within Asset Accounting.

▶ **ABAVN**
This transaction indicates asset retirement by scrapping.

When you use Transaction F-92, you're posting to an asset within a Financial Accounting transaction with the same screens as Transaction FB01. All of the information provided in Section 6.3.2, Posting Acquisitions with Financial Accounting Vendor Invoices, is valid here as well; however, instead of Transaction 100 or something similar, you must use a retirement transaction type.

With Transaction ABAON (Figure 6.53), you post the retirement against an offsetting account specified for the account determination. Follow these steps:

1. Run Transaction ABAON, and specify a company code upon request.

2. In the following screen, take these steps:

▶ Specify the asset to be retired, the document date, posting date, asset value date, and a meaningful text description.

▶ Choose between manually specifying the revenue (the Manual Revenue button) or taking the revenue from the Net Book Value of the asset (the Rev. from NBV button).

▶ Post the transaction, by clicking the Save button.

3. Clear the offsetting account by posting the customer invoice.

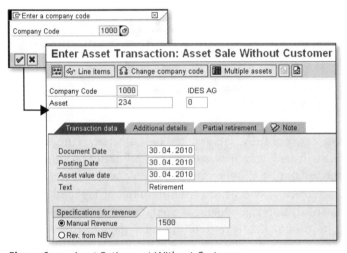

Figure 6.53 Asset Retirement Without Customer

With Transaction ABAVN, you post a retirement by scrapping, without any sale. In this case (Figure 6.54), simply specify the asset number, the sub-number, and the three dates involved in any asset transaction (document date, posting date, and asset value date) Then you can save the document.

The result of all three transactions (F-92, ABAON, and ABAVN) is the following:

▶ An asset document is recorded in Tables ANEK and ANEP.

▶ A general ledger document is created to clear the balance of the acquisition value and of the accumulated depreciation. If the asset isn't completely depreciated (i.e., if the net book value isn't zero), the difference is posted to a cost account that was defined in the customization of account determination.

▶ The deactivation date is set in the asset.

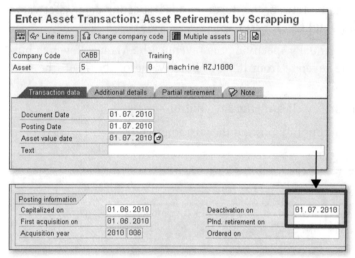

Figure 6.54 Asset Retirement by Scrapping

If the retirement refers to a part of the asset, you can post a partial retirement; in this case, the asset isn't deactivated, and the system writes off only a portion of the acquisition value and the accumulated depreciation. To post a partial retirement in Transaction ABAON or ABAVN, select the Partial Retirement tag, and specify either the amount of the acquisition value that is retired (the Amount field) or the percentage of the acquisition value that is retired (the Percentage field).

6.3.8 Posting an Unplanned Depreciation

Quick Reference

Menu path: ACCOUNTING • FINANCIAL ACCOUNTING • FIXED ASSETS • POSTING • MANUAL VALUE CORRECTION • UNPLANNED DEPRECIATION

Transaction: ABAA

Unplanned depreciation can reduce the net book value of an asset, increasing the amount of the accumulated depreciation by posting a one-time transaction (for example, if an asset has damage that has permanently reduced its productivity). Unplanned depreciation must be allowed in the depreciation areas in which you want it; otherwise, the system issues an error message.

Unplanned depreciation is posted with a specific transaction type; once posted, it's shown in the Asset Explorer as unplanned depreciation in the planned values. After the relevant depreciation run is posted, it's also shown in the posted values.

To post an unplanned depreciation, follow these steps (Figure 6.55):

1. Run Transaction ABAA.

2. Specify the asset, and the document and posting date (❶).

3. In the next screen, define the amount of the unplanned depreciation and the asset value date (❷).

When saving the document, no accounting document is created; the relevant Financial Accounting update occurs with the depreciation run.

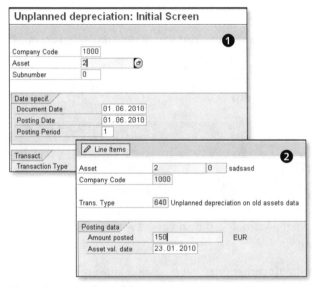

Figure 6.55 Unplanned Depreciation

6.3.9 Changing an Asset Document

You can change or display accounting documents posted against an asset using Transaction AB02, which also allows you to change the asset value date and the text and assignment, if necessary. However, the depreciation start date isn't recalculated from the new asset value date, and the text and assignment aren't automatically transferred to the general ledger document; these changes must be made separately. To see and change the documents for an asset, simply run Transaction AB02, specify the asset, and press Enter. In the resulting screen, the system displays all of the documents posted against the asset. You have, among others, the following options:

▶ 🔖: With this button, you can see and edit the header data of each transaction (e.g., the dates).

▶ ◀ ▶: With these buttons, you can see and edit the values in the other depreciation areas managed in the asset.

▶ Acct Doc. : With this button, you can see an overview of the connected accounting document.

6.3.10 Reversing an Asset Document

Quick Reference
Menu path: Accounting • Financial Accounting • Fixed Assets • Posting • Reverse Document • Other Asset Document
Transaction: AB08

After an asset document has been posted, it can be reversed with Transaction AB08 (Figure 6.56). Follow these steps:

1. Specify the asset to which the document has been posted, and press Enter.

2. In the resulting screen, you see a list of all of the documents posted to the asset. Mark the ones you want to reverse, and click on the Reverse button.

3. Specify a posting date and reversal reason; this information is used in the related accounting document.

4. In the resulting screen, the system displays an overview of the accounting document that is created with the reversal; click on the Post button (🖫) to finalize the reversal.

As a result of the reversal, an Asset Accounting and a Financial Accounting document is created.

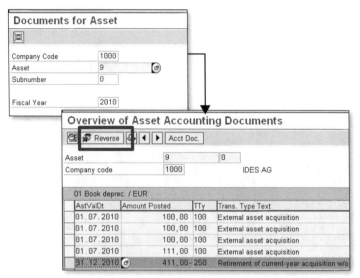

Figure 6.56 Reverse of an Asset Document

6.3.11   Using the Asset Explorer

Quick Reference

Menu path: ACCOUNTING • FINANCIAL ACCOUNTING • FIXED ASSETS • ASSET • ASSET EXPLORER

Transaction: AW01N

The Asset Explorer provides a single-screen comprehensive, interactive view of one asset's values. You can access the Asset Explorer in two ways: by executing Transaction AW01N, or by executing Transactions AS02 or AS03 and then selecting Asset Values.

The Asset Explorer (Figure 6.57) allows you to see the planned and posted values of one specific asset, together with the depreciation parameters. You can browse through the different fiscal years in which the asset has planned values, both in the past and in the future. All of the values displayed refer to exactly one depreciation area. The depreciation areas available for the asset are displayed on the left side; to see the values of another depreciation area, simply double-click it.

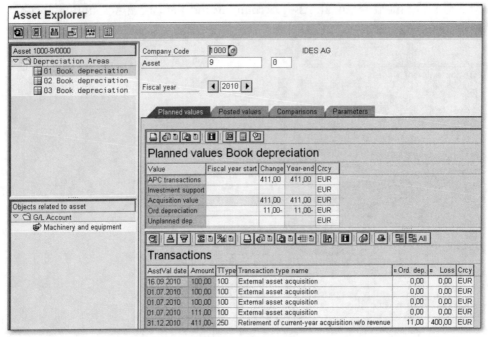

Figure 6.57 Asset Explorer: Planned Values and Transactions

When you click on the Planned Values tab, you can see the depreciations and the interest planned for each month of the chosen year. You can choose any year of the life of the asset, from the first acquisition year up to the last year in which the depreciation is planned, or the year in which the asset has been dismissed.

The planned depreciation and interests are based on the depreciation terms, and on all posted transactions. If you change the depreciation terms and re-open the Asset Explorer, the planned values are automatically adjusted for all open fiscal years. You can also choose a fiscal year in the future; in this case, the system projects future depreciations and interest based on the present available information (depreciation terms and transaction).

The Posted Values tab (Figure 6.58) shows the depreciation and interests for the posting periods in which depreciation runs were already executed.

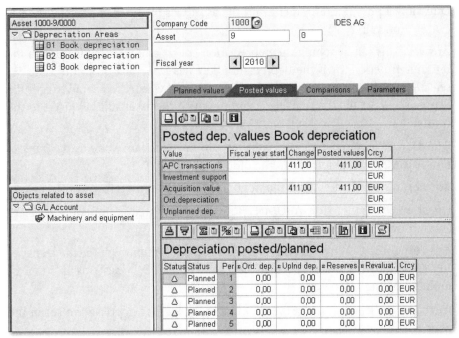

Figure 6.58 Asset Explorer: Posted Values

6.3.12 FAQ and Troubleshooting Tips

Next we answer some frequently asked questions and offer helpful troubleshooting tips.

FAQ

1. **Question:** When I post the retirement of a main asset, are the sub-assets also automatically retired?

   Answer: No. The sub-assets are not automatically retired by posting a retirement to the main asset.

2. **Question:** I posted a retirement, but the asset still appears in reporting, even though I chose to report on a period subsequent to the period in which the retirement took place. Why is this happening?

   Answer: Check the transaction type used; it must have the Deactivate Asset checkbox selected. The system recognizes that an asset no longer belongs to a company when a deactivation date is set in the asset master data.

3. **Question:** I posted a retirement, but the asset was included in the next depreciation run. Why?

   Answer: This can happen if the depreciation covers a period that is prior to the retirement period, or if the depreciation key has Depreciation to the Date Set selected. (In this case, the period in which the asset was retired could trigger the depreciation for the days of the period in which the asset still belonged to the company.)

4. **Question:** When I post an asset transfer within a company code using Transaction ABUMN, what happens to the old asset?

   Answer: It's deactivated, and the net book value listed as zero.

5. **Question:** In Transaction ABUMN, how can the system automatically create another transaction in the receiving asset?

   Answer: There is a customizing setting in the transaction type for the transfer: TTY Offsetting Entry. This specifies the transaction type the systems uses to post in the receiving asset.

6. **Question:** In Transaction ABUMN, when is the start of depreciation set in the new asset?

   Answer: This depends on whether the Transfer Adopting Dep. Start Date option is set in the relevant transaction type. If set, the depreciation start date is copied in the new asset; if not, the asset value date is used (corrected by the period control, as usual).

7. **Question:** In Transaction ABUMN, I don't see the transaction type in the posting screen. How does the system know which transaction type has to be used?

   Answer: This is a customizing setting: FINANCIAL ACCOUNTING • ASSET ACCOUNTING • TRANSACTIONS • SPECIFY DEFAULT TRANSACTION TYPE *or* DETERMINE TRANSACTION TYPE FOR INTERNAL TRANSACTIONS.

8. **Question:** In Transaction ABUMN, I can still see a net book value for the old asset in the Asset Explorer. Why is this the case?

   Answer: This happens if you still have to perform a depreciation run on the old asset; for example, if you transfer the asset with an asset value date of July but haven't yet performed the depreciation for June. After the successful June depreciation, the net book value becomes zero.

9. **Question:** What is the difference between unplanned depreciation and an unplanned run in AFAB?

Answer: Unplanned depreciation is a transaction posted to an asset that increases the depreciation on the asset as a special exception. An unplanned posting run is when you skip a sequence in the periodic posting of a depreciation run (e.g., instead of posting February after January, you post March, and include February). Unplanned posting runs should be carried out only in exceptional cases in a production system, ensuring that the accounting principles followed by your company are fulfilled.

10. **Question:** My company uses a calendar fiscal year variant, and, in July 2010, I discovered that I didn't capitalize an asset in January 2010. Should I use the post-capitalization procedure?

    Answer: No. Post-capitalization is used for assets purchased in closed fiscal years that were not capitalized. Post the acquisition in the current period with a normal transaction for acquisition (such as ABZON), and set the capitalization date as January. Clear the offsetting account against the incorrectly posted expense account. The depreciation not posted from January to June will be posted in the current period (catch-up) or spread in the remaining depreciation periods (smoothing), depending on the setting made in FINANCIAL ACCOUNTING • ASSET ACCOUNTING • INTEGRATION WITH THE GENERAL LEDGER • SPECIFY INTERVAL AND POSTING RULES.

Troubleshooting Tips

1. **Issue:** The following error message appears: "Asset CCCC INTERN-00001-0 is incomplete, check the asset (AAPO184) in Transaction ABT1N (intercompany transfer)."

    Solution: This means that the two company codes have different settings and requirements for the asset master data. To solve this, manually create the destination asset, and select Existing Asset instead of New Asset.

2. **Issue:** When running Transaction ABT1N, error message AA389 appears: "Transaction type 1000 not possible (no affiliated company specified)."

    Solution: Ensure that a company is assigned to each company code involved. Although the message refers to transaction types, the problem is in the company code configuration.

3. **Issue:** Running Transaction ABT1N, error message AAPO129 appears: "Asset XXXX INTERN-00001-0 is incomplete, transaction not allowed."

Solution: Double-click the error message to find out what data is missing; then click on the Master Data button to enter more data, such as the business area and the cost center.

4. **Issue:** In running various reports, error message AU117 appears: "Report date YYYY-MM-DD is invalid." Then the system sends me back to the SAP menu.

Solution: When you run a report in Asset Accounting, you must first consider the report date — you aren't allowed to choose any date. Table 6.6 shows the allowed dates for Asset Accounting reporting.

Fiscal Year	Allowed Dates
Future fiscal years	Last date of fiscal year
Current fiscal year	Last date of each posting period
Old closed fiscal years (in Asset Accounting)	Last date of fiscal year
Old opened fiscal years (in Asset Accounting)	Last date of each posting period

Table 6.5 Allowed Dates for Asset Accounting Reporting

6.4 Depreciation and Other Periodic Postings

There are four types of depreciations:

▶ **Ordinary depreciation**
This is the normal depreciation, calculated according to the accounting principle followed by your company. To activate this type of depreciation in a depreciation area, follow this path: FINANCIAL ACCOUNTING • ASSET ACCOUNTING • DEPRECIATION • ORDINARY DEPRECIATION • DETERMINE DEPRECIATION AREAS.

▶ **Special depreciation**
This is a depreciation calculated according to specific tax rules (in general, the tax rules allow more depreciation in the initial years). To activate this type of depreciation in a depreciation area, follow this path: FINANCIAL ACCOUNTING • ASSET ACCOUNTING • DEPRECIATION • SPECIAL DEPRECIATION • DETERMINE DEPRECIATION AREAS.

▶ **Unplanned depreciation**

This is a depreciation calculated according to exceptional events, so that the normal use and consumption of the asset isn't applicable. To activate this type of depreciation in a depreciation area, follow this path: FINANCIAL ACCOUNTING • ASSET ACCOUNTING • DEPRECIATION • UNPLANNED DEPRECIATION • DETERMINE DEPRECIATION AREAS.

▶ **Transfer of reserves**

Some legislation allows "suspending" the revenue of the sale of assets and taxing it later, when a new asset is purchased as replacement. The suspended profit is posted as a depreciation reduction in the new asset. To activate this type of depreciation in a depreciation area, follow this path: FINANCIAL ACCOUNTING • ASSET ACCOUNTING • SPECIAL VALUATION • TRANSFERRED RESERVES (DEFERRED GAIN) • DETERMINE DEPRECIATION AREAS.

It's important to understand that all four different types are cumulative in a depreciation area; in other words, each of them contributes to reduce the net book value.

In general, depreciation is carried out until the net book value becomes zero. It can happen that in a certain period, if you carry out two or more depreciation types for one asset, its net book value falls below zero. In this case, the system automatically reduces the depreciation. To understand the way the system reduces the depreciation, it's important to know that this is the sequence in which the system carries out the different types of depreciation:

1. Transferred reserves

2. Ordinary depreciation

3. Special depreciation

4. Unplanned depreciation

This means that if a reduction is necessary, it first affects unplanned depreciation, then special depreciation, and so on (the sequence is the opposite than the sequence for depreciation runs). You can choose to switch the sequence between ordinary and special depreciation: FINANCIAL ACCOUNTING • ASSET ACCOUNTING • DEPRECIATION • SPECIAL DEPRECIATION • CALCULATE ORDINARY DEPRECIATION BEFORE SPECIAL DEPRECIATION.

Next you will learn how to run a depreciation run; then we describe another important period-end function, the periodic posting of APC transactions.

6.4.1 Executing Depreciation Runs

To execute a depreciation run, use Transaction AFAB. The selection screen is divided into four sections (Figure 6.59); next we describe the use of each of them. Then we provide some instructions on how to understand the result of the depreciation run.

Parameter

In this section of the selection screen (❶ of Figure 6.59) specify the company code, fiscal year, and posting period. Note that the depreciation area can't be specified; the depreciation run calculates the values and posts for all of the depreciation areas.

Reason for Posting Run

In this section, you have to specify one of the four possible options for the depreciation run; only one of them can be chosen (❷ of Figure 6.59):

▸ **Planned Posting Run**
This is the standard option. This should be used when the last depreciation run was successful, and it's time to carry out the depreciation run as part of the new period-closing process. The system checks that the posting period is the one following the last successfully posted period; this information is then recorded in Table T093D, in the AFBLPE (period) and AFBLCJ (year) fields.

▸ **Repeat**
In this case, the posting period is the same as the last successful one. The system recalculates the depreciation for that period, subtracts the depreciation already posted, and then posts only the difference. This can happen if something has changed in some assets that affect the last posting run, for example, new transactions or changes to depreciation terms.

▸ **Restart**
This option must be used when the last depreciation run was not successful, for

example, if the Financial Accounting posting period was incorrectly closed. In this case, the depreciation run has to be performed again, choosing the same posting period and Restart.

▶ **Unplanned Posting Run**

This option should not be confused with unplanned depreciation. When selected, the system doesn't check whether the specified posting period is the one following the last posting period. This can be a useful option for test purposes, but we don't recommend using it in a productive system. The system calculates all depreciations up to the specified period. In practice, if you want to skip two periods, the system posts depreciation for three periods in one run. Again, as we stated earlier, unplanned posting runs should be carried out only in exceptional cases in a production system, ensuring that the accounting principles followed by your company are fulfilled.

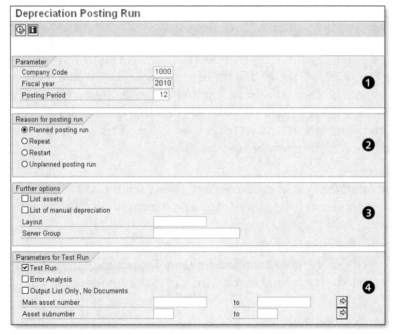

Figure 6.59 Depreciation Run Selection Screen

Further Options

In this section, you can use the following main parameters to influence the type of information that is presented in the list (❸ of Figure 6.59):

449

▶ **List Assets**
If not selected, the list shows summarized data for asset classes; if selected, the depreciation for a single asset is shown.

▶ **List of Manual Depreciation**
Unplanned depreciation is displayed for each asset. With this flag, you can also choose to display the asset document with which the unplanned depreciation was posted.

▶ **Layout**
The list of the depreciations is presented in ALV format; here you can specify an ALV layout that you have already created.

Parameters for Test Run

In this section (Figure 6.59, ❹), you can use some parameters that are only available when you run the report in test mode. The following list describes the most important of these parameters:

▶ **Test Run**
If you select this indicator, the program works just as a report, showing the depreciation that would be posted and the potential errors that would result. If the Test Run option is chosen, you can run it online or in the background. If Test Run isn't chosen, the system calculates the depreciation, updates the relevant tables, and posts to SAP General Ledger. Note that, in test mode, the program processes only a maximum of 1000 assets.

▶ **Error Analysis**
With this indicator, the system carries out a complete simulation of the Financial Accounting document to be generated and produces a list of only the documents in error.

▶ **Main Asset Number/Asset Subnumber**
In test mode, you can use these two fields to limit the depreciation to specific assets that you select. In a productive run, you can't select specific assets.

Result of the Depreciation Run

Usually, you first run the program online. If any issues occur, the system displays a list similar to the one shown in Figure 6.60. In the first column, Status, a red light indicates that the program could not process the depreciation for an asset. Click on the Error List button (📇) to see a list of all of the errors encountered; to get more information about the error message, double-click the error line. We recommend correcting all of the errors displayed in the test run before processing the depreciation in a productive run.

When you're ready to run the depreciation in productive mode, deselect the Test Run flag, and process the program in the background (with the Planned Posting Run option). Check the resulting list with Transaction SP01 (the program run in the background produces a spool list); if some errors still occurred, correct the errors, and rerun Transaction AFAB in productive mode using the Restart option.

> **Note**
>
> No batch input session is created. To improve the consistency and integration between Asset Accounting and SAP General Ledger, the posting to SAP General Ledger automatically takes place in the background. Any errors must be corrected before the run or rerun (restart) of the depreciation run.

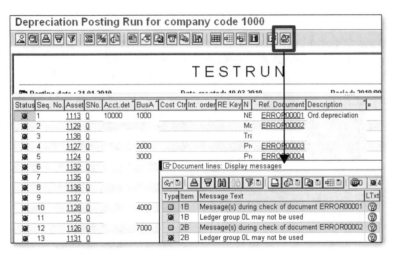

Figure 6.60 Depreciation Error List

6.4.2 Periodic Posting of Transactions

> **Quick Reference**
>
> **Menu path:** ACCOUNTING • FINANCIAL ACCOUNTING • FIXED ASSETS • PERIODIC PROCESSING • APC VALUE POSTING
>
> **Transaction:** ASKB
>
> **Program:** RAPERB2000

One depreciation area posts in real time to SAP General Ledger. In the new SAP General Ledger, this is depreciation area 01, and it posts to the leading ledger and to Controlling. All other depreciation areas post periodically with Transaction ASKB. When you run this transaction, the system doesn't allow you to specify any period; instead, it posts all transactions not yet posted for the relevant depreciation areas.

In the selection screen (Figure 6.61), specify the following:

▶ **Company Code**
You can run Transaction ASKB for only one company code each time.

▶ **Test Run**
The transaction can only run online in test mode; otherwise, you must carry out the function in the background.

▶ **Posting Control**
Specify whether this is a standard posting run or a restart. Restarts are used if, for some reason, the previous run was not okay for all documents selected (e.g., perhaps the posting period was closed). You must first solve any issues with the previous posting run before carrying out the restart.

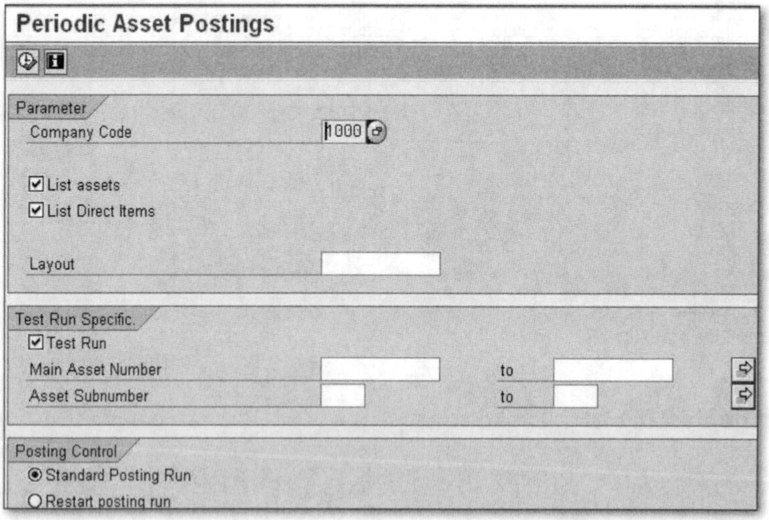

Figure 6.61 Periodic Asset Postings

The system posts the document without creating any batch input transactions; if errors occur, you must first remove the cause of the errors (e.g., unblock accounts or open the posting period) and then rerun the program in restart mode.

6.4.3 FAQ and Troubleshooting Tips

Next we answer some frequently asked questions and offer helpful troubleshooting tips.

FAQ

1. **Question:** How can I get an audit trail of the unplanned depreciations posted?

   Answer: Unplanned depreciation is shown separately in the Asset Explorer; in addition, it's recorded as a transaction and can be retrieved using report RABEWH_ALV01 (asset transactions).

2. **Question:** Are the posting periods coming from the fiscal year variant assigned to the company code, or are they from the alternative fiscal year variant defined in Asset Accounting?

   Answer: The posting periods come from the fiscal year variant assigned to the company code in SAP General Ledger, not from the alternative one in Asset Accounting.

3. **Question:** I ran depreciation in productive mode, and it was unsuccessful. How can I see and analyze the log?

   Answer: The best way is to use Transaction AFBP, which is available in the menu after Transaction AFAB.

4. **Question:** When I run the depreciation with Transaction AFAB, does the system create individual postings to each asset? If not, how can the system post to the accumulated depreciation account that is a reconciliation account?

   Answer: No, the system doesn't post at the asset level; the SAP General Ledger document is summarized. With the depreciation posting, the system puts an asterisk (*) in the asset field. The detail of each depreciation run at the asset level is kept in Table ANLP and available in various reports.

5. **Question:** When is ordinary depreciation calculated in a depreciation area?

   Answer: When the depreciation key in the depreciation area is configured for ordinary depreciation.

Troubleshooting Tips

1. **Issue:** During the transfer of reserves, the following error message appears: "Data inconsistency: Area XX for value takeover is missing (Error AAPO 105)."

   Solution: You can limit the transfer of reserves to some depreciation areas, but this limitation has to be consistent with the derivation rule. For example, if depreciation area 30 is allowed for the transfer of reserves, but it derives its values from area 29, which isn't allowed for transfer of reserves, this results in an error.

2. **Issue:** The following error message appears: "Unplanned depreciation not allowed in area YY (Transaction CCC)."

   Solution: Unplanned depreciation must be allowed in the specific depreciation area in customizing.

3. **Issue:** When running unplanned depreciation, the following error message appears: "In Area XX, you can only post manual depreciation up to the amount of ZZZZ.ZZ."

   Solution: This means that the unplanned depreciation leads to a negative net book value, which isn't allowed in the specified depreciation area.

4. **Issue:** In running Transaction AFAB, the following error message appears: "According to posting cycle, you should post period MMM next."

   Solution: This means that you have chosen the planned posting run, but the period isn't subsequent to the last successful one (recorded in Table T093D).

5. **Issue:** In running Transaction AFAB, the following error message appears: "Posting Period MM/YYYY is not open (message F5201)."

   Solution: This means that the posting period in Financial Accounting isn't open. Check the posting periods with Transaction OB52 for the variant assigned to the company code and account type +, A, and S.

6. **Issue:** In running Transaction AFAB, the following error message appears: "Posting rules in area XX are different from area YY (message AA694)."

   Solution: This means that area YY depends on area XX, or vice versa (one is real; the other is derived). The two depreciation areas must post with the same periodicity and rules to SAP General Ledger. Check the customizing of both areas under FINANCIAL ACCOUNTING • ASSET ACCOUNTING • INTEGRATION WITH GENERAL LEDGER • POST DEPRECIATION TO THE GENERAL LEDGER • SPECIFY INTERVALS AND POSTING RULES.

7. **Issue:** In running Transaction AFAB, the following error message appears: "The depreciation run does not issue any errors in the test run, but fails in productive mode."

   Solution: From our experience, this can be due to number range issues. Check the number range for the document type used in the depreciation postings.

8. **Issue:** In running Transaction AFAB, error message GLT2076 appears: "There is no item category assigned to account XXXX/CCC."

   Solution: This means that document splitting is active in your new SAP General Ledger environment, and this requires the assignment of all of the accounts to an item category. Carry out the assignment with Transaction SM30, view V_T8G17.

9. **Issue:** In running Transaction AFAB, error message AU133 appears: "Account 'Acc. dep. accnt. for ordinary depreciation' could not be found for area XX."

   Solution: This means that the system can't find the account for a specific combination of chart of depreciation (which comes from the company code), account determination, and depreciation area. Carry out the account determination using Transaction AO90. To see which account determination is involved, see to which row the message refers, and then, in the depreciation list, go to the specific row where the account determination is displayed.

10. **Issue:** In running Transaction AFAB, error message AA776 appears: "Create document number range 04 using internal number assignment."

    Solution: Run Transaction FBN1, and specify that the involved number range is internal. If the number range has already been used, remember to identify the last number posted, and set this number in the number range.

6.5 Year-End Activities

At the end of every year, two steps must be carried out: fiscal year change, and fiscal year closing. We discuss both these activities in detail next and also discuss how to reopen a closed year.

6.5.1 Running Fiscal Year Changes

The consequences of a fiscal year change as follows:

▶ You can post to the new fiscal year (it's still possible to post to the old fiscal year).

▶ The values from the old fiscal year are carried forward and displayed as accumulated values at the beginning of the new fiscal year.

No more than two fiscal years can be open in Asset Accounting at the same time. To carry out the fiscal year change, run Transaction AJRW (Figure 6.62), and follow these steps:

1. Specify the company code or codes.

2. Specify the new fiscal year.

3. Select the Test Run option if you want to preview the result of the report; this immediately tells you whether it's possible to carry out the fiscal year change. If the fiscal year change isn't possible, the system provides details about the errors. Note that there is a maximum of 1000 assets when you run the report online. If you have a much larger number of assets, we recommend running the program in the background and in test mode.

4. If you don't want to run the program in test mode, select the background functionality; the fiscal year change in Asset Accounting can only be run online in test mode.

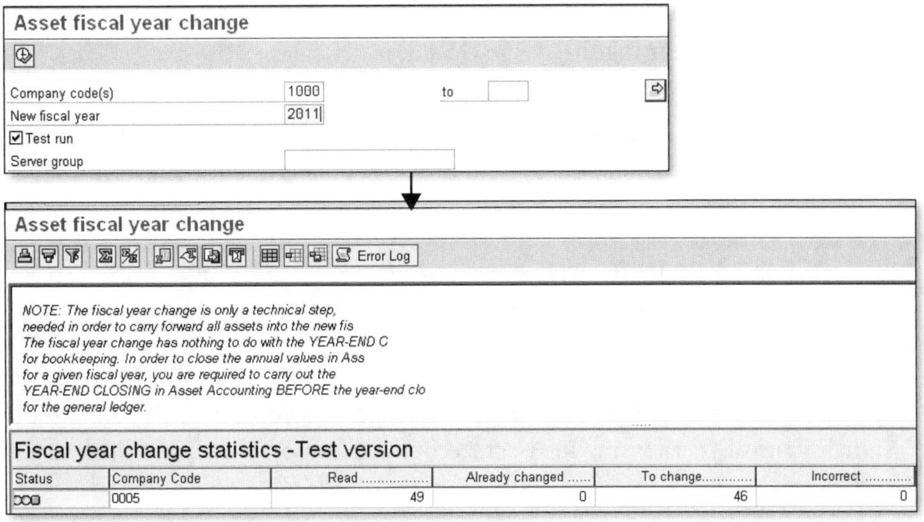

Figure 6.62 Fiscal Year Change in Asset Accounting

The fiscal year change has to be carried out as soon as you start to use Asset Accounting in the first work calendar day of the new fiscal year. If you're using a calendar fiscal year variant, don't forget to run the fiscal year change on the second of January (assuming that the first is a holiday and the second is a working day); otherwise, you won't be able to post any asset transactions with asset value dates in the new fiscal year.

6.5.2 Executing Fiscal Year Closings

> **Quick Reference**
>
> **Menu path:** ACCOUNTING • FINANCIAL ACCOUNTING • FIXED ASSETS • PERIODIC PROCESSING • YEAR-END CLOSING • EXECUTE
>
> **Transaction:** AJAB
>
> **Program:** RAJABS00

The fiscal year closing has to be carried out when you no longer want to post to the old fiscal year. To run the fiscal year closing, use Transaction AJAB (Figure 6.63), and follow these steps:

1. Specify the company code or codes.

2. Specify the fiscal year that has to be closed.

3. Select the Test Run option if you want to preview the result of the report; this immediately tells you whether it's possible to close the fiscal year. If the fiscal year closing isn't possible, the system provides details about the errors.

Note

There is a maximum of 1000 assets when you run the report online. If you have a much larger number of assets, we recommend running the program in the background and in test mode.

---

4. If you don't want to run the program in test mode, select the background functionality; fiscal year closing in Asset Accounting can only be run online in test mode.

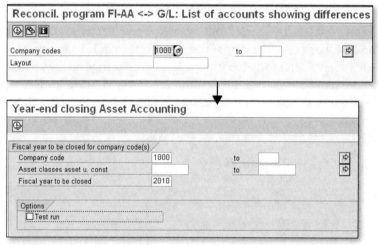

Figure 6.63 Year-End Closing

Tip

Use Transaction ABST2 to reconcile Asset Accounting and SAP General Ledger before the fiscal year closing.

The consequences of the fiscal year closing are as follows:

▶ You can't post any transactions to the closed fiscal year.

▶ Any change to the depreciation terms will have no effect on the closed fiscal year (i.e., no recalculation of the planned depreciation for the closed year).

> **Note**
>
> Unlike the fiscal year change, which is a purely technical activity, fiscal year closing (as well as reopening) has to be run in coordination with your accounting department.

6.5.3 Reopening Closed Fiscal Years

> **Quick Reference**
>
> **Menu path:** ACCOUNTING • FINANCIAL ACCOUNTING • FIXED ASSETS • PERIODIC PROCESSING • YEAR-END CLOSING • UNDO
>
> **Transactions:** OAAQ (entire company code), OAAR (for specific depreciation areas)
>
> **Table/views:** T093B/V_T093B_02 (entire company code), T093B/V_T093B_01 (for specific depreciation areas)

If for any reason you need to post to a closed fiscal year in Asset Accounting, you can reopen the fiscal year. There are two transactions available for this purpose:

▶ **Transaction OAAQ**
This transaction allows you to reopen the fiscal year for the entire company code and then for all of the depreciation areas managed in the company code assets (❶ of Figure 6.64). In this case, specify the last closed fiscal year in the Closed Fiscal Year column.

▶ **Transaction OAAR**
This transaction allows you to reopen the fiscal year just for one or more depreciation areas assigned to the company code (❷ of Figure 6.64). In this case, you first select the company code, and then double-click on the Fiscal Year folder; in the next screen, change the last closed fiscal year only for those depreciation areas where it's needed.

In any case, reopening the fiscal year is an activity that should be carried out in coordination with and under the authorization of your accounting department.

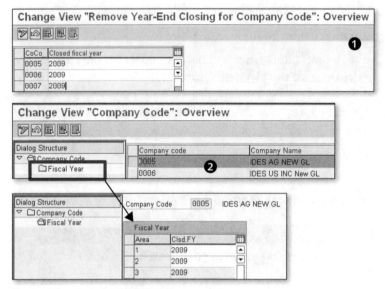

Figure 6.64 Reopen Fiscal Year

6.5.4 FAQ and Troubleshooting Tips

Next we answer some frequently asked questions and offer helpful troubleshooting tips.

FAQ

1. **Question:** What happens if I run Transaction AJRW more than one time?

   Answer: If a fiscal year change was already carried out successfully, the second run has no effect.

2. **Question:** When is the earliest time I can run the fiscal year change?

   Answer: You can run the fiscal year change when the calendar is in the new fiscal year, or in the last month of the old year. You can't perform the change any sooner than this.

Troubleshooting Tips

1. **Issue:** Error message AU070 ("Depreciation not posted completely") appears when running the year-end closing for Asset Accounting.

Solution: The planned depreciation for the fiscal year (Transaction AFAB/AFABN) has to be posted completely. For example, if the depreciation for December has not been done, or it was done with errors, the fiscal year closing will end with errors.

2. **Issue:** Error message AU075 ("Asset balance sheet values not completely posted") appears when running the year-end closing for Asset Accounting.

   Solution: The periodic postings of APC transactions (Transaction ASKB/ASKBN) must be carried out for all of the transactions relevant for the fiscal year, for all depreciation areas that don't post in real time to the general ledger.

3. **Issue:** When running the year-end closing, the system issues an error message stating that there are incomplete assets.

   Solution: You can't have incomplete assets. Use Transaction AUVA to see a list of incomplete assets, and correct the relevant master data before rerunning the year-end closing.

4. **Issue:** Error message AA761 ("Fiscal year change in co.code CCCC possible only after year-end closing YYYY") appears when running fiscal year change Transaction AJRW.

   Solution: You must close the previous fiscal year; for example, if you want to close FY 2009, 2008 must be already closed in Asset Accounting.

5. **Issue:** When running the fiscal year change, error message AA761 appears: "Fiscal year change in co. code XXXX possible only after year-end closing YYYY."

   Solution: You can't have more than two fiscal years open. Close the oldest fiscal year.

6. **Issue:** Error AB059 appears: "Fiscal year change not yet made for Company Code CCCC."

   Solution: Before executing any reporting, ensure that the current fiscal year in the system is also the current fiscal year in Asset Accounting. In other words (supposing that a calendar fiscal year variant is used), if you're working in January 2009, you must have carried out the fiscal year change specifying the new year as 2009. If you haven't done this, you will get an error message every time you run a report in Asset Accounting.

6.6 Summary

With this chapter, we conclude our analysis of the three subledgers: Accounts Receivable, Accounts Payable, and Asset Accounting. In the next chapter, we focus on the functions provide by SAP to manage the integration between Financial Accounting and your banks.

SAP provides many functions to manage the interaction between your company and banks. In this chapter, we explain the most important of these procedures.

7 Banking

In this chapter, we describe the two main types of master data necessary to carry out the bank functionalities in SAP:

- Bank data (bank branches)
- House banks (bank branches where your company has a bank account)

After this discussion of master data, we describe the following main functionalities that SAP provides to facilitate interaction with your banks and the management of cash and bank accounts:

- Bank chains
- Importing electronic bank statements
- Cash journal

> **Note**
>
> Automatic payment functionality is described in detail in Chapter 5, Accounts Receivable and Accounts Payable.

7.1 Bank Data (Database of Bank Branches)

In each country, a bank office (or bank branch) is uniquely identified by a national code, and some may also have an international identification number (SWIFT). In SAP, each bank branch used in the system must be created as a separate bank master record. Your company codes might also keep some accounts in branches known as *house banks,* which are identified with a separate master record. The house banks master data is linked to the bank branch master data.

In this section, we explain how to create bank branch master data, which you can do manually, one by one; or automatically and collectively, with the help of specific programs.

7.1.1 Bank Data Manual Update

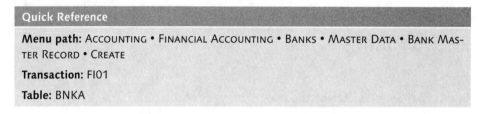

Quick Reference

Menu path: ACCOUNTING • FINANCIAL ACCOUNTING • BANKS • MASTER DATA • BANK MASTER RECORD • CREATE

Transaction: FI01

Table: BNKA

Each branch data is identified by two pieces of information, both of which appear on the screen when you use Transaction F101 to create a new bank (Figure 7.1):

- Country
- Bank key

The bank key format depends on the configuration made in the country to which the bank branch belongs (see Chapter 1, General SAP Configuration for Financial Accounting, for more details about this).

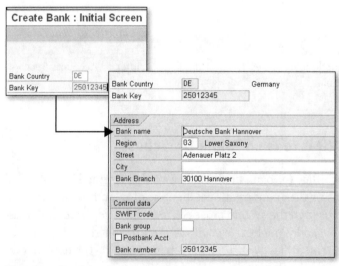

Figure 7.1 Creating a Bank Branch

The following country-specific settings are relevant:

▶ **Bank Key**
Three choices are available (choice number 2 is obsolete):

  ▶ **1:** Bank Number. The bank is identified by the local code used in the country and assigned by the local central bank or banking association. If you choose this setting in the country, the bank key is copied into the Bank Number field (BNKA-BNKLZ), and the Bank Number field can't be changed.

  ▶ **3:** Assigned Internally. The system automatically assigns a progressive number that you can't change. This is a rare configuration.

  ▶ **4:** Assigned Externally. You specify the bank key with the rules that you define in the following point. This configuration choice is generally used in countries where you want to identify the bank with the SWIFT code.

▶ **Length of Bank Key**
Specify the field length; then, in the field at the right of the field length, specify how the system should use the length for control purposes. The following nine choices are available:

  ▶ Maximum Value Length, Without Gaps.

  ▶ Maximum Value Length, Numerical, Without Gaps.

  ▶ Length to be Kept to Exactly, Without Gaps.

  ▶ Length to be Kept to Exactly, Numerical, Without Gaps.

  ▶ Maximum Value Length.

  ▶ Maximum Value Length, Numerical.

  ▶ Length to Be Kept to Exactly.

  ▶ Length to Be Kept to Exactly, Numerical.

  ▶ Check Against Country-Specific Edit Format: See the online help (put the cursor on the field and press F1) to see for which countries specific control rules exist.

Note on the Bank Key Control

If you use the SWIFT code as a bank key in a specific country, we strongly recommend that you set the Bank Data flag on the Further Checks tab in Transaction OY17 (Set Country-Specific Checks). This ensures that the system automatically performs the formal control on the SWIFT code entered in the SWIFT Code field (BNKA-SWIFT) — not on the SWIFT code entered in the bank key.

In Transaction FI01, specify the country to which the bank branch belongs and the bank key, according to the settings of the country. If the bank key is assigned internally, don't specify any bank key (the system assigns the next number available in the country).

When you confirm the information on the first screen, the system takes you to the next screen, where you can specify the following (refer to Figure 7.1):

- **Address**
  - **Bank Name:** Enter the name of the branch.
  - **Region:** This information depends on the country. If you open the match-code, you see all of the regions that are assigned to the country in Customizing.
  - **Street:** Enter the address name without the city.
  - **City:** Enter the city in which the branch is located.
  - **Bank Branch:** Enter the branch name (if you haven't specified the name in the Bank Name field.
- **Control Data**
  - **Society for Worldwide Interbank Financial Telecommunication (SWIFT) Code: Thi**s an internationally-recognized code for identifying banks. SWIFT codes are commonly used to identify the banks involved in an international wire transfer.
  - **Bank Group:** You can use this field to optimize payments by identifying banks belonging to the same group.
  - **Postbank Acct:** Flag if this is a post account.
  - **Bank Number:** This is where you enter the number with which the bank branch is identified in its country, according to the central bank or national bank association rules. Note that if the bank key is the same as the bank number (discussed previously), you can't change the content of this field; it's automatically copied from the bank key.

If you click on the Address button, you can specify additional address information.

7.1.2 Mass Update with Local Database

Menu path: ACCOUNTING • FINANCIAL ACCOUNTING • BANKS • MASTER DATA • BANK MASTER RECORDS • TRANSFER BANK DATA

Transaction: BAUP

Program: RFBVALL_0

Table: BNKA

Instead of creating bank master records manually, you can use Transaction BAUP to collectively upload all of the banks of one specific country at the same time, or to automatically update the existing ones (changes to name, closed branches, new branches created, etc.). This transaction, unlike the one described in the following section, is designed to work with the bank database created by the local central banks or the local bank association. In other words, every country-specific database is different.

SAP Note 132012

The prerequisite for this functionality is to get access to a database of the bank branches in a specific country. See SAP Note 132012 for details, or contact your bank to find the file that lists all of the banks.

Run Transaction BAUP, and you see the selection screen displayed in Figure 7.2.

Figure 7.2 has four main areas: country data, file data, updating options, and list display options. We explain each of these in more detail here:

- **Country data**

  In this area, you specify the country and format. Select a country, and click on the matchcode of the Format field; the formats supported for the specific country are displayed. If more than one format is displayed, find out from the source of the file (whether it's your local bank or the bank association) which format you should choose.

- **File data**

  In this area, you select the path where the file that contains the list of the banks is located. If you select the Presentation Server radio button, you can select all of the directories on your PC, CD, or DVD, using the Multiple Selection button (⇨); if you select the Application Server radio button, you must manually specify the directory. To find a list of the directories available in your SAP server, use Transaction AL11, or contact your SAP Basis expert.

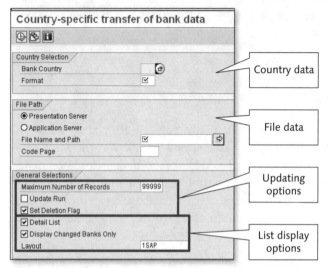

Figure 7.2 Selection Data for Transaction BAUP

▶ **Updating options**

  ▶ **Maximum Number of Records:** This field is filled with 99999 by default, which means that all records in the file will be imported, even if there are more than 99999. If you specify a different value, the system stops the import when it has reached that value. You can use this field for test purposes.

  ▶ **Update Run:** If you select this checkbox, the system updates the bank master records (only Table BNKA); if you don't select it, you'll get only a list of bank master records.

  ▶ **Set Deletion Flag:** If you check this box after you've selected Update Run, the banks that are present in the country (in SAP) but not contained in the file are marked for deletion. (How the system matches the bank in SAP and the bank in the file is explained following this list.)

▶ **List display options**

  ▶ **Detail List:** If selected, a list of all of the updated bank branches is displayed; if not selected, only a summary is displayed.

▶ **Display Changed Bank Only:** If selected, in the detail list, all of the unchanged banks (those for which the SAP data matches the data in the file) aren't displayed.

▶ **Layout:** The detailed list is an ALV list. You can create your layout and specify it here.

If this program is run in productive mode, the program matches the banks in the file with the banks in the SAP database. *The match criteria are the bank number in the file and the bank key in the SAP master data.*

Four cases are possible:

1. The bank details in the file and in the SAP database are exactly the same; in this case, no changes are made.

2. One bank exists in the file and doesn't exist in the SAP database (remember, the program searches for banks with bank keys equal to the bank number in the file records); in this case, the bank is added to the SAP database.

3. One bank exists in the file and in the SAP database, but some details are different; in this case, the program updates the details in the SAP database.

4. One bank exists in the file but not in the SAP database; in this case, the bank is marked for deletion, but only if the Set Deletion Flag checkbox has been selected.

7.1.3 Mass Update with the BIC Database

Quick Reference

Menu path: ACCOUNTING • FINANCIAL ACCOUNTING • BANKS • MASTER DATA • BANK MASTER DATA • TRANSFER BIC FILE

Transaction: BIC

Program: RFBVBIC_0

Table: BNKA

The BIC database is a database of banks for a very large number of countries that contains the basic information needed to create bank branches in SAP; for example, the SWIFT code (if available), the local bank identification number, and the address (plus other information not relevant for SAP master data).

The database allows you to extract a flat file for one or more countries, and the program described in this section is designed to read this file and update the SAP bank master data with the information contained in it. (Refer to the documentation that comes with the BIC database to learn how to generate the flat file.)

The selection screen for Transaction BIC is displayed in Figure 7.3 and is very similar to the one for Transaction BAUP.

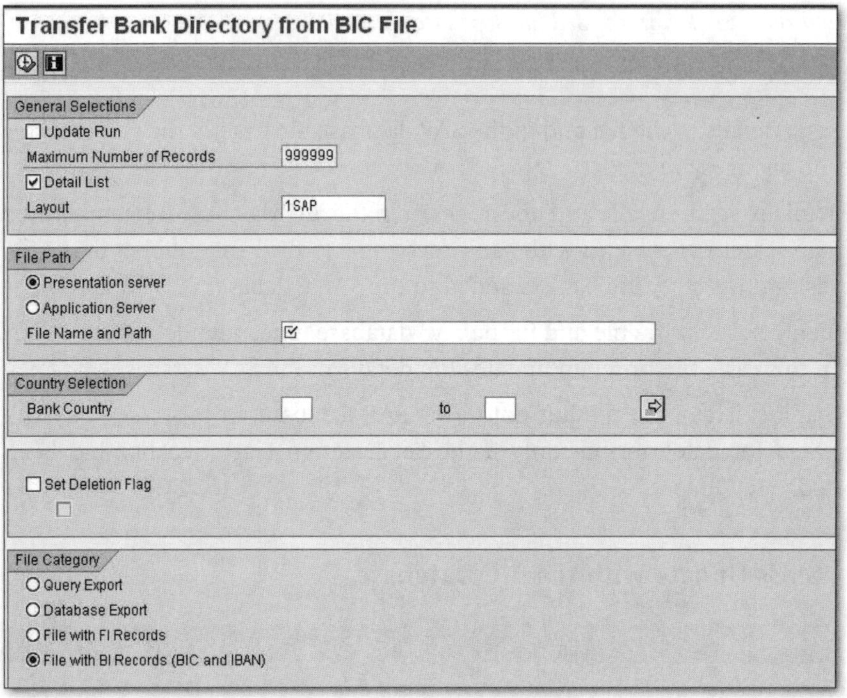

Figure 7.3 Selection Screen for Transaction BIC

There are a few significant differences, however:

▶ **Bank Country**
In this field, you can specify more than one country because the technical format of the data is the same for all of the countries, and there is no reason for the Format field.

▶ **File Category area**
The file format depends on the function you used in the BIC database to create the file. The standard function is the query export.

Note that the BIC database has more fields than the ones you can update in the SAP bank master data. Next we list the details of the mapping between the BIC database fields and the SAP bank master data fields:

▶ The first 60 bytes of the Bank Name field are transferred to field BNKA-BANKA.

▶ The first 27 bytes of the City field and the first 8 bytes of the Postal Code field are transferred to field BNKA-ORT01. If the postal code has more than eight characters, only the first 35 bytes of the City field is transferred (in other words, the postal code isn't transferred).

▶ The first 35 bytes of the Street field is transferred to field BNKA-STRAS.

▶ The Bank Key field is transferred to field BNKA-BANKL.

▶ The Bank Number field is transferred to field BNKA-BNKLZ; if the bank number is selected as the bank key, it's also transferred to BNKA-BANKL.

▶ The SWIFT field is transferred to field BNKA-SWIFT; if the SWIFT code is selected as the bank key, it's also transferred to field BNKA-BANKL.

▶ The first 40 bytes of the Branch field is transferred to field BNKA-BRNCH, if contained in the input file.

Recall that two possible fields uniquely identify the bank — the SWIFT code and the local bank code — and that the bank master records are created in the following two ways, depending on the country settings:

▶ If, in the country-specific settings, the bank key is external (option 4, Assigned Externally), the SWIFT code is used.

▶ If, in the country-specific settings, the bank key is the bank code (option 1, Bank Number), the local bank code is used.

The countries that are to be updated using the BIC database are affected by these two options. To decide which is appropriate, follow these steps:

1. Check the content in the BIC database. If the local code is present, use option 1, Bank Number. The bank will be identified with the local code; if the SWIFT code is available, it will be placed on field BNKA-SWIFT.

2. If the local code isn't present, but the SWIFT code is present and always unique to the country, use the SWIFT code as the bank key (option 4, Assigned Externally).

3. If neither the local code nor the SWIFT code are present, don't use the BIC database for automatic upload.

The way the system updates bank master data for all other fields follows the same logic as Transaction BAUP.

7.1.4   Bank Branch Data Deletion

Quick Reference
Program: SAPF023 and SAPF061

It's possible to delete bank data (Table BNKA) in two ways:

▶ **Program SAPF023, Reset Bank Data**
This program deletes all bank data in a specified country. The program doesn't check the usage of bank data in customers, vendors, and house bank accounts; all of the country's banks are deleted, no matter whether the deletion flag is set in the bank master record. For these reasons, the program must be used carefully.

▶ **Program SAPF061, Archiving Bank Data**
This program archives the bank master records that have the deletion flag set. All other bank master records are untouched. You should discuss this option with the team in your company that takes care of data archiving. (This program is no longer available in SAP ERP 6.0.)

7.1.5   FAQ and Troubleshooting Tips

Next we answer some frequently asked questions and offer helpful troubleshooting tips.

FAQ

1. **Question:** Is it possible that the same bank key exists more than one time in the system?

   Answer: Yes, but the same bank key can exist just once in one country.

2. **Question:** Where can I update the IBAN information?

   Answer: The IBAN information is specific to each bank account, not to each bank branch. Therefore, you can update the IBAN each time you specify the bank account, for example, in the vendor master data, customer master data, and house bank account data.

Troubleshooting Tips

1. **Issue:** Error message AR102 appears: "Specify field Bank Key with length 08."

   Solution: You've entered a Bank Key field length that doesn't respect the rules you've set up for the country to which the bank belongs (see Chapter 1, General SAP Configuration for Financial Accounting). Verify the length of the bank key, and specify a bank key that respects the rule fixed for the country.

2. **Issue:** Error message BF00323 appears: "Error reading file *C:\....*"

   Solution: First check the document path, and try to put the file in a path that is shorter than 45 characters (including the file name). For example, put the file in the directory *C:\temp*. If the error persists, select another format in the Format field and try again.

3. **Issue:** Warning message BF00257 appears: "Bank number is not defined as the bank key in country XX."

   Solution: This is a warning message. Remember, the system uses the local bank number as a bank key, and places it in the Bank Number field. This warning indicates that the bank key isn't defined with option 1 (Bank Number), so the bank number can be manually changed afterwards. If option 1 *is* selected, the system automatically ensures that the bank key and bank number are always the same. We strongly recommend that, if you use a local database to update the banks in one specific country, you use option 1.

7.2 House Banks and House Bank Accounts

House banks are the banks of your company; each house bank refers to a physical bank branch in which your company keeps a current account. They are mainly used in Financial Accounting for automatic outgoing and incoming payments.

The following two sections describe how to create house banks and the related bank accounts. Unlike bank branches, house banks are updated in customizing.

7.2.1 Defining House Banks

Quick Reference

Menu path: IMG • FINANCIAL ACCOUNTING • BANK ACCOUNTING • BANK ACCOUNTS • DE-FINE HOUSE BANKS

Transaction: FI12

Table/view: T012/V_T012

To create house banks, use Transaction FI12 (to directly update house banks) or FBZP (to update all of the settings for automatic payments, including house banks) (Figure 7.4). Each house bank belongs exactly to one company code; therefore, the first information the system asks you is to specify the company code.

After entering the company code (❶ of Figure 7.4), select New Entries in the following screen, and specify the identification code of the house bank (a maximum of five digits) (❷ of Figure 7.4). Next (❸ of Figure 7.4), specify to which correspondent physical bank branch the house bank belongs; if you specify an existing combination of country/bank key, the system automatically displays all of the details of the bank branch (bank name, region, street, etc.).

> **Note**
>
> It's also possible to create a new bank branch in this screen. However, we recommend creating the bank branch separately, according to the naming convention rule for the specific country.

The following additional information can be added (❸ of Figure 7.4):

▶ **Details of the contact in the bank branch**
This includes the tax code of the branch, contact person, and telephone number.

▶ **EDI details**
This information can be used if you exchange the information to/from the bank with EDI technology.

▶ **Data medium exchange details**
This information can be transferred to a DME (data medium exchange) file with relation to automatic payments. See the discussion of automatic payments to vendors in Chapter 5, Accounts Receivable and Accounts Payable, for more details on the creation of a DME file.

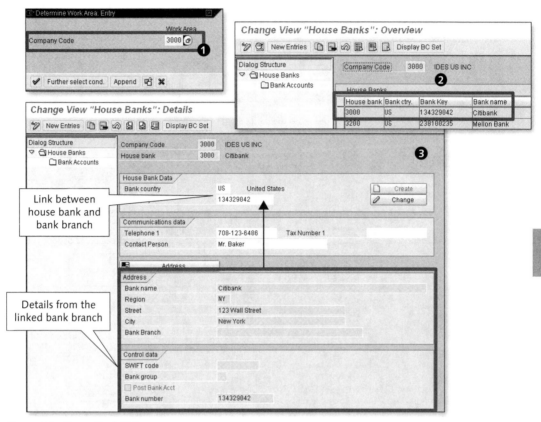

Figure 7.4 House Bank Data

7.2.2 Defining House Bank Accounts

Your company can keep one or more current accounts in one bank branch, in the same or in different currencies. These bank accounts can be created in customizing using the same transaction code to create house banks (Transaction FI12).

Follow these steps (Figure 7.5):

1. In the list of the house banks of a specific company code, select exactly one house bank.

2. Double-click on the Bank Accounts folder on the left side of the screen.

3. Specify an ID of the bank account, according to your naming convention, and the following additional data:

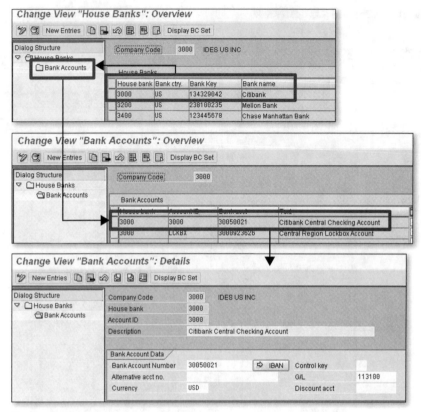

Figure 7.5 House Bank Account Details

▶ **Description:** Your own description of the bank account.

▶ **Bank Account Number:** Be extremely precise here because this information will be used in many processes and in the IBAN generation.

▶ **Control Key:** This information is used in some countries to trigger a control among the bank number, the bank account number, and the control key.

▶ **Alternative Acct.No.:** An alternative account number is needed only if, in the same house bank, two house bank accounts have the same account number, and the only difference is the currency. In this case, your bank assigns an alternative account number to each of them; the alternative account number is then used in the electronic bank statement update to identify the correspondent house bank account in SAP.

► **G/L:** Here you assign a general ledger account to your bank account. Always assign exactly one general ledger account to the bank account. This information is used in the electronic bank statement upload.

► **Currency:** This is the currency of the bank account. This currency is used by the electronic bank statement to post.

7.2.3 FAQ and Troubleshooting Tips

Next we answer a frequently asked question and offer a helpful troubleshooting tip.

FAQ

1. **Question**: Can I use the same house bank key in multiple company codes?

   Answer: Yes. For example, you can create house bank 0001 in company code 1000, house bank 0001 in company code 2000, and so on. However, we recommend defining a naming convention for the house banks. If, for example, the companies in your group all work with Barclays, Citigroup, and HSBC, you could reserve the first digit to identify the institute (e.g., Barclays = B), and the remaining digits could be a progressive number to identify different branches of the same bank (e.g., B001 could be Barclays London, and B002 Barclays Manchester). Discuss the naming convention with your accounting and treasury department.

Troubleshooting Tip

1. **Issue:** When I create a house bank account, I want to specify the IBAN number. I see that in some countries, the system automatically proposes the IBAN based on the bank key and account number; however, this function isn't available for other countries that use the IBAN. Why this different system behavior?

   Solution: To see the countries for which the described functionality is active, use Transaction FIBF; then, from the menu, select Settings P/S Modules...of an SAP Application. Go to event 00003030, which provides a list of all conversion rules (from bank account to IBAN) active for the countries. Event 00003040 provides the inverse conversion rules (from IBAN to bank data), that is, bank key and bank number. If the country isn't in the list, check the availability of the function module (Transaction SE37) in the system: CONVERT_BANK_

ACCOUNT_2_IBAN_XX, where XX is the ISO code of the country (use CON-VERT_IBAN_2_BANK_ACCOUNT_XX for the inverse conversion rule). If you find the function module, make a new entry for the relevant country (copy one of the existing records, and change the country and the function module). If you can't find the function module in your system, check in SAP Notes for its availability; if it was developed later, you may find the ABAP code and the instructions on how to import in your system. (Get the assistant of an ABAP developer to perform this task.)

7.3 Bank Chains

Bank chains are used in automatic payments. When making payments abroad and to specific countries, it's sometimes necessary to have more than just a receiver bank and bank account; you may also require some intermediary banks to complete the transfer of money. The bank chain is the list of these intermediary banks. For each payment, SAP allows you to specify up to three different intermediary banks; each intermediary bank is classified as one of four possible bank types in the chain:

- Sender's correspondent bank
- Intermediary bank
- Recipient's correspondent bank
- External house bank (used for in-house cash payments only)

Next we describe how to customize and maintain bank chains, and then we discuss how they affect payments.

7.3.1 Customizing Bank Chains

To use bank chains, you must perform the following two steps in customizing:

- Define the bank chains scenario.
- Activate the bank chains scenarios.

If no scenario is activated, you'll see error message PZ876 ("Bank chains are not active") every time you try to create a bank chain.

Creating and Defining the Scenario

The first step to using bank chains in SAP is to create and define the scenario, which is the search strategy for the bank chain. The search strategy answers the following question: When should a bank chain be found and assigned to a payment? In other words, the search strategy allows you to define a certain, specified combination of factors that, when it appears in a payment, automatically result in that payment being assigned to a specific bank chain. (Although the scenario affects the search of the bank chain, the transactions that allow the creation of a single bank chain aren't themselves affected. This concept is described in more detail in Section 7.3.2, Maintaining Bank Chains.)

Use the menu path in the Quick Reference box to create and define the scenario. Keep in mind that you can create many scenarios, but only one can be activated in your client.

Create the scenario by selecting the New Entries button, and specify a scenario code (four digits long, starting with Z or Y), scenario description, and one or two of the following options (see Figure 7.6):

▶ Gen. Search (general search)

▶ Rec. Search (receiver-specific search)

Searches are based on a number of factors, which we discuss in more detail later in the chapter.

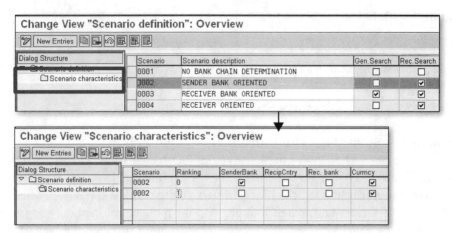

Figure 7.6 Defining Bank Chain Scenarios

The receiver-specific search rules aren't created in customizing but in the application menu. (See Section 7.3.2, Maintaining Bank Chains, for more details.)

Both searches can lead to up to three intermediary banks selected for a single payment. If both searches are selected, the system first performs the receiver-specific search; then, if this search isn't successful, the system performs the general search.

After you've created the scenario with the information just described, save your data and select the corresponding row (see Figure 7.6, where the scenario 0002 has been created and its record selected). Double-click on the Scenario Characteristics folder, and define which of the following information should be taken into consideration when searching the bank chain (the rules apply to both the general and receiver-specific search):

- Ranking
- Sender bank detail
- Receiver country of the receiver bank
- Receiver bank
- Currency
- You can create more than one search strategy for each scenario, each of which is identified by a ranking (from 0 up to 9).

Activating the Scenario

Use Transaction FIBD (Figure 7.7) to activate exactly one scenario in your system. Remember, it's not possible to activate more than one scenario; in fact, Table TBCHAINC0 contains just two fields:

- The client (key field)
- The active scenario

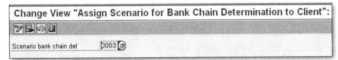

Figure 7.7 Activating a Bank Chain Scenario

7.3.2 Maintaining Bank Chains

Depending on the active bank chain scenario, you may need to maintain only the general rules, only the partner-specific rules, or both. (Keep in mind that if both the rules are active, the partner-specific rules take precedence.) We discuss the maintenance of these rules next.

Maintaining General Bank Chains

The general search is potentially based on the following factors (but you can decide to use only some of them):

- Currency
- Bank country of the sender bank
- Sender bank key
- Bank country of the receiver bank
- Receiver bank key
- Supplement payment method

To create a general bank chain search, there are two steps (Figure 7.8):

1. **Create a bank chain with up to three correspondent banks.**
   - Select the Bank Chain folder, and click on New Entries.
   - Specify the bank chain ID, the progressive number of the correspondence bank (from 1 to 3), and the type of the correspondent bank (open the match-code to find the four possible alternatives; check with your bank colleagues about their meaning and usage).
   - Specify the bank branch that plays the role of the correspondent bank in the chain, supplying the bank country and bank key.

2. **Assign the created bank chain to a search strategy.**
   The possible factors in a search strategy are the following:
   - Currency
   - Bank country of the sender bank
   - Sender bank key
   - Bank country of the receiver bank
   - Receiver bank key
   - Supplement payment method

Use just the dimensions that are active in the active scenario. If you search records with more information than the scenario, these records are ignored. For example, in Figure 7.8, a search record with only the currency and the receiving bank has been created because just the currency, and the receiving country and bank are available in the scenario; all of the other possible dimensions (like the sending country and the sending bank) have been left blank.

1. Create the chain

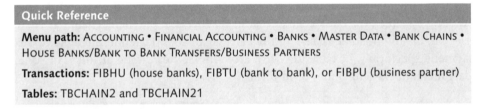

2. Assign the chain

Figure 7.8 Maintaining General Bank Chains

Maintaining Receiver-Specific Bank Chains

The receiver-specific bank chains work in the same way as the general bank chains. There are, however, three main differences:

▸ The receiver bank account can be used just in the partner-specific bank chains, meaning that you can create specific bank chains for each receiving bank account. However, remember that the receiver bank account must be activated in the active scenario.

▸ The general bank chains are updated in customizing and need to be transported, while the partner-specific bank chains are updated in the application menu in the productive SAP system.

▸ With the general bank chain, you can freely define the search strategy based on the available factors that are active in the scenario; in the partner-specific chain, you must always start from the bank details of a business partner (customer or vendor) and complete the bank chain from those details.

When you use one of the three transactions listed in the Quick Reference box (FIBHU, FIBTU, or FIBPU), you have to specify either a house bank account or a customer or vendor; the bank information found in one of the three objects becomes the starting point of the bank chain. This starting point can be the information of the receiver bank or of the sending bank, depending on whether you choose an ingoing or outgoing payment.

7.3.3 Bank Chains in Payments

Quick Reference

Menu path: Accounting • Financial Accounting • Accounts Payable • Periodic Processing • Payments

Transaction: F110

Table: REGUH

Use Transaction F110 for making automatic payments to your vendors (the details on how to use this transaction are provided in Chapter 5, Accounts Receivable and Accounts Payable). If a bank chain scenario is active and one bank chain has been selected, the intermediary banks of the bank chain are updated in the table of the payment (specifically, in Table REGUH). From there, they can be included in DME (data medium exchange) files or in forms.

Note

Intermediary banks aren't included in lists of payments (program RFZALI20); follow the instructions in SAP Note 842128 to include the bank chain in the list (you'll need the help of an ABAP expert).

The intermediary banks are placed in Table REGUH (which is the header table for automatic payments performed with Transaction F110) in the following fields:

▶ **BTYP1:** Type of bank in a bank chain (correspondent, intermediary)

▶ **BNKS1:** Bank country key

▶ **BNKL1:** Bank key

▶ **BNKN1:** Bank account number

▶ **BTYP2:** Type of bank in a bank chain (correspondent, intermediary)

▶ **BNKS2:** Bank country key

- **BNKL2:** Bank key
- **BNKN2:** Bank account number
- **BTYP3:** Type of bank in a bank chain (correspondent, intermediary)
- **BNKS3:** Bank country key
- **BNKL3:** Bank key
- **BNKN3:** Bank account number

From there, the information can be transferred to your bank for the execution of the automatic payment. For example, it can be included in a DME file.

7.3.4 FAQ and Troubleshooting Tips

Here we answer some frequently asked questions and offer helpful troubleshooting tips.

FAQ

1. **Question**: Should I also use bank chains in local bank payments?

   Answer: There's little reason to use bank chains to perform payments between two bank accounts located in the same country. In general, the local bank number and the bank account are sufficient (though in countries that adhere to the IBAN standard, the IBAN number could also be required).

2. **Question**: Can I assign more than three banks to a bank chain?

   Answer: No. The maximum number of correspondent banks that SAP can update for one bank payment is limited to three.

Troubleshooting Tips

1. **Issue**: I have created a bank chain, but it hasn't taken payments into consideration.

   Solution: Make sure that you create bank chains with exactly the information that is required in the search strategy of the scenario. For example, if your active scenario has just one search strategy based on the receiving country and on the currency, don't create bank chains with more information — they will simply be ignored by the system.

2. **Issue**: When creating a bank chain, error message PZ876 appears: "Bank chains are not active."

Solution: This means that no scenario is active in your client. Define and activate one scenario, as described in Section 7.3.1, Customizing Bank Chains.

7.4 Electronic Bank Statements

In this section, we explain how to configure electronic bank statements and import them into SAP.

7.4.1 Configuring Electronic Bank Statements

Quick Reference

Menu path: IMG • FINANCIAL ACCOUNTING • BANK ACCOUNTING • BUSINESS TRANSACTIONS • PAYMENT TRANSACTIONS • ELECTRONIC BANK STATEMENTS • MAKE GLOBAL SETTINGS FOR ELECTRONIC BANK STATEMENTS

Transaction: FMLGD_H_ELKO

In just one step, you can carry forward all of the settings necessary to allow the importing of electronic bank statements into SAP. Execute Transaction FMLGD_H_ELKO, and, upon prompting, supply the chart of accounts (Figure 7.9). Then follow the steps in the order described next.

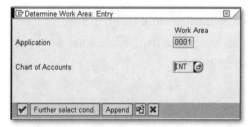

Figure 7.9 Specify Chart of Accounts to Customize the Electronic Bank Statement

Creating Bank Statement Transaction Types

Quick Reference

Transaction: FMLGD_H_ELKO

Table/view: T028V/V_T028V

A transaction type groups together rules to interpret each transaction in a bank statement. This can be very useful if you receive many bank statements for accounts that use the same format and transactions in the file; if you assign each bank account to the same transaction type, the interpretation rules have to be defined just once. However, even if you have just one bank account, you still must create a transaction type.

The creation is very simple (Figure 7.10):

1. Select the Create Transaction Type folder.

2. Select the New Entries button.

3. Specify the transaction type ID (maximum of eight digits) and the description.

4. Save your entries, and go to the next step.

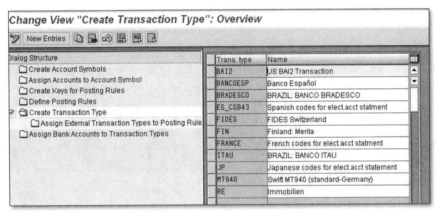

Figure 7.10 Bank Statement Transaction Types

Assigning House Bank Accounts to Bank Statement Transaction Types

Quick Reference

Transaction: FMLGD_H_ELKO

Table/view: T028B/V_T028B

After you define a transaction type, you must assign the transaction type to one or more house bank accounts. Follow these steps (Figure 7.11):

1. Double-click on the Assign Bank Accounts to Transaction Types folder.

2. Select New Entries.

3. Specify the bank key and bank account of your house bank account. Don't specify the house bank ID and the house bank account ID.
4. Specify the transaction type the bank account belongs to. You must have first created the transaction type, as described previously.
5. Specify a currency class only if the bank statement doesn't use the currency ISO code.
   - Specify a currency class in customizing under FINANCIAL ACCOUNTING • BANK ACCOUNTING • BUSINESS TRANSACTIONS • PAYMENT TRANSACTIONS • ELECTRONIC BANK STATEMENT • CREATE CURRENCY CLASS.
   - Assign a currency code to a currency class in customizing under FINANCIAL ACCOUNTING • BANK ACCOUNTING • BUSINESS TRANSACTIONS • PAYMENT TRANSACTIONS • ELECTRONIC BANK STATEMENT • DEFINE CURRENCY CLASS.
6. Specify the company code to which the bank account belongs, and save your entries.

The system uses the entries made in this customizing step to understand, when uploading the bank statement, which rules has to be applied to translate the bank transactions contained in the statement into Financial Accounting postings.

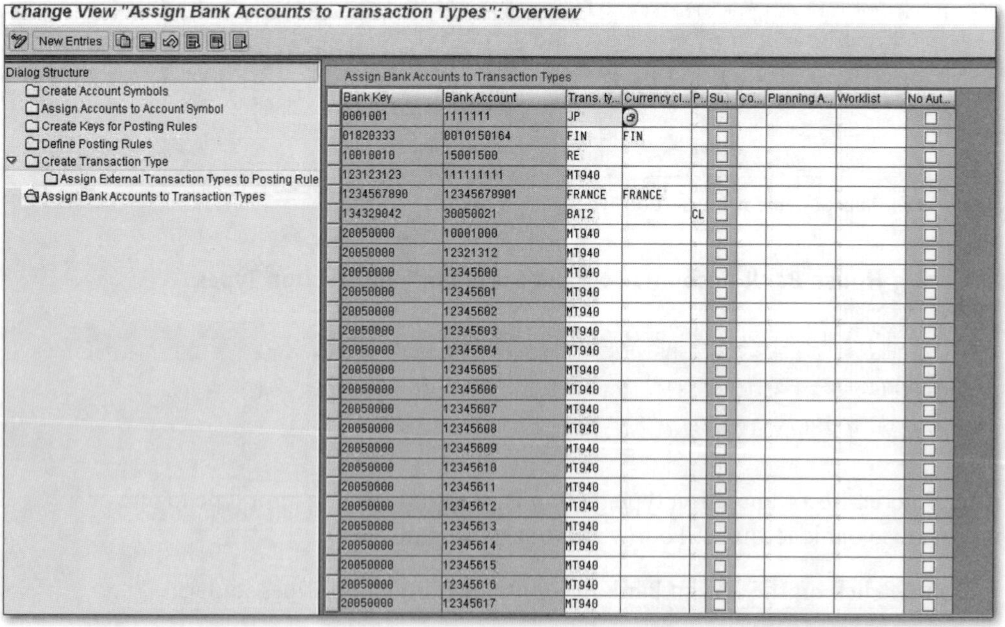

Bank Key	Bank Account	Trans. ty...	Currency cl...	P...	Su...	Co...	Planning A...	Worklist	No Aut...
0001001	1111111	JP							
01820333	0010150164	FIN	FIN						
10010010	15001500	RE							
123123123	111111111	MT940							
1234567890	12345678901	FRANCE	FRANCE						
134329042	30050021	BAI2		CL					
20050000	10001000	MT940							
20050000	12321312	MT940							
20050000	12345600	MT940							
20050000	12345601	MT940							
20050000	12345602	MT940							
20050000	12345603	MT940							
20050000	12345604	MT940							
20050000	12345605	MT940							
20050000	12345606	MT940							
20050000	12345607	MT940							
20050000	12345608	MT940							
20050000	12345609	MT940							
20050000	12345610	MT940							
20050000	12345611	MT940							
20050000	12345612	MT940							
20050000	12345613	MT940							
20050000	12345614	MT940							
20050000	12345615	MT940							
20050000	12345616	MT940							
20050000	12345617	MT940							

Figure 7.11 Link Between House Bank Accounts and Bank Statement Transaction Types

Creating Account Symbols

Account symbols simplify the management of accounting rules. Say, for example, that you have 50 bank accounts, each of which has a clearing account for incoming payments. If the clearing account is the same as the bank account except for the last digit (say a 5 instead of a 0), you can use the account symbol technique to define a rule that is valid for all 50 accounts by automatically replacing the bank account's last digit with a 5. If the account symbol technique was not available you would need to perform 50 customizing entries, instead of a single entry.

Follow this procedure to create the account symbols (Figure 7.12):

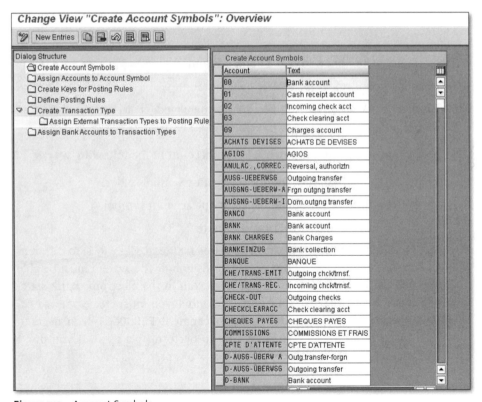

Figure 7.12 Account Symbols

1. Select the Create Account Symbols folder.

2. Select the New Entries button.

3. Specify an account symbol ID (maximum 15 digits) and a short description.

4. Save your entries.

The next step is to create the rules that transform the account symbol into a real general ledger account.

Link Between Account Symbols and General Ledger Accounts

> **Quick Reference**
>
> **Transaction:** FMLGD_H_ELKO
> **Table/view:** T033GI/V_T033G_EBST

In this step, you tell the system how to use account symbols. The general ledger bank account is the starting point of the account determination; the logic for this is as follows:

1. Each account statement refers to a bank account.

2. Each bank account refers to a house bank account.

3. Each house bank account is linked to a general ledger account (see Section 7.2.2, Defining House Bank Accounts).

Link the account symbol to the general ledger account in the following way:

1. Double-click on the Assign Accounts to Account Symbol folder.

2. Select the New Entries button, and specify one account symbol.

3. Specify the following additional details (Figure 7.13):

  ▶ **Acct Mod. (account modification):** Use free text (e.g., CLEAR_1) to differentiate account determination for an account symbol. The system must be able to match particular information that is present in the electronic bank statement with the account modification. To do this, you must create a user exit. Use Transaction CMOD, and select enhancement FEB00001 (you need to work together with an ABAP developer to perform this step). If you don't need this functionality, leave the field blank or enter "+".

- **Currency:** You can differentiate the general ledger accounts based on the currency of the transaction. If you don't need this functionality, leave the field blank or enter "+".

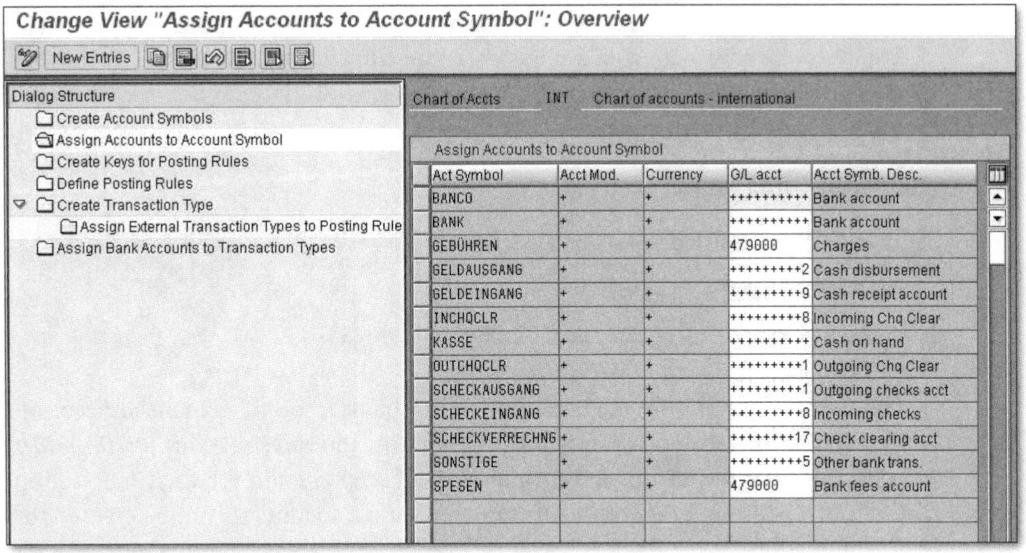

Act Symbol	Acct Mod.	Currency	G/L acct	Acct Symb. Desc.
BANCO	+	+	++++++++++	Bank account
BANK	+	+	++++++++++	Bank account
GEBÜHREN	+	+	479000	Charges
GELDAUSGANG	+	+	+++++++++2	Cash disbursement
GELDEINGANG	+	+	+++++++++9	Cash receipt account
INCHQCLR	+	+	+++++++++8	Incoming Chq Clear
KASSE	+	+	++++++++++	Cash on hand
OUTCHQCLR	+	+	+++++++++1	Outgoing Chq Clear
SCHECKAUSGANG	+	+	+++++++++1	Outgoing checks acct
SCHECKEINGANG	+	+	+++++++++8	Incoming checks
SCHECKVERRECHNG	+	+	++++++++17	Check clearing acct
SONSTIGE	+	+	+++++++++5	Other bank trans.
SPESEN	+	+	479000	Bank fees account

Figure 7.13 Account Symbols and General Ledger Accounts

- **G/L Acct:** Enter a specific account or put a rule that leads to a different general ledger account, starting from the general ledger account associated with the house bank account. If, for example, you want to post to an account that is the same as the general ledger account associated with the house bank account except for the last digit, which is 9, enter "+++++++++9". This indicates that the initial 9 characters are the same as the general ledger account associated with the house bank, except for the last digit, which is a 9. (Keep in mind that if the account is numeric and not alphanumeric, you must consider the leading zeros of each general ledger account. If your account is 6 numbers long, you have to add 4 leading zeros so it's 10 digits. To have account 113000 become 113009, use +++++++++9, not +++++9.)

After you defined the account symbols and the rule to translate the account symbols into general ledger accounts, you're ready to define the posting rules, in which the account symbols and not the real general ledger accounts are used. The posting rules, as the last step in the electronic bank statement configuration, are linked to the external transactions present in the bank statement file.

> **Special Account Symbol for the House Bank General Ledger Account**
>
> Don't forget to create a special account symbol to post directly to the general ledger account associated with your house bank account (after every successful electronic bank statement import, the balance of this general ledger account should always be equal to the final balance of the electronic bank statement). When assigning the general ledger account to this special account symbol, create an entry like the one for the BANK account symbol in Figure 7.13.

Defining Posting Rules

> **Quick Reference**
>
> **Transaction:** FMLGD_H_ELKO
>
> **Tables/views:** T028D/V_T028D and T033F/V_T033F_EBST

Each time an amount is debited or credited in a bank account, a Financial Accounting document is created (or two, as described in the next section). *Posting rules* specify the structure of the accounting document(s) created for each transaction present in a bank statement (one or two accounting documents can be created for each transaction).

To begin, create a posting rule key (four digits long) and description by selecting, in Transaction FMLGD_H_ELKO, the Define Posting Rules folder (Figure 7.14), creating a new entry, and specifying the posting rule key and description. Save and go to the next step.

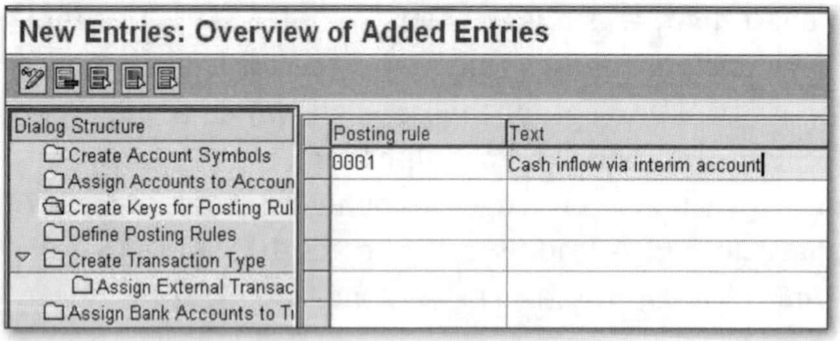

Figure 7.14 Creating Keys for Posting Rule

In the second step, define the posting rule in detail, determining the structure of the financial document that the posting rule generates. For each posting rule, two entries are possible: one for posting area 1, and one for posting area 2. In general, you use posting area 1 to post to the house bank account general ledger account (the account defined in the house bank account configuration) and to an offsetting general ledger account (such as bank charges or a clearing account for posting area 2. Posting area 2 is generally used to post to a customer account. Always use posting area 2 together with a record for posting area 1; both the records post to a bank clearing account. The reason for this is that the posting in posting area 1 is the most simple, booking just to general ledger accounts, so it's very likely that you won't encounter any errors. This posting updates the bank general ledger account, which can be quickly reconciled with the bank account balance. The posting in area 2, on the other hand, is designed to clear a customer account and therefore is more prone to error in automatic processing; a successful automatic clearing depends on the quality of the information the customer has in the note to payee (text information contained in the bank statement that has been entered by the customer to facilitate the retrieval of the invoices that are paid; for example, the note to payee can contain the invoice number).

Follow the next steps to define the posting rule (Figure 7.15). Remember that each row in this table contains the rule for exactly one Financial Accounting document.

1. Select the Define Posting Rules folder.

2. Select New Entries, and specify the posting rule and the posting area. As described previously, create a record in posting area 2 only after you've created the same record in posting area 1. The same clearing account must be present in the two posting areas, once on the debit side and once on the credit side.

3. Specify the posting key for the account on the debit side: field PKey (D). If the posting has to take place to a customer account with clearing open items, leave the field blank because the transaction is a clearing transaction, and the posting key is automatically determined by the system when clearing. Specify 40 for general ledger accounts and 15 for posting to customer account without clearing (for an incoming payment).

4. In column DCInd (D), specify a special general ledger indicator for posting to a customer account without clearing. In this case, the posting key has to be 09; normally, though, this field should be left blank and compiled only if you want to post down payments with a special general ledger indicator.

5. In the Acct (Debit) field, specify the account symbol (only if you're not posting to a customer account).

6. Specify the same information as described in the three points above for the correspondent credit line:

- PKey (C): Posting key for the credit line
- DCInd (C): Special general ledger indicator for the credit line
- Acct (Credit): Account symbol (if you aren't posting to a customer account)

7. Define the document type that will be used to post to accounting.
8. Specify the posting type:
   - 1: Post to G/L account
   - 2: Post subledg.acc deb
   - 3: Post subldg.acc cred
   - 4: Clear debit G/L acct
   - 5: Clear credit G/L act
   - 7: Clear deb.subledg.ac
   - 8: Clear cred.subl.acct
   - 9: Reset & rev. clear
9. Save your entries. The posting rule is complete and can be assigned to the external transaction, as described next.

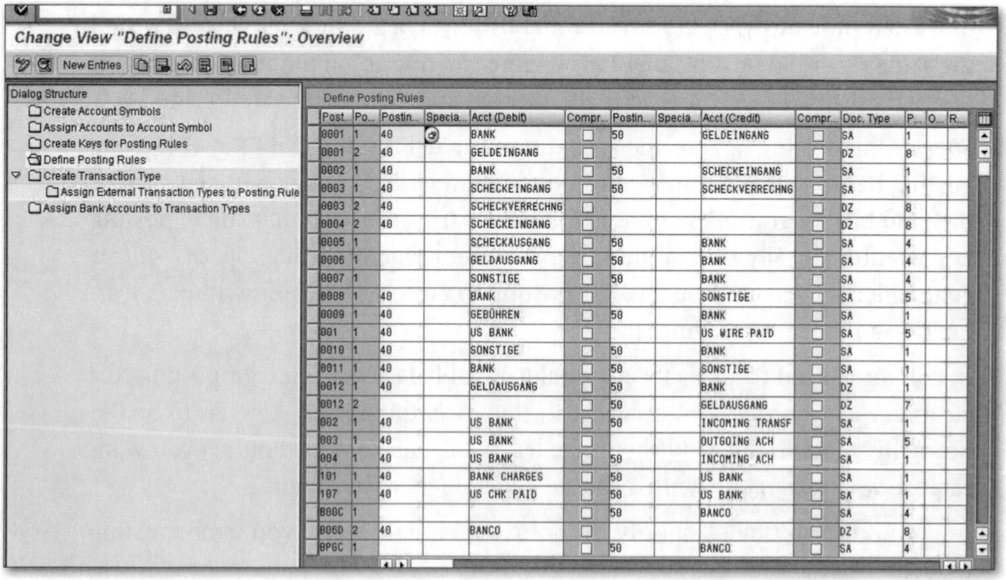

Post...	Po...	Postin...	Specia...	Acct (Debit)	Compr...	Postin...	Specia...	Acct (Credit)	Compr...	Doc. Type	P...	O...	R...
0001	1	40		BANK	☐	50		GELDEINGANG	☐	SA	1		
0001	2	40		GELDEINGANG	☐				☐	DZ	8		
0002	1	40		BANK	☐	50		SCHECKEINGANG	☐	SA	1		
0003	1	40		SCHECKEINGANG	☐	50		SCHECKVERRECHNG	☐	SA	1		
0003	2	40		SCHECKVERRECHNG	☐				☐	DZ	8		
0004	2	40		SCHECKEINGANG	☐				☐	DZ	8		
0005	1			SCHECKAUSGANG	☐	50		BANK	☐	SA	4		
0006	1			GELDAUSGANG	☐	50		BANK	☐	SA	4		
0007	1			SONSTIGE	☐	50		BANK	☐	SA	4		
0008	1	40		BANK	☐			SONSTIGE	☐	SA	5		
0009	1	40		GEBÜHREN	☐	50		BANK	☐	SA	1		
001	1	40		US BANK	☐			US WIRE PAID	☐	SA	5		
0010	1	40		SONSTIGE	☐	50		BANK	☐	SA	1		
0011	1	40		BANK	☐	50		SONSTIGE	☐	SA	1		
0012	1	40		GELDAUSGANG	☐	50		BANK	☐	DZ	1		
0012	2				☐	50		GELDAUSGANG	☐	DZ	7		
002	1	40		US BANK	☐	50		INCOMING TRANSF	☐	SA	1		
003	1	40		US BANK	☐			OUTGOING ACH	☐	SA	5		
004	1	40		US BANK	☐	50		INCOMING ACH	☐	SA	1		
101	1	40		BANK CHARGES	☐	50		US BANK	☐	SA	1		
107	1	40		US CHK PAID	☐	50		US BANK	☐	SA	1		
B00C	1				☐	50		BANCO	☐	SA	4		
B06D	2	40		BANCO	☐				☐	DZ	8		
BPGC	1				☐	50		BANCO	☐	SA	4		

Figure 7.15 Definition of Posting Rules

Assigning External Transaction Types to Posting Rules

Quick Reference
Transaction: FMLGD_H_ELKO
Table/view: T028G/V_T028G

An external transaction describes the way each transaction in the bank statement is identified by the bank, according to its internal rule and classification system. For example, transaction type 100 can be bank charges, transaction type 101 can be bank interest, and so on. These transactions must be translated into a posting rule to automatically generate Financial Accounting documents.

Define the external transactions and their links to the posting rules under the transaction type that you defined earlier (Step 1: Creating Bank Statement Transaction Types). Start by selecting the Create Transaction Type folder, and, in that folder, selecting one of the existing transaction types. Then double-click on the Assign External Transaction Types to Posting Rules subfolder, which you can find under the Create Transaction Types main folder. Then follow these steps (Figure 7.16):

1. Select the New Entries button.

2. In the Ext Trans column, type the external transaction type of the bank. You can get the list and meaning of all transaction types from the bank that provides the electronic bank statement.

3. In the +/ – column, specify the sign of the amount. For the same external transaction with positive and negative amounts, you should specify different posting rules.

4. In the Post. Rule column, assign the combination of external transactions and the sign of the amount to a posting rule already created.

5. The Int Algthm column is used for posting area 2 to specify the rule that has to be used to match the transaction with a customer open item (the information in the note to payee is used). For cases in which the posting rule doesn't clear open items, select 0 000: No Interpretation. If clearing is needed, the usual rules are 20 020: Document Number Search (which matches the note to the payee with the Financial Accounting document number BKPF-BELNR) and 21 02: Reference Document Number Search (which matches the note to the payee with the Financial Accounting reference field BKPF-XBLNR).

6. Save your entry and repeat this process for all external transactions in the bank statement.

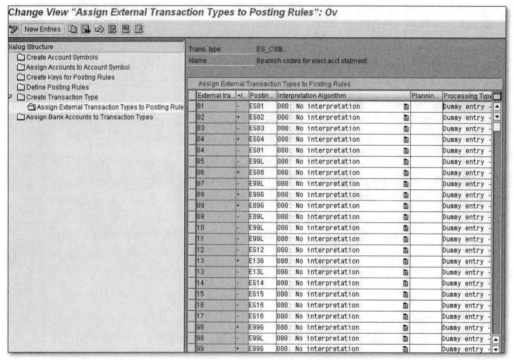

Figure 7.16 Linking Between External Transaction Types and Posting Rules

7.4.2   Importing Electronic Bank Statements into SAP

Now let's discuss the process of importing electronic bank statements into SAP.

Converting Files

Quick Reference

Menu path: ACCOUNTING • FINANCIAL ACCOUNTING • BANKS • INCOMINGS • BANK STATE-MENT • CONVERT

Transaction: FEBC

Program: A list of the available standard programs for your release is listed when you run Transaction FEBC.

When you run Transaction FEBC, the system displays a list of the available programs to convert your bank statement to the MultiCash format. (However, you may not need to perform this step if your bank statement format is supported by the bank statement upload program (Transaction FF_5).) Find a program suitable to convert your file format to the MultiCash format.

All of the conversion programs have the same basic structure, with the path for the source file to be converted and the path for the created converted file. Figure 7.17 show an example selection screen of program RFEBDK00, which is used for files with Denmark's specific format. As your destination directory, select whatever directory is read by the bank statement upload (Transaction FF_5).

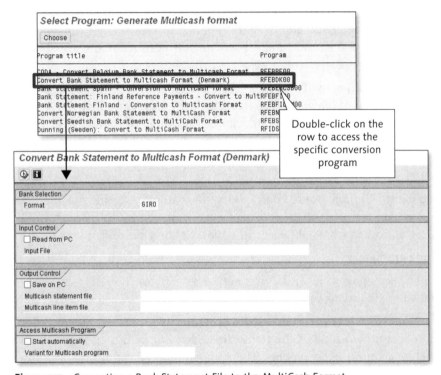

Figure 7.17 Converting a Bank Statement File to the MultiCash Format

Carefully read the instructions of each program and, if necessary, search for additional information (such as an ABAP code) in the SAP support notes. As a last resort, you could be forced to create a brand new custom program. Work with the sourcing bank and with your ABAP developer to identify an optimal solution.

Importing Bank Statements

Run Transaction FF_5 to import the bank statement into your SAP system.

Specify the following parameters in the selection screen (Figure 7.18):

▶ **File path and format**

  ▶ **Import Data flag:** If you don't flag this option, this is just a test run; you get only a preview of the result, and the statement isn't stored in the bank buffer or posted to Financial Accounting.

  ▶ **Elect. Bank Statement Format:** Select the format that corresponds to the technical format of the file that contains the bank statement. If you've generated the file with Transaction FEBC, choose the option M MultiCash (format: AUSZUG.TXT and UMSATZ.TXT). The format is needed to allow the system to find various information in the file (amount, transaction key, value date, etc.).

  ▶ **Statement File/Line Item File:** Specify the path where the statement is located (and the path for the line item file in case of a MultiCash format); if you're uploading from a PC, select the Workstation Upload flag.

▶ **Posting parameters**

  You can directly post to Financial Accounting with Transaction FF_5 by choosing one of the following options (instead of Do Not Post):

  ▶ **Post Immediately:** The system tries to post directly using the call transaction technique, in which all of the transactions that can be posted immediately generate accounting documents. There may be some postings that can't be posted because not all of the Financial Accounting controls are respected (e.g., one general ledger might be blocked for posting); these must be reprocessed with Transaction FEBAN (which we discuss later in the chapter).

  ▶ **Generate Batch Input:** The system generates one or more batch-input sessions to be processed with Transaction SM35. In this case, reprocessing with Transaction FEBAN isn't possible.

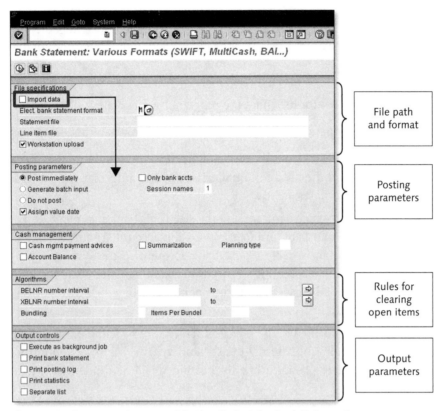

Figure 7.18 Program to Import and Optionally Post the Bank Statement

- **Rules for clearing open items**

  - **BELNR Number Intervals:** Here you specify a range of document numbers (usually customer invoices) that the system should use to interpret the information in the note to payee.

  - **XBLNR Number Intervals:** Here you specify a range of reference numbers (usually customer invoices) that the system should use to interpret the information in the note to payee.

  - **Bundling/Items per Bundle:** This section is useful if you want to group the transactions in the statement for postprocessing reasons; the grouping affects both the batch input session creation and the postprocessing screen in Transaction FEBAN. If you select 1, all of the transactions to clear open items are grouped together according to the accounting clerk in the customer master data (if found). If you select 2, the transactions are grouped together in groups of "n" transactions. The "n" value is specified in the Items per Bundle field.

▶ **Output parameters**
Here you control the list (or lists) that the program can generate.

This is how the system operates when it imports an electronic bank statement:

1. The system uses the electronic bank statement format you specify in the selection screen to interpret the file and to understand where information is stored (sender bank, amount, dates, etc.).

2. The system searches to which bank account the electronic bank statement refers; this is a combination of a bank number and a bank account. Then the system matches this information with the house bank account, so the system understands to which house bank account the electronic bank statement belongs, and then to which general ledger account it corresponds, and in which currency the postings must be made.

3. Based on the format specified in the selection screen, the system identifies each transaction and the relevant external transaction type; each transaction in the file becomes one or two postings (one for posting area 1, and potentially one for posting area 2).

4. To decide how each transaction is posted, the system searches for the connection between the external transaction and the posting rule. From the bank account, the system retrieves the transaction type. Then, with the transaction type and the external transaction type determined, it can determine the posting rule.

5. The system must find the accounts for the posting rule. If the posting area is 2, and the system has to search for a customer account, the search strategy is used with the information in the note to the payee; in any other case, the general ledger account of the house bank account is used (this can be modified by the account modification rule).

After the file is imported, it's stored in the bank buffer (Tables FEBKO and FEBEP).

If you choose the Do Not Post option, you must perform Transaction FEBP (discussed next).

Posting Imported Statements

Use this transaction to post a bank statement that has been uploaded in the tables of the bank buffer but hasn't yet been passed to Financial Accounting; this applies to bank statements that are uploaded using Transaction FF_5 and the Do Not Post option.

Select the account statements to be posted using the selection criteria displayed in Figure 7.19. For all other parameters in the selection screen, refer to the section titled Importing Bank Files, which describes the functionality of Transaction FF_5 (Importing Bank Statements).

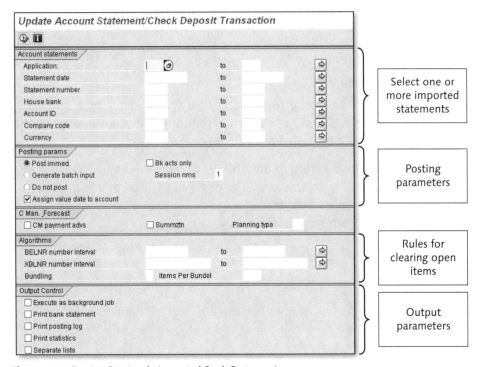

Figure 7.19 Posting Previously Imported Bank Statements

Reprocessing (or Postprocessing) of Imported and Partially Posted Bank Statements

Use Transaction FEBAN when you've posted the electronic bank statement using the Post Immediately option. This displays the content of the transaction already posted to Financial Accounting (the accounting document number is displayed; double-click on the field to branch to the overview of the financial document). It also allows you to reprocess transactions to correct errors. Fill in the selection screen with the data necessary to identify the bank statements to be reprocessed, and run the program.

The program displays a screen like the one shown in Figure 7.20; on the left side of the screen, the following are displayed in hierarchical order:

1. The house bank

2. The house bank account to which the statement refers

3. The statement number

4. The transactions that belong to the statement (green status means that the transaction has been posted to Financial Accounting; red status means that the transaction could not be posted due to errors)

If you click on the Other Display button, all of the transactions are displayed in a flat list, instead of in hierarchical form. The way you perform the reprocessing of the transactions is exactly the same, regardless of which view you choose.

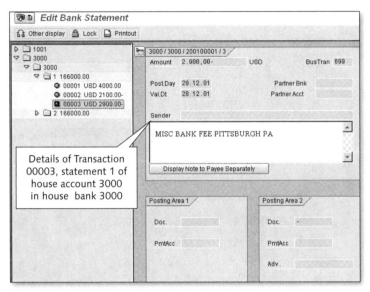

Figure 7.20 Details of Unposted Transactions

Perform the reprocessing of the transactions one by one. To start the reprocessing, double-click on the transaction, and select the Save button. If no error occurs (because the error has already been solved outside Transaction FEBAN), the transaction is posted, the status changes to green, and the accounting document number is displayed in the transaction details. If the error is still present, the system simulates the Financial Accounting document and opens the posting screen where the error is occurring.

Figure 7.21 shows an example of a transaction that has been reprocessed; here you can see that the system has to post to a P&L account that requires the assignment to a real controlling object. In such a case, you usually specify the cost center. If the transaction involves the clearing of customer open items, you go through a clearing transaction in which you may be asked to specify the customer number and the documents to be cleared; the information available in the note to payee will help you in the identification process.

After all of the transactions are green, the selected bank statement has been completely posted to Financial Accounting.

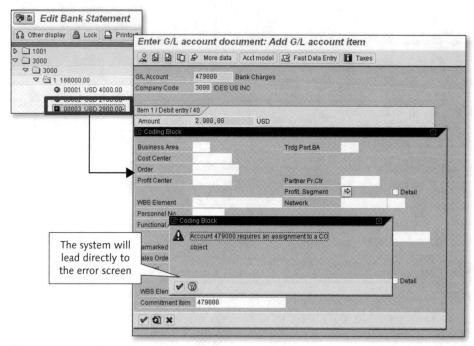

Figure 7.21 Reprocess a Transaction

7.4.3 FAQ and Troubleshooting Tips

Next we answer some frequently asked questions and offer helpful troubleshooting tips.

FAQ

1. **Question**: How can I get enough information on the format of the bank statement and on the external transaction types contained?

   Answer: When customizing the electronic bank statement upload, one of the most time-consuming steps is the mapping of the external transaction types contained in the bank statement against posting rules in SAP. In general, this is done in collaboration with the bank that provides the file. Discuss the technical aspects of the bank file with an expert at your bank; integration of the bank statement with SAP is quite a common project, and the bank may have the expertise to help you.

2. **Question:** Why do the electronic bank statements in MultiCash formats have two files?

   Answer: The MultiCash format consists of two files, AUSZUG.TXT and UMSATZ. TXT. The AUSZUG.TXT file contains the header information for the account statements; the UMSATZ.TXT file contains the item information.

3. **Question:** Why is Transaction FEBP available if it's possible to post directly when importing the bank statement with Transaction FF_5?

   Answer: With Transaction FF_5, you can import the file and subsequently post with Transaction FEBP, or you can import and post all at once. Your approach here depends on the segregation of duties within your company; it may be, for example, that the bank activities must be performed by a team that isn't allowed to post to Financial Accounting.

Troubleshooting Tips

1. **Issue:** Using Transaction FF_5 or Transaction FEBP, error message F5263 appears: "The difference is too large for clearing." What is the problem?

   Solution: This error generally occurs in posting area 2, when the system tries to clear a customer open item; the possible issue is that there isn't enough information in the note to payee. In this case, postprocess the transaction in error with Transaction FEBAN, identify which invoice the payment refers to (you may need to contact the customer to do this), and manually specify the customer or document number to be paid in the screen of Transaction FEBAN.

2. **Issue:** When running Transaction FF_5, error message FV626 appears: "Incorrect input file: No ; separator exists in AUSZUG.TXT format." What is the problem?

   Solution: This means that you've selected the MultiCash format, but the file isn't in MultiCash format. Convert the file to MultiCash format with Transaction FEBC, or change the format in the selection screen of Transaction FF.5.

7.5 Cash Journal

A *cash journal* is a SAP tool used to keep track of and to post all of the transactions that are performed by cashiers. (Even though in most companies the usage of cash is quite rare, there are still some expenses that must be paid in cash.) In this section, we discuss some of the most important concepts of the cash journal: cash journal customizing, cash journal postings, and cash journal reporting.

7.5.1 Customizing Cash Journals

Next we discuss the following aspects of customizing a cash journal:

- Defining cash journals
- Creating business transactions
- Creating number ranges for documents

Defining Cash Journals

> **Quick Reference**
>
> **Menu path:** IMG • Financial Accounting • Bank Accounting • Business Transactions • Cash Journal • Set Up Cash Journal
>
> **Transaction:** FBCJC0
>
> **Table/view:** TCJ_C_JOURNALS/V_TCJ_C_JOURNALS

Create the cash journal using Transaction FBCJ0 (Figure 7.22). Select New Entries, and specify the company code and the cash journal ID (four digits long) (❶ of Figure 7.22). Remember that every cash journal is assigned to exactly one company code. Figure 7.22 lists the settings that are possible for each cash journal:

- **G/L Account (❷)**
  This is the account in which the first row is posted in Financial Accounting. The offsetting account depends on the cash transaction you use, as well as on the single posting. We strongly suggest creating exactly one general ledger account for each cash journal.

- **Currency (❸)**
  This is the currency in which the cash journal and all corresponding Financial Accounting documents are managed. A cash journal can be managed in one and only one currency.

- **CJ Closed (❹)**
  You can use this flag to deactivate a cash journal; all of the existing postings won't be affected.

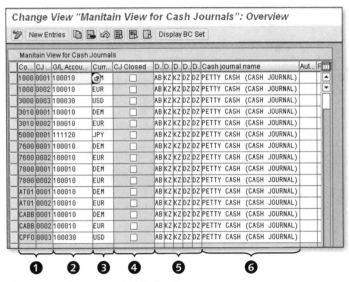

Figure 7.22 Cash Journal Main Settings

- ▶ **DT G/L Act (⑤)**
  This is the document type used to post to the general ledger offsetting account, debit and credit.

- ▶ **DT Disb (⑤)**
  This field is only used in Russia.

- ▶ **D.Tpe: Vept (⑤)**
  This is the document type used to post to the vendor offsetting account, debit.

- ▶ **D.Tpe: Vept (⑤)**
  This field has the same column heading as the previous one but a different meaning. It's the document type to post to vendor offsetting accounts, credit.

- ▶ **D.Tpe: Cupt (⑤)**
  This is the document type used to post to customer offsetting accounts, debit.

- ▶ **Doc: Cus. Pt (⑤)**
  This is the document type used to post to customer offsetting accounts, credit.

- ▶ **Cash Journal Name (⑥)**
  In this field, enter the name for the cash journal.

- ▶ **Additional optional data**
  - ▶ **Authorization Group:** You can use this field to segment the access of users to cash journals; for example, you may want user DINCAS to be able to

access cash journal 0005 in company code 1000. Discuss this issue with your SAP authorizations expert.

▶ **Person 1, Person 2, and Additional Text:** These fields have been added by SAP to be used only in specific countries; they have no effect on the standard functionalities of the cash journal, but they can be used in reporting.

Creating Business Transactions

> **Quick Reference**
>
> **Menu path:** IMG • FINANCIAL ACCOUNTING • BANK ACCOUNTING • BUSINESS TRANSACTIONS • CASH JOURNAL • CREATE, CHANGE, DELETE BUSINESS TRANSACTIONS
>
> **Transaction:** FBCJC2
>
> **Table/view:** TCJ_TRANSACTIONS/V_TCJ_TRANSACT

After you've created the necessary cash journals for your company code, the second step in the cash journal configuration is to create the business transactions. As with the cash journals, the business transactions are also dependent on the company code.

Using Transaction FBCJC2, select New Entries, and specify the company code. The system automatically sets the transaction number (the last number created in the company code plus 1) (❶ of Figure 7.23). The following settings are then available (Figure 7.23):

▶ **Business Transaction Type (❷)**
This setting is the most important in the transaction definition because it controls whether you can post to customer or vendor accounts, or whether you post to a balance sheet account or to a P&L account. (In this last case, don't forget that an additional account assignment object is necessary if, as usual, the P&L account is created as a cost element in the controlling area assigned to the company code.) The following six business transaction types are possible:

▶ **C: Receipt from bank account.** Posts debit to the cash journal account. The offsetting account is a balance sheet general ledger account, and you can only use the postings in the Cash Receipt area.

▶ **B: Payment to bank account.** Posts credit to the cash journal account. The offsetting account is a balance sheet general ledger account, and you can only use the postings in the Cash Payment area.

- ▶ **R: Revenue. Posts debit to the cash journal account.** The offsetting account is a P&L general ledger account, and you can only use the postings in the Cash Receipt or Check Receipt areas.

- ▶ **E: Expense. Posts credit to the cash journal account.** The offsetting account is a P&L general ledger account, and you can only use the postings in the Cash Payment area.

- ▶ **D: Customer posting.** Posts credit to the cash journal account. The offsetting account is a customer account, and you can use the postings in all areas: Cash Payment, Cash Receipt, or Check Receipt.

- ▶ **K: Vendor posting.** Posts credit to the cash journal account; the offsetting account is a vendor account, and you can use the postings in all areas: Cash Payment, Cash Receipt, or Check Receipt.

▶ **G/L Account (❸)**

In this column, specify the offsetting general ledger account for the transaction.

▶ **Tax (❹)**

If the general ledger account to be posted requires a tax code, then you can specify a default tax code here.

▶ **Cash Journal Business Trans. Description (❺)**

Provide a meaningful description of the business transaction.

▶ **BusTraBlkd (business transaction blocked) (❻)**

If you don't want to use a specific business transaction, but you want to keep it in the system for auditing reasons, simply block it using this indicator; this ensure that the business transaction can't be used to create new postings.

▶ **Acc.Mod (account modifiable) (❼)**

If you set the Acc.Mod indicator, this account is modifiable when you create a specific cash journal posting. No general ledger account need be specified if the business transaction type is D or K because you must specify the customer account or the vendor account at the time of the posting.

▶ **Tax Mod. (tax code modifiable) (❽)**

If you select this indicator, the default tax code specified in the Tax field can be overwritten by the user at the time of the posting.

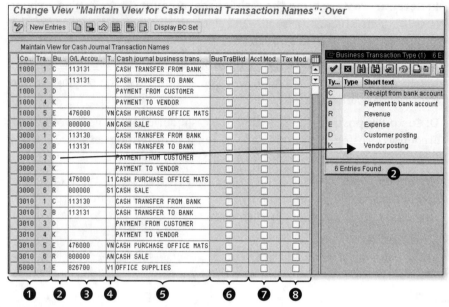

Figure 7.23 Creating Business Transactions

Creating Number Ranges for Cash Journal Documents

Quick Reference

Menu path: IMG • Financial Accounting • Bank Accounting • Business Transactions • Cash Journal • Define Number Range Intervals for Cash Journal Documents

Transaction: FBCJC1

Table: NRIV (object name CAJO_DOC2)

Cash journal documents have their own number range, which is different from the number range of the linked accounting documents. Create the cash journal number range using Transaction FBCJC1 (Figure 7.24).

To create the number range, specify the company code, and select the Intervals button (❶ of Figure 7.24). The system requires the number range 01 created as the internal number range, so specify the number range 01 and the initial and final number (no specific bindings; create a large number range to avoid maintaining it in the coming years) (❷ of Figure 7.24). Don't select the Ext flag, which would make it an external number range; cash journal transactions require an internal number range.

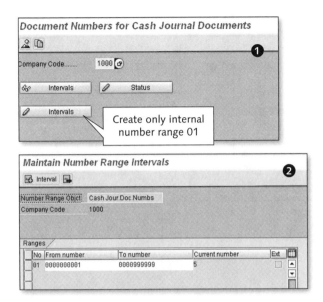

Figure 7.24 Cash Journal Documents Number Ranges

7.5.2 Cash Journal Postings

> **Quick Reference**
>
> **Menu path:** Accounting • Financial Accounting • Banks • Outgoing • Cash Journal
>
> **Transaction:** FBCJ
>
> **Tables:** TCJ_BALANCE (cash journal totals records after every transaction), TCJ_DOCU-MENTS (cash journal documents header data), and TCJ_POSITIONS (cash journal documents item data)

Next we describe the way you post a cash journal document and create all of the follow-up functions (post to accounting, deleting, print the receipt, etc.). All actions are performed using Transaction FBCJ.

Posting Cash Journal Documents

To post a cash journal document, always use Transaction FBCJ; see Figures 7.25 and 7.26 to see the working area in which you perform all of the actions for cash journal documents. Begin by specifying the company code and the cash journal. (You can change the cash journal at any time by selecting the Change Cash Journal button.)

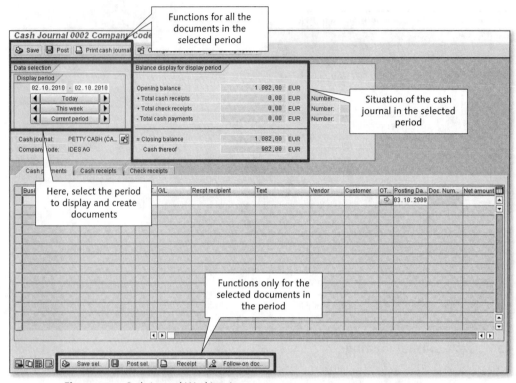

Figure 7.25 Cash Journal Working Area

The cash journal works with periods, which can be one day, one week, or one posting period. By default, the system selects the current day as the working period; all of the cash journal postings belonging to today's date are displayed.

If you click on the This Week button, the working period becomes the week in which today's date falls (from Monday until Sunday). If you click on the Current Period button, the working period becomes the posting period in which today's date falls.

With the left arrow button (◀), you can jump behind in the period (previous day, previous week, or previous posting period). With the right arrow button (▶), you can jump ahead in the period (next day, next week, or next posting period). To create a new cash journal document, follow these steps (refer to Figure 7.26):

1. Specify where you want to post; this determines whether the money is coming in or going out. The following three tabs are available:

   ▶ Cash Payments

- Cash Receipts

- Check Receipts

- Click one of the tabs, and go to the following step.

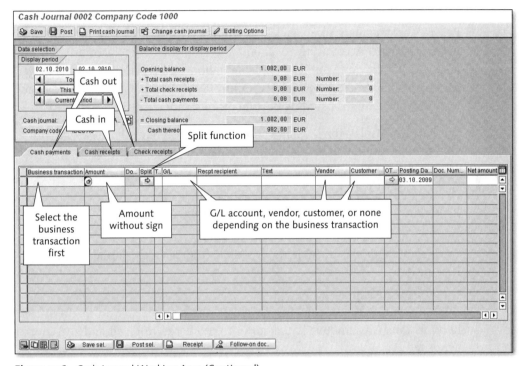

Figure 7.26 Cash Journal Working Area (Continued)

2. Specify the business transaction and the amount. Note that the business transaction must be allowed in the posting area in which you're working; the control is made through the transaction type with which the business transaction is associated. For the permitted combinations of business transaction type and posting area, refer to the Creating Business Transactions section under Section 7.5.1, Customizing Cash Journals.

3. Specify all needed additional data. The required data depends on the offsetting account that you're using and the field status of that account. For example, if you're posting to an account that is also defined as a cost element, you must specify an additional account assignment (a real cost object). As another example, if you post to a general ledger account with the value date manda-

tory according to the field status group, you must specify the value date. If the information contained in the lines doesn't satisfy this rule, you'll get an error message that explains what required information is missing.

4. Save the document in the cash journal with the Save Set button. The document is saved in the cash journal but not in Financial Accounting.

5. Release the document to Financial Accounting with the Post Set button; a connected Financial Accounting document and all of the linked accounting documents (depending on your SAP implementation, you could have special ledger documents, controlling documents, Controlling – Profitability Analysis documents, profit center accounting documents, etc.) are created.

In the Balance Display for Display Period section, you have the following information for the period you've chosen (e.g., today), all in the currency in which the cash journal is managed:

▶ **Opening Balance**
Represents your overall balance, including the checks.

▶ **Total Cash Receipts**
Total amount of the documents posted in the selected period in the Cash Receipts tab.

▶ **Total Check Receipts**
Total amount of the documents posted in the selected period in the Check Receipts tab. This amount is the sum of the checks received and the checks deposited.

▶ **Total Cash Payments**
Total amount of the documents posted in the selected period in the Cash Payments tab.

▶ **Closing Balance**
The closing balance of the cash journal for the displayed period, including both cash and checks.

▶ **Cash Balance**
The closing balance of the cash journal, excluding the balance of the checks.

Note that the cash journal can never have a negative balance.

Managing Checks in the Cash Journal

If you receive a payment with a check, you can manage the check receipt and the cash deposit in the bank with the cash journal in the Check Receipts tab. The posting area has a description that can be misunderstood; remember, it's used both to receive checks and to deposit checks at the bank. *Do not* use the Cash Payments tab to deposit checks at the bank!

Follow these steps to post the receipt of checks (see Figure 7.27 for an example of a check receipted and deposited at the bank):

1. Select the Check Receipts tab.
2. Specify a business transaction, which must be one of the following types:
   - R (revenue)
   - D (customer posting)
   - K (vendor posting)
3. Specify the amount, and all of the needed information about the check (remember that the relevant information is printed in the check lot you'll use to deposit the checks by the bank):
   - Check number
   - Check issuer
   - Bank data of the check
4. In the case of transaction type D or K, specify the customer or the vendor from whom you've received the check.
5. Save the transaction, and post to Financial Accounting.

The following steps explain how to deposit checks to a bank (see Figure 7.27 for an example of a check receipted and deposited at the bank):

1. Select the Check Receipts tab.
2. Select the items of the checks you want to deposit together (i.e., in a lot).
3. Select the Deposit Checks button. The system asks you the business transaction you want to use; you can only select type B (payment to bank account).
4. Confirm your choice, and save the document in the cash journal with the Save Selected Entries button; to post to Financial Accounting, use the Post Selected Entries button (🖫).

5. Print the list of the checks that you've posted with the Check Lot button; you need the printed list when you go to the bank to deposit the checks.

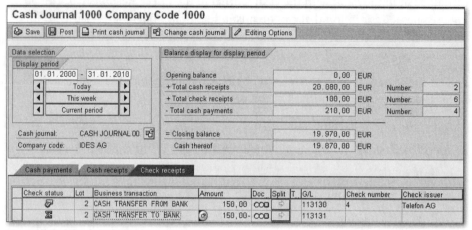

Figure 7.27 Check Received and Deposited

Releasing Cash Journal Documents to Financial Accounting

There are several options for posting documents to Financial Accounting. You can post the following:

▶ **One specific cash document**
Select the row corresponding to the document you want to post, and then select the Post Set button in the bottom of the screen.

▶ **All of the cash documents on the screen (except those that have a Deleted or Posted status)**
Simply select the Post Set button in the upper part of the screen.

To show the linked Financial Accounting and Controlling documents, select one row and click the Follow-On Doc. Button (❶ of Figure 7.28); then double-click on one of the documents listed (❷ of Figure 7.28); the system will display the overview of the associated Financial Accounting or Controlling document (see ❸ of Figure 7.28, where the overview of the connected Financial Accounting document is displayed).

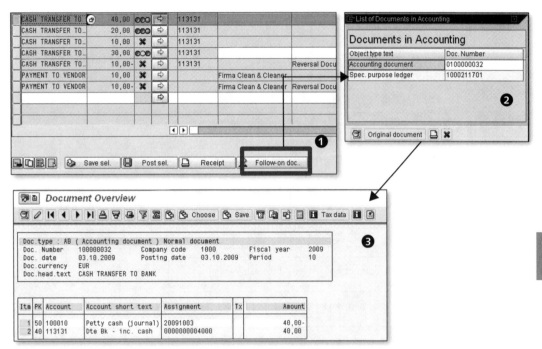

Figure 7.28 Displaying the Accounting Documents Linked to the Cash Journal Documents

Deleting a Document Not Released to Financial Accounting

If necessary, it's possible to delete a document saved in the cash journal and not released to Financial Accounting. The document disappears from the cash journal area, but it can be retrieved by selecting EXTRAS • DELETED DOCUMENTS. The document isn't physically deleted from the database. To actually delete the document, select the corresponding row in the cash journal area, and click on the Delete button.

Deleting a Document Already Released to Financial Accounting

If necessary, it's possible to delete a document saved in the cash journal and released to Financial Accounting. The document doesn't disappear from the cash journal area but will receive a specific status, as shown in Figure 7.29.

As a result of the "deletion," an equal document with opposite signs is created in Financial Accounting. However, if the original document contained customer, vendor, or general ledger open items, the open items aren't cleared automatically; they must be cleared separately in Financial Accounting. To delete the document, select the corresponding row in the cash journal area, and click on the Delete button.

Figure 7.29 displays all of the possible statuses that a document can have in cash accounting.

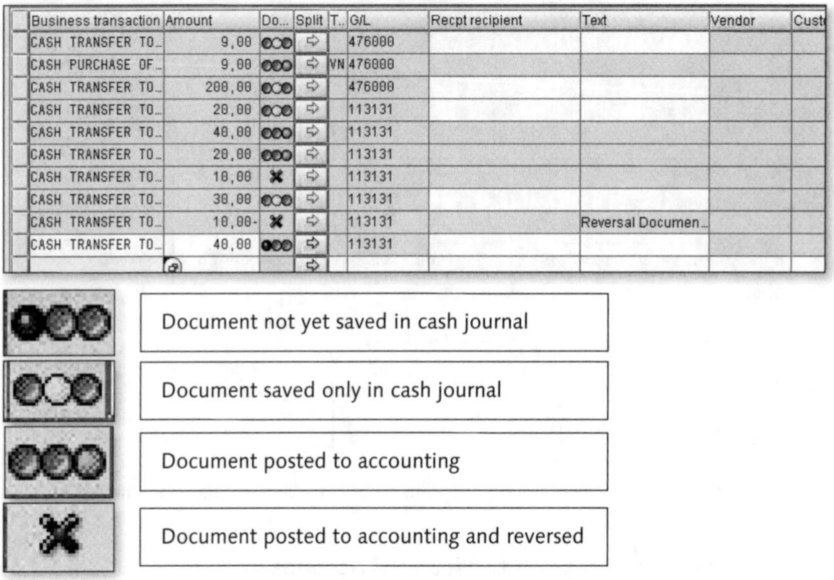

Business transaction	Amount	Do...	Split	T...	G/L	Recpt recipient	Text	Vendor	Cust
CASH TRANSFER TO...	9,00	●○●	⇨		476000				
CASH PURCHASE OF...	9,00	●○●	⇨	VN	476000				
CASH TRANSFER TO...	200,00	●○●	⇨		476000				
CASH TRANSFER TO...	20,00	●○●	⇨		113131				
CASH TRANSFER TO...	40,00	●○●	⇨		113131				
CASH TRANSFER TO...	20,00	●○●	⇨		113131				
CASH TRANSFER TO...	10,00	✖	⇨		113131				
CASH TRANSFER TO...	30,00	●○●	⇨		113131				
CASH TRANSFER TO...	10,00-	✖	⇨		113131		Reversal Documen...		
CASH TRANSFER TO...	40,00	●○●	⇨		113131				
		⊕	⇨						

●●●	Document not yet saved in cash journal
○●●	Document saved only in cash journal
●●●	Document posted to accounting
✖	Document posted to accounting and reversed

Figure 7.29 Status of Cash Documents

7.5.3 Cash Journal Reporting

Quick Reference

Menu path: ACCOUNTING • FINANCIAL ACCOUNTING • BANKS • INFORMATION SYSTEM • PRINT CASH JOURNAL

Transaction: S_ALR_87012309

Program: RFCASH00

You can print a list of cash journal entries using report RFCASH00, which you can run in two ways:

▸ **From the cash journal working area**
In this case, the system prints only the entries that are contained in the selected period (Figure 7.30).

▶ **From the menu**

In this case, select Transaction S_ALR_87012309.

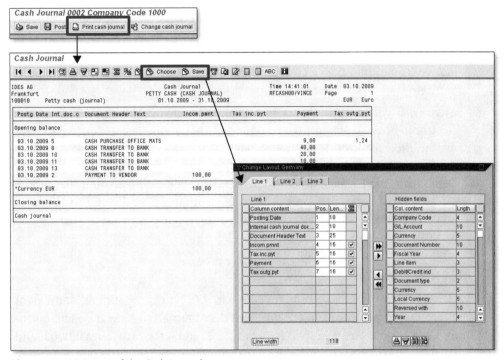

Figure 7.30 Printout of the Cash Journal

7.5.4   FAQ and Troubleshooting Tips

Next we answer some frequently asked questions and offer helpful troubleshooting tips.

FAQ

1. **Question:** Must I update the number ranges every year?

   Answer: No. The number ranges for cash accounting documents aren't year dependent.

2. **Question:** Should I create the number ranges in the development system and transport them?

Answer: No. For each application and SAP component, always create the number ranges directly in the productive system, and recreate them in the test and development systems. Don't transport number ranges.

3. **Question:** I'm depositing a check lot to a bank account in which data is uploaded into SAP through an electronic bank statement. In doing so, am I making a double posting to the bank account? For the same check deposit, one posting will come from the electronic bank statement, and a second from the cash journal.

   Answer: If you deposit checks to a bank account for which you manage the electronic bank statement, we recommend that you create a clearing account for the check deposit. Identify the external transaction in the bank statement that posts the check deposit, and link that transaction to a posting rule that posts debits to the bank account and credits to a clearing account. Set up the cash journal business transaction so that it doesn't post directly to the bank account but to the same clearing account to which the electronic bank statement posts.

Troubleshooting Tips

1. **Issue:** I'm creating business transactions in different cash journals, and I want all business transactions in the different cash journals to have the same meaning. I've created business transactions 1, 2, 3, and 4 for cash journal 0001, and I want to create the same business transaction 4 in cash journal 0002. But every time I create a new transaction, the system automatically assigns the first progressive number available, and I can't change it.

   Solution: The only way to have the same business transactions with the same meaning in different cash journals is to create an Excel sheet that defines a master list of the transactions with the relevant settings. Then create all of the transactions in all of the cash journals, and block the transactions that you don't use in one specific cash journal. Remember that every time you create a new transaction, you must create it in all of the cash journals.

2. **Issue:** Error message F5A071 appears: "You can't use accounting transaction type Expense here."

   Solution: You've used a business transaction belonging to transaction type E (Expenses) in the Cash Receipts or Check Receipts areas, which doesn't make sense. Select the Cash Payment tab, and enter the business transaction that belongs to the E type.

3. **Issue:** Error message F5A055 appears: "Payment amount is larger than cash on hand. Change amount."

   Solution: You're making a payment for an amount larger than the amount in cash available in the cash journal. Check the amount: Is it correct? If not, the balance of your cash journal (in cash) doesn't coincide with the amount in cash you actually have. Most likely, there are some cash incomings not posted. Solve this problem and have the cash amount recorded in the system equal to the cash amount physically available before posting the cash payment. (Note that you get this message even if you're posting a transaction in the past, and the outgoing amount will lead to a negative cash balance for the current date.)

7.6 Summary

In this chapter, we went through the major functionalities provided by SAP to support your banking and cash requirements, including the descriptions of the relevant master data and configuration. In the next chapter, we discuss the special ledger component of Financial Accounting.

The special purpose ledger has become somewhat obsolete with the release of SAP ERP 5.0, SAP ERP 6.0, and SAP General Ledger, but many companies still use this component, and will continue to do so until they migrate to SAP General Ledger.

8   Special Purpose Ledger

The *special purpose ledger* allows you to carry out parallel accounting with the general ledger. In most cases, this is to comply with legal requirements. In this chapter, we discuss several aspects of the special purpose ledger: its configuration, its postings, and its functionalities. In the last section of the chapter, we explain total data reporting, which is the type of reporting most commonly used with the special purpose ledger.

8.1   Special Purpose Ledger Configuration

This section provides a step-by-step guide to the creation of a new special ledger. These steps are as follows:

1. Install table groups.
2. Define field movement.
3. Create the ledger.
4. Assign companies or company codes to the ledger.
5. Configure the ledger selection.
6. Configure validations and substitutions.
7. Configure manual special ledger postings.

8.1.1 Installing Table Groups

When you create a new special ledger, you assign it to one (and only one) table group. Each table group is a list of five connected tables where special ledger data is stored. There can be many table groups in the system, but each special ledger can use only the fields that are available in the table group to which it is assigned.

> **Note**
>
> This first step, even though it doesn't require any ABAP knowledge, must be performed by a user with a development key. If you don't have a development key, perform the step with an ABAP developer. (No other steps have this requirement.)

When you need to create a new special ledger, appropriate table groups may already exist; if one of the existing table groups satisfies the requirements of the new special ledger, you can assign the new special ledger to that table group. In any other case, it's necessary to create a new table group.

Run Transaction GCIQ for the creation and management of table groups (Figure 8.1).

In the Table Group field, specify the name of a table group, starting with Z or Y. In the Processing Options area, select Foreground. Then click the Create button.

> **Background Versus Foreground**
>
> If you choose to install in the background, the system creates a local table group that works with company codes. We strongly recommend selecting the other option, Foreground, if you want to choose whether you want to create a local or a global table group. The Foreground option also gives you better control over the creation process.

The system asks you which characteristics you want to manage in the table group and gives you the option to add or delete fields that are to be managed. For example, you can choose the profit center, cost center, business area, and so on. Click the Insert Fields button to see a complete list of the fields you can include in the table group.

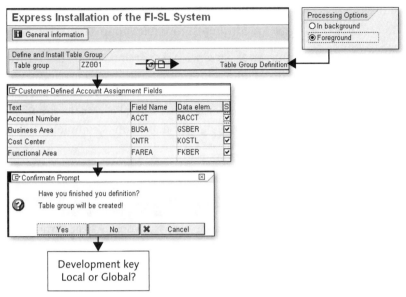

Figure 8.1 Express Installation of Table Groups, Field Movements, and Ledgers

When you've specified all of the fields needed, the system asks you for the development class and the transport request; the next step is to specify whether it's a local table group (i.e., one that works with company codes) or a global table group (i.e., one that works with companies).

When confirmed, the system creates five tables. Each table name is exactly the same, except for the very last letter. The final letters denote the following:

► **T:** Summary table

► **A:** Actual line items

► **P:** Plan line items

► **O:** Object table_1 (object/partner)

► **C:** Object table_2 (transaction attributes)

For example, if you create the table group ZZ001, the following five tables are automatically created:

► **ZZ001T:** Summary table for table group ZZ001

► **ZZ001A:** Actual line items for table group ZZ001

► **ZZ001P:** Plan line items for table group ZZ001

- ▶ **ZZ001O:** Object table_1 (object/partner) for table group ZZ001
- ▶ **ZZ001C:** Object table_2 (transaction attributes) for table group ZZ001

The next step is to decide the number of currencies that are managed. To do this, click the Rework Definition and Installation button; in the next screen, choose the Change processing type. Finally, click on the Tech.characteristics button, and define whether the transaction currency plus two possible additional currencies are to be stored in the table group. With this, the table group definition is complete.

8.1.2 Defining Field Movement

Quick Reference
Menu path: IMG • FINANCIAL ACCOUNTING • SPECIAL PURPOSE LEDGER • BASIC SETTINGS • MASTER DATA • LEDGER • MAINTAIN FIELD MOVEMENTS   **Transaction:** GCF2   **Table:** T888

When you create a table group, two types of fields are created (Figure 8.2):

- ▶ **Fixed fields**
  These fields include Ledger, Version, Period, and so on. These are the fields technically needed by the system for any type of special ledger. You can't choose them; the system creates them automatically.

- ▶ **Customer-defined account assignment fields (custom fields)**
  These are the fields that you can decide to add.

Tip
You can easily see which fields are fixed and which are customer defined by using Transaction GCIN. Select your table group, and click the Change button. Go to the Summary table and to the Actual Line Item table; the fields whose names appear in gray are fixed fields, and the ones that appear in white are customer-defined fields.

The entries for these fields (also called *characteristics*) are supplied in two different ways:

- ▶ The system automatically creates the rules to fill fixed fields. You can review these rules using Transaction GCI4.

- ▶ The rules for custom fields are defined by you, using Transaction GCF2.

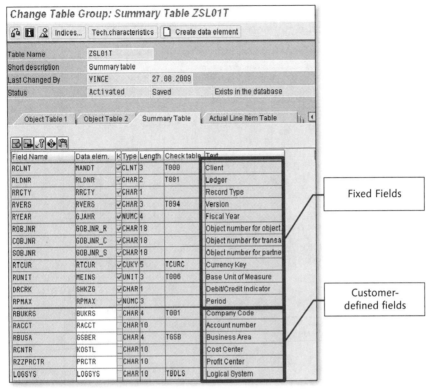

Figure 8.2 Fixed Fields and Customer-Defined Fields

To create rules to feed the custom fields, follow these steps (Figure 8.3):

1. Run Transaction GCF2, and select Field Movement • Create from the menu.

2. In the next screen, specify the name of the field movement, which should be in the form of an alphanumeric four-digit code. It doesn't need to start with Z or Y; you can specify, if available, a field movement to copy from. Press Enter.

3. In the resulting screen, specify the following information:

   ▶ **Field Movement:** Provide a description.

   ▶ **Receiver Table:** This is the total table of your table group.

   ▶ **Sender Table:** Open the possible entries with the matchcode; if you're creating the rules to specify how your customer fields are supplied by the document that creates a general ledger document, select the first row. Figure 8.4 shows the possible sending tables for the field movement.

4. Click on the Proposal button; the system automatically supplies the rules.

5. Review the proposal, make any necessary changes, and save.

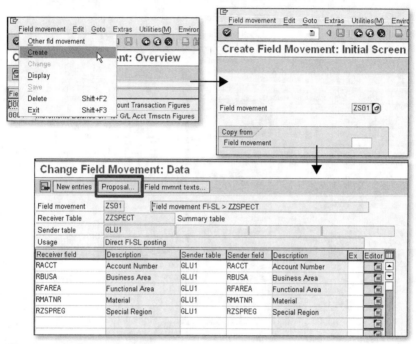

Figure 8.3 Defining a Field Movement

Posting Manually

If you need to post manually to the special ledger, you must create a separate field movement that refers to the GLU1 sender table.

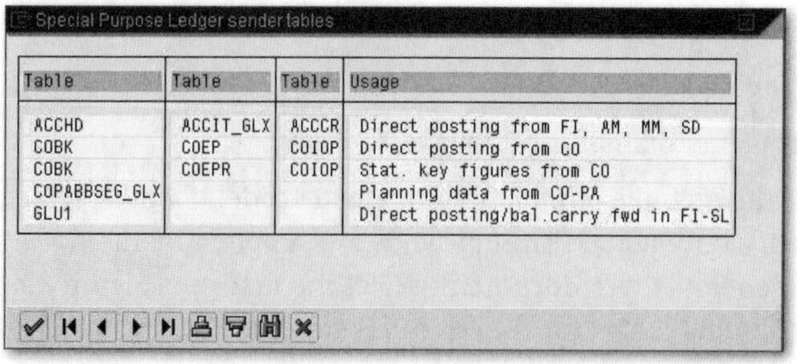

Table	Table	Table	Usage
ACCHD	ACCIT_GLX	ACCCR	Direct posting from FI, AM, MM, SD
COBK	COEP	COIOP	Direct posting from CO
COBK	COEPR	COIOP	Stat. key figures from CO
COPABBSEG_GLX			Planning data from CO-PA
GLU1			Direct posting/bal.carry fwd in FI-SL

Figure 8.4 Sending Tables for Field Movements

If you require complex rules to fill the customer fields, create a user exit in the program by following this menu path: FINANCIAL ACCOUNTING • SPECIAL PURPOSE LEDGER • BASIC SETTINGS • USER EXITS • MAINTAIN CLIENT-SPECIFIC USER EXITS. Use the GIMV area (Variable Field Movement). Then specify the user exit ID you created in the field movement definition.

8.1.3 Creating the Ledger

> **Quick Reference**
>
> **Manu path:** IMG • FINANCIAL ACCOUNTING • SPECIAL PURPOSE LEDGER • BASIC SETTINGS • TABLES • DEFINITION • EXECUTE EXPRESS INSTALLATION
>
> **Transaction:** GCIQ
>
> **Table:** T881

Create the ledger with reference to a table group. The ledger name should be two digits long, letters or numbers, and should not start with Y or Z.

To create the ledger, run Transaction GCIQ and, on the table group definition (express installation) screen, specify the name of the table group and field movement to which you want to assign the ledger (Figure 8.5). Then specify the name of the ledger, and click on the Create button. The system automatically creates the ledger with default characteristics (which you may need to edit, as we discuss later).

Before creation, the system asks for a company code that is assigned to the ledger. After the ledger creation, you can review the ledger settings and, if needed, change them using the Rework Ledger button. This brings you to a screen where all ledgers are listed. Double-click the ledger just created, and you'll see all of the ledger settings (Figure 8.6):

▶ **Summary Table (❶)**
This is the summary table of the table group to which the ledger is assigned.

▶ **Ledger text (❷)**
This field contains the description of the ledger.

▶ **Ledger Post.Allowed (❸)**
If flagged, this means that the ledger allows direct postings or postings coming from other SAP components. Don't flag this checkbox for a rollup ledger.

▶ **Rollup Allowed (❹)**
This indicates whether the ledger can receive data from the rollup functionality.

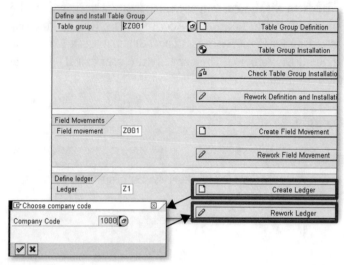

Figure 8.5 Creation of a Ledger

- **Set Up Balance C/F (❺)**
  This indicates that the ledger supports the carryforward of account balances to the new fiscal year.

- **Write Line Items (❻)**
  If you check this box, the system creates line items in the Line Item table for each document posted directly or indirectly. This is of particular importance for reconciliation.

- **Debit/Credit (❼)**
  If this checkbox is selected, the system creates, in the Total table, different totals for debit and credit data. This increases the size of the Total table.

- **Productive (❽)**
  If this flag is checked, the ledger data can't be deleted. If unselected, you can delete ("reset") the ledger data using the functionality described in Section 8.3.4, Deleting and Reposting Data.

- **Transaction Currency (❾)**
  If selected, the transaction currency values are written in the Total and Line Item tables.

- **2nd Currcy (❿)**
  Here you can specify another currency stored in the company code. Click on the 2nd Currcy button, and choose the currency type. The first local currency of the company code is indicated by selecting Currency Type 10.

▶ **3rd Currcy (⑪)**

Here you can specify another currency stored in the company code. Click on the 3rd Currcy button, and choose the currency type.

▶ **Store Quantities (⑫)**

Select this indicator if quantities are to be stored in the ledger. Don't select this indicator if you want to manage just the currency amount.

▶ **Store Add. Quantity (⑬)**

Select this indicator if additional quantities are to be stored in the ledger. Don't select this indicator if you want to manage just the currency amount.

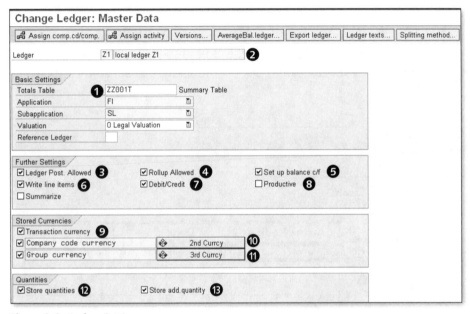

Figure 8.6 Ledger Settings

8.1.4 Assigning Companies or Company Codes to the Ledger

> **Quick Reference**
>
> **Menu path:** IMG • FINANCIAL ACCOUNTING • SPECIAL PURPOSE LEDGER • BASIC SETTINGS • MASTER DATA • LEDGER • DEFINE LEDGER
>
> **Transaction:** GCL2
>
> **Table:** T882

Each ledger can work with company code data or companies but not with both; this depends on which table group the ledger is assigned to. Companies inherit transaction data from the company codes assigned to them. In general, each company code is assigned to exactly one company; however, several company codes can be assigned to the same company. Assign the company codes to companies in customizing: Enterprise Structure • Assignment • Financial Accounting • Assign Company Code to Company. (This process is discussed in more detail in Chapter 2, Organizational Structure: Definition and Assignment.)

Company codes (in the case of local ledgers) or companies (in the case of global ledgers) aren't automatically assigned to a ledger. To do this (Figure 8.7), go to the menu path given in the Quick Reference box, and choose the Assign Comp.cd/ comp button. The system displays two lists:

▸ The company codes or companies assigned to the ledger

▸ The company codes or companies that exist in the system but aren't assigned to the ledger

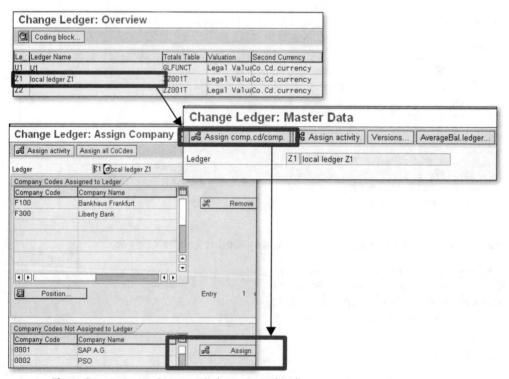

Figure 8.7 Assigning Company Codes to Special Ledger

You can assign a company code or a company to the ledger using the Assign button.

8.1.5 Special Ledger Settings for Company and Company Codes

Quick Reference
Menu path: IMG • FINANCIAL ACCOUNTING • SPECIAL PURPOSE LEDGER • BASIC SETTINGS • MASTER DATA • LEDGER • DEFINE LEDGER
Transaction: GCL2
Table: T882

When you assign a company code or company to a ledger, you can specify the following settings (Figure 8.8):

▶ **Blocking Indicator (❶)**

This indicates whether or not direct posting is allowed. If you choose 0, the company code (or company) in the specific ledger can only receive postings coming from other components (you can't post directly inside the special ledger). If you choose 1, you can also make direct postings; in this case, the direct postings exist only in the special ledger and have no link to documents generated in other components.

▶ **Fiscal Year Variant (❷)**

Here you can specify a fiscal year variant other than the one (or ones, if you're using SAP General Ledger and have more than one ledger with different fiscal variants) specified in the general ledger. Every time a posting comes into the special ledger, the system uses the posting date and reads the fiscal year variant configuration to determine fiscal year and posting period.

▶ **Write Line Items (❸)**

Here you can specify, at the level of company code or company, that line items are written (not just total records). So, for example, you can decide that special ledger S1 doesn't write line items, with the exception of line items for company 1000.

▶ **Always Check (❹)**

Select this indicator if the ledger is to be posted in the background (not online), and the system should check online if it can't post to the ledger.

▶ **Company Code Currency (❺)**

You select this indicator if the second currency isn't updated at the ledger level, and you want to update it at the company code level (lower level). Please note that the system displays the description "Company Code Currency" because this is the second currency used in the ledger; if, for example, the Controlling area currency is used as a second currency, a different description is shown.

▶ **Group Currency (❺)**

You select this indicator if the third currency isn't updated at the ledger level, and you want to update it at the company code level (lower level). Please note that the system displays the description "Group Currency" because this is the third currency used in the ledger; if, for example, the Controlling area currency is used as a third currency, a different description is shown.

▶ **Validation Type (❻)**

Here you specify which chart of account is used by the company code in the ledger. Generally, you transfer operative accounts to the special ledger. However, you can instead choose to transfer the alternative account, the group account, or accounts that belong to a different chart of account (this last option is very rare, but technically allowed). The system uses this information to validate the accounts entered in the postings (both direct and indirect), and to determine the retained earning account for the balance carryforward of the P&L accounts. Note that if you choose 9, you must specify the chart of accounts.

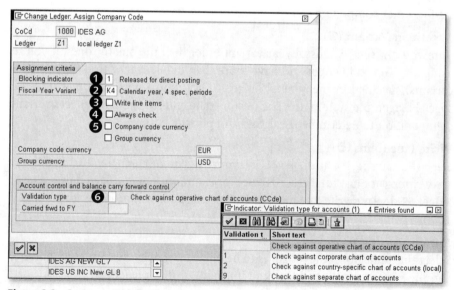

Figure 8.8 Company Code Settings for the Ledger

8.1.6 Assigning Activities to the Special Ledger

Menu path: IMG • FINANCIAL ACCOUNTING • SPECIAL PURPOSE LEDGER • BASIC SETTINGS • MASTER DATA • LEDGER • DEFINE LEDGER

Transaction: GCL2

Tables: T886A (a combination of ledger and company/company code) and T886B (ledger, valid for all companies/company code)

Special ledgers are updated by the following:

▶ Documents created in other components

▶ Documents created directly in the special ledger (these are known as *direct postings*)

Other components provide information to a special ledger if the correspondent *activity* is assigned to that ledger. An activity is a *tag* that identifies each source that can update the special ledger.

You can assign activities at two levels (Figure 8.9):

▶ **At the ledger level**
Using Transaction GCL2, double-click on your ledger, and choose the Assign Activity button; then click the Activity Groups button. Select one or more of the groups, specify the field movement, and, if needed, select the Line Items flag. Confirm the selection. In the next screen, all activities related to the group are displayed.

▶ **At the company code/company level**
Using Transaction GCL2, double-click on your ledger and choose the Assign comp.cd/comp button; the system displays all of the company codes/companies assigned to that ledger. Click once on the row of one company code or company, and choose the Assign Activity button; in the upper part of the screen, the system displays the activities assigned to the specific company code or company. In the lower part of the screen, the system displays the activities assigned to the ledger, and then to all organizational units.

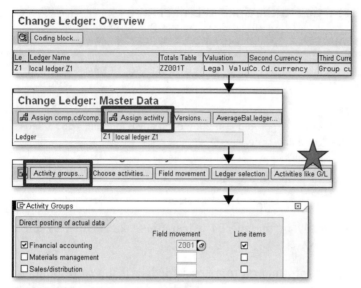

Figure 8.9 Assign Activities to Ledger

Note

If you want the special ledger to be updated every time the general ledger is updated, select the Activities Like G/L button; this ensures that all updates to the general ledger will also be made to the special ledger.

For each activity, regardless of whether it's assigned at the ledger level or at the company code/company level, the following specifications are required:

- Field movement
- Posting indicator
- Check independent of posting
- Write line items
- Required posting

The activities that you assign to ledgers are predefined by SAP. It can be difficult to understand exactly which activities must be assigned to each ledger; generally, you want to ensure that all of the postings from a specific component update your special ledger.

To ensure that all of the documents of a particular component are assigned to the ledger, click the Activity Group button, and choose the appropriate SAP component. All of the activities belonging to that component are automatically selected; you can then review the list and remove activities that you don't want to assign to the ledger.

The following activity groups are available:

- Actual data
  - Financial Accounting
  - Material Management
  - Sales/Distribution
  - Human Resources
  - Controlling
  - CO Stat. Key Figures
  - Spec.Purpose Ledger (i.e., actual data manually entered directly into the special ledger)
- Plan data
  - Controlling
  - CO Stat. Key Figures
  - Spec. Purpose Ledger (i.e., plan data manually entered directly into the special ledger)

8.1.7 Configuring the Ledger Selection

Quick Reference

Menu path: IMG • FINANCIAL ACCOUNTING • SPECIAL PURPOSE LEDGER • BASIC SETTINGS • MASTER DATA • LEDGER • DEFINE LEDGER

Transaction: GCL2

If you don't want all of the documents belonging to a certain activity to update a special ledger, you can create a condition rule that specifies the conditions the document must fulfill to update the ledger. The condition rule is valid for a group of activities (not for a single activity). See Section 8.1.6, Assigning Activities to the Special Ledger, for a complete list of the groups of activities.

To create a condition rule, call Transaction GCL2, and follow these steps (Figure 8.10):

1. To maintain the ledger, Choose Assign Activity and then Ledger Selection.

2. Position the cursor on one line, and choose the Ledger Selection button. The system automatically recognizes the group of activities to which the activity belongs.

3. Click on Rules. Give a short and long name to your rule, and then click on Rule Definition.

4. Define the *Boolean rule*. Each document that belongs to the activity group must satisfy this rule to post to the ledger.

5. Save the rule, and go back to the Ledger Selection screen. Here the new rule is available in the matchcode. Save the ledger selection and proceed, if needed, with the other activity groups.

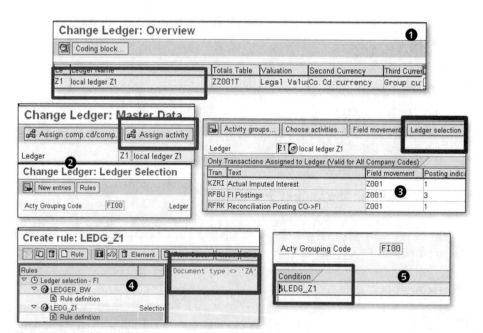

Figure 8.10 Ledger Selection

8.1.8 Configuring Validations and Substitutions

You create validations and substitutions in the special ledger with the same technique described in Chapter 3, General Ledger Configuration. This section describes only information that is specific to special ledger validations and substitutions:

▶ There are two callup points (the moment in a posting when the validation is triggered) in special ledger validations and substitutions: the document header, and document line items. Unlike general ledger validations and substitutions, the level for the "complete" document isn't available in the special ledger (this check is triggered when all of the line items are entered, and the document is ready to be posted).

▶ The fields from structure GLU1 can be used in special ledger validations and substitutions. Structure GLU1 is automatically generated by the system and contains all of the fields used in all of the special ledgers present in the system.

▶ Validations and substitutions are assigned to company codes or companies, not to table groups.

▶ You can use user exits that were defined in customizing and stored in the program by accessing the following menu path: FINANCIAL ACCOUNTING • SPECIAL PURPOSE LEDGER • BASIC SETTINGS • USER EXITS • MAINTAIN CLIENT-SPECIFIC USER EXITS.

▶ Following are the application areas:

  ▶ GBLR (validations)

  ▶ GBLR (substitutions)

Figure 8.11 shows an example of a special ledger validation; Figure 8.12 shows an example of a special ledger substitution.

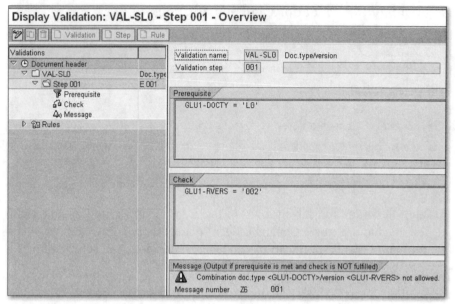

Figure 8.11 Example of Special Ledger Local Validation

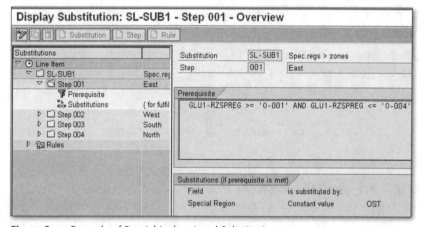

Figure 8.12 Example of Special Ledger Local Substitution

8.1.9 Configuring Manual Special Ledger Postings

You can make postings directly within the special ledger by performing the following customizing steps:

- ▶ Define the versions for actual data.
- ▶ Set up the document types for manual special ledger postings.
- ▶ Configure special ledger number ranges.
- ▶ Set up and maintain special ledger posting periods.

We discuss each of these steps in more detail next.

Defining Versions for Actual Data

Quick Reference

Menu path: IMG • FINANCIAL ACCOUNTING • SPECIAL PURPOSE LEDGER • ACTUAL POSTINGS • MAINTAIN ACTUAL VERSIONS

Transaction: GCVI

Table/view: T894/V_T894

For direct postings, it's possible to create different versions for actual data postings; actual postings that come from other SAP components are always posted to version 1. If you don't want to use different versions for actual data, you don't need to perform this customizing step.

You can create the versions for actual data using Transaction GCVI. Choose New Entry, and specify the following (Figure 8.13):

- ▶ **Ld**
  This is the ledger for which the actual version is created.
- ▶ **Ver**
  This is the version code (two digits, numerical).
- ▶ **Activate Version**
  To activate a version, select this checkbox. If you don't activate a version, it remains in the system, but it can't be used in new postings. Typically, you deactivate a version if there is historical data posted to it, but it won't be used in the future.
- ▶ **Version Description**
  Provide a brief description of the version.

Save your data. This isn't a customizing setting.

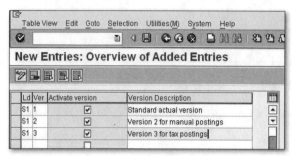

Figure 8.13 Versions for Actual Data

Setting Up Document Types for Manual Postings

To manually post in the special ledger, you must create at least one document type. For each document type, use Transaction GCBX to define the following settings (Figure 8.14):

- ▶ **Doc. Type**
  Two digits, alphanumeric, free.

- ▶ **Transactions to be managed**
  Specify which currencies the document type can manage (TC stands for "transaction currency"; C2 stands for "second local currency"; C3 stands for "third local currency").

- ▶ **Bal. Check**
  In SAP General Ledger, you can't post a document that doesn't balance to zero. In the special ledger, however, you can decide if the document must balance to zero. You have the following three options for each document type:

- ► **0:** The system issues an error message if the document doesn't balance to zero.

- ► **1:** The system issues a warning message if the document doesn't balance to zero.

- ► **2:** The system doesn't issue any message if the document doesn't balance to zero.

► **Description**
Specify the long description of the document type.

Change View "Valid Document Types": Overview

Doc. Type	TC	C2	C3	Bal. check	Local	Global	Description
A0	☑	☑	☑	1	01	01	FI-SL direct posting actual
A2	☐	☐	☑	2	01		
AF	☑	☑	☑	0		01	FI-LC Addit. fields actual
G0	☑	☑	☑	1		03	Global document entry
L0	☑	☑	☑	1	04		Adjustment posting (GB01)
PC	☑	☑	☑	2	01		Profit Center Accounting
V0	☑	☑	☑	2	03	01	Allocation of actual

Figure 8.14 Document Types for Special Ledger

Note that the assignment of the number range to the document type is performed using Transaction GB04 or Transaction GB05. This is discussed in more detail next.

Defining and Assigning Number Ranges for Actual Postings

Quick Reference

Menu path: IMG • FINANCIAL ACCOUNTING • SPECIAL PURPOSE LEDGER • ACTUAL POSTINGS • MAINTAIN LOCAL NUMBER RANGES

OR

IMG • FINANCIAL ACCOUNTING • SPECIAL PURPOSE LEDGER • ACTUAL POSTINGS • MAINTAIN GLOBAL NUMBER RANGES

Transactions: GB04 (local number ranges) or GB05 (global number ranges)

Create the number ranges for special ledger documents in two steps:

1. Define a group and a number range for a company code and one or more years.

2. Assign special ledger document types to the group.

We discuss both of these steps in more detail next.

Defining a Number Range Group

To create new number range groups, follow these steps (Figure 8.15):

1. Run Transaction GB04, and select the button for maintaining groups (⊘ Groups).

2. Select GROUP • INSERT, or press F6; if you need to view or change an existing group, select the group from the list, and click the Maintain button (⊘).

3. Specify the company code, and click Continue.

4. In the following screen, maintain the number range interval for the combination group/company code. Specify the year (9999 for a year-independent number range), the first number of the interval, and the last number of the interval.

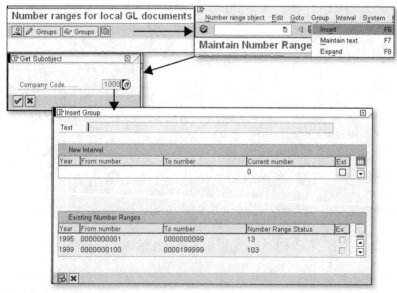

Figure 8.15 Definition of Number Range Group

5. Select the Ext button if you want to specify that this is an external number range; then, when you post directly into the special ledger, you'll need to specify the document number manually. In general, however, there is no need to use external number ranges in the special ledger.

6. Save your entries.

> **Technical Note on Special Ledger Number Ranges**
>
> The special ledger number ranges are stored in Table NRIV with object GL_GLOBAL (Number ranges for global GL documents) and GL_LOCAL (Number ranges for local GL documents).

Assigning Special Ledger Document Types to the Group

From the Maintain Number Ranges Groups screen, follow these steps (Figure 8.16):

1. Position the cursor on one of the document types that appear at the bottom of the list as Not Assigned. Click the Select Element button (![select element icon]).

2. Select one of the groups, and click on the Element/Group button.

3. Save your entries.

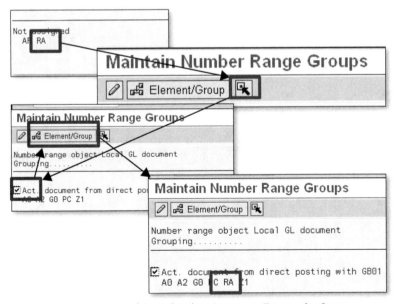

Figure 8.16 Assignment of Special Ledger Document Type to the Group

Opening and Closing Special Ledger Posting Periods

> **Quick Reference**
>
> **Menu path:** ACCOUNTING • FINANCIAL ACCOUNTING • SPECIAL PURPOSE LEDGER • ENVIRON-MENT • CURRENT SETTINGS • LOCAL POSTING PERIOD
>
> **OR**
>
> ACCOUNTING • FINANCIAL ACCOUNTING • SPECIAL PURPOSE LEDGER • ENVIRONMENT • CURRENT SETTINGS • GLOBAL POSTING PERIOD
>
> **Transaction:** GCP1 (local posting periods) or GCP2 (global posting periods)

You assign each company code to a posting period variant in the general ledger using Transaction OB37; the posting period variants defined in Transaction OB37 are used in the special ledger as well. You open and close posting periods in the special ledger for direct posting to company codes (local posting periods) using Transaction GCP1 (upper half of Figure 8.17):

- Specify the posting year variant to which the company code belongs.
- Create up to two ranges of opened posting periods.
- Save your entries.

You open and close posting periods in the special ledger for direct posting to companies (global posting periods) using Transaction GCP2 (lower half of Figure 8.17):

- Specify the single company.
- Create up to two ranges of opened posting periods.
- Save your entries.

Note that, unlike company codes, you don't use the posting period variant to open and close posting periods for companies. The reason for this is that many company codes can be assigned to one company, and they can have different posting period variants.

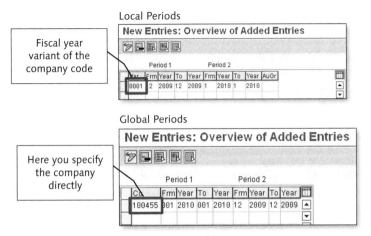

Figure 8.17 Special Ledger Posting Periods

8.1.10 FAQ and Troubleshooting Tips

Next we answer some frequently asked questions and offer helpful troubleshooting tips.

FAQ

1. **Question:** Can I create a table group for both company codes (local) and companies (global)?

   Answer: No. A table group is either a local table group (for company codes) or a global table group (for companies).

2. **Question:** How many ledgers can use the same table groups?

   Answer: There is no maximum number of ledgers you can assign to a table group.

3. **Question:** Can I create the table groups directly in the productive system?

   Answer: No, you must perform the creation of table groups in a development system.

4. **Question:** What are Tables GLU1 and GLU2? What should be done on them?

   Answer: GLU1 and GLU2 are structures, not transparent tables. Therefore, no data is stored in them in the database. GLU1 is dynamically used by the system when actual data is updated in the special ledger. GLU2 is dynamically used by the system when working with plan data and rollup. In general, no action is required with regard to these structures.

5. **Question:** What is the difference between field movements and *fixed* field movements?

   Answer: When you create a table group, the system automatically creates fixed field movements. They can't be changed because they ensure the basic consistency of the special ledger data. For example, the company code is inherited from the BKPF-BUKRS field.

6. **Question:** What is the relationship between the currencies in the company code configuration and the currencies in the special ledger?

   Answer: When you create the table group, you specify how many currencies can be managed in the group; you can choose the transaction currency plus two additional currencies. However, the creation of the table group doesn't involve configuring the relationship between the currencies of the special ledger and the company code currencies; you decide this when you're assigning single ledgers to the table group. For example, assume your table group is set up to manage just one local currency, and ledger S1 and S2 are assigned to the table group. In the ledger definition of S1, you can specify that it manages the company code in the local currency (Currency Type 10). In the ledger definition of S2, you can decide that it manages the hard currency (Currency Type 40).

7. **Question:** Can I assign both company codes and companies to the same ledger?

   Answer: No. The ledger is assigned to a table group. The table group definition specifies whether it works with company codes or companies. Table groups, and therefore ledgers, can't work with both.

8. **Question:** Can I post directly to a company in SAP?

   Answer: This is possible only in special purpose ledger with the manual postings you can perform using Transaction GB11. All other special ledger documents posted to a specific company are generated by posting in other components to the company codes assigned to that company.

9. **Question:** If an activity is assigned to a special ledger after documents have been posted, what happens to these documents? Is it possible to post them subsequently?

   Answer: Yes. This can be done using the programs RGUREC10 (Transfer Data from Financial Accounting), RGUREC30 (Transfer Data from Materials Management), RKEPCU40 (Transfer Data from Sales and Distribution), and RGUREC20 (Transfer Data from Controlling).

10. **Question:** What happens if a document doesn't respect the ledger selection rule and isn't posted to my special ledger? Does the system issue an error or a warning message?

    Answer: No, no message is issued. As a result, the accuracy of the ledger selection is very important.

11. **Question:** I changed the ledger selection today; however, I would like all of the documents posted from the beginning of the month to respect the new ledger selection. How can I manage the documents posted before the change?

    Answer: If there are documents not posted due to the old ledger selection, repost them with the appropriate program, as described in Section 8.3.3, Actual Data Transfer. If some documents have been posted but they didn't respect the ledger selection, you can delete them and also correct the total data with program RGUREP03.

12. **Question:** I'm posting a document in the general ledger. What happens if the special ledger validation fails? Is it possible to post the Financial Accounting document, or does the system block its creation?

    Answer: Yes, the document will be created, as will the special ledger document. The validations in the special ledger affect only the documents posted directly, not those coming from other components

13. **Question:** What is the difference between the ledger selection and the special ledger validation?

    Answer: The ledger selection applies to all documents that are posted from other components outside the special ledger; the special ledger validations specify the rules that must be fulfilled by the documents directly posted inside special ledger accounting (e.g., using Transaction GB01).

14. **Question:** To which version are the documents that come from other SAP components posted?

    Answer: All of the postings coming from other applications (Financial Accounting, Sales and Distribution, Materials Management, Human Resources, Controlling) are automatically posted to version 1.

15. **Question:** To which version are the documents manually created in the special ledger posted?

    Answer: You choose the version when you make the posting. You can choose version 1 or any other actual version available.

16. **Question:** Can a version be used for both plan and actual data?

    Answer: Yes.

17. **Question:** Can I use the same version in different ledgers?

    Answer: Yes. But you must create the version for each ledger you want to assign it to.

18. **Question:** In the Line Item table, the Document Type field is always filled, even when the documents come from other components. How is the document type determined in these cases?

    Answer: In this case, the document type is the document type of the corresponding general ledger document. When the table group is installed, the system automatically creates a fixed field movement from field BKPF-BLART to field DOCTY in the special ledger Line Item table.

19. **Question:** Can the same document type be used for both plan and actual data?

    Answer: Yes. However, even though the plan data and the actual data are marked differently in the database, we don't recommend it. For the sake of clarity, we suggest that you use different document types for actual and plan data.

20. **Question:** How can I block a special ledger document type without deleting it?

    Answer: Create a special ledger validation that discontinues the use of that document type. See Section 8.1.8, Configuring Validations and Substitutions, for more information on validations.

21. **Question:** Can the same document type be used for both local and global postings?

    Answer: Yes.

22. **Question:** In the special ledger, is it possible to create number ranges for each fiscal year?

    Answer: Yes. The number ranges in the special ledger are year dependent. However, if you want to use year-independent number ranges, create the number range for the year 9999.

23. **Question:** Do the local and global posting periods affect both the postings coming from other components *and* the documents directly posted to the special ledger?

Answer: No. They affect only the documents directly posted to the special ledger using Transaction GB01 or GB11.

24. **Question:** What condition must a special ledger fulfill to pass the period check?

    Answer: The posting date of the special ledger document must be contained in at least one of the ranges of open periods.

25. **Question:** How is the posting period determined in the special ledger — through the general ledger fiscal year variant, or the special ledger fiscal year variant?

    Answer: The fiscal year variant assigned to the company code in the special ledger determines the period in the special ledger. See Section 8.1.5, Special Ledger Settings for Company and Company Codes, for more details.

Troubleshooting Tips

1. **Issue:** I received an error message that refers to the GLU1 (or GLU2) structure.

   Solution: To correct an error with the GLU1 structure, run Transaction GCGG. To correct an error with the GLU2 structure, run Transaction GCU2. Carefully read and follow the instructions provided by the system.

2. **Issue:** I received error message GG414, "No activities can be assigned to ledger LR."

   Solution: In the definition of the ledger, make sure you've selected the Ledger Post Allowed option. This should always be selected in cases where the ledger should accept direct postings or postings from other components, and it's generally only deselected if the ledger is just used for rollup.

3. **Issue:** I updated the prerequisite in a validation step, and the syntax looks correct. However, when I click on the Check tab, the system pulls me back to the prerequisite without any message.

   Solution: This is a frequent problem that occurs with the Validation Editor. It often happens when you move from the expert to the not-expert mode, or when you perform deletions within the expert mode. Don't lose time in trying to understand the technical cause of the problem; simple recreate the validation step. Before restarting, copy the formula entered, and paste it into a text editor. Then paste again within the expert editor.

4. **Issue:** I transported the validation, but there was a generation error.

   Solution: Run program RGUGBR00 with Transaction SA38 or SE38. Mark the choices for validations (or substitutions), and choose the application area FI-SL.

The program will issue a pop-up with the error found. Typical errors include the following:

- **The validation or substitution rule refers to a set that doesn't exist in the client.** In this case, create the set and regenerate the validation or substitution
- **The validation or substitution rule refers to a user exit that doesn't exist in the client.** In this case, transport the user exit, and regenerate the validation or substitution.

5. **Issue:** I received a message saying that the number range is already assigned.

   Solution: Check the number ranges using Transaction GB04 or GB05, and you'll see that all of the available numbers in the range have been used. Enlarge the number range, or change the first and last number, thus assigning a new range of unused document numbers.

6. **Issue:** I closed the posting period for the special ledger, but the postings coming from the general ledger have been transferred to the special ledger. Why haven't they been blocked?

   Solution: The special ledger posting periods affect only the direct postings in the special ledger, performed with Transaction GB01 (local postings) or GB11 (global postings).

8.2   Special Ledger Postings

In this section, we discuss special ledger postings, focusing on the following topics: postings from other SAP components, postings within the special ledger, and actual allocations in the special ledger.

8.2.1   Posting from Other SAP Components

> **Quick Reference**
>
> **Transactions:** GCU1 (transfer data from Financial Accounting), GCU4 (transfer data from Materials Management), GCU5 (transfer data from Sales and Distribution), GCU3 (transfer data from Controlling)
>
> **Programs:** RGUREC10 (transfer data from Financial Accounting), RGUREC30 (transfer data from Materials Management), RKEPCU40 (transfer data from Sales and Distribution), RGUREC20 (transfer data from Controlling)

Special ledgers are typically updated by documents created in other components. Every document created in other components belongs to an *activity*; if the activity is assigned to the ledger or to the company code/company in the ledger, the document updates the ledger. For example, an invoice created in Sales and Distribution updates your ledger only if the SD00 activity is assigned.

When you assign the activity, you also decide *when* the document updates the ledger. Three options are available, as shown in Table 8.1.

Updating Mode	When Does the MM, SD, or FI Document Update the SL?	Which Action Is Required to Have the SL Updated?
0 – Online	Immediately.	Nothing.
1 – In Background	When you run the programs.	Schedule the updating program (or programs) in the background.
2 – Online and in Background	Immediately, but if needed you can also use the program.	Nothing, but you can use the updating programs if necessary (e.g., to correct single postings).

Table 8.1 Posting from Other SAP Components

If you choose to update in the background, you must schedule one or more of the reports listed in Section 8.3.3, Actual Data Transfer. These are the same reports that you use for a data transfer. If you decide not to perform the update online, work with your SAP Basis colleagues to schedule the programs for the updating of the special ledger. However, it's the job of the SAP Financial Accounting expert to identify which programs should be scheduled and the relevant job variants. This depends on the information that your special ledger stores.

That being said, we can make the following recommendations:

▶ If, as a general principle, the special ledger should be updated by all of the postings that are assigned to update the general ledger, use only program RGUREC10 (Figure 8.18) and select Document from Materials Management and Sales and Distribution. If, on the other hand, some types of documents are to be excluded, use the Ledger Selection tool to properly filter the data (see Section 8.1.7, Configuring the Ledger Selection).

► In addition to program RGUREC10, you can use program RGUREC20 to transfer secondary postings from Controlling.

► If your special ledger should only be updated from Materials Management or Sales and Distribution data, don't schedule program RGUREC10. Instead, use programs RGUREC30 and/or RKEPCU40.

► To ensure that all appropriate documents are transferred, schedule the programs with a variant that takes into consideration the entry date of each document. The entry date should be *(today's date – 1)*.

► To ensure that no document is transferred more than one time, always select the Check for Existing Records checkbox. When checked, the system automatically excludes documents already posted to the special ledger.

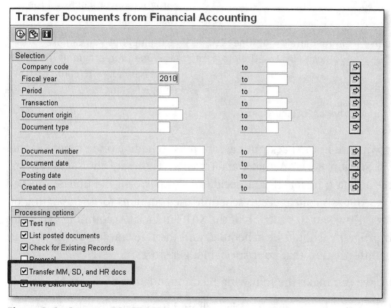

Figure 8.18   Program RGUREC10

To see the original document while displaying a special ledger document, follow these steps (Figure 8.19):

1. Run Transaction GD23 to display one or more special ledger documents.

2. Specify the document number or numbers, and press F8.

3. Single-click the row of the special ledger document, and choose Environment/Relationship Browser. The system displays the source document and the accounting document linked to the special ledger document. From this list, you drill down and display the source documents.

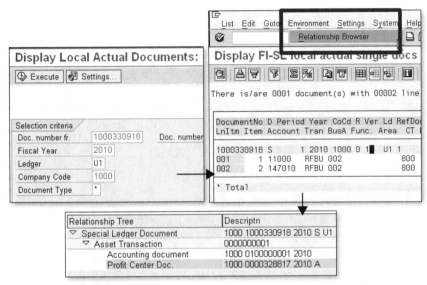

Figure 8.19 Browsing from Special Ledger Document to Original Document

To see the special ledger document from within the general ledger document, choose Environment/Accounting Documents from the Document Overview. To see the special ledger document linked to a Materials Management document, choose Accounting Documents from the material document display screen. (You can see a Materials Management document using Transaction MB03). All of the linked accounting documents, including the special ledger documents, are displayed; double-click the row corresponding to the special ledger document, and the system displays the overview of the special ledger document. To see the special ledger document linked to a Sales and Distribution invoice, select Accounting from the Sales and Distribution invoice overview (which you can view using Transaction VF03). All of the accounting documents, including the special ledger document, are displayed; you can drill down to see each document in the list.

8.2.2 Posting Within the Special Ledger

> **Quick Reference**
>
> **Menu paths**: Accounting • Financial Accounting • Special Purpose Ledger • Actual Posting • Local Documents • Enter
>
> **OR**
>
> Accounting • Financial Accounting • Special Purpose Ledger • Actual Posting • Global Documents • Enter
>
> **Transactions**: GB01 (local documents) or GB11 (global documents)

You can use manual posting in the special ledger if the following activities are assigned to the ledger or to the company code/company in the ledger:

▸ **RGL0:** FI-SL Act. Local Post (GB01)

▸ **RGG0:** FI-SL Act. Global Post (GB11)

There are different transactions to post to the company code (Transaction GB01) and to the company (Transaction GB11), but the process is the same. The following instructions are for posting to the local ledger (company code), but the same steps apply for postings to the global ledger (company).

Use the menu path specified in the Quick Reference box or Transaction GB01. In the resulting screen, fill in the following information (❶ of Figure 8.20):

▸ **Company Code**
The special ledger doesn't allow you to make a cross-company code posting; you specify exactly one company code.

▸ **Posting Date**
This is the date used by the system to determine the posting period and fiscal year in the special ledger.

▸ **Transaction Currency**
Here you specify the document currency.

Many special ledgers can be assigned to one company code. You have two options:

▸ You can post to all of the special ledgers assigned to the company code.

▸ You can post to a specified ledger.

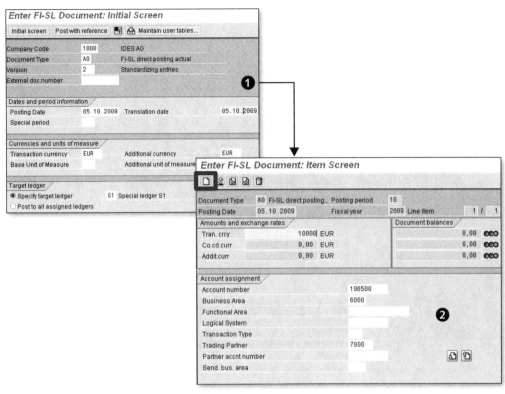

Figure 8.20 Posting Within the Special Ledger (Part 1)

Press Enter, and you see the next screen (❷ of Figure 8.20), where you specify the amount, account, and additional account assignment of the first line item. Click the Enter New Item icon ( ) to create another line item, and the screen shown in ❸ of Figure 8.21 appears. Add your line items, remembering to include a negative sign in front of the amount if you post negative values. After all of the line items have been entered, click the Overview button to see a preview of the overall document that will be created (❹ of Figure 8.21) and then click on the Save button; the system immediately issues the number of the created document (❺ of Figure 8.21).

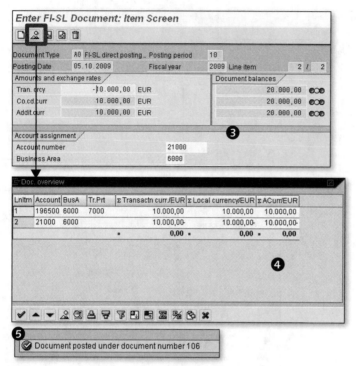

Figure 8.21 Posting Within the Special Ledger (Part 2)

8.2.3 Actual Allocations in the Special Ledger

Allocations commonly take place in the Controlling component and can then be transferred to the special ledger if the corresponding activities are assigned to the ledger. (The same principle applies to Profit Center Accounting allocations.)

These are the activities that must be assigned to the ledger to be updated by Controlling and Profit Center Accounting allocations:

► RKIU CO Actual Assessment

► RKIV CO Actual Distribution

► RKPU CO Assessment Planning

► RKPV CO Distribution Planning

Allocations in special ledger accounting are created and executed in a similar way as Controlling allocations, but there are a few differences:

▶ In the assessments, you don't need to use a cost element with cost element type 42; instead, you can use any account as the assessment account. Balance sheet accounts can also be used.

▶ You can't use statistical key figures as tracing factors.

Refer to a Controlling manual to find all of the instructions on how to create and run allocations, as a more detailed discussion of this topic is beyond the scope of the book. However, for the sake of completeness, Table 8.2 lists the most important transactions to be used for configuring, creating, and executing allocations in the special ledger.

Activity	Transaction	Type *
Maintain field usage for assessment	GCA1	CT
Maintain field usage for distribution	GCA6	CT
Create actual assessment	GA11	AT
Change actual assessment	GA12	AT
Execute actual assessment	GA15	AT
Create plan assessment	GA27	AT
Change plan assessment	GA28	AT
Execute plan assessment	GA2B	AT
Create actual distribution	GA31	AT
Change actual distribution	GA32	AT
Execute actual distribution	GA35	AT
Create plan distribution	GA47	AT
Change plan distribution	GA48	AT
Execute plan distribution	GA4B	AT

* CT = customizing transaction; AT = application transaction

Table 8.2 Transactions for Configuring, Creating, and Executing Allocations

8.2.4 FAQ and Troubleshooting Tips

Next we answer some frequently asked questions and offer helpful troubleshooting tips.

FAQ

1. **Question:** I'm using the updating programs to update the special ledger. How can I ensure that the system doesn't post the same Financial Accounting, Materials Management, or Sales and Distribution document to the special ledger twice?

   Answer: All of the updating programs have a Check Double Postings option. If you manage line items in your ledger, you can use this option. For each special ledger document, the system remembers the original document, so double postings can be avoided. However, if you don't have line items in your ledger, only total data, the system can't help; in this case, in the selection screen, you must specify the selection criteria necessary to identify only the documents not posted.

2. **Question:** How can I distinguish manual postings from automatic postings (coming from other components)?

   Answer: If you need this functionality, we recommend creating a new version for actual data using Transaction GCVI. All actual data that is automatically posted flows to version 1, so you can create version 2 to store manual postings and retrieve them separately. When reporting, you can easily merge data from the two different versions.

Troubleshooting Tips

1. **Issue:** We started using the Materials Management component. The system creates the Financial Accounting documents but doesn't create the corresponding special ledger document; nor does it update the total data. No error message is issued.

   Solution: In Transaction GCL2, check that the activities for the Materials Management postings are assigned to the ledger or company code.

2. **Issue:** Documents posted with a specific general ledger transaction don't generate any special ledger documents. How can I easily understand what is wrong or missing in the configuration?

   Solution: Use Transaction GCD1 to simulate the Financial Accounting posting or to find why a specific general ledger document can't be posted to the special ledger (use the Troubleshooting button). You can also try to post the general ledger document using Transaction GCU1, and then use the log to understand the cause of the missed special ledger update.

3. **Issue:** Error message GI558 appears: "Period PPP in year YYYY is not open for posting."

   Solution: This means that the posting period in the special ledger is closed. In general, the opening and closing of posting periods is assigned to a specific group or person in the company, to ensure that no postings are made in periods that have been already reported internally or externally. Refer to Section 8.1.9, Configuring Manual Special Ledger Postings, to find the instructions on how to open and close posting periods in the special ledger.

4. **Issue:** Error message GI192 appears: "No ledgers assigned."

   Solution: There are two possibilities here:

   ▶ The activity RGLO or RGGO for manual postings isn't assigned to the ledger or to the company/company code in the ledger. Make the assignment by following the instructions in Section 8.1.6, Assigning Activities to the Special Ledger.

   ▶ You have specified a second currency that doesn't correspond to the second currency of the company code in the ledger. Solve this by specifying the correct currency.

5. **Issue:** Error message GI505 appears: "Check number range maintenance."

   Solution: You're using a document type that isn't assigned to a number range. Perform the assignment as described in Section 8.1.9, Configuring Manual Special Ledger Postings.

8.3   Main Special Ledger Functionalities

In this section, we discuss a number of the most helpful and common functionalities in the special ledger: balance carryforward, reconciliation between ledgers, actual data transfer, deletion and reposting of data, and reconciliation between total data and line items.

8.3.1   Balance Carryforward

For each ledger, you can decide whether or not to manage balance carryforward. (Specify this by selecting the appropriate indicator in the ledger master data; see Section 8.1.3, Creating the Ledger, for more details.) To use the carryforward functionality, you must define the retained earning account in the special ledger customizing screen and, optionally, create a field movement rule to specify special rules on how the data from account assignment objects (such as the transaction type or the business area) are carried forward. Next we discuss both of these topics, as well as the actual process of running the balance carryforward.

Defining the Retained Earning Account

For each chart of account and P&L statement account type, you must specify a retained earned account. This customizing must be done in the special ledger and can be different from the corresponding customizing that is set in SAP General Ledger, Transaction OB53.

To define the retained earnings account in the special ledger, use Transaction GCS6 (for local ledgers) and GCS7 (for global ledgers). For each combination of chart of accounts and P&L statement account type, specify the correspondent retained earnings account where the balance of the P&L accounts should be carried forward (Figure 8.22).

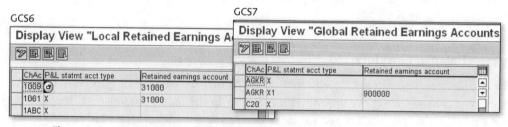

GCS6

GCS7

Display View "Local Retained Earnings A...

Display View "Global Retained Earnings Accounts

ChAc	P&L statmt acct type	Retained earnings account
1009		31000
1061	X	31000
1ABC	X	

ChAc	P&L statmt acct type	Retained earnings account	
AGKR	X		
AGKR	X1	900000	
C20	X		

Figure 8.22 Retained Earnings Accounts in Special Ledger

Field Movement for the Balance Carryforward

Quick Reference

Menu path: IMG • FINANCIAL ACCOUNTING • SPECIAL PURPOSE LEDGER • PERIODIC PROCESSING • BALANCE CARRYFORWARD • ASSIGN FIELD MOVEMENT

Transaction: GCS5

Table/view: T884C/V_T884C

In the process of balance carryforwards, each balance sheet account is carried forward with all its additional account assignments. For example, if the special ledger manages the business area as additional information for the balance sheet account, and account 10000 has a balance of 4000 with business area A001 and 6000 with business area A002, the carryforward retains the business area information; in period 0 of the new fiscal year, account 10000 will have a balance of 4000 with business area A001 and 6000 with business area A002. If this rule has to be changed (e.g., if you want to carry forward all of the balance sheet accounts with a dummy business area), you have to create a specific field movement for the carryforward.

Follow these steps (Figure 8.23):

1. Create a field movement with Transaction GCF2 (see Section 8.1.2, Defining Field Movement, for detailed instructions).

2. Assign the field movement to each ledger in Transaction GCS5.

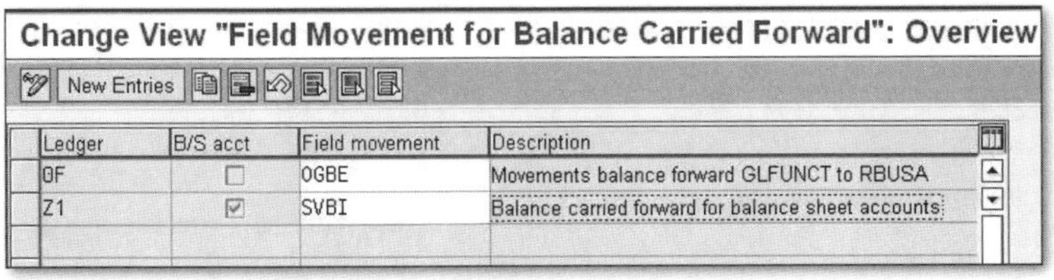

Change View "Field Movement for Balance Carried Forward": Overview

	Ledger	B/S acct	Field movement	Description	
	0F	☐	0GBE	Movements balance forward GLFUNCT to RBUSA	
	Z1	☑	SVBI	Balance carried forward for balance sheet accounts	

Figure 8.23 Assigning Field Movement for Carryforward

Running the Balance Carryforward

Quick Reference

Menu path: ACCOUNTING • FINANCIAL ACCOUNTING • SPECIAL PURPOSE LEDGER • PERIODIC PROCESSING • BALANCE CARRYFORWARD

Transaction: GVTR

Program: SAPFGVTR

You should run the carryforward at the beginning of each fiscal year, and you can run the program more than one time. You don't need to re-run the carryforward if you make postings in the old fiscal year; all of the balances in the new fiscal year will be updated automatically (provided you've run the carryforward in a calendar date that falls in the new year, not in the old).

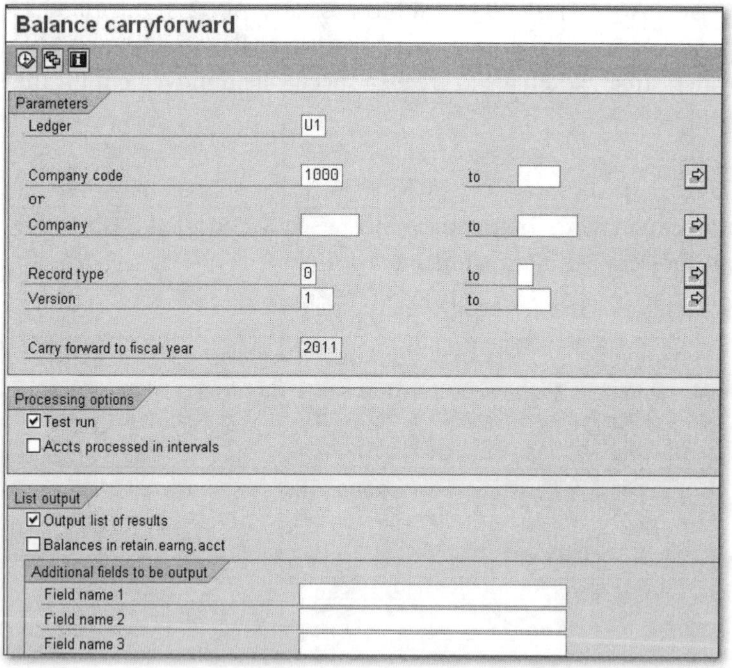

Figure 8.24 Balance Carryforward Program for Special Ledger

When you run the carryforward, specify the following (Figure 8.24):

- One ledger (mandatory).

- The company or company codes — leave these fields blank to run for all companies and company codes (optional).

- The record type: 0 for actual and 1 for plan (mandatory).

- The version (optional).

- The new fiscal year (mandatory).

- You can also run the program in test mode, a function that can be executed online or in the background.

8.3.2 Reconciliation Between Ledgers

Quick Reference

Menu path: IMG • FINANCIAL ACCOUNTING • SPECIAL PURPOSE LEDGER • TOOLS • COMPARE LEDGERS

Transaction: GCAC

Program: RGUCOMP4

You can reconcile the total data (not the line items!) between two special ledgers, between one special ledger and the profit center ledger (in which case the profit center ledger is fixed at 8A), and between one special ledger and one general ledger.

Reconciliation by period makes sense only if the fiscal year variant is the same in the two ledgers to be reconciled. Reconciliation by year makes sense only if the fiscal year variants are the same or, though different, have the same start and finish date.

To carry out the reconciliation, run Transaction GCAC, and specify the following in the selection screen (Figure 8.25):

- **Base Ledger Selection Data area**
  Specify the first ledger and version to be compared. Enter the company code or the company; you can leave these fields empty if you want to carry out reconciliation for all of the entities managed in the ledger. Specify the fiscal year and the posting period ranges to be compared.

- **Comparison Ledger Selection Data area**
  Specify the second ledger and version to be compared.

- **Common Selection Data area**
  Specify the record type with these possible values:

- ▸ **0:** Actual

- ▸ **1:** Plan

- ▸ **2:** Actual assessment/distribution

- ▸ **3:** Planned assessment/distribution

If you want to limit the reconciliation to a specific set of accounts, enter these account numbers.

▸ **Key Figures for Comparison area**
Finally, indicate whether the reconciliation is for the currency values or for quantity values (if quantity values are managed in the ledgers).

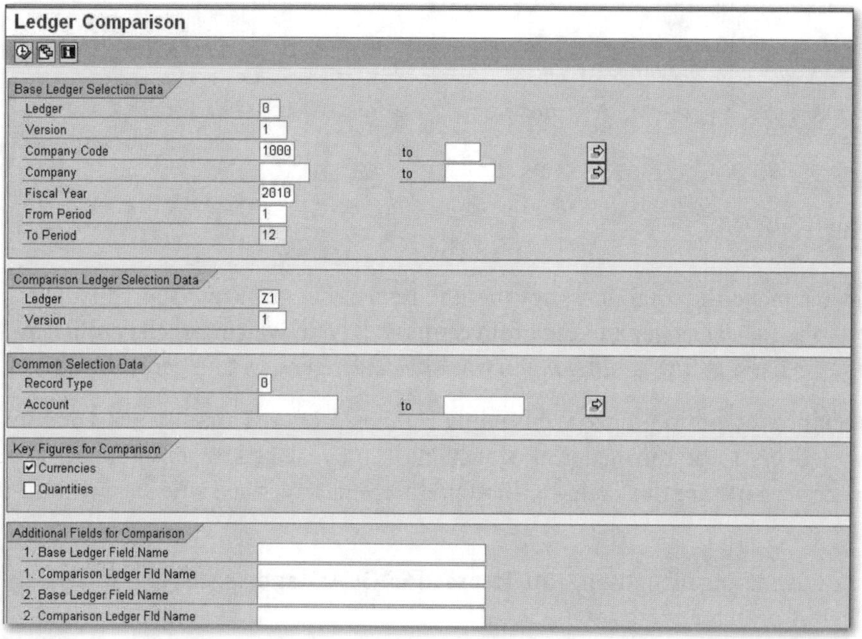

Figure 8.25 Program to Compare Ledgers (Selection Screen)

Run the report. For each combination of company code, account, currency, and fiscal year, the system displays the amount in the first ledger, the amount in the second ledger, and the difference.

You can also use report ZZ_SL_ANALYZE_RELEASE46 to analyze in-depth differences between the special ledger and the general ledger. Refer to SAP Note 764523 to download the code and all of the details.

8.3.3   Actual Data Transfer

Quick Reference
Menu path: IMG • Financial Accounting • Special Purpose ledger • Basic Settings • Production Start-Up Preparation
Transactions: GCU1 (transfer data from Financial Accounting), GCU4 (transfer data from Materials Management), GCU5 (transfer data from Sales and Distribution), GCU3 (transfer data from Controlling)

You can use the programs for data transfer in two situations:

▶ **Mass update**
This case is applicable if you've activated the special ledger after the other SAP components, and you want to load the historical data into the special ledger. If you've decided not to post online to the special ledger, use the listed programs for the periodic background update.

▶ **Single or selected update**
In this case, you want specific documents to update the special ledger. For example, say you've discovered that one Materials Management document has incorrectly updated the special ledger; delete the related special ledger document, and use the function described here to repost the document to the special ledger.

Next we discuss the selection options for all of the available programs for data transfer.

Transferring Data From Financial Accounting (GCU1)

Follow these steps to transfer the data from Financial Accounting (Figure 8.26).

1. Run Transaction GCU1.

2. In the Selection area of the screen, fill those fields that are necessary to identify exactly which general ledger documents have to be transferred to the special ledger. For example, you may want to specify the company code, fiscal year, and document type.

3. In the Processing Options area of the selection screen, make appropriate selections for the following flags:

   ▶ **Test Run:** Select this indicator to see a report without updating the special ledger.

- **List Posted Documents:** Select this option to get a detailed list of the documents that are posted. Documents that can't be posted are listed in detail.

- **Check for Existing Records:** Select this option to avoid the risk of posting a general ledger document to the special ledger more than one time.

- **Transfer MM, SD, and HR Docs:** If you select this indicator, all of thee Financial Accounting documents — regardless of whether they are posted directly in Financial Accounting or are from Materials Management, Sales and Distribution, or Human Resources — are transferred to the special ledger. (Only the Financial Accounting data of the document is read, however, not the data of the original document.) If the flag isn't selected, only the documents directly posted into Financial Accounting are transferred.

4. In the Target Ledger field, specify the special ledger that should be updated with the program.

Run the program with the Execute button. If you're in test mode, you'll only get a list of documents that can or can't be posted; if not in test mode, the update occurs.

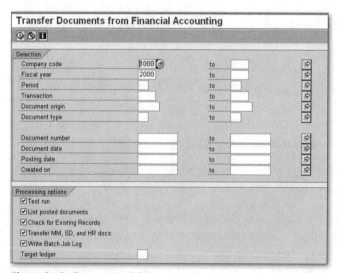

Figure 8.26 Transaction GCU1

Transferring Data from Materials Management (GCU4)

Execute Transaction GCU4 (Figure 8.27). The instructions for filling this screen are the same as those for Transaction GCU1.

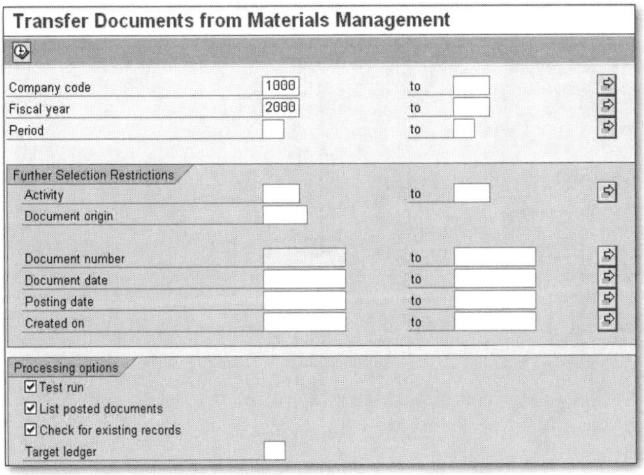

Transfer Documents from Materials Management

Company code	1000	to		
Fiscal year	2000	to		
Period		to		

Further Selection Restrictions

Activity		to	
Document origin			

Document number		to	
Document date		to	
Posting date		to	
Created on		to	

Processing options

☑ Test run
☑ List posted documents
☑ Check for existing records
Target ledger

Figure 8.27 Transaction GCU4

Transferring Data from Sales and Distribution (GCU5)

Execute Transaction GCU5 (Figure 8.28). The instructions for filling this screen are the same as those for Transaction GCU1.

Post SD Billing Documents

Company Code	1000	to	
Sales Organization		to	
Distribution Channel		to	
Division		to	

Billing Document

Billing Document Number		to	
Billing Date		to	

Processing Options

☑ Test Run
☑ Log
☑ Check for Existing Records
Target Ledger

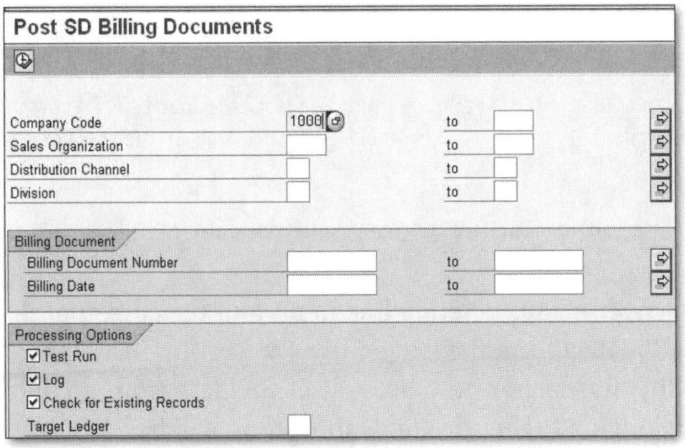

Figure 8.28 Transaction GCU5

Transferring Data from Controlling (GCU3)

Execute Transaction GCU3 (Figure 8.29). The instructions for filling this screen are the same as those for Transaction GCU1.

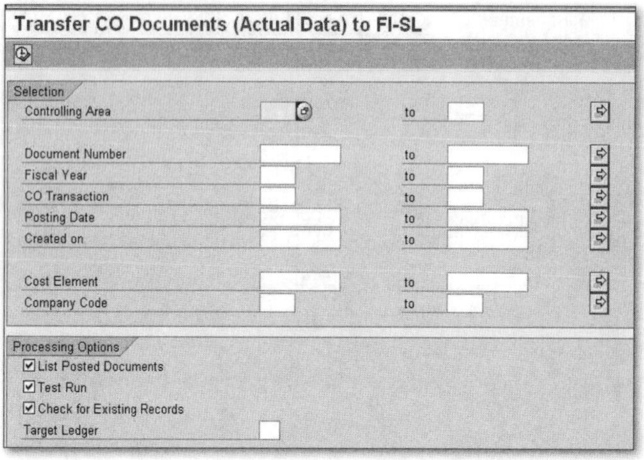

Figure 8.29 Transaction GCU3

8.3.4 Deleting and Reposting Data

Here we discuss how to delete and repost special ledger data.

Deleting Special Ledger Data

Quick Reference
Menu path: IMG • Financial Accounting • Special Purpose Ledger • Tools • Delete Transaction Data (Mass Deletion)
Transaction: GCDE (mass deletion)
Programs: RGUDEL00 (mass deletion) or RGUREP03 (for specific documents deletion)

Deleting data from a special ledger means deleting line items and the corresponding total data. To delete all of the data from the ledger, use Transaction GCDE (Figure 8.30). You can also use this transaction to delete all of the data from a table group; this way, all ledgers belonging to the specified table group will have all data deleted. You can use this transaction only if the ledger doesn't have a productive status (see Section 8.1.3, Creating the Ledger).

To delete the data for a ledger, select the Delete the Data of One Ledger tab in the selection screen. Then specify the ledger. If you only want to perform a partial deletion of the data (not recommended), fill out the following fields:

- The record type
- The version
- The company code or the company
- The logical system to delete only the data supplied by a specific SAP system or by a specific external system
- The range of accounts
- The fiscal year
- The posting periods

You can further specify the type of record to be deleted (for mass deletion, we recommend that you delete all data):

- Total records
- Actual line items
- Plan line items

You can run the program in test mode or in productive mode; in the latter, the data is actually deleted from the ledger.

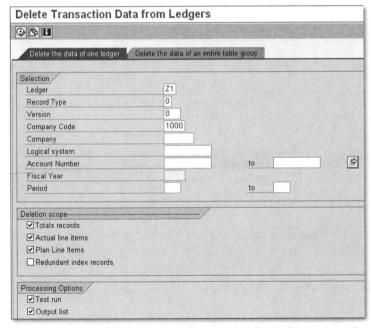

Figure 8.30 Program to Delete Data for Special Ledger (Selection Screen)

To delete specific documents from one ledger, use program RGUREP03 (Figure 8.31). You need to specify the exact special ledger document number to be deleted (one or more). Note that only the special ledger document is affected. For example, if the document was generated from a general ledger posting, the relevant general ledger account isn't affected at all.

To execute the function, run Transaction SE38 or SA38; specify the program RGUREP03, and click on the Execute button. In the selection screen, specify the necessary data to exactly identify the special ledger document (at least the fiscal year and the document number of the special ledger document). Don't select the Test Run flag if you want to actually delete the document from all of the special ledger tables.

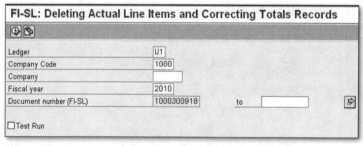

Figure 8.31 Program to Delete Specific Special Ledger Documents

As an alternative to the deletion, you can reverse a special ledger document. In this case, a new special ledger document is created, which contains opposite amounts than the ones in the document being reversed. This could be required for audit reasons. Use Transactions GB06 (local documents) or GB16 (global documents) to perform reversals.

Reposting to Special Ledger

For the reposting of documents to the special ledger, you can use one of the programs listed in Section 8.3.3, Creating the Ledger. Refer to that section for all of the necessary details.

8.3.5 Reconciliation Between Total Data and Line Items

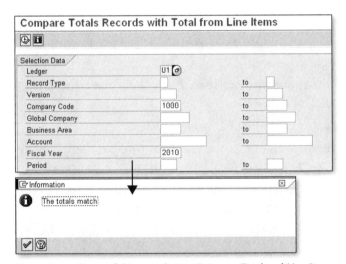

Figure 8.32 Successful Reconciliation Between Total and Line Items

You can perform periodic reconciliation between line items and total records in special ledger accounting. To perform a full reconciliation, specify only the ledger and the fiscal year. If the data is fully reconciled, and no difference arises, you see a short message (Figure 8.32). Otherwise, the system displays a list of the records that aren't reconciled. In this case, follow these steps:

1. Identify exactly which line items have led to inconsistency.

2. If some documents have incorrectly updated the total records, delete and repost the corresponding line items (as described in Section 8.3.4, Deleting and Reposting Data).

3. Re-run the report to reconcile line items and total records.

8.3.6 FAQ and Troubleshooting Tips

Next we answer some frequently asked questions and offer helpful troubleshooting tips.

FAQ

1. **Question:** Are the secondary cost elements carried forward?

   Answer: No. Only the general ledger accounts (primary cost elements) are carried forward. However, you can create a user exit with Transaction CMOD and enhancement GVTRS001 to add this functionality.

2. **Question:** If I use program RGUREP03 to delete one special ledger document, will the total table be adjusted as well?

   Answer: Yes, the deletion of one or more special ledger documents results in the adjustment of the total table as well.

3. **Question:** Can I repost a document that has been reversed?

   Answer: Yes, you can repost with one of the programs listed in the following section. However, you have to deselect the Check If Already Exists checkbox.

4. **Question:** What happens if I delete all of the data in the general ledger? Is the productive status of the special ledger taken into consideration?

   Answer: No. The data from the special ledger is deleted even though the ledger is in a productive status.

Troubleshooting Tips

1. **Issue:** A carryforward was not performed for one account. What should I do to correct the error?

   Solution: Re-run the carryforward. The system will update the balance of the account in the new year.

2. **Issue:** When re-running the balance carryforward, error message GI251 appears: "Ledger XX, chart of accts. CCC, PL type ZZ: No entry available."

Solution: This means that the customizing for the balance carryforward isn't completed. Perform the necessary settings described in Section 8.3.1, Balance Carryforward.

3. **Issue:** Error message GI732 appears: "Your ledger is not assigned."

   Solution: This means that the document hasn't yet been posted to the ledger, according to the existing settings for the ledger. Possible reasons for this include the following:

   ▶ The activity linked to the document isn't assigned to the ledger or to the company/company code in the ledger (see the instructions in Section 8.1.6, Assigning Activities to the Special Ledger).

   ▶ The ledger can only be assigned online. You can change this setting for every activity assigned to the ledger or to the company/company code in the ledger (see the instructions in Section 8.1.6, Assigning Activities to the Special Ledger).

   Run Transaction GCD1 to perform a complete diagnosis of the issue.

4. **Issue:** When running Transaction GCDE, error message GU779 appears: "You cannot delete the transaction data of table XXXX."

   Solution: You're using Transaction GCDE to delete all of the data from the table group. However, this error message means that at least one of the ledgers assigned to the table group has a productive status. If you need to delete the data from another special ledger assigned to the table group, use the program to delete only the data for that ledger, not all of the data from the table group.

5. **Issue:** When running Transaction GCDE, error message GU780 appears: "Ledger XX is set as productive."

   Solution: If you need to delete all of the data from the ledger, change the ledger settings. Delete the productive status. If you need to delete only some selected data, then use program RGUREP03 instead.

8.4 Total Data Reporting

In this section, we describe total data reporting, the most common type of reporting in special ledger accounting.

Note

Instructions on Report Painter and Report Writer are beyond the scope of this book.

Quick Reference

Menu path: ACCOUNTING • FINANCIAL ACCOUNTING • SPECIAL PURPOSE LEDGER • INFORMA-
TION SYSTEM • PROGRAMS FOR SPECIAL PURPOSE LEDGER • TOTAL RECORD DISPLAY

Transaction: GD13

Program: SAPLGD13

Transaction GD13 is the most common tool used to control the total data in a special ledger. Data is output in an ALV list.

When you run the transaction, the system takes you through two selection screens.
In the first selection screen (Figure 8.33), you specify the ledger (one and only one)
and the following two parameters:

▶ **Optimize Column Width**
If this checkbox is selected, the system automatically reduces the width of the
column as much as possible (so that no valid value is hidden).

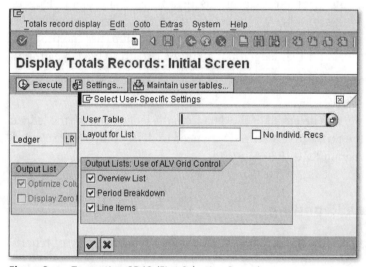

Figure 8.33 Transaction GD13 (First Selection Screen)

▶ **Display Zero Records**
If this checkbox is selected, the system displays the records in the system that have zero values.

As shown in Figure 8.33, you can use the Maintain User Tables button to specify the following user-specific settings. These are saved for your user ID until you change them:

▶ User Table

▶ Layout for List

▶ Output Lists: Use of ALV Grid Control

When you select the Execute icon (⊕), you see the second selection screen (Figure 8.34). In this screen, the fields for selection depend on the special ledger. All of the characteristics available in the special ledger you specified in the first screen are displayed and available as selection parameters. Fill in the selection screen with the selection restrictions you want, and run the report with the Execute icon.

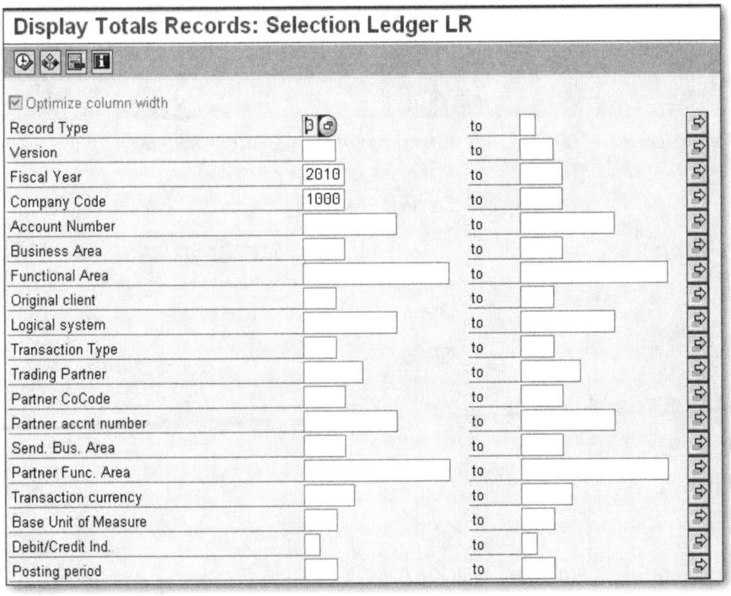

Display Totals Records: Selection Ledger LR		
☑ Optimize column width		
Record Type	▷ 🖻	to
Version		to
Fiscal Year	2010	to
Company Code	1000	to
Account Number		to
Business Area		to
Functional Area		to
Original client		to
Logical system		to
Transaction Type		to
Trading Partner		to
Partner CoCode		to
Partner accnt number		to
Send. Bus. Area		to
Partner Func. Area		to
Transaction currency		to
Base Unit of Measure		to
Debit/Credit Ind.		to
Posting period		to

Figure 8.34 Transaction GD13 (Second Selection Screen)

If you haven't specified a list layout in the user-specific settings, a standard list is displayed. All of the dimensions available in the special ledger are displayed, but not the period; in other words, Transaction GD13 displays only total data per fiscal year. If you want to see the amounts broken down by period, simply double-click on one row. If you want to see the special ledger line items, double-click on one row corresponding to one period.

8.5 Other Special Ledger Functionalities

This section briefly describes two functionalities that are less common in special ledger accounting:

▸ Planning in special ledger

▸ Setting up and executing rollups

8.5.1 Plan Data in the Special Ledger

Planning is a typical functionality of the SAP Controlling component. Although a complete description of the planning functionality isn't within the scope of this book, Table 8.3 provides a list of the transactions needed to configure and use the planning tools within the special ledger.

Activity	Transaction/path	Type *
Planning Layout Definition	FINANCIAL ACCOUNTING • SPECIAL PURPOSE LEDGER • PLANNING • DEFINE PLANNING LAYOUT	CT
Planning Profile Definition	FINANCIAL ACCOUNTING • SPECIAL PURPOSE LEDGER • PLANNING • DEFINE PLANNING PROFILE	CT
Local Plan Periods Open/Close	GCP5	CT
Global Plan Periods Open/Close	GCP6	CT
Plan Versions Definition	GCVP	CT
Local Version Parameters	GCP3	CT
Global Version Parameters	GCP4	CT
Document Types for Planning Definition	GCBA	CT
Distribution Keys Definition	GP32	CT
Activate Local Line Items	GCLE	CT

Table 8.3 Planning in Special Ledger

Activity	Transaction/path	Type *
Activate Global Line Items	GCGE	CT
Local Number Ranges Maintenance	GB32	CT
Global Number Ranges Maintenance	GB03	CT
Set Planner Profile	GLPLSET	AT
Planned Values Enter	GP12N	AT
Planned Values: Upload from Excel	GLPLUP	AT
Search for Planning Documents	GD02	AT
Copy Local Model Plan	GP52	AT
Copy Global Model Plan	GP62	AT
Report: Display Totals	GD13	AT
Local Plan Documents Display	GD43	AT
Global Plan Documents Display	GD44	AT
Plan Assessment: Create	GA27	AT
Plan Assessment: Execute	GA2B	AT
Plan Distribution: Create		AT
Plan Distribution: Execute	GA4B	AT
* CT = customizing transaction; AT = application transaction		

Table 8.3 Planning in Special Ledger (Cont.)

8.5.2 Rollup

With the rollup functionality, you summarize data from a source ledger to a destination ledger. In the summarization process, you can select only some fields from the source ledger; only the data relevant for these fields is transferred to the destination ledger, and all other fields and content are ignored.

Using the rollup tool involves the following steps:

1. Perform customizing settings specific for the rollup functionality.

2. Create a rollup.

3. Execute the rollup.

We discuss each of these steps in more detail next.

Customizing Settings

Quick Reference

Menu path: IMG • FINANCIAL ACCOUNTING • SPECIAL PURPOSE LEDGER • PERIODIC PROCESSING • ROLLUP

The customizing activities necessary for the rollup functionality are as follows:

1. **Maintain field movements (Transaction GCR2).**

   Specify the mapping between the fields in the sending table and the fields in the destination table (Figure 8.35). All of the fields not listed here are ignored by the rollups that use this field movement. Note that you can assign only the field movements created with this transaction to a rollup.

   You create the field movements for the rollup in the same way as you create the field movements for the ledger; refer to Section 8.1.2, Defining Field Movements, for step-by-step instructions.

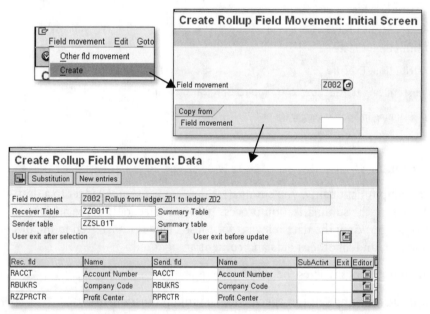

Figure 8.35 Field Movement Creation for Rollup

2. **Maintain substitution (Transaction GCR5).**

   This is an optional activity; you use substitutions in a rollup to replace the content of one field from the sender table with a constant value. Figure 8.36 shows an example of a substitution. To create a new substitution for the rollup, run Transaction GCR5, and choose the New Entries button to create a new substitution. Then specify the following:

▶ **SubActivty (substitution activity):** This is a freely definable four-digit ID that identifies a new substitution. Within the substitution activity, you can create more sequence numbers (the No. column) to create more substitutions steps that will be performed in the sequence.

▶ **Totals Table:** Enter the totals table that will be affected (receiver total table).

▶ **Receiver Field:** Enter the field in the receiver table that is affected by the substitution.

▶ **Constant Value:** Enter the value that the Receiver field will take as a consequence of the substitution. Alternatively, enter the user exit (in the Exit column) for more complex substitution logics; the user exit must be contained in the program specified in Transaction GCX2 (application area GBRU).

▶ **Rule:** Optionally, enter the rule that must be fulfilled for the substitution to be triggered. If you don't specify any rule, the substitution is always performed. The rules are created with Transaction GCVZ.

Change View "Rollup Substitution": Overview

New Entries

SubActivty	No.	Totals Table	Receiver field	Constant value	Exit	Rule
2A01	001	GLT1	RACCT	0000100000		X12A01001
2A01	002	GLT1	RACCT	0000200000		X12A01002
SAD1	001	FILCT	RVERS	100		
ZRSU	001	ZZSL01T	RACCT	0000422222		ZROLLRACCT1
ZRSU	002	ZZSL01T	RACCT	0000433333		ZROLLRACCT2

Figure 8.36 Rollup Substitutions

3. **Maintain valid document types (Transaction GCBR).**

Here you create a specific rollup document type and assign to it a number range.

The document type is necessary because the rollup creates documents and line items in the receiving ledger.

To perform this step, run transaction GCBR, and specify (Figure 8.37) the following:

▶ The document type for the rollup (two digits, alphanumeric)

▸ The number range that is used by the document type (see the next section)

▸ A brief description of the document type

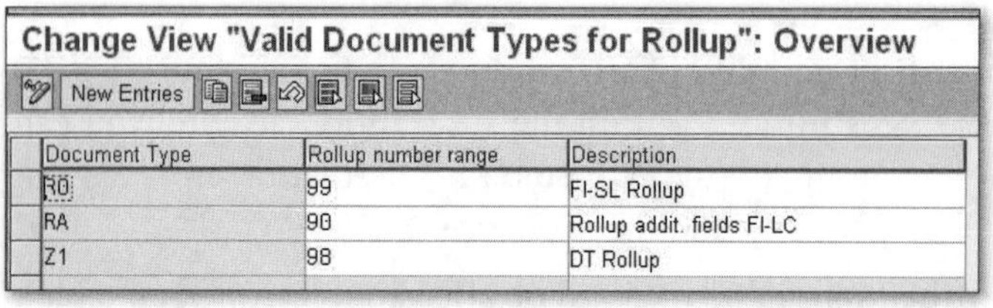

Document Type	Rollup number range	Description
R0	99	FI-SL Rollup
RA	90	Rollup addit. fields FI-LC
Z1	98	DT Rollup

Figure 8.37 Document Types for Rollup

4. **Maintain number ranges (Transaction GL20).**

Here you create a number range that you'll assign to a rollup document type. To perform this step (Figure 8.38):

▸ Run transaction GL20.

▸ Click on the Change Intervals button.

▸ In the next screen, click on the Insert Interval button, and specify the number range (two-digit ID) — the initial and final number of the range.

▸ Set the number range as internal (don't select the Ext flag).

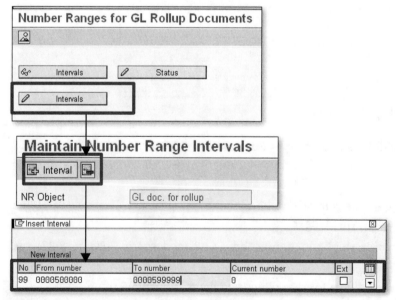

Figure 8.38 Number Ranges for Rollup Documents

Creating a Rollup

Quick Reference

Menu path: ACCOUNTING • FINANCIAL ACCOUNTING • SPECIAL PURPOSE LEDGER • PERIODIC PROCESSING • ROLLUP • CREATE

Transaction: GL21

Tables: T807H (rollup header) or T807 (rollup sequences)

Run Transaction GL21 to create a rollup in a special ledger (Figure 8.39). Three types of rollup are possible: standard, hierarchy, and export. The following step-by-step instructions apply to the standard rollup, which is used in the majority of cases:

1. Run Transaction GL21, specify the rollup name (eight digit, free alphanumerical definition), choose Standard, and press Enter.

2. In the resulting screen (shown in Figure 8.39), specify the following:

   ▶ **Title** (mandatory): Long description.

   ▶ **Sender Table** (mandatory): This is a total table for a special ledger (or any other ledger, including ledgers from Profit Center Accounting and SAP General Ledger).

   ▶ **Receiver Table** (mandatory): This is the total table of the table group to which your ledger belongs.

   ▶ **Reset Set** (optional): If you want to delete only some data in the receiving table, create a multidimensional set with all of the characteristics that should be used to select the data to be deleted in the receiving table.

   ▶ **Rollup Set** (optional): This is a multidimensional set that you can use to limit the data to be sent to the receiving table.

3. Select the Rollup Sequence button to go to the next screen of the rollup. In this screen (shown in Figure 8.39), specify one or more rollup sequences and indicate the following:

   ▶ **Sequence Set** (optional): This has the same function as the rollup set but applies only to the specific sequence. You can further limit the data to be selected with the sequence set.

▶ **Rule** (optional): This is a condition that the data must satisfy to be extracted and sent to the receiving ledger.

▶ **Field Movement** (mandatory): The field movement contains the rules that run the transfer of data (from field to field); see the previous section for more details.

▶ **Ledger** (mandatory): This is the destination ledger in the destination table. You can specify only one ledger for each sequence; if you want to transfer the same data for more than one ledger in the same table group, you can create two rollups, or, alternatively, one rollup with two sequences.

▶ **Blocked** (optional): Here you can deactivate the sequence.

▶ **Description** (optional): Here you can enter text for the sequence.

4. Save.

Creating a rollup isn't customizing, so the system doesn't ask for a transport request.

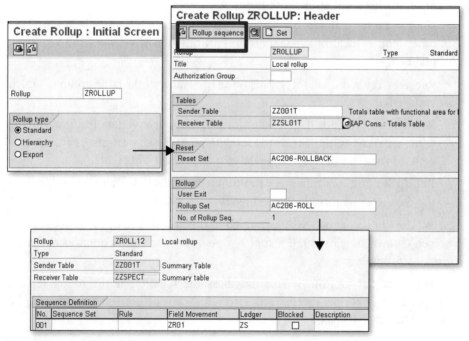

Figure 8.39 Creating a Rollup

Executing a Rollup

Menu path: ACCOUNTING • FINANCIAL ACCOUNTING • SPECIAL PURPOSE LEDGER • PERIODIC PROCESSING • ROLLUP • EXECUTE

Transactions: GL25 (execute) or GL26 (reverse)

Program: SAPMGLRV

To execute a rollup, follow these steps (Figure 8.40):

1. Execute Transaction GL25.
2. Specify the rollup, and click the Execute button (or press F8).
3. If there are variables in the rollup set or in the reset set, the system presents a pop-up where you must specify the values for each variable. Do so.
4. In the resulting screen (Figure 8.40), specify the following:

   ▶ The periods and the fiscal year: You can execute the rollup for exactly one period or for a range of consecutive periods.

   ▶ Whether the rollup is performed in the background or online.

   ▶ Whether line items are written in the destination ledger.

   ▶ The document type (only if the Write Line Items option is selected).

   ▶ Whether the rollup will add or replace the values in the destination ledger.

   ▶ Whether zero-value records are transferred.

   ▶ Whether a detailed log list is issued at the end of the execution.

When you reverse a rollup, you just specify the following:

   ▶ The periods and the fiscal year: You can reverse the rollup for exactly one period or for a range of consecutive periods.

   ▶ Whether the rollup is performed in background or online.

   ▶ The document type.

   ▶ Whether a detailed log list is issued at the end of the execution.

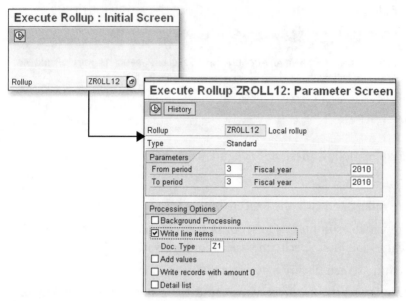

Figure 8.40 Executing a Rollup

8.5.3 FAQ and Troubleshooting Tips

Next we answer a frequently asked question and offer helpful troubleshooting tips.

FAQ

1. **Question:** Is it possible to execute the rollup in test mode?

   Answer: No. If the data from a rollup execution must be deleted, execute the reverse with Transaction GL26.

Troubleshooting Tips

1. **Issue:** When executing a rollup, error message GL304 appears: "Include dimension RLDNR in set ...."

   Solution: There are certain dimensions that technically must be present in the rollup selection set: ledger, version, fiscal year, period, and record type (this identifies actual or plan data). Modify the rollup selection set with Transaction GS02, and add sets with the missing dimensions.

2. **Issue:** When creating or executing a rollup, warning message GL136 appears "Ledger LL is not just a rollup ledger, you can also post to it."

   Solution: This is only a warning message. Do you really want to post documents and to execute rollups in the specified ledger? Consider the risk of overwriting existing posted data in the ledger that receives the rollup.

8.6 Summary

In this chapter, we discussed how to build a special purpose ledger from scratch, and we then discussed in detail how a ledger is posted. We then covered specific special purpose ledger functionalities and reporting, such as balance carryforward, total data reporting, and rollups.

Appendices

A   Tables and Views

Table	Description
T005	Country and Country-Specific Checks
T005E	County
T005G	City
T005S	Regions
TCURC	Currency Codes
TCURD	Max. Exch. Rate Differences for Postings in Foreign Currency
TCURE	Expiring Currencies
TCURF	Translation Ratios Between Currency Pairs
TCURR	Exchange Rates
TCURV	Exchange Rate Type
TCURX	Currency Decimal Places

Table A.1   General Configuration Tables

View	Description
V_005_B	Country-Specific Checks
V_CURC	Currency
V_CURX	Currency Decimal Places
V_T005	Country
V_TCURF	Translation Ratios Between Currency Pairs
V_TCURR	Exchange Rates
V_TCURR	Exchange Rates with Worklist
V_TCURV	Exchange Rate Type
V_T005S	Regions

Table A.2   General Configuration Views

Table	Description
T001	Company Code
T001K	Valuation Area (By Rule Plant)
T001K_ASSIGN	Assign Plant to Company Code
T014	Credit Control Area

Table A.3   Organizational Structure Tables

Table	Description
T500P	Assign Personnel Area to Company Code
T880	Company (Trading Partner)
TFKB	Functional Area
TGSB	Business Area
TGSBK	Consolidation Business Area
TKA01	Controlling Area
TKA02	Assign Company Code to Controlling Area
TKEB	Operating Concern
TVKO	Assign Sales Organization to Company Code

Table A.3 Organizational Structure Tables (Cont.)

View	Description
V_001_X	Assign Company Code to Credit Control Area
V_001_Y	Assign Company Code to Company
V_GSB_A	Assign Business Area to Consolidation Business Area
V_T001	Company Code
V_T001K_ASSIGN	Assign Plant to Company Code
V_T014	Credit Control Area
V_T500P	Assign Personnel Area to Company Code
V_T880	Company (Trading Partner)
V_TFKB	Functional Area
V_TGSB	Business Area
V_TGSBK	Consolidation Business Area
V_TKA01_ER	Assign Controlling Area to Operating Concern
V_TKA01_GD	Controlling Area
V_TKA02	Assign Company Code to Controlling Area
V_TVKO_ASSIGN	Assign Sales Organization to Company Code

Table A.4 Organizational Structure Views

Table	Description
BKPF	G/L Document Header Data
BSAS	Secondary Index for G/L Cleared Items (Only if Account is Managed on Line Item Basis)
BSEC	One-Time Account Data for Line Item

Table A.5 General Ledger Tables

Table	Description
BSEG	G/L Document Item Data
BSEG_ADD	New G/L Document Item Data (Documents Not Posted to the Leading Ledger)
BSET	Tax Data in G/L Document
BSIM	Secondary Index for Material Documents
BSIS	Secondary Index for G/L Open Items (Only if Account is Managed on Line Item Basis)
CEPC	Profit Centers
CSKA	Cost Element (Chart of Accounts Data)
CSKB	Cost Element (Controlling Area Data)
CSKT	Cost Element (Description)
FAGL_ACTIVEC	New General Ledger: Document Splitting Fields
FAGL_BELNR_LD	New General Ledger: Document Types and Number Range for General Ledger View
FAGL_DOCNR_LD	New General Ledger: Document Types and Number Range for Entry View in a Ledger
FAGL_LEDGER_SCEN	New General Ledger: Fields Assigned to the Scenario
FAGL_SCEN_FIELDS	New General Ledger: Assignment of Scenarios to Ledgers
FAGL_SCENARIO	New General Ledger: Scenarios
FAGL_SEGM	New General Ledger: Segment
FAGL_SEGM_CUST	New General Ledger: Settings for Segment Maintenance and Derivation
FAGL_SPLIT_FIELD	New General Ledger: Document Splitting Activation
FAGL_T8A30	New General Ledger: Default Profit Center
FAGL_TLDGRP	New General ledger: Ledgers Assigned to the Ledger Group
FAGL_TLDGRP_MAP	New General Ledger: Ledger Group Definition
FGALFLEXA	New G/L Actual Line Items
FGALFLEXT	New G/L Plan Total Data
FGALFLEXT	New G/L Total Data
GLPCA	Profit Center Line Item (Classic Ledger)
GLPCT	Profit Center Total Data (Classic Ledger)
GLT0	Classic G/L Total Data by Company Code, Business Area, Year, Period and Account
GLT3	Classic G/L Consolidation Preparation Ledger
SKA1	G/L Account Only Chart of Accounts Data

Table A.5 General Ledger Tables (Cont.)

Table	Description
SKAT	G/L Account Description in Different Languages
SKB1	G/L Account Only Company Code Data
SKM1	Sample Account
SKMT	Sample Account Names
T001A	Parallel Currencies for Company Code
T001B	Permitted Posting Periods
T001D	Validation in General Ledger
T001O	Cross-System Company Codes (ALE)
T001Q	Substitutions in General Ledger
T001U	Clearings Accounts Between Company Codes
T003	General Ledger Document Types
T003A	Document Types for Posting with Clearing
T003D	Document Types for Enjoy Transactions
T004	Chart of Accounts
T004F	Field Status Groups of Each Field Status Variant
T004M	Data Transfer Rules for Sample Accounts (Field by Field)
T004R	List of Rules for Sample Accounts
T004V	Field Status Variant
T007A	Tax Codes
T009	Fiscal Year Variant
T009B	Posting Periods of the Fiscal Year Variant
T009Y	Shortened Fiscal Year Variant
T030	Automatic Account Determination
T030A	Transaction Keys for Automatic Account Determination
T030H	Exchange Rate Difference Accounts
T030HB	Exchange Rate Difference Accounts for Valuation Area
T030K	Account Determination for Taxes
T030U	Account Determination for Balance Sheet Transfer Postings
T041C	Reason for Reversal Postings
T043	Assignment of Tolerance Groups to Users
T043S	Tolerance Groups for G/L Accounts
T043T	Tolerance Groups for Employees
T044A	Foreign Currency Valuation Method

Table A.5 General Ledger Tables (Cont.)

Table	Description
T054	Run Schedule for Recurring Documents
T074	Special G/L Accounts
T074U	Special G/L Indicator
T077S	G/L Account Group
T856	Consolidation Transaction Types
T856X	Consolidation Transaction Types Groups
T881	Ledgers
T882	Assignment of Company Codes to Ledgers
T882C	Company-Ledger Assignment in Special Ledger
T882G	Fiscal Year Variant and Parallel Currencies in Non-Leading Ledgers New G/L)
T8G12	New General Ledger: Classification of G/L Accounts for Splitting
T8G17	New General Ledger: Classification of Document Types for Splitting
TBAER	Rules for Changing Fields in Documents
TBSL	Posting Keys
TF123	Rules for Clearing Open Items
TKSKA	Automatic Creation Cost Elements: Configuration

Table A.5 General Ledger Tables (Cont.)

Views	Description
V_001_B	Company Code Detailed Settings
V_FAGL_ACTIVEC_2	New General Ledger: Document Splitting Fields
V_FAGL_BELNR_LD	New General Ledger: Document Types and Number Range for General Ledger View
V_FAGL_DOCNR_LD	New General Ledger: Document Types and Number Range for Entry View in a Ledger
V_FAGL_SCE_FIELD	New General Ledger: Assignment of Scenarios to Ledgers
V_FAGL_SCENARIO	New General Ledger: Scenarios
V_FAGL_SEGM	New General Ledger: Segment
V_FAGL_SPLIT_FLD	New General Ledger: Document Splitting Activation
V_FAGL_T881	New General Ledger: Ledger Definition
V_FAGL_T882G	Settings for Non-Leading Ledgers (Fiscal Year Variant and Parallel Currencies)

Table A.6 General Ledger Views

Views	Description
V_T003	General Ledger Document Types
V_T004	Chart of Accounts
V_T030H	Exchange Rate Difference Accounts
V_T077S	G/L Account Group
V_T856	Consolidation Transaction Types
V_T8G12	New General Ledger: Classification of G/L Accounts for Splitting
V_T8G17	New General Ledger: Classification of Document Types for Splitting
V_TBAER	Rules for Changing Fields in Documents
V_TF123	Rules for Clearing Open Items
V_TKSKACSKB	Automatic Creation Cost Elements: Configuration

Table A.6 General Ledger Views (Cont.)

Tables	Description
BSAD	Secondary Index for Customer Cleared Items
BSAK	Secondary Index for Vendor Cleared Items
BSID	Secondary Index for Customer Open Items
BSIK	Secondary Index for Vendor Open Items
BSIP	Secondary Index to Check Double Postings of Vendor Invoices
BSIW	Index for Customer Bill of Exchange
INTITHE	Interest Calculation Header
INTITIT	Interest Calculation Line Item
INTITPF	Interest Calculation Forms
KNA1	Customer General Data
KNAS	Customer Additional VAT Registration Number in Different Countries
KNB1	Customer Company Code Data
KNB5	Customer Dunning Data
KNBK	Customer Bank Data
KNBW	Customer Withholding Tax Data
KNC1	Customer Total Transaction Data
KNC3	Customer Total Transaction Data (Special G/L Transaction Figures)

Table A.7 Accounts Payable and Accounts Receivable Tables

Tables	Description
KNKA	Customer Credit Management: Central Data
KNKK	Customer Credit Management: Control Data
KNVV	Customer Sales Area Data
LFA1	Vendor General Data
LFAS	Vendor Additional VAT Registration Number in Different Countries
LFB1	Vendor Company Code Data
LFBK	Vendor Bank Data
LFC1	Vendor Total Transaction Data
LFC3	Vendor Total Transaction Data (Special G/L Transaction Figures)
LFM1	Vendor Purchasing Organization Data
MAHNS	Accounts Blocked by the Dunning Selection
MHND	Dunning Data at Customer Level
MHNK	Dunning Data at Document Level
T001S	Accounting Clerk
T003D	Default Document Type for Enjoy Transactions
T008	Payment Block Reasons
T030H	Accounts for Exchange Rate Valuation
T030HB	Accounts for Exchange Rate Valuation with Valuation Area (New G/L)
T033	Valuation Areas
T033F	Posting Configuration with Account Symbols
T033I	Account Symbols
T040	Dunning Keys
T040S	Dunning Blocks
T042	Sending Company Code (Automatic Payments for Configuration)
T042A	House Bank Selection (Automatic Payments Configuration)
T042B	Paying Company Code (Automatic Payments Configuration)
T042D	Available Amounts per House Bank Account (Automatic Payments Configuration)
T042E	Payment Method per Company Code (Automatic Payments Configuration)

Table A.7 Accounts Payable and Accounts Receivable Tables (Cont.)

Tables	Description
T042I	House Bank Account Selection (Automatic Payments Configuration)
T042Z	Payment Method per Country (Automatic Payments Configuration)
T043	Assign Accounting Clerks to Tolerance Groups
T043G	Tolerance Groups for Customer/Vendors
T044A	Foreign Currency Valuation Method
T044G	Value Adjustment Key
T047	Company Code Dunning Configuration
T047A	Dunning Procedures
T047B	Dunning Levels
T047C	Dunning Charges
T047E	Form Selection for Dunning Letters
T047H	Dunning Minimum Amounts
T047M	Dunning Areas
T047R	Grouping Rules of Dunning Notice
T048	Correspondence Types
T048B	Report Assignment for Correspondence
T048V	Correspondence Procedure
T052	Payment Terms
T052S	Payment Terms – Installments
T056	Interest Indicator
T056A	Time-Dependent Interest Rates
T056P	Interest Rates for Reference Rate
T056R	Reference Interest Rates
T056U	Interest Indicator Settings
T077D	Customer Account Group
T077K	Vendor Account Group
TACC_BWBER_PR	Assign Valuation Areas and Accounting Principles

Table A.7 Accounts Payable and Accounts Receivable Tables (Cont.)

Views	Description
V_077D_B	Assign Number Ranges to Customer Account Groups
V_FAGL_TRGT_LDGR	Check Assignment of Accounting Principle to Ledger Group
V_FAGL_TRGT_LDGR	Assignment of Accounting Principle to Ledger Group
V_T001S	Accounting Clerk
V_T008	Payment Block Reasons
V_T033	Valuation Areas
V_T040S	Dunning Blocks
V_T044A	Valuation Method
V_T047M	Dunning Areas
V_T052	Payment Terms
V_T052S	Payment Terms – Installments
V_T056	Calculation Types
V_T077D	Customer Account Group
V_T077K	Vendor Account Group
V_TACC_BWBER_PR	Assign Valuation Areas and Accounting Principles

Table A.8 Accounts Payable and Accounts Receivable Views

Tables	Description
AAACC_OBJ	Activation of CO Objects for Posting in Asset Accounting per Company Code
ANEA	Asset Line Items for Proportional Values (in Case of Retirement)
ANEK	Asset Document Header
ANEP	Asset Document Line Items
ANKA	Asset Class Definition
ANKB	Asset Class per Depreciation Area
ANLA	Asset Master Record Segment (for example: description, asset class)
ANLB	Asset Depreciation Terms
ANLC	Asset Value Fields (for example, cumulative APC values up to the current fiscal year)
ANLV	Asset Insurance Data
ANLZ	Asset Time-Dependent Data
T030B	Specify Posting Key for Asset Posting
T082A	Screen Layout Rules – Asset Master Data

Table A.9 Asset Tables

Tables	Description
T087	Evaluation Groups (4-Character)
T087G	Evaluation Groups (8-Character)
T090	Calculation Keys
T090A	Period Control for Depreciation
T090NA	Depreciation Keys
T090NAZ	Assignment of Calculation Methods to Depreciation Keys
T093	Depreciation Areas Definition
T093_ACCOBJ	Generic Activation of CO Objects for Posting in Asset Accounting
T093A	Real Depreciation Area
T093B	Company Code Related Depreciation Area Settings
T093C	Company Code in Asset Accounting
T093D	Posting Rules for Depreciation
T093SB	Substitutions for Asset Master Data
T093V	Validation for Asset Master Data
T095	Asset Balance Sheet Accounts
T095A	Account Determination in Asset Accounting
T095B	Asset Depreciation Accounts
T095P	Asset Special Reserves
T096	Chart of Depreciation Definition
T099	Insurance Types
TABW	Asset Transaction Types
TABWA	Asset Transaction Types in Depreciation Areas
TABWD	Default Asset Transaction Types for Transactions
TABWG	Asset Transaction Types Groups
TABWQ	Define History Sheet Groups

Table A.9 Asset Tables (Cont.)

Views	Description
V_AAACC_OBJ_01	Activation of CO Objects for Posting in Asset Accounting per Company Code
V_ANKA_00	Asset Class Definition
V_ANKB_00	Deactivation of Depreciation Areas in Asset Classes
V_ANKB_XSPEB	Asset Classes Deactivation in Chart of Depreciation
V_T082A_01	Screen Layout Rules – Asset Master Data

Table A.10 Asset Views

Views	Description
V_T082A_10	Screen Layout Rules – Asset Master Data (Details for Each Field)
V_T087	Evaluation Groups (4-Character)
V_T087G	Evaluation Groups (8-Character)
V_T093_00N	Depreciation Areas Definition
V_T093_ACCOBJ	Generic Activation of Controlling Objects for Posting in Asset Accounting
V_T093A_03	Depreciation Area: Adoption of APC Values from Another Depreciation Area
V_T093A_04	Depreciation Area: Adoption of Depreciation Terms from Another Depreciation Area
V_T093B_01	Reopen of Closed Fiscal Year – For Specific Depreciation Areas
V_T093B_02	Reopen of Closed Fiscal Year – Entire Company Code
V_T093B_05	Depreciation Area Currency
V_T093C_00	Assignment Chart of Depreciation to Company Code
V_T093C_01	Document Type for Depreciation
V_T093D_00	Posting Rules for Depreciation
V_T093SB	Substitutions for Asset Master Data
V_T093V	Validations for Asset Master Data
V_T095_MASTER	Asset Balance Sheet Accounts
V_T095A_01	Account Determination in Asset Accounting
V_T095B_MASTER	Asset Depreciation Accounts
V_T095P_MASTER	Asset Special Reserves
V_T096_00	Chart of Depreciation Definition
V_TABWQ	Define History Sheet Groups

Table A.10 Asset Views (Cont.)

Tables	Description
BNKA	Bank Master Data
BNKAIN	Bank Master Data Additional Fields
FEBEC	Clearing Data for Electronic Bank Statement
FEBEP	Electronic Bank Statement Items
FEBKO	Electronic Bank Statement Header
FEBRE	Reference Record for Electronic Bank Statement Items
T012	House Banks Definition

Table A.11 Banking Tables

Tables	Description
T012A	Allocation of Payment Terms to Bank Transactions
T012K	House Bank Accounts
T028B	Assignment of House Bank Accounts to Bank Statement Transaction Types
T028D	Electronic Bank Statement Posting Rule (ID and Text)
T028G	External Transaction Types to Posting Rules Assignment (Electronic Bank Statement)
T028V	Bank Statement Transaction Types
T033F	Posting Rule (Assignment of Accounts)
T033GI	Link Between Account Symbols and General Ledger and Sub-Ledger (Customer and Vendor) Accounts
T033I	Account Symbols
TBCH0	Bank Chain Scenarios
TBCH1	Bank Chains Scenario Details
TBCHAIN0	General Bank Chains
TBCHAIN1	General Bank Chain Details
TBCHAIN2	Bank Chains (Receiver-Specific)
TBCHAIN21	Bank Chains (Receiver-Specific) Details
TCJ_BALANCE	Cash Journal Totals Records after Every Transaction
TCJ_C_JOURNALS	Cash Journal Definition
TCJ_DOCUMENTS	Cash Journal Documents Header Data
TCJ_POSITIONS	Cash Journal Documents Item Data
TCJ_PRINT	Parameters for the Cash Journal Receipt
TCJ_TRANSACTIONS	Cash Journal Business Definition

Table A.11 Banking Tables (Cont.)

Views	Description
V_T012	House Banks Definition
V_T012K	House Banks Account
V_T028B	Assignment of House Bank Accounts to Bank Statement Transaction Types
V_T028D	Posting Rule (ID and Text)
V_T028G	External Transaction Types to Posting Rules Assignment
V_T028V	Bank Statement Transaction Types

Table A.12 Banking Views

Views	Description
V_T033F_EBST	Posting Rule (Assignment of Accounts)
V_T033G_EBST	Link Between Account Symbols and General Ledger and Sub-Ledger (Customer and Vendor) Accounts
V_T033I_EBST	Account Symbols (Bank Statement)
V_TBCH0	Bank Chains Scenario
V_TBCH1	Bank Chains Scenario Details
V_TBCH2	General Bank Chains
V_TBCH3	General Bank Chains Details
V_TCJ_C_JOURNALS	Cash Journal Definition
V_TCJ_PRINT	Parameters for the Cash Journal Receipt
V_TCJ_TRANSACT	Cash Journal Business Definition

Table A.12 Banking Views (Cont.)

Tables	Description
T807	Rollup Sequence – Special Ledger
T807H	Rollup Header – Special Ledger
T881	Ledgers
T882	Companies or Company Codes Assignment to Ledgers
T884C	Field Movement for the Balance Carry Forward (Special Ledger)
T886A	Activities Assignment to Combination of Ledger and Company/Company Code
T886B	Activities Assignment to Ledger (Valid for all Companies/Company Codes)
T888	Field Movement Definition
T889	Document Types for Special Ledger Manual Postings
T894	Versions for Special Ledger Actual Data

Table A.13 Special Ledger Tables

Views	Description
V_T030_GL	Retained Earnings Account – Special Ledger Local (Company Code)
V_T030C	Retained Earnings Account – Special Ledger Global (Company)
V_T884C	Field Movement for the Balance Carry Forward (Special Ledger)
V_T889	Document Types for Special Ledger Manual Postings
V_T894	Versions for Special Ledger Actual Data

Table A.14 Special Ledger Views

Tables	Description
APQI	Batch Input Sessions
CDHDR	Change Documents – Header Data
CDPOS	Change Documents – Line Item Data
DD02L	Tables
LDBD	Logical Database
NRIV	Number Ranges
REPOSRC	Programs
T000	Clients Within the Instances
T002	Language Key
T006	Unit of Measure
T100	Messages
TSTC	Transaction Codes

Table A.15 General Tables

B Transaction Codes

Transaction Code	Description
OB07	Exchange Rate Type
OB08	Exchange Rates
OBBS	Translation Ratios Between Currency Pairs
OY01	Country
OY04	Currency
OY17	Country-Specific Checks
TCURMNT	Exchange Rates with Worklist

Table B.1 General Configuration Transaction Codes

Transaction Code	Description
KEKK	Assign Controlling Area to Operating Concern
KEP8	Operating Concern Definition
OB38	Assign Company Code to Credit Control Area
OB45	Credit Control Area Definition
OBB6	Assign Business Area to Consolidation Business Area
OCC1	Consolidation Business Area Definition
OKBD	Functional Area Definition
OVX3	Assign Sales Organization to Company Code
OX02	Company Code Definition
OX03	Business Area Definition
OX06	Controlling Area Definition
OX15	Company (Trading Partner)
OX16	Assign Company Code to Company
OX18	Assign Plant to Company Code
OX19	Assign Company Code to Controlling Area

Table B.2 Organizational Structure Transaction Codes

Transaction Code	Description
FAGL_FC_VAL	Foreign Currency Valuation (New)
FAGLGVTR	Balance Carryforward (New)
FAGLF03	G/L Reconciliation (New)
F.03	G/L Reconciliation
F.05	Foreign Currency Valuation
F.07	G/L Balance Carryforward
F.08	G/L Account Balances
F.09	G/L Account List
F.13	Automatic Clearing of Open Items
F.14	Recurring Entries
F.13E	Automatic Clearing of Open Items with Specification of Clearing Currency
F.56	Delete Recurring Entry Documents
F.19	GR/IR (Good Receipt/Invoice Receipt) Account Clearing
F.57	Delete Sample Accounts
F.80	Mass Reversal of Financial Accounting Documents
F.81	Reverse Postings for Accrual/Deferred Documents
F-01	Enter Sample Document
F-02	Basic Transaction for G/L Posting
F-03	Clear G/L Account
F-04	Post with Clearing
F-05	Post Manually Foreign Currency Valuation
F-05	Post Manually Foreign Currency Valuation
FB00	Editing Options
FB02	Change Document
FB03	Change Document
FB03L	Document Display: G/L View
FB03Z	Display Document/Payment Usage
FB04	Document Changes
FB05	Post with Clearing
FAGLB03	Display G/L Balances (New G/L)
FAGLL03	Display/Change G/L Line Items (New G/L)
FB01	Basic Transaction for G/L Posting
FB01L	Basic Transaction for G/L Posting (New G/L)

Table B.3 General Ledger Transaction Codes

Transaction Code	Description
FB08	Reversal of Documents Without Cleared Items
FBV0	Post Parked Document
FB09	Cahnge Line Items
FBS1	Enter Accrual/Deferral Document
FB1S	Clear G/L Account
FB41	Post to Tax Accounts
FBV1	Create Parked Document
FBV2	Change Parked Document
FBV3	Display Parked Document
FB50	G/L Enjoy Transaction
FB50L	G/L Enjoy Transaction (New G/L)
FBL3N	Display/Change G/L Line Items
FBN1	General Ledger Number Ranges
FBM2	Change Sample Document
FBM3	Display Sample Document
FBRA	Reversal of Documents with Cleared Items
FBV0	Post Parked Documents
FS00	G/L Account Chart of Accounts and Company Code Data
FS01	Create G/L Account
FS02	Change G/L Account
FS03	Display G/L Account
FS05	Block G/L Account
FS06	Mark G/L Account for Deletion
FS10N	Display Balances of G/L Account
FS15	G/L Accounts Copy from Company Code: Sending
FS16	G/L Accounts Copy from Company Code: Receiving
FSK2	Data Transfer Rules for Sample Accounts (Field By Field)
FSM1	Sample Account Creation
FSM2	Sample Account Change
FSM3	Sample Account Display
FSM5	Sample Account Deletion
FSP0	G/L Account Only Chart of Accounts Data
FSS0	G/L Account Only Company Code Data
FTXP	Tax Codes

Table B.3 General Ledger Transaction Codes (Cont.)

Transaction Code	Description
FV50	G/L Parking Enjoy Transaction
GS01	Set Creation
GS02	Set Change
GS03	Set Display
KCH1	Profit Center Groups Creation
KCH2	Profit Center Groups Change
KCH3	Profit Center Groups Display
KCH5N	Profit Center Standard Hierarchy Maintenance
KDH1	Account Groups Creation
KDH2	Account Groups Change
KDH3	Account Groups Display
KE51	Profit Centers
KE56	Assignment of Profit Centers to Company Codes
OB03	Maintain Financial Accounting Document Types
OB08	Currency Exchange Rates
OB09	Exchange Rate Difference Accounts
OB13	Chart of Accounts
OB15	List of Rules for Sample Accounts
OB22	Parallel Currencies
OB26	Screen Layout for Creating, Displaying, Changing G/L Accounts
OB28	Validations – General Ledger
OB29	Fiscal Year Variant
OB32	Rules for Changing Header Fields in Documents
OB32A	Rules for Changing Item Fields in Documents
OB40	Accounts for Tax Codes
OB41	Posting Keys
OB52	Open and Close Posting Periods
OB53	Maintain Retained Earnings Account Determination
OB58	Financial Statement Versions
OB67	Assign Company Code to Sample Account Rules
OB74	Rules for Clearing Open Items
OBA0	Tolerance Groups for G/L Accounts
OBA4	Assignment of Tolerance Groups to Users
OBA5	Change Message Control (Error, Warning, Info)

Table B.3 General Ledger Transaction Codes (Cont.)

Transaction Code	Description
OBA7	General Ledger Document Types
OBBH	Substitutions – General Ledger
OBBI	Maintain G/L Account Field Groups
OBC4	Field Status Variant
OBD4	G/L Account Group
OBH1	Copy Number Ranges from Company Code to Company Code
OBH2	Company Number Range from Fiscal Year to Fiscal Year
OBS2	Additional Ledgers in Classic General Ledger
OBYF	Revenue Account Determination
OBY2	Additional Ledgers in Classic General Ledger
OBY7	Copy Chart of Account Dependent Table Entries
OBY7	Delete Chart of Account Dependent Table Entries
OBXZ	Clearing Difference Accounts
OBY6	Company Code Detailed Settings
OC08	Consolidation Transaction Types
OKB2	Automatic Creation Cost Elements: Configuration
OKB3	Cost Elements Mass Creation
OKB9	Automatic Account Assignment

Table B.3 General Ledger Transaction Codes (Cont.)

Transaction Code	Description
F.05	Exchange Rate Valuation in Classic Ledger
F.13	Automatic Clearing of Open Items Without Specification of Clearing Currency
F.12	Advance Return for Tax on Sales/Purchases
F.23	Customer Balances in Local Currency
F.27	Periodic Account Statement
F110	Automatic Outgoing Payments
F101	Grouping of Payables and Receivables for Balance Sheet Reporting
F103	Transfer Postings for Doubtful Receivables
FD32	Customer Credit Data Change
FD33	Customer Credit Data Display

Table B.4 Accounts Payable and Accounts Receivable Transaction Codes

Transaction Code	Description
F13E	Automatic Clearing of Open Items with Specification of Clearing Currency
F150	Dunning Run
F-06	Post Incoming Payment
F-07	Post Outgoing Payment
FBZ1	Post Incoming Payment
FBZ2	Post Outgoing Payment
FBZ3	Incoming Payment Fast Entry
FBZ4	Payment with Printout
F-22	Financial Accounting Outgoing Invoices (Classic Transaction)
F-26	Manual Incoming Payment – Fast Entry
F-27	Financial Accounting Outgoing Credit Memos (Enjoy Transaction)
F-28	Manual Incoming Payment
F-29	Down Payments Received
FB1D	Clear Customer
FB1K	Clear Vendor
F-39	Clearing Down Payments Received
F-41	Financial Accounting Incoming Credit Memos (Enjoy Transaction)
F-43	Financial Accounting Incoming Invoices (Classic Transaction)
FAGL_FC_VAL	Exchange Rate Valuation in New General Ledger
FB60	Financial Accounting Incoming Invoices (Enjoy Transaction)
FV60	Park Incoming Invoices (Enjoy Transaction)
FBA2	Post Customer Down Payment
FBA3	Clear Customer Down Payment
FBA7	Post Vendor Down Payment
FBA8	Clear Vendor Down Payment
FB05	Post with Clearing
FB65	Financial Accounting Incoming Credit Memos (Classic Transaction)
FB70	Financial Accounting Outgoing Invoices (Enjoy Transaction)
FB75	Financial Accounting Outgoing Credit Memos (Classic Transaction)
FV65	Park Incoming Credit Memos (Classic Transaction)
FV70	Park Outgoing Invoices (Enjoy Transaction)

Table B.4 Accounts Payable and Accounts Receivable Transaction Codes (Cont.)

Transaction Code	Description
FV75	Park Outgoing Credit Memos (Classic Transaction)
FBL1N	Vendor Line Items Reporting
FBL5N	Customer Line Items Reporting
FBMP	Define Dunning Procedures
FBZP	Automatic Payments Configuration
FD01	Customer Master Data Creation: General and Company Code Data
FD02	Customer Master Data Change: General and Company Code Data
FD03	Customer Master Data Display: General and Company Code Data
FD04	Changes to Customer Master Records
FD05	Blocking Customer Accounts
FD06	Setting for Deletion Customer Accounts
FINT	Interest Calculation and Invoicing
FINTSHOW	Interest Run Display
FK01	Vendor Master Data Creation: General and Company Code Data
FK02	Vendor Master Data Change: General and Company Code Data
FK03	Customer Master Data Display: General and Company Code Data
FK04	Changes to Vendor Master Records
FK05	Blocking Vendor Accounts
FK06	Marking for Deletion Vendor Accounts
OB05	Accounting Clerk
OB18	Define Dunning Blocks
OB20	Screen Layout for Activities (Customer Master Record)
OB21	Screen Layout per Company Code (Customer Master Record)
OB23	Screen Layout for Activities (Vendor Master Record)
OB24	Screen Layout per Company Code (Vendor Master Record)
OB27	Payment Block Reasons
OB46	Define Interest Calculation Types
OB59	Define Valuation Methods
OB61	Define Dunning Areas
OB81	Define Time-Based Terms
OB82	Prepare Interest on Arrears Calculation
OB83	Define Time-Based Terms (Reference Rate)
OBA1	Prepare Automatic Postings for Foreign Currency Valuation

Table B.4 Accounts Payable and Accounts Receivable Transaction Codes (Cont.)

Transaction Code	Description
OBAC	Define Reference Interest Rates
OBAR	Assign Number Ranges to Customer Account Groups
OBAS	Assign Number Ranges to Vendor Account Groups
OBB8	Payment Terms
OBB9	Payment Terms – Installments
OBD2	Customer Account Group
OBD3	Vendor Account Group
OBR2	Deletion of Customer, Vendor, and G/L Master Data
OBV1	A/R: Calculation of Interest on Arrears (Postings)
OBXR	Define Reconciliation Accounts for Customer Down Payments
OBXT	Define Alternative Reconciliation Account for Vendors (Other)
OBXY	Define Alternative Reconciliation Account for Customers (Other)
OBYM	Define Alternative Reconciliation Account for Bills of Exchange Payable
OBYN	Define Alternative Reconcil.Acct for Bills/Exch. Receivable
OBYR	Define Alternative Reconciliation Account for Down Payments (Vendor)
OBZO	Default Document Type for Enjoy Transactions
XD01	Customer Master Data Creation: General, Company Code. and Sales Data
XD03	Customer Master Data Display: General, Company Code, and Sales Data
XD02	Customer Master Data Change: General, Company Code, and Sales Data
XD06	Customer Master Data Mark for Deletion (All Levels)
XD05	Customer Master Data Block (All Levels)
XD07	Change of Account Group in Customer Master Record
XDN1	Create Number Ranges for Customer Accounts
XK01	Vendor Master Data Creation: General, Company Code, and Sales Data
XK02	Vendor Master Data Change: General, Company Code, and Sales Data
XK03	Vendor Master Data Display: General, Company Code, and Sales Data
XK06	Vendor Master Data Mark for Deletion (All Levels)

Table B.4 Accounts Payable and Accounts Receivable Transaction Codes (Cont.)

Transaction Code	Description
XK05	Vendor Master Data Block (All Levels)
XK07	Change of Account Group in Vendor Master Record
XKN1	Vendor Number Ranges

Table B.4 Accounts Payable and Accounts Receivable Transaction Codes (Cont.)

Transaction Code	Description
AB01	Posting a Generic Asset Document
AB02	Changing an Asset Document
AB03	Display an Asset Document
AB08	Reversing an Asset Document
ABAA	Posting an Unplanned Depreciation
ABAON	Asset Sale Without Customer
ABAVN	Asset Retirement by Scrapping
ABNAN	Post Capitalization
ABMA	Manual Depreciation
ABNV	Asset Document Number Ranges
ABT1N	Transfer Company to Company (in the Same Client)
ABUMN	Transfer Within the Company Code
ABZON	Acquisition with Automatic Offsetting Entry
ABZE	Acquisition from in-House Production
ABZP	Acquisition from Affiliated Company
ABZS	Write-Up
ACSET	Activation of Controlling Objects for Posting in Asset Accounting per Company Code
AFAB	Depreciation Run
AFAF	Asset with Errors
AFAR	Recalculate Depreciation
AFABN	Depreciation Run
AFBN	Include New Depreciation Area for Existing Assets
AFBP	Create Depreciation Posting Log
AFAMA	Depreciation Keys
AJAB	Fiscal Year Closing
AJRW	Fiscal Year Change

Table B.5 Asset Accounting Transaction Codes

Transaction Code	Description
AM05	Asset Classes Deactivation in Chart of Depreciation
AO90	Specify G/L Accounts for APC Posting and Depreciation
AR01	Mass Change to Asset Master Data – Generate Worklist
AR32	Mass Change to Asset Master Data – Edit Worklist
AS01	Creating a Main Asset
AS05	Blocking an Asset
AS06	Deleting an Asset
AS08	Number Ranges for Asset Master Data
AS11	Creating a Sub-Asset
ASKB	Periodic Posting of Transactions
ASKBN	Periodic Posting of Transactions
AW01N	The Asset Explorer
CJ01	WBS Creation
CJ06	Project Definition
CJ30	WBS Direct Budgeting
CJ88	Settlement of Costs from WBS to AuC /Final Asset
EC08	Chart of Depreciation Definition
F-90	Acquisition with Financial Accounting Vendor Invoice
F-92	Asset Retirement with Customer
IM01	IM Program Definition
IM11	IM Creation of Top Position
IM22	IM Program Structure
IM32	IM Program Budgeting
KO01	Internal Order Creation
KO22	Internal Order Budgeting
KO88	Settlement of Costs from Internal Order to AuC/Final Asset
OA02	Substitution for Asset Mass Change
OA81	Maintain Transaction Types – Expert
OA79	Maintain Asset History Sheet Version
OAAQ	Reopen of Closed Fiscal Year – Entire Company Code
OAAR	Reopen of Closed Fiscal Year – for Specific Depreciation Areas
OAB3	Document Type for Depreciation

Table B.5 Asset Accounting Transaction Codes (Cont.)

Transaction Code	Description
OABC	Depreciation Area: Adoption of APC Values from Another Depreciation Area
OABK	Delete Depreciation Area
OABD	Depreciation Area: Adoption of Depreciation Terms from Another Depreciation Area
OABT	Parallel Currencies in Depreciation Areas
OAMK	Change Asset Reconciliation Accounts
OACS	Substitutions for Asset Master Data
OACV	Validations for Asset Master Data
OADB	Depreciation Areas Definition
OAOA	Asset Class Definition
OAOB	Assigning Chart of Depreciation to Company Code
OAPL	Set the Chart of Depreciation for Customizing
OASI	Asset Accounting Simplified IMG
OAV8	Evaluation Groups (8-Character)
OAV9	Define History Sheet Groups
OAVA	Evaluation Groups (4-Character)
OAYH	Depreciation Area Currency
OAYR	Posting Rules for Depreciation
OAYZ	Deactivation of Depreciation Areas in Asset Classes
OBYD	Specify Posting Key for Asset Posting
AO73	Transaction Types for Asset Acquisition
AO74	Transaction Types for Asset Retirement
OAXG	Transaction Types for Capitalization of Asset Under Construction
AO76	Transaction Types for Asset Transfer
OAYA	Limit Transaction Types for Asset Acquisition to Depreciation Areas
OAXB	Limit Transaction Types for Asset Retirement to Depreciation Areas
OAXC	Limit Transaction Types for Asset Transfer to Depreciation Areas
OAZ1	Define Validation for Asset Posting
OABL	Reset Company Code in Asset Accounting
OAGL	Reset Posted Depreciation

Table B.5 Asset Accounting Transaction Codes (Cont.)

Transaction Code	Description
BAUP	Bank Master Data Mass Upload with Country Specific File
BIC	Bank Master Data Mass Upload from BIC Database
FBCJ	Cash Journal Postings
FBCJ3	Display Cash Journal Postings
FBCJC0	Cash Journal Definition
FBCJC1	Number Ranges for Cash Journal Documents
FBCJC2	Cash Journal Business Definition
FBCJC3	Parameters for the Cash Journal Receipt
FEBA_BANK_STATEMENT	Reprocess (or Postprocess) of Imported and Partially Posted Bank Statements
FEBAN	Reprocess (or Postprocess) of Imported and Partially Posted Bank Statements
FEBC	Conversion of Bank Statements to Multicash Format
FEBP	Posting of the Imported Bank Statement
FF_5	Bank Statement Import
FI01	Bank Master Data Creation
FI02	Bank Master Data Change
FI03	Bank Master Data Display
FI04	Bank Master Data Deletion Flag
FI06	Bank Master Data Display Changes
FIBAN	Maintain IBAN
FIBPU	Bank Chains for Partner
FI12	House Banks and House Banks Accounts
FIBHU	Bank Chains for House Banks

Table B.6 Banking Transaction Codes

Transaction Code	Description
GA31	Financial Accounting Special Ledger Actual Distributions
GA11	Financial Accounting Special Ledger Actual Assessments
GA27	Financial Accounting Special Ledger Plan Assessments
GA27	Financial Accounting Special Ledger Plan Distributions
GA15	Actual Assessment: Execute
GA4B	Plan Distribution: Execute
GA35	Plan Assessment: Execute

Table B.7 Special Ledger Transaction Codes

Transaction Code	Description
GA4B	Plan Distribution: Execute
GB01	Posting Directly in Special Ledger (Local, Company Code)
GB03	Global Number Ranges Maintenance
GB04	Special Ledger Number Ranges for Company Code Actual Postings (Local)
GB05	Special Ledger Number Ranges for Company Actual Postings (Global)
GB11	Posting Directly in Special Ledger (Global, Company)
GB32	Local Number Ranges Maintenance
GCAC	Reconciliation Between Ledgers
GCBA	Document Types for Planning Definition
GCBR	Maintain Valid Document Types
GCBX	Document Types for Special Ledger Manual Postings
GCD1	Simulation of Financial Accounting Posting to Special Ledger
GCDE	Mass Deletion of Special Ledger Data
GCF2	Field Movement Definition
GCGE	Activate Global Line Items
GCGS	Reconciliation Between Special Ledger Total Data and Line Items
GCIQ	Table Group Installation (Special Ledger)
GCIQ	Set Up Tables for Special Ledger
GCL2	Special Ledger Definition
GCL2	Companies or Company Codes Assignment to Ledgers
GCLE	Activate Local Line Items
GCP1	Special Ledger Posting Periods for Company Code Postings (Local Posting Periods)
GCP2	Special Ledger Posting Periods for Company Postings (Global Posting Periods)
GCP3	Local Version Parameters
GCP4	Global Version Parameters
GCP5	Local Plan Periods Open/Close
GCP6	Global Plan Periods Open/Close
GCR2	Maintain Field Movements for Special Ledger Rollup
GCR5	Maintain Substitution for Special Ledger Rollup
GCS5	Field Movement for The Balance Carryforward (Special Ledger)

Table B.7 Special Ledger Transaction Codes (Cont.)

Transaction Code	Description
GCS6	Retained Earnings Account – Special Ledger Local (Company Code)
GCS7	Retained Earnings Account – Special Ledger Global (Company)
GCU1	Data Transfer from Financial Accounting to Special Ledger
GCU3	Data Transfer from Controlling to SL
GCU4	Data Transfer from Materials Management to Special Ledger
GCU5	Data Transfer from Sales and Distribution to Special Ledger
GCVI	Versions for Special Ledger Actual Data
GCVP	Plan Versions Definition
GCVV	Special Ledger Local Validations (for Company Codes)
GCVW	Special Ledger Global Validations (for Companies)
GCVX	Special Ledger Local Substitutions (for Company Codes)
GCVY	Special Ledger Global Substitutions (for Companies)
GD02	Search for Planning Documents
GD13	Special Ledger Total Data
GD13	Report: Display Totals
GD43	Local Plan Documents Display
GD44	Global Plan Documents Display
GL20	Maintain Number Ranges for Special Ledger Rollup
GL21	Rollup Creation in Special Ledger
GL25	Rollup Execution – Special Ledger
GL26	Rollup Reverse – Special Ledger
GLPLSET	Set Planner Profile
GLPLUP	Planned Values: Upload from Excel
GP12N	Planned Values Enter
GP32	Distribution Keys Definition
GP52	Copy Local Model Plan
GP62	Copy Global Model Plan
GVTR	Balance Carryforward in Special Ledger
GRR1	Create Report Painter
GRR2	Change Report Painter
GRR3	Display Report Painter
Gr37	Export Report

Table B.7 Special Ledger Transaction Codes (Cont.)

Transaction Code	Description
Gr38	Import Report
Gr51	Create Report Group
GR5G	Generate Report Groups
GS07	Export Set
GS08	Import Set
GS01	Create Set
GS02	Change Set
GS03	Display Set
GR21	Create Library
GR31	Create Report Writer
GR32	Change Report Writer
GR33	Display Report Writer

Table B.7 Special Ledger Transaction Codes (Cont.)

Transaction Code	Description
BALA	ALE Application Distribution
BALM	ALE Master Data Distribution
BD87	Reprocess IDocs in Error or Waiting for Action
GBB0	Validations (All)
GBB1	Substitutions (All)
LSMW	LSMW (Legacy System Migration Workbench)
MASS	Mass Change of Master Data and Documents
PFCG	Role Management (Authorizations)
PPOME	Organizational Structure Definition
SA38	ABAP Program Run
SBWP	SAPOffice Workplace
SCAT	Computer Aided Test Tool (CATT)
SE10	Transport Requests
SE16	Table Entries Display
SE37	Function Module Management
SE38	ABAP Program Maintenance and Run
SE71	Forms
SE80	ABAP Object Navigator

Table B.8 Other Transactions

Transaction Code	Description
SE93	Transaction Codes
SFP	Interactive Forms
SM02	Messages
SM30	Table and View Entries Display
SM35	Process Batch Input Sessions
SMARTFORMS	Smartforms
SO99	Release Notes
SPRO	Customizing
SQ01	Managing and Running Query
SQ02	Infosets Definition
SQ03	Query User Groups Definition
ST22	ABAP Dump Analysis
STMS	Transport Management System
SU01	Users Create, Change, and Display
SW02	Bussiness Object Browser
SWDD	Workflow Builder
SWDD_CONFIG	Business Workflow Configation
SWDM	Business Workflow Explorer
SWI1	Work Items Selection
SWI2_DIAG	Diagnosis of Workflow with Error
SWI5	Workload Analysis
SWPR	Restart Workflow after Error
SWU_EWBTE	Business Transaction Event
SXDA	Data Transfer Workbench
WE05	View IDocs
WE09	IDoc Lists According to Content. Search for IDocs Base on Field Content
WE19	Edi Test Tool. Use to Test Inbound Function Module Changes
WE20	Partner Profile Configuration. Add Partner Detail Together with Inbound and Outbound Relationships
WE30	Create IDoc Extension Type
WE57	Assign Function Module to Logical Message and IDoc Type
WE60	IDoc Type Documentation Tool
WE82	Link Release Detail to Extension IDoc Type

Table B.8 Other Transactions (Cont.)

C   Program Codes

Program	Description
FAGL_ACCOUNT_BALANCE	G/L Account Balance Display
FAGL_ACCOUNT_ITEMS_GL	G/L Account Line Item Display
FAGL_COFI_RECON	Comparison of New General Ledger Accounting with Controlling
FAGL_FC_VALUATION	Exchange Rate Valuation in New General Ledger
FAGL_FSV_CONVERT	Conversion of Financial Statement Versions from Tab. RFDT to FAGL_011*
FAGL_NRIV10	Document Number Ranges: Copy by Company Code (General Ledger View)
FAGL_NRIV20	Document Number Ranges: Copy by Fiscal Year (General Ledger View)
FAGL_RKGALGA15	Actual Assessment: General Ledger
FAGL_RKGALGA2B	Plan Assessment: General Ledger
FAGL_RKGALGA35	Actual Distribution: General Ledger
FAGL_RKGALGA4B	Plan Distribution: General Ledger
RFBABL00	Display of Changed Documents
RFBELJ00	Compact Document Journal
RFBELJ10	Document Journal
RFBIBL00	Post Financial Accounting Documents with Batch Input
RFBILA00	Financial Statement
RFBISA10	G/L Accounts Copy from Company Code: Sending
RFBISA20	G/L Accounts Copy from Company Code: Receiving
RFDAUB00	Recurring Entry Documents
RFITEMGL	Display/Change G/L Line Items
RFNRIV10	Copy Number Ranges from Company Code to Company Code
RFNRIV20	Company Number Range from Fiscal Year to Fiscal Year
RFSABL00	Changes to G/L Account Master Data
RFSEPA01	Recreation of Line Items
RFSEPA02	Recreation of Open Items (No Longer Available in Later Releases)

Table C.1   General Ledger Program Codes

Program	Description
RFSEPA04	Reduced Line Item Display After Master Data Change
RFSKPL00	G/L Master Data List (Chart of Accounts Level)
RFSSLD00	G/L Account Balances
RFSUMB00	Year End Postings
RFSKVZ00	G/L Master Data List (Company Code Level)
RFUMSV00	Tax Reporting
RFUMSV10	Additional List for Advance Return for Tax on Sales/Purchases
RFUMSV25	Deferred Tax Transfer
RFUSVX10	Data Medium Exchange with Disk
RFASLM00	EC Sales List
SAPF010	Carry Forward Receivables/Payables
SAPF011	Carry Forward G/L Balances
SAPF019	Deletion of Customer, Vendor, and G/L Master Data
SAPF020	Deletion of Transaction Data
SAPF070	Reconcile Documents and Transaction Figure
SAPF071	Adjust Balances after Comparing Documents/Transaction Figures
SAPF080	Mass Reversal of Financial Accounting Documents
SAPF100	Exchange Rate Valuation in Classic Ledger
SAPF120	Create Posting Documents from Recurring Documents
SAPF124	Automatic Clearing of Open Items
SAPF180	Post Balance Sheet Adjustments
SAPF181	Profit and Loss Adjustments

Table C.1 General Ledger Program Codes (Cont.)

Program	Description
FAGL_FC_VALUATION	Exchange Rate Valuation in New General Ledger
RFBIDE00	Batch Input for Customer Master Data
RFBIDE10	Copy Customer Master Data from Company Code: Send
RFBIDE20	Copy Customer Master Data from Company Code: Receive
RFBIKR00	Batch Input for Vendor Master Data

Table C.2 Accounts Payable and Accounts Receivable Program Codes

Program	Description
RFBIKR10	Copy Vendor Data from Company Code: Send
RFBIKR20	Copy Vendor Data from Company Code: Receive
RFBISA00	Batch Input for G/L Master Data
RFBISA10	Copy G/L Master Data from Company Code: Send
RFBISA20	Copy G/L Master Data from Company Code: Receive
RFDABL00	Changes to Customer Master Records
RFDKLI10	Customers with Missing Credit Data
RFDKLI30	Credit Limit Overview
RFDKLI50	Credit Limit Mass Change
RFDKVZ00	Reporting on Vendor Master Data
RFDOPR00	Customer Evaluation with OI Sorted List
RFDOPR10	Customer Open Item Analysis by Balance of Overdue Items
RFDOPR20	Customer Payment History
RFDSLD00	Customer Balances in Local Currency
RFDUML00	Customer Sales
RFINTITAR	Interest Calculation and Invoicing
RFINTITDEL	Interest Run Deletion
RFINTITSHOW	Interest Run Display
RFINTITUSEREXT	Enhancement of Item Interest Calculation
RFITEMAP	Vendor Line Items Reporting
RFITEMAR	Customer Line Items Reporting
SAPF019	Deletion of Customer, Vendor, and G/L Master Data
SAPF100	Exchange Rate Valuation in Classic Ledger
SAPF103	Provision for Doubtful Receivables
SAPF110V	Automatic Outgoing Payments
SAPF124	Automatic Clearing of Open Items
SAPF140	Trigger for Correspondence
SAPF150V	Dunning Run

Table C.2 Accounts Payable and Accounts Receivable Program Codes (Cont.)

Program	Description
RAJABS00	Asset Fiscal Year Closing
RAJAWE00	Asset Fiscal Year Change
RAPERB2000	Periodic Posting of Transactions

Table C.3 Asset Accounting Program Codes

Program	Description
RAPERDEL1	Reset Periodic APC Posting Run
RAPOST2000	Depreciation Run
RAPOST2001	Log of Depreciation Run

Table C.3 Asset Accounting Program Codes (Cont.)

Program	Description
RFBVALL_0	Bank Master Data Mass Upload with Country Specific File
RFBVBIC_0	Bank Master Data Mass Upload from BIC Database
RFCASH00	Cash Journal Printout
RFEBKA00	Bank Statement Import
RFEBKA30	Posting of the Imported Bank Statement
RFEBKAP0	Print Bank Statement
RFEBKAT0	Generate Test Data for Multicash
SAPF023	Delete Banks in a Specific Country
SAPF061	Archive Banks with Deletion Flag

Table C.4 Banking Program Codes

Program	Description
RFBILA10	Financial Statement for Special Ledger
RGUCOMP4	Reconciliation Between Ledgers
RGUDEL00	Mass Deletion of Special Ledger Data
RGUGBR00	Generation of Validations and Substitutions
RGUREC10	Transfer Documents from Financial Accounting to Special Ledger
RGUREC20	Transfer Documents from Controlling to Special Ledger
RGUREC30	Transfer Documents from Materials Management to Special Ledger
RGUREP03	Deletion of Specific Special Ledger Documents
RGUSLSEP	Reconciliation Between Special Ledger Total Data and Line Items
RKEPCU40	Transfer Documents from Sales and Distribution to Special Ledger
SAPFGVTR	Balance Carryforward in Special Ledger
SAPLGD13	Special Ledger Total Data
SAPMGLRV	Rollup Execution – Special Ledger

Table C.5 Special Ledger Program Codes

D   Menu Paths and Customizing Paths

Description	Menu Path
Exchange rates with worklist	ACCOUNTING • FINANCIAL ACCOUNTING • GENERAL LEDGER • ENVIRONMENT • CURRENT SETTINGS • ENTER TRANSLATION RATES – ENTER CURRENCY EXCHANGE RATES USING A WORKLIST
Exchange rates	ACCOUNTING • FINANCIAL ACCOUNTING • GENERAL LEDGER • ENVIRONMENT • CURRENT SETTINGS • ENTER TRANSLATION RATES EXCHANGE RATES USING A WORKLIST

Table D.1   General Configuration Menu Paths

Description	Customizing Path
Currency	SAP NETWEAVER • GENERAL SETTINGS • CURRENCIES • CHECK CURRENCY CODES
Exchange rate type	SAP NETWEAVER • GENERAL SETTINGS • CURRENCIES • CHECK EXCHANGE RATE TYPE
Translation ratios between currency pairs	SAP NETWEAVER • GENERAL SETTINGS • CURRENCIES • DEFINE TRANSLATION RATIOS FOR CURRENCY TRANSLATION
Currency decimal places	SAP NETWEAVER • GENERAL SETTINGS • CURRENCIES • SET DECIMAL PLACES FOR CURRENCIES
Country	SAP NETWEAVER • GENERAL SETTINGS • SET COUNTRIES • DEFINE COUNTRIES IN MYSAP SYSTEMS
Country-specific checks	SAP NETWEAVER • GENERAL SETTINGS • SET COUNTRIES • SET COUNTRY-SPECIFIC CHECKS

Table D.2   General Configuration Customizing Paths

Description	Customizing Path
Assign Controlling area to operating concern	ENTERPRISE STRUCTURE • ASSIGNMENT • CONTROLLING • ASSIGN CONTROLLING AREA TO OPERATING CONCERN
Assign company code to Controlling area	ENTERPRISE STRUCTURE • ASSIGNMENT • CONTROLLING • ASSIGN COMPANY CODE TO CONTROLLING AREA

Table D.3   Organizational Structure Customizing Paths

Description	Customizing Path
Assign business area to consolidation business area	ENTERPRISE STRUCTURE • ASSIGNMENT • FINANCIAL ACCOUNTING • ASSIGN BUSINESS AREA TO CONSOLIDATION BUSINESS AREA
Assign company code to company	ENTERPRISE STRUCTURE • ASSIGNMENT • FINANCIAL ACCOUNTING • ASSIGN COMPANY CODE TO COMPANY
Assign company code to credit control area	ENTERPRISE STRUCTURE • ASSIGNMENT • FINANCIAL ACCOUNTING • ASSIGN COMPANY CODE TO CREDIT CONTROL AREA
Assign personnel area to company code	ENTERPRISE STRUCTURE • ASSIGNMENT • HUMAN RESOURCES MANAGEMENT • ASSIGNMENT OF PERSONNEL AREA TO COMPANY CODE
Assign plant to company code	ENTERPRISE STRUCTURE • ASSIGNMENT • LOGISTICS GENERAL • ASSIGN PLANT TO COMPANY CODE
Assign sales organization to company code	ENTERPRISE STRUCTURE • ASSIGNMENT • SALES AND DISTRIBUTIONS • ASSIGN SALES ORGANIZATION TO COMPANY CODE
Operating concern	ENTERPRISE STRUCTURE • DEFINITION • CONTROLLING • CREATE OPERATING CONCERN
Controlling area	ENTERPRISE STRUCTURE • DEFINITION • CONTROLLING • MAINTAIN CONTROLLING AREA
Business area	ENTERPRISE STRUCTURE • DEFINITION • FINANCIAL ACCOUNTING • DEFINE BUSINESS AREA
Credit control area	ENTERPRISE STRUCTURE • DEFINITION • FINANCIAL ACCOUNTING • DEFINE CREDIT CONTROL AREA
Functional area	ENTERPRISE STRUCTURE • DEFINITION • FINANCIAL ACCOUNTING • DEFINE FUNCTIONAL AREA
Company code	ENTERPRISE STRUCTURE • DEFINITION • FINANCIAL ACCOUNTING • EDIT, COPY, DELETE, CHECK COMPANY CODE
Consolidation business area	ENTERPRISE STRUCTURE • DEFINITION • FINANCIAL ACCOUNTING • MAINTAIN CONSOLIDATION BUSINESS AREA
Company (trading partner)	FINANCIAL ACCOUNTING • FINANCIAL ACCOUNTING GLOBAL SETTINGS • COMPANY CODE • ENTER GLOBAL PARAMETERS

Table D.3 Organizational Structure Customizing Paths (Cont.)

Description	Menu Path
Tax reporting	ACCOUNTING • FINANCIAL • ACCOUNTING • GENERAL LEDGER • REPORTING • TAX REPORTS • GENERAL • ADVANCE RETURN FOR TAX ON SALES/PURCHASES
Diplay and change open items; display balances	ACCOUNTING • FINANCIAL ACCOUNTING • GENERAL LEDGER • ACCOUNT
Change and display existing documents in G/L	ACCOUNTING • FINANCIAL ACCOUNTING • GENERAL LEDGER • DOCUMENT
Carryforward G/L balances	ACCOUNTING • FINANCIAL ACCOUNTING • GENERAL LEDGER • PERIODIC PROCESSING • CLOSING • CARRY FORWARD
G/L manual accruals	ACCOUNTING • FINANCIAL ACCOUNTING • GENERAL LEDGER • PERIODIC PROCESSING • MANUAL ACCRUALS
Post recurring entries for recurring document	ACCOUNTING • FINANCIAL ACCOUNTING • GENERAL LEDGER • PERIODIC PROCESSING • RECURRING ENTRIES
Posting transactions for G/L	ACCOUNTING • FINANCIAL ACCOUNTING • GENERAL LEDGER • POSTING
Create reference documents (account assignment model, recurring document, sample document)	ACCOUNTING • FINANCIAL ACCOUNTING • GENERAL LEDGER • POSTING • REFERENCE DOCUMENTS
Display/change G/L line items	ACCOUNTING • FINANCIAL ACCOUNTING • GENERAL LEDGER • ACCOUNT • DISPLAY/CHANGE LINE ITEMS
Reversal of documents with cleared items	ACCOUNTING • FINANCIAL ACCOUNTING • GENERAL LEDGER • DOCUMENT • RESET CLEARED ITEMS
Reversal of documents without cleared items	ACCOUNTING • FINANCIAL ACCOUNTING • GENERAL LEDGER • DOCUMENT • REVERSE • INDIVIDUAL REVERSAL
Mass reversal of Financial Accounting documents	ACCOUNTING • FINANCIAL ACCOUNTING • GENERAL LEDGER • DOCUMENT • REVERSE • INDIVIDUAL REVERSAL
G/L standard reports	ACCOUNTING • FINANCIAL ACCOUNTING • GENERAL LEDGER • INFORMATION SYSTEM
G/L queries	ACCOUNTING • FINANCIAL ACCOUNTING • GENERAL LEDGER • INFORMATION SYSTEM • TOOLS • QUERIES
G/L accounts master mass change	ACCOUNTING • FINANCIAL ACCOUNTING • GENERAL LEDGER • MASTER RECORD • COLLECTIVE PROCESSING
G/L accounts master records copy from company code	ACCOUNTING • FINANCIAL ACCOUNTING • GENERAL LEDGER • MASTER RECORD • COMPARE COMPANY CODE

Table D.4 General Ledger Menu Paths

Description	Menu Path
Sample accounts	ACCOUNTING • FINANCIAL ACCOUNTING • GENERAL LEDGER • MASTER RECORD • G/L ACCOUNT • SAMPLE ACCOUNT
G/L account single maintenance	ACCOUNTING • FINANCIAL ACCOUNTING • GENERAL LEDGER • MASTER RECORD • INDIVIDUAL PROCESSING
Automatic clearing of open items	ACCOUNTING • FINANCIAL ACCOUNTING • GENERAL LEDGER • PERIODIC PROCESSING • AUTOMATIC CLEARING
Tax codes	ACCOUNTING • FINANCIAL ACCOUNTING GLOBAL SETTINGS • TAX ON SALES/PURCHASES • CALCULATION • DEFINE TAX CODES FOR SALES AND PURCHASES

Table D.4 General Ledger Menu Paths (Cont.)

Description	Customizing Path
Automatic creation cost elements	CONTROLLING • COST ELEMENT ACCOUNTING • MASTER DATA • AUTOMATIC CREATION OF PRIMARY AND SECONDARY COST ELEMENTS
Profit centers	ENTERPRISE STRUCTURE • DEFINITION • FINANCIAL ACCOUNTING • DEFINE PROFIT CENTRE
SAP General Ledger: segment	ENTERPRISE STRUCTURE • DEFINITION • FINANCIAL ACCOUNTING • DEFINE SEGMENT
SAP General Ledger: ledger definition	FINANCIAL ACCOUNTING (NEW) • FINANCIAL ACCOUNTING GLOBAL SETTINGS (NEW) • LEDGERS • LEDGER • DEFINE LEDGERS FOR GENERAL LEDGER ACCOUNTING
SAP General Ledger: document types and number range for general ledger view	FINANCIAL ACCOUNTING (NEW) • DOCUMENT • DEFINE DOCUMENT TYPES FOR ENTRY VIEW IN A LEDGER
SAP General Ledger: document types and number range for entry view in a ledger	FINANCIAL ACCOUNTING (NEW) • DOCUMENT • DEFINE DOCUMENT TYPES FOR GENERAL LEDGER VIEW
SAP General Ledger: scenarios	FINANCIAL ACCOUNTING (NEW) • FINANCIAL ACCOUNTING GLOBAL SETTINGS (NEW) • LEDGERS • LEDGER • ASSIGN SCENARIOS AND CUSTOMER FIELDS TO LEDGERS
Definition of non-leading ledgers	FINANCIAL ACCOUNTING (NEW) • FINANCIAL ACCOUNTING GLOBAL SETTINGS (NEW) • LEDGERS • LEDGER • DEFINE AND ACTIVATE NON-LEADING LEDGERS

Table D.5 General Ledger Customizing Paths

Description	Customizing Path
SAP General Ledger: ledgers assigned to the ledger group	Financial Accounting (New) • Financial Accounting Global Settings (New) • Ledgers • Ledger • Define Ledger Group
SAP General Ledger: document splitting fields	Financial Accounting (New) • General Ledger Accounting (New) • Business Transactions • Document Splitting • Activate Document Splitting
SAP General Ledger: document splitting configuration	Financial Accounting (New) • General Ledger Accounting (New) • Business Transactions • Document Splitting • Classify Document Types For Document Splitting
Consolidation transaction types	Financial Accounting • Consolidation • Master Data • Transaction Types • Maintain Transaction Types
Company code detailed settings	Financial Accounting • Financial Accounting Global Settings • Company Code • Enter Global Parameters
Parallel currencies	Financial Accounting • Financial Accounting Global Settings • Company Code • Multiple Currencies • Define Additional Local Currencies
Additional ledgers in the classic General Ledger	Financial Accounting • Financial Accounting Global Settings • Company Code • Multiple Currencies • Define Additional Local Currencies For Ledgers
Rules for changing header fields in documents	Financial Accounting • Financial Accounting Global Settings • Document • Document Header • Document Change Rules, Document Header
General ledger number ranges	Financial Accounting • Financial Accounting Global Settings • Document • Document Number Ranges • Define Document Number Ranges
Rules for changing item fields in documents	Financial Accounting • Financial Accounting Global Settings • Document • Line Item • Document Change Rules, Line Item
Fiscal year variant	Financial Accounting • Financial Accounting Global Settings • Fiscal Year • Maintain Fiscal Year Variant (Maintain Shortened Fisc. Year)
Accounts for tax codes	Financial Accounting • Financial Accounting Global Settings • Tax On Sales/Purchases • Posting • Define Tax Accounts

Table D.5 General Ledger Customizing Paths (Cont.)

Description	Customizing Path
Substitutions: general ledger	FINANCIAL ACCOUNTING • G/L ACCOUNTING • BUSINESS TRANSACTIONS • G/L POSTING • CARRY OUT AND CHECK DOCUMENT SETTINGS • SUBSTITUTION IN ACCOUNTING DOCUMENTS
Validations: general ledger	FINANCIAL ACCOUNTING • G/L ACCOUNTING • BUSINESS TRANSACTIONS • G/L POSTING • CARRY OUT AND CHECK DOCUMENT SETTINGS • VALIDATION IN ACCOUNTING DOCUMENTS
Customizing of account determination for posting from other SAP modules	FINANCIAL ACCOUNTING • GENERAL LEDGER ACCOUNTING • BUSINESS TRANSACTIONS • INTEGRATION
Clearing difference accounts	FINANCIAL ACCOUNTING • GENERAL LEDGER ACCOUNTING • BUSINESS TRANSACTIONS • OPEN ITEM CLEARING • CLEARING DIFFERENCES
Exchange rate difference accounts	FINANCIAL ACCOUNTING • GENERAL LEDGER ACCOUNTING • BUSINESS TRANSACTIONS • OPEN ITEM CLEARING • DEFINE ACCOUNTS FOR EXCHANGE RATE DIFFERENCES
Rules for clearing open items	FINANCIAL ACCOUNTING • GENERAL LEDGER ACCOUNTING • BUSINESS TRANSACTIONS • OPEN ITEM CLEARING • PREPARE AUTOMATIC CLEARING
Screen layout for creating, displaying, changing G/L accounts	FINANCIAL ACCOUNTING • GENERAL LEDGER ACCOUNTING • G/L ACCOUNT • MASTER RECORDS • PREPARATION • ADDITIONAL ACTIVITIES • DEFINE SCREEN LAYOUT FOR EACH TRANSACTION
G/L account group	FINANCIAL ACCOUNTING • GENERAL LEDGER ACCOUNTING • G/L ACCOUNT • MASTER RECORDS • PREPARATION • DEFINE ACCOUNT GROUP
Retained earnings account	FINANCIAL ACCOUNTING • GENERAL LEDGER ACCOUNTING • G/L ACCOUNT • MASTER RECORDS • PREPARATION • DEFINE RETAINED EARNINGS ACCOUNT
Chart of accounts	FINANCIAL ACCOUNTING • GENERAL LEDGER ACCOUNTING • G/L ACCOUNT • MASTER RECORDS • PREPARATION • EDIT CHART OF ACCOUNTS LIST
Defining the rules for the sample accounts	FINANCIAL ACCOUNTING • GENERAL LEDGER ACCOUNTING • G/L ACCOUNTS • MASTER DATA • ADDITIONAL ACTIVITIES • SAMPLE ACCOUNTS

Table D.5 General Ledger Customizing Paths (Cont.)

Description	Customizing Path
General ledger document types	FINANCIAL ACCOUNTING • GENERAL LEDGER ACCOUNTING • G/L POSTING • CARRY OUT AND CHECK DOCUMENT SETTINGS • DEFINE DOCUMENT TYPES
Posting keys	FINANCIAL ACCOUNTING • GENERAL LEDGER ACCOUNTING • G/L POSTING • CARRY OUT AND CHECK DOCUMENT SETTINGS • DEFINE POSTING KEYS
Field status variant	FINANCIAL ACCOUNTING • GENERAL LEDGER ACCOUNTING • G/L POSTING • CARRY OUT AND CHECK DOCUMENT SETTINGS • MAINTAIN FIELD STATUS VARIANTS

Table D.5 General Ledger Customizing Paths (Cont.)

Description	Menu Path
Vendor line items and balance reporting	ACCOUNTING • FINANCIAL ACCOUNTING • ACCOUNTS PAYABLE • ACCOUNT
Posting vendor document (invoices, credit memo, payments, various documents)	ACCOUNTING • FINANCIAL ACCOUNTING • ACCOUNTS PAYABLE • DOCUMENT ENTRY • CREDIT MEMO
Changing and displaying vendor documents	ACCOUNTING • FINANCIAL ACCOUNTING • ACCOUNTS PAYABLE • DOCUMENTS
Reporting on vendor master data and documents	ACCOUNTING • FINANCIAL ACCOUNTING • ACCOUNTS PAYABLE • INFORMATION SYSTEM
Maintain vendor master records	ACCOUNTING • FINANCIAL ACCOUNTING • ACCOUNTS PAYABLE • MASTER RECORDS
Automatic outgoing payments	ACCOUNTING • FINANCIAL ACCOUNTING • ACCOUNTS PAYABLE • PERIODIC PROCESSING • PAYMENTS
Posting customer document (invoices, credit memo, payments, various documents)	ACCOUNTING • FINANCIAL ACCOUNTING • ACCOUNTS RECEIVABLE • DOCUMENT ENTRY • CREDIT MEMO
Reporting on vendor customer data and docuemnts	ACCOUNTING • FINANCIAL ACCOUNTING • ACCOUNTS RECEIVABLE • INFORMATION SYSTEM
Maintain customer master records	ACCOUNTING • FINANCIAL ACCOUNTING • ACCOUNTS RECEIVABLE • MASTER RECORDS

Table D.6 Accounts Payable and Accounts Receivable Menu Paths

Description	Menu Path
Dunning customers	ACCOUNTING • FINANCIAL ACCOUNTING • ACCOUNTS RECEIVABLES • PERIODIC PROCESSING • DUNNING
Interest calculation and invoicing	ACCOUNTING • FINANCIAL ACCOUNTING • ACCOUNTS RECEIVABLES • PERIODIC PROCESSING • INTEREST CALCULATION • ITEM INTEREST CALCULATION
Automatic clearing of open items	ACCOUNTING • FINANCIAL ACCOUNTING • GENERAL LEDGER • PERIODIC PROCESSING • AUTOMATIC CLEARING
Customer and vendor balances carryforward	ACCOUNTING • FINANCIAL ACCOUNTING • GENERAL LEDGER • PERIODIC PROCESSING • CLOSING • CARRY FORWARD
Payables and receivables reclassification	ACCOUNTING • FINANCIAL ACCOUNTING • GENERAL LEDGER • PERIODIC PROCESSING • CLOSING • RECLASSIFY
Exchange rate valuation	ACCOUNTING • FINANCIAL ACCOUNTING • GENERAL LEDGER • PERIODIC PROCESSING • CLOSING • VALUATE
Print customers and vendors correspondence	ACCOUNTING • FINANCIAL ACCOUNTING • GENERAL LEDGER • PERIODIC PROCESSING • PRINT CORRESPONDENCE

Table D.6 Accounts Payable and Accounts Receivable Menu Paths (Cont.)

Description	Customizing Path
Dunning procedure configuration	FINANCIAL ACCOUNTING • ACCOUNTS RECEIVABLE AND ACCOUNTS PAYABLE • BUSINESS TRANSACTIONS • DUNNING
Payment terms: installments	FINANCIAL ACCOUNTING • ACCOUNTS RECEIVABLE AND ACCOUNTS PAYABLE • BUSINESS TRANSACTIONS • INCOMING INVOICES/CREDIT MEMOS • DEFINE TERMS OF PAYMENT FOR INSTALLMENT PAYMENTS
Default document type for enjoy transactions	FINANCIAL ACCOUNTING • ACCOUNTS RECEIVABLE AND ACCOUNTS PAYABLE • BUSINESS TRANSACTIONS • INCOMING INVOICES/CREDIT MEMOS • INCOMING INVOICES/CREDIT MEMOS – ENJOY • DEFINE DOCUMENT TYPES FOR ENJOY TRANSACTION
Payment terms	FINANCIAL ACCOUNTING • ACCOUNTS RECEIVABLE AND ACCOUNTS PAYABLE • BUSINESS TRANSACTIONS • INCOMING INVOICES/CREDIT MEMOS • MAINTAIN TERMS OF PAYMENT
Interest calculation configuration	FINANCIAL ACCOUNTING • ACCOUNTS RECEIVABLE AND ACCOUNTS PAYABLE • BUSINESS TRANSACTIONS • INTEREST CALCULATION

Table D.7 Accounts Payable and Accounts Receivable Customizing Paths

Description	Customizing Path
Payment block reasons	FINANCIAL ACCOUNTING • ACCOUNTS RECEIVABLE AND ACCOUNTS PAYABLE • BUSINESS TRANSACTIONS • OUTGOING PAYMENTS • OUTGOING PAYMENTS GLOBAL SETTINGS • PAYMENT BLOCK REASONS • DEFINE PAYMENT BLOCK REASONS
Configuration of special Accounts Receivable posting type	FINANCIAL ACCOUNTING • ACCOUNTS RECEIVABLE AND ACCOUNTS PAYABLE • BUSINESS TRANSACTIONS • POSTINGS WITH ALTERNATIVE RECONCILIATION ACCOUNT • DEFINE ALTERNATIVE RECONCILIATION ACCOUNT FOR CUSTOMERS
Configuration of special Accounts Payable posting type	FINANCIAL ACCOUNTING • ACCOUNTS RECEIVABLE AND ACCOUNTS PAYABLE • BUSINESS TRANSACTIONS • POSTINGS WITH ALTERNATIVE RECONCILIATION ACCOUNT • DEFINE ALTERNATIVE RECONCILIATION ACCOUNT FOR VENDORS
Assign number ranges to customer account groups	FINANCIAL ACCOUNTING • ACCOUNTS RECEIVABLE AND ACCOUNTS PAYABLE • CUSTOMER ACCOUNT • MASTER DATA • PREPARATION FOR CREATING CUSTOMER MASTER DATA • ASSIGN NUMBER RANGES TO CUSTOMER ACCOUNT GROUPS
Customer number ranges	FINANCIAL ACCOUNTING • ACCOUNTS RECEIVABLE AND ACCOUNTS PAYABLE • CUSTOMER ACCOUNT • MASTER DATA • PREPARATION FOR CREATING CUSTOMER MASTER DATA • CREATE NUMBER RANGES FOR CUSTOMER ACCOUNTS
Screen layout for activities	FINANCIAL ACCOUNTING • ACCOUNTS RECEIVABLE AND ACCOUNTS PAYABLE • CUSTOMER ACCOUNT • MASTER DATA • PREPARATION FOR CREATING CUSTOMER MASTER DATA • DEFINE SCREEN LAYOUT PER ACTIVITY (CUSTOMERS)
Screen layout per company code	FINANCIAL ACCOUNTING • ACCOUNTS RECEIVABLE AND ACCOUNTS PAYABLE • CUSTOMER ACCOUNT • MASTER DATA • PREPARATION FOR CREATING CUSTOMER MASTER DATA • DEFINE SCREEN LAYOUT PER COMPANY CODE (CUSTOMERS)
Accounting clerk	FINANCIAL ACCOUNTING • ACCOUNTS RECEIVABLE AND ACCOUNTS PAYABLE • CUSTOMER ACCOUNT • MASTER DATA • PREPARATION FOR CREATING CUSTOMER MASTER DATA • ENTER ACCOUNTING CLERK IDENTIFICATION CODE FOR CUSTOMERS

Table D.7 Accounts Payable and Accounts Receivable Customizing Paths (Cont.)

Description	Customizing Path
Customer account group	FINANCIAL ACCOUNTING • ACCOUNTS RECEIVABLE AND ACCOUNTS PAYABLE • CUSTOMER ACCOUNTS • MASTER DATA • PREPARATION FOR CREATING CUSTOMER MASTER DATA • DEFINE ACCOUNT GROUPS WITH SCREEN LAYOUT (CUSTOMERS)
Assign number ranges to vendor account groups	FINANCIAL ACCOUNTING • ACCOUNTS RECEIVABLE AND ACCOUNTS PAYABLE • VENDOR ACCOUNT • MASTER DATA • PREPARATION FOR CREATING VENDOR MASTER DATA • ASSIGN NUMBER RANGES TO VENDOR ACCOUNT GROUPS
Vendor number ranges	FINANCIAL ACCOUNTING • ACCOUNTS RECEIVABLE AND ACCOUNTS PAYABLE • VENDOR ACCOUNT • MASTER DATA • PREPARATION FOR CREATING VENDOR MASTER DATA • CREATE NUMBER RANGES FOR VENDOR ACCOUNTS
Screen layout for activities (vendor)	FINANCIAL ACCOUNTING • ACCOUNTS RECEIVABLE AND ACCOUNTS PAYABLE • VENDOR ACCOUNT • MASTER DATA • PREPARATION FOR CREATING VENDOR MASTER DATA • DEFINE SCREEN LAYOUT PER ACTIVITY (VENDORS)
Screen layout per company code (vendor)	FINANCIAL ACCOUNTING • ACCOUNTS RECEIVABLE AND ACCOUNTS PAYABLE • VENDOR ACCOUNT • MASTER DATA • PREPARATION FOR CREATING VENDOR MASTER DATA • DEFINE SCREEN LAYOUT PER COMPANY CODE (VENDORS)
Vendor account group	FINANCIAL ACCOUNTING • ACCOUNTS RECEIVABLE AND ACCOUNTS PAYABLE • VENDOR ACCOUNTS • MASTER DATA • PREPARATION FOR CREATING VENDOR MASTER DATA • DEFINE ACCOUNT GROUPS WITH SCREEN LAYOUT (VENDORS)
Customizing of bill of exchange	FINANCIAL ACCOUNTING • BANK ACCOUNTING • BUSINESS TRANSACTIONS • BILL OF EXCHANGE TRANSACTIONS
Customizing of exchange rate calculation	FINANCIAL ACCOUNTING • FINANCIAL ACCOUNTING GLOBAL SETTINGS • GENERAL LEDGER ACCOUNTING • BUSINESS TRANSACTIONS • CLOSING • VALUATE • FOREIGN CURRENCY VALUATION
Customizing of made down payments	FINANCIAL ACCOUNTING • FINANCIAL ACCOUNTING GLOBAL SETTINGS • GENERAL LEDGER ACCOUNTING • BUSINESS TRANSACTIONS • DOWN PAYMENTS MADE
Customizing of received down payments	FINANCIAL ACCOUNTING • FINANCIAL ACCOUNTING GLOBAL SETTINGS • GENERAL LEDGER ACCOUNTING • BUSINESS TRANSACTIONS • DOWN PAYMENTS RECEIVED

Table D.7 Accounts Payable and Accounts Receivable Customizing Paths (Cont.)

Description	Customizing Path
Customizing of automatic payment program	FINANCIAL ACCOUNTING • FINANCIAL ACCOUNTING GLOBAL SETTINGS • GENERAL LEDGER ACCOUNTING • BUSINESS TRANSACTIONS • INCOMING PAYMENTS • AUTOMATIC INCOMING PAYMENTS
Customizing of special G/L transactions	FINANCIAL ACCOUNTING • FINANCIAL ACCOUNTING GLOBAL SETTINGS • GENERAL LEDGER ACCOUNTING • BUSINESS TRANSACTIONS • POSTING WITH ALTERNATIVE RECONCILIATION ACCOUNT

Table D.7 Accounts Payable and Accounts Receivable Customizing Paths (Cont.)

Description	Menu Path
Managing main asset and sub-asset master data	ACCOUNTING • FINANCIAL ACCOUNTING • FIXED ASSETS • ASSET
The Asset Explorer	ACCOUNTING • FINANCIAL ACCOUNTING • FIXED ASSETS • ASSET • ASSET EXPLORER
Mass change to asset master data	ACCOUNTING • FINANCIAL ACCOUNTING • FIXED ASSETS • ENVIRONMENT • WORKLIST
Reporting on asset master data, transactions, and depreciations	ACCOUNTING • FINANCIAL ACCOUNTING • FIXED ASSETS • INFORMATION SYSTEM • REPORTS ON ASSET ACCOUNTING
Periodic posting of transactions	ACCOUNTING • FINANCIAL ACCOUNTING • FIXED ASSETS • PERIODIC PROCESSING • APC VALUE POSTING
Depreciation run	ACCOUNTING • FINANCIAL ACCOUNTING • FIXED ASSETS • PERIODIC PROCESSING • DEPRECIATION RUN • EXECUTE
Fiscal year change	ACCOUNTING • FINANCIAL ACCOUNTING • FIXED ASSETS • PERIODIC PROCESSING • FISCAL YEAR CHANGE
Reopen of closed fiscal year	ACCOUNTING • FINANCIAL ACCOUNTING • FIXED ASSETS • PERIODIC PROCESSING • YEAR-END CLOSING • UNDO
Fiscal year closing	ACCOUNTING • FINANCIAL ACCOUNTING • FIXED ASSETS • PERIODIC PROCESSING • YEAR-END CLOSING • EXECUTE
Posting acquisitions	ACCOUNTING • FINANCIAL ACCOUNTING • FIXED ASSETS • POSTING • ACQUISITION
Changing and displaying existing asset transactions	ACCOUNTING • FINANCIAL ACCOUNTING • FIXED ASSETS • POSTING • EDIT DOCUMENT

Table D.8 Asset Menu Paths

Description	Menu Path
Posting an unplanned depreciation	ACCOUNTING • FINANCIAL ACCOUNTING • FIXED ASSETS • POSTING • MANUAL VALUE CORRECTION • UNPLANNED DEPRECIATION
Post capitalization	ACCOUNTING • FINANCIAL ACCOUNTING • FIXED ASSETS • POSTING • POST-CAPITALIZATION
Posting a retirement	ACCOUNTING • FINANCIAL ACCOUNTING • FIXED ASSETS • POSTING • RETIREMENT
Reversing existing asset transactions	ACCOUNTING • FINANCIAL ACCOUNTING • FIXED ASSETS • POSTING • REVERSE DOCUMENT
Posting a transfer	ACCOUNTING • FINANCIAL ACCOUNTING • FIXED ASSETS • POSTING • TRANSFER

Table D.8 Asset Menu Paths (Cont.)

Description	Customizing Path
Depreciation keys	FINANCIAL ACCOUNTING • ASSET ACCOUNTING • DEPRECIATION • VALUATION METHODS • DEPRECIATION KEYS • MAINTAIN DEPRECIATION KEY
Asset history sheet configuration	FINANCIAL ACCOUNTING • ASSET ACCOUNTING • INFORMATION SYSTEM • ASSET HISTORY SHEET
Generic activation of Controlling objects for posting in Asset Accounting	FINANCIAL ACCOUNTING • ASSET ACCOUNTING • INTEGRATION WITH THE GENERAL LEDGER • ADDITIONAL ACCOUNT ASSIGNMENT • VALUATION METHODS • ACTIVATE ACCOUNT ASSIGNMENT OBJECT
Activation of Controlling objects for posting in Asset Accounting per company code	FINANCIAL ACCOUNTING • ASSET ACCOUNTING • INTEGRATION WITH THE GENERAL LEDGER • ADDITIONAL ACCOUNT ASSIGNMENT • VALUATION METHODS • SPECIFY ACCOUNT ASSIGNMENT TYPE FOR ACCOUNT ASSIGNMENT OBJECT
Specify G/L accounts for APC posting and depreciation	FINANCIAL ACCOUNTING • ASSET ACCOUNTING • INTEGRATION WITH THE GENERAL LEDGER • ASSIGN G/L ACCOUNTS
Document type for depreciation	FINANCIAL ACCOUNTING • ASSET ACCOUNTING • INTEGRATION WITH THE GENERAL LEDGER • POST DEPRECIATION TO GENERAL LEDGER • SPECIFY DOCUMENT TYPE FOR POSTING OF DEPRECIATION
Posting rules for depreciation	FINANCIAL ACCOUNTING • ASSET ACCOUNTING • INTEGRATION WITH THE GENERAL LEDGER • POST DEPRECIATION TO THE GENERAL LEDGER • SPECIFY INTERVALS AND POSTING RULES

Table D.9 Asset Customizing Paths

Description	Customizing Path
Specify posting key for asset posting	FINANCIAL ACCOUNTING • ASSET ACCOUNTING • INTEGRATION WITH THE GENERAL LEDGER • SPECIFY POSTING KEY FOR ASSET POSTING
Substitutions for asset master data	FINANCIAL ACCOUNTING • ASSET ACCOUNTING • MASTER DATA • DEFINE SUBSTITUTIONS
Validations for asset master data	FINANCIAL ACCOUNTING • ASSET ACCOUNTING • MASTER DATA • DEFINE VALIDATIONS
Screen layout rules: asset master data (details for each field)	FINANCIAL ACCOUNTING • ASSET ACCOUNTING • MASTER DATA • SCREEN LAYOUT • DEFINE SCREEN LAYOUT FOR ASSET MASTER DATA
User fields (and evaluation groups)	FINANCIAL ACCOUNTING • ASSET ACCOUNTING • MASTER DATA • USER FIELDS
Screen layout rules: asset master data	FINANCIAL ACCOUNTING • ASSET ACCOUNTING • ORGANIZATIONAL STRUCTURES • ASSET CLASSES • CREATE SCREEN LAYOUT RULES
Number ranges for asset master data	FINANCIAL ACCOUNTING • ASSET ACCOUNTING • ORGANIZATIONAL STRUCTURES • ASSET CLASSES • DEFINE NUMBER RANGES INTERVAL
Account determination in Asset Accounting	FINANCIAL ACCOUNTING • ASSET ACCOUNTING • ORGANIZATIONAL STRUCTURES • ASSET CLASSES • SPECIFY ACCOUNT DETERMINATION
Chart of depreciation definition	FINANCIAL ACCOUNTING • ASSET ACCOUNTING • ORGANIZATIONAL STRUCTURES • COPY REFERENCE CHART OF DEPRECIATION/DEPRECIATION AREAS
Depreciation area currency	FINANCIAL ACCOUNTING • ASSET ACCOUNTING • VALUATION • CURRENCIES • DEFINE DEPRECIATION AREAS FOR FOREIGN CURRENCIES
Asset classes deactivation in chart of depreciation	FINANCIAL ACCOUNTING • ASSET ACCOUNTING • VALUATION • DEACTIVATE ASSET CLASS FOR CHART OF DEPRECIATION
Depreciation areas definition	FINANCIAL ACCOUNTING • ASSET ACCOUNTING • VALUATION • DEPRECIATION AREAS
Deactivation of depreciation areas in asset classes	FINANCIAL ACCOUNTING • ASSET ACCOUNTING • VALUATION • DETERMINE DEPRECIATION AREA IN ASSET CLASSES

Table D.9 Asset Customizing Paths (Cont.)

Description	Customizing Path
Set the chart of depreciation for customizing	FINANCIAL ACCOUNTING • ASSET ACCOUNTING • VALUATION • SET CHART OF DEPRECIATION
Asset class definition	FINANCIAL ACCOUNTING • ORGANIZATIONAL STRUCTURES • ASSET CLASSES • DEFINE ASSET CLASSES

Table D.9 Asset Customizing Paths (Cont.)

Description	Menu Path
Conversion of bank statements to multicash format	ACCOUNTING • FINANCIAL ACCOUNTING • BANKS • INCOMINGS • BANK STATEMENT • CONVERT
Bank statement import	ACCOUNTING • FINANCIAL ACCOUNTING • BANKS • INCOMINGS • BANK STATEMENT • IMPORT
Posting of the imported bank statement	ACCOUNTING • FINANCIAL ACCOUNTING • BANKS • INCOMINGS • BANK STATEMENT • POST
Reprocess (or postprocess) of imported and partially posted bank statements	ACCOUNTING • FINANCIAL ACCOUNTING • BANKS • INCOMINGS • BANK STATEMENT • REPROCESS
Cash journal printout	ACCOUNTING • FINANCIAL ACCOUNTING • BANKS • INFORMATION SYSTEM • PRINT CASH JOURNAL
Bank chains (receiver specific)	ACCOUNTING • FINANCIAL ACCOUNTING • BANKS • MASTER DATA • BANK CHAINS • HOUSE BANKS/BANK TO BANK TRANSFERS/BUSINESS PARTNERS
Bank master data management	ACCOUNTING • FINANCIAL ACCOUNTING • BANKS • MASTER DATA • BANK MASTER RECORD
Bank master data mass upload with country specific file	ACCOUNTING • FINANCIAL ACCOUNTING • BANKS • MASTER DATA • BANK MASTER RECORD • TRANSFER BANK DATA
Bank master data mass upload from BIC database	ACCOUNTING • FINANCIAL ACCOUNTING • BANKS • MASTER DATA • BANK MASTER RECORD • TRANSFER BIC FILE
Cash journal postings	ACCOUNTING • FINANCIAL ACCOUNTING • BANKS • OUTGOING • CASH JOURNAL

Table D.10 Banking Menu Paths

Description	Customizing Path
House banks and house bank accounts	FINANCIAL ACCOUNTING • BANK ACCOUNTING • BANK ACCOUNTS • DEFINE HOUSE BANKS
Bank chains	FINANCIAL ACCOUNTING • BANK ACCOUNTING • BANK CHAINS
Cash journal business definition	FINANCIAL ACCOUNTING • BANK ACCOUNTING • BUSINESS TRANSACTIONS • CASH JOURNAL • CREATE, CHANGE, DELETE BUSINESS TRANSACTIONS
Number ranges for cash journal documents	FINANCIAL ACCOUNTING • BANK ACCOUNTING • BUSINESS TRANSACTIONS • CASH JOURNAL • DEFINE NUMBER RANGE INTERVALS FOR CASH JOURNAL DOCUMENTS
Cash journal definition	FINANCIAL ACCOUNTING • BANK ACCOUNTING • BUSINESS TRANSACTIONS • CASH JOURNAL • SET UP CASH JOURNAL
Parameters for the cash journal receipt	FINANCIAL ACCOUNTING • BANK ACCOUNTING • BUSINESS TRANSACTIONS • CASH JOURNAL • SET UP PRINT PARAMETERS FOR CASH JOURNAL
Bank statement configuration	FINANCIAL ACCOUNTING • BANK ACCOUNTING • BUSINESS TRANSACTIONS • PAYMENT TRANSACTIONS • ELECTRONIC BANK STATEMENT • MAKE GLOBAL SETTINGS FOR ELECTRONIC BANK STATEMENT

Table D.11 Banking Customizing Paths

Description	Menu Path
Posting directly in Special Ledger	ACCOUNTING • FINANCIAL ACCOUNTING • SPECIAL PURPOSE LEDGER • ACTUAL POSTING
Special Ledger posting periods for company postings (global posting periods)	ACCOUNTING • FINANCIAL ACCOUNTING • SPECIAL PURPOSE LEDGER • ENVIRONMENT • CURRENT SETTINGS • GLOBAL POSTING PERIOD
Special Ledger posting periods for company code postings (local posting periods)	ACCOUNTING • FINANCIAL ACCOUNTING • SPECIAL PURPOSE LEDGER • ENVIRONMENT • CURRENT SETTINGS • LOCAL POSTING PERIOD
Special Ledger total data	ACCOUNTING • FINANCIAL ACCOUNTING • SPECIAL PURPOSE LEDGER • INFORMATION SYSTEM • PROGRAMS FOR SPECIAL PURPOSE LEDGER • TOTAL RECORD DISPLAY

Table D.12 Special Ledger Menu Paths

Description	Menu Path
Ledger total records report	ACCOUNTING • FINANCIAL ACCOUNTING • SPECIAL PURPOSE LEDGER • INFORMATION SYSTEM • PROGRAMS FOR THE SPECIAL PURPOSE LEDGER • TOTAL RECORD DISPLAY
Allocations (plan and actuals; assessment and distribution) in Special Ledger	ACCOUNTING • FINANCIAL ACCOUNTING • SPECIAL PURPOSE LEDGER • PERIODIC PROCESSING • ALLOCATION
Balance carry forward in Special Ledger	ACCOUNTING • FINANCIAL ACCOUNTING • SPECIAL PURPOSE LEDGER • PERIODIC PROCESSING • BALANCE CARRYFORWARD
Periodic posting of transactions	ACCOUNTING • FINANCIAL ACCOUNTING • SPECIAL PURPOSE LEDGER • PERIODIC PROCESSING • DATA TRANSFER
Rollup in Special Ledger	ACCOUNTING • FINANCIAL ACCOUNTING • SPECIAL PURPOSE LEDGER • PERIODIC PROCESSING • ROLLUP
Planning in Special Ledger	ACCOUNTING • FINANCIAL ACCOUNTING • SPECIAL PURPOSE LEDGER • PLANNING
Report painter	ACCOUNTING • FINANCIAL ACCOUNTING • SPECIAL PURPOSE LEDGER • TOOLS • REPORT PAINTER • REPORT
Library	ACCOUNTING • FINANCIAL ACCOUNTING • SPECIAL PURPOSE LEDGER • TOOLS • REPORT PAINTER • REPORT WRITER • LIBRARY
Report writer	ACCOUNTING • FINANCIAL ACCOUNTING • SPECIAL PURPOSE LEDGER • TOOLS • REPORT PAINTER • REPORT WRITER • REPORT
Sets	ACCOUNTING • FINANCIAL ACCOUNTING • SPECIAL PURPOSE LEDGER • TOOLS • REPORT PAINTER • REPORT WRITER • SETS
Report Painter and Writer export/import	ACCOUNTING • FINANCIAL ACCOUNTING • SPECIAL PURPOSE LEDGER • TOOLS • REPORT PAINTER • UTILITIES • TRANSPORT

Table D.12 Special Ledger Menu Paths (Cont.)

Description	Customizing Path
Versions for Special Ledger actual data	FINANCIAL ACCOUNTING • SPECIAL PURPOSE LEDGER • ACTUAL POSTINGS • MAINTAIN ACTUAL VERSIONS
Special Ledger number ranges for company actual postings (global)	FINANCIAL ACCOUNTING • SPECIAL PURPOSE LEDGER • ACTUAL POSTINGS • MAINTAIN GLOBAL NUMBER RANGES
Special Ledger number ranges for company code actual postings (local)	FINANCIAL ACCOUNTING • SPECIAL PURPOSE LEDGER • ACTUAL POSTINGS • MAINTAIN LOCAL NUMBER RANGES

Table D.13 Special Ledger Customizing Paths

Description	Customizing Path
Document types for Special Ledger manual postings	FINANCIAL ACCOUNTING • SPECIAL PURPOSE LEDGER • ACTUAL POSTINGS • MAINTAIN VALID DOCUMENT TYPES
Companies or company codes assignment to ledgers	FINANCIAL ACCOUNTING • SPECIAL PURPOSE LEDGER • BASIC SETTINGS • MASTER DATA • LEDGER • DEFINE LEDGER
Special Ledger definition	FINANCIAL ACCOUNTING • SPECIAL PURPOSE LEDGER • BASIC SETTINGS • MASTER DATA • LEDGER • DEFINE LEDGER
Field movement definition	FINANCIAL ACCOUNTING • SPECIAL PURPOSE LEDGER • BASIC SETTINGS • MASTER DATA • LEDGER • MAINTAIN FIELD MOVEMENTS
Set up tables for Special Ledger	FINANCIAL ACCOUNTING • SPECIAL PURPOSE LEDGER • BASIC SETTINGS • TABLES • DEFINITION • EXECUTE EXPRESS INSTALLATION
Table group installation (Special Ledger)	FINANCIAL ACCOUNTING • SPECIAL PURPOSE LEDGER • BASIC SETTINGS • TABLES • DEFINITION • EXECUTE EXPRESS INSTALLATION
Declaration of programs for user exits	FINANCIAL ACCOUNTING • SPECIAL PURPOSE LEDGER • BASIC SETTINGS • USER EXITS • MAINTAIN CLIENT-SPECIFIC USER EXITS
Declaration of programs for user exits	FINANCIAL ACCOUNTING • SPECIAL PURPOSE LEDGER • BASIC SETTINGS • USER EXITS • MAINTAIN CLIENT-SPECIFIC USER EXITS
Special Ledger validations	FINANCIAL ACCOUNTING • SPECIAL PURPOSE LEDGER • BASIC SETTINGS • VALIDATION
Field movement for the balance carry forward (Special Ledger)	FINANCIAL ACCOUNTING • SPECIAL PURPOSE LEDGER • PERIODIC PROCESSING • BALANCE CARRYFORWARD • ASSIGN FIELD MOVEMENT
Retained earnings account: Special Ledger global (company)	FINANCIAL ACCOUNTING • SPECIAL PURPOSE LEDGER • PERIODIC PROCESSING • BALANCE CARRYFORWARD • RETAINED EARNING ACCOUNT • MAINTAIN GLOBAL RETAINED EARNING ACCOUNT
Retained earnings account: Special Ledger local (company code)	FINANCIAL ACCOUNTING • SPECIAL PURPOSE LEDGER • PERIODIC PROCESSING • BALANCE CARRYFORWARD • RETAINED EARNING ACCOUNT • MAINTAIN LOCAL RETAINED EARNING ACCOUNT
Rollup customizing	FINANCIAL ACCOUNTING • SPECIAL PURPOSE LEDGER • PERIODIC PROCESSING • ROLLUP

Table D.13 Special Ledger Customizing Paths (Cont.)

Description	Customizing Path
Planning customizing	FINANCIAL ACCOUNTING • SPECIAL PURPOSE LEDGER • PLANNING
Reconciliation between ledgers	FINANCIAL ACCOUNTING • SPECIAL PURPOSE LEDGER • TOOLS • COMPARE LEDGERS
Mass deletion of Special Ledger data	FINANCIAL ACCOUNTING • SPECIAL PURPOSE LEDGER • TOOLS • DELETE TRANSACTION DATA
Reconciliation between Special Ledger total data and line items	FINANCIAL ACCOUNTING E193 SPECIAL PURPOSE LEDGER • TOOLS • RECONCILE TOTAL RECORDS WITH LINE ITEM TOTALS

Table D.13 Special Ledger Customizing Paths (Cont.)

E   The Author

**Vincenzo Sopracolle** graduated from Venice University in 1996. In 1999, after three years of working in the accounting and controlling departments of Italian-based companies, he began working with SAP R/3, and after few months of self-teaching, he joined his first project in Greece as an SAP Financial Accounting and Controlling consultant. In 2006, after seven more years working as an SAP Financial Accounting and Controlling expert for Italian-based companies with frequent projects abroad (United Kingdom, Spain, Belgium, and Croatia, among others), he relocated to London to work with one of the biggest multinational companies in the food market. He continued to travel and participate in international projects, including some in Dubai, Switzerland, Germany, and Sweden, where he currently lives with his family in the lake city of Alingsås.

He has worked with SAP for the last ten years, and has no plans to change, as he's still enjoying most of his work!

Index

P

T

W

X

Y

Z

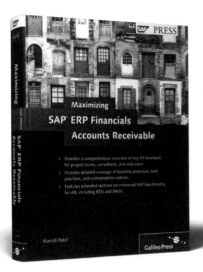

Provides a comprehensive overview of key AR functions for implementation teams, consultants, and end-users

Includes detailed coverage of business processes, best practices, and customization options

Features extended sections on enhanced SAP functionality for AR

Manish Patel

Maximizing SAP ERP Financials Accounts Receivable

Are you using SAP ERP Financials Accounts Receivables to its maximum capability? If not, or you're not sure, this book will give you a roadmap for ensuring that you are whether you're an implementation team member, executive, functional or technical user, or an end-user. The book will teach you how to maximize the use and potential of the Accounts Receivable component and increase the ROI of your implementation. It will also help you develop knowledge and strategies for enhancing the use of the AR component and integrating it with other SAP services and components.

505 pp., 2010, 79,95 Euro / US$ 79.95
ISBN 978-1-59229-303-2

>> www.sap-press.com

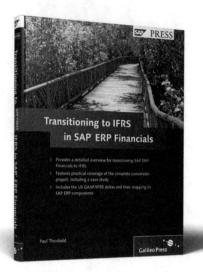

Provides a detailed overview for transitioning SAP ERP Financials to IFRS

Features practical coverage of the complete conversion project, including a case study

Includes the US GAAP/IFRS deltas and their mapping to SAP ERP components

Paul Theobald

Transitioning to IFRS in SAP ERP Financials

This book is the roadmap your conversion project team needs to prepare your SAP ERP Financials systems for conversion to IFRS. It includes detailed coverage of the transition process, an overview of the US GAAP/IFRS deltas and how they are mapped in ERP Financials, and real-world advice from an IFRS conversion project at a large petrochemical company. With this concise guide, you'll give your finance professionals, executives, technical staff, project managers, and consultants a real jumpstart to IFRS projects in upgrade or non-upgrade scenarios.

209 pp., 79,95 Euro / US$ 79.95
ISBN 978-1-59229-319-3

>> www.sap-press.com

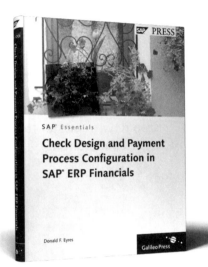

Provides comprehensive, step-by-step instructions for check design and payment process configuration in SAP

Teaches readers best practices for data gathering, payment format options, and seamlessly integrating technology with design

Donald Eyres

Check Design and Payment Process Configuration in SAP ERP Financials

The book will provide finance professionals with the data-gathering strategies, configuration steps, best practices, technical guidance, and case studies for smoothly implementing or optimizing the check delivery and payment processes. Specific sections of the book focus on configuration steps for payment configuration in SAP, designing check and electronic payment strategies centred around a comprehensive data-gathering strategy (internal and external stakeholders), and technical considerations for both printed checks and electronic payments.

340 pp., 2010, 69,95 Euro / US$ 84.95
ISBN 978-1-59229-273-8

>> www.sap-press.com

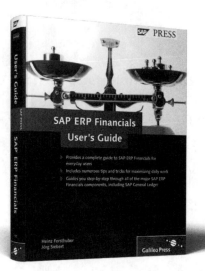

Get to know how to use SAP
Financials in your daily work

Learn step by step how to master the
processes of financial accounting

Up-to-date for SAP ERP 6.0

Heinz Forsthuber, Jörg Siebert

SAP ERP Financials User's Guide

This easy-to-read book will cover all the functionality of SAP ERP
Financials. It will be custom-tailored for users in the Finance and
Accounting departments. Readers will learn how to best use SAP ERP
Financials in their daily work. Using step-by-step descriptions, practical
examples and many figures, it will be easy to follow even for those new
to ERP Financials. The robust appendices help readers provide readers
with additional information: an introduction to the SAP system,
transaction and menu paths, a glossary and two indices. The book is
based on SAP ERP 6.0.

593 pp., 2009, 69,95 Euro / US$ 69.95
ISBN 978-1-59229-190-8

>> www.sap-press.com

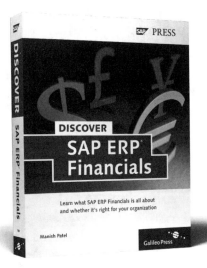

Discover what SAP Financials (FI) is all about and whether it's right for your organization

Lean how this powerful, time-tested tool can improve your financial processes and save you money

Explore the major modules, including receivable and payables, tax accounting, cost accounting, payroll accounting, travel management, and more

Manish Patel

Discover SAP ERP Financials

Business financials are an essential part of every business, large or small. Whether you just need basic accounting or you perform complex financial audits and reporting, your business needs a software tool that meets your needs. Discover SAP Financials explains how SAP can provide this solution. Using an easy-to-follow style filled with real-world examples, case studies, and practical tips and pointers, the book teaches the fundamental capabilities and uses of the core modules of SAP Financials. As part of the Discover SAP series, the book is written to help new users, decision makers considering SAP, and power users moving to the latest version learn everything they need to determine if SAP Financials is the right solution for your organization.

544 pp., 2008, 39,95 Euro / US$ 39.95
ISBN 978-1-59229-184-7

>> www.sap-press.com